SIXTH EDITION

SMALL BUSINESS

AN ENTREPRENEUR'S BUSINESS PLAN

SIXTH EDITION

SMALL BUSINESS

AN ENTREPRENEUR'S BUSINESS PLAN

J.D. Ryan
Irvine Valley College

Gail P. Hiduke
Irvine Valley College

SOUTH-WESTERN
THOMSON LEARNING™

Australia • Canada • Mexico • Singapore • Spain • United Kingdom • United States

SOUTH-WESTERN
THOMSON LEARNING

Editor: John Szilagyi
Development Editor: Debbie Anderson
Marketing Manager: Rob Bloom
Project Manager, Editorial Production: Elaine Hellmund
Print/Media Buyer: Lisa Kelley
Permissions Editor: Marcy Lunetta

Production Service: Graphic World
Text Designer: Jeanne Wolfgeher
Copy Editor: Graphic World
Cover Designer: Jeanne Wolfgeher
Cover Images: © DigitalVision; © Image Club/Eyewire
Cover Printer: Phoenix Color
Compositor: Graphic World
Printer: Phoenix Color

Printed in the United States of America
3 4 5 6 7 05 04 03

For more information about our products, contact us at:
Thomson Learning Academic Resource Center
1-800-423-0563

For permission to use material from this text, contact us by:
Phone: 1-800-730-2214
Fax: 1-800-730-2215
Web: http://www.thomsonrights.com

ISBN: 0-03-033587-6
Library of Congress Catalog Card Number: 2001095660

Asia
Thomson Learning
60 Albert Street, #15-01
Albert Complex
Singapore 189969

Australia
Nelson Thomson Learning
102 Dodds Street
South Melbourne, Victoria 3205
Australia

Canada
Nelson Thomson Learning
1120 Birchmount Road
Toronto, Ontario M1K 5G4
Canada

Europe/Middle East/Africa
Thomson Learning
Berkshire House
168-173 High Holborn
London WC1 V7AA
United Kingdom

Latin America
Thomson Learning
Seneca, 53
Colonia Polanco
11560 Mexico D.F.
Mexico

Spain
Paraninfo Thomson Learning
Calle/Magallanes, 25
28015 Madrid, Spain

Preface

Welcome to the sixth edition of *Small Business: An Entrepreneur's Business Plan.* This book was created for you and thousands of dreamers like you who want to start your own business. Most first-time entrepreneurs start out with little more than an idea. By combining your talents with the practical approach, we will show you how to take your idea and form it into a functional Business Plan.

Every great adventure begins with a map; this book serves as your map and navigator. The Action Steps provide you with direction and tasks to accomplish along the way, while the vignettes give you a first-hand look at the trials, tribulations, and successes of other entrepreneurs.

By following the Action Steps, you will learn how to develop a Business Plan from the inception of the idea, how to find your Target Customers, and how to market to them successfully.

Fasten your seatbelt, and prepare to embark on your great entrepreneurial adventure!

ORGANIZATION

Target the Chapters That Call to You.

The Action Steps are paced out across fifteen chapters from Chapter 1, "Your Great Adventure," to Chapter 15, "Pull the Plan Together."

- Chapters 1, 2, and 3 help you focus on yourself and your ideas; they explain how to develop and test your ideas in the marketplace before you spend your money. If you are just exploring entrepreneurship, concentrate on these chapters and the accompanying Action Steps. You are designing not only your business but also your life.
- Chapters 4, 5, and 6 help you locate the key to success in small business: your Target Customer.
- Chapter 7 helps you find a location—on the street or at a crossroads in cyberspace.
- Chapter 8 plunges you into numbers—how much you will need to start up and how much you will need to keep going. Chapter 9, "Shaking the Money Tree," helps you find the money to take your dream from the drawing board to reality.
- Chapter 10 focuses on copyrights, trademarks, and patents to help you keep control of your intellectual property. This is especially helpful if you are a creative person trying to peddle an invention or book.
- Chapter 11 helps you build a winning team.
- Chapter 12 guides you through insurance, taxes, and ethical dilemmas.
- Chapter 13 offers tips and advice if you want to buy an ongoing business. If you want to join the franchise movement, read Chapter 14 first. There are franchisees around every corner in the United States, but not all of them are happy with their lot. If your goal is to be the "happy franchisee," turn to page 300 now.
- Chapter 15 asks you to gather all of your Action Steps together to form the basis of your Business Plan—your business's launching document.

- Appendix A is a "Fast-Start" plan for a smaller business. A small business has one owner or is a tight partnership with few employees where extra work is contracted out and the loss of investment will not sink your ship.
- Appendix B showcases Annie's Business Plan Proposal for a chocolate and candy store located at Sea World.
- Appendix C contains forms to assist you in your entrepreneurial planning: personal budget, SBA loan forms, and other helpful and time-saving documents.

KEY FEATURES

Action Steps

More than 70 Action Steps take readers through every phase of a startup, from the initial dream to developing marketing strategies and finally to building and implementing the completed Business Plan.

Entrepreneurial Vignettes

Throughout the text we present you with small case studies full of strategies and real world applications providing insight into entrepreneurial minds and ventures. We have modified the stories for simplicity and clarity. Some vignettes are compilations of several case studies, and other vignettes are purely fictional.

Business Plans

Featured Business Plans include "Yes, We Do Windows, a Fast-Start Plan," applicable for very small businesses requiring minimal capital (located in Appendix A), and Annie's, an in-depth Business Plan Proposal for a chocolate store to be located at Sea World (found in Appendix B).

Entrepreneurial Links

Our featured resources page at the beginning of each chapter highlights books, magazines, journals, Web sites, and associations that will help guide you through the entrepreneurial maze to a wealth of information.

NEW TO THE SIXTH EDITION

Community Resources

Recognizing that the entrepreneurial life can be lonely and scary at times, we encourage you to reach out to available community resources for support, guidance, and direction. From young entrepreneurial organizations in Chapter 1, to inventors' associations in Chapter 5, to AngelInvestors.com in Chapter 15, we encourage you to seek out like-minded individuals dreaming the same dream as you.

Passion

In each chapter we highlight a passionate entrepreneur, one who exhibits his or her passion for products, locations, or markets. Not all entrepreneurs are passionate solely about money; in fact, few are. We highlight passionate entrepreneurs like Amilya Antonetti, who developed safe natural soap products to save her chemically sensitive son and in doing so founded Soapworks. Another passionate entrepreneur, Jeff Dantzler, CEO of Comtronic Systems, moved his firm from Seattle to Cle Elum, a town of 1,795, passionately seeking a place to raise his children *and* grow his business.

Planning for Success

The reason we wrote this book was to provide you with a Business Plan workbook. We supply the steps, and you supply the effort to chart a course for your dream business. Writing a Business Plan sharpens your focus. When you sharpen your focus, you see clearer. Seeing clearer raises your confidence. In the big world of small business, as in life, confidence helps you keep going when the going gets tough. There is an adage in the business world: If you fail to plan, then you are planning to fail.

Before you write a Business Plan, you should study the form. From the outside, a Business Plan looks like a stack of paper: for the short plan it is a thin stack; for the long plan it is a thick stack bound together to look like a book. However thick the stack, your plan will be a document with a beginning, middle, and end.

There are two good plans in this book to serve as a guide. There are more good plans floating out there in cyberspace for you to peruse.

We hope you can open one of the three entrepreneurial doorways and find success along with the thousands of others who have followed the Action Steps provided within. Good luck!

We have endeavored to provide current material, but Internet sites will come and go, and government programs will take new forms. Because of the dynamic nature of small business, we urge you to keep up-to-date by checking both the Internet and our Web site and its vast resources at **http://management.swcollege.com.**

Because laws and tax issues are constantly in flux, consult your legal counsel and advisors rather than relying only on the material contained in the text. All forms have been provided as examples only and should not be used without benefit of counsel. Our society is highly litigious and requires diligence on your part to keep you out of court. Never skimp on legal fees!

Instructor's Resource Materials

Instructor's Manual and Test Bank

The Instructor's Manual includes teaching aids such as learning objectives, lecture outlines, and suggestions for guest speakers and class projects. The Test Bank is full of true/false, multiple choice, and short answer questions.

Computerized Test Bank

The computerized version of the printed test bank enables instructors to preview and edit test questions, as well as add their own. The test and answer keys can also be printed in "scrambled" formats.

Videos

Video segments include coverage of themes featured throughout the text. This engaging series is available through Southwestern's custom produced BusinessLink series. Contact your local sales representative for more information and ordering options.

Web site

Visit the book site at **http://management.swcollege.com** to access our complete list of management topics including information on time management and careers.

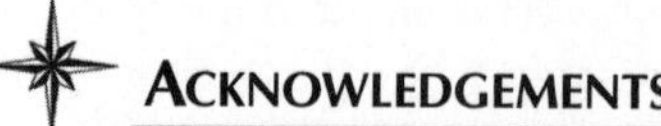

Acknowledgements

First and foremost we want to thank the thousands of entrepreneurs we have met whose grit, determination, passion, and hard work have served as an inspiration to us. Many of their personal stories have been woven throughout this book. In addition, we have attempted to address many of the problems and issues they have faced.

A very special thank-you goes to Josie Rietkerk, Founder and President of Caterina's, LLC, who improved each chapter with her current real-world retailing and franchising experience. Her invaluable insight will save readers thousands of dollars as they embark on their ventures.

We want to extend a thank-you to the reviewers whose insightful comments helped to shape this edition:

William L. Smith	Emporia State University
Rathin Basu	Ferrum College
Harry Domicone	California Lutheran University
David Ackerman	University of Alaska—Southeast

We also thank the book team: Mike Roche, Tracy Morse, Debbie Anderson, Elaine Hellmund, Linda Blundell, and Marcy Lunetta.

We are grateful for Debbie Anderson's assistance and patience.

Last, but certainly not least, appreciation and thanks are extended to Troy and Casey for their patience, support, and unending love. Couldn't have done it without you!

Joe Ryan
Gail Hiduke

Brief Table of Contents

Table of Contents

CHAPTER 1

CHAPTER 2

CHAPTER 3

CHAPTER 4

CHAPTER 5

CHAPTER 6

Marketing Promotions Overview *109*

CHAPTER 7

Location, Location, Location *131*

CHAPTER 8

Numbers and Shoebox Accounting 155

CHAPTER 9

Shaking the Money Tree 183

CHAPTER 10

Legal Issues 205

CHAPTER 14

CHAPTER 15

APPENDIX A

APPENDIX B

APPENDIX C

Your Great Adventure

Exploring the Right Fit

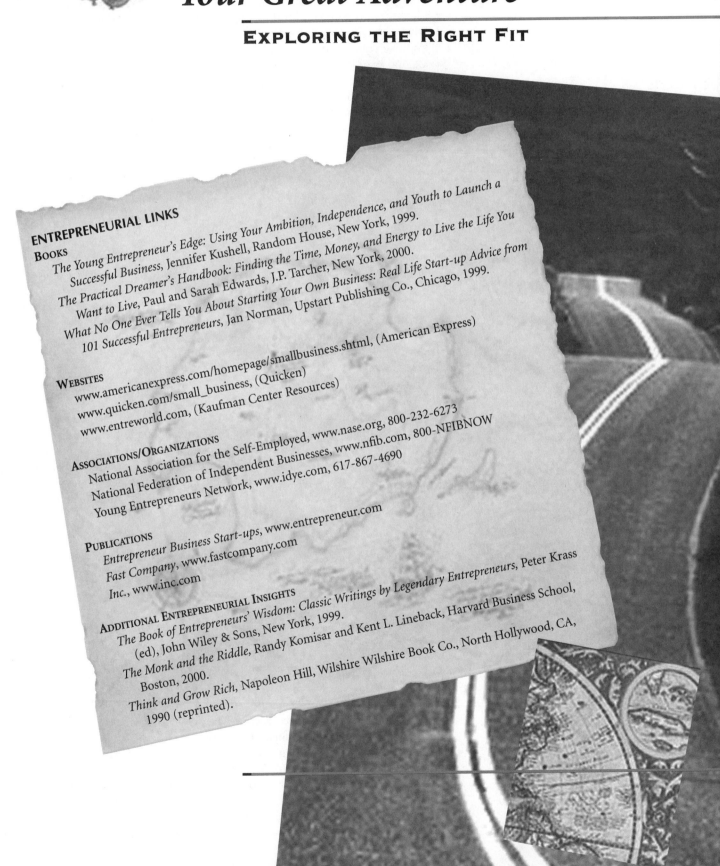

ENTREPRENEURIAL LINKS

Books

The Young Entrepreneur's Edge: Using Your Ambition, Independence, and Youth to Launch a Successful Business, Jennifer Kushell, Random House, New York, 1999.

The Practical Dreamer's Handbook: Finding the Time, Money, and Energy to Live the Life You Want to Live, Paul and Sarah Edwards, J.P. Tarcher, New York, 2000.

What No One Ever Tells You About Starting Your Own Business: Real Life Start-up Advice from 101 Successful Entrepreneurs, Jan Norman, Upstart Publishing Co., Chicago, 1999.

Websites

www.americanexpress.com/homepage/smallbusiness.shtml, (American Express)

www.quicken.com/small_business, (Quicken)

www.entreworld.com, (Kaufman Center Resources)

Associations/Organizations

National Association for the Self-Employed, www.nase.org, 800-232-6273

National Federation of Independent Businesses, www.nfib.com, 800-NFIBNOW

Young Entrepreneurs Network, www.idye.com, 617-867-4690

Publications

Entrepreneur Business Start-ups, www.entrepreneur.com

Fast Company, www.fastcompany.com

Inc., www.inc.com

Additional Entrepreneurial Insights

The Book of Entrepreneurs' Wisdom: Classic Writings by Legendary Entrepreneurs, Peter Krass (ed), John Wiley & Sons, New York, 1999.

The Monk and the Riddle, Randy Komisar and Kent L. Lineback, Harvard Business School, Boston, 2000.

Think and Grow Rich, Napoleon Hill, Wilshire Wilshire Book Co., North Hollywood, CA, 1990 (reprinted).

Learning Objectives

- Determine how you can fit in, survive, and prosper in business.
- Brainstorm a clear picture of success in small business.
- Identify successful and unsuccessful businesses in your community.
- Discover your personal strengths.
- Improve your information-gathering skills.
- Expand your knowledge of small business through interviewing small-business owners.
- Understand your financial and family situation.
- Review the Three Doorways to Entrepreneurship.
- Begin work on an Adventure Notebook and future Business Plan.
- Design your own entrepreneurial lifestyle.

Life is short; you only go around once. So you want to make sure you're getting what you want, having fun, making money, and being the best person you can be.

How do you do that? Some people do it by going into business for themselves. If you are thinking about owning your own business, this book is for you.

Try this line of thought: What do you want to be doing in the year 2010? In 2015? What's the best course of action for you right now? What might be the best business for you? What are your strengths? What do you want out of life? What are your dreams? And most of all what are your passions? This chapter will help you address these questions.

This is the age of the **entrepreneur**. According to the Small Business Administration (SBA), **www.sba.gov**, there are almost 20 million small businesses out there. Each year, more than a million new businesses are started. If you are thinking about starting a small business, you are among the 7 million budding entrepreneurs currently dreaming the same dream. Statistics from the Entrepreneurial Research Consortium, **www.wm.edu/PSYC/erc.html**, show that one in three U.S. households have been involved in small business. Most new jobs in the private sector are created by firms with fewer than 20 employees. Yes, it's a great time for an entrepreneur. You could have the time of your life. Come along with us!

Building Your Road Map

This book, with its Action Steps, can be your personal road map to success in small business. Beginning with Action Step 1, the book will guide you through the bustling marketplace—through trends, Target Customers, and promotion; through shopping malls, spreadsheets, and hushed gray bank buildings; through independent businesses that are for sale; and through franchise opportunities—all the way to your own new venture.

Along the way you will meet fascinating people, have fantastic adventures, and fun. Furthermore, by completing the action steps, you'll be drawing a customized road map for your small business success. The elements for your complete **Business Plan** will emerge to clearly evaluate and illuminate your opportunity for entrepreneurial success. Each action step draws you deeper into your business and will light the way to a final presentable Business Plan.

Entrepreneur A visionary self-starter who loves the adventure of a new enterprise and is willing to risk his or her own money.

Business Plan A blueprint outlining finances and direction for a new start-up or expansion.

You will start your journey by taking a careful look at yourself and your skills. What kind of work pleases you? How secure is your present job? How long does it take you to get organized? What internal drive makes you believe that you are an

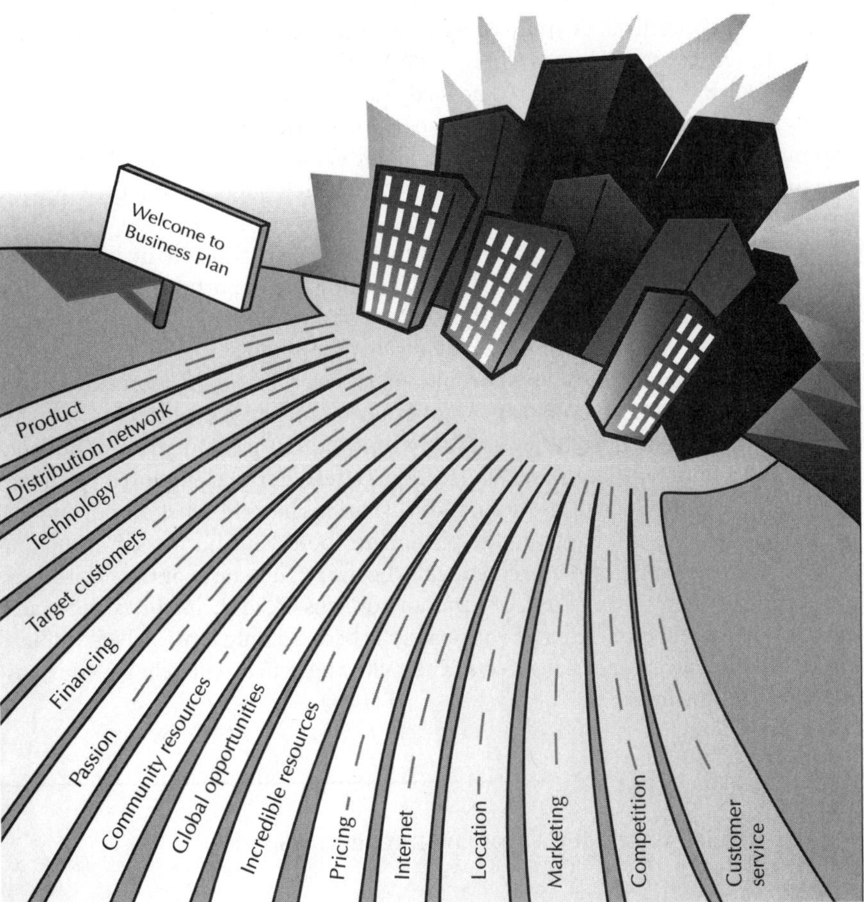

FIGURE 1.1
Entrepreneurial Road Map

entrepreneur? What do you value? What do you like to work with? Who do you like to work with? What are your passions?

Next, you'll step back and look at the marketplace. What's hot? What's cooling down? What's going to last? Where are the long lines forming? What are people buying? What distinguishes the up-and-comers from the down-and-outers?

You will brainstorm a business that will fit into an industry niche, toss around numbers to get a feel for how they turn into money, and keep having fun.

Then it will be time to profile your Target Customer, assess the competition, figure out clever promotional strategies, and scout locations. By that time you will know where you're going and feel that you're in control of your own destiny.

By the time you reach Chapter 15, you will have gathered enough material to write a complete Business Plan for showcasing your business to the world—that is, to bankers, vendors, and lenders, venture capitalists, credit managers, key employees, your family, and your friends. Your finished plan will be a blueprint for your business. It will provide a walk-through of your industry, generate excitement in potential investors, demonstrate your competence as a thoughtful planner, and underline the reasons customers will clamor for your product or service. Your plan will also serve as a means of channeling your creative energies.

Let's think about that for a moment.

One reason you're reading this book is that you're creative. You like to build, to pull things together, to plant seeds and watch things grow, to develop projects, to produce. When your mind is racing, you probably come up with more ideas than you can process. That is when you need a plan to help keep your entrepreneurial energies on track while the creative steam rises. Perhaps you've always dreamed of working for yourself—being your own boss. Well, you can have that dream *if you are prepared.*

Preparing yourself takes time, energy, and the willingness to reach out to the larger business community you will operate within. Once you get started, your engines revved, and you possess basic knowledge about your industry and markets, you can then reach out to entrepreneurs, associations, inventors' forums, and website communities. Throughout the text we highlight Community Resources, which are only the tip of the iceberg. Show your tenacity and search out the best sources for you and your business. You will be glad you did!

We hope to kick-start our readers into thinking internationally by highlighting global information within the Global Village boxes. The opportunities are limitless and few entrepreneurs take the global path. Be a pioneer in your industry or market and reach out to almost 6 billion people outside the United States.

Incredible Resource boxes focus on individual websites, books, associations, and programs that provide excellent sources of information and assistance.

More than anything, we believe strongly that without passion you will not succeed. Ten- to fourteen-hour days, no vacations, stress, tension, employee problems, misplaced cash, bank loan turndowns, and frustrations beyond belief cannot and will not be handled by you unless you are passionate about your business. Throughout the text, we have highlighted entrepreneurs who are passionate about their products and services, employees, markets, or ideas and dreams. Read their stories and search your soul. Believe in yourself and your passions because only those beliefs will lead you to achieve entrepreneurial success. The following article will help get your passionate juices flowing:

Passion

Pinpointing That Critical Entrepreneurial Spark

Those weighing whether they are entrepreneur material should consider the following:

John Preston, the entrepreneurial head of technology transfer at MIT, talks about "passion." Is there the requisite passion to succeed?

Entrepreneurs are driven to succeed. They will figure out ways to go over, under, around, or through obstacles to reach their goal.

Entrepreneurs leave the impression that they are going to succeed, that their train is leaving the station and they will be on it, one way or another.

Prospective entrepreneurs should ask whether they are leaving their current positions because of something there, or because they have the passion to do something innovative.

Can they focus on success and set clear goals and accomplish them?

Because nothing succeeds like success, can the prospective entrepreneur sacrifice the perfect situation to generate some near-term successes that he or she can leverage? Entrepreneurs usually are not distracted by details that are not important to achieving the task at hand. That is usually the opposite of what it takes to succeed in a larger, more rigid organization.

Warning: Those who have this trait should make sure they get someone working with them who will worry about the details without dragging the effort down.

Entrepreneurs, however, probably will have more control over their situation than they did in a larger company.

But they shouldn't look to control for control's sake. They should inquire: "Am I a control maniac?"

If so, prospective entrepreneurs should ask if they would like to work with—and for—somebody like themselves.

Start-ups can be very stressful.

One of my start-up clients is a company founded by a former Digital employee and a former Data General employee, both in their 40s.

Each held very responsible positions with their prior employers and both worked long hours. They admit that they did not really understand stress until they started up their own company.

"At DEC I never woke up in the middle of the night in a sweat, unable to get back to sleep," says the entrepreneur-client.

Not all founders face that level of stress. The point is: Is the founder ready for stress and, perhaps more importantly, are the spouse and children ready?

A roller coaster metaphor is appropriate for several reasons.

A roller coaster provides highs and lows. Is the prospective business owner capable of managing such extremes? The highs and lows of a roller coaster usually come in rapid succession. Start-ups can also face rapid changes, and one should be ready for them.

Are roller coasters risky? Thrilling, perhaps; but not commonly thought of as being risky. Jumping out of an airplane without a parachute—now that is risky!

Although people often say that entrepreneurs are risk-takers, one will find that most of them don't jump out of airplanes.

On the contrary, while they're not afraid to undertake projects that might fail, they also work to minimize risk.

Are they innovators?

Entrepreneurs look at problems and craft new ways of doing things.

Can they build a team?

Entrepreneurs often think and act differently, but the most successful ones are not loners.

MIT Sloan Professor Ed Roberts in his book "Entrepreneurs in High Technology" (Oxford Press), reports on research that shows that entrepreneurial teams of three or more persons have a higher probability of success.

Are they capable of identifying their strengths and weaknesses? Are they capable of finding and motivating persons with complementary skills?

Are the founders control freaks?

Many people leave larger companies because they want to be their own boss. The simple fact is that no one is really their own boss. An entrepreneur must answer to many people, including customers, investors, and employees.

For those who have answered these questions to their satisfaction and are not dissuaded from starting a new venture, here are some homework assignments:

1. Hang out with people interested in entrepreneurial ventures.
2. Read extensively about entrepreneurial efforts in newspapers.
3. Join the entrepreneurial network. Talk to people. Get on mailing lists from the Big Three accounting firms, law firms, etc.
4. Read biographies—not only of today's entrepreneurs, but of those who have innovated in the past.
5. Ask what traits the person had that enable him or her to succeed. How did the person handle failure?
6. Above all, constantly plumb the soul and consider motivations.

*By Joe Hadzima and George Pilla, **jhadzima@world.std.com**. Joseph G. Hadzima, Jr. is a partner and co-director at the Boston-based corporate law firm Sullivan & Worcester, where he heads the High Technology/New Ventures Group. He is also a visiting faculty member at the MIT Sloan School of Management.*

INTERNET LINKS

The links in this book hook you into the **Internet**, your key to keeping up with what's happening in business and the world.

All of the links included in our text are listed on our Web page at **http://management.swcollege.com**. Our Internet hot links to business and general publications, statistics, associations, and other resources are available and continually updated through our home page. Throughout the text we will highlight useful sites. Remember the Internet's resources are limited only by the amount of time you have available to surf the "Net."

As you read through this book and work through the Action Steps that lead you to a Business Plan, you can access a wealth of information, ask questions of experts, communicate with fellow entrepreneurs, and discover marketing and financial

Internet (Net) Electronic window to the world.

FIGURE 1.2
Business Plan Outline

SBA Business Plan Basic Outline

Below is a sample outline for a Business Plan.

1. Cover sheet
2. Statement of purpose
3. Table of contents

I. The Business
   A. Description of business
   B. Marketing
   C. Competition
   D. Operating procedures
   E. Personnel
   F. Business insurance
   G. Financial data

II. Financial Data
   A. Loan application
   B. Capital equipment and supply list
   C. Balance sheet
   D. Break-even analysis
   E. Proforma income projections (profit & loss statements)
      Three-year summary
      Detail by month, first year
      Detail by quarters, second and third years
      Assumptions upon which projections were based
   F. Proforma cash flow
      Follow guidelines for letter E.

III. Supporting Documents
   - Tax returns of principals for last three years
   - Personal financial statement (all banks have these forms)
   - In the case of a franchised business, a copy of franchise contract and all supporting documents provided by the franchisor
   - Copy of proposed lease or purchase agreement for building space
   - Copy of licenses and other legal documents
   - Copy of resumes of all principals
   - Copy of letters of intent from suppliers, etc

For more information, see **www.sba.gov/starting/indexbusplans.html** (accessed December 20, 2000).

resources on the Internet. For example, if you had typed in the Internet address **www.sba.gov** previously cited, you would have reached the Small Business Administration's home page, which was active as this book went to press. If you type in an address and come up empty—websites on the Internet come and go at warp speed—persevere and you will find your desired site or one that replaced it.

Web Link Starting Points

- **www.sba.gov**
- **www.entreworld.com**
- **www.brint.com**
- **www.entrepreneurs.about.com**
- **www.allbusiness.com**
- **www.inc.com**
- **www.fastcompany.com**
- **www.nfib.com**
- **www.smartbiz.com**

We'll be linking to the Internet as we move through the phases of the book—personal assessment, trends, location, number-crunching, legal issues, and writing the plan. For example, if you'd like to review sample Business Plans, turn to the last chapter and the appendices in this book; or, you could link to the Internet at **www.business-plan.com** and **www.bplans.com.** The World Wide Web offers numerous examples (some are free, some are for sale) of how to blueprint your business. This book shows you how to sharpen your vision so that you can write the Business Plan you need to achieve success in a fast-changing world. A basic sample Business Plan outline is shown in Figure 1.2. As you follow the action steps, you will be building your own personal Business Plan for your great adventure.

KNOCKING AT THE ENTREPRENEURIAL DOORS

There are three doorways to small business ownership. Doorway I is buying an ongoing business: You search, locate a business that you like, and buy it. Sounds pretty easy, doesn't it? A business broker will make it sound even easier, so beware!

Doorway II is buying a franchise: You find a logo you like—one with national visibility—and buy it. In exchange for your money, the franchisor may (or may not) supply you with inventory, advice, training, buying power, a shorter learning curve, and a product or service that is well-known in the marketplace. Sounds pretty easy, doesn't it? A slick franchisor will make it sound even easier.

Doorway III, our favorite, is starting a new business—a business that is compatible with your interests, skills, and passions, one that is also backed up by careful research that demonstrates strong customer need. Entering the world of small business by any of these doorways demands a carefully designed Business Plan—words and numbers written out on paper that guide you through the gaps, competition, bureaucracies, products, and services. The Action Steps presented in this book will provide you with all the necessary elements to complete a Business Plan. We hope to show you how to have fun as an entrepreneur as you collect the essential pieces for your plan.

What About These Three Doorways?

More than two-thirds of all entrepreneurs enter the world of small business by buying an existing business or investing in a franchise operation. When these people have gained some experience and confidence, many of them decide to start a totally new business from scratch. Few entrepreneurs are happy with just one business. They start up; they sell; they start up again—and they become experts at writing Business Plans.

No matter which doorway you choose, you're going to need a Business Plan. If you buy an ongoing business you may inherit the seller's Business Plan. However, it's advisable to write one of your own. Ask the seller (again and again, if necessary) for the data you need to write your own plan before you finalize the sale. That way—before you commit to a purchase—you can check out those claims of huge potential profits and endless goodwill.

If you invest in a franchise, you'll be buying a Business Plan from the franchisor. But until you see it you won't know for certain if you'll need to prepare one of your own as well. If you don't understand the franchisor's plan, ask questions and, by all means, write your own plan addressing the needs of your particular customers and marketplace. Writing a Business Plan is a lot cheaper than plunking down money on a franchise that may not be successful.

If you start your own business, a Business Plan is a must, an absolute must! That plan stands between you and failure.

The world is changing, and you must assess the changes and act accordingly. You want to survive. You want to have fun. You want your life to have meaning. You want substance and honesty and security and success. So, to decide which road to take, begin your research and keep your eyes and ears wide open.

Personal financial security obtained by employment in large companies continues to wane. Many people are recognizing that self-employment through one of the three doorways described is often the most secure and rewarding career option. This text is written to help you take control of your business and personal life and prepare you to enter one of the three doors.

The Age of the Entrepreneur

If the business world is changing faster and faster—revving up like a high-speed motor—what do you do? If life is not what you imagined it would be when you were in high school, what do you do? If the big firm you targeted as your dream employer is busy downsizing, if the job you trained for is now obsolete, if the position you now have is spoiled by office politics—what do you do?

If you have a great idea for a product but your employer doesn't believe in it, what do you do? If you have found a great location for a small unique restaurant on your

ACTION STEP 1

ADVENTURE NOTEBOOK

If you're a typical entrepreneur, you probably write 90 percent of your important data on the back of an envelope. That might have been okay in the past, but now that you're doing this for real, purchase an organizer and some type of container (a shoebox, a briefcase, a folder) in which to store your information. The best—and recommended way—to organize your data is to compile an **Adventure Notebook**, something with pockets, so that you can keep track of small items such as articles, advertisements, and business cards. For some, utilizing their notebook computers or personal digital assistant (PDA) may work best.

Your **Adventure Notebook** should include:

1. a twelve-month calendar
2. an appointment calendar
3. a priority list of things you need to do
4. your name and phone number (on the front cover, in case you leave it someplace)
5. an idea list (continue to add items to this throughout your search)
6. a "new eyes" list for keeping track of successful and not-so-successful businesses you come across, plus notes about the reasons for their success or failure
7. a list of possible team members (Who impresses you and why? What are their key attributes?)
8. articles and statistics you gather that serve as supportive data for your Business Plan
9. a list of helpful websites
10. a list of possible "taxi squad" members—experts who can serve as resource people when you need them, such as a lawyer, a CPA, bankers, successful businesspeople, and so on
11. a list of potential customers
12. a list of names and phone numbers of contacts for goods and services

Your Adventure Notebook will become the heart of your Business Plan.

Adventure Notebook Storage place for personal, valuable business information.

last vacation in Sun Valley, what do you do? If you saw a great product on your trip to Hungary and think it would sell well in Cedar Falls, Iowa, what do you do?

Get up to speed. Upgrade your computer. Surf the Internet for opportunities. Figure out who you are and what you want from life. Think with your pencil while you figure out how much you're willing to pay for the "good life." How much time are you willing to spend? How much money? How much sweat? How much risk?

REV UP

Small companies (with fewer than 100 employees) employ more than half of the workers in the United States. New start-ups create new jobs. These jobs are created by an absolutely unique partnership—the marriage of money and hard work. The money comes from savings, friends, family, credit cards, second mortgages, bank loans, venture capitalists, and angels. Hard work, faith, and passion come from the driving force of the entrepreneur and from those who trust the entrepreneur. In the first decade of the twenty-first century, entrepreneurship should blossom and grow. The fields—biotechnology, software, short-run manufacturing, telecommunication, and others—are ripe and ready for the harvest, so plant early. The new millennium will certainly be the Age of the Entrepreneur.

Ready to Start?

First, you need to get organized. Action Step 1 will help you to do that. Some people believe that getting organized stifles creativity. Jan Wilkes was like that until she saw the value of using her **Adventure Notebook** in developing a new Internet travel business—Romantic Escapes.

Romantic Escapes—From Adventure Notebook to Internet Business

During her five years working as a travel agent for three different travel agencies, Jan kept a diary form of notebook, listing what seemed to be important elements of the travel business, her contacts, news and magazine articles, ideas, competitors' ads, and business cards. Her Internet guru friend, Pat Perk, tired of working for other people, enthusiastically agreed to be her partner.

With their combined knowledge of the travel business and the Internet, they developed a Net travel business. After reviewing her notes, Jan looked for a gap in the marketplace. She realized that many of her clients were looking for short breakaway escapes. Pat suggested they tap into the Internet by focusing on using websites that offered weekend discounts on cars, hotels, and airfares. After extensive research, Jan and Pat repackaged these deals into great regional weekend escapes. By adding extras such as dinners, flowers, theater tickets, and limousine services, romantic weekend escapes for Southern Californian lovers emerged.

Now they had to determine how to reach their market. They were fortunate in that Jan had retained most of her past clients' phone numbers and addresses. She and Pat sent postcards announcing their new online Internet service and requested all to come online to give them their e-mail addresses and a chance to win a free trip. Surprisingly, 30 percent responded. Once online, they were asked to fill out detailed questionnaires about their travel desires for weekend escapes.

They now had the information they needed—the market and their desires. Every Wednesday at noon, Romantic Escapes posted their weekend escapes. Wednesday through Friday they were busy booking trips. Within six months, they were profitable and customers quickly became repeat customers. Sales rapidly increased due to word of mouth and excellent publicity through a travel column highlighting a couple's recent romantic rendevous. Romance was in the air and money was in the bank for Pat and Jan.

Why Do You Want to Be an Entrepreneur?

For some, becoming an entrepreneur is a lifelong dream, for others it's buying a job. It's the excitement of an unlimited income or a way to pay the bills. It's the dream of never having a boss or the dream of being the boss. It's the desire to leave a legacy. It's the joy of producing the perfect product. It's the thrill of developing a new service. It's the desire to live out your dreams and passions as the following entrepreneurs are.

One entrepreneur opened her retail store to keep an eye on her three teenagers. Ten years later she owns five stores. One of her teenagers (now 27) manages her stores, and the other (now 25) manages the chain's finances. She not only has built a chain of stores but a legacy for her children. Not willing to stop at this point, she and her daughter are already designing a new store concept.

Sam wanted to improve children's lives. He researched businesses that served children and located and purchased a Sylvan Learning Center franchise.

With a love of basketball and kids, Felix developed a summer basketball camp for 8- to 12-year-olds, using his local courts. The successful camp paid for four years of Felix's tuition bills!

Complete Action Step 2 to discover your entrepreneurial motives. Your job situation can change quickly, your life situation may change, or your job and personal desires may change like Sally Honeycutt Binson's did.

Action Step 2

WHY DO I WANT TO BE AN ENTREPRENEUR?
In your Adventure Notebook make a list of all the reasons why you want to become an entrepreneur. Think about your personal, family, financial, and professional lifestyle and your social, spiritual, and ego needs.

Now prioritize your list. Spend a few minutes now and many many hours throughout the next few months reviewing how several businesses would fit into your prioritized list. What fits? What doesn't?

Review your current job situation. Are you happy? Are you excited about going to work each day? Is there something else you'd rather be doing? If money were no object, what would you do?

As you explore various businesses, continue to return to these lists and questions to focus on whether or not your selected business ideas will meet your entrepreneurial focus and passion.

Make a list of all the reasons you do not want to become an entrepreneur. Review the list. What can you do to minimize these issues as you become an entrepreneur? When you honestly review the advantages and disadvantages of being an entrepreneur they are the flip side of each other. Many people want to become entrepreneurs to be their own boss and find out they now have many bosses-employees, customers, suppliers, and investors! Be sure to look realistically at these lists and keep refining them as you seek fulfillment of your passions and dreams.

Marketeer to Writer-Entrepreneur

When she turned 30, Sally Honeycutt Binson took a good look at her life. Sally lived in Charleston, South Carolina; had a good job as a marketing director of a restaurant chain; and earned a good salary. Her home—sunny with a view of the water—was wonderful. But Sally paid a price for the "good life" with endless meetings, squabbles with her boss (a second vice president), and lots of air miles.

To plot her future in the twenty-first century, Sally drew a mind map (Figure 1.4). When she put herself inside a bubble in the center of the page, she didn't get anywhere. When she added "Internet" inside a bubble she found a new career: freelance writer. Sally had a degree in English literature and read many books. As a savvy entrepreneur, Sally created a home office and began to write. Her first effort was rejected by agents and publishers. Sally then researched her local bookstore. She found large sections with romance, mystery, and science fiction. Using her marketing knowledge, she took bookstore managers to lunch and asked: What was selling? What did readers want? What did editors want? Which books received the most promotion?

Armed with information about book sales and target readers, Sally enrolled in a writing course at her local community college. The instructor was a published author. With his guidance, Sally studied the mystery genre.

Before she began writing her second book, Sally checked out websites for anything related to mystery. At ***www.MysteryNet.com*** *she found a homepage for mystery: writing, selling reader's group,* ***webzines****. Sally joined two organizations: Mystery Writers of America and Sisters in Crime. A contact from Sisters in Crime connected Sally to several literary agents.*

As she networked from one hotlink to another, Sally discovered discussion groups, sometimes called ***newsgroups,*** *that gave her information on the latest trends in mystery writing. Her favorite news group was Dorothy L, named for the famous British author, Dorothy L. Sayers.*

A Book Is a Product

With her strong marketing background, Sally visualized her book as a product for the marketplace. Before she developed her product, she engaged in intensive research and development (R&D) by analyzing ten mystery novels.

Webzines Magazines on the Web.

Newsgroups Group of individuals with similar interests on the Net.

FIGURE 1.3
PC and Pixel

SOURCE: **www.pccomix.com** (accessed January 31, 2001).

FIGURE 1.4
Mind Map for Mystery Writer Sally Honeycutt Binson

Mind mapping: Begin with a trigger word, then explore and write down all the words and concepts that come into your mind. Connect similar ideas with lines. Explore the niches and ideas that you discover.

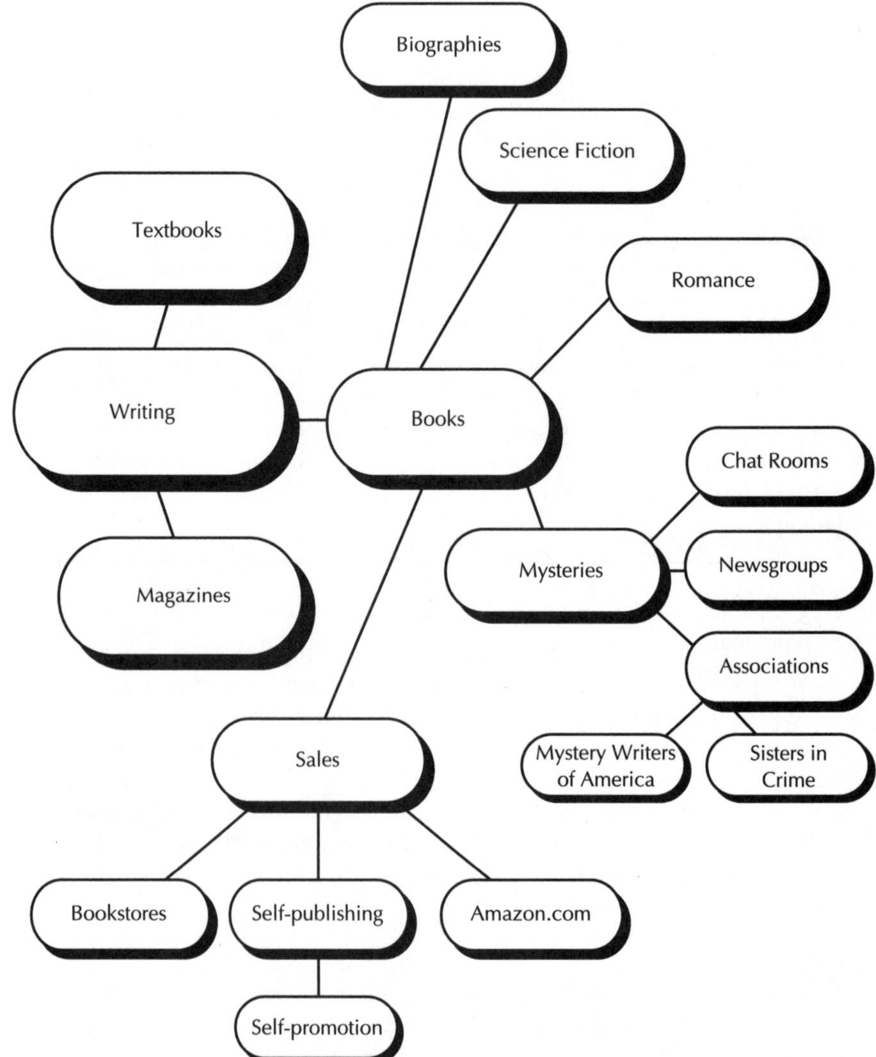

Using the analytical techniques she learned in college, Sally discovered the secret of mystery writing: conceal and then reveal. Following her instructor's advice, the setting of her first mystery was a location Sally was familiar with: an island off the coast of South Carolina. Because she could relate easily to her own gender's thinking patterns, Sally's main characters were female: the sleuth, the victim, and the killer. The police bungle the investigation, leaving a niche for the sleuth.

Sally wrote on weekends and holidays and revised and edited on plane trips. In one year, Sally had a manuscript. Although her agent connections through Sisters in Crime didn't work out, Sally did find an agent through the Internet.

She mailed a plot outline and the first three chapters. The agent sold the book to a publisher. The publisher sold film rights to a film director and Sally consulted on the script. Her first mystery novel, Murder on Drake Island, *became a best-seller and the movie's success gained her access to Hollywood.*

When the royalty checks were enough to pay back her advance from the publisher, Sally tendered her resignation at her office. By then, her second book was underway: Murder on Cannon Beach.

ACTION STEP 3

REVIEW YOUR FINANCIAL AND FAMILY PICTURE

Sit down with your family to discuss how opening your own business may affect the family's financial future. Complete the Personal Financial Statement and Budget, which can be found in Appendix C.

You will need these figures later to determine your financial needs and also to assess the financial contribution you will be able to make to your business.

After completing the above, ask yourself: Can I live on less? How much less? What can I cut from my budget? How long can I continue before feeling too deprived?

Talk with your family about the time and money sacrifices that may be involved in developing your new venture. A business is a living, breathing entity, and it takes time for the golden egg to hatch. Be prepared to wait a while.

The following websites will assist you in preparing budgets and financial planning issues:

www.quicken.com
www.cnnfn.com
www.fidelity.com

WHAT IS YOUR CURRENT FAMILY AND FINANCIAL PICTURE?

Action Step 3 will help you assess your current situation as you prepare for the future. Is your family dreaming the same dream? If so, that's great. If not, ask what they are willing to do to help. Family support is an essential element to achieve a successful entrepreneurial lifestyle.

Review your current financial picture. Complete the personal financial statement and budget in Appendix B. Sit down with your family and review how you can reduce expenses. For many, short-term financial pain is worth long-term gain; for others it is not worth it! Before leaping into the new venture decide what you and your family are willing to sacrifice.

Believing in your dream opens your eyes to endless possibilities. Living at home for an extra year to save cash, working a part-time job to support your fledgling business, or moving to a less-expensive area of the country all become realistic options if one believes in his or her own dream. Amilya Antonetti, founder of Soapworks, and her husband were willing to leave their jobs, sell their home, and risk everything for their dream. What are you willing to give up for your dream?

WHAT DOES IT TAKE TO BE AN ENTREPRENEUR?

To find out if you have what it takes to make it in small business, profile yourself as an entrepreneur in Action Step 4 and complete the questionnaire in Table 1.1. You won't be a perfect fit because there is no such thing.

In following the action steps throughout the text you will benefit more from this book if you mentally immerse yourself in a new and exciting venture. Even if you do not end up following through with your Business Plan, you will have learned the process. One never knows when the entrepreneurial passion will start to burn, and you will already know the process and be able to follow your dream with a Business Plan.

Entrepreneurship isn't for everyone, and even if it is for you, you'll need some help along the way. Keep your mind open and your pencil sharp. The opportunities are unlimited.

Afar Bhide (Harvard School of Business) believes that there is no "ideal" entrepreneurial personality. "Successful founders can be gregarious or taciturn, analytical or intuitive, risk-adverse or thrill-seeking."

ACTION STEP 4

SELF-ASSESSMENT

- Complete the questionnaire in Table 1.1.
- If your entrepreneurial juices are flowing, surf the following:

www.sba.gov/BI/quiz.html Quiz for Small Business Success

new.innonet.ch Are You the Entrepreneurial Type?

www.keirsey.com Myers-Briggs Personality Test

future.sri.com/vals/surveynew.shtml Psychographic Profiling

www.toolkit.cch.com Business Owner's Toolkit

Compile a list of:

- things you love to do.
- skills you have acquired through the years.
- things you are good at.
- the times you were happiest in your life.
- your values.
- your passions.
- your financial dreams.
- your past dreams.

Study your lists and profiles. In Action Step 5, you will be pulling together all your information. Add new items to the lists whenever they occur to you. Keep your lists current and continue to refine the lists as you continue to work on your Business Plan.

TABLE 1.1

25 Questions to Answer to See if You Have What It Takes to Be an Entrepreneur

So you want to start a business on your own, be your own person, be an entrepreneur! To find out more, answer the following 25 questions. If you really have what it takes, you should be able to answer each question, easily, with a "yes!"

1. When you've been disappointed, have you dealt with it and come back with a positive state of mind?
2. Do you like to be the center of attraction, sell yourself or the business you're in?
3. Is it easy for you to be organized?
4. Do you know how to take control of your life and be disciplined?
5. Are you a risk-taker?
6. Do you have a vivid imagination and know how to express your creative side?
7. Are you able to take what seems like a detriment and turn it into an opportunity?
8. Are you courageous and patient?
9. Is your family in a position to cope with the lack of freedom you will experience when you start your new business?
10. Do you know how to fight for what you believe in?
11. Do you like people?
12. Have you ever had any management experience?
13. Do you dread routine?
14. Are you reliable and self-confident?
15. Do you ignore the judgement of others when you really believe in someone or something?
16. Do you have a knack for influencing others?
17. Do others describe you as an enthusiastic person, full of life?
18. Do you like the idea of working alone most of the time?
19. Do you enjoy being on the telephone and talking to strangers?
20. Do you wake up early in the morning with a positive attitude?
21. Is your financial situation stable? (You should have enough money to get by for at least one year before you venture out on your own.)
22. Have you done your homework—studied all materials that cover the business you are going to start?
23. Do you know how to laugh at yourself?
24. Is it easy to control your temper with others?
25. Do you get bored easily?

If these are easy questions, you're a born entrepreneur!

SOURCE: **www.smartbiz.com** (accessed April 4, 2001).

Entrepreneurial Success

Starting one's own business allows a person to design his or her own successful lifestyle. Action Step 5 asks you to design your "entrepreneurial lifestyle." Warren Bennis, author of *Organizing Genius,* developed a four-question test aimed at anyone seeking "success." The questions are:

1. Do you know the difference between what you want and what you're good at?
2. Do you know what drives you and what gives you satisfaction?
3. Do you know what your values and priorities are, what your organization's values and priorities are, and can you identify the differences between the two?
4. Having measured the differences between what you want and what you're able to do, between what drives you and what satisfies you, and between your values and those of your organization, are you able to overcome those differences?

Bennis concludes that the key to success is identifying those modules of talent—unique to you—and then finding the right arena in which to use them.

Success is personal and subjective; whereas income and return on investments are measurable. Success wears many faces. You need to think about this as you start your adventure. Action Step 5, the Success Checklist (see page 13), and a review of the following Killer and Success Factors for Entrepreneurs will help you. Add any other items that signify success to you.

INCREDIBLE RESOURCE

THE ENTREPRENEUR'S MIND

www.benlore.com/index.html

Log on to the Internet and gain access to the minds of successful entrepreneurs. Bertucci's, Mecklermedia, Nantucket Nectars, and id Software have all been profiled recently. Reading about other people who are willing to risk their time and money for their dreams keeps entrepreneurial juices flowing.

The Entrepreneur's Mind (EM) is an Internet resource that presents an array of real-life stories and advice on the many different facets of entrepreneurship and emerging businesses written by successful entrepreneurs and industry experts. Each EM article presents in-depth profiles of entrepreneurs telling how they grew their successful companies, as well as interviews with industry professionals discussing starting and growing new businesses.

Review "The Trade-Off Game" and "Key Strategies for Small Business" presented by Arthur Anderson. Global entrepreneurial ventures are also highlighted on this website to encourage entrepreneurs to stretch outside U.S. borders.

Visit this website on a regular basis for online entrepreneurial pep juice!

For additional success stories, log on to: **www.microsoft.com/business/default.asp**
www.fastcompany.com
www.inc.com

The Ten Killer Factors

1. **Weak Personality:** The lack of sound psychological or emotional strength at the head of a company leads to failure 50 percent of the time. If company founders cannot cope with the many challenges they must confront and if they have private problems as well, a collapse is predetermined.
2. **The Loner Syndrome:** Loners have a difficult life. Because they don't discuss their problems with colleagues or professionals, they lose that critical distance, the perspective, to their projects. They flounder with closed eyes into failure.
3. **Nebulous Business Ideas:** Losers don't know how to make their ideas work. They don't familiarize themselves with the market and don't know their competition or their potential customers.
4. **No Plan:** If a clear concept is missing, one false decision follows another. When requested, a business plan is submitted to the bank, but it seldom has anything to do with reality. It is written just to be convincing.
5. **Too Little Financial Backing:** There are always young entrepreneurs who succeed without beginning capital. But then modesty is called for. Many founders use too much money too early for private purposes. Too little financial substance leads immediately to problems. A general rule of thumb has it that one-third of the balance or two-thirds of the fixed assets should come from one's own capital.
6. **Cash-flow Troubles:** Entrepreneurs without knowledge of business management and who fail to exercise cash-flow management are responsible for their own downfall. Many naively believe that their customers will pay within 30 days. The opposite is true. If salaries and suppliers cannot be paid, then any attempt to save the sinking ship comes too late.
7. **No Marketing Strategy:** According to statistics, one-third of young entrepreneurs disappear from the market because of insufficient marketing. An amateurish market approach undermines credibility. A lack of trust results in a lack of business.
8. **No Controlling:** Ignoring the need for a good evaluation system usually results in realizing too late that something has gone wrong, so it's virtually impossible to turn the situation around and correct it.
9. **The Wrong People:** Hiring the wrong people is the quickest way to lose a lot of money very fast.
10. **Underestimating the Competition:** Good ideas are not the perfect guarantee for getting a good hold in the market. The competition is not sleeping. It takes the offensive and tries to make up for opportunities it missed. New developments that are undertaken without first checking out the chances on the market simply cost a lot of money.

ACTION STEP 5

"INC. YOURSELF"

Mind map your way to a picture of what you want you to become, your product—"YOURSELF" (see Figure 1.4). There is no such thing as a wrong idea or a wrong direction.

So far you have looked at why you want to be an entrepreneur, what success means to you, and have reviewed your skills, accomplishments, and passions. It's now time for you to mind map the life you want.

Review your answers to Action Steps 2-4. Draw a circle in the middle of a piece of paper. Write your name inside the circle. Close your eyes for a few minutes, and allow your imagination to take over. Think of yourself as a product. In 5 to 10 years, where and what do you want to be? What do you want your product to be? What do you want—personally, socially, spiritually, financially, family, friends, hobbies, lifestyle—and what are your material wants and needs? You can predict your future as well as anyone else; all you need to do is mesh information with your imagination and go for it!

If you "Inc. yourself," you'll be ready to explore the many business opportunities available which fit your needs. By meshing your personal desires with your business desires you are more likely to find success.

Success Checklist

Do you measure success in dollars? If so, how many? $__________

Do you measure success in other ways?

- Being able to enjoy a certain lifestyle
- Dealing with friendly customers who appreciate the service
- Power
- Being able to live and work where you want
- Providing employment for others
- Being the best business in your area
- Time to enjoy your children and hobbies
- Participating in teamwork
- Building a legacy
- Early retirement
- Fame
- Making peoples' lives safer
- Recognition
- Helping others
- ________________

Action Step 6

Survey Your Friends About Successful Businesses

The next time you're at a party or with a group of your colleagues and there's a lull in the conversation, pass out paper and pencils and ask them to list three to five small businesses they perceive as successful. Then ask them to list the signs of those firms' success and the reasons for their success.

Group the negative thinkers together in a devil's advocate group and have them list unsuccessful businesses and point out the reasons why those firms are losing.

If you continue to assess businesses in your selected industry and other industries you will begin to recognize many factors that are constant throughout. Keep your eyes and ears open at all times!

The Ten Success Factors

1. **Willingness to Succeed:** Successful entrepreneurs spare no expense. They must be prepared to work 50 to 60 hours a week and give up holidays. For that, they need the support of their families.
2. **Self-Confidence:** Only those who believe in themselves will achieve their goals. That calls for optimism and trust in the future. Founders must take on challenges and confront constant changes and should not be afraid of making mistakes.
3. **A Clear Business Idea:** The idea has to be right. The heads of companies know their strengths and weaknesses and their competition. They know the reason for their success, whether it's because they have better products, better service, or a more intelligent sales and marketing approach.
4. **The Business Plan:** The business plan is the key to building up a company. This instrument, which is always being adapted to the latest developments, makes it possible to proceed with a systematic plan of action, to recognize problems in their early stages so that the proper corrective measures can be taken in plenty of time.
5. **Exact Control of Finances:** A young entrepreneur doesn't have to be swimming in money. But success usually doesn't come as quickly as anticipated. That's why financial resources should be calculated somewhat generously. An entrepreneur must understand something about business management, know how to react quickly, and have finances and cash flow under control. Any profits are reinvested in the company.
6. **Targeted Marketing:** Only entrepreneurs who have a clear concept about how to introduce a product or service to the market will be able to succeed.
7. **A Step Ahead of the Competition:** Success must be worked on constantly. It includes a plan for research and development, so that an advantage in the market isn't lost. Acting instead of reacting will supply the advantage.
8. **Management Support:** Young entrepreneurs' powers increase if they can fall back on the knowledge of experienced entrepreneurs. Possible advisers to call on would be financiers or successful colleagues who are also entrepreneurs. This can also open doors for company founders that might otherwise be closed to them.
9. **Cooperation:** No one is top in every field. Building up a network of cooperation often provides access to additional know-how that would otherwise cost a lot of money.
10. **Clear Company Structure:** A successful company has a clear structure. The employees are motivated and know exactly what their responsibilities are. The customers know who to contact.

Source: **new.innonet.ch** (accessed May 1, 1999).

Defining Business Success

Action Step 6 is optional, but it's fun! Thinking about business success can be stimulating and enlightening. What makes a business successful? Unsuccessful? How do you measure success? How do your friends measure it?

You and your friends can merely speculate about which businesses are doing well financially. Only a detailed examination of each business's books will give the whole picture, but we still urge you to exercise your marketplace intuition. Personal observation is a good way to become more aware of what is happening to small firms in your community and your selected industry. For example, next time you dine out try to estimate:

- the number of customers in the restaurant.
- the total number of customers the restaurant serves each day.
- the average price per meal.
- the number of employees.
- the number of cars in the parking lot.

Then multiply the average per-meal price by the total number of daily customers. Perform your estimations on different days of the week and at different hours. Do

GLOBAL VILLAGE

WORLD ECONOMIC DATA TO PONDER

COUNTRY	GNP PER CAPITA	WORLD RANK
Switzerland	$39,980	3
Japan	$32,350	7
United States	$29,240	10
United Kingdom	$21,410	22
New Zealand	$14,600	36
Hungary	$4,510	71
Jamaica	$1,740	108
Morocco	$1,240	124
China	$750	145
India	$440	161
Ethiopia	$100	206

According to the recent World Bank Group's Development Data, "One-sixth of the world's people produce 78 percent of the world's goods and services and receive 78 percent of the world's income—an average of $70 a day. Three-fifths of the world's people in the poorest 61 countries receive 6 percent of the world's income—less than $2 a day."

As you venture around the world as a potential global entrepreneur, you need to be aware of economic conditions that will preclude your selling medium- and high-ticket items in many countries. However, a huge market for basic products and services, clean water, electricity, communications, and infrastructure exists throughout the world. The global entrepreneur will view the above statistics as an opportunity, not a threat, to their business ventures.

Half of U.S. exporters employ fewer than five people, so explore and find the right opportunity for you. The possibilities are endless!

Based on 1998 Data
SOURCE: **www.worldbank.org/data** (accessed May 1, 2001).

COMMUNITY RESOURCE

Share Your Passions and Your Dreams
The Young Entrepreneur's Resource Guide

by Stephanie Klein
Web exclusive of FSB (Fortune Small Business)

Even would-be dotcom millionaires have to start somewhere. Joining a networking organization can be an easy way to build valuable contacts and expand your business knowledge. Here are some good ones to consider.

Association for Collegiate Entrepreneurs (www.acecanada.ca)
Based in Canada, this not-for-profit international organization has chapters at colleges throughout the U.S. Offering events like annual conferences and contests, it focuses on teaching young people how to thrive in the new economy.

Collegiate Entrepreneurs Organization (www.c-e-o.org)
Partake in leadership training and professional development programs through this national network of young business owners.

Students in Free Enterprise (www.sife.org)
Run by a 25-year-old, international non-profit organization, this site provides mentors to collegiate entrepreneurs.

The Idea Café (www.ideacafe.com)
This hip site is chock full of features designed to appeal to GenX self-starters, ranging from how-to articles to profiles of young entrepreneurs. If you need to vent your business woes, try out the Cyberschmooze message boards.

ACTION STEP 7

INTERVIEW ENTREPRENEURS

Interview at least three people who are self-employed. One should be in your area of interest. If you are a potential competitor, you may need to travel 50 miles or more to find an interview subject willing to help you.

Successful entrepreneurs love to tell the story of how they achieved success. Be up front about the type of information you need and why you want it. Then make appointments with them at their convenience. Look for the passion behind their success.

Prepare for your interviews. Open-ended questions are best because they leave room for embellishment. Some suggestions are:

- What were your first steps?
- How did you arrange financing?
- If you had it to do all over again, would you do anything differently?
- How large a part does creativity play in your particular business?
- Are your rewards tangible? Intangible?
- What was your best marketing technique?
- What proportion of gross sales do you spend on advertising?
- Did you hire more employees than you originally thought you'd need?
- What makes your business unique?
- How did you write your Business Plan?
- Are gross profits all you expected them to be?

Depending on how you relate to your subject, you might be able to think of these first interviewees as sources of marketplace experience. They may help when you begin to assemble your "taxi squad": your lawyer, accountant, banker, and so on.

It is helpful to take notes during interviews. If you use a cassette recorder, be sure to ask permission. Don't worry about evaluations at this stage. The information will assemble into patterns sooner than you think. Be sure to send a personal handwritten thank-you note. You will be amazed at how much help you receive from fellow entrepreneurs.

The National Foundation for Teaching Entrepreneurship (www.nfte.com)
Low-income teens can learn new business skills through school-based programs run by this national non-profit.

Young Entrepreneurs Organization (www.yeo.org)
More than 3,000 young entrepreneurs belong to this well-regarded group, which runs educational forums and support groups for entrepreneurs.

Young Entrepreneurs Network (www.youngandsuccessful.com)
Run by Jennifer Kushell, author of *The Young Entrepreneur's Edge,* this site offers members access to a directory of other business owners, a bartering network, and member discounts on business supplies and services. Non-members have access to a library of resources. YEN also works with Ernst & Young to pick a Young Entrepreneur of the Year.

Young Presidents' Organization (www.ypo.org)
If you're the chairman, CEO, or president of your company, are under 44, and run a company that's big enough to meet YPO's tough standards, this could be an excellent networking venue.

SOURCE: **www.fsb.com** (accessed March 1, 2001).

this for other businesses you patronize as well. Soon you'll begin to get the feel for which businesses are losing and which are winning customers. If you observe small businesses with your new eyes, success factors will begin to emerge.

Now, attempt to develop a business's profit profile. In the course of your interview (see Action Step 7), try to ascertain key numbers, such as gross sales, cost of goods sold, rent, salaries (owner, management), how much is spent on marketing (advertising, commissions, promotions, and so on). You can estimate the other expenses and arrive at a range that will give you perspective when it comes time to work with your own numbers.

For example, let's assume a business with $500,000 in sales. The cost of goods sold (COGS) averages 53 percent; rent is $2000; and total salaries are 15 percent of gross sales. The company spends 6 percent of their gross on marketing. These are the only numbers you acquired from the interview. Based on these numbers, you can estimate benefits, including FICA (social security) costs, at 20 to 30 percent of salaries; and other expenses (supplies, utilities, accounting, legal, auto, entertainment, and so on) at 8 to 12 percent. Combining what you have been given with your estimates yields the profit profile shown below.

On the high side, the profit profile is slightly better than 10 percent, or $51,000. On the low side, it's slightly below 5 percent, or $23,500. (That $23,500 may not be as low as it appears if the owner has already taken salary and auto and entertainment expenses.)

	High Side	**Low Side**
Sales	$500,000	$500,000
Less: COGS (53%)	$265,000	$265,000
Gross Profit	$235,000	$235,000
Less: Marketing (6%)	$30,000	$30,000
Salaries (15%)	$75,000	$75,000
FICA/Benefits	$15,000	$22,500
Rent ($2000/mo.)	$24,000	$24,000
Other Expenses	$40,000	$60,000
Net Profit	$51,000	$23,500

Interviewing Successful Entrepreneurs

Action Step 7 encourages you to interview entrepreneurs primarily within your selected industry—competitors, customers, distributors, suppliers, and wholesalers.

SUMMARY

According to Jim Collins, author of *Built to Last,* one should look at developing a business that looks at the intersection of three circles: (1) What you're good at, (2) What you stand for, and (3) What people will pay you for. You have answered the first two. In Chapter 2, you will be looking at your changing world for opportunities. In later chapters you will discover the right target market: people who possess the dollars to purchase your product or service.

THINK POINTS FOR SUCCESS

Remember:

- We are entrepreneurs. Work is our fun. We seldom sleep.
- Even though you may not be in business yet, you can intensify your focus by writing down your thoughts about the business you think you want to try. Stay flexible.
- Change is accelerating everywhere, and change is what provides you with opportunities to follow your entrepreneurial venture.
- To find the doorway into your own business, gather data and keep asking questions.
- Get reckless on paper before you get reckless in the marketplace.
- Brainstorm.
- Draw mind maps.
- Be sure to confirm your venture with numbers and words before you enter the arena.
- Write a Business Plan.
- Follow your passions.

KEY POINTS FROM ANOTHER VIEW

Top 15 Things I Learned in My First Year in Business

By Evan C. Williams from *Edge Magazine* online

1. I'm not as smart as I think I am.
2. If you don't pay close attention to the numbers, it's like you're running blind.
3. Taking the time and expense to do things right is always cheaper and quicker than doing things in a hurry NOW to buy some time to do things right LATER.
4. It's hard to be passionately committed to seven different projects at once—in fact, two is pushing.
5. There's a limit to the number of things I can do, and do well. Every time you decide to do something new, you have to decide to quit doing something else.
6. Focus. Focus. Focus.
7. I need to think very carefully about what I really want to do before committing to an ongoing, time-obligating project.
8. Make your expectations of those around you very clear; they can't read your mind.
9. Not everyone thinks as I do. (And that's good!)
10. Believe it or not, the rules of success also apply to me.
11. I am much more productive if I balance my life and take care of myself than I am if all I do is work 18 hours a day and eat junk food.
12. If I am floating around, unfocused, unproductive, unenergetic, and in general have a groggy, icky feeling, it is because I don't have a clearly defined worthwhile goal I am excited about. As long as I'm working toward a worthwhile goal, I feel great and accomplish lots.
13. A good way to not make any money is to try very hard to make money.
14. There is a great deal of difference between intellectually understanding something—even if you passionately agree with it—and knowing something. Some things it seems we just choose to learn for ourselves.
15. Knowing the laws of success, the road to riches, and the keys to the universe are not enough. The key lies in exercising the self-discipline to practice what you know.

SOURCE: **www.edgeonline.com** (accessed May 1, 2001).

Spotting Trends and Opportunities

Opening Your Eyes

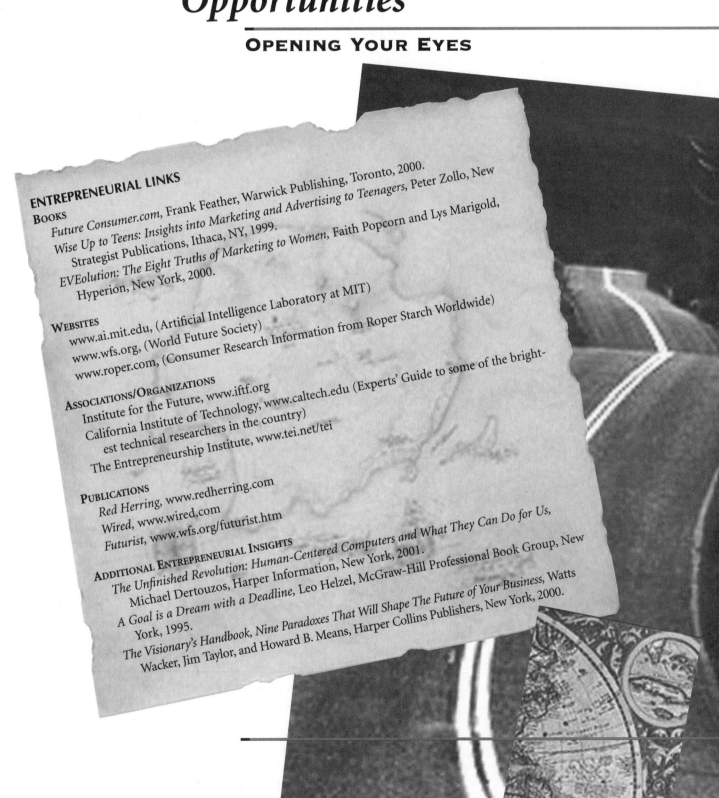

ENTREPRENEURIAL LINKS

Books

Future Consumer.com, Frank Feather, Warwick Publishing, Toronto, 2000.

Wise Up to Teens: Insights into Marketing and Advertising to Teenagers, Peter Zollo, New Strategist Publications, Ithaca, NY, 1999.

EVEolution: The Eight Truths of Marketing to Women, Faith Popcorn and Lys Marigold, Hyperion, New York, 2000.

Websites

www.ai.mit.edu, (Artificial Intelligence Laboratory at MIT)

www.wfs.org, (World Future Society)

www.roper.com, (Consumer Research Information from Roper Starch Worldwide)

Associations/Organizations

Institute for the Future, www.iftf.org

California Institute of Technology, www.caltech.edu (Experts' Guide to some of the brightest technical researchers in the country)

The Entrepreneurship Institute, www.tei.net/tei

Publications

Red Herring, www.redherring.com

Wired, www.wired.com

Futurist, www.wfs.org/futurist.htm

Additional Entrepreneurial Insights

The Unfinished Revolution: Human-Centered Computers and What They Can Do for Us, Michael Dertouzos, Harper Information, New York, 2001.

A Goal is a Dream with a Deadline, Leo Helzel, McGraw-Hill Professional Book Group, New York, 1995.

The Visionary's Handbook, Nine Paradoxes That Will Shape The Future of Your Business, Watts Wacker, Jim Taylor, and Howard B. Means, Harper Collins Publishers, New York, 2000.

LEARNING OBJECTIVES

- Train your eyes, ears, and intuition to read market forces that forecast future needs.
- Understand the "big picture" and its effect on trends and opportunities.
- Learn to become your own "Futurist."
- Understand the changing family structure and its impact on businesses.
- Gain an awareness of the splintering of the mass market and cultural changes.
- Research technological changes and their impact on your industry.
- Understand how to access the vast secondary resources available.
- Become excited about brainstorming techniques.
- Learn how to conduct "new eyes" research.
- Analyze the potential for small business success by applying the life-cycle yardstick to industries.

OPENING YOUR EYES AND MIND TO VAST OPPORTUNITIES

Where can you find a business idea that will really pay off? One that fulfills your passions? One that will make you rich? One that will make you famous? What are the best ventures to pursue today?

Only you can answer these questions because the best opportunity for you is one that you will enjoy, and one that makes money. The best business for you uses those experiences, passions, skills, and aptitudes that are unique to you. The Action Steps in this book are designed to help you discover what is unique about you: Who are you? What are your skills? What turns you on? What special knowledge do you have that distinguishes you from other people?

Look around; check out the new businesses in your town or industry. Which new firms are operating in your selected industry? What new target markets are developing? What could you sell on the Internet? How can you meet the needs of the aging **baby boomers**? What about the **echo boomers**?

As you seek opportunities and formulate your business, consider if your business opportunity possesses *Forbes ASAP*'s following six leading success factors:

1. **Responsiveness to Change**: How well can your company respond to market change?
2. **Market Opportunity**: How big is the potential market for your company's products?
3. **Marketing Expertise**: How good will your company be at selling and marketing into the previously mentioned opportunity?
4. **Human Capital**: Can you build strong management, marketing sales, and support?
5. **Alliances and Partnerships**: Can you build strong partnerships and relationships?
6. **Prospects for Growth**: How fast is the company growing and can it continue to ramp up quickly?

Baby boomers Persons born between 1946 and 1963.

Echo boomers Persons born between 1977 and 1997.

Market segments Identifiable slices of market.

Chapter 2 is designed to help you recognize opportunities in **market segments** so you can define the gaps in the marketplace. You want to be sure your business serves a need; that you will enter the marketplace from a position of strength. It's time to look at your changing world and selected industry to spot trends and opportunities.

Be a trend-spotter and you can ride your way to a successful business. Don't forget to add blood, sweat, tears, energy, enthusiasm, money, passion, and a good idea!

When we began working with entrepreneurs some 20 years ago, we handed out sage advice like "Just find a need and fill it." Now we say, "Examine the marketplace thoroughly for flaws and opportunities and use technology to keep track of your customer's needs continually." We also used to say, "If you're doing business now the same way you did three years ago, you're probably doing many things wrong." Now we say, "If you're doing business today the same way you did six months ago, you should think about a new strategic plan."

Use your marketplace radar to choose a growth segment of a growth industry; to ride the crest of the wave. Choosing the hot growth sector is usually the right way to begin before the trend turns down. Occasionally, however, the trend sours quickly. Twenty years ago one could ride a trend for 5 to 10 years, but now that time is greatly compressed and reaching a profit sooner than later is essential for continuing your business.

If you are already in a small business, or thinking about getting into one, make it easy on yourself by first identifying industries in the growth phase of their **life cycle**. Play "marketplace detective."

Look around you. When you focus in on a particular business, do you sense growth over the long term? Or is it involved with a fad that won't last? For your business, you want a growth industry that will generate new customers quickly, allowing you to build a repeat customer base.

As a small-business owner, one of the things you must have going for you is fast footwork, so you can adjust to change quickly. It's one of your best weapons in the marketplace. But you can benefit from fast footwork only if you operate from a position of knowledge: stay in touch with customers, and keep your ear tuned to the marketplace.

Look before you leap. Brainstorm with your family, friends, colleagues, competitors, and interview your potential customers. Study the marketplace. Read industry journals. Use your **new eyes**. With trained eyes you'll be able to see the big picture. When conducting your research, start with the big picture and work down into your industry and then your competitors and specific marketplace. To jump-start your mind, complete Action Step 8. You may not open a business after taking this class or reading this text, but by keeping an open mind and training your intuition over the next few years an incredible opportunity may be placed in front of you. Allow yourself to dream.

Life Cycles Stages—from birth to death—of a product, business, service, industry, location, target market, and so on.

New eyes Observation with intuition.

Passion

Build Your Future, Inc.

Redefining a Life and Living with Passion

For years Patti Moir dreamed of her **own** business with her **own** schedule, with her **own** office, and her **own** clients. When she turned 55 years old, Patti knew it was time for her to spread her wings and fly into a new life where she would not only help high school students build their futures but she also would build her new future. It would be a future that would include time for herself, her grandchildren, exercising, and most of all time to enjoy the few sun-filled days in Lake Oswego, Oregon. Patti was passionate about finding the correct fit and a balance in her life. After passionately teaching, tutoring, and counseling for more than 30 years and with a secure pension in hand, Patti's vast experience and reputation at one of the leading high schools in the country spurred her on to open an educational counseling service business.

Patti's passion for helping teenagers find their way through the college planning process was a welcome relief to parents and teens. With the trend toward stiffer admission requirements and a much more competitive atmosphere, many parents and teens require a specialist like Patti to maneuver the maze. Patti has definitely found her passion for sunlight and students and as a side benefit has increased her income substantially.

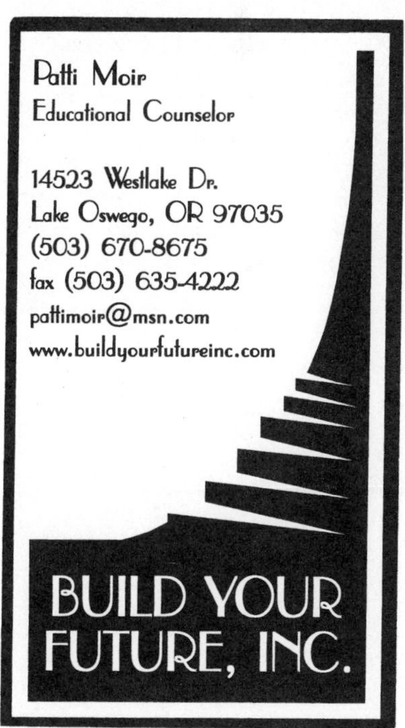

Patti Moir
Educational Counselor
14523 Westlake Dr.
Lake Oswego, OR 97035
(503) 670-8675
fax (503) 635-4222
pattimoir@msn.com
www.buildyourfutureinc.com
BUILD YOUR FUTURE, INC.

ACTION STEP 8

OPENING YOUR MIND TO NEW INFORMATION

Your community and workplace are your marketing labs. It is time to open your mind to all the information around you. Time to head out!

First stop (Large bookstore with lots of magazines): Select and read five distinctly different magazines that you have never read before. What did you learn? Did you read about a target market that you didn't know existed? Next review the top 10 best sellers: fiction, nonfiction, children's, trade, and paperbacks. What does this tell you about your current world?

Second stop (Music store): What's hot? What's not?

Third stop (Local mall): What new stores are opening? Which department store has the best service? Highest prices? Best selection? Which food places are hot? Where are the longest lines?

Fourth stop (Visit your favorite store): Compile a list of all the products and services that were not there 2 years ago (if you are visiting a computer store, shorten the time to 3 or 6 months). Can you guesstimate shelf velocity? What's hot?

Fifth stop (television time): Spend 1 hour watching CNN World Report. Make a list of the stories. Did any surprise you? Are there any opportunities?

Final stop (Log on): Surf the Internet for at least 2 to 4 hours on topics you know nothing about.

Your brain should now be in high gear—and suffering from information overload! Use this information as you continue to explore opportunities.

GLOBAL VILLAGE

WHY GO GLOBAL? LOOK AT THE NUMBERS!!!

World Population by Region

REGION MID 2000 EST.	POPULATION	PERCENT
Africa	784,445,000	13.00
Asia	3,682,550,000	61.00
Europe (inc. Russia)	728,887,000	12.00
Latin America & the Caribbean	519,143,000	9.00
North America	309,631,000	5.00
Oceania	30,393,000	<1.00
Total World	6,055,049,000	

Our world has grown from 3 billion to more than 6 billion in only 40 years! China and India currently comprise almost 40 percent of the world's population. Only one of 20 people in the world live in the United States. Is it any wonder why huge multinational firms are heading off to the rest of the world? You can too!

Which products and services will those who live outside of the United States need? What resources are available? What cultural, financial, and legal obstacles must be overcome to meet the needs of 2050's estimated 9 billion people (two-thirds who will live in urban areas). Potential international customers are being born each minute. Is it time for you to search out opportunities overseas?

To find out, resources on the Internet will be most helpful to you because they are constantly updated. Try the following sites to begin your international search:

- **www.tradeport.org** (assists in searching international markets)
- **www.gcc.net** (in-depth information by country)
- **www.hg.org** (excellent extensive checklists for global ventures and in-depth country information)
- **www.doingbusinessin.com** (Ernst & Young's Passport Online: accounting, business, tax, and investment advice for individual countries)

In addition to Internet resources, search out federal and state trade offices, local colleges with international programs, consulates, embassies, and international chamber of commerce organizations.

SOURCE: United Nations Population Fund, "World Populations Prospects: The 1998 Revision," **www.xist.org** (accessed January 2, 2001).

It's a Dynamic World

- Today's computer chips are 20,000 times faster than chips of 25 years ago.
- Computers and telecommunications have created a global village.
- Software is being developed in 8-hour shifts in three countries: India, the United States, and Ireland.
- Industry deregulation has created incredible opportunities.
- Competition is everywhere and intense.

Environmental Variables

Changes within the business and social world occur within five major environmental variables and examples of those changes follow. Your challenge is threefold: 1) constantly be aware and follow the big picture, which consists of the five major variables; 2) recognize the changes occurring within each variable; and 3) identify opportunities for products or services.

1. Technology—biotechnology, miniaturization, Internet, nanotechnology, genomics, telecommunications, etc.
2. Competition—deregulation, impact of "box stores," international
3. Social/cultural—immigration, single parents, religion, ethnic shifts
4. Legal/political—who is in power, tax laws, changing regulations
5. Economics—recessions, inflation, changing income levels, cost of housing, food prices, energy

Each change within the environmental variables and subsequent trends affect how products are manufactured, marketed, and delivered to customers. Buy and read *Newsweek, Time,* industry journals, newspapers, and any other magazines and begin

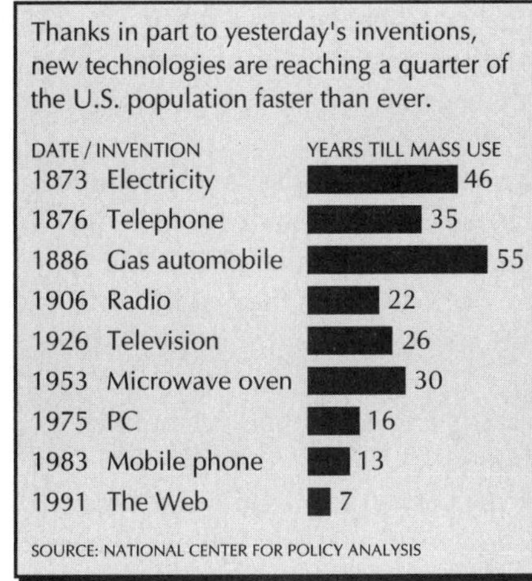

Thanks in part to yesterday's inventions, new technologies are reaching a quarter of the U.S. population faster than ever.
DATE / INVENTION
YEARS TILL MASS USE
1873 Electricity 46
1876 Telephone 35
1886 Gas automobile 55
1906 Radio 22
1926 Television 26
1953 Microwave oven 30
1975 PC 16
1983 Mobile phone 13
1991 The Web 7
SOURCE: NATIONAL CENTER FOR POLICY ANALYSIS

FIGURE 2.1
Reeling in the Years

SOURCE: "Reeling in the Years," *Newsweek,* April 13, 1998, p. 14. Copyright © 1998 Newsweek, Inc. All rights reserved. Reprinted by permission.

ACTION STEP 9

CHANGES=TRENDS=OPPORTUNITIES

Environmental Variables	Changes /Trends	Opportunities
Social/Cultural		
Competition		
Technology		
Legal/Political		
Economics		

Pick up the last six issues of *Time* or *Newsweek* (your local library should have copies), your notes from Action Step 8, and start reading. What is happening in the world? Fill in the chart with the areas that are changing within each environmental variable. If you are fortunate and have done your research, you will spot the changes before trends start to develop. Being at the forefront of trends has made business-savvy people rich. Remember when the biotechnology industry began only a few short years ago? If you had spotted the changes within this technology, hopped on the truck, and rode the opportunities to success, where would you be today?

to learn how to spot the changes. Action Step 8 opened your mind to new information and now it's time to evaluate the information and search for opportunities. Action Step 9 will help you to do this.

Changing Families

How does your world differ from the world your parents experienced? How will your children's world differ from yours? You recognize how your world differs from your parents, but opportunities reside in how your children's world will differ from yours.

The "Beaver Cleaver" family of a working dad, stay-at-home mom, and two children, exists for very few today. The opportunities to serve the diverse family structures that exist are vast: day care, after-school care, recreation programs, shopping help, and career college selection services. If you compiled a list of all the services June and Ward Cleaver provided to keep their household running, you would discover that all those services are still needed today; but service-oriented businesses are doing them, not June and Ward.

Who else is in need of these services? The elderly? Single parents? Disabled? Chronically ill? Grandparents raising grandchildren? Dual working couples? All time starved! In fact, many say real wealth today is time.

In 2000 more than 60 percent of our 6 trillion-dollar economy was spent on services. People are buying time. Do you see a need for a service? Do any of your friends or colleagues have the same need? Are people willing to pay for this service? Can you provide this service and get the word out? If you answered yes, go for it! In many instances service-oriented businesses can begin as home-based, with low capital investment, few employees, and a great idea that fills a need. According to Andrew Carnegie, "Making money shouldn't be your first goal. Fill a need, and if you're good enough at it, the money will come."

People are marrying later, having fewer children and having them later; divorcing in greater numbers; remarrying and reformulating new families. Eighteen percent of homes today are purchased by single women, something almost unheard of just 30 years ago. Are there any opportunities here for you? Each change and trend in our society represents threats and opportunities to current businesses. If current businesses don't expand and change, new businesses will move in. Your firm's success depends on **you** recognizing changes and capitalizing on them.

Can You Help Us? Please! (The Family Today)*

- The workforce has changed dramatically. Today's workforce is more racially and ethnically diverse (20 percent is non-white), older (the median age is

*SOURCE: **www.familiesandwork.org** (accessed May 1, 1999).

nearly 40), and composed of more women (48 percent) than it was 20 years ago. The study also found that higher proportions of workers have college degrees (31 percent) and hold managerial and professional jobs (34 percent).

- **The vast majority (85 percent) of workers have day-to-day family responsibilities at home.** Some 78 percent of married employees have spouses and partners who are also employed, compared to 66 percent in 1977. A full 46 percent of workers have children under 18 who live with them at least half-time. Nearly one in five employed parents is single, and surprisingly, 27 percent of single parents are men.
- **The roles of married men and women are changing.** Although employed married women spend more time on chores than employed married men do, this gap has narrowed substantially over the past 20 years. On workdays, men spend 2.1 hours on household chores (an increase of nearly 1 hour) compared to the 2.9 hours (a half-hour decline) women spend. Both men (1.6 hours per workday) and women (1.3 hours per workday) have less personal time.
- **When it comes to child care, two-thirds of all employed parents with pre-kindergarten children rely on partners and relatives as the primary source.** When one member of a dual-earner couple has to take time off to care for a child, 83 percent of employed mothers say they are more likely to take time off while 22 percent of fathers make this claim.
- **Today's jobs are more demanding than ever.** Employees today spend an average 44 hours per week working—6 more than they are scheduled to work. Among employees who work at least 20 hours a week, the hours spent on the job each week has increased an average of 3.5 (from 43.6 to 47.1) since 1977. In addition, many workers say they have to work very fast (68 percent) and very hard (88 percent). One in three employees bring work home at least once a week, an increase of 10 percent over the past 20 years. The number of employees who would like to work fewer hours rose 17 percentage points over this time.
- **Many workers experience stress and negative spillover from work.** Nearly one-fourth of all employees often or very often felt nervous or stressed; 13 percent often or very often had difficulty coping with the demands of everyday life; 26 percent often or very often felt emotionally drained by their work; 28 percent often or very often have not had the energy to do things with their families or others; and 36 percent often or very often felt used up at the end of the workday.

After reading the previously mentioned information, what opportunities do you see? What gaps are there in the marketplace? How can you help? What do these families and individuals need? The changing family is only one social change; there are many others, such as people living longer, rising incomes, teenagers with large spendable incomes, etc. What other changes do you see? What opportunities open up? Read in following how one entrepreneur parlayed his love of chess into a business focusing on after-school programs for the children of working parents.

Checkmate!

Chess had changed Sammy Wong's life and he wanted to change others' lives too. At most local grade schools chess isn't considered a trendy game. But Sammy knew he could make chess "cool." After graduating from college, he worked with local elementary schools volunteering his time to teach chess with four free half-hour lessons. After providing incredibly fun lessons—bishops being conked on the head, three-foot-tall chess pieces, double chessboards, and lots of laughter, Sammy was ready to launch after-school chess classes at $5 per class per child. In some schools more than 30 percent of the kids took his classes! Currently, several thousand children are involved in his programs.

Yes, Sammy wrenched kids away from Nintendo and Playstation2! Parents were thrilled. They had been looking for an activity without a keyboard that would challenge their children's minds. Few envisioned chess would be the answer! Sammy was riding the trend of parents seeking alternatives to television, computers, and video games.

Many of the moms and dads in the upscale community where Sammy lived were programmers, engineers, and scientists who had played chess as children but couldn't find the time to teach their own kids. Sammy came to the rescue. In addition, Friday night chess tournaments, traveling chess teams, chess camps, and chess champs were born from listening to his customers—parents and kids!

Sammy started his business for less than $1,000. Can you do the same? Action Step 10 asks you to explore the business opportunities open to you if you had only $1,000 and a working car or truck. In good times and bad times there are **always** opportunities to make money. Not everyone has a nest egg or a rich uncle; most entrepreneurs are just regular people. After completing this assignment you may discover an opportunity you never recognized before, or at the least you will have a list ready and waiting for the next friend who complains he/she doesn't have any money. Your list can show them the way to green dollars! As students share their lists in class, we have seen light bulbs go on! One student with less than $200 started an incredibly successful window-washing business. Two students joined together using their interior design skills to offer computerized interior designs in addition to their monthly trips to the Furniture Mart with their clients. Complete Action Step 10 after you have finished reading the chapter.

Action Step 10

$1000 and a Working Vehicle

Quickly, can you think of a business to start with little capital and no employees? Place yourself in the position of having to make money within 1 week. You have to start a business and only have $1000. You have a working car or pickup truck, an apartment, and a phone. Remember, the business must be legal!

Start looking by asking friends what they need, driving through local neighborhoods, and reading. Find out what other people are accomplishing with what appears to be a small investment.

Can you purchase products at a warehouse for resale at a swap meet? Could you tap a skill you already possess? Remember Felix's basketball skills in Chapter 1? Sammy's chess skills?

Compile a list of all the business opportunities you have discovered and share them with your friends or potential customers. What are they willing to pay for your products/services? How often would they purchase? Who are your competitors?

P.S. Apple Computer started with $1350. Dell Computer started with $1000. Nike started with $1000.

P.P.S. Go for it! Remember, Walt Disney started in his garage!

Boomer Explosion

Baby boomers, who have been a major economic and social force in our society for decades, are aging. As they approach their fifties and sixties, they are redefining aging and retirement. What products will they need and want? Where will they buy them? How can you reach them?

Soon boomers (29 percent of the population) will control more than 75 percent of the nation's assets and 50 percent of its discretionary income. By 2030 half of all U.S. adults will be 50 or greater. According to many sources, the boomers will **not** "go gently into that good night." They will fight the aging process with every dollar they have!

One can't look at past generations to predict the buying habits of this group. They are wealthier, more educated, have fewer children, and are in "new family" structures. Firms are going to the source—the boomers—and asking them what they want. The boomer research of Del Webb, a premier developer of retirement communities, showed not only a need for retirement communities in sunny climates, but also the need for retirement communities in the East and Midwest to serve boomers who choose to retire closer to home.

Scrutinize boomers—from the tops of their heads to the bottoms of their feet—to determine if you can develop products or services to make money. Brainstorm away! If you are twenty-something look at your folks; if you're forty-something look in the mirror. Be as creative and wild as you can! The following should help get you started:

- Hair—toupees, hair implants, wigs, great hats, special sunscreen for bald spots
- Eyes—eyedrops, cool magnifiers, trifocals, eye surgery
- Face—plastic surgery, skin creams, skin cancer checkups, facial exercise classes, facial massages, makeup

Every doctor, dentist, lawyer, accountant, travel agent, and financial planner is waiting in the wings for the boomers to break down their doors. Opportunities are enormous for those who want to capitalize on and meet the boomers' needs.

ACTION STEP 11

SPOTTING TRENDS IN YOUR SELECTED TARGET MARKETS

Select a target market of your choice—Generation Y, Generation X, the over-80, frail, elderly, soccer kids. Search the net for statistics and information. Start with census data at www.census.gov and continue using search engines. Try www.easidemographics.com, and www.awool.com/index.html. Using your statistics, intuition, and knowledge of the target market, work back through the baby boomer exercise or go through a day in the lives of your selected target market. What trends do they identify with? What products and services will your target market desire? How can you best meet their needs?

Next, review the list of products, ideas, and services the baby boomers identified with. Compile a similar list for your Target Customer.

As you continue through this book, you will learn how to refine your target market.

Modern Maturity, the largest distributed subscription magazine (distributed free to American Association of Retired Persons (AARP) members as part of their membership dues), is targeted at those over age 50, and may have one of the hottest websites of the future: **www.aarp.org/mmaturity**. Legally and politically those over age 50 have always been a very strong political force. With the power of the Internet, real social, political, and economic change is not only possible but also inevitable.

After reading the following about the boomers, complete Action Step 11 to explore your chosen target market and try to spot the emerging trends and opportunities.

About Boomers*

- In the U.S. between the end of World War II and 1964, 78 million baby boomers were born and now are part of the "Boomers" generation.
- Boomers are now entering middle age and changing the demographics of the total population. Four of ten households are between ages 35 to 54 and the numbers of households ages 45 to 54 increased 20 percent from 1995 to 2000.
- As empty nesters, boomers have more money to spend because the median income bracket for boomers is $47,300 annually.
- The average household headed by boomers age 35 to 54 spends $12,000 annually for housing.
- The number of couples without children between the age of 45 and 60 will increase from 8 million in 1980 to 16 million in the year 2010.
- Every 7.5 seconds, a boomer turns 50!
- Generation identified with Iron Curtain, Berlin Wall, Cold War, Sputnik, transistor radios, calculators, computers, man on the moon, hula hoop, "Leave It To Beaver," Mousketeers, doo-wop, R & B, "American Bandstand," Elvis, Little Richard, Chuck Berry, Motown, Beach Boys, Haight-Ashbury, hippies, PEACE, VW Bug, LOVE, LSD, Woodstock, California Dreamin', hot tubs, TM, platform shoes, bell-bottoms, miniskirts, hot pants, bikinis, tie-dyed, flower power, communal, Nehru jackets, The Beatles, Rolling Stones, Chelsea, King's Road, Carnarby Street, bohemians, The Mods, The Rockers, Liverpool, Twiggy, the fall of the Berlin Wall, Pan Am, and $5.00 a day in Europe.

Are all boomers alike? Not according to Yankelovich's Monitor MindBase. There are two major groups of boomers—one group is the "Renaissance Elders who are mature but still involved in the world and enjoying life with their deep pockets" and the other group is the "Retired from Life who are mature but uninvolved, somewhat sedentary, and tend to see technology as a threat." The opportunities to capitalize on all boomers' needs are vast! Go for it!

Three menopausal women recognized the huge market of 50 million women entering menopause during the next 10 years. They developed "As We Change" (Figure 2.2), a 32-page catalog of products to address the needs and concerns of a very large and growing market.

Many firms, such as Victoria's Secret, Sharper Image, and Gateway, start with mail order or online retailing and move to storefront retailing as momentum builds for their products. Are retail stores in the future for As We Change? What about online retailing? Do you see any other avenues?

The Splintering of the Mass Market

Today's consumers are informed, individualistic, and demanding. Their buying habits are often difficult to isolate because they tend to buy at several levels of the market. For example, some may purchase copiers direct from Xerox but the paper from Staples. High-fashion, high-income consumers may patronize upscale boutiques but buy their household appliances at Wal-Mart or Costco.

For the consumer, three key factors have splintered the mass market:

*SOURCE: **hometown.aol.com/boomersint/bindex.html** (accessed July 23, 2001).

FIGURE 2.2
As We Change: Catalog Products

SOURCE: *As We Change Catalog,* 1999; 800-203-5585. Used with permission.

Get a better look.

Elegant sterling silver rimmed pendant doubles as a fashionable magnifier for those times when you need to see better quickly. Optical quality 1⁷/₈" diameter glass magnifies 3 times and 6 times for super magnification. Sterling silver 24" chain with 3" drop, accented with onyx, freshwater pearls.

Magnifier Necklace

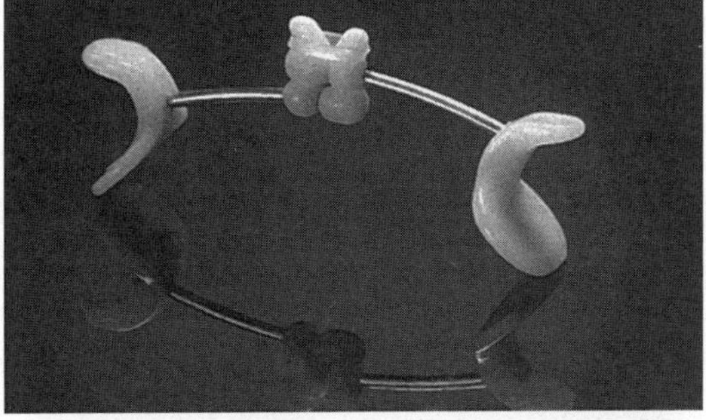

Tone and tighten your facial muscles.

Here's a completely natural way to noticeably improve facial skin tone and firmness. Facial Flex® Ultra provides a mini-workout for the muscles that support the skin of your mouth, cheeks and chin—areas that tend to sag over the years. Significant results in just 2 to 3 minutes twice daily over a 60-day period. Comes with instructional video and 2 strengths of replacement elastic bands.

Facial Flex® Ultra

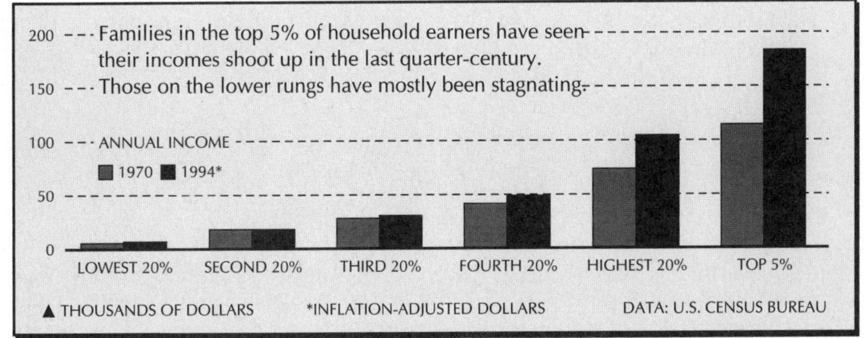

FIGURE 2.3
The Rich Get Richer

SOURCE: *Business Week,* March 17, 1998.

1. A shrinking middle class—the wealthiest fifth of the populations' income has grown by 21 percent and the poorest 60 percent have stagnated or dipped according to U.S. census data (Figure 2.3). In 1996, 20 percent of all children in the United States were poor, which was classified as a family of four with an income below $16,036. Two distinct marketing strategies are developing to reach customers at both ends of the population: satellite phone services offering $2000 phones and $2-a-minute charges versus prepaid phone cards for those with no phone service.
2. The size of age and ethnic groups is shifting (Figure 2.4). Latinos are the largest minority group with more than 30 million people. The Latino market tends to be younger and more demographically centered. The greater Los Angeles area, already the most ethnically diverse population in the world, has television stations available in Spanish, English, Farsi, and Vietnamese. In one school district the students speak more than 50 languages. In addition, ethnic diversity is rapidly expanding throughout the United States.

FIGURE 2.4
Changing Work-Age Population

SOURCE: *Los Angeles Times,* March 25, 1998.

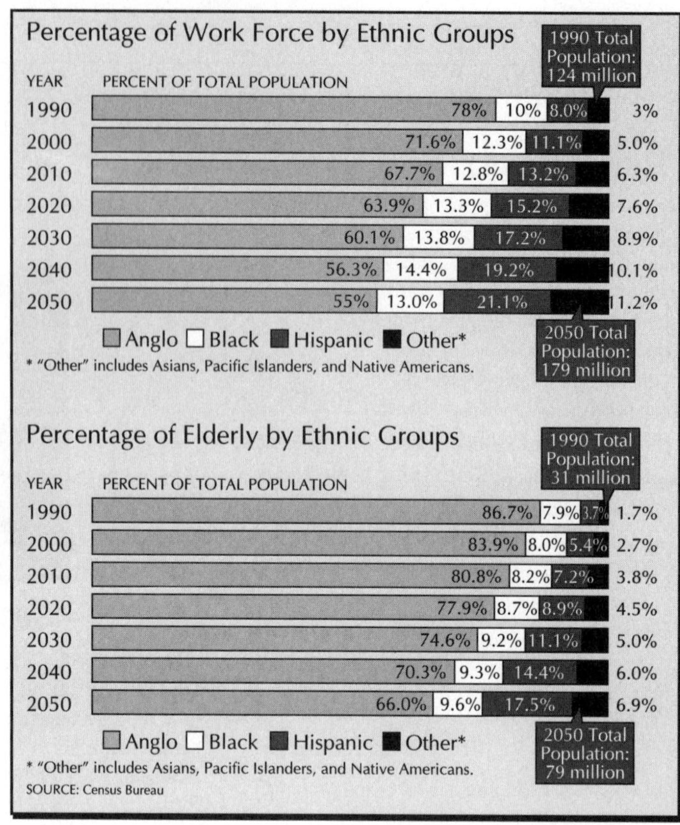

3. Living arrangements are changing and evolving: stepfamilies, dual-career families, single parents, grandparents raising grandchildren, grandparents living with children, increasing population of frail and elderly, and children returning to the nest.

If you look with "new eyes" you can see additional major segments emerging, growing, and becoming more powerful: affluent 80-year-olds, Asians (5 percent of the population), pre-teen consumers (Figure 2.5), Silicon Valley billionaires, and so on. Take a few minutes to surf **www.mediafinder.com** and **www.srds.com**. Within minutes, you will discover hundreds of very narrow target markets reached by magazines. One of the latest, INTERRACE, addresses the concerns of interracial and multiracial couples, families, and singles. For the first time, the year 2000 census collected multiracial data, which may provide information to enable entrepreneurs to reach other niche markets.

Today's technology allows us to define ever-smaller target markets. With the power of the Internet and the right software, we achieve one-to-one target marketing. If you order product B and 50 percent of customers who order product B also order product Z, product Z will pop up on your screen automatically. Basically, a salesperson in a box. Amazon.com's incredible software provides an excellent example of instant marketing and sales promotion.

Information Overload

The average person today receives more information from their big-city Sunday newspaper than a Middle-Ages person received in their entire lifetime! Human wants and needs of the American consumer are screaming: faster, pare it down, earn lots, save money, train me, quality over quantity, and pile on the excitement! **Generation X** does not take their tents to the mountains and veg out for the week. They take their

Generation X Individuals born between the early 1960s and the mid 1970s.

FIGURE 2.5
Teenager's Buying Power Statistics

Teenagers' Buying Power Statistics

The spending children influence, according to James McNeal's calculations:

- It comes close to $520 billion annually.
- From age 4 to 14, they influence at least $20 billion in new car purchases. They influence the model, the brand, the size, the color, and the shape.
- Children of today, particularly "tweens," children 8 to 11 years old, are ready to buy on the Internet.
- It is believed the average 10-year-old has memorized 300 or 400 brand names.
- McNeal's most recent study shows that when kids make requests for their parents to buy anything, the requests are made by brand name 92 percent of the time.
- In 1997, American children aged 4 to 12 saved an estimated $4.5 billion.

mountain bikes, snowboards, and cross-country skis. No vegging out allowed! REI, a major outdoor retailer, is there to meet their needs.

Our private lives and work lives are converging. We spend less time at home and more time at work. Becoming more dependent on the workplace to provide us with parenting, financial-planning classes, travel services, company concierges, dry cleaning, child and adult day care, and so on. Each change becomes an opportunity for the enterprising entrepreneur. How can you reduce the information overload of your customers?

ACTION STEP 12

HAVE SOME FUN WITH IDENTIFYING PROBLEMS

Form a focus group of your friends or colleagues and ask them about their wants and needs. Hopefully you will discover gaps in the marketplace. Don't judge their answers; you're just seeking information and the more they provide, the better. Ask them to respond to questions such as the following:

- What frustrates you most about your daily life? Shopping? Banking? Dating? Living? Buying a car? Grocery shopping? Clothing shopping?
- What products or services do you need or want but can't find or get?
- What products or services would enhance your quality of life?
- How could you increase your productivity without working more hours?

If you are dealing with a nonconsumer product, change the questions to fit your market.

Make a list of the gaps that the group identifies. Then project the list out as far as you can into the marketplace and follow the wants, needs, and frustrations of your friends. Are any of their needs national in scope? Global?

Remember the women from the *As We Change* catalog. They not only discovered a 50-million-strong national market, but an international market as well. They listened to their friends and customers!

Additional Thoughts

The World Future Society recently published a list of "50 Trends Now Changing the World" and shaping life in the twenty-first century. We have highlighted seven of these trends. Your job is to review the changes and discover the opportunities available to you as a potential entrepreneur.

1. As the pace of technological change accelerates, many industries will face much tighter competition. At the same time entry-level and low-wage workers will be scarce.
2. Values are changing rapidly. Society will increasingly take its cue from Generation X and dot-com, rather than the baby boomers.
3. The work ethic is declining. Tardiness is increasing and the abuse of sick leave is common. The erosion of the work ethic could have a negative impact on future corporate performance.
4. Time will become the world's most precious commodity. American workers already spend about 10 percent more time on the job than they did a decade ago.
5. The emphasis on preventive medicine is getting stronger. People will be more inclined to control stress as they realize that 80 to 90 percent of all diseases are stress-related.
6. The worldwide loss of biodiversity will be a growing worry for decades to come. Half of all drugs used in medicine are derived from natural sources, including 55 of the top 100 drugs prescribed in the United States.
7. The former Soviet Union and India will emerge as the fastest-growing new markets.

SOURCE: World Future Society, "50 Trends Now Changing the World," **www.wfs.org** (accessed December 20, 2000).

Have some fun now with a group of people and complete Action Step 12. Remember, the more problems you spot, the more opportunities arise. With each problem you are closer to your business plan.

Franchisers Respond to Cultural Changes

Take a look at the top 10 new franchises for 2001 according to *Entrepreneur* and see how they are meeting the needs of a changing society. Ace America's Cash Express is targeted at the needs of lower income people who are cash starved. Express One, Quick Internet, and Worldsites all capitalize on the Web's growth. Because of an increase in spendable income and a desire to eat out frequently, there are Wetzel's, Friendly's Restaurants, and New York Burrito-Gourmet Wraps.

Entrepreneur's Top 10 New Franchises for 2001

ACE America's Cash Express
Wetzel's Pretzels
Friendly's Restaurants Franchise Inc.
Express One
Quik Internet
New York Burrito-Gourmet Wraps
Window Gang
Sears Carpet & Upholstery Care Inc.
Christmas Décor Inc.
Worldsites

The following list includes *Entrepreneur's* fastest-growing franchises based on straight growth in the number of franchises from 1998 to 1999 verified in *Entrepreneur's* annual *Franchise 500®* listing. With four of the leading franchises being fast food outlets, you again can see the unending desire for food on the go. No time to cook! No time to sit and eat! No time to shop!

According to *Entrepreneur,* "The following list is not intended to endorse any particular franchise but simply to provide a starting point for research. Perhaps after a careful investigation of these franchises, you may find a franchise that can put you on the fast track to success."

*Entrepreneur's Top 10 Fastest-Growing Franchises for 2001**

McDonald's
Coverall North America Inc.
Taco Bell Corp.
Subway
Jani-King
Mail Boxes, Etc.
Quizno's Corp., The
ByeByeNow.com, Travel Inc.
Jiffy Lube Int'l Inc.
Curves for Women

Technology Revolution

The $5 microchip that runs a 2001 Nintendo cost $1000 in 1993 and powered high-end servers. The computer has changed every facet of every life. We rarely reach a human being when we telephone a business. When frustrated, we look up their website and send an e-mail message. Computer-to-computer communication is now a way of life. Long handwritten letters seem to be a thing of the past. We use videophones, teleconferencing, and send new jokes via e-mail messages to our best friends. What impact will technology have on your business? What opportunities are just waiting for you to exploit?

The Human Genome project mapped the 40,000 genes that make up human DNA. Possibilities for products and services are mind-boggling and will come at an incredible pace. Will there be genetic testing centers cropping up in every city? Will people go to one of these centers before getting married to have potential mates evaluated? Will these centers be franchised?

Embedded microchips are common in veterinary medicine, giving veterinarians instant access to a pet's medical history. Will it be long before people also have embedded microchips? Can you discover any other new uses for embedded chips? What

*SOURCE: **www.entrepreneurmag.com** (accessed June 1, 2001).

about in appliances? Clothing? Furniture? Sports equipment? Keep up on technology news by watching technology-oriented programs on television; surfing the Internet; reading *Forbes ASAP, Scientific American*; and checking out MIT's and CalTech's websites.

With artificial body parts and transplanted organs an everyday occurrence, will cancer, Parkinson's, Alzheimer's, and heart disease become a distant memory with the advances in biotechnology? If these diseases were cured, what could you do with the empty doctor's offices? Medical buildings? Equipment? One enterprising entrepreneur in Southern California follows the changes in medical equipment and then scoops up the "old" technology equipment, services it and sells it into third-world countries.

Surgeons provide online instructions in real-time to operating rooms throughout the world. When a patient's chest is open and a surgeon must cut in the exact spot, Dr. Melia from Syracuse is ready to assist—not only for his own patients in Syracuse but also to doctors and patients in places like Bolivia. Doctors monitor patients at home with products previously available only at a hospital. This saves untold hospital bed space and doctor visits. Do you know someone with a chronic illness? How could technology be of help to him or her?

New high-tech materials from the aerospace industry allow Flex-Foot of Aliso Viejo, California, (**www.flexfoot.com**) to design and market innovative lower-limb prosthetic devices for amputees constructed of 100 percent carbon fiber. New materials used creatively have allowed many new businesses to produce products for industry and consumers. People with disabilities have been greatly aided by technology, and the future holds even more promise.

In our last edition we listed *Forbes ASAP's* "25 Cool Things You Wish you Had . . . and Will." Amazingly many, which seemed incredible just 4 short years ago, are now available such as powerful personal digital assistants, wearable computers, and e-books. Some of the other items on that list included toxin testers, common cold detectors, earthquake survivor detectors, and digital spines. Which of these will be common in the next 3 years?

Recent MIT gurus listed the following as emerging technologies for the next 20 years:

- Biometrics
- Flexible Transistors
- Microphotonics
- Microfluidics
- Advanced Robotics
- Brain-Machine Interfaces

In addition to MIT's list mentioned previously, scholars at George Washington University created a "top ten" list of developing technologies for the next 10 years.

TOP TEN TECHNOLOGIES for 2001-2010

Portable information appliances rival PCs. By 2003, 30 percent of industrialized nations will use portable devices to surf the Internet, send e-mail, watch video, and more.

Fuel-cell powered cars hit the streets. Toyota and Ford should introduce experimental fuel-cell automobiles by 2004.

Precision farming becomes ultra-efficient. Satellite data and computerized tractors should boost crop yields within a decade.

Millions of consumers buy customized merchandise online instead of visiting stores. Virtual shopping could account for one-third of the U.S. economy by 2007.

"Teleliving" becomes the lifestyle of choice by 2010. People at home and work will access streams of information through large wall monitors.

Virtual assistants handle routine chores. By 2007 sophisticated software will create computerized helpers to file, screen calls, and write letters.

ACTION STEP 13

NEW TECHNOLOGIES

If you are a tech expert, share your insights with others. Bring them up to speed! Technology affects every aspect of small business today—distribution, marketing, products, and so on. If you are not tech savvy, it's time to get up to speed!

1. Read *Wired* (www.wired.com) either online or in hard copy.
2. Surf the Internet or visit the library and find five articles on new technologies. Can you discover any trends developing? Future opportunities? Share your findings with others. A technological breakthrough in one industry will often lead to a breakthrough in another industry.
3. Read several copies of *The Futurist, Science,* or high-tech magazines in your selected industry. List all the new, developing technologies. Can you spot any trends and opportunities?

With the previously mentioned information in hand, you will be better prepared to focus on the opportunities within these changing technologies.

Market research Collection and analysis of data pertinent to current or potential future of a product or service.

Primary research Interacting directly through interviews, observations, experimentation, questionnaires, and so on.

Secondary research Reading someone else's published (primary) research.

Genetically designed species of plants and animals enter the mainstream by 2008. Biotechnology will improve crop production to feed a more-populated world.
Computers take over healthcare tasks. By 2009 more-powerful hardware and software systems will keep medical records, fill prescriptions, and monitor patients.
Alternative energy challenges carbon-based fuels. Within a decade, alternative energy sources—wind, solar, geothermal, biomass, hydroelectric—will meet 30 percent of all energy needs.
Smart robots take on sophisticated jobs. Decision-making robots that do complex factory work and assist the handicapped will arrive by 2010.

SOURCE: **www.gwforecast.gwu.edu** (accessed March 1, 2001).

Some individuals make a business of trend-watching such as leading trend-watchers Nicholas Negroponte of the MIT Media Lab (**www.media.mit.edu**), author of *Being Digital;* Faith Popcorn, author of *EVEolution*; and Sherry Turkle, author of *Life on the Screen: Identity in the Age of the Internet.* Faith Popcorn's firm follows more than 500 magazines and newspapers to predict trends. Jennifer James, an urban cultural anthropologist, studies language and symbol shifts with a keen eye on television programs.

Locate your "industry gurus" and read **everything** they write. In addition to individual trend-watchers, major market research firms Roper Starch Worldwide, Nielsen, and Burke, provide extensive studies, many of which are available on the Net. Action Step 13 asks you to explore new technologies in depth.

INFORMATION IS EVERYWHERE

Hopefully, the information presented so far has your juices flowing and you want to learn more and explore several opportunities and markets. If that is the case, you will need **market research**, creativity, and intuition to discover the right opportunity for you. Conducting research is easier with the advent of the greatest information source ever—the Internet. Research data previously available only to large corporations with big R&D budgets are now available free to you—or, for a few dollars—Internet access to thousands of dollars of research can be yours. By keeping your eyes wide open, your intuition and creativity will blossom.

Secondary Research

Researching industries and markets takes three forms—**secondary**, **primary**, and "new eyes" research. Secondary research should be your starting point. When

INCREDIBLE RESOURCE

ABBOTT WOOL'S MARKET SEGMENT RESOURCE LOCATOR

www.awool.com: If you want to follow the demographic and economic trends of African Americans, teens, singles, Hispanics, Asian Americans, and those over age 50, this site provides a good start. While not a comprehensive list, the related links can start you on the never-ending Internet search for your specific target market.

The site provides listings of advertising agencies, marketing and research services, media, and government and academic associations involved with each specific market.

Examples from the teen link:

- Thorne Creative Research: Qualitative Research
- Yankelovich Youth Monitor: Attitudes and Values Study
- Media: *Empowered Young Women* (female teens), *Web Magazine, Nomad, The Brat Journal* (teens in military families), **www.WhatNext.com** (teens considering college) and *Latingirl Magazine* (Hispanic teen girls).

you read what someone else discovered and published, you're carrying out secondary research. Using the Internet and asking Yahoo! to search for census data, locating newspaper articles containing information you think will be helpful—both are forms of secondary research. For instant access to U.S. and international newspapers and other publications, use **www.newspapers.com** or **www.newsdirectory.com**.

Conducting good thorough secondary research will prepare you to perform targeted primary research as you will now know the right questions to ask and can get to the heart of any issue much quicker. Also, by continuing to flood your brain with information you will start to build your intuition and your "new eyes" will grow.

Get online and learn what's happening in the rest of the world: products you could import or export, service businesses that might do well in your community, new markets for you to reach.

Contact **trade associations** (Figure 2.6) for industry, supplier, distributor, and customer information. Trade associations conduct research, publish trade journals, and offer books and courses. They also provide data to project how much money one can net in small business. Good research techniques here will save lots of footwork. Never underestimate the information available through associations. Their primary goal is the success of their members, so they listen and are attuned to their members' information needs. Many times early on in your research, national and local association chapters can provide you with invaluable contacts for further primary research. At the library begin with the *Encyclopedia of Business and Professional Associations.* Also ask people in the industry which associations they belong to and which magazines they read.

Next, move on to the *Directory of Periodicals* or click on **www.mediafinder.com** to find magazines that reach your **target market** or are part of your industry. Also, use a search engine to locate various associations for your business. Many have online access to their research and periodicals. Some associations provide student memberships at a reduced cost.

Magazines develop **media kits**, which provide statistics on their readership, for their advertisers. This is one of the quickest ways to get a quick read on the marketplace. Reading magazines and media kits will show you competitive products, what interests your customers, and trends, and it will provide extensive **demographic** and **psychographic** information.

Trade associations Groups dedicated to the needs of a specific industry.

Target market Segment of market most likely to purchase the product or service. Desire, dollars, and authority.

Media kits Readership profiles, ad information, and market research developed by magazines for potential advertisers.

Demographics Quantifiable data on population, race, age, education, income, gender, and so on.

Psychographics Descriptive features on lifestyles, values, and attitudes.

FIGURE 2.6
NAMM Home Page

SOURCE: **www.namm.com** (accessed June 15, 2001).

ACTION STEP 14

LAUNCH YOUR INDUSTRY RESEARCH

1. Use the *Encyclopedia of Business and Professional Associations* or the Internet to locate the names of trade associations your business would be part of and make note of the addresses, phone numbers, and websites. Contact the associations and request information. Because you are a potential member, they should send you an enormous amount of information and provide membership details. If you mention you are a student conducting research, they may be surprisingly helpful. You can go further on this assignment by contacting associations your suppliers and customers may belong to. Combining this information will provide you with an incredible amount of data to sift through.
2. Locate a chapter of a national association and attend a meeting as a guest.
3. Use **www.mediafinder.com** or the *Directory of Periodicals* to locate (a) magazines or journals within your selected industry, (b) magazines or journals that reach your target customers, and (c) magazines or journals for your suppliers. Spend some time on the Net or in the library researching your list and delving deeper into the information.
4. After you have thoroughly done your industry research, select at least one magazine or journal from each of the categories and request a media kit. The media kits will provide you with an excellent start on your specific research. Complete this Action Step before moving on, as you will need the information to complete the Action Steps in Chapters 3-5.

Sometimes highly technical journals are not easy to locate online or in any stores. If this is the case, ask your library to locate the corporate libraries within your area and industry. Most corporate libraries will allow individuals access to their facilities. In addition, their trained librarians can be an invaluable resource.

In fact, as you begin your research, locate the best research librarian in your college or local library. In many universities individual libraries exist within certain specialties such as pharmacy or biomedical engineering. Many college librarians may be able to direct you to faculty members who are involved in projects and areas where you need further information. Check the Internet to locate faculty members throughout the world who may be conducting research applicable to your business venture.

Begin your industry research with Action Step 14.

Primary Research

After you acquire the basics about your industry, customers, suppliers, and competitors through secondary research, you are ready to conduct primary research, interacting with the world directly by talking to people—and perhaps interviewing them.

It is time to find out exactly what your potential customer wants. Don't make assumptions! Don't give him or her what you want to give them; *give them what they want.* Go out and ask questions:

- What do you wish your local music store would carry?
- How likely are you to use the Internet to purchase clothing?
- How much do you usually spend each month on fast-food meals?
- How would your ideal automobile dealer behave?
- What would you buy on the Internet?

Vendors and suppliers are asked questions such as: What advertising works best in businesses like ours? What products are hot? What services are being offered? Small-business owners are asked: With whom do you bank? Where did you obtain your first financing? What percentage of sales do you spend on advertising? How do you encourage repeat customers? What are the biggest problems in the industry?

"New Eyes" Research

"New eyes" research provides a variety of fresh ways to look at a business. Based on your knowledge, experience, and intuition, play detective. You might become a "mystery shopper" to check out your competition. You might sit in your car and take telephoto pictures of a business you're thinking about buying; when **Target Customers** appear, photograph them so that you can profile them later.

Stand in a supermarket aisle and, trying not to look nosy, observe what's in people's shopping carts. For example:

Hamburger + chips + ice cream + apples + *Family Circle* = family with young active children

Protein bars + pasta + *Runner's World* + *GQ* + chicken = single man who is athletic, clothes- and weight-conscious.

Profiling your Target Customer demographically and psychographically is necessary for you to gain a handle on your customer's needs and wants. Profiling will be covered thoroughly in later chapters, but to start training your observation faculties, have some fun and complete Action Step 15.

New eyes research is fun. Combined with books, magazines, trade journals, publications (*The Wall Street Journal,* for example), and talking to people, it will get you

Target Customers Persons who have the highest probability of buying a product or service.

Community Resource

www.associationcentral.com

Seeking out opportunities and tracking down trends becomes much easier if you locate the right associations for your industry. The perfect resource to begin your search is a click away at **www.associationcentral.com.** Entering sports in the keywords' box brought up 200 associations out of the 135,000 associations listed. The first ten follow:

American College of Sports Medicine
American Orthopaedic Society for Sports Medicine
National Alliance for Youth Sports
National Intramural-Recreational Sports Association
Sporting Goods Manufacturers
Sports Turf Managers Association
American Sport Fishing Association
Association of Surfing Professionals
Billiard Congress of America
National Athletic Trainers' Association

SOURCE: **www.associationcentral.com** (accessed March 1, 2001).

Locate several associations with which your potential customers, suppliers, and competitors might be affiliated. Contact the organizations for information or peruse their websites. The national associations provide many of the following: legislative updates, industry research, publications, industry news, workshops, market intelligence, online training, tradeshows, message boards, and chat rooms. After reviewing the national associations' information, select those that you think might be most helpful to you and contact the local associations in your area. Attend meetings as a guest.

Action Step 15

Decode the Secrets of the Shopping Cart

Use your new eyes to uncover the lifestyle of your customer by analyzing the contents of a supermarket shopping cart. Play detective the next time you're in a supermarket and make some deductions about lifestyles as you observe the behaviors of shoppers.

Give each subject a fantasy name, perhaps associated with a product (Chad Cereal, Steve Steak, and Sally Sugar) so that you can remember your insights. What can you deduce about each shopper's lifestyle? What do their shoes say? Their clothes? Their jewelry? Their hairstyle? Their car? Put these deductions together with a demographic checklist (sex, age, income, occupation, socioeconomic level), and then decide if any of these shoppers are potential target customers for your business.

Trained marketers look for a category of buyer known as a "heavy user." A heavy user of apples would eat 7 to 10 apples a week. A heavy user of soda would drink four a day. A heavy user of airlines—called a "frequent flyer"—flies 10 to 30 times a year. Who are the heavy users in your business?

all the way to your Business Plan. And the Business Plan will either make you a success or show you that your idea isn't worth any more of your time. Better to waste time than money!

Train your mind. Remain open to new ideas, new information, new statistics, new people, and a changing world. Observe everything. Keep your ideas in your Adventure Notebook. The more ideas that pour in, the more likely you are to find the right fit for you and your target market. The founder of the largest audio-books firm in Switzerland said he kept a notebook, and when he had 200 ideas he sat down and reviewed them all before launching his firm. Chapter 3 will help you sort through your ideas.

The Big Picture

A Business Plan begins with the "big picture"—the industry overview. Industries go through life cycles (see Figure 2.8). Products and services within industries also progress through the cycles—embryo, growth, maturity, and decline. Target markets in addition experience major changes. The industry overview in your Business Plan helps you gain perspective on your **"niche"** and helps the reader (lender or investor) understand why you have chosen to pursue this segment of the market.

To be successful in small business you need to know what business you are really in, and where your business is placed on the life-cycle yardstick. Entrepreneurs tend to be in a big hurry. They want to push on, to get on with it, to throw open the doors to customers, and read the bottom line; and that's not all bad. But before you charge into the arena, step back and examine what's going on in your **industry segment.**

Niche A small, unique slice of an industry.

Industry segment Potential slice of industry market share.

Where are the lines? In what part of your community do you see "Going Out of Business" signs? Where are the start-ups? What's hot? What's cooling down? Which business segments will still be thriving three years from now? If you opened the doors of your new business today, how long would it be before your product or services were no longer valuable or wanted?

Let's back up and get the big picture. Before the Industrial Revolution, most people were self-employed. Farmers and sheepherders were risk-takers because they had to be; there were few other options. The family functioned as an entrepreneurial unit.

The growth of megacorporations should not be viewed as a threat to the small venture, but as an opportunity. First, most large corporations are dependent on small business to produce support products and services. Second, bigger isn't always better. Many small businesses—even those whose markets are expanding rapidly—are barely noticed by large corporations. And therein lies the opportunity! If you're lucky, you'll hit on a high-tech idea and be bought out for millions by Bill Gates!

So, look before you leap; **brainstorm** with your family, friends, colleagues, and suppliers. Interview potential customers. They will tell you what they want and need. If you have done your research, your "new eyes" will be in full gear, and you will be able to recognize the opportunities and understand the risks. Continue to study the marketplace with your "new eyes." Read! Read! Read!

Brainstorm Your Way into Small Business

Snowboard Express

Annie and Valerie loved to snowboard. For 7 years, they snowboarded every chance they had—Mammoth, Vail, Tahoe, Snowbird. They kept looking for ways they could make a living snowboarding.

At school Annie and Valerie discovered the technique of mind mapping—a method of note-taking using clusters and bubbles—to let information flow along its own course. They just knew they could mind map their way into the snowboarding business!

In the center of a large sheet of paper they wrote "snowboarding." In a bubble next to "snowboarding " they wrote, "travel." Momentum built up. They wrote "beginners," "pros," "teens," "girls," and "parents." Then they wrote "clothes," "gloves," "pants," "sunglasses," "boots," and "shoes." Then they let their imaginations go even further and wrote "the West," "the East," "the Alps," "contests," "lessons," "trips," "fun," "exciting," "skateboarders," "transportation," "buses."

"This is great fun!" Annie said.

"This smells like money and fun!" Valerie exclaimed.

The two friends kept on mapping until they developed an idea for their business—Snowboard Express—roundtrip weekend bus transportation to mountain ski resorts from five local pickup points surrounding Salt Lake City. Different resorts were selected each weekend.

Two or three weeks after they began booking their trips, they went back to their mind map and the word "clothes" jumped out at them. They went to one of the major manufacturers and bought out their seconds and sold them all to Snowboard Express' customers at 100 percent over cost within the next 4 weeks.

After they were in business for only 2 months, a few women asked if Valerie and Annie could provide weekday trips so they could have the mountains to themselves while their small children were in school. A new market segment was uncovered! A gap was filled! They listened to their customers and began "Slope Thursdays."

Sometime in April the riders were asking what Annie and Valerie were going to do for the summer, they responded by asking, "What are you doing this summer?" The answer they kept hearing was, "I'm going mountain-biking." Valerie and Annie were off to explore the regional mountain bike trails. Afterwards they talked

Brainstorm Unlocking your brain.

FIGURE 2.7
Snowboard Express Mind Map

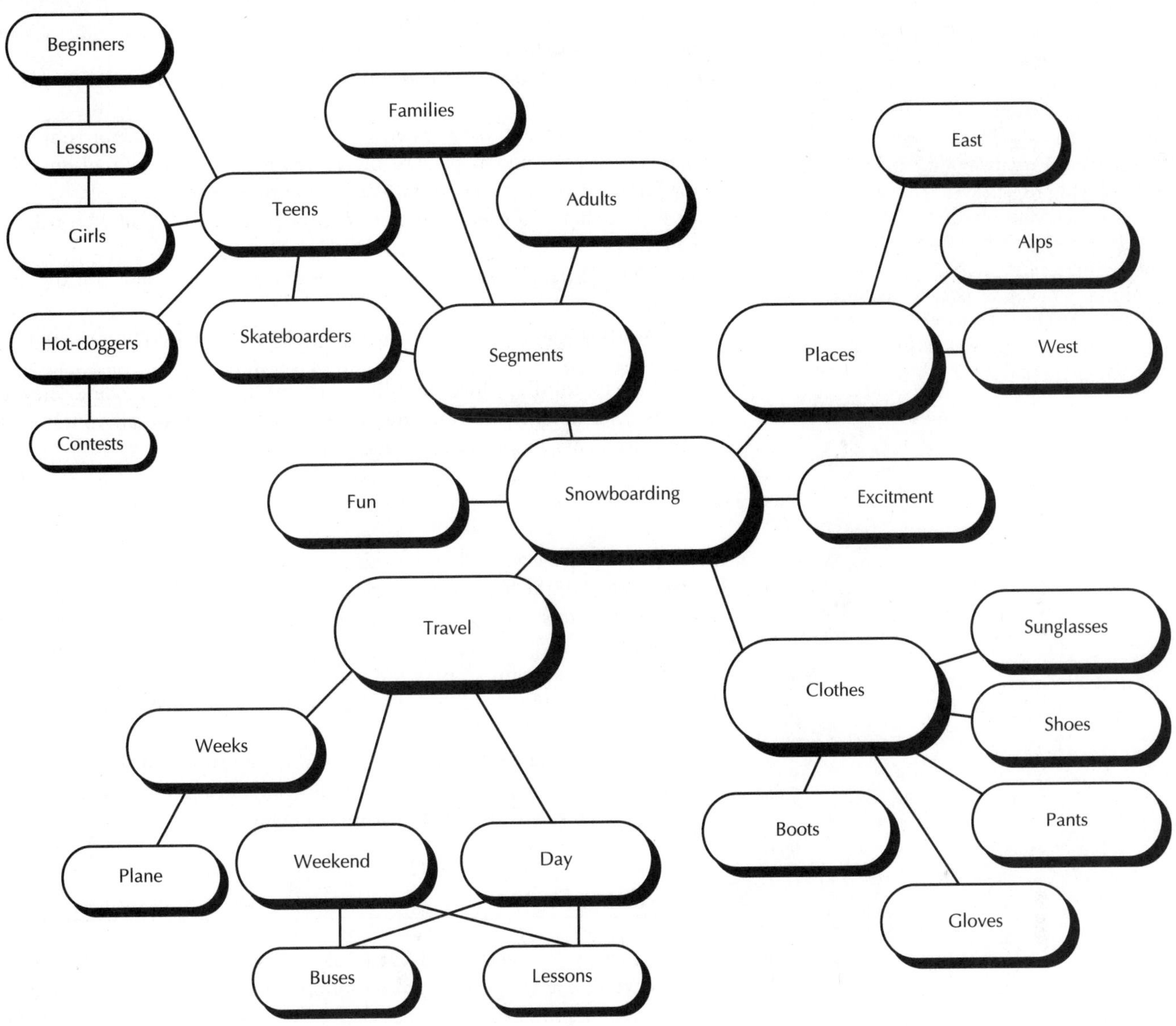

to their bus drivers to determine how they could transport all the bikes on the buses. With their answers in hand and market research completed, "Mountain Bike Express" was born.

Brainstorming Techniques

The point of the examples is to show what can result from a simple exchange of ideas. If you gather people around you with wit, spark, creativity, positive attitudes, knowledge, and good business sense, the result will almost always surprise you, and could lead to company growth, expanded profits, or perhaps the formation of a new industry. The possibilities are limitless, but the trick is to structure brainstorming sessions in a way that maximizes creativity. A few suggestions follow.

When gathering participants and planning your meeting:

ACTION STEP 16

PLACING TRENDS ON THE LIFE CYCLE

Throughout this chapter you have hopefully discovered many trends. Review Figure 2.8 and take the time to place the trends you have identified on the life cycle. How many did you find in the Embryo/Birth stage? In the Growth stage? In the Maturity stage? It's now time to move forward and to try to discover opportunities that are hopefully within the Embryo or Growth stage. If you are entering a Mature or Declining market, be ready to meet and beat the competition head on!

1. Try to find imaginative people who can stretch their minds and who can set their competitive instincts aside for a while.
2. Remember, in brainstorming sessions, there's a no-no on no's. You're not implementing yet. Skepticism will kill a session.
3. Find a neutral location. Eliminate interruptions.
4. Encourage the members of the group to reinforce and believe in each other; challenge ideas.
5. Use helpful equipment like a cassette recorder, paper and pencil, or your laptop. If you haven't mind mapped before, review *Use Both Sides of Your Brain* by Tony Buzan or *Writing the Natural Way* by Gabriele Rico.
6. Pick a time that is convenient and not rushed (relaxed) for all who will be involved.
7. Invite 10 to 15 people (some will drop out and you should allow for the no-shows).
8. Schedule the starting time. Relax and serve some food, and begin after about a half-hour.
9. Allow time for self-introduction(s). Tell participants not to be modest. They're winners, and they want to come on like winners. Have them talk in terms of accomplishments, problems, activities, and interests.

Tips:

- Have everyone arrive with a business idea or a problem.
- Before the close of the first meeting, select two or three hot ideas (cast a vote) and ask participants to prepare a one-page checklist summarizing and analyzing the ideas.
- Get together again within 2 weeks and brainstorm the hot ideas. Make it clear that the basic purpose is to get energy rolling, not to form a huge partnership.
- The best brainstorming sessions occur when you come brain-to-brain with other creative, positive people. It helps remind you that you've still got it. Brain energy is real and you need to keep tapping it.

LIFE-CYCLE STAGES

Economically, socially, technically, and financially our world is changing at incredible speed. The world is at warp speed—a revolution. There are Internet coffeehouses in Africa with telecommunication satellites circling, China is opening its doors, there are Russian capitalistic entrepreneurs, and the United States is benefiting by providing services and products to all.

Product life cycles are measured in terms of months and years rather than decades and generations. This offers great opportunity but also increased risk if you make the wrong decision. The market doesn't give you years to test your product or idea.

Review past Action Steps and make a list of all the trends, products, services, and markets you unearthed. Divide these into four groups according to the stage of their life cycle (Figure 2.8). If a trend is just beginning, and is in its formative stage, label it Embryo. If it's exploding, label it Growth. If it's no longer growing and is beginning to wane, label it Mature. If it's beyond maturity and is feeling chilly, label it Decline. Think through these life-cycle stages often. Everything changes—products, needs, technology, and neighborhoods. Complete Action Step 16.

Market signals are everywhere—in the newspaper (classified ads, bankruptcy notices, display ads), in the queue lines at the theater, in the price slashing after Christmas, and in discount coupons, rebates, closings, and grand openings. With practice, you can follow a product or target market through its life cycle. Which items have

FIGURE 2.8
Life-Cycle Stages

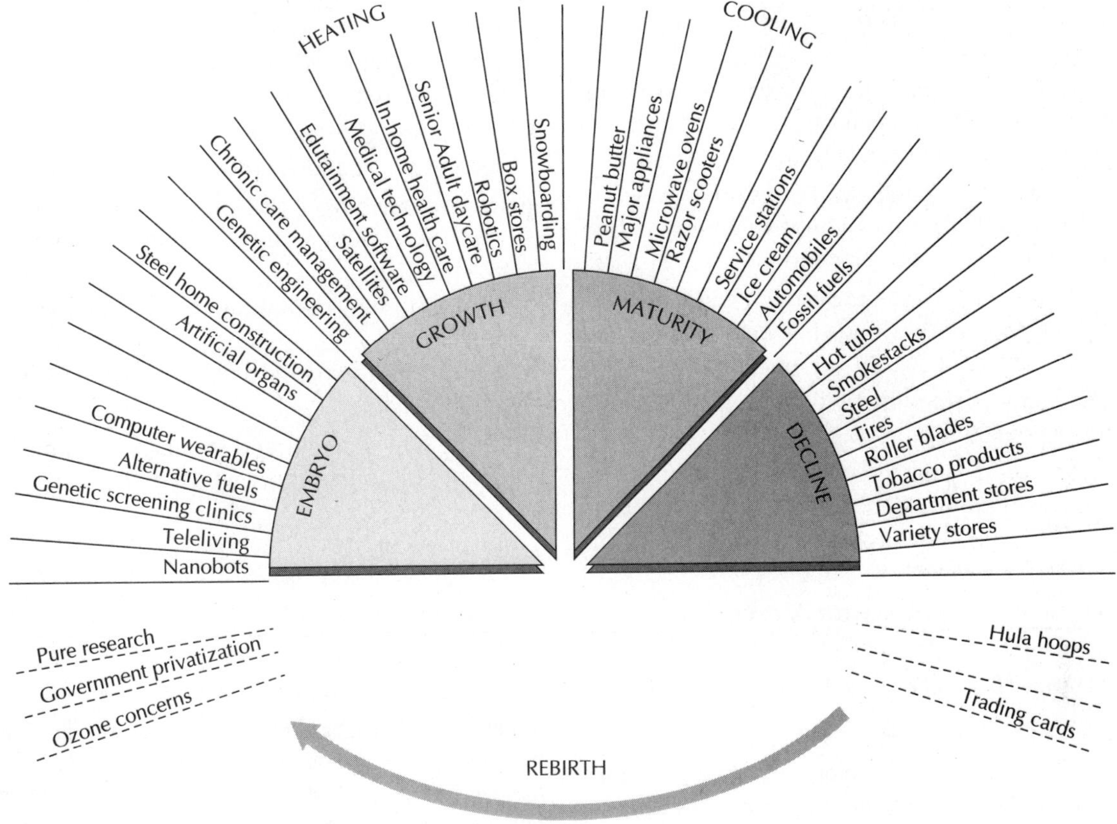

you seen go through their life cycle from upscale out of sight to deep discounts? Looking at the life-cycle diagram, you can see that the auto industry as a whole is very mature. Nonetheless, some of its segments remain promising; for example, convertibles and upscale imports—and the VW Beetle is back! In the suburbs you see Yuppie moms driving Volvo and Chrysler convertibles. Despite traffic jams, people are still driving, but the cars they drive reflect changing lifestyles.

You have looked at who you are and what you want in Chapter 1. You became a trend-spotter in this chapter. Now it is time for you to put your research and ideas together to generate the right opportunity for you.

SUMMARY

Two tools will help you chart trends: researching—secondary, primary, and new eyes (that is, playing marketplace detective); and applying the life-cycle yardstick to products, industries, and so on. A life cycle has four phases: embryo, growth, maturity, and decline. Before you open the doors of your small business, you need to be aware of what phase your product is in.

Information on trends is all around you—on the freeways, in the headlines and classifieds, at government agencies, and in the many trade associations. This information can give you the big picture if you know how to seek it out.

For your Business Plan you will need to demonstrate your knowledge and understanding of the business opportunity you will pursue. Investors look for opportunities within growth segments of growth industries, and you should too!

Think Points for Success

- The most valuable tool you have for charting trends is new eyes research combined with extensive secondary and primary research.
- Keeping your eyes open, to not only your own selected industry, but also developments in other industries that may impact yours, will keep you one step ahead.
- The life-cycle yardstick helps you discover a growth industry, decide what business you're really in, and uncover promising gaps and segments.
- Trends don't usually develop overnight. The signs are out for all to read, months, and sometimes years, in advance.
- Try to latch onto a trend that will help you survive (in style) for the next 3 to 5 years.
- Keep your eyes posted for new trends at all times. Don't ever assume that because you have caught one trend, that another won't be down the road nipping at your heels.
- Once you know what segment you're in, you can focus your research.
- Save time and money by accessing valuable resources, such as associations and trade periodicals.
- Read everything you can, and talk to everyone you can. The opportunities will appear endless.
- Trends are like customers. You can spot some by standing outside and others by staring through a window. Still others won't show up until you're in business, working and sweating away, wondering whether or not you'll make it.
- You're now a great trend-spotter, so it's time to analyze the opportunities you have unearthed.

Key Points from Another View

Twenty Things That will be Obsolete in Twenty Years

By Eric Haseltine

Like waves at sea, waves of technology are always out there somewhere, relentlessly heading for an impact. And they can be detected while still far from shore. We even ought to be able to see them coming when they're 20 years away.

Perhaps the most interesting thing about change is what it carries with it. So follow me into the future to discover not only what the semiconductor, genomic, and energy-conservation waves will sweep away as they pound the shore but also what surprises they will bring.

VICTIMS OF MOORE'S LAW

Many forms of mechano-electric technology will vanish, leaving in their place more reliable, purely solid-state devices. Storage media—such as CDs, DVDs, VCRs, and cassette tapes—will disappear as continued advances in data compression technology cram music and videos into even less memory space and the capacity of solid-state memories to hold these media grows exponentially. MP3–type storage devices of 20 years from now will store 128 megabytes (today's capacity) times 10,000, which is 1.28 terabytes. That's enough to hold more than 200 feature-length movies. Even high-definition video, with its huge appetite for memory, will not put a significant dent in the ability

FIGURE 2.9
The Benefits of Interacting

SOURCE: *The Economist,* **www.economist.com/editorial/freeforall/21-9-97/tel9.html** (accessed March 1, 1998).

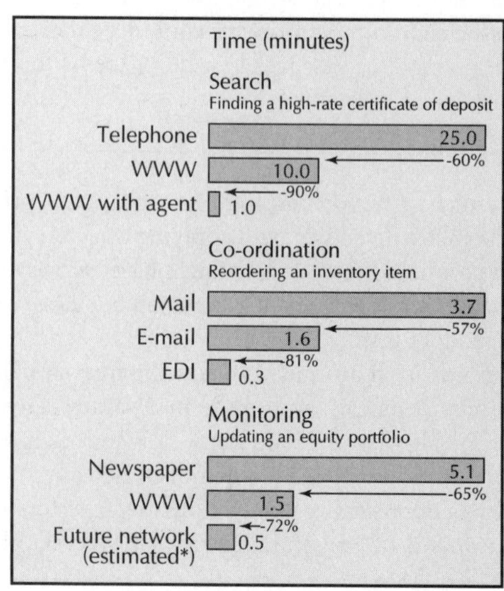

of solid-state devices to satisfy almost everyone's need for archiving movies. Film movie cameras and projectors will be out of the picture, too, as high-resolution digital imaging and digital light modulators—with no moving parts—replace their counterparts. It's a good bet that still-film cameras and slide projectors will be curiosities better suited to antique stores. Odds are that mechanical push buttons on a wide range of appliances from television remotes to telephones will go away as voice-activated controls, made possible by inexpensive, high-performance signal processors, take over.

Writing your signature on a legal document will be considered quaint because of ubiquitous biometric IDs, including iris, fingerprint, and voice-recognition systems. In effect, you'll become your own irreproducible ID.

Film scores played by real orchestras will be found only in archives as computer-synthesized music, which has already made major inroads into motion pictures, completely drowns out the real thing. The majority of choral music in movies will also arise from electronics, not singers.

Nielsen ratings will be gone because most televisions will be linked to broadband two-way network connections that tell broadcasters how many viewers are watching at any given instant. In addition, biometric ID technology could make it possible for broadcasters to find out exactly who is watching and what they do with their remotes (scary, huh?).

Many analog devices will vanish as more powerful digital devices replace them. Analog TVs and radios will join the vacuum tubes on the shelves of electronic surplus stores. Digital broadcasting, providing more than 10 times the channel capacity of the analog spectrum, will be the norm. Digital television and radio will also have much better quality. The market for analog cathode-ray tubes will implode as various sorts of more compact, power-efficient flat panel displays come to dominate. Incandescent light bulbs will give way to much longer-lived LED lighting sources that consume little power. Analog cellular phones and phone modems will be disconnected forever as high-performance digital systems replace them. Although it would be great if mobile phone service got more reliable as a result, the likely scenario is that cellular services will be as flaky as today, only they'll move a lot more data, including video. Unfortunately, decreased reliability seems to be a pervasive side effect of progress, which explains why your PC crashes a lot more often than your television.

We'll wonder why we ever patronized video, record, and software stores. Broadband connections will be a much simpler way to distribute movies, music, and software. Network distribution of content will also be considerably cheaper: no manufacturing, no middleman, and no inventory to stock.

Wires on headphones, even for the cheapest portable stereo devices, will be gone because low-cost radio links will replace them. It will also be hard to find anyone who holds a cell phone to his ear because it will be much more convenient to put the guts of the phone on a wrist or waist and have it wirelessly link to a small earpiece and microphone.

Getting lost will take real creativity in an era where an embedded GPS receiver will enable personal electronic devices such as cell phones, personal digital assistants, and wristwatches to know where they are to within a few yards.

Junk mail will no longer show up. Advertisers will print their messages in your home or office using your online connection without troubling themselves with postage and printing costs. You won't call it junk mail because advertisers will know so much about you from monitoring your purchase patterns and online behaviors that the advertisements will be for items you probably will want to buy anyway. Postal meters will also be stamped out in an era in which secure remote printing of postage in homes and businesses becomes commonplace.

Stunt doubles in action-packed television shows and motion pictures will have ridden off into the sunset because incredibly realistic computer animation of actors will be much safer and cheaper to produce. Similarly, the Screen Actors Guild probably won't have extras on its roster in 20 years.

VICTIMS OF GENE-BASED THERAPIES

Hemophilia medicines that now come from limited supplies of donated blood will be replaced by safe proteins synthesized outside the body or by coagulation factors produced by genetically modified cells within the body.

Baldness treatments will thin out dramatically as dermatologists learn how to make scalp tissue grow hair follicles. Antigraying formulas may also fade away as gene therapies restore melanin pigments to older scalps. Although genetic baldness treatments are in the very early stages of development, the revenues that could be generated from effective treatments will no doubt guarantee that significant research dollars will be focused on getting to the root of the problem.

These days more than 600,000 coronary bypass procedures are performed annually, but such painful and debilitating surgery will be passe when cardiologists begin to use their genetic arsenal to grow new blood vessels in place of those that are blocked. Promising early results from clinical trials of vascular endothelial growth factor 2 suggest that stimulated blood-vessel growth may be a viable treatment option both in the heart and in the limbs well before 2020.

Patients with diabetes mellitus will finally be able to say good-bye to insulin injections. The better alternative: Doctors will routinely implant healthy islet of Langerhans cells into the pancreas.

Genetic diseases can arise from mutations of either single genes or multiple genes acting in concert. The first genetic diseases to be eliminated will most likely be the single-gene variety because doctors can more precisely target the locus of the disorder. Illnesses falling in this category include cystic fibrosis, familial hypercholesterolemia, Huntington's chorea, sickle-cell anemia, Duchenne (a form of muscular dystrophy), and Tay-Sachs disease. To some extent genetic research has already provided a type of treatment for these cases, in that individuals carrying the mutations can be identified and counseled on the risks of passing on the disorder to their offspring.

Immunosuppressants to prevent rejection of transplanted organs won't be needed in a world where doctors grow new organs from a patient's own tissues.

Chemotherapies that are toxic to both healthy and malignant cells are likely to become less important for attacking cancers when more precise gene-based treatments emerge. Techniques in development include: infecting tumors with recombinant viruses that make cancer cells vulnerable to antiviral and antibiotic agents; designing antibodies that attack cancers; and taking tumor cells out of the body, genetically altering them, and injecting them back into the body as vaccines that stimulate the immune system.

DROWNED IN OIL

Internal combustion engines won't be found on any sales lots because cars and trucks will be powered by battery-driven electric motors, hybrid gas/electric engines, or gas/fuel-cell engines. Even with improved fuel efficiency, long-haul trucking in the United States is likely to dwindle as it has in Europe, where gas prices are already high.

Cooling towers on industrial buildings will be eliminated because they throw off too much waste heat. They'll be replaced by natural-gas–powered absorption chillers similar to technology found on old gas refrigerators. Radiated energy will be recaptured to warm water and generate electricity.

Plastic wrap and many plastic utensils will be found only in landfills. Replacing plastics will be an entire family of biopolymers made from cornstarch. Some are already available but still too costly compared with compounds made from temporarily cheap petrochemicals.

BEYOND 2020

Let's ride our wave metaphor out to sea, past the swells of Moore's Law, genomics, and oil prices to longitudes where tomorrow's tsunamis are but today's gentle undulations. In these waters we'll find disturbances arising from nanotechnology, optical computing, bionics, and nuclear fusion, giving us glimpses of a future more interesting than we can guess.

SOURCE: Eric Haseltine, *Discover*, October 2000, pp. 84-87.

Opportunity Selection

Filtering Your Ideas

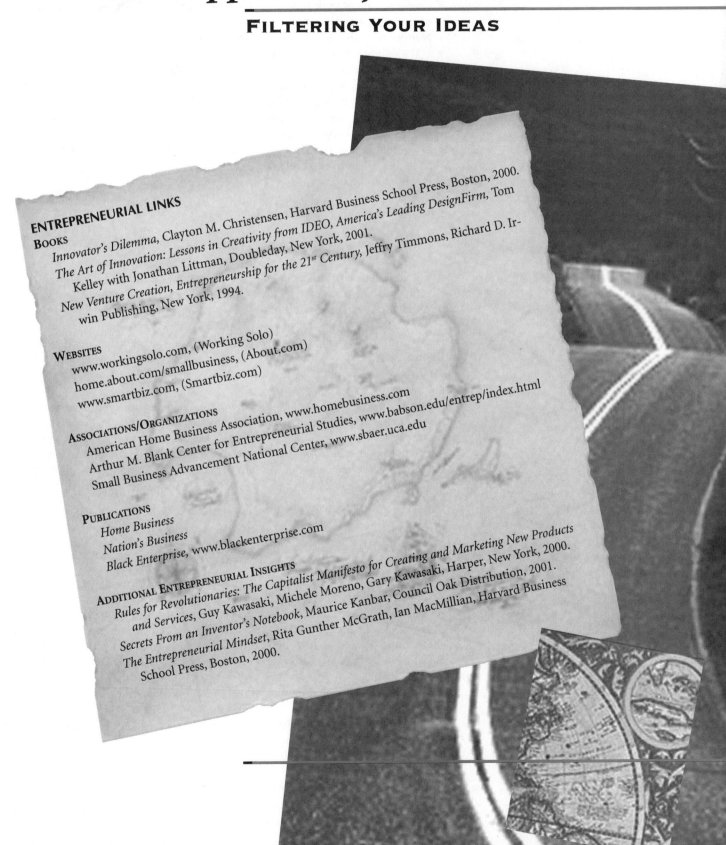

ENTREPRENEURIAL LINKS

Books

Innovator's Dilemma, Clayton M. Christensen, Harvard Business School Press, Boston, 2000.

The Art of Innovation: Lessons in Creativity from IDEO, America's Leading DesignFirm, Tom Kelley with Jonathan Littman, Doubleday, New York, 2001.

New Venture Creation, Entrepreneurship for the 21st Century, Jeffry Timmons, Richard D. Irwin Publishing, New York, 1994.

Websites

www.workingsolo.com, (Working Solo)

home.about.com/smallbusiness, (About.com)

www.smartbiz.com, (Smartbiz.com)

Associations/Organizations

American Home Business Association, www.homebusiness.com

Arthur M. Blank Center for Entrepreneurial Studies, www.babson.edu/entrep/index.html

Small Business Advancement National Center, www.sbaer.uca.edu

Publications

Home Business

Nation's Business

Black Enterprise, www.blackenterprise.com

Additional Entrepreneurial Insights

Rules for Revolutionaries: The Capitalist Manifesto for Creating and Marketing New Products and Services, Guy Kawasaki, Michele Moreno, Gary Kawasaki, Harper, New York, 2000.

Secrets From an Inventor's Notebook, Maurice Kanbar, Council Oak Distribution, 2001.

The Entrepreneurial Mindset, Rita Gunther McGrath, Ian MacMillian, Harvard Business School Press, Boston, 2000.

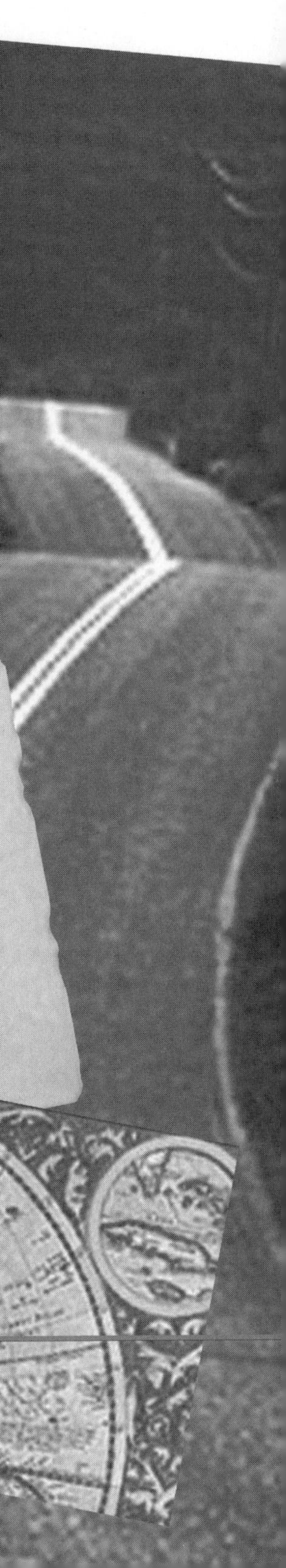

Learning Objectives

- Mesh your personal and business objectives with one of the many opportunities in the marketplace.
- Understand that your business objectives provide a positive and unique thrust to your business.
- Narrow your industry research until viable gaps appear.
- Gain insight into using the life-cycle yardstick.
- Discover how problems can be turned into opportunities.
- Understand how to use SIC and the new North American Industrial Classification System (NAICS).
- Research your favorite industry using secondary data and the Internet.
- Brainstorm creative solutions with mind mapping.
- Use a matrix grid for blending your objectives with your research findings to produce a portrait of a business.
- Define your business.

As you head for one of the doorways to small business, you may feel weighed down with information; that's part of life in the "Information Age." Hopefully, you may also be feeling exhilaration! Opportunities exist that were unheard of 2 years ago and, in some instances, 2 days ago. The speed of change is overwhelming. If you've done the research in Chapter 2, you understandably are experiencing information overload. Despite the fact that you're a creative, wound-up, and ready-to-charge person, unless you live vigorously for 200 years, you'll never be able to follow up on all the changing trends you have discovered.

What you need is a "filtering" system, something like a wine press or a Mouli mill (the kitchen machine that turns apples into applesauce) to get rid of peels (segments that aren't growing), stems (markets where barriers to entry are too high), and seeds (opportunities that don't mesh with your personal objectives). After completing the Action Steps in Chapter 3, you will have amassed valuable information and identified several well-defined business opportunities, and you will be further along on your Business Plan.

Welcome to Opportunity Selection

Conducting research will help you exploit gaps, that is, segments in the marketplace. Research shows you what new skills you will need to develop. It aims the power of your mind at a particular segment and opportunity. It opens up the world!

If you've been doing each Action Step as you read through this book, you're now ahead of the game. If you are not doing the Action Steps, go back and start. Here's a quick preview of the seven steps needed to achieve effective opportunity selection:

1. Keep personal and business objectives in mind throughout the filtering process.
2. Learn more about your favorite industry.
3. Identify three to five promising industry segments.
4. Identify problems that need solutions through research.
5. Brainstorm for solutions.
6. Mesh possible solutions with your objectives.
7. Concentrate on the most promising opportunity.

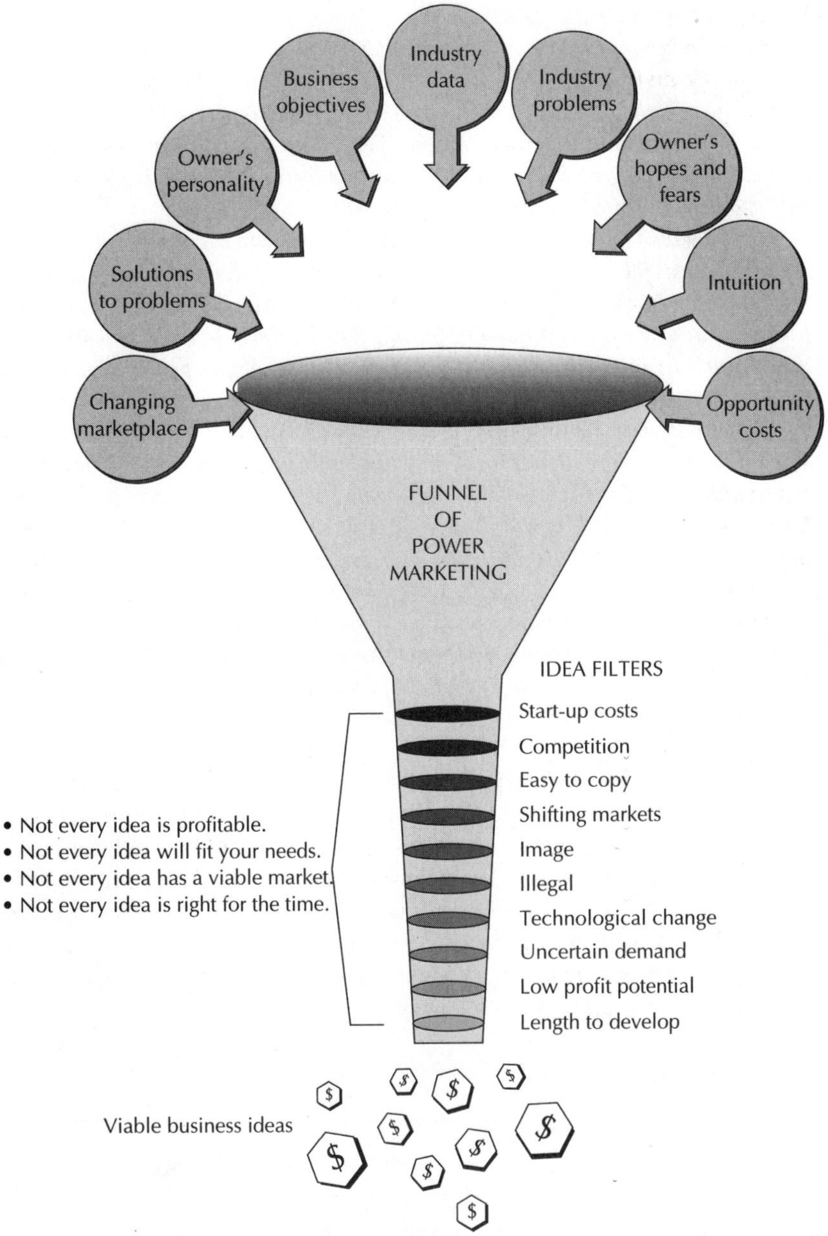

FIGURE 3.1
Opportunity Selection Funnel

At this point you have just begun to plan. The marketplace is open, filled with excitement and confusion. The most important thing is not to lose your momentum. Momentum is related to confidence, and confidence helps you win. The first step, keeping your personal and business objectives in mind, means that you have decided why you want to be an entrepreneur.

Opportunity selection is like a huge funnel equipped with a series of idea filters (Figure 3.1). You pour everything into this funnel: goals, personality, problems, hopes, fears, industry data, research, and intuition. And, after you narrow the choices, viable businesses filter through to the bottom. Carrying out this process gives you the knowledge of where you're going. And knowledge is power.

International Freelancer and Soloist

After Eric Duke graduated from law school, he freelanced as a lawyer while planning his wedding and yearlong European and Asian honeymoon with his new wife, Christy, who had just earned her accounting degree from the University of Minnesota. While planning the trip, Eric and Christy realized their true dream was to live overseas for several years. They figured now was the time to experience overseas living—no kids, no mortgage, and no car payments!

They saw the Opportunity Selection Funnel and began their search. On researching the overseas job market, Eric and Christy recognized that continuing to freelance might be the best choice. Eric spent a great deal of time on the Internet and in the library researching opportunities. One day he found an article about a nearby conference for private investment abroad. Eric signed up, and after paying $1000, he was ready to begin his primary research.

At the conference he came into contact with 50 lawyers from around the world. Eric made the best use of every meeting and break by finding out each lawyer's interests and needs. By the end of the meeting he had set up three meetings for the following week. In addition, Eric had a handshake deal with a Greek lawyer and a new idea for one of his current clients for an international office. His $1000 was well spent!

Without the international research background information and his goals clearly in his mind, Eric would have not been able to respond to the opportunities. Although it may seem that some people fall into opportunities, most "lucky" people are fully prepared!

Before you begin your industry research, review Action Step 5, which asked you to "Inc. Yourself." Think back to what is important to you. Keep this picture in the front of your mind at all times. Stay focused on what you want your life and your business to become. As you begin to explore the vast opportunities within your selected industry, you discover that some will mesh better than others. Making your business work for you and your customers will bring you the most satisfaction. Hold your business objectives, personal skills, passions and strengths in the forefront as you begin to follow the unending research threads.

INDUSTRY RESEARCH

Searching for trends in Chapter 2, you probably found a half-dozen industries that sounded interesting. You will be brainstorming, mind mapping, funneling, and matrixing ideas and opportunities throughout this chapter. It is time now to focus in on one industry in more depth and, by the end of the chapter, to define your main business idea. The industry that interests you most might be genetics, robotics, infotainment, food service, travel, education, publishing, **e-tailing**, construction, small manufacturing, or information services. Remember that it must be something that creates great interest and passion in you!

As you moved through your favorite industry collecting information from your previous Action Steps, what were the problems? What were the solutions? Where can you take these solutions?

While Chapter 2 focused on the broader picture—trends and problems, the focus of Chapter 3 is on the industry and opportunity you select. Chapter 4 asks you to profile your target market, and Chapter 5 looks at **competition.**

What you're now looking for is an accurate picture of opportunities in your selected industry. Conducting secondary and primary research does not eliminate risk but it does definitely reduce it. You need to learn what's breaking, what's cresting, and what's cooling down. You also need to be aware of potential industry changes on the horizon. Action Step 14 in Chapter 2 asked you to start researching by finding at least one association and one periodical associated with a selected industry. Now it's time to explore your selected industry in greater depth:

E-tailing Retailing on the Internet.

Competition A contestant in the same arena who is fighting for the business; everyone is fighting for customers' dollars.

Community Resource

Small Business Innovation Research (SBIR)—Research and Development Funding

The SBIR program is a highly specialized form of funding for small firms (less than 500 employees) to perform cutting-edge R&D that addresses the nation's most critical scientific and engineering needs. These needs span the technology spectrum—from aviation and agriculture to medicine and manufacturing.

SBIR is a federal government program administered by 10 federal agencies with $1.2 billion in funds for the purpose of helping to provide early stage Research and Development funding to small technology companies (or individual entrepreneurs who form a company). Solicitations are released periodically from each of the agencies and present technical topics of R&D, which the agency is interested in funding.

Companies are invited to compete for funding by submitting proposals answering the technical topic needs of the agency's solicitation. Each of these 10 agencies has various needs and flavors of the SBIR program, and you can learn more about them by visiting their sites. A list of SBIR Federal Agency links follows. In addition to these sites, contact your local SBA office, Economic Development Center, or SBDC to lead you to local and state offices, which can help you further explore the SBIR opportunities within your state.

Air Force SBIR/STTR: **www.afrl.af.mil/sbir/index.htm**
Army SBIR/STTR: **www.aro.army.mil/arowash/rt**
BMDO SBIR Program Home Page: **www.winbmdo.com**
DARPA SBIR Program Home Page: **www.darpa.mil/sbir**
DOC-NOAA SBIR Page: **www.rdc.noaa.gov/~amd/sbir.html**
DOC-NIST Home Page: **www.nist.gov/sbir**
DOD SBIR Home Page: **www.acq.osd.mil/sadbu/sbir**
DOD Defense Technical Information Center (DTIC): **www.dtic.mil/dtic/sbir**
DOD Special Operations Acquisition Center (SOAC): **soal.socom.mil/smallbus04.htm**
DOE SBIR Home Page: **sbir.er.doe.gov/sbir**
DOT SBIR Home Page: **www.volpe.dot.gov/sbir**
ED (Dept. of Education): **www.ed.gov/offices/OERI/SBIR**
EPA SBIR Home Page: **es.epa.gov/ncerqa/sbir**
NASA SBIR Home Page: **sbir.nasa.gov**
Navy SBIR/STTR: **www.navysbir.com**
NIH SBIR Home Page: **grants.nih.gov/grants/funding/sbir.htm**
NSF SBIR Home Page: **www.eng.nsf.gov/sbir**
SBA SBIR Home Page: **www.sbaonline.sba.gov/SBIR**
USDA SBIR Home Page: **www.reeusda.gov/sbir**

Source: National SBIR/STTR Conference Center, **www.zyn.com/sbir** (accessed May 1, 2001).

- What role is technology playing in the industry?
- Who are the key players?
- What are the trends?
- Are there barriers to entry? If so, what are they?
- What are the niches?
- Where are the gaps?
- What is the cost of **positioning** yourself?
- Are there distribution changes underway?
- Who are the industry leaders? What makes them successful?
- What is required to succeed?
- Can the market handle another player?

Positioning Where a firm or product lies in the buyer's mind compared to other products.

ACTION STEP 17

DETERMINE NAICS OR SIC CODES

Find the NAICS or SIC codes for your:

- Industry segment (i.e., retail candy store)
- Suppliers
- Wholesalers
- Customers (if applicable)

Determine through your research the size of your market in dollars and volume.

Locate future sales projections for your industry. What is the growth rate? Are you in a growth segment?

- Is the industry regulated?
- How long does it take to bring a product to market?

Later, after you have gathered the data, you can use these and other emerging questions as idea filters for the Opportunity Selection Funnel (see Figure 3.1). In addition, you are building background information and statistical data for your Business Plan. Remember, bankers and investors want to see backup data; your research will provide facts and figures that demonstrate the need for your product or service in your selected industry or area.

One of the reasons you were asked to look at the big picture in Chapter 2 was to be sure you kept your eyes open to technology and changes throughout the business world. For example, bookstore owners and **www.amazon.com** have to be looking over their shoulders at the new breakthrough with e-books—small computers that look and function much like a book. With an initial investment of about $200 for the computer, individuals can download books directly from the Internet to their e-book computers, completely eliminating the need for traditional books, bookstores, and shipping costs. What will happen to textbook manufacturers, local bookstores, writers, graphic artists, and paper manufacturers? MP3 and Napster changed the music world. Keep your eyes wide open, or be left in the dust!

The point is to find an industry segment where there is room for growth. While driving down a street, you see a shopping mall being renovated. You suspect that the facelift is an attempt to move the mall from a mature or declining phase back to its initial growth phase.

In addition to growth, look for industry **breakthroughs**. What in your selected industry or segment is really humming? Early computers' memory banks filled large rooms and read data from punched cards. The first industry breakthrough was the printed circuit, the second was the microchip processor, and the third was the Internet. What is the fourth? What breakthroughs are now occurring in your selected industry? Does your business idea capitalize on these latest advances in technology and imagination?

CONDUCTING SECONDARY RESEARCH FOR YOUR SELECTED INDUSTRY

Chapter 2 introduced secondary, primary, and new eyes research. You may have stumbled across a wonderful opportunity with your new eyes, and now it's time to develop industry-specific knowledge. Is someone else already conducting a similar business? Is there a market? Are you in a **growth industry?** Will people pay for your product or service? What do you need to know before leaping? The first place to start is with secondary research. If you are lucky, it will provide you with free, excellent background information.

RESEARCH USING NAICS/SIC CODES

Almost all government statistics, business research, and tracking will use the North American Industry Classification System (NAICS). NAICS will replace the U.S. Standard Industrial Classification (SIC) system. NAICS provides comparable statistics throughout businesses in North America. To locate your selected industry's NAICS code and those of your potential customers and suppliers, refer to the government's NAICS manual (available at your library) or contact the NAICS Association at **www.naics.com**. For some time, both systems will be in use. NAICS is a numerical system that assigns a number to almost every identifiable industry. The structure of the new system is:

XX	Industry Sector (20 major sectors)
XXX	Industry Subsector
XXXX	Industry Group
XXXXX	Industry
XXXXXX	U.S., Canadian, or Mexican national specific industry

Breakthrough A new way through, over, under, or around an obstacle.

Growth industry Annual sales increase well above average.

Growth segment An identifiable slice of an industry that is expanding more rapidly than the industry as a whole.

North American Industry Classification System

An example of this coding system follows:

31	Manufacturing
315	Apparel Manufacturing
3151	Apparel Knitting Mills
31511	Hosiery and Sock Mills
315111	Sheer Hosiery Mills
315119	Other Hosiery and Sock Mills
31519	Other Apparel Knitting Mills
315191	Outerwear Knitting Mills
315192	Underwear and Nightwear Knitting Mills
3152	Cut and Sew Apparel Manufacturing
31521	Cut and Sew Apparel Contractors
315211	Men's and Boys' Cut and Sew Apparel Contractors
315212	Women's and Girls' Cut and Sew Apparel Manufacturing
31522	Men's and Boys' Cut and Sew Apparel Manufacturers
315221	Men's and Boys' Cut and Sew Underwear and Nightwear Manufacturing
315222	Men's and Boys' Cut and Sew Suit, Coat, and Overcoat Manufacturing
315223	Men's and Boys' Cut and Sew Shirt (except Work Shirt) Manufacturing
315224	Men's and Boys' Cut and Sew Trouser, Slack, and Jean Manufacturing
315225	Men's and Boys' Cut and Sew Work Clothing Manufacturing
315228	Men's and Boys' Cut and Sew Other Outerwear Manufacturing

NAICS and SIC codes help you:

- Discover what industry you are in for statistical purposes.
- Define the boundaries of that industry.
- Locate customers, suppliers, and competitors.
- Reach out to other industries thoughtfully and systematically.
- Track customer sales.

Once you have researched your NAICS codes, you are ready to use all the resources available. Action Steps 17 and 18 should be reviewed now and worked on throughout the chapter.

ACTION STEP 18

RESEARCH YOUR SELECTED INDUSTRY SEGMENT THROUGH SECONDARY DATA

Which segment really attracts you? What magnetic pull can't you resist? To help you get started, recall what you discovered in Action Steps 8, 9, 11, 12, 13, and 15.

Keep your views wide-angled by looking at two or three segments that are promising and interesting segments to YOU.

After you've decided on "your" segment, research in depth. It will help to organize your research if you categorize trends, target markets, competition, industry breakthroughs, and market share. For now, while looking for opportunities, focus primarily on the segment and its changes, and be sure to file all extraneous data for upcoming Action Steps.

If you're working alone, write an industry overview. If you're working with a team, there will be less confusion if each team member writes an overview, and later shares his or her perspective with the others.

This is a never-ending Action Step. Once you are in business you have to be as diligent in keeping up with the segment as you were in your initial research. Only it's more important because now your money is on the line!

Libraries

The first research stop is your public or school library. Many large cities offer libraries focused on business with excellent technical expertise available—librarians can help people find needles in a haystack. An excellent reference librarian can be one of your best resources and save you an incredible amount of research time. Always ask lots of questions.

Technical and specialized journals may be available only through private corporate libraries. Use your local library's computer to generate a list of these. Also, certain trade groups and associations have private libraries. When researching the horse racing industry, one student located a private library in Los Angeles. With one phone call and a plea, he was in!

In addition, more than 1300 federal depository libraries, which offer a wealth of free information, are available throughout the United States. Find the one closest to you at **www.access.gpo.gov/su_docs/locators/findlibs.**

Trade Associations

Your next research stop should be the trade associations within your selected industry as discussed in Chapter 2. Detailed information about these associations is provided in the *Directory of Associations*. Select four or five associations that look the most promising, and request information. Many of their products are available only to members, and membership fees for start-ups are usually low. Associations provide vast resources—you usually can't go wrong looking for data there.

Throughout the text we have highlighted many of the resources available through one association, the National Association of Music Merchants (NAMM), **www.namm.com**, which services the music product industry. Be aware that many other associations provide similar, incredible resources for your particular industry. Do **NOT** fail to seek out your associations.

Do you want to learn about the Czech Republic's music marketplace? NAMM will sell you a report for $50, which is probably less than the cost of two international calls. Secondary information always provides you with a starting point. After reading a report on the Czech marketplace, your primary research will be much easier. Your questions to those in the industry will become focused, targeted, and productive. Secondary information sharpens intuition as well.

Music USA (Figure 3.2), published annually, renders data on 18 product categories and provides general social and economic indicators for the music products industry. For $45 this information can be in your hands. Fortunately, most of your potential competitors may not be accessing this data. Get a leg up and know the industry upside down before you leap.

For specific training opportunities, NAMM presents classes throughout the United States (Figure 3.3) that help entrepreneurs to get up and running quickly and efficiently and to save time, money, sweat, and tears. If you can't attend classes through the association, check out possible online courses, such as those offered through NAMM U, or seminars offered regionally or at trade shows. In addition, many associations offer start-up manuals with incredibly detailed and well-researched advice and information. Some would-be entrepreneurs are cocky and won't take advice from others. Don't make this mistake! Developing expertise takes time, energy, and money. Be open and willing to learn from others.

Trade Shows

Another way to research your selected industry is to attend trade shows—events where manufacturers and corporations in a common industry demonstrate their wares to potential customers. While there, research your competition, pick up literature, talk to everyone you can, and soak it all in. Most trade shows are open only to

FIGURE 3.2
NAMM Music USA

Music USA is NAMM's annual statistical review of the music products industry. It contains data on units shipped from manufacturers to retailers for 18 product categories and social and economic indicators affecting the industry. Music USA is available to both members ($15) and nonmembers ($45) of NAMM.

Features

- Industry Revenue at a Glance
- Segment Data
  - Fretted Products
  - Sound Reinforcement
  - The Piano Market
  - School Music Market
  - Printed Music
  - General Accessories
  - Microphones
  - Percussion Market
  - Multi-Track Market
  - Portable Keyboards
  - Signal Processing
  - Karaoke Market
  - Electronic Musical Instruments
  - Computer Music Products Market
- Cables
  - Organ Market
  - The DJ Market
  - The Music and Sound Industry
- Import/Export Statistics
- Gallup Survey
- Music Retailing
  - Excerpts from NAMM's Cost of Doing Business Report
  - Salaries, Wages, & Benefits
- Profile of the American Music Dealer

SOURCE: **www.namm.com** (accessed March 1, 2001).

FIGURE 3.3
NAMM University

NAMM University currently offers 28 courses at various locations across the United States in addition to online courses through NAMM U.

Sample Course Listings
SALES

- Sales Training Institute
- Real World Sales for Music Product Professionals
- Road Kill for Retailers
- Road Kill III-Selling to Retailers
- Road Kill-Road Warriors

MANAGEMENT

- Survival Skills for Supervisors & Managers
- Low-Budget/High Impact Marketing
- Managing Killer Service
- Financial Management for Music Product Retailers
- Managing Gen-X Employees
- Profits in a Changing Industry

NAMM University's mission is "to provide high quality professional developmental products and programs to the music products industry, providing performance-based, measurable results through flexible formats and effective instructive design, for both retail and commercial courses."

NAMM University's goal is to develop and enhance members' professional competitiveness, serving the strategic interests of both companies and employers by strengthening their competitive advantage in a changing industry environment.

For more information and current listings, see **www.namm.com**.

SOURCE: **www.namm.com** (accessed March 1, 2001).

GLOBAL VILLAGE

USA TRADE ONLINE, WWW.USATRADEONLINE.GOV

USA Trade Online provides access to specific U.S. export and import information on more than 18,000 commodities worldwide. Foreign marketing intelligence can help guide you in selecting international marketing opportunities. The service provided by STAT-USA and the Foreign Trade Division of the U.S. Census Bureau is available online for $50 a month or an annual subscription of $300.

USA Trade Online customers can use the information to:
Discover existing and emerging export markets for your products
Compare your product exports with related products
Determine your market share of export markets for specific products
Monitor trends in specific products, markets, and countries

USA Trade Online has 2- through 10- digit HS detail for commodities in the following data tables:

Exports—current month and previous month
Exports—cumulative year to date, current year and prior year
Exports—annual 2 year, historical
Imports—current month and previous month
Imports—cumulative year to date

firms within the industry. Ask your industry friends to take you as a guest. To locate trade shows for your industry, go to **www.tsnn.com**. Search by industry, month, or city. A sample listing that follows represents just a few of the food and beverage trade shows to be held in September 2001:

Fine Food Australia 2001: Sydney
International Exposition for Food Processors 2001: Las Vegas
Interfood: Gothenburg
SETOUCHI Total Food Fair: Hiroshima
Food China 2001: Shanghai

Each trade show listed is hyperlinked, enabling you to access further data. Additionally, **www.tsnn.com** will help you locate associations and publications affiliated with individual industries. Locate your trade shows, put your most comfortable shoes on, attend, open your eyes, listen to everyone you meet, and ask many questions. The knowledge you gain from visiting trade shows will be immeasurable.

Additional Resources

Newspapers—Several trend-watchers monitor more than 6000 regional and daily newspapers. Study your local newspapers for business and other news. For a bigger picture, read *The Wall Street Journal* or *The Christian Science Monitor.* Thousands of daily, weekly, national, and college papers are linked at **www.ajr.newslink.org**. If you are exploring a service business, research other towns' papers to see if someone is currently providing such a service, phone the owners, and ask questions! Remember, people love to talk about their "business baby."

Magazines—Reviewing magazines keeps one up to date. The ads tell you what's hot and where the money is flowing. Visit **www.mediafinder.com** or **www.ajr.newslink.org**.

Trade Journals—These are valuable resources once you know the industry you want to enter. Many journals are also available online.

Banks—Banks make money by "renting" or loaning money. Large corporate banks have staffs of economists, marketing experts, and others who research and write forecasts and reports of economic trends. Request copies of these reports.

Brokerage Firms—These service-oriented companies have staff analysts who survey specific industries. The analysts gather earnings statistics, attend corporate and stockholder meetings, read annual reports, and publish reports about individual companies and industry overviews. Reports, which predict the direction an industry is taking, are available to clients of the firms and sometimes are available at libraries. In addition, you can contact the report authors for further information and insight.

Planning Offices—Cities and counties employ planners to chart and plan future growth. Check the city and county offices' listings in the phone book to locate these offices. For the best service, however, you'll need to visit the office, make friends with the staff, and be pleasant and patient. If you are planning a retail establishment or a manufacturing facility, these visits are essential. You also may need to attend city council meetings or at least read all of the meeting minutes to be aware of upcoming changes and long-range planning.

Reports from Colleges and Universities—State universities publish annual and semiannual reports on economic conditions in the state where they are established. You probably can access copies of these by writing to the university publications office. Reports are also published by private institutions of higher learning with special interests. A vast amount of technical research is conducted at universities throughout the world. Search directly on the Internet and talk directly with cutting-edge leaders.

Real Estate Firms—Large commercial and industrial real estate firms have access to developers' site research. The more specific your request, the easier it will be for these firms to help you. Familiarize yourself with the dynamics of the area. Which firms are going into business? Which firms are relocating? Where is expansion occurring?

SBA—The Small Business Administration of the U.S. government has an excellent website: **www.sba.gov**. This website provides access to hundreds of resources, including franchising, financing, start-up costs, and federal and state programs.

INCREDIBLE RESOURCE

STATE OF THE NATION

www.stat-usa.gov, 1-800-STAT-USA, (202) 482-1986

STAT-USA's State of the Nation scours the government information vaults, assembles that information in one location, and delivers it via advanced computer technology. The information is available by subscription online for $175 a year or $75 a quarter. In addition, individual reports can be purchased without a subscription. For free access to the information, locate your local federal depository library at **www.access.gpo.gov/su_docs/fdlp/index.html,** and complete your research. State of the Nation data is compiled by the Economics and Statistics Administration within the Department of Commerce.

Historical and current economic and financial data are both available. This impressive collection of data is easy to use and provides excellent statistical backup data for a Business Plan. Remember bankers live and die by numbers, and here is where you can find the numbers to back up your ideas and dreams.

In the Consumer Price Index (CPI), housing, employment, manufacturing, economic policy, and general economic indicators are available.

U.S. Department of Commerce (**www.doc.gov**)—This department publishes the annual *U.S. Industrial Outlook* that forecasts growth rates for the coming year. Check your local chamber for additional information and support.

www.census.gov—This website provides access to 100 current industrial reports on more than 5000 manufactured products and is a treasure chest of data.

Bureau of Labor Statistics (**stats.bls.gov**)—Economic and employment statistics can be obtained in hard copy or downloaded from its website.

www.marketingtools.com—Consumer trends and demographic changes are tracked on this website.

www.brint.com—One of the most extensive general business sites on the Internet. It searches the Internet for forums, books, articles, announcements, comprehensive indexes of magazines, journals, and publishers.

Websites—To locate industry information on the Internet, begin searching under your selected industry and follow the never-ending thread. About 1000 sites are added each day. Go to your competitors' websites to find general industry information. In Chapter 5 we will delve deeper into researching competitors.

Standard & Poor's Industry Surveys—Provide an overall review of industry and major players and are available at your local library.

Company Directories on the Web—Hoover's covers 10,000 firms (**www.hoovers.com**); Dun & Bradstreet provides free, brief profiles (**www.dnb.com**); Thomas Register has information on manufacturers (**www.thomasregister.com**).

Predicasts, Wall Street Journal Index, Find-SVP, *Small Business Sourcebook, Encyclopedia of Business Information Sources*—Excellent information tools.

LOCATING PRIVATE DATABASE VENDORS

A number of private database service firms have emerged, and many of them are frequent advertisers in *Marketing Tools* and *American Demographics Magazine.* (Contact American Demographics, Inc. at 127 West State, Ithaca, New York 14850 or **www.marketingtools.com.**) Also, many metropolitan newspapers now sell specialized research studies at modest prices. Some vendors specialize in niche markets, such as boomers, healthcare, teens, and Internet users. Others provide data for manufacturers, site selection, and locating foreign markets. A list of potential vendors and a short synopsis of their capabilities follows. Many of these vendors supply free analyses in addition to their paid studies, research, and data CD-ROMs.

ACTION STEP 19

NET RESEARCH ASSIGNMENT

Action Step 19 asks you to complete several industry-specific research assignments.

1. Research at least three associations in your industry. What services do they offer? What classes and publications do they offer? What research can they provide? What is the cost to join?
2. Click on www.tsnn.com to locate trade shows for your selected industry.
3. Using www.ajrnewslink.org, research your industry and customers. If you have a technical product, you will need to research it through specific databases found in the library and online.
4. Prepare a list of the best magazines and trade journals for your selected industry. Try to read at least four or five. This is time very well spent. If they are not readily available, locate someone in your desired line of business and ask if they will loan copies.
5. Go to www.sba.gov. What sources on the SBA site do you think will be most helpful?
6. Go to www.census.gov and explore applicable census data.
7. Using *Standard and Poor's, Hoover's Online,* or *Dun and Bradstreet,* profile several of your competitors.
8. Locate "virtual communities" or newsgroups for your business on the Internet.

Virtual community Online group of individuals within an industry sector.

1. Roper Starch Worldwide (**www.roper.com**) provides marketing, public opinion, advertising, and media research in the United States and around the world.
2. Easy Analytic Software, Inc., (**www.easidemographics.com**) provides excellent demographic information and franchise potential data.
3. Claritas (**www.claritas.com**) and CACI (**www.demographics.caci.com**) are both excellent sources for additional demographic information on potential customers.
4. Mediamark Research (**www.mediamark.com**) provides research on Internet usage.
5. InfoUSA (**www.infousa.com**) can help you generate sales leads and mail and telemarketing campaigns.

Searching the Internet is an adventure because you never know what you will encounter. Many researchers and writers can be reached directly via the Internet. University websites lead you to researchers in your specific field, crucial for those involved in high-tech or manufacturing. First, visit home pages, if they are available. Your questions may be answered there. Additional links to sources also may aid you. If not, send an e-mail requesting information.

You may be lucky and find an online community such as **www.foodonline.com**, a site that provides a virtual community and marketplace for professionals and vendors in the food equipment and ingredients industries. This website saves time in locating products, employees, proposals, and regulations and provides online chat rooms in which to locate additional information. Jump on the Internet and locate your "**virtual community**," which will give you access to possibly thousands of experienced people. Start tossing out questions in the chat rooms, and you may gain access to "free consultants."

Janet Shore, a successful entrepreneur, had only 3 days to complete a retail store proposal requiring only California products. She jumped on the Internet, completed the proposal, and won the contract. After awarding Janet the contract, the vendor asked how she was able to get the proposal together in 3 days. Hard work, diligence, experience and THE INTERNET!

It is time for you to head onto the Internet and complete Action Step 19.

If you are developing a product and need patent information, read Chapter 10 before going further.

PRIMARY RESEARCH ON YOUR SELECTED RESEARCH

After spending days or weeks researching your favorite industry, whittle down the opportunities to two or three by using the Opportunity Selection Funnel. Use the questions on the funnel to help you.

Get off the Internet and out of the library! It is time to step out and talk directly with people involved in the industry: salespeople, developers, manufacturers, competitors, suppliers, and customers. You now have a strong knowledge base and a million questions. Ask away! Take notes. Now is the time to set your ego on the shelf. Listen to everything people say. Remember, your goal is to provide a service or product that your market needs and wants, not a product you want to give them!

Primary research can be conducted via telephone, mail, and face-to-face interviews. Depending on your needs, time, and available money, select the research methods that are best for you. When conducting personal interviews, listen carefully and read between the lines. Ask intelligent follow-up questions. Probe your potential customer's psyche. Action Step 20 helps you to define your opportunity further.

It's time to start sharing your business ideas with others. This may be a scary time. Many entrepreneurs are afraid to share their idea for fear someone will steal it. It can happen. But if you don't share your idea, how can you turn it into a business? In Appendix C you will find a confidentiality agreement that may make you feel more comfortable.

Industry Segmentation and Gap Analysis

Industry segmentation breaks down potential markets into as many "digestible" segments as possible, just as is done with NAICS codes. The more you learn about an industry, the further you'll be able to go. This procedure helps you isolate opportunity gaps and see combinations of gaps that may constitute markets. Figure 3.4 illustrates a mind map that "explodes" one segment of the food industry. This is the kind of thinking we want you to do in Action Step 21. This is another brainstorming activity, so have fun with it.

Healthy Gourmet

Susan and John Johnson, founders of Healthy Gourmet, searched for gaps and opportunities by taking a look at a major, far-reaching trend—the meal replacement market. People want fresh, high-quality food, but they don't want to cook! The "time bind" is fueling this market change.

Frozen dinners have been available since 1953, but these can't be compared to the freshly-prepared, nutritionally-balanced meals from Healthy Gourmet. These include grilled chicken with couscous salad, peach dressing, and fresh fruit or grilled flank steak, parmesan potatoes, and cider carrots.

After coming home to face cooking one time too many, Susan realized that there had to be many other busy individuals hoping for a hot, wonderful gourmet meal as they opened their front doors. With unemployment less than 5 percent, there were many others with the same need and available cash!

Researching their selected industry, Susan and John recognized that no one was producing fresh, made-from-scratch, calorie-controlled gourmet meals that met the guidelines of the American Heart Association, the American Cancer Society, and the American Dietetic Association. Others merely produced frozen meals, diet replacement drinks, take-out food, and so on.

Quality meals that were convenient and nutritionally balanced represented a gap the Johnsons knew they could fill. With a 3000-square-foot kitchen, a varied menu of 1 to 21 meals per week, and delivery to one's door or to several pickup points twice a week, they developed a product and service that met their customers' needs.

Healthy Gourmet was located in the heart of a leading and growing high-tech community whose demographics included the "young" and "highly educated." Chapter 4 delves deeper into the Johnson's target market.

Five years after opening their doors they are grossing more than $1,650,000 and have expanded their business to include Los Angeles and San Diego counties in addition to Orange County.

In business one needs to segment markets and then differentiate products or services to meet one's target market's needs. By requiring no minimum orders the Johnsons enabled busy people to access their product on their own terms without preset requirements.

Find gaps in the marketplace, and take advantage of those gaps by developing products and services that fulfill the needs of the marketplace. Listen closely to your customers. They will lead you in the right direction.

Wrap your product around your target market through pricing, product development, marketing, advertising, and location. Many times, opportunities in the market exist, not because there is a need for a new product or service, but because there are new target markets. As a result, a product can be delivered differently, priced lower, or offered in combination with another product or service.

When you write your Business Plan, explain why you have selected a particular industry segment (gap). If you have chosen a promising segment and have communicated your excitement about it, you will have developed a "hook" for the banker or venture capitalist who will read your plan.

Action Step 20

Brainstorming Solutions

Okay, here's where you need to get creative. Brainstorm solutions with everyone you meet. If your business idea is fairly well developed, you should be presenting it to people and asking them to brainstorm with you as to its fit in the marketplace.

You will generate better ideas and solutions now that you have completed your secondary research. Have fun at this stage as you continue to develop your ideas. Write down everyone's input. You may want to take a tape recorder. After brainstorming ideas, ask yourself the following questions:

- Which niches can you own?
- Which niches might be the most profitable?
- Which niches will be easiest to reach?
- What can you do to be unique?

Action Step 21

Mind Mapping Your Business

Narrow the Gaps; Watch Your Target Customer Emerge

Consider all the secondary and primary information you have gathered. Take out paper and pencil and start a mind map (see Figure 3.4). Review all the ideas you have researched. Sketch out your mind map focusing on the specific segment that you have chosen.

You need to stay with this segment until you know whether or not it will work for you.

Ideas will come together as you place opportunities next to each other. You will be able to identify the most promising gap in your selected industry.

FIGURE 3.4
Healthy Gourmet Mind Map

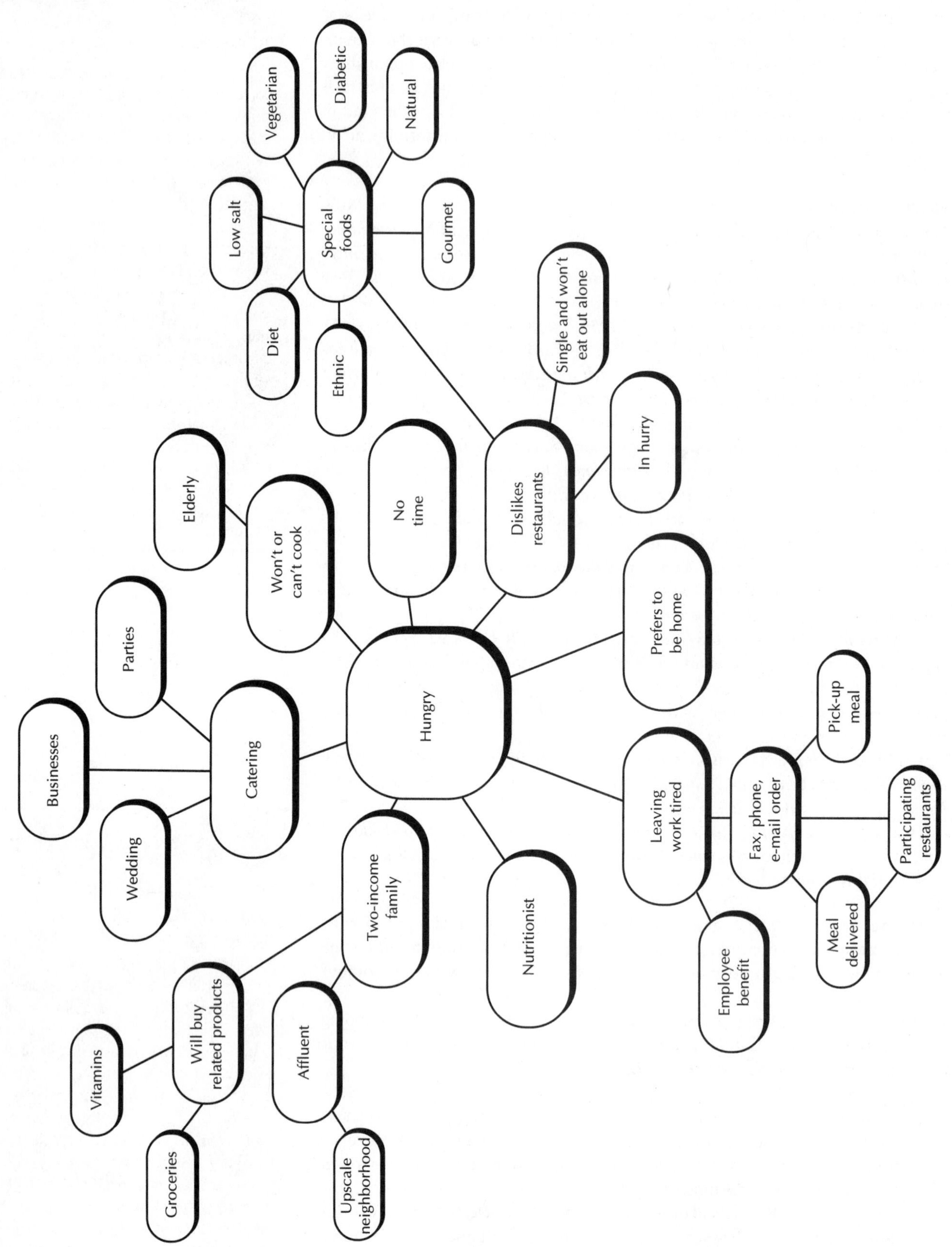

More Brainstorming for Possible Solutions

Brainstorming is a process used by many groups—think tanks, middle management, small businesses, and major corporations—to generate fresh ideas. The goal is to come up with many ideas, some that may seem far out or even erroneous, and then, to see how concepts develop as momentum grows. The key to brainstorming is to reserve judgment initially so that creativity is not stifled.

What follows is a recap of a brainstorming session held by the Info Team, the founders of the Software School, when they began to transform problems into business opportunities. As you read, consider not only the information you gather but also the process involved.

Software School

Before they began, three friends listed ideas for businesses that had come to them during the earlier steps of the opportunity selection process. One wanted to start a company to design computer games, and go into head-to-head competition with Microsoft and Sony. Another, a graphic designer with game design experience, said he could certainly help with the artwork.

On a flipchart, Derek wrote "Design Computer Games."

"Here's another," Robert said. "Let's take over Oracle!"

For a half hour they transferred their ideas—game design, leveraged buyouts, software design, retailing, end-user training, and marketing—onto the flip chart. Robert, who was turning into a mad inventor, wanted to design a computer program that boiled down all election data into a single voter, who then made the decision on who became president. The 2000 election had gone on too long for Robert!

Phil Carpenter suggested a takeover of all Chinese hardware manufacturers.

"Time for a break," Derek said.

When they came back from their break, Phil flipped to a clean sheet on the chart and proceeded to draw a mind map. As Phil developed the mind map, five areas for a business emerged: hardware manufacture, software manufacturing (including game design), retailing (both hardware and software), training (taking advantage of the speed of change in the industry, which left users in the dust), and marketing and promoting software products.

Further refinements of the mind map brought training and marketing into the foreground while retailing hardware and software receded into the background.

Excitement built up in the room as the ideas flowed, and soon all three friends were standing at the flipchart, adding their ideas and amendments to the mind map. As the brainstorming session wound down, they had identified two areas to explore.

The first area was computer training taking up where software makers left off. They could start in one location and then do on-site training in businesses and corporations.

The second area was marketing and promotion. Robert, who had worked for Microsoft, knew there were many small companies—bootstrap operations run by dreamers whose basic skills did not include targeting customers, promotions, or building an image.

"You could consult," Phil said. "You love that."

"I'd love to do the promotions!" Robert said.

There was a silence.

"So," Derek said, "We've got two options that look pretty good. How do we decide?"

"How about a matrix?" Derek said.

"A what?"

"It's a way of weighing what you really want. I learned about it from one of my inventor buddies. He called it an Opportunity Matrix."

"Let's try it," they said.

It's helpful to summarize after a brainstorming session so that you can identify the most useful ideas. Let's summarize what happened in this session:

1. *Using the mind-mapping device, the team identified problems and possible solutions.*
2. *They decided all ideas were good ideas.*
3. *The two ideas that looked best were computer training and software marketing and promotion.*
4. *They asked whether they could do both at once, or if one would have to go on the back burner.*

MATRIX ANALYSIS

Whereas some people like to use lists, mind maps, or opportunity funnels for arriving at conclusions, others prefer a more systematic numeric method. A **matrix grid** can provide a desired structure to serve as another type of filter. After you have brainstormed some possible solutions, you need to improve your focus on them and evaluate them. The matrix grid in Figure 3.5 helped the Info Team do this.

At their next meeting they rated each possible solution on the objectives, which they had designated earlier. On review the software school received the highest total of points from the group. The key people saw this as an area where their teamwork skills within a fast-growing industry could be used best. In addition, the cost to develop a school was relatively low compared to other choices. The opportunity gap seemed wider, there was little competition, and the barriers to entry (cost) were very low in comparison.

As trainers, they would have to:

Solve problems. Businesspeople have problems to solve and tasks to perform. Computers reduce the workload. All one needs is an open mind and the right software.

Provide clarity. Software documentation can be confusing. The school would devise a clear, streamlined, space-age teaching system.

Matrix grid Measurement tool where ideas are screened and evaluated in order to find solutions.

FIGURE 3.5
Opportunity Matrix Grid for Software School

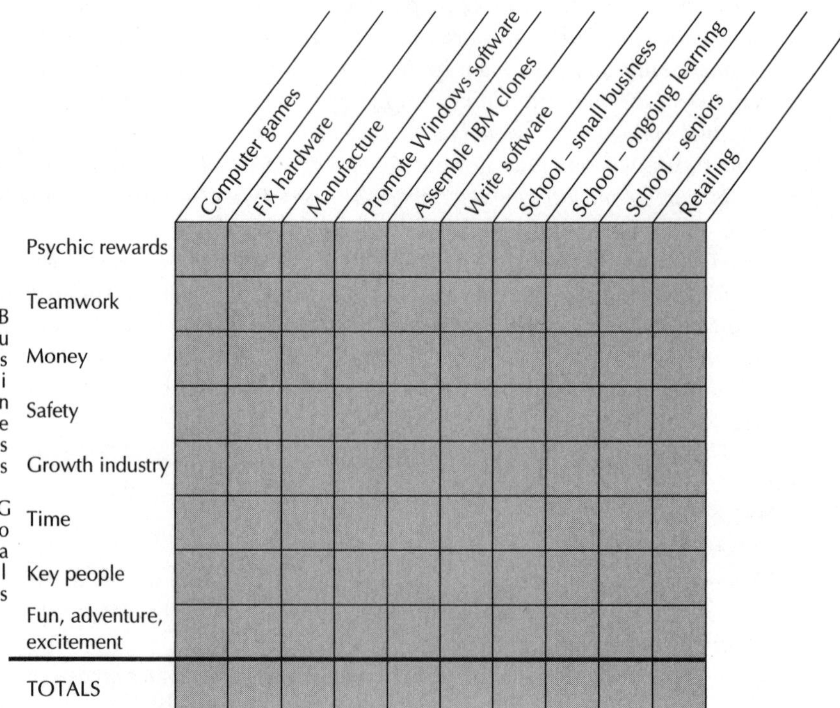

Offer speed. Businesspeople are in a hurry—time is money. Could the school teach software in a week? a day? a half day?

Build a psychological cushion. The founders would start a club. Once a student had taken a course, he or she would be a software club member for life and be entitled to take the course again at no charge. In addition, the instructors would provide online assistance as needed for the first 6 months after the students attended the class.

Charge reasonable fees. Research studies showed that businesspeople would pay $250 a day to learn a software program's intricacies.

Enjoy yourself. If clients are having fun learning, they'll relax and learn more. If they learn more, they'll spread the word about the school.

Review Figure 3.5 and prepare a matrix grid to help you focus on the best course of action for your opportunity. Action Step 22 tells you how to do it.

ACTION STEP 22

MATRIX GRID

MESH POSSIBLE SOLUTIONS WITH OBJECTIVES

A matrix analysis helps you focus, especially if you're working with a group and have diverse objectives to satisfy. Prepare a large grid, and put it on the wall, so all members of the team can participate.

Down the left side, list business goals brainstormed earlier. Along the top, list the business opportunities you have discovered. Select a rating system to use for evaluating the match of each possible solution with each objective. It could be a 10-point scale or a plus-zero-minus system:

Plus (+) = 3

Zero (0) = 2

Minus (−) = 1

When you've rated all the combinations, find the total for each column. The totals will indicate your best prospect. The rest is up to you.

Taking Stock

What have you learned about opportunity selection? Before you answer this, take a minute to rethink what you want to achieve with your business. If you feel a little uneasy about how fast you've run the last couple of laps, perhaps it's because you haven't identified your industry or the right opportunity for you. If it doesn't feel like home, you should sense it now. Have you used the Opportunity Selection Funnel (see Figure 3.1)?

Have you whittled down the list from hundreds of trends to industry segments to the one opportunity that emerged through all your research? Does it feel like home? If so, you are ready to define your new business.

DEFINE YOUR BUSINESS

Watch a painter working at an easel. She works close to the canvas, layering the paint with brush and spatula. But at regular intervals, the painter steps back for a long view of the work. Up close, the artist can see only brushstrokes and colors, but from a few feet away, the entire painting can be seen. From a few more feet, the entire landscape being painted becomes apparent.

What business is the painter in?

Watch a carpenter framing a new house. He works close to the wood, nailing with quick strokes of his hammer. However, to get a view of the total house—the structure that will become someone's home—he must walk across the street. He has to step back from his detailed work to see the shape of the whole.

What business is the carpenter in? Is he in the nail-driving business, the framing business, or the home-building business? Or is he in the business of satisfying the age-old dream of home ownership?

Only by stepping back can you answer this very important question, "What business am I in?" Once you know who your customers are and what satisfies their internal and external needs you can move forward. Mary Clark's stable experience illustrates the importance of understanding exactly what business one is really in.

Clark's Stables

Mary Clark, a 30-year-old software engineer, had always been more interested in riding her prize-winning quarter horses than in programming. When her grandmother died and left her $500,000, Mary made a down payment on a boarding stable and left the corporate world forever—or so she thought.

The boarding stable was run-down. It had stalls for 50 horses, but only 25 stalls were occupied. Mary did everything she could think of to make the place better for

Psychological cushion A unique, untouchable rung on the ladder in your target customer's mind.

horses. She spent $200,000 rebuilding, painting, and grading, which made Clark's Stables a very attractive place. She bought the highest quality of feed and gave the horses the best care money could buy.

When owners began to move their horses to other stables after 9 months, Mary couldn't understand. She had not increased her fees, and she treated the horses like friends. After 12 months, only six paying customers remained. After 15 months, she was behind on her mortgage payments. In her eighteenth month Mary sold the stable at a great loss. Luckily, she was able to return to her old programming job.

Mary had made the simple mistake of thinking horses were her customers. Her real target customers were young girls between age 7 and 14 and their parents. Mary thought she was in the business of stabling horses. She should have seen that she was in the business of providing girls a fun, social activity. Parents viewed the stables as a safe after-school activity for their daughters. The girls wanted recreation, training, and social events. Mary's customers left because other stables provided parties, barbecues, and horse shows with lots of ribbons and trophies. The girls wanted prizes, but Mary was more interested in satisfying her horses than the young girls and their parents.

What Business Are You Really In?

Now that you have defined a specific industry segment, it is time to define what you do. Naming anything is a game of words, and a small business is no exception. The following examples can help you define your business. If you're hesitant about defining at this early stage, remember what happened to Clark's Stable. When defining your business, ask yourself why people buy the product. People do not buy products or services; they buy what the product or service will do for them: enhance their lives or make life easier, safer, and more fun. Cosmetics firms frequently say they are in the business of selling "hope in a jar." Use the following examples to help zero in on defining what business you're truly in.

If You're a	Try Saying
personal financial planner	I'm in the peace-of-mind business.
small-business teacher	I'm in the dream-to-reality business.
cosmetic plastic surgeon	I'm in the don't-grow-old business.
Porsche car salesperson	I'm in the ego-gratification business.
gourmet cookware salesperson	I help people be Martha Stewart.
personal fitness trainer	I keep you young and buff.
coffeehouse owner	I provide a place to see and be seen.

Passion

Passion for Listening to Customers

Being a rebellious teen is tough work, but it's murder without the right accessories. That's where Elizabeth McLaughlin comes in. The Hot Topic chief executive peddles $8 dog-collar chokers, $30 neon-blue wigs, and $84 black vinyl gowns to kids determined to stand out from the crowd. Apparently there are a growing number of them: The 11-year-old retail chain now boasts 262 stores, up from 212 last January, and posted sales of $240 million this year, up 42 percent. McLaughlin ships new merchandise to each store daily and uses domestic manufacturers to keep her order cycle less than 60 days. Most retailers need to wait 90 days before new product hits the stores. McLaughlin also realizes that antifashion is as capricious as mainstream tastes. Prodded by employees who scout out rock concerts, the chain moved from Marilyn Manson-style gloom fashions into the baggy-pants look sported by bands like Limp Bizkit. "Pleasing customers is easy," she says. "You ask them what they want, and then you give it to them."

SOURCE: "200 Best Small Companies: Hot Topic," *Forbes*, 116(12): October 30, 2000, p. 200.

Keep honing your definition of your business. Your **business definition** should be a work in progress as you further explore your target market and competition. Check your definition with your potential target customers because they may perceive your business differently. You may have new stationery printed after you talk to them, but as business expenses go, that's a small price to pay to overcome customer confusion. Three of our favorite business definitions or mission statements are:

Fast Company—"Fast Company is where best practice meets big ideas; new talent meets innovative tools; the emerging business community meets the emerging conversation about the future of business."

Deux Amis Needlepoint—"We believe there is nothing so beautiful as an exquisitely painted canvas, or the enjoyment, satisfaction, and relaxation derived from fine handwork and stitching a lovely design with beautiful threads on fine canvas."

Chicken Soup—"We're selling stories that encircle the heart and penetrate the soul and cuddle up to make you feel better."

Dazzle your consumer with the best business definition you can by completing Action Step 23.

Being in business today is all about satisfying needs and providing benefits. You find a need, you satisfy it, and then you translate the results into a benefit for your customer. This new era of knowledge-based and experienced-based marketing involves two key principles. First, all of a firm's efforts should be focused on satisfying the needs of a customer at a profit. Second, the name of the game is to create or develop your own pie; that is, own the market as opposed to sharing it with competitors. You create and develop your market niche or segment by constantly changing your product or service as dictated by the customer. Marketing today emphasizes networking, creativity, associations, and partnerships and requires:

1. Integrating customers' needs and desires and your strategies into the development of the product. Market needs drive the product.
2. Focusing your knowledge and experience on a specific and targeted customer segment or niche. The idea is to own this niche. The old concept of sharing a market is obsolete for small business ventures.
3. Creating customer, supplier, and even competitor relationships that will sustain and grow your customer base. Cooperation is the key.

Marketing encompasses everything a business does to get products and services from the manufacturer to the customer so that the consumer is satisfied and the seller has met his or her objectives.

ACTION STEP 23

DEFINE YOUR BUSINESS

1. Brainstorm what business you're really in. Let your mind play at this. Remember your customers' comments when you were probing their psyche.
2. Think of yourself riding up 50 floors in an express elevator. You have 30 seconds to explain to a stranger what your business is about. What will you say? Can you dazzle him or her, so they will ask for more? Include your product or service's benefits, your target market, distribution, and why customers will buy from you.

Keep working and refining your "elevator speech" throughout the semester.

SUMMARY

You've found the industry that interests you. You've applied the life-cycle stick to learn what stage the industry is in and how long you've got to make your business go. If your skills don't exactly guarantee success, you're sure of at least three things: you know where to acquire the skills you need, you know how long it will take to get them, and you're exploring the marketplace.

You have brainstormed your business objectives and reviewed the interlocking concepts—life cycle, competition, and industry breakthrough. A business idea should be starting to mesh for you. Continue to explore the gaps in the marketplace.

Nobody wants to hear about a "me too" business. Stress your differentiation and your position and translate features into market-hungry benefits. It is important to show how you have an edge over the competition. Try to think in terms of a "personal niche monopoly."

Business definition A clear picture of the enterprise.

FIGURE 3.6

SOURCE: *Orange County Register,* November 16, 2000.

"It's an OK concept but not worth talking about at 15 cents a minute."

THINK POINTS FOR SUCCESS

- Build your business around your likes, strengths, and passions.
- Direct the power of your mind toward a particular industry segment through Opportunity Selection.
- Spend time early on learning about the industry, its major players, and its trends.
- Use all secondary data available, so when you move out to conduct primary data research, you will come from a position of knowledge and strength.
- Find a gap and take advantage of it. This is much easier and brings more success than being a "me too" competitor. If someone else owns the niche, find another—unless you are willing to hold on and fight the competition with your deep pockets.
- Recognize that not all opportunities are equal.
- Acknowledge that not all opportunities can be profitable.
- Don't fall in love with a product or a market.
- Know that there has to be a compelling reason for the customer to change.
- Dare to be different in your approach.
- Define your business. Dazzle in 50 words or less. Make them beg for more.
- Research! Research! Research! And *Never* Stop!

KEY POINTS FROM ANOTHER VIEW

Benchmark: Encourage Wild Ideas

By Tia O'Brien

IDEO Product Development is the world's most celebrated design firm. Its ultimate creation is the process of creativity itself. For founder David Kelley and his colleague, work is play, brainstorming is a science, and the most important rule is to break the rules.

Walk into the offices of IDEO Product Development, and you quickly appreciate how many ways there are to describe new products. Computer screens display intricate designs embedded in software. Long rolls of butcher paper, spread out over conference tables, record doodles, scribbles, and notes. Prototypes are everywhere and in every medium: cardboard, foam, wood, plastic.

Standing in the middle of things, admiring the creative chaos, is David M. Kelley, 45, IDEO's founder. Kelley describes IDEO as "a living laboratory of the workplace." The company "is in a state of perpetual experimentation," he says. "We're constantly trying new ideas in our projects, our work space, even our culture."

IDEO is arguably the world's most influential design firm. About 250 people work in a network of offices stretching from San Francisco to London to Tokyo. They create 90 new products a year, including some that have become familiar parts of our daily lives: Levolor blinds, Crest's Neat Squeeze toothpaste container, and telephones and answering machines from AT&T. Others are icons of the digital age: cutting-edge laptop computers, virtual reality headgear, and even automatic teller machines. But the firm's defining creation is the process of creativity itself. To understand how IDEO works, you have to see how it looks.

The company's main offices are spread over seven low-rise buildings in downtown Palo Alto, the heart of California's Silicon Valley. The people here (about 140 in all) work under tight deadlines and intense pressure, but you wouldn't know it from the feel of the place. Kelley is adamant that people can't be creative without heavy doses of freedom and fun. Therefore there are no "bosses" or job titles at IDEO; all work is organized into project teams that form and disband in Chicago or Tokyo if they can find a colleague willing to switch.

"The most important thing I learned from big companies," Kelley says, "is that creativity gets stifled when everyone's got to follow the rules."

That same spirit infuses the offices, which display many funky touches and clever twists. Consider the small matter of bicycles. It seems nearly everyone at IDEO bikes to work, so "parking" is a problem. The solution? An intricate system of hangers and pulleys that allows people to wheel their bikes to their cubicles, raise them to the ceiling, and retrieve them as needed. It's a bicycle rack in the sky.

There's also the matter of noise. The firm's twenty-somethings like to play music while they work, which can drive the others crazy. So IDEO created a special area for the youngsters—dubbed the Spunk Space—complete with a DC-3 aircraft wing that pivots on a pole to serve as a room divider.

Of course, all this fun and freedom is in the service of something tangible: radical new ideas that become important new products. Kelley says the primary "engine for innovation" at IDEO is its distinct approach to brainstorming—the only part of company life where strict rules do apply.

Sessions are held in spaces dubbed (not-so-creatively) Brainstormer Rooms. There are three such rooms in Palo Alto, and they all have the same main features. Participants can draw almost anywhere: on whiteboard-covered walls, on conference tables covered with butcher paper. Multimedia tools—a television, VCR, computer projector, and video screen—allow for in-depth presentations or sensory stimulation. To help maintain the right spirit, IDEO's five principles of brainstorming are emblazoned on the walls: (1) Stay focused on the topic, (2) Encourage wild ideas, (3) Defer judgement, (4) Build on the ideas of others, and (5) One conversation at a time.

Project leaders call a brainstorm at the beginning of a new assignment or when they feel stumped. A typical session involves eight participants from a mix of disciplines: industrial design, engineering, and human-factors analysis. Invitations are sent via e-mail, and attendance is voluntary, but no one takes brainstorming lightly.

These sessions generate a frenzy of activity. In fact, their very productivity creates a challenge: how to record all the ideas. So each Brainstormer Room has a clever device (sort of a hybrid camera-copier) that photographs every drawing on the whiteboards and every artifact on the walls. The project team selects the most promising ideas and moves quickly to develop them.

The key word is quickly. Kelley encourages his designers to model their ideas (usually from simple materials like foam or cardboard) within days of coming up with them. As an idea becomes more robust, it goes to the company's machine shop where powerful computer-controlled machine tools generate prototypes from plastic or metal within hours of receiving software files from a designer's computer. In creative work, Kelly believes, enlightened trial and error beats careful planning every time.

Indeed, one of the most popular slogans at IDEO is "Fail often to succeed sooner." Which is why the company's designers store their diagrams, mockups, and prototypes on large metal racks outfitted with wheels. When it's time to begin a new project, designers just grab an oversized roll of plastic wrap, seal their belongings, wheel them down the hall or across the street, and join their colleagues.

Can this formula for creativity work in other places? Some of the world's leading companies certainly think so. In a separate (and super-secret) building in Palo Alto, IDEO has opened a lab with Samsung, the Korean electronics conglomerate, where the two company's product developers can rub shoulders. In January, Steelcase, the office-furniture giant, made an equity investment in IDEO and named Kelley its vice president of technical discovery and innovation.

"Companies are coming to us and saying, 'How can you make us more innovative?'" Kelley says. "They want us to help change their corporate culture to make it as creative as we are."

SOURCE: Tia O'Brien, "Encourage Wild Ideas," *Fast Company*, 2:April/May 1996, p. 83.

CHAPTER 4

Profiling the Target Customer

ENTREPRENEURIAL LINKS

BOOKS

The Clustered World: How We Live, What We Buy, and What it all Means About Who We Are, Michael J. Weiss, Little, Brown, & Company, New York, 2000.

Positioning: The Battle for Your Mind, Al Ries and Jack Trout, McGraw Hill Professional Publishing, New York, 1993.

The $100 Billion Allowance: How to Get Your Share of the Global Teen Market, Elissa Moses, John Wiley & Sons, New York, 2000.

WEBSITES

www.mediafinder.com, (Mediafinder, Oxbridge Communications)

www.easidemographics.com, (The Right Site)

future.sri.com, (Business Intelligence Center)

ASSOCIATIONS/ORGANIZATIONS

American Marketing Association, www.ama.org

Direct Marketing Association, www.the-dma.org

SBA's Office of Women's Business Ownership, www.sba.gov/womeninbusiness

PUBLICATIONS

Advertising Age, www.adage.com

Edge, www.edgeonline.com

American Demographics, www.demographics.com

ADDITIONAL ENTREPRENEURIAL INSIGHTS

Start Small, Finish Big: Fifteen Key Lessons to Start and Run Your Own Successful Business, Fred DeLuca, Warner Books, 2001. *Permission Marketing*, Seth Godin and Don Peppers, Simon and Schuster, New York, 1999.

The Origin and Evolution of New Businesses, V. Bhide, Oxford University Press, New York, 2000.

Learning Objectives

- Draw a magic circle around your customer.
- Understand your key to survival in small business is your Target Customer.
- Learn how to use media kits to profile Target Customers.
- Identify primary and secondary Target Customers.
- Interview, observe, and survey to gain insight into your Target Customer.
- Understand lifestyle factors.
- Explore various profiling systems.
- Develop your customer profiling ability into a reflex.
- Picture your Target Customer by preparing a Target Customer collage.

Chapters 4 and 5 go together. Your best strategy is to read both chapters quickly, grasping the heavy connection between competition (Chapter 5) and your Target Customer (Chapter 4). Then read the chapters again, taking notes, doing research, and completing the Action Steps for both chapters. Your Target Customer is the lifeblood of your business—your resource base. You provide customers a product or a service, and they in return support your business by purchasing your product or service.

Competition occurs when someone else—another entrepreneur corporation—wants your resource base enough to wage war. This could be a price war: Your competitor cuts the price of the same or competing product or service to steal away your Target Customers. This could be a quality war: The competitor has a superior product or better service. The war could be waged with a smear campaign: Your product is not environmentally sound, so the competition toots its horn about cleaning up the planet.

The best defense against competition is to know your Target Customer. Chapter 4 focuses on profiling your Target Customer through secondary, primary, and "new eyes" research.

By conducting ongoing market research you will:

- minimize the risk of doing business
- uncover opportunities
- identify potential problems and solutions
- be guided to customers

Your prime concerns in Chapter 3 were: "Do I have a product or service that is in a growth segment of a growth market?" and "Are the business goals consistent with my own personal goals?" Hopefully, by now you have some pretty solid ideas as to what products are hot for you. Now it's time to establish whether or not there is a market for those products. If there is a market, are buyers willing to pay for it? Chapter 6 will focus on how to reach your Target Customers through marketing efforts.

Passion

Passion For Child's Health Drives Entrepreneur

How'd They Do That? The Mothers of Invention

It's one mom's crusade. Amilya Antonetti proves necessity truly is the mother of invention. A mystery illness in her family put Amilya on the path to corporate success. It's an incredible story that made us ask, How'd she do that?

For Amilya Antonetti and Dennis Karp, the incredible birth of their son, David, quickly turned to pain.

"Screaming . . . Just that chilling scream. I'm talking lengthy hour upon hour to where my child couldn't cry anymore, and he'd pass out," says Amilya. Even after 30 trips to the emergency room, they had no answers. David's rashes, asthma, and ghostly color worsened. Doctors told the couple to prepare for the worst.

"If the medical community that I was dealing with had given up on him, I wasn't. I was not prepared to give up on him," she says.

How would she determine what was making David sick? Amilya basically became a detective and started keeping a journal.

"It took me really looking at my journal to realize that when I cleaned the floors or cleaned the oven with a powerful cleaner, in the next 2 hours he'd have a major reaction. It was burning his lungs, and he woke up in pain. The enemy in my home was a very common item, and it happened to be that his biggest reaction is to ammonia," Amilya explains.

Now that Amilya had identified the culprit, how'd she find cleaning solutions that wouldn't harm her son? Books and experts on natural remedies helped and so did talking to other moms with similar problems. But as it turned out, Amilya's grandmother had the answers she needed. Words of wisdom from grandma were: Keep it simple: baking soda, vinegar, soda ash, borax, lemons, and grapefruit. Citrus are wonderful when it comes to grease.

"And she started cleaning the house with it, the house looked great, and David stopped crying," Dennis remembers. "This really worked." It worked so well that neighbors started wanting it too.

"I was making products for different people, and I couldn't believe how news spread by word of mouth," says Amilya.

It spread so fast that Amilya found herself at a crossroad. "I came home, sat down with my husband, and said, 'I really want to do this. I want to be the mom amongst the shelf of big companies.'"

How'd they do that? "We liquidated everything we had to put into this business idea," says Amilya. "My husband gave up his career. Talk about commitment."

So Amilya created Soapworks, and Dennis left his law practice to join. They hired expert formulators to perfect Amilya's all-natural cleaning products. Amilya revised the formulas based on other parents' input. In less than 3 years Amilya's business has grown into a $10 million dollar enterprise headquartered in San Leandro, California, with offices and warehouses nationwide. Soapworks offers a dozen cleaning products in 3000 stores and is growing.

"I took my mothering skills and applied them to business, which is much easier than taking business skills and applying them to parenthood," Amilya believes.

And what about the little boy who inspired all this? David is now 6 years old and says he doesn't get sick from products anymore. Through it all, Amilya never lost sight of her most valued treasure.

"When everything's said and done, my greatest accomplishment is my son," she says.

SOURCE: **www.extratv.com/cmp/spotlight/2000/05_15c.htm** and **www.soapworks.com** (accessed February 15, 2001).

THE POWER OF PROFILING

Your Target Customer is your key to survival in small business. Profiling draws a "magic" circle around your Target Customer. Placing the customer in the center of that circle transforms the whole arena into a target at which you can aim your product or service. Nothing happens without customers; every segment of your business plan must begin with a complete understanding of their wants and needs. Profiling is the instrument used to uncover the wants, needs, and behaviors of your customers. Generating this profile requires a combination of demographics (the statistical analysis) and psychographics (the firsthand intuitive insight into lifestyle, buying habits, patterns of consumption, and attitudes). In this chapter we focus on specific profiling techniques and sources to help you get a handle on that elusive customer.

It's often useful to ask prospects, "If you could make one wish, what could be improved?" If you talk to enough people, a gap will emerge and so will your Target Customers. Effective market research can help you target rich niches and avoid stagnant ones. For example, a plumber who was ready to leave his day job with a construction company asked his friends what would make them more likely to use his plumbing services. Their replies were almost universal: "Can you come during evening or weekend hours, so I won't have to stay home from work?" In response, he called himself the "Midnight Plumber." He worked from 6 to 12 PM every day without charging overtime rates. He was an immediate success because he had profiled his customers and found a **market niche** with his positioning.

Two social workers found a niche by listening to their clients who were unable to visit their loved ones in prison. The clients had limited resources, no access to cars, and no access to any public transportation that served the prison. Visits to husbands, wives, and children were therefore nearly impossible. The social workers believed, as did the families, that frequent contact was necessary for future rehabilitation of the prisoners and for keeping the family together.

On locating a used 15-passenger van, the social workers began "Family Express." They offered weekend roundtrips to the prison for $20 a passenger. Not only were they supplying a service, they were also providing a community for their riders, in the same way that AOL's online chat rooms provide a community for its various targeted customer groups. Developing relationships beyond the product or service is essential in today's hotly competitive marketplace.

With more than 1.7 million people in the U.S. prison and jail system today, the opportunity to serve family needs is vast. What other needs can you envision? How could you meet them?

A market segment profile identifies similarities among potential customers within a segment and explains the unique needs among the people and firms in differing segments.

Business-to-business profiling is unlike the segmentation of consumer markets. It is most effectively performed using geographic factors, customer-based segmentation, size of company, and end-user applications.

When profiling for a Target Customer, it is likely that several different prospective segments will be discovered. Further analysis will be required to focus on only the most worthy. These should then be separated by sales estimates, competitive factors, and the costs associated with reaching each segment.

Identifying the unfilled need (your niche) and clearly explaining the market potential for your concept can make or break a business plan. Before we get to profiling in depth, let's take a look at the different kinds of Target Customers. We will focus on primary and secondary Target Customers. These are the only customers that you can see right now. However, once you open your business, a new customer may arrive on the scene, and you must always be ready to change so that you can take advantage of new market opportunities.

THREE TYPES OF TARGET CUSTOMERS

Entrepreneurs tell us to watch for at least three Target Customer (TC) groups.

1. **Primary**. This TC group is perfect for your business and could be a heavy user. They possess the resources to purchase your product, have a need or desire (or you can create the need or desire), and have the authority to purchase the product.
2. **Secondary**. This one almost slips away before you can focus the camera. Sometimes your secondary TC group will lead you to the third customer—who is invisible at first.
3. **Invisible**. These customers appear after you have the courage to open the doors.

Market Niche A small focused area of a market segment.

What Can We Learn from Media Sources?

An easy way to understand the power of profiling is to analyze media sources that are aimed at different target markets. For example, what would you find if you contrasted information on the readers of three different surfing magazines?

Most, if not all, of the major media sources have conducted extensive research on the demographic and psychographic profiles of their Target Customer. In many cases these profiles are available through media kits from the advertising departments of the media sources.

A media kit includes a copy of the magazine, reader profile, distribution figures, **rate card** (specifications for advertisements and costs), editorial calendar (monthly proposed content schedule), and an audited magazine circulation statement (ABC statement).

If your Target Customer is travel-oriented, request media kits from specific travel-related magazines. The key here is to know which media sources your Target Customer reads, listens to, and watches. You can obtain in-depth profiles from these media companies because they compile these data for potential advertisers who are aiming their products and services at your target market.

For an example of how specific and targeted magazines can be, read Key Points from Another View at the end of the chapter, and discover how three magazines target "ferret owners."

In this chapter we will focus primarily on magazines. However, you can take advantage of almost any media—especially commercial ones—because of the useful information contained in ads. We could just as easily expand our discussion to include TV programs, radio stations, Internet sites, and, to a lesser extent, books and movies.

We often walk past magazines without giving them a sideways glance. That's unfortunate because magazines hold the answer to many questions about customers. One way to view a magazine is as a glossy cover wrapped around pages of advertisements and editorial copy. With new eyes, however, you can see that a mass-market magazine exists because it is a channel to the subconscious of a certain type of reader.

That knowledge is power! What can you learn about target markets, consumption patterns, and buying power from the advertisements in a magazine?

Put yourself in an analytical frame of mind. Begin by counting the advertisements. Then note the types of products that dominate the advertisements; these advertisements are probably aimed at the heavy users of those products. Next, study the models; they are fantasy images that the Target Customer is expected to identify with, connect with, and remember. The activities pictured in the advertisements enlarge the fantasy, and the words link it to real life. A good advertisement becomes a slice of life—a picture that beckons the customer inside toward the product.

We took an issue of *Surfing* and did a new-eyes analysis. After we looked at the articles and the advertisements, we completed a trial profile. We developed categories as we went along. (One of the nice things about new-eyes research is that you can expand the model as you collect data.) What we looked for was:

- Total number of advertisements, half page or larger
- Advertisements aimed at heavy users (type of products that are advertised the most)
- Large advertisements (two or more pages)
- Demographics of models (estimated age, occupation, sex, and lifestyle)
- Main activities depicted in advertisements
- Content of magazine articles

Rate Card Magazine's advertising prices and details for ad placements.

Reviewing the Media Kit

The issue of *Surfing* we studied contained 160 pages, 90 of which were advertisements. These advertisements, mostly full page and two-page spreads, covered almost 60 percent of the magazine. There were four main categories: clothing, surfboards, sunglasses, and shoes.

The advertisements predominantly depict the surfer lifestyle. Professional surfers were showcased in several of the advertisements. The remaining models were primarily blond, surfer types between age 15 and 20. Text, content, and advertisements almost meld together.

After our initial profiling, we reviewed the following information supplied by *Surfing's* advertising department:

Sex

Male	86%
Female	14%

Age (years)

Median	17.5
Average	20.5
Under 16	30%
16–20	32%
21–24	12%
25–30	11%
31–40	11%
41+	4%

Average Household Income

$57,135 (most live at home with parents, almost half in Hawaii and California—high-income states)

Average Years Surfing

6.7 years

Surf More Than 2 days a Week

76% (Southern California high schools have surf teams)

In or Graduated from College

44%

Other Sporting Activities

Skateboarding	53%
Snowboarding	47%

Own or Have Access to a Computer

88%

Have Purchased Surf-related Items through the Internet

93%

From the previous reader profile (provided by *Surfing* magazine), the magazine's content, and what we know about their customer, we agree with *Surfing's* following customer profile:

> They shun the pretension of the 1980s for innovation and excellence, astutely seeking both value and "the latest." Upwardly mobile, educated or being educated, idealistic, and stoked on their number-one passion (surfing), they are the first to try new maneuvers, new music, or new technologies they deem appropriate. Fashion and change leaders, they are the ones others turn to for advice.

The next step in profiling your Target Customer is to compare the profiles of the readers of all the surfing magazines aimed at your target market to determine which best represents your customer. Look not only at demographics and psychographics

GLOBAL VILLAGE

THE WORLD'S BIGGEST VALUE GAPS

According to a recent study, "Remapping the World of Consumers," by Roper Starch, "Some values exhibit hugely polarizing trends from culture to culture, giving a great amount of insight to those countries and cultures." Understanding the culture of a country is vital before an entrepreneur enters the global marketplace.

CULTURAL VALUE	WHERE IT'S IN (Rank out of 60)	WHERE IT'S NOT (Rank out of 60)
Respecting ancestors	Vietnam (1)	Germany (46)
Faith	Indonesia, Egypt, and Saudi Arabia (1)	France (45)
Friendship	Germany (1)	South Africa (46)
Freedom	Argentina, France, Italy, and Spain (2)	China (40)
Knowledge	India (2) and Singapore (3)	Egypt (34)
Stable relationships	U.K. and Japan (3)	Venezuela (43)
Self-reliance	Mexico (3) and Russia (4)	Saudi Arabia (33)
Ambition	Egypt (6) and Saudi Arabia (7)	Italy (55)
Romance	Thailand (9)	India (56)
Looking good	Egypt (13)	Japan and China (54)

SOURCE: **www.americandemographics.com/publications/ad/00_ad/ad0010roper.htm** (accessed December 11, 2000).

but the spirit of the reader as well. One editor defined his target reader as the "soul-surfer, one who lives to surf!"

Complete Action Step 24 to focus more clearly on your Target Customer.

Changing Profiles

In the past we discussed segmenting the market like slicing a pie. Each business tried to aim their products at their slice. Slicing the pie was primarily based on demographic segmentation. As technology advanced and media outlets conducted extensive research on customers, we suggested to our readers that they try to aim for a single blueberry in a slice of blueberry pie. With the Internet and the explosion of relatively inexpensive independent target-market studies, we now suggest you aim for the seeds in the blueberry. If you add your intuition, demographics, psychographics, and extensive observation of your target market, you will accomplish **"one-to-one marketing"**: meeting the needs of the "seeds."

ACTION STEP 24

MEDIA KIT ASSIGNMENT—TARGET CUSTOMER

Choose five magazines that you believe your Target Customer reads. Return to Action Step 14 in Chapter 2 for the list you researched. Use **www.mediafinder.com** or Standard Rates and Data Services listings from the library to contact the publishers, and request a media kit that includes reader profiles.

Compare the magazines when they arrive. First compare the content of the magazines and the advertisements using your "new eyes," and profile the Target Customer. Next compare your "new eyes" profile with the demographic and psychographic information provided. Then rank the five magazines from one to five with number one being the one that best targets your customer.

At the beginning you may not be able to advertise in these magazines because of cost, but you may very well be able to keep an eye on your competitors and your market by following these magazines.

If none of these magazines profile your Target Customer, begin again.

INCREDIBLE RESOURCE

NATIONAL ASSOCIATION OF HISPANIC PUBLICATIONS' MEDIA KIT & RESOURCE BOOK

If you are trying to reach the 33 million Hispanics in the United States through print media, the *National Association of Hispanic Publications' Media Kit & Resource Book* should be your first stop. It provides a treasure trove of more than 211 U.S. Hispanic publications servicing more than 57 individual and national markets. In addition, the publishers have completed a readership survey of more than 37,000 readers, which provides a wealth of information on Hispanic consumers and their reading and buying habits.

According to recent U.S. Census and economic projections, Hispanics now make up about 12 percent of the population with 65 percent native-born U.S. citizens. Thirty-three percent of the total U.S. population is projected to be Hispanic by the year 2010. The Hispanic purchasing power has increased 28 percent from 1990 to 2000 reaching $348 billion. How can you capitalize on the growing Hispanic market's needs and desires?

One-to-one Marketing Meeting customer's needs on a very personal and individual basis.

Thirty years ago there was usually only one bookstore owner in town, and he knew exactly what each of his customers wanted. He was in the business of one-to-one marketing. Today we have **www.amazon.com** conducting one-to-one marketing. The bookstore owner's brain is replaced by the computer's CPU.

Society's fragmentation allows you to focus directly on the needs of your particular market segment. No longer focusing only on age segmentation, you now also look for lifestyle segments such as the difference between the purchases of 40-year-old first-time parents and the purchases of 40-year-old parents who just sent their youngest child off to college.

Market segmentation is easily understood if one looks at how various industries such as hotels, cars, tennis shoes, and pizza have aimed at specific niches. Your goal is to find a market that can be dominated easily and is more profitable than others.

Focus your efforts on your carefully selected blueberry seed!

Profiling in Action

Susan and John Johnson made a decision to locate their Healthy Gourmet business in Orange County, California. Let's review many of the secondary data resources available to aid the Johnsons to profile their target consumer market. Many of the sources are available both on the Internet and in print form at libraries.

Healthy Gourmet actually serves the Tech Coast of Orange County, San Diego, and Los Angeles. For illustration purposes, we focus on their customers in the Newport Beach coastal area of Corona Del Mar (zip code 92625). Chapter 7 discusses additional issues in Healthy Gourmet's choice of physical location. Healthy Gourmet's initial research identified Orange County as an excellent location as a result of its high-income demographics, a high level of dual-career couples, and a propensity for large expenditures on restaurant meals. In addition, this location is centralized between Los Angeles and San Diego. The Johnsons would be able to use the Orange County location as their main commissary kitchen, serving areas both to the north and to the south.

First we focus on the demographics and psychographics of their Corona Del Mar customers.

The first stop is U.S. Census data, **www.census.gov** (the last Census figures available are for 2000). You can search the database by hundreds of different variables, from education, employment, family household size, income, race, sex, age groupings, and so on.

Your next stop is **www.easidemographics.com,** one of the easiest online databases to use. Searching on Newport Beach, California, produces a report on relevant variables based on 2000 Census data (Figure 4.1). Using Claritas' PRIZM lifestyle segmentation systems online database, **www.claritas.com**, allows you to search by zip code. PRIZM "defines every neighborhood in the United States in terms of demographically and behaviorally distinct types or clusters." Sixty-two clusters of Target Customer profiles focus on lifestyle, retail, financial, and media variables. The three major clusters for 92625 (Corona Del Mar, an area adjacent to Newport Beach) are Blue-Blood Estates, Winner's Circle, and Executive Suites, as shown in Figure 4.2.

Another excellent source for demographic information, DemographicsNow.com, **www.demographicsnow.com**, provides an excellent Executive Demographic Report as shown in Figure 4.3.

The Johnson's could also review Roper Starch's view of "how people naturally 'group' around certain sets of values." The Roper Values Segments (**www.roper.com**) divide people psychographically (rather than demographically) as follows:

CREATIVES are "Renaissance people" who are deeply involved in all areas of life.

FUN SEEKERS are "party people" who stress social hedonistic pursuits.

INTIMATES are "people people" who value relationships above all else.

FIGURE 4.1
Significant Variables Report & Analysis

NEWPORT BEACH, CA

City Code:	0651182
City Name:	NEWPORT BEACH, CA
County Name:	Orange, CA
County FIPS Code:	06059
Area Code:	714
State Abbreviation:	CA
State Name:	CALIFORNIA
Metropolitan Area Code:	5945
Metropolitan Area Name:	Orange County, CA
TV Market Code:	803
TV Market Name:	LOS ANGELES
Bureau of Economic Area Code:	161
Bureau of Economic Area Name:	Los Angeles-Riverside-Orange County, CA
Division Name:	PACIFIC
Region Name:	WEST

Description	Value	EASI Score	EASI Rank (of 3733)
Head of Household < 25 Income $50K–75K	413	A	1
Male Non-Family HH not Living Alone:	4,066	A	2
Occupations - Sales:	8,737	A	3
Rent $1000+:	5,961	A	3
Head of Household 25–34 Income $100K+:	1,233	A	5
B - Young and with Money (US Ave=100):	200	A	5
B - Luxury Priced Product Market (US Ave=100):	200	A	5
B - Single & Money (US Ave=100):	200	A	5
B - Sales Jobs (US Ave=100):	200	A	5
P - Luxury Rent (US Ave=100):	200	A	5
Median Value - Owner Occupied:	500,000	A	6
B - Median Home Value (US Ave=100):	200	A	6
Education, College (age25+):	20,893	A	8
Median with Mortgage Costs:	2,000	A	9
B - Homeowner Expenses with Mortgage (US Ave=100):	200	A	9
Employees - Finance, Insurance, Real Estate:	6,986	A	10
Total White Collar Occupations:	33,101	A	10
Value - Owner Occupied $500000+:	7,728	A	13
Self-Employed Workers:	5,683	A	16
B - Working Singles (US Ave=100):	199	A	19
B - Divorced (US Ave=100):	199	A	19
B - Higher Priced Product Market (US Ave=100):	199	A	19
B - White Collar Employment (US Ave=100):	199	A	19
B - Self Employed (US Ave=100):	199	A	19
B - Finance-Insurance-Real Est. Jobs (US Ave=100):	199	A	19
P - Singles with Jobs (US Ave=100):	199	A	19
P - Young with Jobs (US Ave=100):	199	A	19
P - Few Young Children (US Ave=100):	199	A	19
P - Divorced (US Ave=100):	199	A	19
P - Expensive Homes (US Ave=100):	199	A	19

EASI Rank: based on the concentration of the variable with a "1" being the highest rank and the number of areas in a geography being the lowest rank. (ZIP codes=29,467; Cities=3,733; Counties=3,141; Sectional Postal Centers=881; Metropolitan Areas=318; TV Markets=211; Bureau of Economic Areas=174; Area Codes=122).
EASI Score: arranges EASI Rank into a quintile frequency distribution ranging from "A" (the highest concentration group and top 20%) through "E" (the lowest concentration group and bottom 20%).
"(US Ave=100)" indicates an index value that has a range of 0 (low) to 200 (high).
All data are derived from the U.S. Census and other official government sources.
B in a variable description means it is a Business Profile.
P in a variable description means it is a Personal Profile.
SOURCE: The Right Site, Easy Analytic Software, Inc., **www.easidemographics.com** (accessed June 1, 2001).

STRIVERS are "workaholics" driven by a desire for status and wealth.

DEVOUTS are "traditionalists" who have strong convictions about faith, modesty, duty, and respect for the past.

FIGURE 4.2
Claritas' PRIZM Lifestyle Segments for Corona Del Mar

Top Three PRIZM Segments in ZIP Code 92625

PRIZM: Blue-Blood Estates

Demographics: Elite, super-rich couples, ages 45 to 64, professional household income of $135,900 (1.2% of U.S. households belong to this PRIZM cluster).

Lifestyle: Belong to a health club, visit Eastern Europe, buy classical music, watch "Wall Street Week," and read *Architectural Digest.*

Geography: Scottsdale, AZ; Lake Forest, IL; New Canaan, CT.

PRIZM: Winner's Circle

Demographics: Executive suburban couples, ages 45 to 64, professional household income of $90,700 (2.26% of U.S. households belong to this PRIZM cluster).

Lifestyle: Have a passport, shop at Ann Taylor, have Keogh plan, watch "NYPD Blue," and read Epicurean magazines.

Geography: Northbrook, IL; Dunwoody, GA; Vienna, VA.

PRIZM: Executive Suites

Demographics: Upscale white-collar couples, ages 45 to 64, professional household income of $68,500 (1.25% of U.S. households belong to this PRIZM cluster).

Lifestyle: Belong to a health club, visit Japan and other parts of Asia, have an airline travel card, watch "Friends," and read *Entrepreneur.*

Geography: Irvine, CA; Aurora, IL; Mount Laurel, NJ.

SOURCE: **www.dellvader.claritas.com/yawyl/** (accessed March 5, 2001).

FIGURE 4.3
Executive Demographic Report

Geography: 92625 Corona Del Mar Date: February 2, 2001

Population

The current year population in your selected geography is 17,834. The population has changed by 42.77% since 1990. It is estimated that the population in your area will be 19,299 five years from now, which represents a change of 8.21% from the current year. The current population is 47.77% male and 52.23% female. The median age of the population in your area is 45, compare this with the U.S. average which is 36. The population density in your area is 7,279.18 people per square mile.

Households

There are currently 8,346 households in your selected geography. The number of households has changed by 42.74% since 1990. It is estimated that the number of households in your area will be 9,057 five years from now, which represents a change of 8.52% from the current year. The average household size in your area is 2.14 persons.

Income

The current year median household income for your selected geography is $116,815, compare this with the U.S. average, which is currently $39,618. The median household income for your area as changed by 58.48% since 1990. It is estimated that the median household income in your area will be $145,283 five years from now, which represents a change of 24.37% from the current year.

The current year per capita income in your area is $84,297, compare this with the U.S. average, which is $24,219. The current year average household income in your area is $180,029, compare this with the U.S. average, which is $62,563.

Race & Ethnicity

The current year racial makeup of your selected area is as follows: 95.76% White, 0.19% Black, 0.13% Native American and 3.92% Asian/Pacific Islander. Compare these with U.S. averages, which are: 82.35% White, 12.72% Black, 0.87% Native American, and 4.05% Asian/Pacific Islander.

People of Hispanic origin are counted independently of race. People of Hispanic origin make up 4.50% of the current year population in your selected area. Compare this with the U.S. average of 11.52%.

Housing

The median housing value in your area was $533,994 in 1999, compare this with the U.S. average of $114,168 for the same year. In 1990 there were 3,695 owner-occupied housing units in your area. At that time the median housing value for the area was $499,223 and the median monthly mortgage payment was $1,975. Also in 1990 there were 2,141 renter-occupied housing units in your area. The median rent at the time was $973.

Employment

For the current year there are 7,495 employees in your selected area, this is also known as the daytime population. For this area in 1990 89.09% of employees were employed in white-collar occupations and 10.91% were employed in blue-collar occupations. In 1990 unemployment in this area was 1.81%. In 1990 the average time traveled to work was 22.0 minutes.

Current year data is for the year **2000,** 5-year projected data is for the year **2005.** Demographic data copyright 2000 by MapInfo Corporation, Crime data copyright 2000 by Applied Geographic Solutions. Shopping Center data copyright 2000 by Directory of Major Malls. Traffic Count data copyright 2000 by DataMetrix. All rights reserved.
SOURCE: **www.demographicsnow.com** (accessed March 5, 2001).

ALTRUISTS are "humanitarians" who place relatively higher value on social values and the world at large.

SOURCE: **www.roper.com** (accessed May, 1, 2001).

Most likely the majority of Healthy Gourmet's customers come from the strivers' segment. If this is true, then the marketing and promotion material should be focused specifically on meeting the needs of time-strapped and status-oriented individuals.

Continuing on with the search for data brings one to Sri's Values and Lifestyles Segment Profiles (VALS) on the Web at **future.sri.com**. A quick check of the VALS segmentation diagram (Figure 4.4) shows eight profiles of customer/buyers: Actualizers, Fulfilleds, Achievers, Experiencers, Believers, Strivers, Makers, and Strugglers. Read through each of the profiles on the website to determine which segment needs your product or service.

Each of these segments defines adult consumers who have "different attitudes and exhibit distinctive behavior and decision-making patterns." Looking at the neighboring types with similar characteristics will aid you in defining your primary and secondary target markets.

The Actualizer Profile, **future.sri.com/vals/VALS.segs.html**, seems like a close fit for Healthy Gourmet—"sophisticated, active, 'take-charge' people with high self-esteem and abundant resources." The profile sharpens when you hot link to the Actualizers' activities page where you find arts associations, dinner parties, cruises, foreign cars, and golf as their main interests.

ACTUALIZERS

Various Other Actualizer-Related Products and Activities

Category	Index	Category	Index
Membership in Arts Association	382	Cruise Ship Vacation in Past 3 Years	230
Visit Art Museum in Past Year	302	Swim 201 Days in Past Year	218
Cross-Country Skiing Past Year	291	Own Import/Foreign Car	202
Own Elect. Espresso/Cappuccino Maker	268	Bought Custom-Made Furniture Past Year	195
Give Dinner Party 1 Month or More	240	Own Hot Tub/Spa	189
Foreign Travel in Past 3 Years	240	Play Golf	175
		Own Personal Computer at Home	175
		Bought Sheet Music	168

Category	Index
Have Wood-Burning Stove/Heater	79
Used 151 Plastic Garbage Bags in Past Month	69
Use Powder-Form Pain Relievers	61
Use Cinnamon-Flavor Toothpaste	58
Watch Professional Wrestling on TV	54
Own a Motorcycle with a 300-649cc Engine	44

These categories represent a sample of some consumer activities that involve Actualizers either markedly more (high index) or less (low index) than the population at large.

Index numbers indicate the relative purchase of products and services by each VALS group. For example, an index of 100 means that the product is used by the segment on an average with the rest of the U.S. adult population. An index of 120 indicates that the segment's purchase of a product is 20 percent higher than the average of all segments. Indexes less than 100 indicate the group is relatively uninvolved with the category. Indexes more than 120 indicate that the group is heavily involved with the product category.

SOURCE: SRI Consulting, **future.sri.com/VALS/actualizers.shtml** (accessed March 1, 2001).

FIGURE 4.4
The VALS™ Segment Profiles

SOURCE: SRI Consulting. "VALS™ Segment Profiles" VALS is a trademark of SRI International.

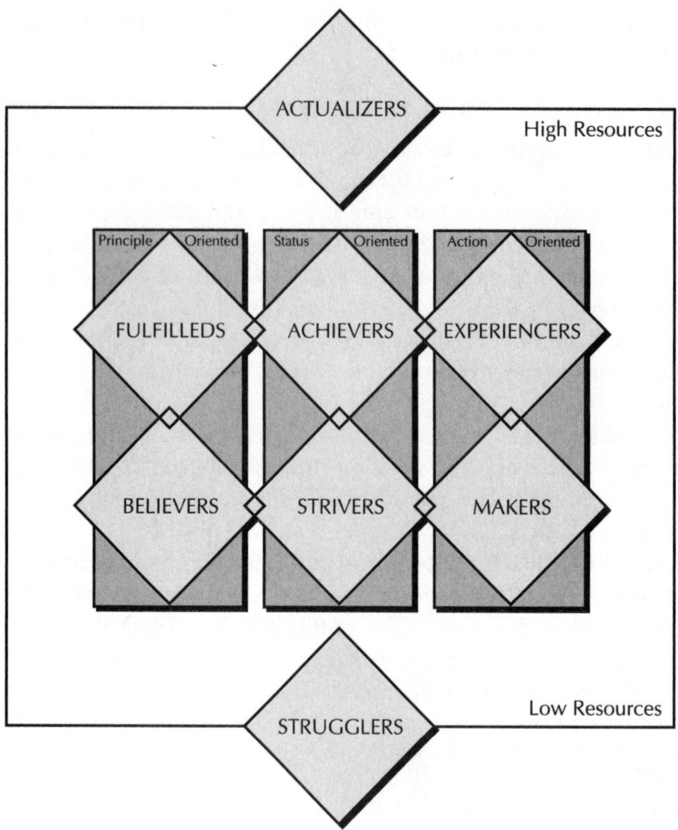

Take the profile test yourself, and ask several people whom you see as your Target Customers to take the test. Always be careful to target your product to the needs of your customers and not your own needs.

Standard Rates and Data Services (SRDS) also offers an insight into Healthy Gourmet's customer. Figure 4.5 includes SRDS's Lifestyle Market Profiles for Orange County. These profiles are available free in many regional or college libraries. The index figures are available for you to compare your target market to the overall marketplace and to contrast it with several different market areas. With 100 being the average throughout the United States, SRDS demonstrates that Orange County again is a high-income area with people traveling and participating in sports at a very high level.

The Johnson's describe their primary customer briefly as follows:

- sophisticated
- knowledgeable and concerned about their health
- age 30 to 60
- baby boomers that are in excellent shape and interested in retaining their health
- professionals, entrepreneurs, and others who work very long hours and are active physically
- highly educated
- expect the best
- purchase products to save time and energy and thus require high-level service and consistency

Healthy Gourmet also reaches two secondary markets—those over age 70 (many whose children purchase food for their parents) and dieters. Both have different needs and requests, and require a different marketing and sales effort.

FIGURE 4.5
SRDA—Market Profiles

Los Angeles, CA- Orange County,CA

Demographics
Base Index US = 100

Total Adult Population 1,960,499

Occupation	Population	%	Index
Administrative	333,285	17.0	133
Blue Collar	107,827	5.5	54
Clerical	148,998	7.6	88
Homemaker	237,220	12.1	88
Professional/Technical	570,505	29.1	115
Retired	268,588	13.7	74
Sales/Marketing	170,563	8.7	161
Self Employed	74,499	3.8	136
Student	52,933	2.7	113

Education (1990 Census)			
Elementary (0-8 years)	136,019	9.0	87
High School (1-3 years)	148,109	9.8	68
High School (4 years)	303,776	20.1	67
College (1-3 years)	503,270	33.3	134
College (4+ years)	420,147	27.8	137

Race/Ethnicity			
White	1,135,129	57.9	79
Black	33,328	1.7	14
Asian	243,102	12.4	365
Hispanic	541,098	27.6	263
American Indian	5,881	0.3	43
Other	1,960	0.1	100

Total Households 892,485

Age of Head of Household	Households	%	Index
18-24 years old	46,409	5.2	98
25-34 years old	192,777	21.6	113
35-44 years old	215,981	24.2	108
45-54 years old	181,174	20.3	113
55-64 years old	106,206	11.9	95
65-74 years old	82,109	9.2	76
75 years and older	68,721	7.7	73
Median Age	**44.6 years**		

Sex/Marital Status			
Single Male	203,487	22.8	113
Single Female	207,949	23.3	96
Married	481,049	53.9	97

Children At Home			
At Least One Child	273,993	30.7	98
Child Age Under 2	44,624	5.0	116
Child Age 2-4	81,216	9.1	111
Child Age 5-7	71,399	8.0	99
Child Age 8-10	66,044	7.4	91
Child Age 11-12	45,517	5.1	88
Child Age 13-15	63,366	7.1	84
Child Age 16-18	58,904	6.6	86

Home Ownership			
Owner	537,276	60.2	92
Renter	355,209	39.8	114

Stage in Family Lifecycle	Households	%	Index
Single, 18-34, No Children	125,840	14.1	118
Single, 35-44, "	66,936	7.5	125
Single, 45-64, "	88,356	9.9	110
Single, 65+ "	63,366	7.1	78
Married, 18-34, "	49,087	5.5	120
Married, 35-44, "	33,914	3.8	115
Married, 45-64, "	116,916	13.1	96
Married, 65+ "	74,969	8.4	76
Single, Any Child at Home	67,829	7.6	92
Married, Child Age Under 13	131,195	14.7	111
Married, Child Age 13-18	75,861	8.5	87

Household Income			
Under $20,000	132,980	14.9	57
$20,000-$29,999	99,958	11.2	77
$30,000-$39,999	105,313	11.8	91
$40,000-$49,999	107,098	12.0	103
$50,000-$74,999	206,164	23.1	120
$75,000-$99,999	114,238	12.8	156
$100,000 and over	125,840	14.1	199
Median Income	**$50,022**		

Income Earners			
Married, One Income	205,272	23.0	89
Married, Two Incomes	274,885	30.8	103
Single	411,436	46.1	104

Dual Income Households			
Children Age Under 13 years	76,754	8.6	106
Children Age 13-18 years	49,979	5.6	82
No Children	148,153	16.6	111

Age By Income			
18-34, Income under $30,000	91,926	10.3	88
35-44, "	33,914	3.8	62
45-64, "	41,054	4.6	53
65+ "	66,936	7.5	52
18-34, Income $30,000-$49,999	63,366	7.1	109
35-44, "	50,872	5.7	93
45-64, "	58,012	6.5	87
65+ "	40,162	4.5	100
18-34, Income $50,000-$74,999	47,302	5.3	129
35-44, "	58,012	6.5	114
45-64, "	76,754	8.6	118
65+ "	23,205	2.6	124
18-34, Income $75,000 and over	36,592	4.1	186
35-44, "	73,184	8.2	178
45-64, "	111,561	12.5	181
65+ "	18,742	2.1	140

Credit Card Usage			
Travel/Entertainment	184,744	20.7	153
Bank Card	726,483	81.4	106
Gas/Department Store	326,650	36.6	114
No Credit Cards	103,528	11.6	71

340 **Market Profiles** The Lifestyle Market Analyst 1997

FIGURE 4.5
SRDA—Market Profiles—cont'd

Lifestyles

Base Index US = 100

Los Angeles, CA- Orange County,CA

The Top Ten Lifestyles Ranked by Index

Snow Skiing Frequently	171	Wines	141
Foreign Travel	164	Real Estate Investments	141
Tennis Frequently	156	Running/Jogging	138
Use an Apple/Macintosh	151	Travel for Business	131
Frequent Flyer	150	Casino Gambling	131

Home Life	Households	%	Index
Avid Book Reading	320,402	35.9	**97**
Bible/Devotional Reading	141,013	15.8	**83**
Flower Gardening	261,498	29.3	**86**
Grandchildren	151,722	17.0	**72**
Home Furnishing/Decorating	193,669	21.7	**97**
House Plants	232,046	26.0	**82**
Own a Cat	222,229	24.9	**95**
Own a Dog	252,573	28.3	**83**
Shop by Catalog/Mail	227,584	25.5	**86**
Subscribe to Cable TV	570,298	63.9	**98**
Vegetable Gardening	129,410	14.5	**64**

Good Life			
Attend Cultural/Arts Events	162,432	18.2	**116**
Fashion Clothing	144,583	16.2	**117**
Fine Art/Antiques	109,776	12.3	**111**
Foreign Travel	209,734	23.5	**164**
Frequent Flyer	292,735	32.8	**150**
Gourmet Cooking/Fine Foods	194,562	21.8	**121**
Own a Vacation Home/Property	113,346	12.7	**121**
Travel for Business	239,186	26.8	**131**
Travel for Pleasure/Vacation	369,489	41.4	**109**
Travel in USA	341,822	38.3	**105**
Wines	170,465	19.1	**141**

Investing & Money			
Casino Gambling	156,185	17.5	**131**
Entering Sweepstakes	103,528	11.6	**76**
Moneymaking Opportunities	120,485	13.5	**113**
Real Estate Investments	83,001	9.3	**141**
Stock/Bond Investments	181,174	20.3	**107**

Great Outdoors			
Boating/Sailing	116,023	13.0	**123**
Camping/Hiking	221,336	24.8	**102**
Fishing Frequently	132,088	14.8	**60**
Hunting/Shooting	71,399	8.0	**51**
Motorcycles	70,506	7.9	**104**
Recreational Vehicles	82,109	9.2	**106**
Wildlife/Environmental	138,335	15.5	**94**

Sports, Fitness & Health	Households	%	Index
Bicycling Frequently	201,702	22.6	**125**
Dieting/Weight Control	182,067	20.4	**91**
Golf	199,024	22.3	**112**
Health/Natural Foods	170,465	19.1	**114**
Improving Your Health	229,369	25.7	**109**
Physical Fitness/Exercise	383,769	43.0	**118**
Running/Jogging	143,690	16.1	**138**
Snow Skiing Frequently	117,808	13.2	**171**
Tennis Frequently	82,109	9.2	**156**
Walking for Health	292,735	32.8	**98**
Watching Sports on TV	318,617	35.7	**93**

Hobbies & Interests			
Automotive Work	119,593	13.4	**92**
Buy Pre-Recorded Videos	157,077	17.6	**95**
Career-Oriented Activities	103,528	11.6	**125**
Coin/Stamp Collecting	55,334	6.2	**91**
Collectibles/Collections	96,388	10.8	**86**
Community/Civic Activities	62,474	7.0	**77**
Crafts	194,562	21.8	**80**
Current Affairs/Politics	160,647	18.0	**108**
Home Workshop	192,777	21.6	**83**
Military Veteran in Household	174,927	19.6	**84**
Needlework/Knitting	102,636	11.5	**74**
Our Nation's Heritage	41,947	4.7	**94**
Self-Improvement	193,669	21.7	**118**
Sewing	120,485	13.5	**80**
Supports Health Charities	141,905	15.9	**83**

High Tech Activities			
Electronics	117,808	13.2	**114**
Home Video Games	102,636	11.5	**93**
Listen to Records/Tapes/CDs	473,017	53.0	**105**
Own a CD Player	626,524	70.2	**118**
Photography	172,250	19.3	**109**
Science Fiction	85,679	9.6	**107**
Science/New Technology	99,958	11.2	**123**
Use a Personal Computer	498,007	55.8	**131**
Use an Apple/Macintosh	124,055	13.9	**151**
Use an IBM Compatible	420,360	47.1	**126**
VCR Recording	166,002	18.6	**96**

The Lifestyle Market Analyst 1997 **Market Profiles** **341**

SOURCE: Standard Rates and Data Services Lifestyle Market Analyst, *SRDS and Equifax.*

After being in business for 4 years and keeping records diligently, Healthy Gourmet now knows exactly who comprises their target market. But for those just starting a business, using the previous resources gives a good head start on defining Target Customers. By knowing your target market you can focus your promotional and marketing efforts on their needs and desires.

Continue to refine your profile as you work through the remainder of the Action Steps. Before continuing, be sure to complete Action Step 25.

ACTION STEP 25

INITIAL CUSTOMER PROFILE

Based on what you know to date, profile your Target Customer using the following:

- **www.census.gov**
- **www.claritas.com**
- **www.easidemographics.com**
- **future.sri.com/**
- SRDS Lifestyle Market Analyst (available in libraries)
- Any additional databases that you can locate on the Internet or in the library.

For business-to-business customers, access the customers' SIC codes or NAISC codes using the books available in the library or at various sites on the Internet. Use the following to profile your business-to-business customer:

- **www.abii.com**
- **www.hoovers.com**
- **www.dnb.com**
- **www.edgar-online.com**

Search the library and the Internet for directories that address your market.

How large is the market in terms of numbers of customers? How large is the market in terms of potential sales? Who are the major players? List your top 10 prospects.

Focus on your Target Customer throughout the remainder of the chapter. As you recognize variables to add, or questions to be asked, jot them down. Action Step 27 entails further profiling.

Profiling Business-to-Business Customers

Business-to-business markets include a wide range of customers. You need to look at your customer based on demographics (size, geographic location), customer type, end-use application, and purchasing situation.

End-user profiling concentrates on how a product or service is used. Small firms often thrive in specific niches because larger firms may ignore such markets. Selling replacement parts for compressors is an example of a profitable niche market. Geographic profiling is used when customers are concentrated in a specific geographic area. Some examples include furniture in North Carolina, film-making in Hollywood, and biotechnology in San Diego. Such users have narrow and specific needs. If an industry leader is opening a plant in a different location, a new support business may do well because of less competition in the new area. If you were to follow the exodus of businesses to Las Vegas, you would be able to provide innumerable services to a growing industrial base.

Segmentation of business markets can include the following:

- NAISC or SIC codes
- Sales revenue
- Number of employees
- End-use application
- Location
- Purchasing method (i.e., bidding, low bid only, single sourcing)
- Credit risk
- Years in business
- Type of ownership: public, private, federal or state government, non-profit organizations
- International versus U.S. sales
- Ability to reach decision maker
- Purchase decision: group or individual
- Economic and technological trends affecting various industries
- Competitive nature of particular segments
- Barriers to entry in various segments

Use business information to help you:

Check a firm's financial stability.

Compare firm's sales to number of employees.

Discover ownership of firm or subsidiaries.

Locate specific companies.

Search specific industries.

Size up current and new markets by using multiple selection criteria.

Search potential prospects or prospective employers in a targeted market.

Identify decision makers so you can reach them directly.

(A sample listing from D & B Million Dollar Database appears in Figure 4.6.)

FIGURE 4.6
D&B Million Dollar Database Company Record Sample

D-U-N-S Number	80-480-0217		
Company Name	Gorman Manufacturing Company		
Street Address	492 Koller St		
City	San Francisco		
State	CA		
ZIP Code	94110		
County	San Francisco		
Phone Number	(415) 555-0000		
Latest SEC Information	Latest 10-Q, All Filings, Management's Discussion, People, Balance Sheet, Cash Flow, Income Statement, Latest Proxy (Officer Info)		
Sales	$10,600,000	(ESTIMATED)	
Employees Here	100		
Employees Total	105		
Location Type	SINGLE LOCATION		
Line Of Business	COMMERCIAL PRINTING		
Primary SICs	27520000	COMMERCIAL PRINTING, LITHOGRAPHIC	
Ownership Date	1965		
Metropolitan Area	SAN FRANCISCO-OAKLAND, CA		
State of Incorporation	CA		
Import/Export	IMPORTER		
Parent D-U-N-S	00-123-4567		
Parent Name	Gorman Holding Limited View		
Subsidiary Status	N/A		
Public/Private	PRIVATE		
Ticker Symbol			
Bank	FIRST SECURITY NAT BNK OF NEV*		
Accountant	ABC ACCOUNTING		
URL	www.gorman.com		
CEO	☐ Leslie Smith	Pres	
Executives	☐ Mr Kevin J Hunt	Sec-Treas	
Executive Biographies	LESLIE SMITH year of birth: 1926 Graduated from the University of California, Los Angeles, in June 1947 with a BS degree in Business Management. 1947-65 general manager for Raymor Printing Co, San Francisco, CA. 1965 formed subject with Kevin J Hunt. KEVIN J HUNT year of birth: 1925 Graduated from Northwestern University, Evanston, IL in June 1946. 1946-65 was general manager for Raymor Printing Co, San Francisco, CA. 1965 formed subject with Leslie Smith.		

Continued

HELP / INFORMATION U.S. CUSTOMERS	HELP / INFORMATION CANADIAN CUSTOMERS
For Sales Questions / Trials 1.800.526.0651	**For Sales Questions / Trials** 1.800.463.6362
For Information Questions 1.800.234.3867	**For Information Questions** 1.800.463.6362
For Technical Assistance 1.800.234.3867 or 1.800.526.0651	**For Technical Assistance** 1.800.463.6362
Email Feedback customerservice@dnb.com	Email Feedback cic@dnb.com

FIGURE 4.6—CONT'D

SOURCE: **www.dnb.com** (accessed February 8, 2001).

In addition to the variables and information previously mentioned, personal traits of the individual buyers within each firm become important. Getting to know the hobbies, activities, and lifestyles of the people to whom you are selling may be as important as the listed demographic and geographic variables. Relationships tend to be long term in business-to-business markets, and your ability to break into new markets may depend on your ability to break long-term relationships. Do not underestimate how difficult this may be.

Primary Research Is Absolutely Necessary!

Secondary sources of demographic and psychographic information, especially media sources, may provide enough data to allow you to gauge a fairly accurate profile of your Target Customer. Chances are, though, that you'll need to test your profile against reality. Field interviews, surveys, and observation are three primary tools that will provide you a more accurate profile of your Target Customer.

Field Interviews

Sometimes people enter into small businesses because of personal circumstances rather than an initial grand desire. Often, they have to learn new skills and learn them fast. Fortunately, entrepreneurs tend to be bright, creative, and hard-working people. Julia Gonzales is a good example. When Julia discovered that she would have to work for herself, she quickly began to research her Target Customers by conducting field interviews.

Baby Store?

It was no secret that Julia Gonzales was distressed when her husband was transferred. She couldn't blame him for wanting the transfer; she would have wanted it, too. But Julia had a terrific job as regional manager of a full-line baby furniture and bedding store chain, and to keep both job and husband she would have to commute more than 150 miles, 5 days a week. Julia chose to relocate with her husband to a lovely town with affordable housing.

She missed the store, and it was hard living on one salary when they had gotten used to two. She also missed the excitement of retailing and customer contact. When Julia started to look for work, she found that her reputation had preceded her. The two local baby store owners knew of the chain where she'd worked and were pretty sure that the only reason she wanted to work for them was to get a feel for the area so that she could open a store of her own and compete with them.

This gave Julia an idea. She hadn't considered doing that. But when she couldn't find work, Julia decided to go for it—to go ahead and compete with them. Their fear gave Julia confidence!

One thing Julia had learned on her way up the managerial and sales ranks was that it pays to know one's customer. So, in the mornings after sending her children off to school, she'd drive to various baby stores, park her car a block away, and when customers came out of the store, strike up conversations with them and conduct ***interviews****.*

"Hi!" she'd say. "My name is Julia Gonzales, and I'm doing market research in this area. I'm wondering if you might have a minute to answer a few questions about babies."

Her enthusiasm must have helped—she liked people and babies, and it showed. Being a mother helped her understand other mothers. She always dressed up a bit and carried a clipboard. Julia asked obvious questions like:

- *What do you like about this store?*
- *How close is this store to your home?*
- *What items did you buy?*
- *Was there anything you wanted and couldn't find?*
- *Were the people helpful and courteous?*
- *How frequently do you shop here?*
- *At what other stores do you shop for baby items?*

Sometimes Julia parked in an alley to research the arrival and unloading of the delivery trucks. From experience she was able to estimate the store's purchases.

Julia developed a separate list of questions for pregnant women:

- *Have you had a baby shower?*
- *Which gifts did you like best?*
- *Which gifts seemed most useful?*
- *What things are you buying before your baby comes?*
- *What things are you waiting to buy?*
- *How are you going to decorate the baby's room?*
- *What do you really need the most?*
- *What services would be most helpful to you?*

After completing 60 time-consuming interviews, Julia had an abundance of information to make sound decisions concerning her Target Customer. She also knew the strengths and weaknesses of her competition. Many times entrepreneurs just look for their competitors' weaknesses, but an entrepreneur can learn just as much from their competitors' strengths. Never underestimate the power of those strengths and the time and energy that went into developing them. Capitalize on the strengths of your competitors and take advantage of their weaknesses.

Observing Target Customers

In addition to interviewing, Julia was involved in **observing** her customers. This is the least expensive but one of the most effective forms of market research. You must put personal biases and intuition aside and truly listen to and observe your Target Customer. Put away all you know about your product or service and Target Customer. Observe how your Target Customer truly behaves and remember actions speak louder than words.

Julia Gonzales' Target Customers shared that they bought all their children's clothing at up-scale stores, but on observation she realized that more than half of the kids were dressed in Target and K-Mart clothing. People often say one thing but do another. Also, people themselves don't always know why they make purchase decisions unless they spend some time thinking about their actions. They might not even recognize a need, but when presented with a new product or service based on your

Interviews Planned conversations by phone, mail, face-to-face, or the Internet with another person or group of persons for the purpose of eliciting specific information.

Observing Using "new eyes" to learn about Target Customers.

observations, it may be just what they wanted. Julia also observed that the local stores focused on selling not only to mothers but also to the very large and lucrative market of doting grandmothers and aunts.

Private Phone Room Idea
Observation Pays Off
One supplier of a check-cashing service in a low-income Latino immigrant community also provided long-distance phone services. Each Saturday and Sunday large families—aunts, uncles, brothers, sisters, and grandchildren—came to call their loved ones in Mexico and Central and South America. The owner observed how difficult it was to have a private conversation in the open phone rooms and decided to partition off rooms to allow for private conversations. Additionally, he provided one large room where entire families could talk to their loved ones and celebrate birthdays with a song from all.

Use curiosity as you observe and interview. Ask as many open-ended questions as possible.

When Julia Gonzales wrote down her interview responses, she also made notes of the following information:

- Makes and years of cars the women drove
- Attitudes toward their children
- Clothing worn by the children and their moms
- Types and brands of strollers
- Children's snacks
- Hairstyles and grooming of the mothers and children
- Amount spent on their own children versus gifts for others

In addition, Julia decided to go to the local playgrounds and snoop around. She borrowed her friend's two babies, and off she went to ask questions. Julia could not believe how much more open people were to her when she was accompanied by a child rather than looking like a professional interviewer.

Julia combined the information she gathered from **www.easidemographics.com**, *Standard Rates and Data Services Lifestyle Market Analyst* (available at the library), and VALS with her observations, interviews, and secondary data. She was then able to focus in on her target market and make it the center of her dartboard.

Where can you spend some time observing your Target Customer?

In Chapter 5, when we research competition, we'll return to interviewing and observing. Here, we'll use another skill—surveying to reach a more refined picture of a Target Customer.

ACTION STEP 26

INTERVIEW AND OBSERVE PROSPECTIVE TARGET CUSTOMERS

Now that you've profiled several Target Customers via computer and media kit research, it's time for you to take a big step—time to move from the world inside your head to the arena of the marketplace. It's time to rub elbows with the people who'll be buying your product or service.

You know where your Target Customer hangs out and his or her habits, income, sex, personality, and buying patterns. You can guess this customer's dreams and aspirations. Now you're going to check out your assumptions directly by interviewing your potential Target Customers through additional research and observation.

First, observe your customer in the marketplace. Remember Julia Gonzales and the steps she took.

Next prepare for interviews. Develop questions in advance; most should be open-ended and call for more than just simple yes or no answers. Remember, the most important part of your research will be for you to keep an open mind!

Those of you who are Internet-savvy may also research by contacting newsgroups and posting questions or by reading previous postings. The Internet is an excellent research choice as the Internet community basically believes in the free flow of information.

Surveys

When Julia Gonzales and Patti Hale decided that they were going to work for themselves, they quickly began to research their Target Customers. The methods they chose were observation, interviewing, and surveying. You can do the same for your marketing research. Action Step 26 and Patti Hale's experience in the following paragraphs will guide you in conducting a survey for your potential business.

Designing and Conducting a Survey
Patti Hale, a supervisor at a textile plant, decided to leave the plant and turn her love of food and people into a business: a restaurant. For some time, Patti had been developing her business skills. She had taken several courses in restaurant and bar management and an evening small-business course at a local college. In an attempt to gain a handle on her Target Customer, Patti read many studies on the dining habits

of people in the Southeast. But how did these translate to her local market? Although the secondary research was very revealing, Patti couldn't risk her future on someone else's research.

Patti decided to do her own survey. She studied survey design and received advice from her professor, an experienced surveyor.

She considered surveying customers at Joe's Joint, one of the most popular eating spots in town. Patti often had a bite to eat there and got to know Joe, the owner, quite well.

She told Joe about her dream to open a small restaurant some day and about how much she was learning in her small-business course. Patti convinced Joe to let her do a survey of his customers. After all, the price was right. Patti would do the survey free of charge and would give Joe her results—a classic win-win proposition.

Patti spent the next few weeks designing her survey method. How many customers should she survey? When should she do the survey? How should she conduct herself? There was so much to do. She launched a week-long written survey of Joe's customers. To Joe's surprise, customers wanted to fill out the questionnaire.

To Patti's surprise, she overheard Joe explaining to someone that he thought it was about time he learned a bit more about what the customer wanted. From her survey she determined her target market saw no need or desire for additional restaurants in the town and in fact were actually cutting back on the amount they spent to eat out. This was a rude awakening for Patti.

MAKE CUSTOMER PROFILING A REFLEX

We're trying to help you make customer profiling a reflex. Predicting the needs of every customer is almost impossible to accomplish with 100 percent accuracy. New previously **invisible customers** will emerge with needs that have not been anticipated. An alert entrepreneur will listen carefully to unexpected requests and be quick to respond to these opportunities. The following case is a typical example.

Invisible Customers

Some people go into business for themselves because they can't work for someone else. Some are mavericks who don't like to take orders. Others are dreamers who love their own ideas. Still others, like Fred Bowers, have a physical handicap that makes them prefer self-employment to getting a job with a large firm.

Sometimes customers "come out of the woodwork," as Fred's experience in following illustrates.

Soccer City

Revealing "Invisible Customers"

Fred Bowers had planned to be a career Marine until he was injured in a fall from a training helicopter. He could still walk, painfully, but his military career was finished. With a medical discharge in his pocket, Fred looked around for work, but none was to be found.

"I'd always loved soccer," Fred said. "I'd been a pretty fair player, and my coaching experience had given me a good understanding of kids and their parents. I thought there might be a place for a soccer specialty shop in our community, but before I went for financing, I spent several months checking it out."

Using the Internet, Fred found 20 sporting-goods shops located within a 20-mile radius of his desired site. If he wished, for a small fee he could access customer profiles, credit ratings, and credit reports on each of his potential competitors by conducting a search at ***ListBazaar.com*** *and* ***www.abii.com.***

When Fred began profiling his Target Customers, he came up with two easy targets:

- *Primary target: boys, age 6 to 17, and their parents*

Invisible Customer Surprise customers; usually a great find.

- *Secondary target: girls, age 6 to 17, and their parents*

He also gathered the following information:

- *Household income: $60,000–$100,000/year*
- *Level of parents' education: college-educated*
- *Interests: sports, video games, computers, movies, and music*
- *Cars: Ford Expeditions, Ford Explorers, Volvos*

Then Fred segmented the youngsters into two groups: members of school soccer teams and members of American Youth Soccer Organization (AYSO) teams.

Because of Fred's knowledge of the game and helpful demeanor, his store prospered. Schools counted on him for an honest deal, and parents of players counted on his advice for equipment. "I had thought I'd just be selling," Fred said. "What I was really doing was providing a service."

After being in business a year, a third market began to emerge. The customers in this third group were adults, mostly foreign-born, from countries such as Great Britain, Germany, Mexico, and Brazil. They had grown up playing soccer and loved the game. To them, it was a fiercely fought national sport they loved to play. These heretofore-invisible customers would drive 50 to 75 miles to Fred's store for equipment they couldn't find elsewhere. He agreed to sponsor several adult teams, and his business continued to grow each year.

The next year, the local Boys and Girls Club started an indoor soccer league for 1200 kids. Fred offered to sponsor all of the team photos. Needless to say, his business grew by supplying special indoor soccer shoes and knee and shin pads.

Fred now serviced AYSO and boys' high school soccer in fall, indoor soccer in winter, girls' high school soccer in spring, and adult leagues that played primarily in spring and summer.

"If I hadn't opened up, I wouldn't have known about the adult players. Now they make up at least 30 percent of my business. One day they weren't there; the next day they were. I like that. I like it a lot. It makes this whole adventure more interesting. Also, they really help with the cash flow as the previous summers were awful slow. In addition, keeping busy during all seasons makes it much easier for me to be in the store day after day."

Visualizing Your Target Customer

To this point, you have researched, surveyed, and observed your Target Customer. Now read about how Louie Chen from Seattle was able to visualize his customer. Soon you will be able to do the same.

Louie Chen and His Dreams

Louie Chen, born in Seattle, grew up playing baseball but switched to tennis. This was a good choice because he became a professional on the tennis circuit for 3 years.

Worn down by constant travel, Louie Chen left the pro tour and returned to Seattle and a comfortable life as a stockbroker. He was a member of the chamber of commerce and several organizations for Asian Americans. Because of his tennis, Louie did a lot of business at the country club. Louie was looking around for a new opportunity when he met Jiangli Chang, a recent immigrant to America.

Jiangli Chang, a middle-aged tennis player with a terrific backhand, was part of the Hong Kong exodus. His business consisted of importing objects of art from Japan, China, and Southeast Asia.

Jiangli expressed to Louie his difficulty in establishing a good banking relationship. Jiangli's problem started Louie Chen thinking. More and more Asians were coming to the Pacific Northwest. In the 10 years between 1990 and 2000, the Asian population in Washington had jumped 50 percent, from 215,000 to 323,000. With such growth, Louie Chen smelled opportunity.

ACTION STEP 27

TARGET MARKET COLLAGE

Gather up all the information from the past three action steps. It is time to visualize your data!

Develop a collage—a composite symbol of your Target Customer. Look through magazines and select at least 20 pictures, phrases, and possibly statistics, which represent your Target Customers and their lifestyles.

Make a list of your Target Customer's favorite television shows, movies, restaurants, activities, stores, radio channels, music, and books, and attach it to the back of your collage.

After you complete the collage, hang it up wherever you work on your business plan. Eat, sleep, and drink your Target Customer. The Target Customer collage should always be in your line of sight as you prepare to hit the market with your product or service.

Include your collage in your business plan to enable the reader to have a clear idea of your Target Customer.

If you have a business-to-business product, complete your collage with NAISC/SIC codes, a list of 10 best prospects, pictures of the types of people you will be selling to, their lifestyles, and so on.

FOCUS! FOCUS! FOCUS!

Louie enrolled in a local community college entrepreneurship course. His instructor was Grace Rigby, a marketing specialist, whose favorite tool was the Customer Profile.

"Profile your Target Customer. When you sleep, dream profiles. You'll have fun. You won't go wrong," said Grace Rigby.

With the help of Grace Rigby, Louie profiled his Target Customer. One of Grace's key teaching techniques was the Target Customer collage.

"The collage combines all your data and observations into a visual presentation," Grace said. "The idea is to clip pictures, statistics, phrases, and advertisements from magazines that represent your Target Customer. Then arrange all the pieces to form a collage. Hang the collage on the wall near your desk. When you become stuck writing your business plan, focus on the collage. It should bring you right back into focus. Your sole purpose is to solve the needs and wants of your Target Customer."

Louie Chen's collage included the following pictures:

- *Six Asian men and women in business suits*
- *A private jet*
- *Bank of Hong Kong*
- *Sushi*
- *An expensive leather briefcase and fine luggage*
- *Fine gold and diamond jewelry*
- *A laptop, Palm Pilot, and cellular phone*
- *An Asian man in shirtsleeves*
- *A man in a hardhat studying blueprints at a construction site*
- *An Asian man in golf gear teeing up at an expensive resort*
- *Asian families traveling together*
- *Stock market tables*

The collage centered Louie on his Target Customer. Because he had an A1 credit history, a well-developed business plan, and a keen sense of his Target Customer, venture capitalists were eager to finance Louie's bank. Louie chose the name, Shanghai American Bank of Credit (SABC), for his bank located in the international district adjacent to downtown Seattle.

Specializing in the Asian market, Louie hired greeters such as Maryann Wu, who was fluent in Mandarin Chinese and Korean and spoke enough Japanese to get by. Maryann was studying Thai as well. She shook hands with customers and then directed them to the manager who spoke their language or was very familiar with their country of origin.

One day, while sitting at his desk Louie saw an Asian male in his early fifties in the lobby. He wore an expensive tailored suit, carried a briefcase, and looked just like one of the men in his original collage. Louie hurried out of his office and greeted the gentleman, Sam Song, who subsequently deposited $1 million in his new SABC account.

Louie never stopped focusing on his Target Customer collage and had been adding to it during the past year in business. In fact, it was hanging in his office. But now he knew the person he wanted to celebrate with was Grace Rigby. Without Grace's insistence on focusing and refining his target market, he knew SABC would not have been a success.

Sam Song was probably an Actualizer on the VALS scale. An Actualizer is a person of high esteem who takes charge and is attentive to his/her image in the world. Louie's Target Customer collage reflected business leaders with resources and deep interests in music and art. Louie found out later that one reason Sam Song immigrated to Seattle was for access to the Seattle Art Museum and the Pacific Northwest Ballet. If you hot link from the VALS Internet page to the Activity page, you'll see that visiting museums ranks high on the Actualizer's preferred activities lists.

It's now time for you to complete your own Target Customer collage following the instructions in Action Step 27. Start to visualize your customer. Keep the picture of your Target Customer in the forefront as you move into evaluating your competition and promoting your product.

Community Resource

ENTREPRENEURSHIP CENTERS AT YOUR SERVICE

With more than 100 entrepreneurship centers throughout the United States, most individuals are within a short distance of incredible resources. Many of the centers are headquartered at universities and may include small-business development centers (SBDCs), small-business innovation research centers (SBIRs), innovation institutes, and franchise management institutes. Other centers operate individually.

Each center operates to serve the needs of a certain community, and thus they vary greatly. Workshops, consulting, short-term coursework, competitions, degree programs, and specialized programs are available at reasonable costs.

Check out the listings at the National Consortium of Entrepreneuship Centers, **www.nationalconsortium.org**. Also, **entrepreneurs.about.com** provides an excellent listing of centers, several of which we have highlighted in following:

DePaul University Entrepreneurship Program
College of Commerce
DePaul University
Address: 1 East Jackson, Suite 7000
Chicago, IL 60604
Phone: (312) 362-8353
E-mail: hwelsch@wppost.depaul.edu
Programs and activities: degree programs, research, Annual Private Enterprise Network Symposium (PEN), Annual Creative Idea Competitions, DePaul Entrepreneurship Group (DEG), Entrepreneurship in the Arts, student internships, Small Business Institute (SBI), Collegiate Entrepreneurs Organization

Midwest Entrepreneurial Education Center
College of Business
Ball State University
Address: 2000 University Avenue, Muncie, IN 47306
Phone: (765) 285-5327
Fax: (765) 285-9003
E-mail: dkuratko@gw.bsu.edu
Programs and activities: degree programs, corporate entrepreneurship training, YESS! (Youth Empowerment and Self-Sufficiency) Mini-Society, EntrePrep, Mother and Daughter Entrepreneurs in Teams (MADE-IT), executive education.

Institute for Rural Community Entrepreneurship
Center for Sustainable Systems
Address: P.O. Box 12083
Lexington, KY 40580
Phone: (888) 440-7845
Fax: (859) 252-9255
E-mail: cgrowers@mis.net
Programs and activities: educational and training programs on rural entrepreneurship, with a particular focus on agricultural entrepreneurship; policy advocacy with federal, state, and local agencies and decision-makers concerning rural and community entrepreneurship; research and publications on the role of cooperatives in rural community entrepreneurship; establishment of the Kentucky Center for Cooperative Development to advocate and train rural cooperatives in entrepreneurial strategies; grant and micro-loan program for agricultural entrepreneurs and cooperatives.

The Kauffman Center for Entrepreneurial Leadership
Ewing Marion Kauffman Foundation
Address: 4801 Rockhill Road

Kansas City, MO 64110-2046
Phone: (816) 932-1000
E-mail: info@emkf.org
Programs and activities: agri-entrepreneurship, The Denali Initiative, Entrepreneur Invention Society, Entrepreneur Of The Year Institute, EntrePrep, EntreWorld, FastTrac, The Kauffman Center, ERIC Clearinghouse, Kauffman Fellows Program, Kauffman Gathering of Entrepreneurs, MADE-IT (Mother and Daughter Entrepreneurs in Teams), Making a Job, Mini-Society, National Commission on Entrepreneurship, Not-for-Profit Entrepreneurial Leadership Initiatives, School-to-Career Entrepreneurship Partnership.

SOURCE: **entrepreneurs.about.com** (accessed May 5, 2001).

SUMMARY

Before your open your doors, profile your Target Customer at least five times. After your doors are open, continue to gather data through surveys, interviews, and observation and refine the profile yearly.

A profile combines demographic data (age, sex, income, education, residence, cultural roots, etc.) with psychographic insight (observations of lifestyle, buying habits, consumption patterns, attitudes, etc.). The magazines read by your Target Customers will reveal a fairly well-drawn profile.

Questions you need to answer through profiling your Target Customer are:

1. Who are my Target Customers?
2. How can I best reach my Target Customers?
3. What need will my product or service fill? (For example, landscaping is not just mowing grass and trimming shrubs. Its major selling points are enhancing the appearance of property and providing its owner free time.)
4. Where and how can I communicate my message with a minimum of confusion?
5. What additional services does my Target Customer want?
6. What quality of service or product do my customers desire, and what are they willing to pay?
7. Who else is after my Target Customers?
8. Why do my Target Customers act the way they do?

THINK POINTS FOR SUCCESS

- Psychographics is derived from "psyche" and "graphos," the Greek words for "life" or "soul" and for "written," respectively. Thus psychographics is the charting of your customer's life, mind, soul, and spirit.
- Segmenting is discovering the piece of the pie you should focus on. As you go deeper into your research, you will discover that perhaps you could reach the blueberries in the pie, and if you go further, you will reach the seeds—your true Target Customer. In essence, your collage developed in Action Step 27 should represent the blueberry seeds.
- You can save a lot of steps by using market research that has been conducted by others.
- To discover your target market, use everything available: media kits, demographic studies, lifestyle segmentations, and census data.
- Use NAISC or SIC codes to begin your research for business-to-business customers.
- FOCUS! FOCUS! FOCUS on your Target Customer.

Key Points from Another View

Professor Finds Life of Variety in Magazines

By Ted Anthony

He has enough *Time* on his hands to be a real *Details* man. He's got *Allure,* and he's completely in *Vogue*—a real *Cosmopolitan* kind of guy. His *People* skills are formidable. He has a good sense of *Self,* has a *Spin* for everything, and knows all about *Us.*

Got it yet? Samir Husni is a maestro of magazines, a potentate of periodicals who has parlayed his interest into a career of academics, consulting, and just plain reading. And the University of Mississippi journalism professor's travels and page-turning have led him to a conclusion that counters a loudly-spoken notion: that in a world of video and cyberspace, print is dying. In fact, it's thriving in many different ways—not in spite of new media, but because of it.

Husni loves it all. "*Seventeen* has two different covers this month!" he exclaims, his arms full of reading material during a recent buying trip to Manhattan, Mecca of magazinedom.

For magazine lovers, the golden age is back. According to Husni, 5200 consumer magazines were distributed nationally last year, up from just 2500 in 1985. And the survival rate, he says, is a respectable 4 out of 10.

He would know. His yearly book, *Samir Husni's Guide to New Consumer Magazines,* is a must-read in the industry. He uses magazines as textbooks in his journalism classes. His appetite sometimes costs $1500 a month—only some of which Ole Miss will reimburse.

In his office in Oxford, Mississippi, Husni sits surrounded by hip-deep stacks of printed arcana, smiling broadly. In a back room are thousands more; his wife, declaring that the magazine presence had reached critical mass in the Husni household, ordered all issues but the ones he's reading exiled to the campus.

"You could sit in here and read for months," marvels Charles Doudy, Hunsi's teaching assistant.

For Hunsi's collection takes *ad obscurum ad infinitum.* Consider the titles he has amassed: *Pool and Spa Living, Great Escapades of World War II, Naturally Nude, Gentleman Farms, Silicon India, Turkey Hunting, Golf Digest, Retirement Planner, Canoe Journal, Biblical Archaeology Review, Lotto World, American Cheerleader, Wine X* (a Generation-X wine magazine), *Leonardo DeCaprio Magazine,* and *Atlanta Baby.* There are also scores of porn magazines with titles as risqué as their pictures.

Then there's the trio of ferret magazines—*Ferret USA, American Ferret,* and yes, *Modern Ferret.*

"I guess that's as opposed to your traditional ferret," Husni says.

"When we reach this stage, when we have three magazines for ferret lovers, you know magazines are doing well," he says. "If I watch mud wrestling on ESPN and want to see more, I get a magazine. TV's fueling it all."

Newsstands today feature all manner of specialty magazines. Internet sites—"Web 'zines"—are gathering readers online, then launching physical editions of their magazines. "Mr. Food" is a cooking and recipe magazine based on the popular syndicated television gourmet. Introduced as a quarterly last year to ride a wave of viewership, its circulation has already reached 400,000.

"We got such great response to viewers writing in for recipes, and they wanted more. It just seemed like a natural transition," says Howard Rosenthal, Mr. Food's publicist. "People are so loyal to TV, and you can only get so much time on TV. And people always want to know more."

Why is this happening? The Internet and cable television have driven a demand for more information on more obscure things. So, as niche marketing is carried further, magazines become "more human," Husni says.

While TV provides the viewership to feed the readership, the Internet—where niche marketing is far easier because distribution is cheap—is feeding a Balkanization of interests. And amateur 'zines, once almost guerrilla publications, are now entering the mainstream as desktop publishing becomes easier and the number of national distributors increases.

In short, everyone thinks *his or her* hobby-craft-obsession should have its own magazine.

Source: Ted Anthony, "Professor Finds Life of Variety in Magazines," *The Orange County Register Business Monday,* June 22, 1998, p. 18.

Reading and Beating the Competition

ENTREPRENEURIAL LINKS

BOOKS

E-Business Intelligence: Turning Information into Knowledge into Profit," Bernard Liautaud and Mark Hammond, McGraw-Hill Professional Publishing, New York, 2000.

Leading the Revolution, Gary Hamel, Harvard Business School Press, Boston, 2000.

The Sourcebook to Public Record Information: The Comprehensive Guide to County, State and Federal Public Record Information, Michael Sankey, James Flowers, and Peter Weber, BRB Publications, Tempe, Ariz., 2000.

WEBSITES

www.dellvader.claritas.com, (Claritas Express)
www.globaledge.msu.edu, (globalEdge)
ciseek.com, (The CI Resource Index)

ASSOCIATIONS/ORGANIZATIONS

Society of Competitive Intelligence Professionals, www.scip.org
National Retail Foundation, www.nrf.com/home.asp
Center for Entrepreneurial Leadership, www.celcee.edu

PUBLICATIONS

Competitive Intelligence
Small Business Journal, www.tsbj.com
Minority Business Entrepreneur, www.mbemag.com

ADDITIONAL ENTREPRENEURIAL INSIGHTS

Digital Capital: Harnessing the Power of Business Webs, Don Tapscott, David Ticoll, and Alex Lowy, Harvard Business School Press, Boston, 2000.

Differentiate or Die: Survival in Our Era of Killer Competition, Jack Trout and Steve Rivkin (Contributor), John Wiley and Sons, New York, 2000.

Online Competitive Intelligence: Increase Your Profits Using Cyber-Intelligence, Helen Burwell, Facts on Demand Press, 1999.

LEARNING OBJECTIVES

- Define competition in terms of size, growth, profitability, innovation, market leaders, market losers, and potential competitors.
- Discover your Target Customer's Touchpoints.
- Understand the value of positioning in relationship to competitors.
- Evaluate competitors using primary, secondary, and "new eyes" research.
- Develop skills as a marketplace detective.
- Evaluate the competitive landscape broadly.
- Use a competitor test matrix.
- Create uniqueness.
- Create skills to become a lifelong scanner of the landscape.
- Prosper in a rapidly changing competitive marketplace.
- Become the best marketplace detective you can be.

Only a few years ago, the subject of competition conjured up warlike terms such as "beat the competition," "disarm your competitor," "take a piece of their market," and so on. This market-sharing mentality assumed that when one went into business he or she would take a piece of the action away from someone else. In a steady-state environment in which industries changed at a slow and predictable pace, the focus was on attacking the competition—after all, there was little change going on, and this strategy seemed to be the only way to drum up new business.

The knowledge-based economy, technology, and the new informed customer have changed the way business views competition. Learning from and dancing with your competition is what the new economy is all about. Create your own market niche and continually change and improve your product or service as the customer dictates. Today competition is healthy (not easy), and it's there to help you change and respond to the market.

In the previous few chapters we've learned about trend spotting, opportunity selection, and profiling target customers. We've focused your business toward growth industry segments and customer needs. This chapter explains how your perceived competition can help you further define your specific niche—and it all starts with the customer.

Debbee and Steve Pezman, founders of *Surfer's Journal,* a high-quality quarterly journal targeted to surfers over 30, are guided by the following principle: "Identify your target customer, and serve them with a plus that is hard to copy." As the Pezmans review new opportunities, they proceed only if they can answer "yes" to the following questions: "Is this a plus for our customer?" and "Is this something our competitors will find difficult to copy?"

As you read through Chapter 5, complete the Action Steps, and develop your business idea, continually ask the Pezmans' two questions to keep you on track and your customer in focus.

WHY THE NEW MARKET RESEARCH?

Inc. asked Roger D. Blackwell to help make sense of the impact that accelerating product cycles has had on market research. As professor of marketing at Ohio State University and as an independent consultant to companies such as Victoria's Secret and J.C. Penny, Blackwell spends his time studying consumer behavior and the retail sector.

INC: Why is it more important than ever for companies to speed up their market research?

BLACKWELL: Fierce competition. There are too many companies chasing too few consumers, and the survivors are getting better and better at providing what consumers want. In the past many companies faced competition from great, average, and bad companies. But the bad and the average are being eliminated rapidly, and we are left with only top-notch companies that are more likely to strive to have what the consumer wants. That puts pressure on all the surviving corporations, whatever their size, to conduct precise and speedy market research, so they can offer products that match consumers' desires sooner than the competition.

Product cycles have shortened in part because new products and product improvements have come from countrywide chains. A good idea in one part of the country quickly rolls out across the landscape. Local companies no longer have the luxury of waiting years before their competitors come up with better ideas. Now new products that have been tested elsewhere—including other countries—quickly become competitive with local products. Honda, for example, has cut conception-to-production time from years to a matter of months. Technological advances in product design and development also have greatly sped up the pace of new-product offerings.

INC: Does consumer opinion change more rapidly today?

BLACKWELL: For sure. Information now travels so quickly that consumers learn about new products and competitive improvements almost immediately. If Intel has a problem with a new chip, the information flies over the Internet in nanoseconds.

INC: Does information that flies around so quickly force the company owner to make faster decisions?

BLACKWELL: It increases the penalty for making wrong decisions. In the past you might have corrected a problem long before very many people knew about it. But that era is history. Today there's real pressure to have dead-on market research. You've got to get it right because the whole world will know instantly if you've got it wrong. And they may never forgive you for a major mistake.

SOURCE: Joshua D. Macht, "The New Market Research," *Inc.*, July 1998.

WHO IS YOUR COMPETITION?

Think back to Chapter 3 when we talked about defining your business, not in terms of products, but in terms of benefits—not selling a book per se, but selling information, enjoyment, or pleasant memories. If your business was selling ice cream, "old thinking" would ask you to list other ice cream vendors and manufacturers. In the new school of thought your competition is anyone who does or could provide the same benefit. If the benefit for your target customer is an afternoon treat, then your potential competitor is anyone who provides treats! Customers only have so many dollars and everyone wants those dollars, so your customer could stop and buy flowers, specialty coffee drinks, yogurt, sweet rolls, or cookies. Other ice cream stores and yogurt stores in your area would be considered your primary or direct competitors, with the other businesses being your indirect competitors. Never underestimate the power of your indirect competitors. When exploring your competition, define it as broadly as possible at the beginning and then work through the industry, direct, and then indirect competitors.

Your competition is not necessarily who YOU think it is (although your views are important). Your customers define the competition in terms of those who can best satisfy their needs.

If you have truly listened to your customer as you completed the previous Action Steps, you may already be on your way to developing a profitable market niche.

CUSTOMER TOUCHPOINTS

As we have said before, people today are not just purchasing products or services, they are also buying what the products and services do for them. The customer's cry is "What's in it for me? How does it make my life better, easier, more effective, and fun?" To get you started on evaluating your competition, first you need to recognize what is of value to your customer.

ACTION STEP 28

EVALUATING CUSTOMER TOUCHPOINTS

Investigate your customer's perception of the competition and what benefits are important to them. As you look for a niche in the marketplace, you must review your competitors' actions and products.

Work with a group of your potential target customers and walk through the "experience of purchasing your competitors' products." Make a long list (at least 60-80 items) of each time the customer comes in contact with any facet of the competitors' business. Each facet makes up the entire product—the jewel. The more you know about the jewel, the more you can make it shine!

Before beginning the assignment review the chapter's Healthy Gourmet Customer Touchpoints example in the text.

After listing the Touchpoints, ask the target customers to select and rank the five most important Touchpoints.

You need to consider which facets are worth going head to head with, which are not worth dealing with, and in which areas you can supersede your competition.

Keep your Touchpoints handy because you will return to them in Chapter 6. When writing your Business Plan, capitalize on the Touchpoints that make you stand out in the crowd!

Ask them!

Gather together a small group of your potential target customers for a "group think" on your competitors. Walk together through the entire experience your customers encounter with your competition. We like to call this process "evaluating customer Touchpoints." Each Touchpoint represents when the customer has contact with anything affiliated with a firm—from advertising, product, packaging, public relations, receptionists, salespeople, or the clean floor they walk on. Making a list of all the Touchpoints allows you to focus on areas where your competitors are weak. In addition, recognizing your competitors' strengths may indicate areas where you should not try to compete or where competition will be very intense. Make a list of these Touchpoints and prioritize their importance to your target customer.

Where do openings exist? Can you successfully compete in those openings? What needs aren't being met? What area could you capitalize on? Where do you see yourself being strong or weak? What images are your competitors projecting? What image will you project?

Do you recall the Johnsons and Healthy Gourmet from Chapter 4? Let's walk through the Touchpoints for the Johnsons' Healthy Gourmet customers. (Many more Touchpoints could be added to the following list!)

- Receives advertisement in the mail
  - What is the quality of the advertisement? Is it mailed first class? Is it addressed to the right person? How many mailings does the person receive before he or she responds?
- Responds to advertisement
  - How quickly is the phone answered? Is the receptionist pleasant? How long does the customer wait on hold for a salesperson? Is the on-hold music appropriate? Is the salesperson knowledgeable and helpful? If the customer asks a question, how quickly does he or she receive a response? Is the program explained clearly? Are the customer's dieting and health concerns addressed fully?
- Places order
  - Is the order form easy to fill out and understand? Is the form attractive? Is pricing clear? Are alternatives clearly spelled out? Is ordering online easy and quick? Is there a live human to call if the customer has problems ordering online?
- Customer receives order
  - Is the correct order received at the right time and place? Is the meal attractively presented? Are heating directions clear? How does the meal taste?
- Customer calls to complain or change order
  - How are complaint calls or changed orders handled and problems resolved? How long is the person placed on hold? Is it done politely? Is the problem solved in a timely fashion? Are follow-up calls made to ensure the customer's problem has been rectified?

Discover the "customer Touchpoints" in your business by completing Action Step 28. Later you will complete a **competitor matrix** to continue to evaluate your competitors.

To compete you need to stand out! Develop a **distinctive competency**. Own a niche. Success in business is not based merely on obtaining customers; success is achieved by retaining customers. So, as you seek out your competitors' strengths, look for those features that encourage customer loyalty by continually reviewing your Touchpoints and exceeding your competitors' offerings. Remember to focus on the benefits your customers receive.

Competitor Matrix A grid used to get a clear picture of competitors' strengths, weaknesses, and other attributes.

Distinctive Competency Area of greatest strength in the marketplace.

COMPETITION AND POSITIONING

Basically, competition is a mind game played out in customers' minds, where buying decisions are made. Inside customers' minds are many "ladders"—ladders for products, ladders for services, and ladders for sports figures, television programs, banks, and rental cars. To compete for a position at the top of one of these ladders, a business must first get a foothold and then wrestle with other businesses to improve its position. It's that simple.

Looking at competition from this perspective helps you focus on the mind of the target customer. To explore this idea further, read the classic *Positioning: The Battle for the Mind* by Al Ries and Jack Trout.

The name of the competitive game is "change." It is the constant process of positioning your product or service to meet the changing needs of customers and markets. You will use your **positioning strategy** to distinguish yourself from your competitors and create promotions that communicate that position to your target customers.

Another way to look at your competitors is a form of analysis put forth by Larry Kahaner, author of *Competitive Intelligence: From Black Ops to Boardrooms.* Kahaner encourages entrepreneurs to focus on their own and their competitors' Strengths, Weaknesses, Opportunities, and Threats (SWOT). You can develop a competitor matrix by focusing in on each of these areas.

Complete Action Step 29 to help you get a foothold and improve your position on your customer's ladder.

ACTION STEP 29

SCOUTING COMPETITORS AND FINDING ONE'S POSITION ON THE COMPETITIVE LADDER

Part A

Complete secondary research on competitors. Don't worry if your list of competitors gets too long. The more competitors you detect, the more you can learn.

Part B

Using your Touchpoints and past research, develop a competitor review sheet for each competitor. Go out on the streets and snoop! Evaluate each competitor on each variable, and rate them from 1 to 10. If you can't move inside without blowing your mystery shopper disguise, send in a friend with your checklist, or do some cagey telephone shopping. You can elicit valuable information from a phone call survey that's prepared in advance. Interview everyone who will talk to you. Keep this Action Step handy because you will need it to complete Action Step 30.

HOW CAN YOU DISTINGUISH YOURSELF?

There are several different strategies for companies to look at as they research competitors and try to find an area where they can excel. In *The Discipline of Market Leaders: Choose Your Customers, Narrow Your Focus, Dominate Your Market,* Michael Treacy presents the natural advantages small businesses have and how to capitalize on those advantages when meeting the Goliaths. He distinguishes three value disciplines:

1. Operational excellence such as Wal-Mart and Federal Express
2. Product leadership such as Intel
3. Customer intimacy such as Airborne Express and Nordstrom

No company can excel in all three, so focus on a value that differs from your major competitors. Review of your customer Touchpoints and competitor information and completion of a competitor matrix (at the end of the chapter) will help you focus further on your "distinctive competency" in the marketplace.

Scouting the Competition

Seek and Ye Shall Find

Now achieve an in-depth understanding of your competitors to visualize better the position of your company in the grand arena of the marketplace. Action Step 30, which appears later in this chapter, will help you dig.

Remember, work from your strengths; strengths are built on knowledge. Knowing your competitors will increase your confidence. Then you can win.

Secondary Research

Before you begin your primary competition research, start with secondary data by using the library and the Internet. In addition to the resources we have already introduced, the list of resources (following) provides a great start on your research. Many of these sources are also available on the Internet.

Positioning Strategy Where you try to place a product in the customer's eye through pricing, promotion, product, and distribution.

RESOURCES

Library and Net References for Company and Industry Information

Is the company publicly owned or is it privately owned/closely held?

1. *Security and Exchange Commission's EDGAR database,* **www.edgar-online.com**

Does the company have a parent company or subsidiaries?

1. *Directory of Corporate Affiliations*
2. *International Directory of Corporate Affiliations*
3. *D & B's America's Corporate Families*

Do you need to know the company's type of business, executive officers, number of employees, and annual sales?

1. *Standard & Poor's Register of Corporations*
2. *D & B's Million Dollar Directory*
3. *Ward's Private Company Profiles*
4. *Career Guide: Dun's Employment Opportunities Directory*
5. *Standard Directory of Advertisers*

Do you need the company's corporate background and financial data?

1. *Standard & Poor's Corporate Records*
2. *Moody's Manuals*
3. *Walker's Manual of Western Corporations*
4. *Corporate Information,* **www.corporateinformation.com**

Is the company newsworthy?

1. *Predicasts F&S Index*
2. *Business Periodicals Index*
3. Wall Street Research Net, **www.wsrn.com**
4. *PR Newswire,* **www.prnewswire.com**

Is the company listed in a specialized directory?

1. *Thomas Register of American Manufacturers*
2. *Best's Insurance Reports*
3. *Standard Directory of Advertising Agencies*
4. *U.S.A. Oil Industry Directory*
5. *World Aviation Directory*
6. *Medical and Healthcare Marketplace Guide*

How does the company rank in the industry?

1. Annual issues of *Fortune, Forbes, Business Week,* including *Fortune 500, Global 500,* and *America's Most Admired Companies, 100 Best Companies to Work For*
2. *Dun's Business Rankings*
3. *Price's List of Lists*

SOURCE: Linda Pinson, *Anatomy of a Business Plan,* Chicago, 1999, Dearborn.

Using Internet sources can turn up the most helpful resource: the names and phone numbers of people involved in your industry and those who may have conducted research in your area. Now you have to be able to reach out and touch to verify information and conduct interviews. You can also access fee-based services, as discussed in Chapter 3. Additional sources, such as the Science and Technical Information Network (**stinet.dtic.mil**), provide incredibly detailed information for a very low cost. Private database vendors are invaluable and necessary for anyone in a technical field.

Remember, when using the Internet, *you can't believe everything you read.* Act with caution before proceeding on information based solely on the Internet. Before proceeding, track down the source to verify the information.

GLOBAL VILLAGE

INTERNATIONAL INTERNET BUSINESS RESOURCES

How do you find the Asian-Indian Chamber of Commerce, business opportunities in India, or the Apparel India Trade Center? Rush to your library and check out an excellent new book by Lewis-Guodo Liu, *Internet Resources and Services for International Businesses.* In addition to very detailed country-specific websites, the author provides a wide range of general international business sites that can whet your appetite for the global marketplace. Countries around the world are waiting for you to export your products. Find the right country, the right market, and the right product, and your business will grow rapidly.

To do further research and understand how to use international competitor information, turn to Fuld's International Intelligence site, **www.fuld.com/chap6.html**, where you will find an entire chapter devoted to international competitive intelligence.

According to Jan P. Herring, a former employee of the CIA and current owner of Herring and Associates, "People's expectations about what they can find on the Internet are too high." He shared the following counterintelligence advice with Fast Company.

The Best Things in Life Aren't Free.

Free information is usually secondary information, and the problem with secondary information is that everyone else has access to it. It doesn't give you an advantage. You won't gain an advantage over other people unless you spend more time and money than they do. That means subscribing to syndicated services and databases—and in some cases paying people to work those databases. But ultimately you want information that can't be found in any database.

Human Intelligence Beats Machine Intelligence.

Most information never gets written down—it's just floating in people's heads. The only way to access that information is to talk to people. That's why the most valuable network is the human network. If you find an interesting paper on the Internet, don't just download it—call the author after you read it. Attending conferences is still the best way to make connections and gather intelligence. You'll hear things that never make it onto the Internet. And remember: The best information on your competitors comes from your customers.

Group Intelligence Beats Individual Intelligence.

Tracking the competition is everyone's job. The more closely people work together, the better they do. For example, companies often send 15 or 20 people to a big trade show. But how often do those people bother to compare notes? Companies should do what's called "quarterbacking." At several points during the show, get into a huddle and ask: What have we learned? What else do we need to know? Eventually that quarterbacking mentality becomes an everyday thing.

SOURCE: Gina Imperato, "Intelligence Tips," *Fast Company*, April 1998, p. 269.

12 RELIABLE SOURCES FOR INTELLIGENCE

Tracking the competition is no different from any other part of business life. The quality of your analysis can't exceed the reliability of your information. When it comes to finding reliable sources, nobody does it better than Helene Kassler (hkassler@fuld.com), 48, director of library and information services at Fuld & Comkpany. That firm is the CIA of business intelligence—and she is its master operative. Her title is a cover for a fascinating job: unearthing information that no one else can find. With her help *FAST COMPANY* assembled a list of reliable sites for you to use.

Website	What It Is	Helene's Hint
CEO Express **www.ceoexpress.com**	A fabulously comprehensive directory of links to major newspapers and trade magazines, custom news feeds, government agencies, and IPO alerts.	"My one-stop information shop. It has a truly remarkable collection of resources, and it's a great place to start a search."
Deja News **www.deja.com**	A web-based search engine that monitors Usenet discussion forums. The site tracks more than 50,000 different newsgroups.	"Discussion groups aren't moderated, so many of the participants can be uninformed. It's up to you to validate what you find."
Northern Light **www.northernlight.com**	A search engine on steroids. Its real treasure is its "special collection" of nearly 3000 books, magazines, journals, news wires, and reviews.	"Northern Light gets rave reviews for being easy to use. It has a database of some really obscure publications."
WhoWhere? (business and investing) **www.whowhere.lycos.com**	*The* place to start when you want to track down a person. WhoWhere? also lets you create a "Hotlist" of companies that it will watch for you.	"Great for alerting you to new information. You can have it send you an e-mail alert when one of your 'hot' companies submits a filing to the SEC."
Corporate Information **www.corporate information.com**	One of the few sites that offer in-depth information on companies outside the United States—an important feature in global economy.	"The other day, I clicked on 'United Kingdom' and discovered a bunch of really valuable sources. I recommend the site highly."
Career Builder.com **www.careerbuilder.com** Monster **www.monster.com**	CareerBuilder.com posts classified advertisements from newspapers. The Monster Board lets companies post openings and job-seekers post resumes.	"I spend a fair amount of time on these sites—not because I'm looking for a job but because job openings can be a great source of intelligence."

SOURCE: "He's Got Some Counterintelligence," from Gina Imperato, "Intelligence Tips," *Fast Company,* Issue 14, April 1998. All Rights Reserved.

INCREDIBLE RESOURCE

FULD COMPETITIVE INTELLIGENCE CENTER

ask.djinteractive.com/fuld: Do you need help with pricing and cost structure, new product rumors, competitor positioning, or core competencies? Fuld's website is a treasure chest! For 16 different areas, the site reviews the situation, gives advice, and provides a research strategy to gather further information. Fuld teaches one how to turn data into useful analyzed information, also known as "competitive intelligence." Under strategy he not only tells you where to search but also provides search techniques and tactics, which are only gained through years of research experience.

Primary Research

If you've completed the customer Touchpoints assignment and computer and library searches, it's time for you to become a "snoop" at your competitors. This is when your new eyes will come into full alert. If you are going to open a toy store, it's time to visit the toy stores within a 60-mile radius of your home. Take a notebook and write down information at each toy store. If it's easier for you, take a tape recorder and record your comments as you drive to the next store. Compile a list of customers' Touchpoints and rank each store on a scale of 1 to 10. In addition, make a list of anything else you think is vital for success in your selected industry and rank the stores accordingly. Become a paying customer at each store and walk through the total buying experience.

For each business, develop a competitor worksheet that includes all the important Touchpoints and the following: competitor's business name, owner, address, telephone, e-mail address, fax number, length of time in business, market share, target customers, image, pricing structure, advertising, marketing, customer service, return policies, special ordering offerings, cleanliness, stocking, strengths, and weaknesses (adjust the list to fit your business). Take this part of your research seriously because you are discovering your niche in the marketplace by evaluating others.

Entrepreneurs frequently downplay their competitors. *Do not underestimate the power of your competitors.*

Manufacturing and Scientific Competition

The following areas may also need to be addressed in your competitor research, especially if you are in manufacturing or a scientific endeavor.

- Manufacturing facilities
- Distribution channels and facilities
- Patents
- Financial strength
- Profitability
- Ability to acquire expansion capitalization
- Cost of production
- Employees (skilled sales force? great engineers? software designers beyond compare?)
- Service reputation
- Availability of spare parts
- Repair costs

Additional Snooping

You also may want to conduct some snooping with suppliers. They can and will provide a great insight to your competitors and the big picture. Beware and remember those suppliers who provide you with confidential information—they will provide the same information about you to your competitors in the future!

Attending trade shows and asking questions provides excellent market information. If you go with a friend or partner, split up so you can cover the entire show. Compare insights later.

No one knows an industry better than the salespeople who live in the trenches. The more of your competitors' salespeople you encounter, the more you will learn.

Half the battle of succeeding is to understand the obstacles and to be on top of developments—to take advantage of all opportunities. Never underestimate your target customers' loyalty, fickleness, or resistance to change. You must give them strong reasons to try your product and even stronger reasons to continue to use it.

The Competition's Life Cycle

Like everything else in life and business, competition has a four-stage life cycle: embryo, growth, maturity, and decline. In this chapter we examine these stages and look at ways you can use them to meet and beat your competition. Briefly, the four stages of the competition life cycle are as follows:

1. In the *embryonic* stage the arena's empty. There's just you and your idea for a product or service and a tiny core market. Being the first mover in a market does not assure success.
2. As your industry *grows,* competitors smell money and attempt to **penetrate the arena**—to take up positions they hope will lead to profit. Curious target customers come from all directions. You have visions of great success.
3. As the industry *matures,* competition is fierce, and you are forced to steal customers to survive. **Shelf velocity** slows. Production runs get longer. Prices begin to slide.

Penetrate the Arena Calculated thrust into the marketplace to secure market share.

Shelf Velocity The speed at which a product moves from storage to shelf to customer.

4. As the industry goes into *decline,* competition becomes desperate. Many businesses fail; weary competitors leave the arena, which is now silent except for the echoes of battle.

As discussed previously, competitive life cycles have greatly changed over the past few years. For example, a few years ago the embryonic stage for a computer software package might have lasted up to 2 or 3 years. The new economy has changed all that. Today movement from one phase to another can occur at blinding speed.

It's not unheard of for a product to go through these four cycles in a matter of months. In the high-tech business, for example, a common rule of thumb is 3 to 6 months—that is, you've got 3 to 6 months from the birth of an idea to product penetration. After that time period, competitors have already entered the market, and the product begins to enter the decline phase.

What all this means is that to survive you must constantly be in touch with the market and compete vigorously.

Where is your selected industry and segment on the competition life cycle? What does this mean to you if you're a start-up venture? What are the implications for your survival? When your industry enters maturity and decline, will you be ready with Plan B? Are you going to be a one-product wonder? The following information will help you get a further feel for each stage.

COMPETITION LIFE CYCLE

The Embryonic Stage

The embryonic stage is marked by excitement, naive euphoria, thrust, clumsiness, a high failure rate, and much brainstorming. Pricing is high and experimental. Sales volume is low because the market is very small, and production and marketing costs are high. You need to locate your core customer and stress the benefits. Educating the customer may be necessary and costly. Competition has not yet appeared. It's difficult to find distributors, and resellers demand huge gross margins. Profit is chancy and speculative. Shrewd entrepreneurs, however, can close their eyes and divine the presence of a core market. Keep trying! The writers of *Chicken Soup for the Soul* went to more than 30 publishers before they found **the one** that propelled their multimillion dollar empire.

The Growth Stage

Product innovation, strong product acceptance, the beginnings of brand loyalty, promotion by media sizzle, and ballpark pricing mark the growth stage. Distribution becomes all important. Resellers who laughed during the embryonic stage now clamor to distribute the product. Strong competitors, excited by the smell of money, enter the arena of the marketplace, as do new target customer groups. Profit percentages show signs of peaking. Brand loyalty begins as you try to establish your unique position. Media responses start to sizzle.

The Mature Stage

Peak customer numbers mark the mature stage. Design concentrates on product differentiation instead of product improvement. Competitors are going at it blindly now, running momentum even as shelf velocity slows. Production runs get longer, so firms can take full advantage of capital equipment and experienced management. Resellers, sensing doom, cool on the product. Advertising investments increase in step with competition. Some firms go out of business. Prices are on a swift slide down. Competition is very heavy. One needs to enter only if one has a unique twist on the product or truly provides a better product. But first ask yourself, "Can you realistically convey this message to your target customer?"

The Decline Stage

The decline stage is marked by extreme depression and desperation in the marketplace. A few firms still hang on. Research and development cease. Promotion vanishes. Price wars continue. Opportunities emerge for entrepreneurs in service and repair. Diehards fight for what remains of the core market. Resellers cannot be found; they've moved on.

Competition and Positioning in a Mature Market

Sometimes it becomes clear to a lone entrepreneur or a big business think tank that making a **change in the arena** can spell opportunity in a mature market. Although we have encouraged you to aim for growth markets and growth industries, that is not always possible or desirable for an individual. But competing in a mature market takes even more creativity. The change may be very small—a slight change in some aspect of the product or service—but the effect on the market can be very large indeed. The world of business—large and small—is filled with stories of such breakthroughs, and the common thread of these stories is the discovery of an **area of vulnerability** in the existing product or service. Entrepreneurs love to hear these stories, and it's no wonder; the stories contain lessons and inspiration. That's why we include several here.

If you're in a mature industry, you're going to have to win customers away from competitors to survive. The name of the game is dictated first and foremost by your customers, and second by your competitors. Continually learn from your competitors and customers so that you can adjust your product or service to meet the needs and wants of the market. You can guide your business back into growth segments and thus create your own niche by using three major thrusts:

1. Beat the competition with superior service.
2. Create a new arena.
3. Create uniqueness by continually changing your product or service.

Action Step 30

Construct a Competitor Matrix

The purpose of Action Step 30 is to rank your competitors and to visualize the positioning of each in the marketplace. Whenever you unearth some hard data, compare it with industry averages. Keep looking for those areas of vulnerability.

Now that you have a good picture of your major competitors and your target customers' desired benefits, you are ready to complete a competitor matrix. Pull out Action Step 29.

List all of your major competitors on the vertical axis; list all of the important benefits to your target customers and vital elements for operational success of your business in rank order on the horizontal axis.

Rank each competitor on a scale of 1 to 10 for each category (with 10 being the best). Total for each competitor. Next, place and rank your new venture on the matrix, and rate yourself. Note that the competitive marketplace is imperfect. Sometimes a few miles or a few hundred miles can make a significant difference in how competitive a business must be. If a mature marketplace is saturated, keep exploring other areas. You may find an under-served market that will welcome you instantly with warmth and healthy profit margins. By the time you have finished Action Step 30, you will have an excellent overview of your competitors, and opportunities will be in your hands.

Beat 'em with Superior Service

Tire Pro

James Grenchik was in the retail tire business serving a large farming community. His father had died a few years back, and James was left with the opportunity to carry on the family business. With tires lasting longer, he became quite concerned with the viability of his business. James tried price promotions and distress sales in an attempt to drive his competitors out of business, but these old techniques just didn't seem to work any more, and profits declined.

In fact, every time James looked around, there seemed to be a new competitor setting up shop in his market. Costco became a major competitor as well. Discouraged, James finally decided that this was no way to do business or, for that matter, to live. He had two choices—get out of business or change. Before he went any further, he needed to analyze his competitors. He sat down with his employees and a few customers and developed a competitor matrix (Figure 5.1). In Action Step 30 you will complete a matrix for your business.

After months of soul-searching, family discussions, networking, brainstorming, and reviewing his matrix, James finally decided to go for it:

1. *He created a partnership with two key groups. First, he sold 25 percent of his business to a major tire manufacturer and retailer who he knew was the best in the market. His major competitor would now be his partner.*
2. *James sold 24 percent of his business to his key employees. They had been with him a long time, and he knew they were hungry to own a piece of his pie. Now his best employees were also his partners.*
3. *He created uniqueness by changing his product through service add-ons. These new services were the result of cooperative brainstorming by everyone in the firm after completing a thorough analysis of competitors' offerings. In addition, for 3 weeks each employee was to question each customer about additional services they might like to see Tire Pro offer. Tire Pro's implementation of customer suggestions and competitor intelligence follow:*
   a. *Tire Pro now offers an installment plan for farmers who need tires early in the growing season when they experience cash flow problems. This*

Change in the Arena Transform a product or service by adding a benefit that has immediate customer appeal.

Area of Vulnerability Competitor's soft underbelly or Achilles' heel—a weakness ready for you to exploit.

FIGURE 5.1
Tire Pro Competitor Matrix

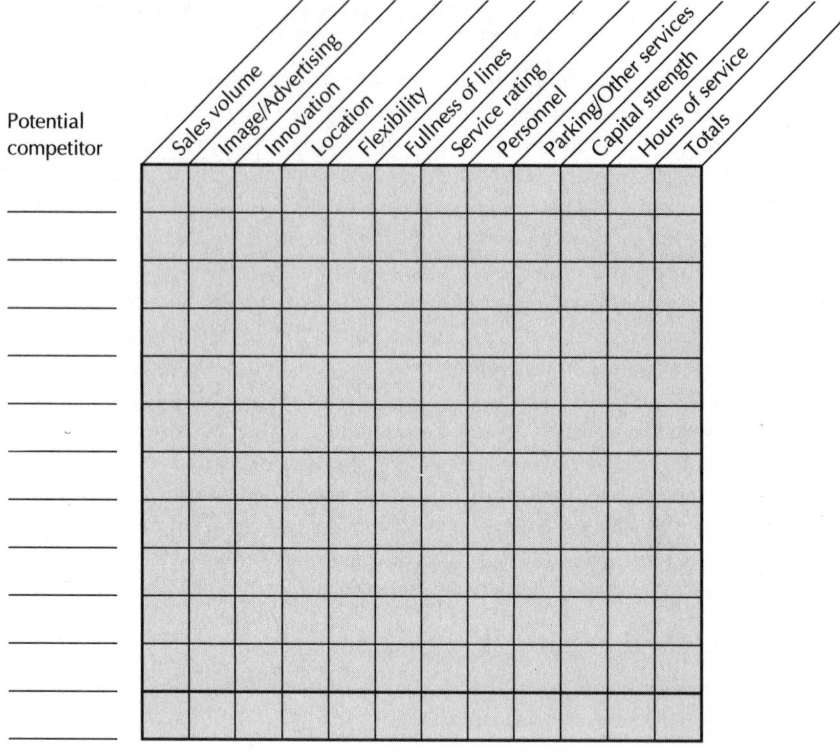

action also created a new profitable arena—finance. With the financial clout of his new manufacturing partner, Tire Pro entered the finance business.

b. All tire customers are given a free 6-month rotation on their cars and trucks. At the same time they get a free report card on potential trouble spots. This new service strategy has changed their product from just tires to "tires with a free rotation and inspection." Reminder postcards are mailed to each customer every 6 months, which keeps Tire Pro's name in front of their customer while providing a welcome service.

c. Tire Pro has another new customer service strategy. Customers who want a tire repaired can also pick up coffee and doughnuts and log on to the Internet for the latest commodities report. A bulletin board for used farm equipment was installed in the waiting room, now filled with farm, business, and kids' magazines. Puzzles and coloring books were also added for the children. (One California car dealer now offers a putting green for its customers. This may not be the best marketing tool for South Dakota farmers, but it is just right for the Mercedes-driving entrepreneurs of Orange County, California!)

d. Everyone at Tire Pro now answers the phone with their first name and a pleasant hello—much easier now that they're making money again! The tire installers wear beepers and headsets so they can hear phone calls; as a result, distractions in the tire bays for both the employees and customers have been reduced greatly.

James and his new partners are now making money by providing the best products and services. But be aware that most of the previous steps involve labor or marketing expenses, which must be recouped through increased profit and sales. His **core product** is tires, but James is also in repair and safety training—the rapidly growing service sector. Tire Pro is now ready to open a second outlet. Changes in financing, personnel, and competitive techniques rescued Tire Pro from a declining sector and propelled it into a growth arena.

Core Product Item possessing perceived needs that best fit customers' needs.

However, even if you start out in a growth market, there's one thing for sure. One day your market will enter a mature stage and eventually a declining one. You must adjust your product or service regularly to market changes, which may happen almost overnight.

Create a New Arena

Let's see how Jackson George, owner of Home Office Havens, successfully changed the arena by developing a niche for himself in a very mature construction market.

Home Office Havens
Positioning Your Business

Jackson George's family had been in the new home construction business for 20 years. After a falling out with his family, Jackson knew he wanted to remain in the same type of business but wanted to specialize and find a niche for himself.

Many of his friends were purchasing computers and developing home offices. At parties Jackson's friends complained that their home-office situations were not ideal. There weren't enough electrical outlets, too much noise was entering the room from other rooms, and they needed more shelves and bookcases for their books and materials. In addition, they desired custom-designed workspaces to fit their individual family's needs.

Jackson kept listening and started scouting the area to see if anyone specialized in home offices. He found firms specializing in bathrooms, closets, kitchens, family rooms, and media rooms, but no one was in the home office market.

*He sat down with five of his friends and brainstormed about home offices. After about 5 hours, the information indicated to Jackson that his friends were willing to spend about $20,000 each for a customized home office. Jackson went into high gear, reading every home office magazine, contacting Soho-Online (**www.soho.org**), visiting furniture and office supply stores, and calling potential suppliers.*

His best friend's sister, Susan Pollack, became his first customer. Susan agreed to show her remodeled office for 3 months to prospective customers in exchange for an extra desk.

To keep the competition at bay for a short time, Jackson limited his advertising and built his first home-office projects through word of mouth. Once he was established, Jackson developed his advertising and marketing with a professionally photographed portfolio of his projects. Because no other competitors had developed expertise in working within the home-office segment, Jackson was a tough competitor. Knowing the benefits his customers desired gave him the edge when competitors came knocking and bidding. On realizing two years later that he owned the market, he contacted a franchise developer. Within 5 years Home Office Havens became a successful franchiser.

Create Uniqueness by Continually Changing Your Product or Service

Change is the most predictable element of competition. Because of this, the entrepreneur needs to keep one eye on the market and the other eye on Plan B.

For a dozen years Ford Johnson has been in the mail order business, which allows him considerable freedom to be creative. Before going into business for himself, Ford trained as an electrical engineer and spent 20 years in the aerospace industry.

Always Ready with Plan B
Inventor Ford Johnson

Ford developed and marketed more than 200 products—from a Mylar heat sheet (for pets) to Engine Coat (a motor lubricant using Teflon) to space monkeys (dried shrimp eggs that hatch when dropped into water). He's also developed a hundred strategies for handling his competitors. The best one is how he competes with himself. Here's the way it works:

Community Resource

United Inventors Association (UIA): www.uiaus.org

The United Inventors Association (UIA) provides leadership, support, and services to inventor support groups and independent inventors. Members include inventors and others who provide reputable service and support to the inventor community. The UIA is an affiliate of the Academy of Applied Science.

Contact UIA to order their excellent Inventor's Resource Guide, which will provide you with an extensive list of websites for inventors. In addition, articles such as "Invention Record Keeping," "Red Flags of Unscrupulous Companies," and "Prototyping 101" will guide you through the invention process.

Best of all, through UIA you will have access to their member organizations throughout the United States. At this writing there are more than 50 members including the Tampa Bay Inventors Council and the Inventors Associates of Georgia. Most members offer monthly meetings, which include guest speakers, individual inventor's presentations, and critiques. In addition, many member organizations offer yearly all-day inventor training workshops. Join fellow passionate inventors, and support people who can help you take your dream from the workbench to the marketplace.

First Ten Commandments of Invention

- Stay away from invention marketing firms that advertise on radio and late night television. They're out to fatten their wallets and empty yours!
- Keep good records about your idea. Some day they may be the back up you need to prove YOUR idea is YOURS!
- Go to a patent depository library, and do your own patent search. If you find your invention is already patented, there's no need to go to a patent attorney.
- Build a model. There's no need to get fancy at first; use cardboard, white glue, balsa wood, and off-the-shelf parts. No matter how simple the idea, prove it works.
- Have your invention evaluated by a non-biased professional. (Even if your mom is in the business, go to someone else!)
- Read all you can about new product development. Go to your local bookstore or library. Others have gone before you—don't re-invent the wheel.
- Network with other inventors. Join a local investors' organization.
- If your patent search looked promising (see previous suggestion), make an appointment with a patent attorney. Show your attorney the results of your search, and follow the advice he or she gives you.
- Do what you do well, and hire pros to do the rest.
- Don't fall in love with your invention—but if you're really sure you've got a winner (see previous suggestion), hang in there! Even overnight successes take a while!

Source: *Inventors' Digest,* Nov/Dec 1995.

Ford introduces a quality product into the marketplace. It retails for $12, which nets him a reasonable profit after overhead. Because he deals with established mail-order houses (they ship to tens of thousands of customers), Ford knows someone out there will copy his idea and try to ace him by bringing out a lower-quality product for less money.

So, for the first couple of runs, Ford manufactures a quality product, using the best materials available. He charges full price for it, and waits for the phone to ring. When it does, he knows it's the buyer from the catalog house, telling him there's a competitor waiting in the wings with an ***inferior product*** *that will retail for $6—half of what Ford's costs. So Ford has a cheaper one ready to roll.*

"When do you need them, and how many can you handle?" Ford asks.

"Wait," the buyer says. "What kind of numbers are we looking at?"

"Mine will retail for $5.75," Ford says. "And I can have 10,000 on your loading dock 2 weeks from tomorrow."

"You're kidding," the buyer jokes. (He's new on the block. Other buyers have watched Ford work before.)

"Can you move 20,000?" Ford asks.

"Ten for sure," the buyer says. "And if we need more, I'll get back to you in 2 weeks."

"Over and out," Ford says. "It's great doing business with you."

You Can Do It!

We have provided you with a number of studies about entrepreneurs who worked with and learned from competitors and brought about big changes in the marketplace. It's altogether possible that some day we may be telling such a story about you. Yes, you too can do it. You just need to do the following:

- Know what business you are in.
- Know your target customers.
- Know your competition.
- Know the benefits of your product or service.
- Develop strategies to capture and maintain your position.
- Give rein to your creativity and your entrepreneurial spirit.

Go for it! Surprise us! Surprise yourself! Action Step 30 will help you.

Passion

Find a Problem and Solve It!

Save Me from the Sharks!

Han Chin and Nick Van Nugteren were both avid big-game fishermen, passionate about their hobby but not passionate about the many gashes and cuts obtained through years of unhooking barracudas and sharks. The last straw came when Nick hooked a barracuda, and the fishhook slipped, causing a large gash that required a hospital visit. Many stitches later, he knew he had to find a solution so that this would never happen again.

Nick worked with Han Chin, who had 12 years experience in engineering and manufacturing, and they developed and patented the "Hook Retriever"—the ultimate hook remover for all types and sizes of freshwater and saltwater fish. Han and Nick have marketed the "Hook Retriever" through the Internet at **www.sharkdundee.com** and at fishing shows throughout the country.

Nick and Han's passion drove them to find a solution to their problem. Fortunately, a great deal of others shared the same problem. Thus a great deal of hands on deck are now safe!

Summary

Now that you have identified your target customers and evaluated your competition, it's time to ask yourself, "Is this a plus for our customer? Is this something our competitors will find difficult to copy?" Customers do not change their habits easily, and businesses do not switch suppliers without extensive analysis. Unless you can offer something the other guys don't, you will struggle.

Inferior Product Something that is lower in quality than to what it's being compared.

Competing on price alone is a very tough road. The big guy can almost always hold out longer than you and put you under quicker than you can ever expect or believe.

Today, products and services cycle through the four life cycle stages rapidly. Being on top of your customers' needs and competitive changes in the marketplace is more important than ever. Use computer research; close contacts with customers, suppliers, and salespeople; and constant evaluation of your competitors to stay on top of the curve. Learn from your customers and competitors to help guide your business into a growth market. That's where the action is.

Think Points for Success

- Do it smarter.
- Do it faster.
- Do it with more style.
- Provide more features.
- Adjust your hours.
- Provide more service.
- Treat your target customers like family; consider their needs.
- Be unique.
- Change the arena through innovation.
- Know your niche.
- Keep your image in the prospect's mind.
- Compete with yourself if necessary.
- Disarm the competition by being better, faster, safer, and more user friendly.
- Remember that a new firm cannot win a price war.
- Know that old habits are hard to break; give your target customer several reasons to switch over to you.
- Develop your own monopoly.
- Talk to your target customer constantly and truly listen.
- Thrive, don't just survive!

Key Points from Another View

Check Out the Competition

For anyone trying to grow a business, one of the first tasks is to map the competitive landscape. With a good understanding of the competition facing your company, you'll be able to spot and exploit opportunities as they develop. These dozen points should help you draw and refine your map, beginning with your earliest efforts to plan your new venture and continuing as long as you stay in business.

1. **Be a customer.** Bring a notepad and pencil to competing establishments, and ask a lot of questions. Testing a firm's ability to serve you will reveal much about their business. Don't just pretend to shop from competitors. Buy something. It's the only way to gain firsthand experience with the company's products and services.
2. **Find out as much as you can about the people who run competing businesses.** Where did they go to school? Where have they worked? How long have they been in the business? What are their strengths and weaknesses? This information can help you anticipate your competition's moves. For example, a lifelong farmer will run an Indiana seed company very differently than will a young MBA.
3. **Buy stock in your competitors.** If you're competing against a publicly-traded firm, consider buying a few shares of its stock. That way you'll receive regular updates on the firm's financial results and business strategies.
4. **Talk to your competitor's customers.** Why do they buy from your competitors? Is it because of the quality of the product or service, the price, the location, or the customer support? What do they dislike about the company? What do they wish that company would provide? Why don't they buy from you?
5. **Use the Internet.** Online services such as Dow Jones Interactive (**www.djinteractive.com**) allow you to search through thousands of publications for information about your competitors, especially if they include large companies. Searches are free, but you'll have to pay a fee for articles on Dow Jones or for a monthly subscription. You also can learn a great deal about competing businesses simply by going to their websites.
6. **Check public filings.** As an entrepreneur, you already know that companies must disclose information to government agencies. Such disclosures are required to undertake public offerings, receive building permits, and register for patents or trademarks. Many of those filings are public record and contain information about the company's goals, strategies, and technologies.
7. **Get to know local librarians.** Many are virtuoso researchers and can save you a great deal of time and effort. Your library also will have local publications that may have information on competitors in your area.

8. **Attend industry conferences and trade shows.** Your competitors' representatives will be pounding their chests about their firms' products or services. Take advantage of the opportunity to familiarize yourself with their product offerings and strategies and how they sell themselves.
9. **Assess the competition's goals.** A competitor trying to increase its market share might lower prices, a firm attempting to increase profits may cut costs, and a business that wants to accelerate sales growth might kick off a marketing campaign. If you know your competitors' goals, you'll be better able to anticipate their strategies.
10. **Be aware of the potential for new competition.** These days, the competitive landscape can change faster than Internet stock valuations. A national chain may not have entered your region yet, but what if it does? Likewise, companies that don't currently compete with yours might shift their focus and pit themselves against your firm.
11. **Don't delegate the job of keeping up with competitors.** You might appoint someone to work with you on the task, doing research and the like. But as the entrepreneur, you're in the best position to appreciate and act on information about your competitors.
12. **Define the competitive landscape broadly.** Your competition includes anything that could draw customers away from your business. For example, movie theaters compete not only with other cinemas but also with restaurants, live music venues, theater, and even cable TV, video rentals, and video games.

SOURCE: **www.allbusiness.com** and **about.allbusiness.com/cmt/information/general.jhtml?fname=289** (accessed May 1, 2001).

Marketing Promotions Overview

Connecting with the Customer

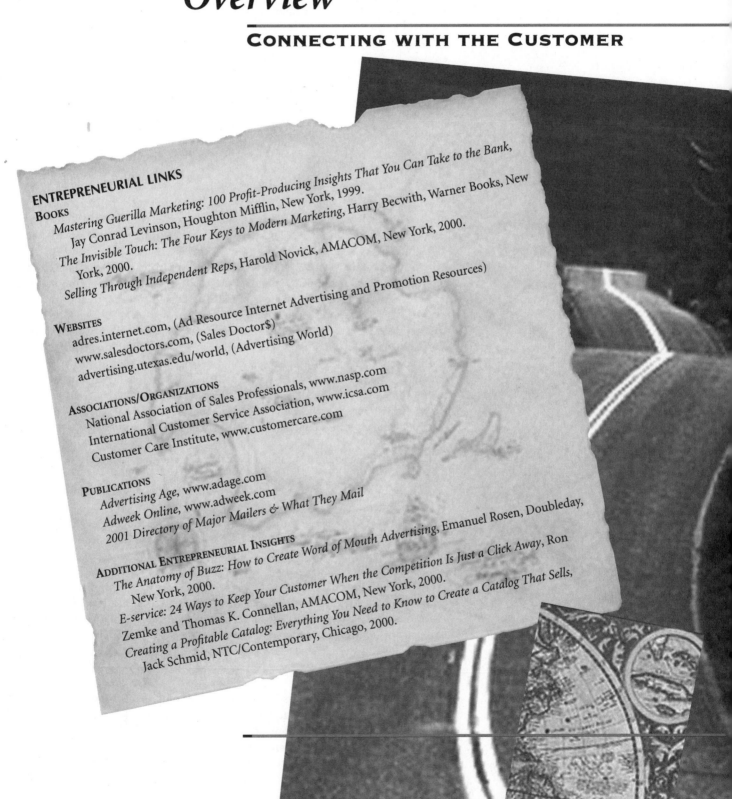

ENTREPRENEURIAL LINKS

Books

Mastering Guerilla Marketing: 100 Profit-Producing Insights That You Can Take to the Bank, Jay Conrad Levinson, Houghton Mifflin, New York, 1999.

The Invisible Touch: The Four Keys to Modern Marketing, Harry Becwith, Warner Books, New York, 2000.

Selling Through Independent Reps, Harold Novick, AMACOM, New York, 2000.

Websites

adres.internet.com, (Ad Resource Internet Advertising and Promotion Resources)

www.salesdoctors.com, (Sales Doctor$)

advertising.utexas.edu/world, (Advertising World)

Associations/Organizations

National Association of Sales Professionals, www.nasp.com

International Customer Service Association, www.icsa.com

Customer Care Institute, www.customercare.com

Publications

Advertising Age, www.adage.com

Adweek Online, www.adweek.com

2001 Directory of Major Mailers & What They Mail

Additional Entrepreneurial Insights

The Anatomy of Buzz: How to Create Word of Mouth Advertising, Emanuel Rosen, Doubleday, New York, 2000.

E-service: 24 Ways to Keep Your Customer When the Competition Is Just a Click Away, Ron Zemke and Thomas K. Connellan, AMACOM, New York, 2000.

Creating a Profitable Catalog: Everything You Need to Know to Create a Catalog That Sells, Jack Schmid, NTC/Contemporary, Chicago, 2000.

Learning Objectives

- Learn how to communicate with target customers using both conventional and creative promotional methods.
- Explore various promotional strategies.
- Promote your business through free ink/free air.
- Understand the value of sales reps and agents.
- Develop the best promotional mix for your business.
- Discover the importance of networking.
- View customer service as a key to promotion.
- Attach price tags to promotion ideas.
- Determine the dollar value of your customer.
- Understand the value of personal selling and sales strategies.

Promotion is the art and science of moving the image of your business to the forefront of a prospect's mind. The word promotion comes from the Latin verb "movere," which means, "to advance, or to move forward." It's an aggressive word, so learn to say it with passion!

Now that you have visualized your customer with your target customer collage and gained a sense of competition and market niches, it's time to plan a promotional strategy that is tailored to fit *your* customer. Each business is unique, and you don't want to waste money on promotional schemes that won't work. For example, if your target customer is a college-educated, suburban female age 45 to 55 who earns more than $100,000, owns three cars, rides horseback 10 hours a week, and reads *Practical Horseman* and *Performance Horseman,* your best chance of reaching her is with direct mail. If, on the other hand, your target customers are male and female, age 18 to 25, with a high-school education and incomes under $25,000, you'll achieve better results with mass-market advertisements such as radio or television.

Developing a promotional plan requires five steps:

1. Determining your sales and marketing goals. (Increase sales by 10 percent this year.)
2. Developing strategies to achieve a goal. (Increase repeat business of best customers.)
3. Creating a specific promotional method for carrying out one or several of the strategies and having measurable objectives. (Mailer for special Christmas shopping night with a goal of selling $20,000 worth of merchandise during the evening.)
4. Detailing and enacting a program involving the specific promotion chosen following a predetermined budget. (Gold embossed mailer sent to 300 best customers in November for special Christmas shopping night with free cookies, pastries, cider, and gift-wrapping at a cost of $1,750.)
5. Evaluating the effectiveness of your promotional vehicles and adjusting as needed.

Tie your promotional efforts into creating an overall image and presence consistent with your target market and business definition. Remember to stress customer benefits and your "distinctive competency."

Promotional Mix All the elements that are blended to maximize communication with your target customers.

Any promotion or **promotional mix** that advances the image of your business is worth considering. Survey some of the more common and traditional means of promotion before you decide on your promotional strategy, and be sure you remain

GLOBAL VILLAGE

OPENING YOUR EYES TO THE NORTH: CANADA

Canada, as the United States' largest trading partner, provides an easy entry into international trading. Travel is easy, language barriers are few, and a similar social and economic structure make Canada an excellent choice for your first international venture. With the North American Free Trade Agreement (NAFTA), opportunities are even wider.

Three great sources on the Internet provide an excellent starting point:

- CanadaOne, **www.canadaone.com**, provides access to banks, business publications, chambers of commerce, media sources, legal issues, and much more.
- Statistics Canada, **www.statcan.ca**, is Canada's national source for Canadian data, including demographic, social, and economic, with many links to Canadian organizations and agencies.
- Doing Business in Canada, **www.dbic.com**, offers comprehensive information on how to trade with Canada.

open to all options. It is essential to keep an open mind as you brainstorm for strategies, examine promotional campaigns, and come to understand the importance of planning ahead. You will then be able to make wiser decisions on how to connect with the customer.

Several things are critical to your campaign: what is appropriate for your target customer; what you can afford to spend (your budget); and your own prior experience. Most important, though, is what is *most likely* to give you "the biggest bang for your buck." Creativity, consistency, and repetition are the key elements to achieving a successful result.

PROMOTIONAL STRATEGIES

The Promotional Mix

The key to connecting with customers is to consider a wide variety of promotional strategies and then to choose the right one. Some of the potential elements of that mix are:

- paid media advertising
- point-of-purchase displays
- packaging
- catalogs/catalog houses
- direct mail
- money-back guarantees
- free ink/free air
- personal selling
- trade shows
- industry literature
- working visibility
- specialty advertising/promotional products
- website and Internet advertising
- web pages
- mailing lists
- sales reps
- networking
- exceptional customer service

These allow an advertiser to pick and choose to combine various elements. You may use several at one time or to promote one product, and others at another time or to promote a different product or attract a different target market. For a closer look at each of these strategies, read on.

Potential Strategies

Paid Media Advertising

A surefire way to reach out is to advertise on radio and television, and in newspapers, magazines, and trade journals. Advertising tickles the target customer's imagination. With a good ad you can reach right into your target customer's mind and create the desire to buy from you.

If you are targeting consumers age 14 to 25, radio advertising is one of the best mediums. Contact your local radio stations for rate information. Creativity is essential in radio advertising.

Figure 6.1 provides print advertising rate information from the Standard Rates and Data Services (SRDS) available in your library. Most entrepreneurs do not recognize the enormous cost for paid advertisements. We suggest you access the SRDS books, which cover radio and television advertising as well, to get a handle on rates.

Advertising has some obvious drawbacks: (1) it can be very expensive to create an effective ad, (2) you must spend even more money to ensure that the ad gets enough exposure, (3) **preferred placements** are reserved for the big spenders, and (4) costly repetition is essential for success.

Advice: Be sure that a large percentage of the listeners, viewers, and readers are in one of your target customer groups, otherwise your message will be wasted. Your practice with profiling in previous chapters should make you much wiser in this respect than the average entrepreneur.

Stock photographs are available for print ads. Look in the Business-to-Business Yellow Pages for stock photo providers. You describe what you want—for example, two in-love Midwestern 18-year-olds on a movie date. They find the photograph and for a royalty payment you are allowed to use it. Professional photographers supply these studios with hundreds of thousands of photographs. Stock photography firms also ply their trade on the Internet or CD-ROMs. Check out one site at **www.stockmarketphoto.com** that offers free photographs and those with royalties.

Stock television and radio commercials are also available through firms that lease previously produced and successful local television commercials. For a fee, you can lease the commercials for introduction into your local market—for example, a successful furniture commercial produced and aired in Spokane could have the firm's name replaced with your own and shown in Topeka. Be sure the commercial you select is aimed at the same target customers.

Contact your local cable television stations to determine the cost of advertising there. It may be surprisingly low. Many stations provide production services, which enable you to create original commercials. If you have a product requiring a lengthy demonstration to convince your customer, purchasing a 10- to 60-minute cable time slot may be the best option.

WIZARD OF ADS

No Cash for TV Ads? Have We Got a Cream Puff of a Used Commercial for You.

Eight years ago Randy Hecht was producing award-winning ads for J. Walter Thompson when he saw gold in commercial syndication: Why not buy the rights to successful local TV campaigns and lease them to smaller firms in different markets? Add a catchy voice-over and logo, and you've got a brand-new ad in the can.

Small businesses benefit from the market research done by larger companies and are assured a quality presentation. Best of all, it's easy on the wallet. "Our clients will pay anywhere from $1,000 to $10,000 to use our ads, as opposed to paying $200,000 to make something from scratch," Hetch says. His company, AdvantEdge, has stockpiled more than 1,500 celluloid gems.

Preferred Placements The best locations within a publication, a store, or a business area; or the best time slots on TV or radio.

FIGURE 6.1

SRDS Information

SOURCE: *SRDS Consumer Magazine Advertising Source.*

Outside

MAGAZINE

ABC MPA

Location ID: 8 MLST 30 **Mid 000227-000**

Published monthly by Mariah Media, Inc., 400 Market St., Santa Fe, NM 87501. Phone 505-989-7100. Fax 505-989-4700.

For shipping info., see Print Media Production Source.

PUBLISHER'S EDITORIAL PROFILE

OUTSIDE is edited for adults who lead active year-round lifestyles. Outside's articles and features cover participatory sports, travel, adventure, people, politics, art and literature of the world outside. Rec'd 5/6/99

1. PERSONNEL

Editor-in-Chief—Lawrence J. Burke.
Pub—Scott Parmelee.
Adv Prod Mgr—Kathy Huff.
Editor—Hal Espen.
Mktg Mgr—Sara Rettig, 312-222,1100.

2. REPRESENTATIVES and/or BRANCH OFFICES

Chicago, IL 60611—Karen Fenske, 444 N. Michigan Ave., Ste 840. Phone 312-222-1100. Fax 312-222-1189.
El Segundo (Los Angeles), CA 90245—Jeff Griffith, Pacific Corporate Towers, 222 N. Sepulveda Blvd., Ste. 2000. Phone 310-335-2055. Fax 310-335-2045.
San Francisco, CA 94133—Kate Parker, Laura Hudman, 535 Pacific St., Ste. B. Phone 415-398-2627. Fax 415-362-6247.
New York, NY 10170-0078—Robert Z. Feiner, Eric Zinczenko, Liz Brown, 420 Lexington, Ste. 440. Phone 212-972-4650. Fax 212-949-7538.
Birmingham (Detroit), MI 48009—187 S. Old Woodward Ave., Ste. 206. Phone 248-433-0277. Fax 248-433-0306.
Santa Fe, NM 87501—Casey Vandenoever, Outside Plaza, 400 Market St. Phone 505-989-7100. Fax 505-989-4700.
Boston, MA 02116—Carol Burroughs, 581 Boylston St., Ste. 304. Phone 617-262-5788. Fax 617-262-1963.

3. COMMISSION AND CASH DISCOUNT

15% to recognized agencies. Net 30 days. 1% interest charge for bills over 30 days. Invoices issued on the date of printing.

4. GENERAL RATE POLICY

Rates and regulations are subject to change without notice and are guaranteed for one issue only. Publisher reserves the right to reject all advertising which he feels is not in keeping with the publication's standard.

ADVERTISING RATES

Effective July 1, 2001. (Issue/Card 34)
Confirmed December 2000.

5. BLACK/WHITE RATES

	1 ti	3 ti	6 ti	9 ti	12 ti
Spread	97,850.	93,940.	91,000.	88,070.	85,130.
1 page	48,925.	46,970.	45,500.	44,035.	42,565.
2/3 page	35,005.	33,605.	32,555.	31,505.	30,455.
1/2 page	28,605.	27,460.	26,605.	25,745.	24,885.
1/3 page	20,045.	19,245.	18,640.	18,040.	17,440.
1/4 page	15,640.	15,015.	14,545.	14,075.	13,605.
1/6 page	11,260.	10,810.	10,470.	10,135.	9,795.

6. COLOR RATES

	1 ti	3 ti	6 ti	9 ti	12 ti
2-Color:					
Spread	103,280.	99,150.	96,050.	92,950.	89,850.
1 page	51,640.	49,575.	48,025.	46,475.	44,925.
2/3 page	36,950.	35,470.	34,365.	33,255.	32,145.
1/2 page	30,195.	28,985.	28,080.	27,175.	26,270.
1/3 page	21,155.	20,310.	19,675.	19,040.	18,405.
1/4 page	16,510.	15,850.	15,355.	14,860.	14,365.
1/6 page	11,885.	11,410.	11,055.	10,695.	10,340.
	1 ti	3 ti	6 ti	9 ti	12 ti
4-Color:					
Spread	108,720.	104,370.	101,110.	97,850.	94,590.
1 page	54,360.	52,185.	50,555.	48,925.	47,295.
2/3 page	38.895.	37,340.	36,170.	35,005.	33,840.
1/2 page	31,785.	30,515.	29,560.	28,605.	27,655.
1/3 page	22,270.	21,380.	20,710.	20,045.	19,375.
1/4 page	17,380.	16,685.	16,165.	15,640.	15,120.
1/6 page	12,510.	12,010.	11,635.	11,260.	10,885.

7. COVERS

2nd cover .... 62,515. 4th cover .... 72,300.
3rd cover .... 62,515.
Covers contribute toward, but do not earn, frequency discounts.

8. INSERTS

Available.

9. BLEED

Extra 15%

10. SPECIAL POSITION

Positioning of ads is at the discretion of the publisher except where a request for a specific preferred position is acknowledged by publisher in writing.
Guaranteed positions, extra 10%

11. CLASSIFIED/MAIL ORDER/SPECIALTY RATES

THE OUTSIDE MART

By the Line:
Per line (no minimum) .... 120.
Black/White Rates:

	1 ti	3 ti	6 ti	9 ti	12 ti
1 inch	1370.	1300.	1235.	1165.	1095.
2 inch	2630.	2500.	2365.	2235.	2105.
3 inch	3520.	3340.	3170.	2990.	2815.
4-1/4 inch	4415.	4195.	3975.	3755.	3530.

Non-commissionable. Each insertion must be accompanied by advance payment, due 1 day prior to space closing. Prepayment of a 3-time schedule (or larger) earns an add'l 10% discount.

ACTIVE TRAVELER DIRECTORY

Listings for outfitters and expeditions.
Frequency discounts available.

	1 ti	3 ti	6 ti	9 ti	12 ti
5 lines	615.	585.	560.	545.	525.
6 lines	705.	670.	640.	625.	600.
7 lines	795.	755.	725.	710.	675.
8 lines	885.	840.	805.	790.	750.

TRAVEL GUIDE

5 lines	255.	9 lines	420.
6 lines	300.	10 lines	460.
7 lines	335.	11 lines	500.
8 lines	375.	12 lines	540.

Non-commissionable. Each insertion must be accompanied by advance payment, due 1 day prior to space closing. Prepayment of a 3-time schedule (or larger) earns an add'l 10% discount.

PREMIER ACTIVE TRAVELER DIRECTORY

	1 ti	2 ti	3 ti	4 ti
1/9 page	3285.	3185.	3120.	3055.

TRAVEL GUIDE

	1 ti	2 ti
1/9 page	1425.	1330.

Must be pre-paid and non-commisionable. Any advertiser who has pre-paid their ATD listing will receive a 460.00 discount.

13. SPECIAL ISSUE RATES AND DATA

FAMILY VACATION GUIDE

ISSUE & CLOSING DATES:

On Sale	Space	Matls
3/6/01	1/3	1/10

BUYER'S GUIDE

ISSUE & CLOSING DATES:

On Sale	Space	Matls
May 1/01	3/7	3/14

ANNUAL TRAVEL GUIDE

ISSUE & CLOSING DATES:

Issue	Space	Matls
Oct 2/01	8/1	8/8

By the line, per line .... 51.

	1 ti	2 ti	3 ti
1 inch	560.	530.	505.
2 inches	1075.	1020.	970.
3 inches	1500.	1425.	1350.
4-1/4 inches	1810.	1720.	1630.

15. GENERAL REQUIREMENTS

Also see SRDS Print Media Production Source.
Printing Process: Offset Full Run, Cover.
Trim Size: 8-1/4 x 10-7/8; No./Cols. 3.
Binding Method: Perfect.
Colors Available: 4-color process; Matched; GAA/SWOP; 5th cylinder.
Covers: 4-color process; 5th cylinder.

NON-BLEED
STANDARD AD PAGE DIMENSIONS

Sprd	15-1/4	x	9-1/2	1/3 v	2-1/4	x	9-1/2
1 pg	7	x	9-1/2	1/3 sq	4-5/8	x	4-5/8
2/3 v	4-5/8	x	9-1/2	1/4 v	3-3/8	x	4-5/8
1/2 isl	4-5/8	x	7-1/8	1/6 v	2-1/4	x	4-5/8
1/2 h	7	x	4-5/8	1/6 h	4-5/8	x	2-1/4

16. ISSUE AND CLOSING DATES

Published monthly.

Issue:	On sale	Closing (+)	(*)
Jan/01	12/11	10/17	10/24
Feb/01	1/16	11/15	11/22
Mar/01	2/13	12/13	12/20
Apr/01	3/13	1/17	1/24
May/01	4/17	2/21	2/28
Jun/01	5/22	3/28	4/4
Jul/01	6/19	4/25	5/2
Aug/01	7/17	5/23	5/30
Sep/01	8/14	6/20	6/27
Oct/01	9/11	7/18	7/25
Nov/01	10/16	8/22	8/29
Dec/01	11/13	9/19	9/26

(+) Space
(*) Material

Cancellations received after space closing date will not be accepted.

17. SPECIAL SERVICES

A.B.C. Supplemental Data Report released October 1990 issue.

18. CIRCULATION

Established 1976. Single copy 3.95; per year 18.00.
Summary data—for detail see Publisher's Statement.

A.B.C. 6-30-00 (6 mos. aver.—Magazine Form)

Tot. Pd	(Subs)	(Single)	(Assoc)
569,224	506,764	62,460	...

Average Non-Analyzed Non-Paid Circulation (not incl. above):
Total 16,669

TERRITORIAL DISTRIBUTION 4/00—571,831

N.Eng.	Mid.Atl.	E.N.Cen.	W.N.Cen.	S.Atl.	E.S.Cen.
33,237	67,841	76,816	50,026	88,883	18,544
W.S.Cen.	Mtn.St.	Pac.St.	Canada	Foreign	Other
39,607	61,316	111,874	19,461	3,009	1,217

Advertising rate base: 550,000.
% above/below rate base: 3.5.

If a syndicated ad sounds right for you, contact a broker such as New York-based AdvantEdge (800-558-8237) or San Francisco-based AdExchange (800-243-2339), or call your local ad agency.

Aidan McNulty

SOURCE: Aidan McNulty, "No Cash for TV Ads?" *Success,* April 1998.

Check with vendors. Ask for advertising copy, **co-op advertising** dollars, and help on layouts.

Ask for help, advice, and information from marketing departments of newspapers, and radio and television stations. Be sure to check out circulation figures and analyze the cost of various media. Newspapers often offer targeted advertising in special supplements at reduced cost. The offers often include free editorial copy.

Don't be afraid to **piggyback**. Let Madison Avenue build the market. Then use your promotional mix to tell the target customer to buy at your place.

Start small and test, test, test!

Consider classified ads in highly selective markets. Read publications on how to write an effective classified ad. This is an art and a science. Considerable research has determined the most effective wording, size, colors, etc. Hire an expert.

Check out Internet advertising opportunities; **www.wilsonweb.com** provides an excellent web marketing information center with links to sources on web branding, banner ads, design and pricing, web demographics, and more. Another useful website is **www.e-land.com**, which provides a wide range of Internet statistics. Because the web business changes so rapidly, we have provided you with numerous sources throughout the text that will enable you to access the most current business opportunities and offerings.

Point-of-Purchase Displays

A point-of-purchase (P-O-P) display encourages impulse purchases of last-minute items like paperbacks, pantyhose, candy, magazines, and flowers. A sharp **P-O-P** must perform all of the selling tasks for you, serving as a tireless silent salesperson, always on duty. A good P-O-P can be used for customer education. If your product is difficult to use or the benefits are unclear to the target customer, these silent salespeople can deliver your message. There are, however, problems with these displays: (1) you can't use them to sell large items because they crowd customers at the cash register, (2) merchants have limited floor space available and don't always want to use it for P-O-Ps, and (3) the display must sell itself and the product. A tacky P-O-P turns prospective customers off instead of on.

Advice: Do weekly evaluations of all P-O-Ps. Make certain your silent salespeople are doing their job. Consider hiring professional designers if this is your only distribution venue.

Packaging

For P-O-P displays, packaging may be the only method of marketing, but don't forget how important the packaging of any product is to your customers. Review your competitors' packaging by purchasing their products and checking out the cost and effectiveness of their product packaging. What can you do better? What can you do more efficiently? What could you do more cost effectively? How could the packaging be made more attractive? Professionals in the packaging and distribution fields will be able to work with you on the proper sizing of packages and provide you with their years of expertise. One entrepreneur tried to sell her homemade sauces in 48-oz. jars until one of her retail accounts suggested she sell them in 24-oz. jars and spiff up her packaging by including her start-up story on the label to distinguish herself in the

Co-op Advertising A manufacturer's cosponsorship or contribution to a retailer's cost of advertising.

Piggyback A technique that allows one to coordinate a local ad campaign with the hoopla generated by national advertising.

P-O-P "Point-of-Purchase"—a display that acts as a silent salesperson for a specific product.

marketplace. Sales of her gourmet sauces tripled as more accounts were willing to stock the smaller jars because they fit on the shelves much better.

Advice: Consider the following packaging points from a recent *Guerilla Marketing Communique:**

1. environmental issues
2. balancing function with appearance
3. appropriateness for target market and position
4. safety in opening
5. legal requirements for export markets
6. ability to attach promotional material
7. physical protection of product
8. filling process required
9. company's production capabilities to handle the pack
10. hygiene
11. graphics and labeling
12. convenience in opening and resealing
13. effectiveness in delivering the product to the consumer
14. acceptance by the distribution network
15. package cost in relation to selling price

Catalogs

Catalogs are just right for isolated shoppers and shoppers in a hurry. Because we are so "time poor," even general items are now being purchased via catalogs. Customers can shop at their convenience and not have to worry about store hours, parking, or traffic. If you attempt to print your own catalogs, however, several problems can occur: (1) the costs associated with design, artwork, photography, and mailing can be *very* expensive—especially if you attempt a four-color catalog; (2) your product may not show well in print; (3) the reader may not easily grasp the products' benefits; and (4) it takes time and extensive resources to develop a successful mail-order catalog business. Catalogs can be considered another kind of silent salesperson, but one recent books-on-tape catalog retailer shared that each customer costs him $300 in marketing costs.

Catalog Houses

Catalog houses such as Lillian Vernon don't usually manufacture what they sell, so they are always looking for good products. To locate potential catalog retailers, search the *Directory of Mail Order Firms* published by the Chain Store Guide. Each listing covers the product lines, mailings per year, sales, and contact information. Write or call each of the catalog houses you feel are aimed at your target market and ask for details about their product submission process. Follow the process exactly. Products in catalogs are marked up (retailed) three to seven times what the catalog houses pay (wholesale) for them. Determine first if you can make a profit in dealing with these houses based on the products and prices in their current catalogs. Look into QVC-type programs as well. Television shopping networks search for items that they can sell in the tens of thousands. Their research is extensive and they *know* what will move.

Advice: There are now many online catalogs, which may also meet your needs. Let major catalog houses do your promotion, but make sure you can deliver if your product takes off. Ask for feedback from each catalog house to which you submit your **product description**. If your product does not fit their needs, they may help you locate a better fit. Their feedback will be invaluable. Listen; it comes backed with years of experience.

Product Description A list of features and benefits.

*Source: *Guerilla Marketing Communique,* **www.gmarketing.com** (accessed December 28, 2000).

Direct Mail

This promotional tool lets you aim your brochures and flyers where they will do the most good. **Direct mail** is very important for small business because it can go to the heart of your target market. Direct mail is also used extensively by business-to-business customers. Direct mail advertising is a science. If you are going to undertake writing the content for direct mail pieces, read the Direct Marketing Association's material before undertaking the effort. Per prospect reached, direct mail is very expensive. Check out the website **www.dmworld.com** for an excellent library of information on direct mail advertising. If, after reading the material, you want to hire a professional direct mail expert, consider asking them to write your piece for a percentage of sales. A terrific experienced writer may achieve excellent results if he or she believes strongly in your product, and the two of you may hit a gold mine.

The success of direct mail depends on your ability to define the target market and develop an appropriate direct mail campaign. If the market is too fragmented for you to do this, direct mail is not for you.

Advice: Stay up nights if you have to, but define, refine, and refine again your target customer. If you aim wrong you have wasted all of your money! Develop customer lists. Check out mail list vendors in your Business-to-Business Yellow Pages. A vendor such as Polk will rent you the right to mail to the names on a list of your choice one time and one time only. Mail list vendors work with you to select the proper mailing list or compilation of lists to meet your needs. Contact The Direct Marketing Association for further information at **www.the-dma.org**.

Money-Back Guarantees

If you haven't considered offering a guarantee as a form of promotion, consider it now! You can reach security-minded customers by emphasizing the no-risk features of your product. The problem is that you must back up your guarantee with time and money. Sally Jones purchased a kitchen remodeling business and found out that the former owners had treated several previous customers horrendously. She decided to make good on their contracts and won not only their loyalty but the respect of everyone they told. It was an expensive and risky initial move but was money well spent.

Advice: Figure 5 percent into your pricing to cover returned goods. If the product is fragile or easily misused—and people have been known to misuse just about everything—build in a higher figure. Be sure all employees understand and honor guarantees. One employee not abiding by your policy may have long-term adverse consequences. Remember bad word of mouth always travels like wildfire!

Free Ink and Free Air

Reviews, features, interview shows, **press releases**, and newspaper columns cost nothing and are tremendously effective. **Free ink** and **free air** are both excellent promotional methods as they establish your company in a believable way. Target Customers are likely to attach more credence to words that are not in the form of paid advertising. You need to locate and convince a media person to believe your business is newsworthy.

Advice: Determine which media reaches your target customer and contact the writers and reporters who cover your type of business. Often publications are seeking out new businesses and clever ideas. Every business is newsworthy in some way. Dig until you find something—news, charity, controversy, photo opportunities, or humor. Call, write, or fax with your information. Make your press kit information visual—send accompanying photographs of your principals, your facility, and your product or service in use.

Direct Mail Advertisement or sales pitch that is posted directly to target customers.

Press Release A news item written and sent to the media in an attempt to get cost-free advertising (free ink).

Free Ink/Free Air Information about a business that is published or broadcast free of charge.

INCREDIBLE RESOURCE

JOHN F. BAUGH CENTER FOR ENTREPRENEURSHIP AT BAYLOR UNIVERSITY INNOVATION EVALUATION CENTER

Over 1,500 products have been scrutinized for potential market success by a team of evaluators with extensive business backgrounds and experience at Baylor University. If you have a product, which does not include medicine, toys, games, or foods, evaluators will review your product and within 4 to 6 weeks forward a thorough evaluation of the market potential for your product.

For a nominal fee of $150, which covers administrative costs, an unbiased team analyzes the commercial potential of an inventor's new product or idea through the knowledge of in-house experts in marketing, manufacturing, finance, and other fields. The invention or idea is evaluated according to more than 30 different criteria.

- legality
- safety
- environmental impact
- societal impact
- functional feasibility
- production feasibility
- stage of development
- investment costs
- payback period
- profitability
- marketing research
- research and development
- potential market
- potential sales
- trend of demand
- stability of demand
- product life cycle
- legal protection
- competitiveness in market place
- customer learning requirements
- customer needs satisfied
- dependence on complementary products
- visibility of advantages
- promotional requirements
- distribution requirements
- service needs
- appearance
- function
- durability
- price
- competition (existing)
- competition (new)

The data is analyzed by a specially designed computer program and processed to give three different scores. These scores are compared to the scores received by earlier innovations that were successfully introduced into the marketplace.

The program gives the inventor objective data on the product's strengths and weaknesses, which may be used to determine the likelihood of commercial success before committing capital to fully develop and market the product. A good score could help secure a development loan by increasing credibility with banks and by encouraging an inventor to pursue the invention with a business plan and patent.

A low score could warn an inventor to reconsider any further investment.

SOURCE: **hsb.baylor.edu/entrepreneur/default.asp?lev3=100** (accessed March 28, 2001).

Personal Selling

It doesn't matter if you've never sold before; no one is a better salesperson than you. You are the business! It is your baby and hopefully you will sell with more passion than anybody else! If you listen carefully, your target customers will tell you how to sell your product or service to them. That's why a good salesperson is a creative listener, not a fast talker. Most customers love to talk with the owner of the business. Use that to your advantage.

Unfortunately, **personal selling** is expensive, especially if you have to pay others to do it, and it will boost your overhead unless you pay your salespeople on a commission-only basis. And if you try to do it all yourself, you may not have the time and energy for other things that only you can do. In the beginning some entrepreneurs do not have many options. One inventor worked all night in his shop, took a nap, and then changed clothes for 8 hours of selling on the road, only to return to his shop again at five to begin his design work. His firm is now valued at $40 million and customers still love to see him in the field. Building and maintaining relationships is essential for any small business.

Personal Selling Client service calls made by an individual sales person or business owner.

Advice: Make everyone in your business a salesperson: delivery people, warehouse people, computer programmers, bookkeepers, and clerical workers. Never underestimate the importance of the person who is hired to answer the telephone. Reinforce a positive attitude in all employees by reminding them that if nothing sells, they're out of a job; your target customers need a lot of tender loving care.

Consider locating and hiring professional **sales reps** who will work on a percentage-of-sales basis. Keep cheerleading. Reps need encouragement too. Be sure to never get so big that you can't personally go on some sales calls. If you lose touch with your customers, they may lose touch with you.

Trade Shows

These shows display your product or service in a highly intensive way. Trade shows develop a carnival and county-fair atmosphere. Your trade show appearance asserts your position in your selected industry. However, if the trade show is not local, you'll have transportation costs. Booths are also expensive. Furthermore, unless you're careful and study the layout, you could rent a space that is thin on **traffic**, and if you haven't participated previously, you may not be offered a choice location.

Advice: Share booth space with another small-business owner or with a complementary business. Combine functions by doing market research while you're promoting. Study the trade show's floor plan and try to position yourself in a high-traffic area.

Industry Literature

Become a source of information in your industry by producing brochures, newsletters, handbooks, product documentation, annual reports, newspaper columns for the layperson, or even the "bible" for your industry. Become a recognized expert in your field. We believe this is one of the best promotional devices around. If you're not handy with words, it can be an obstacle, but it's not an insurmountable one. Remember, expertise is admired and sought out by others.

Advice: If you put your thoughts down on paper, you're two steps ahead of the talkers. If your writing skills aren't strong, hire a professional writer.

Working Visibility

Develop and maintain a presence. Make yourself stand out from your competitors. One pool-cleaning business owner required all his pool cleaners to wear spotless white laboratory coats on their routes. In addition, the business paid for their cleaners' trucks to be washed each week. Because of the employees' professional appearance, sales skyrocketed.

Many service firms display their presence as they work—they put signs on everything: their business, their trucks, and their work sites. Wherever they're busy, they let people know it. They make themselves visible. The drawback here is similar to one of the drawbacks with P-O-P displays. If the presence you maintain doesn't sell itself—if it is unattractive, or if it calls attention to an unsavory part of your business—you will lose rather than gain potential customers.

Advice: Exploit your public activities with signs that tell people who you are. Review your displays frequently. Be sure the message is working. Walk around with a sandwich board—until someone stops you.

Sales Reps Independent salespeople who sell a number of noncompeting but complementary products and services in a specific geographic area on a commission-only basis.

Traffic The numbers of potential buyers who pass by, view, or stop at one's booth in a trade show; vehicles or pedestrians that move past a business site in the course of a normal day.

SPECIALTY ADVERTISING/PROMOTIONAL PRODUCTS

Specialty advertising, now known as promotional products, is a targeted, cost-efficient means of promoting a company's products or services. For the small business, this can be a very effective use of marketing dollars.

Promotional products break through communications clutter and leave a lasting impression. In addition to client marketing, many companies use promotional products for internal marketing to their employees, via recognition and employee motivation programs.

Promotional products keep a company's name or message in the front of a customer's mind. They can be used as a thank you, a trade show traffic builder, a goodwill builder, a customer or employee loyalty reward, or a new product/service introduction tool.

The cost of promotional products ranges from pennies to several hundred dollars. When selecting an item, key considerations are: budget, quantity needed, time frame, the audience receiving it, and, of course, the goal. What are you trying to achieve?

When used to build trade-show traffic, an item that involves the recipient can be effective at keeping a prospect at the booth, which allows time to qualify the prospect and generate interest in your products. An example is a stress-testing card, which requires the user to place his or her thumb on a stress indicator patch for 10 seconds. After completing the test, the person often shows the result and asks the trade-show staffer to take it, allowing even more time to build a relationship.

Pre-show mailings also can be used to build traffic. An eyeglass case can be mailed with an invitation to stop by and pick up a free pair of sunglasses. Or a long-distance telephone card can be mailed, but activated only if the recipient brings it to the booth and perhaps fills out a short marketing questionnaire. Drawings for prizes and gifts can be used to develop a mailing list or ask market research questions.

Sound chip cards have proved an effective way to open doors or introduce new products and services. From a ringing phone to applause, these cards and their messages have impact and generate interest, helpful in reaching hard-to-reach prospects.

Continuity advertising programs can be developed where several gifts are sent over time, often with a theme. A baseball theme campaign could include a stadium cushion, baseball, cap, pennant, ticket-shaped key chain, bat-shaped pen, cap-shaped paperclip dispenser, sound chip card that plays "Take Me Out to the Ball Game," and a package of peanuts.

SOURCE: Lesley Ronson Brown, Lee Wayne Company, *Powerful Promotional Merchandise*, 630-752-0922.

ACTION STEP 31

BRAINSTORM A WINNING PROMOTIONAL CAMPAIGN

Disregard all budgetary restraints. Pretend that money is no object. Close your eyes, sit back, and develop the ideal campaign for connecting with your target customers. It's okay to "get crazy" with this because excellent, workable solutions often develop out of bizarre mental activity!

- If your product or service needs a multimillion-dollar advertising promotion with endorsements by your favorite movie star, fantasize that it's happening now.
- If you need a customer list created in marketing heaven, specify exactly what you need and it is yours.
- If you are looking for the services of a first-class catalog house, just whisper the name three times and you are in business.
- If your business at its peak could use a thousand delivery trucks with smiling drivers who make your target customers feel terrific, write down "1000 smiling delivery people."
- If your product is small, brainstorm the perfect point-of-purchase device, perhaps one with slot machines whose money tubes are connected to your private bank vault. Watch the money roll in.

This chance to ignore costs won't come around again. (Reality is right around the corner.) But for now, have fun.

Earlier we said that if you fail to plan, you're planning to fail. When it comes to promotion, if you fail to plan you're planning to keep your business a secret.

One way to avoid keeping your business a secret is to brainstorm an ideal **promotional campaign** with no holds barred and no worries about costs. Action Step 31 makes sure you consider all of your creative ideas before discarding them as unrealistic. Save the ideas you come up with in Action Step 31 because you will use them later. We hope you will apply ingenious and cost-effective solutions to your promotional needs. Do not be afraid to put your passion for your business into your promotional ideas and campaigns. Creativity and passion can go a long way to promote your business.

As you'll see throughout Chapter 6, the entrepreneurs who succeed are the ones who have the best fix on their target customers. They are also the ones who understand the importance of market research and tracking their advertising expenses.

WINNING PROMOTIONAL STRATEGIES

Choosing the right promotional strategy for your business may prove to be a big win. The examples that follow show how several entrepreneurs discovered their winning strategies. While reading what these entrepreneurs have to say, you may discover your own winning strategy. Look for inspiration.

Earth to Air Travel, Inc.

Newsletter

Two years ago we missed the ironclad deadline for getting our ad in the Yellow Pages, so we tried to make up for that by placing fun-type ads in community newsletters

Promotional Campaign A sales program designed to sell a specific product or service or to establish an image, benefit, and point.

within a 10-mile radius of our agency. The ads didn't cost much, and we hoped they would help to keep our visibility high. Our best response came from a large residential retirement community less than a mile away. It's a gold mine of upper income retirees who dearly love to travel frequently. We offered monthly travel seminars at the retirement community, where we introduced new trips and our clients could share their travel experiences. For the cost of wonderful pastries and gourmet coffee, we usually close on 10 to 20 trips with our clientele throughout the next few weeks at an average of $2,500 each. An excellent return on our investment!

By studying community and travel newsletters, we came up with our own format, and now send out our own monthly agency newsletter. On the front page of our newsletters, we picture our employees. The pictures help us connect, especially with first-time customers. They see our smiling faces, and most feel they know us when they walk through our door. We're already on the way to being friends.

In addition, we encourage our travelers to write stories for the newsletters. Usually they are humorous and a great addition to the newsletter. We also offer a "travel partner wanted" column.

The Software School
Direct Mail

When we started the Software School, we quickly discovered the major local newspaper covered the northern half of the county, while the entrepreneurial market we'd targeted lived in the southern half. The one way to reach the center of our target market was with a direct mail piece. Our strategy was to rent a list from a magazine whose readers matched our profile—in this case, Inc.*—and then to send out our brochure.*

The response was terrific. We generated enough business for a healthy start-up, and after that, satisfied customers sold for us by talking up our 1-day teaching system.

Direct mail allowed us to go right to the heart of our target market. When you're just starting out in a new venture, that kind of accuracy is worth every penny it costs.

Garment District Guides
Free Ink

When my partner and I got the idea for guiding shoppers through the Los Angeles garment district, we thought it would be so exciting we wouldn't have to do much except stop once a week to make bank deposits.

Were we ever wrong!

We ran a good-sized ad in our local paper. We filled a couple of buses, but then our market ran out because those customers didn't need a return trip to LA for shopping on the bus. We had some flyers printed up and covered every car in every parking lot in our community. Two thousand flyers and sore feet netted us half a bus.

Then a feature story appeared in the "View" section of the Los Angeles Times about a tour to Hollywood and Beverly Hills. On an impulse we called the reporter and told her about Garment District Guides.

It worked.

On the next trip, the reporter came along, and brought a staff photographer. Two weeks later, our story was on the front page of the "View" section—a beautiful third of a page—and customers began calling us! Our local papers followed a month or so later with features about the service, and after we got bigger, a television reporter profiled us for one of the evening newsmagazines.

Now business is great. We haven't had to pay to advertise for 18 months. When times are slow, we increase our ***networking*** *activities and try to book group trips. We also started targeting groups with special trips, such as the Back to School Bus, Santa's Sleigh, Spring Fling, and Mother-Daughter Mother's Day Specials. With each trip being unique we get more free press. When people ask me what kind of promotion I believe in, I tell them free ink!*

Networking Communicating via person-to-person channels in an attempt to exchange information.

Passion

Got eMoo? Carbonated Milk for Kids?

Yes! MaryAnn Clark and her husband of Clark Farms believe there is a market for their newly-developed product eMoo, carbonated milk! After years of watching kids down more sodas and less milk, they knew there had to be a way to make kids drink more milk. Well, the answer was simple—make milk more like a soft drink! Give kids what they want!

Luckily, they headed to Cornell University's Food Science program for assistance, where they hooked up with Eric Hallstead, a food scientist, who helped them develop recipes and bottling procedures for eMoo. With recipes in hand they are now seeking bottlers and distributors. Their passion for their product shines through when they announce, "We want to become the Ben & Jerry's of milk." With product flavors such as creamsicle, cookies and cream, raspberry chocolate, and bubble gum, they just might!

Trystan's Toys

Customer Mailing Lists

The toy business is seasonal, and with all the people coming through the door, I wanted to make sure I developed a solid customer base. So, for three weeks, I hired the most wonderful authentic Rent-a-Santa I could find and a professional photographer. Every child who came into my store was photographed and the parents filled out information cards with their child's name, age, toy preferences, and date of birth. As an added bonus, I made the negatives available to parents, many of whom ordered Christmas cards picturing their child talking to Santa.

At the end of 3 weeks I had developed a fine customer list and one valuable piece of information—the birthday of more than 500 children. Every time a birthday rolled around, I mailed a small inexpensive toy and a discount coupon.

As my mailing list grew, I came up with another idea.

I was at the cash register one day when I noticed five customers in a row who spent more than $100. I kept those checks and credit card slips separate, and at the end of the day I copied them and started a Big Spender list. Today, my Big Spender list has grown to several hundred customers, and I've developed a special mailer aimed just at them. These customers keep me going throughout the year and help to smooth out the seasonality of the toy business.

And to think it all began with a Rent-a-Santa!

We hope you found inspiration by reading about these entrepreneurs who, through planning, perseverance, or luck found successful promotional strategies. You may not need a Rent-a-Santa, but you do need a well-organized promotional campaign. Be sure to gather **customer files**. With good files information becomes useful. Organized information is power.

Sales Reps as Connectors

Suppose you have a new product that has immediate sales potential across the country. How can you connect with the whole United States? Should you hire your younger brother to take care of it for you, or should you seek out a professional sales rep that acts like a commissioned salesperson?

An army of trained professional sales reps awaits your call. However, a rep is not a rep is not a rep; select your reps carefully. Exercise caution because the reputation of your sales reps will become your reputation.

Customer Files Lists of persons or firms that have already made purchases.

The best way to find good reps is to interview potential buyers of your goods. Ask them to recommend reps who they consider the very best in their field and who they enjoy working with. When the same names surface several times, you will know who to start calling. In addition, contact the rep associations listed in this chapter.

Trade associations, shows, and journals also provide information on rep associations. Reps attend trade shows to discover new products to carry; so if you have a booth, actively try to reach reps at your show. Also, aggressive reps may contact you if you have a "hot product."

To determine the prevailing practices for commissions, territories, and termination agreements for your selected industry contact the associations listed in following. Hire reps based on their knowledge of the industry, established customer base, and ability to sell to your customers effectively and efficiently. You are in essence paying the reps for immediate access to the market. Ask yourself how long it would take and how much it would cost you to set up a sales force to have similar characteristics to the independent sales rep organizations. Also, you may decide to use your own sales force for certain markets and independent sales reps for other market niches.

Reps must sell because they work solely on commission; you are assured of a fairly aggressive, experienced sales team to promote your product or service. Reps allow you risk-free exploration of new markets as well.

Ask the reps:

- How many salespeople are in your firm?
- What is your background and experience?
- What geographic territories do you cover?
- What complementary lines do you represent?
- What ideas do you have for trade show presentations?
- Would you work with us on a regional rollout, while we prepare for national coverage?
- May I participate in sales meetings and help train the reps on my product line?
- What sales call reports can I expect?
- What performance guarantees do you offer?
- What results have you achieved for similar companies?

Provide all the encouragement and support to your reps that you can; never stop being a cheerleader. Insist on sales call reports that will keep you informed on what is going on in the field; pack your bags and make some calls with the reps. Write monthly sales letters and encourage feedback from both your reps and their customers. Feedback helps you to evaluate your product line and your reps. Provide your reps with materials such as brochures, testimonials, and samples. In addition, conduct any training necessary for your product. Also, be willing to share information you gather on recent sales and competition.

SALES REP RESOURCES

Manufacturer Representative Associations

Manufacturers Agents National Association
www.MANAonline.org
Box 3467
Laguna Hills, CA 92654-3467
(949) 859-4040

North American Industrial Representative Association
www.nira.org
175 N. Harbor Drive, Suite 1205
Chicago, IL 60601
(312) 240-0820

Electronics Representatives Association
www.era.org
444 N. Michigan Ave. Suite 1960
Chicago, IL 60611
(312) 527-3050

To locate sales representatives in foreign countries, call the embassy or consulate for each country and speak to a trade expert. The Department of Commerce and resources cited throughout the chapter also provide trade information.

COMMUNITY RESOURCE

SCORE Free Assistance: Advice from the Start

A nonprofit association, SCORE was formed 34 years ago to provide education for entrepreneurs and to encourage small companies. Headquartered in Washington, D.C., it is sponsored by the U.S. Small Business Administration.

Through SCORE, more than 12,000 retired and active business owners and executives serve as volunteer counselors, offering advice on topics such as writing a business plan, managing cash flow, and obtaining capital. There are 389 SCORE chapters and 450 additional branch locations around the country.

About 300,000 entrepreneurs received counseling or attended SCORE workshops last year.

Without her SCORE counselors, "I wouldn't be here," says business owner Lindsay H. Frucci of Elkins, N.H. "There's absolutely no way I could have accomplished what I have accomplished without them."

Frucci started No Pudge! Food, Inc., which makes fat-free brownie mixes, in 1995. Even before launching the company, she turned to the nearby SCORE chapter in Lebanon, N.H., for guidance.

She was assigned to two counselors, Robert Y. Fox of Hanover, N.H., who was a vice president and associate general counsel of General Foods, and Jason K. "Jay" Albert of Tetford Center, Vt., a former small-business owner and president of a specialty food company. They have worked with Frucci as a team, meeting with her in 2-hour sessions about 50 times over nearly 3½ years.

"They taught me everything from the ground up," says Frucci, 46, whose company, a home-based enterprise, brought in more than $250,000 last year, its second full year of business.

"The big thing we helped her accomplish was to get this business started without spending a great deal of money," says Fox. Instead of doing the manufacturing herself, for example, Frucci took her counselors' advice and found another company to make the mixes.

In addition, Fox and Albert guided her through getting a line of credit at the bank, doing a trademark search, registering her company name, setting up her corporate structure, finding distribution channels for her products, and helping her with all the other tasks associated with starting a business. "They both brought just volumes of knowledge, just amazing knowledge," says Frucci.

Here are some tips from business owners and SCORE staff members and counselors for getting the most out of SCORE:

Don't wait. Seek SCORE's help before you take steps that might become expensive mistakes. "We have too many people coming to us who have already signed leases and bought things," says Fox. "They shouldn't do that until they've got their business plans ready and their cash-flow projections lined up."

Now and then people are already in trouble when they go to SCORE. "We work hard to try to get them out of it, but sometimes that's not possible," says Fox, who has counseled about 70 business owners since joining SCORE 6 years ago.

Be choosy. If the first SCORE counselor assigned to you does not seem right for you or if you are uncomfortable with the person, ask to be assigned to someone else. "People need to go in and almost interview the counselor," says Frucci. "If they're hooked up with someone they're not comfortable with, they need to be free to say, 'Is there someone else within this SCORE office that you think might be suited to what it is I'm trying to do or that might have experience in the business I'm in?'"

Check out other SCORE programs. SCORE chapters offer modestly priced seminars and workshops on topics such as starting a business, developing a business plan, and protecting your invention. Such programs can help you frame questions for discussion with your counselor and make the counseling sessions more useful.

Take full advantage of the full counseling. You'll get more out of it, says Yancey, if you let SCORE become a mentor. He advises visiting your SCORE counselor regularly so the counselor can get to know your business well. One restaurant-owning couple has had nearly 90 sessions with their counselor, according to SCORE.

"If you're a counselee at SCORE, suck us dry," says Albert.

Look for teamwork. Many SCORE chapters emphasize team counseling so clients can receive the benefit of different types of expertise offered by different counselors.

If you think you need specific knowledge that your counselor lacks, you can request that someone with that knowledge be brought in to help.

At SCORE's website, **www.score.org**, there's a new feature: the opportunity to get counseling via electronic mail from about 240 participating volunteers. In addition, the site answers questions about SCORE, provides profiles of successful SCORE clients, and finds the SCORE locations nearest you. (You can also determine the nearest SCORE chapter by calling the national SCORE office at 1-800-634-0245.)

Even though Lougheed has an MBA degree and has been a brand manager for major corporations, she says, "If you're starting a new business and you don't check out SCORE, it's just silly."

She emphasizes, however, that "this is someplace where people aren't just going to tell you what you want to hear." And that's good, she says, because if your business idea is not viable, it's better to find out up front.

For SCORE's Yancey, the bottom line is this: "We want to help people make better-quality business decisions."

SOURCE: Adapted from "Coaching the Women's Team," *Nation's Business,* May 1998, pp. 70–72.

NETWORKING

Another source of promotional power is networking, which carries the image of your business to a support group. An expert on networking, Susan Linn, defines the term broadly: "Networking is using your contacts to get what you want. Commonly, networking is used to refer to group situations in which business people can interact. It's a current buzzword for the age-old principle 'It's not what you know but who you know.'"

Networking gives you confidence and allows you to pass on helpful information to people who aren't directly competing with you—and to receive helpful information.

Networking for Success and Survival

When Dorothy and Dan Gray decided to go into business, they looked around for more than a year. Dorothy had some training in graphics and Dan was good with numbers. They finally decided on a franchised mailbox operation. They paid a flat fee and agreed to pay the franchiser a percentage of their gross. The franchiser provided assistance and a well-developed business plan.

What they didn't tell Dorothy and Dan about was networking.

When you are in the mailbox business, giving good service is how to forge ahead. They knew they had to promote their image and tried everything—brochures, leaflets, flyers, and half-page display ads in the local newspapers. But the business didn't start rolling in until Dorothy joined her first network.

It was a Lead's Club, and the membership varied: a real estate broker, an insurance agent, the president of a small bank, the owner of a coffee service, a printer, a sign manufacturer, the owner of a chain of service stations, a sporting goods storeowner, a travel agent, two small manufacturers, and a contractor. At the breakfast meetings held once a week, members were required to bring at least one sales lead for another club member. If they were remiss, a $5 contribution was made to the kitty. Dorothy and Dan generated more business from the club than from all other promotional efforts combined. So she joined another network club and used the contacts she made to build her own network.

Business has been good ever since. Dorothy and Dan opened a second mailbox shop last April, put in two new computers, a laser printer, and added web design services. They continue to network their way to even more business and are planning to open a third shop 10 miles south of their present location by this time next year.

Why You Should Network

You've probably been networking all your life. In school you networked for information about teachers and courses. When you moved into a new community, you networked for information about doctors, dentists, car service, babysitters, and bargains—all the life-supporting details that make up existence. On the job, you networked your way to sales leads, brainstormed your way to better design, or got in a huddle with some fellow manager or co-workers to solve problems.

As a small-business entrepreneur, you can network your way to a surprising number of new customer connections, which can spell success in big letters. Develop your network and build **core groups** of people within it. Some networks grow naturally from the loose association of people you already know, and because you are at the center of the net, it has to help you.

Networking Organizations

The bottom line for networking is that people do business with people they know and are most comfortable with. So get out there and meet people who can help develop your business. When others spread the word about you, it is like having your own private unpaid sales force working for you! This doesn't just happen. Joining a networking organization is not enough. You must decide to become an active member of the organization. Take positions of leadership. Get to know everyone you can. Do things for others. Make networking a way of life. Be sure you have your elevator speech from Action Step 23 down pat because you will have many chances to present it. Before you join an organization, ask yourself:

What is the purpose of this organization?

What type of people do I enjoy being with?

Do I want to make a political or social statement with this involvement?

Am I participating solely for business purposes?

Most organizations will allow you to attend at least one meeting free, with no obligation to join. We suggest you attend various organizational meetings to determine which best fit your personal and business needs.

What kind of networking groups are out there?

Core Groups Clusters of influential, key individuals who share a common area of interest.

ACTION STEP 32

EXCEPTIONAL SERVICE THROUGH TOUCHPOINTS

Pull out Action Step 28 on your customer touchpoints. With list in hand, brainstorm away and develop a way to make each touchpoint a memorable point for your target customer. In building exceptional customer service you can't just meet your customers' service needs; you have to exceed them!

- If you are sending a package, what could you include to brighten their day?
- If you are serving them a fast-food meal, what could you do to make it quicker?
- If you are sending architectural drawings for review, how could you help them to better understand the drawings?
- If you own a candy store, what extra could you give each time a customer came in the door?

Some things you come up with will not be possible as a result of time or money constraints, but those you can incorporate will be greatly appreciated by your customers and you'll be on your way to being an exceptional business.

Keep refining your touchpoints.

ACTION STEP 33

WHAT IS YOUR CUSTOMER WORTH AND HOW CAN YOU AND YOUR EMPLOYEES REMEMBER THEIR VALUE?

Review the bookstore customer example on page 127.

Now it's time for you to determine the value of your customer.

Determine approximately how much your customer will spend in one year at your business. Multiply that number for 5 or 10 years. Now that you have that dollar figure, design a creative and memorable way for you and your employees to remember that figure. Your firm is in business to make a profit. You need to convince your employees that the only reason they receive a paycheck is because customers return.

Trade organizations focus on a particular industry and provide an opportunity to share primarily with your peers. An excellent place to make contacts to find suppliers, attorneys, accountants, and so on. Involvement at the local level can lead to positions at the national level, which will widen your exposure further.

Sales leads clubs such as the one Dorothy and Dan belonged to generally meet on a weekly basis for breakfast, lunch, or dinner to share leads. One national group is Leads Club, P.O. Box 279, Carlsbad, CA 92018, 800 783-3761. Another is LeTip International, P.O. Box 178130, San Diego, CA 92117-9926, 800 25-LETIP, **www.letip.com**.

Political clubs such as Democratic and Republican clubs provide excellent opportunities to expose your business widely.

Women's organizations such as American Association of University Women (AAUW), Women in Communications (WICI), and National Association of Women Business Owners (NAWBO) focus on social, trades, or business efforts.

Chambers of Commerce are excellent sources of local business contacts. One does not have to live or work in a city to join and participate in its Chamber of Commerce.

Local social and community groups offer the power of community participation to reach a local customer. Many mortgage brokers and real estate agents have found their local PTA participation has paid off handsomely by increasing their client pool.

Visit many, join several, and heavily participate in a few that will have the best payoff for you.

During the recession of the early 1990s, one marketing consultant, Nancy Hopp, continued to network in eight organizations. At one point she was donating 20 to 30 hours of her time to keep busy. As the recession wound down and the good times started to roll, her business skyrocketed. Her community contacts were back in business and so was she! Nancy has never advertised and has relied totally on word of mouth and community contacts for customers. Networking doesn't cost anything but time and can yield incredible results for those willing to develop relationships.

EXCEPTIONAL CUSTOMER SERVICE AS PROMOTION

Another low-cost promotional tool is customer service. Exceptional customer service provides your firm with three vital ingredients for growth: relationships, reputation, and references. Early in the development of a small business, building relationships is essential. From strong relationships will come a good name and qualified referrals.

Take the time and effort early on to get to know everything you can about your target customers. The closer you are to customers the more likely you will be able to meet their needs. If you are passionate about your customers, you may be lucky enough to breed passionate customers who care about your success. Customers who want to continue doing business with you will tell you how to improve and provide constant feedback. Listen to these passionate customers and encourage their participation in your business. Out in the community or in your selected industry, they will be your unpaid, and quite possibly strongest, salespeople. This is a sales force no money could buy!

Gaining a new customer costs fives times the cost of retaining a customer. Do *all* you can to retain your customers and practice continuous customer service improvement.

Remember, people are buying solutions to a problem and want an exceptional and memorable experience. Always be mindful of making the experience one they will want to share with friends and colleagues. You have studied your competitors and target markets extensively and should know what benefits and customer service levels are not only desired but also expected. Exceptional customer service increases the bottom line. Complete Action Step 32 by returning to Action Step 28 on touchpoints and determining how you can make each touchpoint a memorable and exceptional experience. You want your customers to shout your company name from the rooftops. Study premiere companies in customer service—Neiman Marcus, Nordstrom, and Dell Computers. If possible, implement the best of their service strategies into your business.

To be effective everyone in the organization must practice exceptional customer service and this service must be rewarded. It has to be a way of doing business at all times. Employees must know their responsibilities:

- Proactively serve the customer. ("How can I help you?")
- Display the power to act. ("How can I solve the problem?")
- Provide information. Educate and communicate with customers. ("No, we no longer sell Item B, but let me show you Item C, which we now carry, and how it compares favorably.")

When developing your customer service credo for your firm consider what is most important to your customers and honor that variable first. Remember you cannot be everything to everyone and be careful not to give away the store by offering more than you can provide profitably.

What Is Your Customer Worth?

Take a moment to determine how much your customer is worth. If you own a bookstore and your average customer purchases $25 of books a week, your customer is worth $1,300 (25 × 52) annually. If you plan on keeping that customer over the next 10 years, he or she now becomes a $13,000 customer.

Would you and your employees treat customers differently if you envisioned them with the figure $13,000 emblazoned on their forehead? The answer for most of us is a resounding yes! Taking it out further, what if that $13,000 customer brought in, on average, three new customers to your store each year. Is that customer now a $52,000 customer?

The trick here is for everyone in your firm to truly realize the dollar value of each potential customer they serve. How can you get everyone to remember the $13,000/$52,000 figure? Put it on the cash register? Sales slips? Order forms? Paychecks? An employee contest for a new Mercedes convertible based on the $52,000 figure?

Action Step 33 asks you to determine the dollar value of your customers and creative ways to make that figure memorable to all your employees.

You have reviewed the importance of networking, customer service, and an integrated promotional campaign. It's time to develop your ideas into a promotional strategy. Remember you can hire an ad agency to create great advertisements that bring in customers, but only excellent customer service and products will bring them back and make your business profitable over time.

Attach Price Tags to Your Promotional Strategies

You are ready now to make decisions about your promotional mix. Look at the ideal promotional strategies you came up with in Action Step 31, pick the top four or five elements you can realistically do at this point, then determine the price of each. Action Step 34 walks you through this process. Continue to focus your promotions on the target customer from your collage.

Action Step 34

Attach a Price Tag to Each Item of Your Promotional Package

What will your customer connection cost? To get some idea, go back to Action Step 31, list the top four or five connections you want with your customers, then research the cost of each.

Let's imagine that you have chosen the following promotional mix:

Magazine Ads. This choice assumes you know which magazines your target customers read. Good. Contact the display ad department of the magazines and request their media kit.

Direct Mail. Look up mail list brokers under Direct Mail in the Business-to-Business Yellow Pages. Discuss the business you are in and which markets you want to reach. Ask them for recommendations on appropriate mailing lists and strategy tips. Also, contact the magazines previously listed and ask for their mailing list rental rates for the geographic areas you want to reach.

Press Releases. Visit the marketing department of local newspapers for information on targeting its readers. Use this information to angle your release. Make sure you catch the reader's attention. Keep the message simple. Be sure to wield the five W's of journalism: who, what, where, when, why, and the noble H (how).

Personal Selling. If you cannot reach customers personally, you will need to budget for someone who can. If you are planning on personally selling, locate networking opportunities and start building new contacts. Allocate a portion of your salary and expenses as a promotional cost. If you are going to use sales reps locate and determine their cost.

Once you know the cost of each item of your promotional package, you can decide which you can afford. Remember to always consider "What is the message I want my target customer to receive?" and "How can I best reach my target customer effectively and cost efficiently?"

Don't be discouraged if cost knocks out part of your ideal promotional mix. That's why we've filled Chapter 6 with so many inexpensive promotional ideas. And, in the meantime, you have used the power of your imagination to brainstorm the best possible promotional effort for your business.

When bankers review business plans they will definitely want to know how and at what cost you are going to reach your customers. A well-thought-out marketing and promotion plan will demonstrate to your reader that you have done your homework and recognize the costs involved in promoting your product or service.

Summary

Promotion is the art and science of moving the image of your business into the prospect's mind and keeping it there. Anything that will advance the image is a good tactic to consider. We recommend that you survey the whole range of promotional strategies available and then choose the promotional mix that will work best for your unique business and financial resources. Potential strategies include paid media advertising, free ink and free air, personal selling, trade shows, industry literature, networking, and exceptional customer service.

We also recommend that you seek creative solutions to the problem of small-business promoting. New businesses can take creative license and stretch the limits early on in getting their business off the ground. If you are not creative, hire people who are to help you stand out from the crowd.

A coordinated marketing plan focused on target customers is essential for long term success.

Think Points for Success

- Be unique with your promotions. Instead of Christmas cards, send Ground Hog's Day or St. Patrick's Day cards.
- Stand in your target customer's shoes. Think like your target customer. Find the need. Always refer back to your target customer collage to keep the customer in the center.
- Maintain a presence.
- A world in transition means opportunities for entrepreneurs. Fast footwork can keep you in the game.
- To launch your mailing lists, give away something. In return, potential customers will give you their names and addresses.
- Create excitement because excitement sells. Rent a Santa, a robot, or a hot-air balloon.
- Remember to promote the *benefits* of your product or service. People buy solutions!
- People also buy experiences. Make them memorable! Make them want to come back for more. Make them want to send their friends and family.
- Keeping a customer is far cheaper than finding a new one. Make the customer happy. Solve problems. Ask the customer, "**How** can I solve the problem?"
- Make customer service a passion.
- Passionate customers become walking billboards! They care passionately and in their desire for you to succeed they will make you better.
- When you think you have it made, don't let your guard down—keep connecting with that customer! You will never be so big that you can afford to disconnect. Remember this and it will make you rich.
- Creativity! Creativity! Creativity!

Key Points from Another View

His Invention Is Anything But Old Hat

A machine-tool sales rep, Bret Atkins would be out on a work site pitching the product when a metallic voice would intone over the yard loudspeaker: "Yo, Bret. OSHA rules. Put on your hard hat."

Atkins would have to go grumbling back to the pickup to rummage through his safety bag for the ugly dome-shaped headgear. Worse, sometimes his fingers were grimy from handling machinery, and when he'd remove the $100, immaculate, white straw cowboy hat he always wore, he'd get grease marks on the brim.

Finally, he'd had enough. He slammed into the kitchen after work one day and announced to his wife, Julie: "I'm gonna invent a cowboy hard hat."

"Yeah right," she said. "We all get these million-dollar ideas."

But for Atkins it was the beginning of an obsessive three-year journey that would take him through many failures and to the brink of bankruptcy before he produced the Western Outlaw, an OSHA-approved hard hat that looks exactly like a cowboy Stetson.

It's become the hottest item to hit industrial fashion since steel-toed boots.

Because of the Outlaw, Atkins was named inventor of the year at the 12th Annual Invention Convention held on the Queen Mary in Long Beach in April, beating out 400 competitors. And since start-up a year ago, his feisty little company has sold 150,000 cowboy hard hats, and has 1,000 distributors worldwide.

Although a construction worker can pick up an Outlaw for $30 in an Orange County safety products store, out on the Louisiana oil rigs they go for $75, and in Saudi Arabia they bring $250 each to the customs-dodging roughneck who smuggles them in from the United States a dozen at a time in a duffel, Julie Atkins says.

Chris Nielsen, owner of Bakersfield Glove & Safety, says the cowboy hard hat, which comes in six colors, including international orange, is the only excitement in what usually is a very boring business. "It's been our biggest topic of conversation."

But success for the 43-year-old Atkins was at the end of a long dusty trail.

On the very day he got the idea, he made a model for the Outlaw in his garage, modeling it after the straw Stetson he'd been wearing around Bakersfield since childhood.

The fiberglass model looked good. Exactly like a cowboy hat. But with any safety product, the crucial hurdle is approval by the Occupational Safety and Health Administration. And to get that, the Outlaw would have to meet stringent demands of the American National Standards Institute.

Ten times his hat was tested by ANSI. Ten times it failed. Each test cost Atkins $8,000. All of his credit cards were maxed out. To save money, Atkins began testing each new version at home before sending it on to the ANSI lab.

He'd get up on the garage roof and drop a large steel plumb bob through a pipe to see if he could bust the top of the Outlaw. He set the Outlaw on fire with a welding torch. He wrapped the hat in dry ice and stuck it in a freezer chest overnight to see if it would crack.

"At first I thought he'd just give up," his wife says. "But after each failure he'd just go back out again in the garage and start again."

Although skeptical at first, she admired his gumption and grew to share his vision, even when they were up to their eyeballs in debt.

Atkins had the same kind of patience and persistence he had employed in a younger day as a bow hunter of big game. He'd be shivering on a stand in a tree, but wouldn't quit. And then, the trophy buck would step into the clearing.

On the eleventh try, Atkins got the recipe right. The Outlaw passed ANSI with the highest rating, and won OSHA approval.

"At a trade fair in Atlanta an engineer said I obviously must have an advanced degree to figure this out. Obviously, I don't," says the laconic Atkins. "I didn't even go to college at all."

Atkins quit his job and began making the hats in a small workshop, at the rate of 15 a day.

"I'm not a great businessman," Atkins says, "I figured I could make a little bit selling them around Bakersfield."

Fate, however, had bigger plans. A friend of his wife's took a hat with her when she attended a physical therapy convention in New York. She was wearing it one morning when she was part of the crowd in front of the studios of NBC's "Today" show. Host Katie Couric came out to chat, took a liking to the Outlaw, and wore it on the air for 6 minutes. "It's an OSHA-approved Western hard hat," Couric said plainly to a nationwide audience.

"We didn't even have a regular office," Atkins says. "We didn't have our own phone. Orders were pouring in, and I had maybe a dozen hats."

It was the once-in-a-lifetime knock, and Atkins was home. He quickly found a manufacturer, hired a staff of ten to field the calls. He lined up distributors all over the United States. "The thing went right through the roof," he says.

His company just got an order from an Australian distributor for 10,000 hats. The Australian Cancer Society likes the hats because of the sun-shielding broad brim.

"In the West, the white and straw colors are the big sellers," he says. "In Texas and Louisiana the black is popular." Nobody likes the orange, but Atkins keeps a few in stock for road crews.

Friends have suggested that Atkins now broaden the line by inventing a Greg Norman-style golf hard had with a shark on it, but he isn't interested. Getting one ANSI approval was hard enough.

Besides, he doesn't golf.

SOURCE: *Orange County Register*, July 12, 1998, p. 1.

Location, Location, Location

Analyzing Alternatives

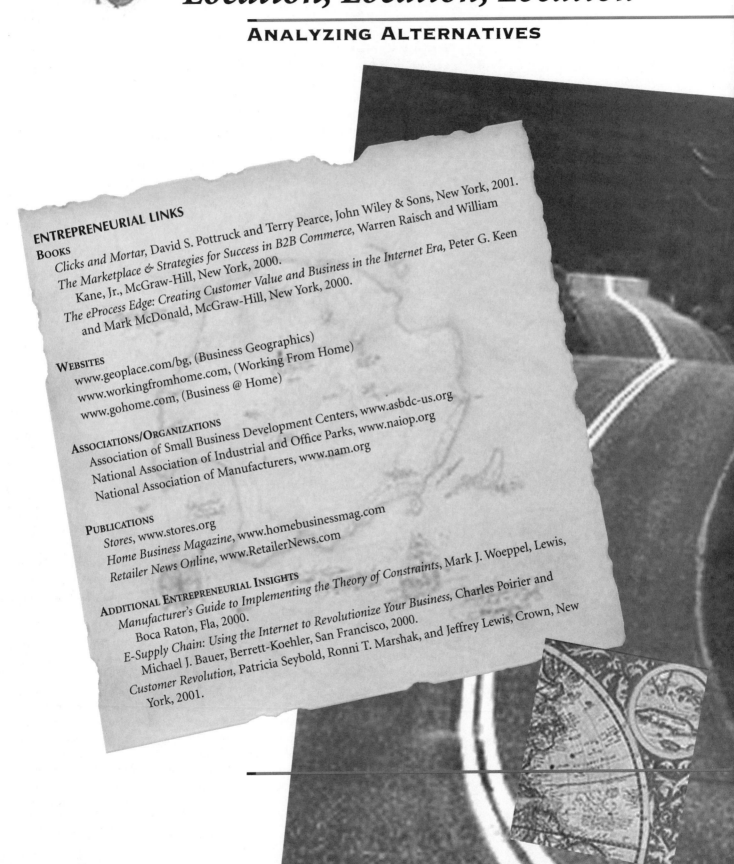

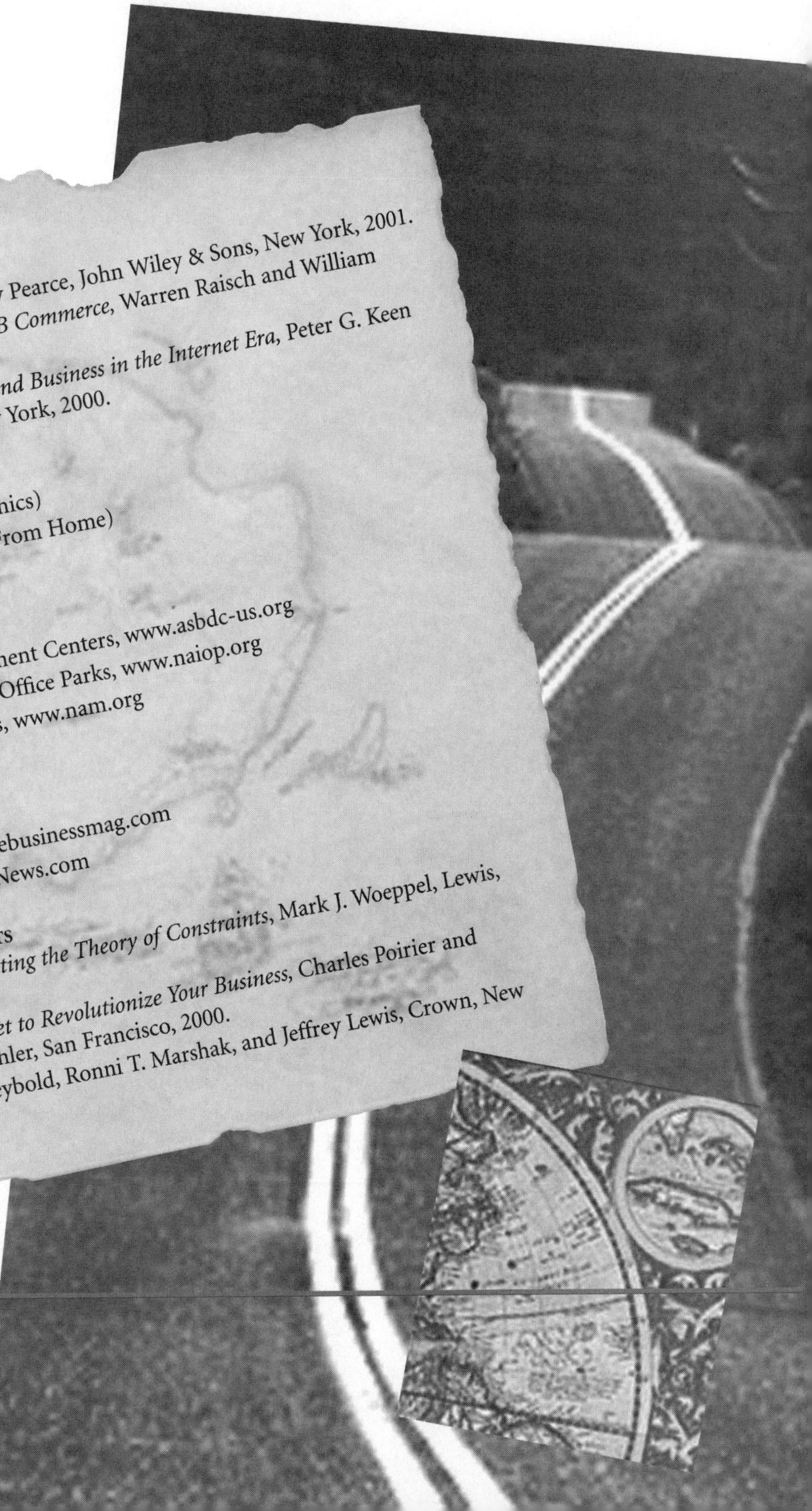

ENTREPRENEURIAL LINKS

Books

Clicks and Mortar, David S. Pottruck and Terry Pearce, John Wiley & Sons, New York, 2001.

The Marketplace & Strategies for Success in B2B Commerce, Warren Raisch and William Kane, Jr., McGraw-Hill, New York, 2000.

The eProcess Edge: Creating Customer Value and Business in the Internet Era, Peter G. Keen and Mark McDonald, McGraw-Hill, New York, 2000.

Websites

www.geoplace.com/bg, (Business Geographics)

www.workingfromhome.com, (Working From Home)

www.gohome.com, (Business @ Home)

Associations/Organizations

Association of Small Business Development Centers, www.asbdc-us.org

National Association of Industrial and Office Parks, www.naiop.org

National Association of Manufacturers, www.nam.org

Publications

Stores, www.stores.org

Home Business Magazine, www.homebusinessmag.com

Retailer News Online, www.RetailerNews.com

Additional Entrepreneurial Insights

Manufacturer's Guide to Implementing the Theory of Constraints, Mark J. Woeppel, Lewis, Boca Raton, Fla, 2000.

E-Supply Chain: Using the Internet to Revolutionize Your Business, Charles Poirier and Michael J. Bauer, Berrett-Koehler, San Francisco, 2000.

Customer Revolution, Patricia Seybold, Ronni T. Marshak, and Jeffrey Lewis, Crown, New York, 2001.

Learning Objectives

- Find a 100 percent location for your business.
- Understand the contribution of location to small business retail success.
- Recognize the uniqueness of your business location needs.
- Develop a checklist for evaluating potential sites.
- Use primary and secondary research to refine customer profile and select location.
- Consult commercial real estate brokers in your search for a location.
- Review major points in leasing agreements.
- Explore running your business from home.
- Investigate using the Internet as a distribution avenue.
- Review small-business incubators and enterprise zones.

One of the most important decisions an entrepreneur has to make is where to locate his or her business. The age-old axiom "location, location, location" has been touted as the three most important reasons for business success. To some extent, and especially in retail, this philosophy has a great deal of merit. For example, if you're planning to rent a location for a number of years, good site selection is critical, and most retail leases reflect this importance in their length (usually 5 to 10 years) and complexity (50 to 75 pages is not unusual).

Chapter 7 will lead you through the processes of finding a good location for your business using primary and secondary research and, if necessary, negotiating a lease that will serve you well.

A cautionary note is in order, however. What you believe will be a good location is certainly relevant, but more important is what your target customer thinks is a good location. You have to be able to climb inside your customer's mind to answer the basic question, "What is the *best* location?"

What happens, then, if you want to operate your business out of your home? First, congratulations! This is a growth market and you may just be on the right track. In this updated version of the cottage industry, more and more of us will be working out of the home. All kinds of services and products are now provided by home-based businesses. Principal Technical Services Inc., number 143 on *Inc.* magazine's top 500 companies for the year 2000, operates out of a home with the president and her son sharing his old room and three other full-time employees working out of their homes. Staff meetings are held at the kitchen table. With the growth in service- and knowledge-based industries, chances are that one day you will be operating some sort of business out of your home. In planning to set up your business at home, however, your location analysis is still important.

There are a number of critical location questions you're going to have to consider: Do local laws allow me to operate a home-based business? How do I balance my family and work life? Do I need a separate telephone line? In this chapter we'll also encourage you to consider all the pros and cons of locating your business outside of the home and help you establish your location strategy.

A new venue to consider for many will be the Internet. Can you sell your product or service online? Can you make a profit? How will people find you? Should you join one of the many online malls? Can your firm stand out from the many other businesses all vying for the same dollars?

The Importance of Location

What Is the Perfect Location?

The perfect location differs for every enterprise. If you're in the house-cleaning business, you can work out of a station wagon equipped with a cellular telephone. If you're in the mail-order business, you can work out of a "cocoon" or a post office box. Action Step 35 asks you to brainstorm the perfect location for *your* business.

A good location can make everything easier for a new business. A highly visible building that's easy for your customers to reach may save you advertising dollars. Once you've been discovered and your customer base is well established, however, location may be less important. Nonetheless, for a retailing firm, a good location is absolutely essential.

Action Step 35

Fantasize Your Perfect Location

Sit down where you won't be disturbed and brainstorm the ideal location for your small business. Get pencil and paper and let yourself dream. Draw a mind map, or use a list format; the idea is to get your thinking on paper.

For example, if opening a candy/cigarette/cigar stand, you might want to locate in the center of New York's Grand Central Station, where 10,000 people pass by every hour. Or if you were opening an extremely upscale boutique, you might visualize a location at Water Tower Place in Chicago.

Once you have the general idea of the type of neighborhood you have in mind, write down what else is terrific about this location. Writing down everything will give you a starting point as you move out to explore the world.

A Location Filter

Before you charge out to scout possible locations for your business, you need to decide what you really need. This checklist will help you zero in on your ideal business location. Use a scale of 1 to 10 to rate the relative importance of each item on this list. When you finish scoring, go back and note the high numbers, anything above 5 or so. Then, after you've read the rest of the chapter, come back to this list if your priorities have changed and focus the rest of your research on these factors.

Target Market

How far will your customers be willing to travel to get to you? Can your business travel/deliver to the customers (flowers, dry cleaning, plumbing, pizza, etc.)? If so, how far can you travel and still make a profit? Will fax and e-mail suffice to keep in touch with clients? Will you need to travel long and inconvenient distances to meet or sell to clients?

Transportation Lines

How much will your business depend on trucks, rail, buses, airports, or shipping by water? If you're in manufacturing or distribution, you'll need to determine your major transportation channel. It's also a good idea to have a backup system. A good technique here is to make a diagram of the location and all the lines of transportation your business will use. (Common-carrier rate listings may help.) Is public transportation available for your employees?

Neighbor Mix

Who's next door? Who's down the street? Who's going to help pull your retail target customers to the area? Which nearby business pulls the most customers? If you're considering a shopping center, who's the anchor tenant (the big department store or supermarket that acts as a magnet for the center)?

Competition

Do you want competitors miles away or right next door? Think about this one. If you're in the restaurant business, it can help to be on "restaurant row." (A good example of a working "competitor cluster" is San Diego's well-known Mile of Cars; having Nissans, Dodges, Chevrolets, Toyotas, and others all in one area cuts down customer driving time and allows for easy comparison shopping.) Does your competition have a stronghold on the market? Is there room for additional competitors?

Security and Safety

How safe is the neighborhood? Is it as safe as a nursery at noon but an urban nightmare at midnight? Is there anything you can do to increase security? Are you willing

Neighbor Mix The industrial/commercial makeup of nearby businesses to be the first in an area to try to turn it around? What can you do to mitigate any problems?

Labor Pool and Education

Who's working for you, and how far will they have to commute? Does your business require more help at certain peak periods of the year? How easy will it be to find that kind of help? Will you need skilled labor? If so, where's the nearest pool of it? Is the site near a bus, train, or subway stop? Will you need technical people? How far will they travel? Don't overlook the potential of part-timers, teens, seniors, and homemakers. Is affordable housing available? Are educational facilities available for training and research? How are the local schools rated? Do local universities offer entrepreneurial assistance?

Restrictions and Opportunities

What local rules (state, county, city, merchants' association, homeowners' associations, etc.) will affect your location? For example, what are the restrictions on signs, hours of business, parking, deeds, zoning, covenants, and employee parking? Is there a reasonable cost of energy?

Services

What is included in the rent (e.g., police and fire protection, security, trash pickup, sewage, maintenance) and who pays for those services that are not?

Costs

Costs include the purchase price if you're buying; otherwise, they are the rent or lease costs. (We advise against buying property and starting a business at the same time because it diverts precious energies and capital that you need for the business.) Also keep in mind things like taxes, insurance, utilities, improvements, association dues, and routine maintenance—you need to know who pays for what. Can you negotiate a few months' free rent? (Always have an experienced leasing attorney look at the lease before you sign it.)

Ownership

If you're still planning to buy property, who will advise you on real estate matters? Consider a lease with an option to buy, and insist the contract be reviewed by a real estate attorney.

Past Tenants

What happened to the past tenants? What mistakes did they make, and how can you avoid those mistakes? If at all possible, contact past tenants and listen to what they have to say. Experience is a great teacher.

Accessibility to Customers

Will your target customers—lured by your terrific promotions—find you easily and then have a place to park when they get there? Consider highway access, construction, and other potential obstacles that could make coming to your place of business inconvenient or unpleasant. Check out plans for potential road construction and closings that might affect your business in the future.

Space

If you need to expand, can you do it there, or will you have to move to a new site? Moving is very expensive.

History of the Property

How long has the landlord owned this property? Is it likely to be sold while you're a tenant? If the property is sold, what will happen to your business? What will happen

Labor Pool Qualified people who are available for employment near one's business location

Restrictions City/county laws governing business locations to your tax obligations? What is the lease status of the other tenants? If the property goes on the market, do you want the first right to meet an offer?

Physical Visibility

Does your business need to be seen? If so, is this location easily visible? Can you make alterations to increase its visibility? Check with the city and the landlord regarding the signs you can post (size, location, fees, etc.).

Life-Cycle Stage of the Area

Is the site in an area that's embryonic (vacant lots, open space, emptiness), growing (high-rises, new schools, lots of construction), mature (building conversions, cracked streets, sluggish traffic), or declining (vacant buildings, emptiness)? What will the area be like in five years? What effect would that have on your business? What do the municipal planners have in mind for the area? What is the quality of life?

Funding Opportunities

Is venture capital funding available? Is a strong entrepreneurial support community available? What economic-development incentives exist?

Image

Is the location consistent with your firm's image? How will nearby businesses affect your image? Is this an area where your customers would expect to find a business like yours? (Look for a place that reinforces your customers' perception of your business.)

GREAT CITIES FOR ENTREPRENEURS

Each year *Inc.* magazine selects the top cities in the United States for entrepreneurs to start and grow companies. The cities are selected based on having a significant number of start-up companies and the city's ability to support the growth of a high proportion of them.

INC.'S 2000 HOT CITIES, HOT SITES

Top 10 Best Large Metro Areas for Entrepreneurial Businesses

1. Phoenix, AZ
   Rapid population growth means more customers and more workers, particularly for high-tech companies, while a renovated art museum, four major sports franchises, and the sunny climate attract residents.
2. Salt Lake City/Provo, UT
   The host city of the 2002 Winter Olympics prides itself on its affordable lifestyle and young, educated, often multilingual workforce (reflecting the influence of the Church of the Latter Day Saints).
3. Atlanta, GA
   Still the capital of the New South, Atlanta has a range of resources for the entrepreneur: universities, a major airport, a large and educated workforce, and access to venture capital and other funding.
4. Raleigh/Durham, NC
   The home of three powerhouse universities (Duke, University of North Carolina, and North Carolina State) and software/pharmaceutical stronghold Research Triangle Park has a strong entrepreneurial infrastructure.
5. Indianapolis, IN
   Established local industries such as pharmaceuticals and auto racing are spinning off start-ups in biotech, software, and other technical areas.
6. Dallas/Fort Worth, TX
7. Charlotte, NC-SC
8. Memphis, TN-AR-MS

9. Washington, DC-MD-VA
10. Orlando, FL

Top 10 Best Small Metro Areas for Entrepreneurial Businesses

1. Las Vegas, NV
   Las Vegas offers a low-tax environment and a market of more than 33 million tourists annually.
2. Fargo/Moorhead, ND-MN
   Because of low crime rates, a strong commitment to education, and the availability of labor (as the agricultural sector has declined), this area provides a solid base for companies like Great Plains Software.
3. Sioux Falls, SD
   A pro-business environment (no corporate or personal income taxes), a family-friendly quality of life, and relatively low labor costs have helped Sioux Falls companies like Gateway thrive.
4. Reno, NV
   No personal or corporate income taxes, an outdoors lifestyle, and easy access to transportation (air, rail, and road) have made Reno a regional-distribution and back-office-processing hub.
5. Austin, TX
   The live-music capital of the world is now home to a host of hardware, software, and Internet companies, thanks to an active venture-capital community and ready pool of talent from the University of Texas's giant flagship campus.
6. Charleston, SC
7. Wilmington/Jacksonville, NC
8. Montgomery, AL
9. Columbia, SC
10. Baton Rouge, LA

SOURCE: *Best Cities: The Lists,* **www.inc.com** (accessed December 1, 2000).

If you are not sure where to locate your business, every state and local economic development office throughout the United States will be more than happy to send you vast amounts of data on their area. Tax breaks, tax incentives, job training, reduced utilities, and infrastructure such as roads and utilities are just a few of the jewels counties and cities will dangle in front of you. Many low-income areas—including inner-city locations—are anxious to lure new enterprises and will offer incentives to employers willing to hire and train as few as ten people.

To explore site selection further, read *Business Geographics,* a magazine that focuses on the use of geographical information systems (GIS). You can also visit their website at **www.geoplace.com**.

After viewing and analyzing all of the data available, you may choose to locate your business based primarily on personal factors or passions like one of the following: remaining near your family, fly-fishing in the river near your home, your community and church, your children's school, living near the beach, or living out in the middle of nowhere. Remember you are trying to not only grow a business but to grow a life based on your dreams. Do them both with passion.

Passion

How Small Entrepreneurs Make It to the Big Time

Consider Paul Orfalea. He doesn't read very well, has a short attention span, suffers from dyslexia, and he struggled to get through school. But one day, without any business experience and with hardly any money, he leased a small space in a garage, leased a copy machine, and launched the business that we know today as Kinko's Inc.

Through trial and error, and by following many of the lessons for microentrepreneurs, Mr. Orfalea was able to turn a profit and eventually expand his business. Having started with just $5,000, Kinko's, based in Ventura, California, has opened more than 1,000 business centers worldwide. Mr. Orfalea started small, and now he's finishing big.

Although this story sounds incredible, it is actually quite typical. I know because I started Subway with $1,000. My story shares many similarities with the stories of Mr. Orfalea and many other microentrepreneurs. We all started with small amounts of money, and you, too, may be able to start small and finish big.

Around the world, and especially in the United States, there are plenty of people who start tiny businesses with less than $10,000 (often much less). We call these enterprises *microbusinesses* and the people who start them *microentrepreneurs.*

Microentrepreneurs Make an Impact

Since the beginning of time, people have started businesses with small amounts of money. They begin modestly, without fanfare and often without great expectations. Today no one knows for sure how many microbusinesses exist or how many are started each year, but the U.S. Small Business Administration reports that first-time entrepreneurs are responsible for 60 percent of business start-ups. Furthermore, the National Federation of Independent Business, an organization based in Washington, D.C., reports that people under the age of 35 launched 1.9 million businesses in 1996, representing nearly half of the businesses started in the United States that year. Three-quarters of these young entrepreneurs started from scratch with almost nothing.

There are few prerequisites for microentrepreneurs. Basically, they need an idea, a little bit of money, and most importantly the desire to get started. There's nothing complicated about what they do. You're not likely to read about them in the newspapers. They don't announce the start-up of their businesses on radio and television, or even on the Internet. They simply start. And regardless of how many people these microentrepreneurs employ initially, how much money they generate annually or how many locations they start with, they all have the potential to grow and finish big.

When I started Subway in 1965, no one told me that I couldn't succeed with just a little bit of money. Of course, at the time, I was just a teenager, recently graduated from high school. I really didn't know much about running a business. I knew nothing about making sandwiches, nor the food industry. I knew nothing about franchising. One day, when a family friend encouraged me to start a business, I became one of those millions of people who think about starting a business at any given time. But I also became one of the few who took the first bold step.

Getting Started

At any given moment in the world millions of people are thinking about starting a business. They are people like you and me, motivated by the desire to be their own boss and to become financially independent. Some want the freedom and the flexibility of self-employment, others want to make more money, and some are tired of making money for others. A business of their own, frightening though it may be, sounds like a logical next step. An exciting next step. If only they can get started.

Unfortunately, few take the first bold step to actually start a business. Few can muster the energy and commitment to begin.

The Keys to Success

Conventional wisdom offers little hope to those who dare to try what so many say can't be done, but based on my personal experiences as a microentrepreneur, I've learned 15 lessons that can help small-business owners start small and finish big:

Start small. It's better than never starting at all.

Earn a few pennies. It's good practice before you earn those dollars.

Begin with an idea. There's probably a good one right under your nose.

Think like a visionary. Always look for the big picture.

Keep the faith. Believe in yourself and your business, even when others don't.

Ready, fire, aim! If you think too much about it, you may never start.

Profit or perish. Increase sales, decrease costs. Anything less and your business will perish.

Be positive. The school of hard knocks will beat you down, but not if you keep a positive attitude.

Continuously improve your business. It's the best way to attract customers, and generate sales and profit.

Believe in your people. Or they may get even with you!

Never run out of money. It's the most important lesson in business.

Attract new customers every day. Awareness, trial, and usage work every time.

Be persistent: Don't give up. You only fail if you quit.

Build a brand name. Earn your reputation.

Opportunity waits for no one. Good or bad, breaks are what you make them.

These are the lessons I learned while building Subway, and they're the same lessons that many other microentrepreneurs have learned and applied, too. No one lesson is sufficient to build a successful business. It's a combination of these lessons, if not all of the lessons, that allows you to start small and finish big.

By Fred DeLuca with John P. Hayes. Fred DeLuca and John P. Hayes wrote Start Small, Finish Big *(Warner Books, 2000), from which this article is adapted.*

WHERE TO GO FOR LOCATION INFORMATION

Businesspeople tend to stay in a location for a while because it's expensive to pack up and move. Selection is a *very* important decision. You need to make sure you're in the heart of your target market or are able to reach your target market from your site. Where do you go for that information?

Previously, we discussed using the Census Bureau, city and county data, and independent research firms such as Claritas and Easy Analytic Software. In addition, we suggest you look to state and local economic development groups and utility services for location assistance. If you are involved in manufacturing, your search should also include association information, Chamber of Commerce, Department of Commerce, and government assistance. You will also need to look extensively into your competition, suppliers, and employee pool.

Targeting by Census Tract

Every 10 years the government gathers together massive amounts of census data. The data from the 2000 U.S. Census is available online at **www.census.gov** or at Federal Depository Libraries. For updated information and projections, contact the fee-based information services.

Census data is broken down from large areas such as a state, to small areas such as a city block. Figure 7.1 illustrates the geographic breakdown for Blair County, Pennsylvania. Locate your county–city tract and go to work.

For researching your retail or service location, you want data that gives you a picture of the lifestyles of your target customers: income, occupation, education, and housing. In addition to census data, fee-for-service and software programs combine census and various other research data to provide a much more thorough and updated evaluation of your potential customer both demographically and psychographically.

Review the sample location worksheet that follows. It highlights site selection factors and their weighting for an appliance repair business. Site location experts and sometimes associations develop various worksheets and analyses of locations and demographics. If you are opening a business that is highly dependent on foot or car traffic, we suggest you hire an expert to assist you. At this time review the worksheet and try to adapt the worksheet for your business location.

FIGURE 7.1
Census Breakdowns

The U.S. Census subdivides metropolitan areas into tracts, block groups, and blocks.

Geographic Subdivisions in a Metropolitan County

AREA

Metropolitan Statistical Area (MSA) and Component Areas (central city and the surrounding metropolitan county(s); the Altoona, PA, MSA has only one county – "Blair" – part of which is shown here)

Census Designated Place

Incorporated Place (central city)

Urbanized Area (all shaded areas)

Incorporated Place

Minor Civil Division (MCD) or Census County Division (CCD)

Census Tract (small, homogenous, relatively permanent area; MSA's are subdivided into census tracts)

Block Group (BG; subdivision of census tracts or block numbering areas)

Block (identified throughout the country; always identified with a 3-digit number, and some have an alphabetic suffix)

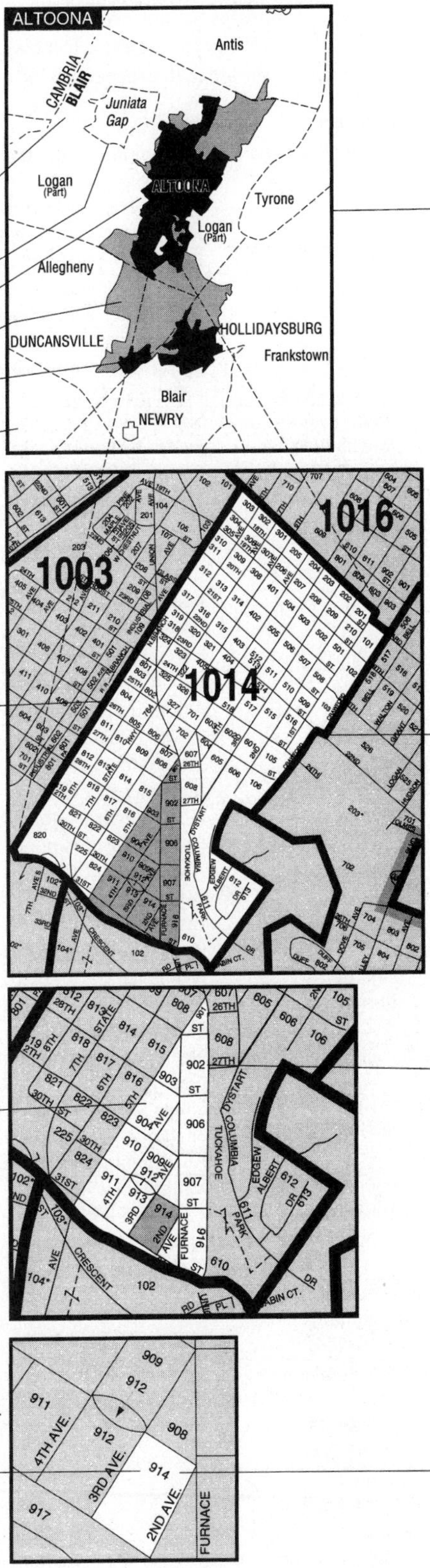

POPULATION SIZE

These areas vary greatly in population size

Average 4,000

Average 1,000

Average 85

SOURCE: The U.S. Census has several helpful services: **www.census.gov**, 301-457-4100 for customer service. Dept. of Commerce, P.O. Box 277943, Atlanta, GA 30384-7943 (for mail orders).

SAMPLE LOCATION WORKSHEET

Often a trade association will help you develop a scoring system that is helpful for a specific type of business location. Here is a 10 category worksheet that will allow a score to be developed for each prospective location for an appliance repair business.

Category	Conditions	Points
Traffic Flow	If two-thirds of the traffic is on the same side of the street as the location	+10
	If there is an even distribution of traffic	+7
	If two-thirds of the traffic is on the opposite side of the street	+5
Building	Free standing and close to road	+15
	Free standing away from road	+10
	Strip center with at least 5 stores	+5
	Strip center with more than 5 stores	−5
	Strip center with end cap location	+10
	Location within a mall	−10
Identification [Signage]	Signs visible for 300 feet	+12
	Signs visible for 150 feet	+6
	Flush mounted signs	+2
	No signage permitted	−10
Parking	5 or more spaces directly adjacent to store	+10
	3 to 4 spaces in front of store	+7
	All parking away from store front (no more than 50 feet)	+5
	Street parking in front of store	+1
	Street parking in front of store with parking meters	−2
	No parking within 50 feet of store and on street meters	−5
Vehicle Traffic	Under 5,000 cars (during business hours)	0
	5,000 to 7,500 cars (during business hours)	+5
	7,500 to 10,000 cars (during business hours)	+8
	10,000 to 15,000 cars (during business hours)	+10
	More than 15,000 cars (during business hours)	+15
Speed Limit	No stoplight or stop sign	+15
	Passing speed is under 25 mph	+10
	Passing speed is 25 mph to 35 mph	+7
	Passing speed is 35 mph to 45 mph	+5
	Passing speed is 45 mph to 50 mph	+2
	Passing speed is more than 50 mph	0
Nearby Businesses	Near Wal-Mart, Kmart, Sears, department store	+15
	Near large appliance dealers	+10
	Near a strong business area	+5
	Near small and medium appliance dealers	+3
	Near bars, pawn shops, liquor stores	−10
Area Demographics	Single-family homes, 15 years or older, within 3 miles	+10
	Single-family homes, 10 years or older, within 3 miles	+5
	Apartment neighborhood	−5
Population of Trading Area	More than 25,000	+9
	15,000 to 25,000	+7
	5,000 to 15,000	+5
	Less than 5,000	0
Economic Conditions	Medium-high to upper income nearby	+5
	Medium income nearby	+4
	Low to medium income nearby	+3
Miscellaneous	Near well-known landmark	+5

Categories	Points	Categories	Points	Rating
Traffic flow	_____	Speed Limit	_____	90+ = Superior
Building	_____	Nearby Businesses	_____	80–89 = Excellent
Identification	_____	Area Demographics	_____	65–79 = Good
Parking	_____	Population	_____	60–65 = Marginal
Vehicle traffic	_____	Economic Conditions	_____	
Total	_____	Grand Total	_____	

A similar format could be used for a service or retail business. This type of worksheet should be placed in the appendix of your business plan and a summary of your findings should be included in the body of your business plan.

GLOBAL VILLAGE

GENERAL EXPORT COUNSELING AND ASSISTANCE

The Trade Information Center's excellent online Export Program Guide provides an incredible source for entrepreneurs exploring the option of exporting. The guide covers general, industry-specific, and country-specific counseling and assistance programs, market research, trade contacts, technical assistance, export finance, insurance and grants, agriculture export and finance programs, export licenses and controls, and food, health, and safety inspection.

General Export Counseling and Assistance
2001 Edition produced by the
Trade Information Center
U.S. Department of Commerce
Washington, DC 20230
1-800-USA-TRADE

International Trade Administration (ITA)/U.S. Department of Commerce—The International Trade Administration is dedicated to opening markets for U.S. products and providing assistance and information to exporters. ITA units include: 1) 104 domestic Export Assistance Centers and 158 overseas commercial export-focused offices in the U.S. and Foreign Commercial Service network; 2) industry experts and market and economic analysts in its Trade Development unit; and 3) trade compliance and market access experts in its Market Access and Compliance offices. The units perform analyses, promote products, and offer services and programs for the U.S. exporting community, including export promotion, counseling, and information programs listed elsewhere in this booklet.

Contact: 1-800-USA-TRAD(E) (1-800-872-8723); Internet home page: **www.trade.gov**

Trade Information Center (TIC)/ITA/U.S. Department of Commerce—The Trade Information Center is the first stop for companies seeking export assistance from the federal government. TIC trade specialists: 1) advise exporters on how to find and use government programs; 2) guide businesses through the export process; 3) provide country and regional business counseling on standards and trade regulations, distribution channels, opportunities and best prospects for U.S. companies, import tariffs/taxes and customs procedures, and common commercial difficulties; 4) direct businesses to market research and trade leads; 5) provide information on overseas and domestic trade events and activities and 6) supply sources of public and private export financing. The TIC trade specialists also direct businesses to state and local trade organizations that provide additional assistance. Country information available on Western Europe, Asia, Western Hemisphere, Africa, and the Near East.

The Trade Information Center website provides a variety of information, including the most frequently asked questions and answers on exporting, the National Export Directory of international trade contacts for each state, a directory of foreign trade offices in the United States, an alternative finance guide, an Internet guide to export trade leads, and the most up-to-date Export Programs Guide. Extensive regional and country market and regulatory information is also available, including assistance with NAFTA Certificate of Origin forms and tariff and border tax rates.

Contact: TIC staff, 1-800-USA-TRAD(E) (1-800-872-8723); fax (202)482-4473; e-mail: tic@ita.doc.gov; Internet home page: **tradeinfo.doc.gov**

www.export.gov—This new interagency trade portal brings together U.S. government export-related information under one easy-to-use website, organized according to the intended needs of the exporter. Whether a company is exploring the possibility of doing international business, searching for trade partners, seeking information on new markets, or dealing with trade problems, this website can help. Additionally, the site has easy links to information on advocacy, trade events, trade statistics, tariffs and taxes, market research, NAFTA Rules of Origin, export documentation, financing export transactions, and much more. Contact: Internet home page: **www.export.gov**

U.S. and Foreign Commercial Service (US&FCS)/ITA/U.S. Department of Commerce—The mission of the US&FCS is to promote the export of goods and services from the United States, particularly by small- and medium-sized businesses, and protect United States business interests abroad. The 1,800 trade experts in the US&FCS work in more than 100 Export Assistance Centers conveniently located throughout the country and in more than 80 overseas posts.

Contact: For information on the US&FCS and its programs, call 1-800-USA-TRAD(E) (1-800-872-8723) or consult the US&FCS home page at: **www.usatrade.gov**

The Export Assistance Center Network (USEACs/EACs)/ITA/U.S. Department of Commerce—The U.S. Department of Commerce, the U.S. Small Business Administration (SBA), the Export-Import Bank (Ex-Im), the U.S. Agency for International Development (USAID), and the U.S. Department of Agriculture (USDA) have formed a unique partnership to establish a nationwide network of Export Assistance Centers (EACs). EACs are located in over 100 cities throughout the United States and serve as one-stop shops that provide small- and medium-sized American businesses with hands-on export marketing and trade finance support.EACs work closely with federal, state, local, public and private organizations to provide unparalleled export assistance to American businesses seeking to compete in the global marketplace. EACs are responsible for providing in-depth, value-added counseling to U.S. firms seeking to expand their international activities, as well as to companies that are just beginning to venture overseas. EAC Trade Specialists provide global business solutions by: (1) identifying the best markets for their clients' products; (2) developing an effective market entry strategy based on information generated from overseas commercial offices; (3) facilitating the implementation of these strategies by advising clients on distribution channels, key factors to consider in pricing, and relevant trade shows and missions; and (4) providing assistance in obtaining trade finance available through federal government programs, as well as access to state, local, public and private sector entities.

Several initiatives have been designed by the EAC network to meet the international trade goals of traditionally under-served communities. The Rural Export Initiative provides companies in rural areas with better access to export assistance and global market research by facilitating their access to international trade services and increasing the number of companies in rural areas engaged in exporting. The Global Diversity Initiative provides minority businesses with the international trade information and industry connections that can make their product or service successful in the global marketplace. The Women in International Trade Initiative offers the expertise, network, and experience of the Commercial Service to meet the needs of women in international trade. The Commercial Service piloted several E-Commerce products through these initiatives that are now available to all Commercial Service clients. These E-Commerce products and services include Video Market Briefs, Video Conferences, Video Gold Keys, and E-Expo USA, a virtual trade show.

Contact: For the address and phone number of the Export Assistance Center nearest you, see the Apendix, call 1-800-USA-TRAD(E) (1-800-872-8723), or consult the web site at **www.usatrade.gov**

USA Trade Center/U.S. Department of Commerce—Emphasizing customer service and seamless assistance, the USA Trade Center brings together key components of the Department of Commerce to serve as a single source in Washington, D.C., for a complete range of export-related products and information. The USA Trade Center, located in the Ronald Reagan Building and International Trade Center in our nation's capital, offers general export counseling, country-specific information and counseling covering the globe, access to extensive market research and online trade leads, innovative e-commerce programs, and a trade reference assistance center.

Contact: 1-800-USA-TRAD(E) (1-800-872-8723); e-mail: tic@ita.doc.gov; Internet home page; **usatc.doc.gov**

District Export Councils (DECs)/ITA/U.S. Department of Commerce—DECs are organizations of leaders from local business communities whose knowledge of international business provides a source of professional advice for local firms. Closely affiliated with the Export Assistance Centers, the 55 nationwide DECs combine the energies of over 1,500 volunteers to supply specialized expertise to small- and medium-sized businesses in their local community who are interested in exporting. For example, DECs organize seminars that make trade finance understandable and accessible to small exporters, host international buyer delegations, design export resource guides, help design Internet home pages, and create export assistance partnerships to strengthen the support given to local businesses.

Contact: For more information on DECs, consult the DEC website at **www.usatrade.gov/dec** or contact your local Department of Commerce Export Assistance Center (EAC). For the address and phone number of the EAC nearest you, see the Appendix, call 1-800-USA-TRAD(E) (1-800-872-8723), or visit the Internet website: **www.usatrade.gov**

Office of International Trade (OIT)/Small Business Administration (SBA)—The Office of International Trade works in coordination with other federal agencies and public and private sector organizations to encourage small businesses to expand their export activities and to assist small businesses seeking to export. OIT directs and coordinates SBA's export finance and export development assistance. OIT's outreach efforts include regional initiatives with Russia, Ireland, Argentina, Mexico, and Egypt. In addition, OIT develops how-to and market-specific publications for exporters. OIT oversees the SBA's loan guarantee programs to small business exporters, including the Export Working Capital Program, which is available to exporters through the U.S. Export Assistance Centers (USEACs) and SBA field offices across the country. The office also spearheads a program, through the USEAC network, called E-TAP (Export Trade Assistance Partnership), which focuses on small groups of export-ready companies, teaches assistance needed to develop export markets, acquire orders or contracts, and provides access to export financing in preparation for a trade mission or show overseas.

Contact: Office of International Trade, (202) 205-6720; fax (202) 205-7272; Internet home page: **www.sba.gov/oit**

Export Legal Assistance Network (ELAN)/Small Business Administration (SBA)—The Export Legal Assistance Network is a nationwide group of private law firm attorneys experienced in international trade that provides free initial consultations to new-to-export businesses on export-related matters.

Contact: The ELAN service is available through SBA district offices, Service Corps of Retired Executives (SCORE) offices, and Small Business Development Centers (SBDCs). For the address and phone number of the SBA office nearest you, call 1-800-U-ASK-SBA; or contact Judd Kessler, ELAN National Coordinator, (202) 778-3080, fax (202) 778-3063, e-mail: jkessler@porterwright.com; Internet home page; **www.fita.org/elan**

Minority Business Development Agency (MBDA)/U.S. Department of Commerce—The Minority Business Development Agency (MBDA) provides management and technical assistance, as well as access to domestic and international markets. MBDA's mission is to promote the establishment and growth of minority-owned business enterprises in the United States. Consequently, it is constantly seeking to create new and innovative ways to engage U.S. minority firms in the international business arena. MBDA assists minority firms in gaining international access in many ways, including: trade missions, matchmaker programs, one-on-one client counseling, seminars, and special international program events.

Contact: MBDA International Trade Office, (202) 482-5061; fax (202) 501-4698; Internet home page: **www.mbda.gov**

Source: **infoserv2.ita.doc.gov/ticwebsite/tic.nsf/6a5f1120d49f8ae1852566330051f340/2293f68ac84bc73985256633005ff4d0!OpenDocument**

BEFORE YOU SIGN A LEASE

When you decide to rent a store location, the property owner's lawyer will draw up a **lease** document. Although its language is very specific, the terms spelled out are *provisional;* that is, the terms are proposed as a starting point for negotiation. Nothing you see in the contract is cast in stone . . . unless you agree to it. Obviously, the terms proposed will favor the property owner. Assume nothing when it comes to leases. Review the proposed lease seriously with your own real estate attorney, with others who have experience with leases, and possibly with some of the tenants if located in a center or multi-use building. Determine how best to begin the negotiation. The following information will guide you through this process. *Do not sign any lease without the assistance of an experienced real estate attorney!*

ACTION STEP 36

SEEK PROFESSIONAL HELP IN FINDING A LOCATION

Visit a commercial real estate office to gain information. Commercial real estate firms have access to planning reports and demographic information that will tell you a lot about growth in the community. Have your plan well in mind and make an appointment beforehand. Dress conservatively.

And leave your checkbook at home!

COMMERCIAL REAL ESTATE

Agents/Commercial Brokers

There is so much to know and analyze when making location decisions and an *experienced* commercial real estate agent can save you time and money. He or she can guide you through the maze of what is available and advise you on leases, prices, taxes, terms, financing, zoning, and public transportation.

Selecting the right broker can be as simple as asking for recommendations from friends or business people in your networking group. Another way would be to note the names of brokers posted at the sites you've been considering as possible locations. Newspaper commercial real estate ads are usually paid for by brokers. Their names and phone numbers appear in the ads. When you call to get information about a particular ad, you'll be connected to the listing agent. If you like what you hear about the property, but don't feel comfortable with that particular agent, don't be concerned. Any agent or broker can show you any listed property; he or she does not have to be the listing agent. Keep in mind, however, if an agent shows you property and then you choose not to use that agent to complete the transaction, there may be problems.

Commercial brokers are paid primarily by the landlord or seller and earn their commissions only when a deal is final and money changes hands. Don't let yourself be rushed, but bear in mind that brokers are an excellent source of free market information. Brokers affiliated with large commercial firms have extensive research departments at their disposal. You can save an agent a lot of time if you have already defined your needs. If you compare each site against your ideal location, you will probably have several workable alternatives. Typically, on-site leasing people have different objectives because they are employees of the developer. They want to fill the building. Most developers also cooperate with commercial brokers, so a broker can take you almost anywhere you want to go and, if asked, might help you negotiate more favorable terms.

If your business requires leasing or purchasing a site, complete Action Step 36.

Anticipate the Unexpected

Bette Lindsay always had a soft spot for books, and when she finally chose a business, it was a bookstore in a shopping center. She had researched everything—trends, census data, newspapers, reports from real estate firms, suppliers—but she failed to anticipate an important potential pitfall, dependency on an **anchor tenant**.

Few small businesses are themselves "destination locations." They must count on anchor tenants to draw traffic. Bette made an assumption that the anchor tenant in her center would be there forever. This case study shows the importance of having Plan B ready.

Lease A legal contract for occupancy

Anchor Tenant A business firm in a commercial area that attracts customers

My husband and I researched small-business opportunities for almost two years, and my heart kept bringing me back to books. I've read voraciously since I was 7 years old and love a well-written story. So when a new shopping center was opening a mile from our home, I told my husband, "This is it."

Everything looked perfect. They had a great anchor tenant coming in—a supermarket that would draw lots of traffic. The real estate agent we'd been working with during most of our search showed us the demographics of the area, which documented that we were smack in the middle of a well-educated market. According to statistics put out by the federal government, a bookstore needs a population of 27,000 people to support it. Our area had 62,000 people, and the closest bookstore was more than 5 miles away.

Everything else looked good, too. We had lots of parking. The neighbors (three hardy pioneers like ourselves) were serious about their businesses and pleasant to work with.

We wanted to be in for the Christmas season because November and December is the peak season for bookstores, so we set a target date of mid-October. The contractor was still working when we opened a month later.

We started off with an autograph party and we ran some bestseller specials. Even though construction work from our anchor tenant blocked our access, we had a very good Christmas that year. We started the New Year feeling very optimistic.

One day in mid-January, construction work stopped on our anchor tenant's new building. The next day we read in the paper that the company had gone bankrupt.

Well, the first thing I did was call the landlord. He was out of town, and his answering service referred me to a property management company. They said they knew nothing about what was happening and that all they do is collect the rent. January was slow. So were February and March. In April, two of our neighbors closed down. The construction debris was blocking customer access. It was a mess.

In May I finally succeeded in getting in touch with the owner and tried to ***renegotiate the lease****, but his story was sadder than mine.*

Fourteen months after we moved in our anchor tenant finally opened! I only wish my lawyer had suggested including a provision in our lease that would have provided reduced rent until the anchor tenant moved in. That expensive mistake does not bear repeating.

How to Rewrite a Lease with Your Lawyer's Assistance

You live with a lease (and a landlord) for a long time. If you're successful in a retail business, your landlord may want a percentage of your gross sales receipts. If you're not successful or if problems develop, you're going to want several Plan Bs and a **location escape hatch**. For example, your lease should protect your interests:

- if the furnace or air-conditioning system breaks down
- if the parking lot needs sweeping or resurfacing
- if the anchor tenant goes under
- if the building is sold
- if half the other tenants move out

The possibility of such grief-producing eventualities needs to be dealt with in precise words and precise numbers in the lease.

Always negotiate free rent until the anchor tenant opens for business and make the lease itself contingent on the anchor's leasing and opening. Also, you will want an escape clause stating that if and when the anchor tenant leaves you may leave also.

You also want to ensure that if the building is sold you are protected and that other tenants cannot disturb your business operations.

Renegotiate a Lease Obtaining a new or modified contract for occupancy

Rewrite a Lease Alter the wording of a lease to make it protect one's interests

Location Escape Hatch A way to cancel or modify a lease if the landlord fails to meet the specified terms

Read the lease slowly and carefully. When you see something you don't understand or don't like, draw a line through it. Feel free to rewrite the sentences if you need to. It's *your* lease, too.

Always hire a real estate lawyer to review and advise you before signing any lease. And make sure that the owner (or the leasing agent) indicates his or her agreement with your changes by initialing each one.

Here's a checklist to start you on your rewrite.

1. **Escape clause.** If the building doesn't shape up or the area goes into eclipse, you will want to get out fast. Be specific. Write something like "If three or more vacancies occur in the center, tenant may terminate lease."
2. **Option to renew.** Common leases today are for 5 years, unless you are a major player like Pier I, in which case the lease might be for 10 years. Options to renew are usually for 2 to 5 years. You should be planning for at least a 5-year run for retail. If you are too afraid to sign for 5 years, rethink your commitment.
3. **Right to transfer.** Circumstances might force you to sublet. In the real estate trade this is called "assigning." Usually assigning requires landlord approval of the new tenant. Be sure the lease allows you to transfer your lease hassle-free if such circumstances arise.
4. **Cost-of-living cap.** Most leases allow the property owner to increase rents in step with inflation according to the Consumer Price Index (CPI). To protect yourself, insist on a cost-of-living cap so that your base rate doesn't increase faster than your landlord's costs. Try for half of the amount of the CPI increase; if the CPI rises 4 percent, your rate will go up only 2 percent. Such an agreement is fair because the owner's costs won't change much. Major tenants in your center will insist on a cap, so you should be able to negotiate one also. Proceed with confidence.

INCREDIBLE RESOURCE

ENTREPRENEURIAL ASSISTANCE FOR THE DISABLED

Entrepreneurs with a disability such as Jan Midori, who suffers from narcolepsy and runs a $20-million direct-marketing art company, can find assistance from the following sources:

Disabled Businesspersons Association
www.disabledbusiness.org
SDSU-Interwork Institute
5850 Hardy Avenue, Suite 112
San Diego, CA 92182-5313

President's Committee on Employment of People with Disabilities
www.pcepd.gov

The Seed Institute
www.seedinstitute.org
Provides training classes, mentors, and an online small-business planning class.

Many people have physical or mental disabilities that make working in a traditional setting difficult. For many disabled, and also for the able, developing a business allows one to gain control over one's time and workplace setting.

For many disabled individuals, insurance and possibly workmen's compensation benefits, tax issues, and health benefits are important variables and need to be discussed thoroughly with the appropriate parties involved.

Alice Weiss Doyel's book, *No More Job Interviews! Self-Employment Strategies for People with Disabilities,* provides an excellent resource as one navigates self-employment. In addition, new federal regulations through Rehabilitation Services and state Voc-Rehab offices provide assistance and possible loan guarantees for disabled small-business owners. For information on adaptive devices contact IBM at (800) 426-4832.

Option to Renew A guaranteed opportunity at the end of a lease to extend for another specific period of time

Cost-of-living Cap An agreement that the rent from one year to another cannot be increased by more than the CPI for that period

5. **Percentage lease**. Percentage leases are common in larger retail centers. They specify that the tenant pays a base rate plus a percentage of the gross sales. Example: $3 per square foot per month plus 5 percent of gross sales more than $500,000 per year. It is important that you make realistic sales projections because the natural break-even point (the maximum amount of gross sales before percentage rent kicks in) is negotiable. The percentage rent itself is also negotiable.
6. **Floating rent scale**. If you're a pioneer tenant of a shopping center, negotiate a payment scale based on occupancy. For example, you may specify that you'll pay 50 percent of your lease payment when the center is 50 percent occupied, 70 percent when it's 70 percent occupied, and 100 percent when it's full. You can't build traffic to the center all by yourself, and motivation is healthy for everyone, including landlords.
7. **Start-up buffer**. There's a good chance you'll be on location fixing up, remodeling, and so on, long before you open your doors and make your first sale. Make your landlord aware of this problem and negotiate a long period of free rent. The argument: If your business is successful, the landlord, who's taking a percentage, will make more money. If your business doesn't do well or if it fails, the landlord will have to find a new tenant. You need breathing space. You've signed on for the long haul. By not squeezing you to death for cash, the landlord allows you to put more money into inventory, equipment, service, and atmosphere—the things that make a business go.
8. **Improvements**. Unless you're a super fixer-upper, you don't want to lease a place with nothing more than a dirt floor and a capped-off cold-water pipe. With most retail sites, however, a plain vanilla shell with very few tenant improvements is the norm. If the economy is slowing down or in a recession, tenant improvements will be easier to negotiate. Find space that does not require extensive and expensive remodeling if cash is tight. Do not go under before getting up!
9. **Use clauses**. If you own a camera store and part of your income derives from developing film, you don't want a Fotomat booth to move into your center. Sam's Videos' lease included a clause that precluded any other video stores from the center. However, the clause did not cover the empty pad, which soon sprouted a Blockbuster store. Build use clauses into your lease to protect yourself. Use clauses must be worded *very carefully.* Catarina's, an ice cream and candy store, had included the word *beverages* in her use clause, which the landlord approved. The landlord came back later to Catarina's owner and told her she could not sell smoothies or coffees. Fortunately, the owner showed the lease to the landlord and pointed out the word *beverages* and no more was said. Additionally, the storeowner had inserted into the lease that she would not sell "soft-serve yogurt." When she began to sell hard-packed yogurt the landlord came calling. Again, she pulled out the lease. Wording your lease properly can mean the difference between success and failure.
10. **CAM (Common Area Maintenance)**. These clauses cover gardeners, building repairs, trash, and so on. Know the CAM charges before leasing. CAM charges can vary greatly from $.25 to more than $1 per square foot. Make sure your CAM charges are based on your square footage. If a portion of the center is empty, be sure the landlord—not you—pays the CAM charges for the empty square footage!

OFFICE/BUSINESS/RETAIL LOCATION ALTERNATIVES

Alternative business locations are available depending on your needs and resources. If you have a business that requires employees to come to your site, your alternatives will be more limited. Find out if delivery services will deliver and pick up at your home. They may be willing to deliver but only to the door and not inside your home. This may pose a problem if you have large heavy deliveries or cannot leave packages outside.

COMMUNITY RESOURCE

Incubate Your Baby for Success

With more than 800 incubators around the country, the opportunity to grow your business surrounded by like-minded entrepreneurs and expertise may provide you with the impetus you need to make your dream a success. The National Business Incubation Association, **www.nbia.org**, suggests entrepreneurs screen incubators just as incubators screen prospective clients by asking the following questions to find the right match:

Does the incubation program offer the services and contacts you need?

What services do you need to make your venture successful? Business plan development, legal and accounting advice, marketing, Internet access, manufacturing facilities?

Is access to a particular market critical? Then consider finding an incubator that specializes in that market. Be sure the program offers what you need or can connect you to service providers who can meet those needs.

Do you meet the incubator's criteria?

Find the incubator's qualifications for accepting clients before applying. For example, some incubators expect prospective clients to have fully developed business plans, whereas others require a less developed idea and offer business plan development assistance.

Is the program's fee structure right for you?

Most for-profit incubators exchange space and services for an equity share in their client companies, whereas most non-profits charge fees for space and services. If a large cash infusion and speed to market are essential for your business success, then giving up equity in your company in order to secure quick cash may be right for you. But if you believe you have the skills to raise your own funding (with some assistance), don't want to give up any equity in your venture, and are willing to build your company more slowly, then paying fees for services and space may be a better choice.

How well is the program performing and what is the success rate of past clients?

SOURCE: "Incubation Search Guidelines," Copyright © 2000 National Business Incubation Association (NBIA). Reprinted with permission of NBIA. **www.nbia.org** (accessed February 28, 2001).

Consider a Just-in-Time Location

Most cities have a wide selection of executive office suites available at modest prices. Services can include the part-time use of a corporate-style executive boardroom, a shared receptionist, phone service, mail receiving, photocopy equipment, fax, and a part-time or permanent office. Such situations may work well for consultants, sales representatives, architects, and owners of virtual companies. Many people choose to use office suites after working out of their home for some time. Also, for retailing seasonal products a just-in-time location may be perfect. Empty retail store fronts can be rented on a short term basis.

Storefront mailbox services work well for some, but you may get a higher level of service for less money by simply renting a U.S. Post Office box. If a private mailbox service closes or moves you are suddenly out of an office.

Business Incubators

Incubators nurture young firms by helping them to survive and thrive during the sometimes-difficult start-up period. More than 800 incubators provide trained professional assistance in marketing, financing, and technical support. You will usually share office space, access to equipment, and storage or production areas. Generally your firm will remain in an incubator for one to three years.

Some incubators serve all types of clients: service businesses, light manufacturing, technology, and research. Other incubators specialize in specific areas such as biotechnology, software development, and retailing. Contact the National Business Incubation Association at **www.nbia.org** to locate an incubator in your state. Several incubator profiles follow.

INCUBATORS—SURVIVE AND THRIVE!

Tucson Technology Incubator, Tucson, AZ

TTI is a nonprofit business incubator, affiliated with the University of Arizona, devoted to the development of technology-based, high-growth companies from industries such as aerospace, biomedicine, biotechnology, environmental technology, information technology, advanced composites/plastics, optics, and others. TTI provides support services, one-on-one guidance, and expertise to entrepreneurs, innovators, and researchers who are creating the new technology companies of today and tomorrow.

Advanced Science and Technology Commercialization Center at the University of Kentucky, Lexington, KY

The Advanced Science and Technology Commercialization Center (ASTeCC) is the University of Kentucky's incubator for multidisciplinary collaborations and start-up ventures. This $17 million, 80,000-square-foot facility, completed in 1994, is located in the heart of the University of Kentucky campus in Lexington. ASTeCC provides research space and an extensive array of modern research instruments to UK faculty, their students (undergraduate, graduate and post-doctoral), staff, and scientists and engineers from new, for-profit, high-technology businesses. Twenty-four faculty-led research groups explore research problems in areas including biopolymers, computational sciences, materials sciences, molecular biology, and biopharmaceutical engineering. ASTeCC is also home to ten for-profit high-technology businesses that lease space in the building from Kentucky Technology, Inc., the University's wholly-owned for-profit subsidiary. The ASTeCC Program has two objectives: first, to combine the experience of scientists and engineers from various disciplines to encourage high-quality, collaborative research of intellectual and commercial value; and second, to foster the commercial development of discoveries made by UK's scientists and engineers.

Biotechnology Development Institute, University of Florida, Alachua, FL

The Sid Martin Biotechnology Development Institute (BDI) at the University of Florida is a full-service business incubator designed specifically to support biotech start-up companies and to facilitate technology transfer from the State University System of Florida to the private sector. The BDI provides a wide array of support services to biotechnology-based start-up companies including state-of-the-art infrastructure support, common use scientific equipment, a fermentation facility, a self-contained greenhouse, and extensive business support services. The BDI can also assist companies with access to seed-stage venture capital through its affiliation with Caerus First Round Partners.

SOURCE: National Business Incubation Association, **www.nbia.org** (accessed February 28, 2001).

Home Offices

Home offices can be an excellent place to start a business; some entrepreneur ventures have been able to grow to multi-million-dollar businesses while based at home. Staying in your home takes planning. Recommendations include hiring babysitters for children, keeping your home and office separate, arranging for back-up equipment, designing office space that works for you with comfortable furniture and adequate computer equipment and telephone lines, and designing your daily work schedule with breaks so you don't become a hermit.

Dorothy Folte, a professional writer, drives to Starbucks each morning to signify that her workday has begun. Casey Trout, a financial planner, has a routine of officially closing the office for the day at 6:00 PM by walking out the back door and walking in the front door.

You need to learn to manage your work time so *all* your time does not become work time. The lure of the computer and work continue to pull on you, and it is sometimes 14 hours later when you realize you haven't seen the light of day.

Home Office

Gloria Brookstone's home-based business began when her handbag was stolen in Venice, Italy where Gloria was traveling with her husband. They were crossing an arched bridge on their way to breakfast when two young men zoomed by on a motorbike. The tailpipes puffed blue smoke. Gloria felt a tug at her shoulder. She saw the teeth of the rider on the bike and her shoulder bag clutched in his fist, the strap swinging free. In his other hand was a pair of tin snips.

The ensuing paperwork stole the entire morning. A policeman interviewed Gloria and her husband. "Have you ever thought of a money belt?" the policeman asked. "So many purses are stolen here."

Gloria tried a money belt. It didn't feel right. She borrowed her husband's safari vest. It was handy, all those pockets, but it didn't look like Gloria. "I am not on safari," she said. "And this vest swallows me up. It's too big."

When she returned home to Indianapolis, she heard of other purse thefts. For her birthday, Gloria received a safari vest that fit. She wore the vest on their next trip. During her trip she had a dream about the perfect vest; one with gold buttons instead of a zipper. It had secret inside pockets to place money and valuables, and beautiful rich colors. It fit like a dream.

The dream vest haunted Gloria all the way home. When she got back to her real estate office, she contacted garment makers in Chicago and Knoxville. They were happy to take her money ($10,000 up front) and Gloria sat up nights designing her Women's Travel Vest.

The first vests (400 for $10,000) looked shabby and cheap. When Gloria complained, the garment maker said, "Business is business." Gloria threatened to sue, but the money was gone. Working with a large manufacturer taught her a lesson.

Brainstorming on paper, she discovered what she wanted to do. Down deep, Gloria was a dreamer and was tired of selling real estate. One thing she did not want to do was to finance her dream-venture by putting in overtime in the real estate market. What Gloria did want to do was work with cloth.

On her travels, she had gathered cloth from Bhutan, the Kashmir, China, Turkestan, Tadjhikistan, Kenya, and Madagascar. Instead of thousands of vests for a faceless mass market, she would create one vest at a time while envisioning a woman traveling the world wearing her vest.

Gloria used the Internet to locate the perfect seamstress–designer. She found an artists' newsgroup. Several women were interested. She used her scanner to scan designs. She sent the designs directly to the women via modem. Before giving up her precious and very expensive cloth, Gloria paid each woman to create a test vest. When the test vests were accepted, Gloria met with each seamstress before she handed over the cloth.

To market the vests, Gloria contacted friends who traveled extensively internationally. She invited each of them to bring two or three friends to her first trunk show in a hotel suite in downtown Indianapolis. French pastries and espresso were served as the women tried on the vests and discussed their travels. There were 50 vests, each unique, with special buttons, fabric, and pockets. Forty-five vests were sold for prices ranging from $150 to $500. Gloria also took several special orders.

Gloria sold her real estate business and started working from her home. The walls of her design room were covered with drawings, photos, and bits of cloth. She purchased a computerized clothing design program. A techie friend helped her re-tool the

Action Step 37

Is a Home Business in Your Future?

Before starting a business at your home, answer the following questions: "What are the benefits?" "What are the negatives?"

1. List reasons to work at home. Start with the obvious: low overhead, close to snacks, an easy commute, familiar surroundings. If you have children and want to be near them, working at home is one solution. Keep listing.
2. List the problems of working at home: How do you handle interruptions? How do you show that you are serious? How do you focus amidst clutter? If you have clients, where do they see you? What's the zoning situation in your neighborhood? Keep listing.
3. List solutions to the problems raised in number 2. If you're being interrupted, you need to get tough. Set up a schedule and post a notice: "Mom's working from 9–11. Lunch will be served at noon. If Mom does not work, there's no lunch!"
4. Go technical. What will it cost you? Consider expenses such as a computer, scanner, modem, printer, answering machine, and so on. Use e-mail to connect with your customers.
5. Where will your workspace be? Garage? Basement? Bedroom? Den? How can you keep it YOURS?
6. Check out your home insurance. What does it cover?
7. Check out health insurance if needed. Can you qualify? What will be the cost?

program for vests. At work in her design room she came up with a company name: QuestVest.

She used e-mail to communicate with her seamstresses. Two lived in Chicago, two in Indianapolis, and two in France. The seamstress in France had sold two vests to a customer in Versailles, outside Paris, who in turn opened her home for the first international trunk show for QuestVest. Gloria was off to Versailles!

*Working daily at the computer gave Gloria a sore wrist. When she checked the Internet, she found a website devoted to repetitive stress injuries, **www.hoaa.com/HOCstress.htm**, which she quickly shared with her seamstresses. The recommended exercises helped keep the women working happily and without pain.*

Gloria discovered that "niches bring riches." Take a tip from Gloria Brookstone and follow your dream. If you have always dreamed of working at home, complete Action Step 37.

Health insurance is a major problem for self-employed people working out of their homes. For insurance information and special group rates, contact the National Association for the Self-Employed, **www.nase.org**, and **800-232-6273.** In addition, chambers of commerce, trade associations, and business organizations may offer group health insurance rates. Insurance is absolutely necessary in today's high-cost healthcare environment. If you cannot afford the initial policy quoted, look into high deductible health insurance. Do not forego health insurance.

Review your homeowner's coverage with your insurance agent. If you have customers coming to your home, your present insurance may not be adequate. Additional information on insurance for home-based businesses is available in Chapter 12.

The following Internet sites will provide the answers to most of your questions about working at home:

Working from Home, **www.paulandsarah.com**

Working Solo, **www.workingsolo.com**

Small Office.com, **www.smalloffice.com**

Home Office Association of America, **www.hoaa.com**

American Home Business Association, **www.homebusiness.com/ahba**

Swap Meets

In many parts of the country incredible opportunities for retailing are provided through weekly or weekend swap meets. For example, Thursday Night's street fair in Palm Springs draws retailers from Arizona and New Mexico weekly. In Southern California many retailers and craftspeople net more than $100,000 a year working only two days a week at the Orange County Swap Meet. For many small retailers, starting at the swap meet or selling through a retail kiosk in a shopping area can provide an excellent way to test the market and pricing. In addition, swap meets and fairs offer incredible opportunities for seasonal businesses as well.

Internet Location

As retail and business-to-business sites on the Internet continue to undergo vast changes, we suggest you explore the option of using the Internet as a channel of distribution and as a way to market your business or service. The Internet can serve as a channel of distribution but all of the functions which go into a successful business—marketing, pricing, advertising, target marketing— are still required (see Key Points at the end of the chapter). In addition, the Internet can be an excellent way for you to maintain contact with your clients by keeping pricing, product, delivery, guarantee, and servicing information online.

ADAM By BRIAN BASSET

Business-to-business e-commerce opportunities are vast with estimates by the Boston Consulting Group of revenues exceeding $4 trillion by 2004. Opportunities for success in the B2B space seem far greater than the retail side. Retail online sales are estimated at $125-$250 billion by the middle of this decade.

Because of the open nature of the Internet, an incredible amount of current information is available on various sites. We suggest you visit several of the following sites as you explore the limitless possibilities of the Internet:

www.ecommercetimes.com
www.ibm.com
www.microsoft.com
www.zdnet.com
www.commerce.net
www.emarketer.com
www.thestandard.com

Enterprise Zones

Certain areas of the United States, many in the inner city, have been designated by the government as Rural Empowerment Zones and Enterprise Communities. Incentives are available to firms willing to locate in primarily economically depressed areas. In the recent tight labor market many firms have discovered ready and eager employees in these areas. In addition to finding employees, the financial incentives and generally lower rents can be of great benefit to a start-up firm.

To gather further information, contact your local economic development office or visit **www.ezec.gov**.

A Success Story

We close this chapter with Charlene Webb's success story because it illustrates very well the things we've discussed. You could almost use this case study as a checklist for small-business success.

"My partner and I were both in education, so carrying out a lot of research for our gourmet cookware store didn't seem unnatural. We hoped to open in October in order to capitalize on the holidays, so we spent our week of spring vacation talking to owners of gourmet cookware shops in the Los Angeles area—where it seems there's one on every corner.

"We spent 5 days and visited an average of 10 shops a day. The owners we talked to were helpful—because they knew our store would be 60 miles away and we would not be drawing from the same pool of target customers.

"When spring vacation was over, we went back to our teaching jobs with our minds loaded with information and our hearts full of hope. Time pressures were heavy. If we were going to open in October, we knew we had to spend the summer on

layout, image, and atmosphere. That meant we needed to find a good location very soon.

"Three days before the end of the school year we found a site—in a very safe and secure center near a convenient freeway off-ramp. Our nearest competition was 6 miles away, and a population study told us there were 55,000 people in the surrounding area to support us. It was perfect. All we had to do now was negotiate a lease we could live with.

"Perhaps it's because I was an English teacher, or because my dad's a lawyer, but whenever I came across a passage in the lease document I didn't like or didn't think was fair to us, I crossed it out. Several places I rewrote entire passages. When it was all over—after the landlord and I had discussed all my changes and we had both initialed the ones we agreed on—my lawyer finalized the lease agreement. I had made four changes that really gave our business some flexibility and breathing space.

1. *We got a 1-year lease with option to renew for the next 2. I knew if we were going to go under, it would be in the first year, and we certainly wouldn't want to have to continue paying a lease if our shop went under.*
2. *We got 3 months' free rent. I was very straightforward with the landlord on this. I said, "Look here, we can pay you 3 months' rent out of what cash we have left after fixing up the interior, or we can put that money into inventory that will help our start-up. I think it would be a benefit to both of us if we put that money into inventory." The landlord agreed.*
3. *We got a 10 percent cost-of-living cap on the percentage the landlord can raise our rent each year. If I ever negotiate another lease, I'll go for 5 percent.*
4. *We refused to let the landlord or his representative look at our books."*

Charlene and her partner's shop started off nicely, with a **grand opening** party for 200 friends and friends of friends. To bring in business, she started a cooking school.

Charlene has developed a customer list of 4,500 names, and remains visible in the community by being actively involved in music activities, the Chamber of Commerce, and the bank (she's now on the Board of Directors) and by writing a cooking column for the newspaper.

Summary

Location decisions are one of the more difficult to make. If you need to move, heavy expenses are usually involved. So exercise caution! Research locations and target markets extensively. Legal advice is essential before signing leases or purchasing a building.

Explore the opportunities of home offices, Internet locations, and incubators. Staying in your office or garage can help you conserve cash for many years, or possibly forever.

Before making decisions, reconsider your personal preferences, the availability of target customers, taxes, and available resources.

Some short journeys will help you see how extremely important location is to retail businesses. First, walk up and down the main business street of your town. Walk it on different days (weekend, weekdays) and at different times of the day (midmorning, noon, afternoon, and evening rush hour). Take some notes on what you see happening.

Second, explore a local shopping center on weekends, weekdays, and different hours. Where is the action at these various times? Observe both vehicle and foot traffic, and what people are buying. Locate the dead traffic zones. A poor location can kill a new retail business. Location is probably the most important decision a retailer can make.

Grand Opening A splashy celebration announcing one's entry into the market arena

Think Points for Success

- The irony of the search for a retail or business start-up location is that you need the best site when you can least afford it.
- Take your time selecting a location. If you lose out on a hot site, keep looking. Don't give up. There are always more places to go. Compromising may be an extremely costly decision.
- Do not locate on a very busy street where traffic goes by too fast—potential customers will not see you and will keep on going.
- Begin with a regional analysis that will allow you to compare neighborhoods.
- A site analysis should include everything that is unique to a specific building or space. Many successful centers have some dead traffic areas. Hire a retail specialist for insight and recommendations.
- Who are your neighbors? Are they attracting *your* type of customers or clients? What will happen if they move or go out of business?
- Know the terms and buzz words—net, gross, triple net, and so on—and be aware that they may mean slightly different things in each contract or lease agreement.
- Everything is negotiable: free rent, signage, improvement allowances, rates, maintenance. Don't be afraid to ask; $1 saved in rental expenses can be worth more than $10 in sales.
- Talk to former tenants; you may be amazed at what you learn.
- *Never* sign a lease without consulting a lawyer who is experienced in lease negotiations.

Key Points From Another View

Profits Pipe Dreams for Many E-Tailers

By James Miller, Special to CNBC

The harshly competitive environment makes it unlikely that many e-tailers will ever find what has become the Holy Grail for all Internet companies: profits. Why? The key for e-tailers is to differentiate themselves from rivals, but they aren't set up to do this.

The problem is that e-tailers sell much of the same merchandise that is offered by their rivals. This is a double whammy of too much competition and the negative effect of not being able to build a brand name because these companies already sell *other* brand-name products.

And while consumers may love e-tailers because they can save billions by shopping online, the companies and their investors see very little benefit. In any business the greater the competition, the more likely it is that profits will dissipate as prices are driven down to the level of costs. Because e-tailers compete against each other far more than brick-and-mortar firms do, profits for e-tailers may always lag behind their traditional retail cousins.

In the traditional retailing world, location in addition to price plays a factor. For instance, there are two pretzel stores in my local mall. Because they are on opposite sides of the shopping center, they don't directly compete for customers. Few shoppers would walk across the mall for a slightly cheaper pretzel. However, it is easy to "walk" from Amazon.com Inc. to BUY.COM Inc. While a single mall can support two stores that sell the same product, the entire Internet might not be able to support, for example, even a handful of profitable bookstores.

Internet firms that sell identical products are therefore unlikely to achieve sustainable high profits. Unless an e-tailer can distinguish itself among customers, it is unlikely to ever be able to charge prices that bring it even moderate profits. Thus, when you evaluate an Internet company, you shouldn't focus merely on what that business can do. Rather, you should focus on what the company can do that its (potential) competitors can't. Unfortunately, it is very challenging for e-tailers to differentiate themselves.

Establishing a brand name seems like an obvious way for Internet firms to separate themselves from the rest of the pack. Brand names can be very important on the Internet because they can signal quality and trust to customers who can't touch goods before buying them. Unfortunately, brand names are only of limited benefit to e-tailers, which sell other companies' branded goods.

If you contemplate buying a PlayStation at BUY.COM you would look toward Sony, not BUY.COM, for quality assurance. The only benefit an e-tail brand provides, aside from price, is an increased likelihood that the good will be shipped in a timely manner. As people become more comfortable shopping on the Internet, even this benefit will dissipate. Furthermore, if having a trusted brand name meant Internet gold, then there are a number of brick-and-mortar companies that would jump into the game, thus increasing competition for pure e-tailers even further.

An e-tailer might try distinguishing itself by having a superior website. Many traditional retail stores are able to charge premium prices because they offer superior services. Traditional retailers that follow this strategy, of course, run the risk of having customers take advantage of their services but at a competitor's lower prices. This risk is multiplied for e-tailers because of the ease of moving from one website to another. For instance, there is obviously nothing stopping you from reading

Amazon.com's book reviews but buying your books from a lower-cost competitor.

One way e-tailers can differentiate themselves is by using the information they gather on their customers. Unlike traditional retailers, Internet sellers can record not just what their customers buy but also what items their customers look at and even, with cookies, what other stores their customers visit. The greatest value of this information would seem to be that it would allow retailers to charge less-price-sensitive customers more.

Unfortunately, Amazon.com's recent attempt at charging different customers separate prices resulted in a minor public relations disaster and a promise by the company to not repeat the mistake. One of e-tailer's best chances to achieve profitability was thus lost.

SOURCE: James Miller, **cnbc.com/commentary** (accessed October 10, 2000).

Numbers and Shoebox Accounting

Keeping Track of the Money Trail

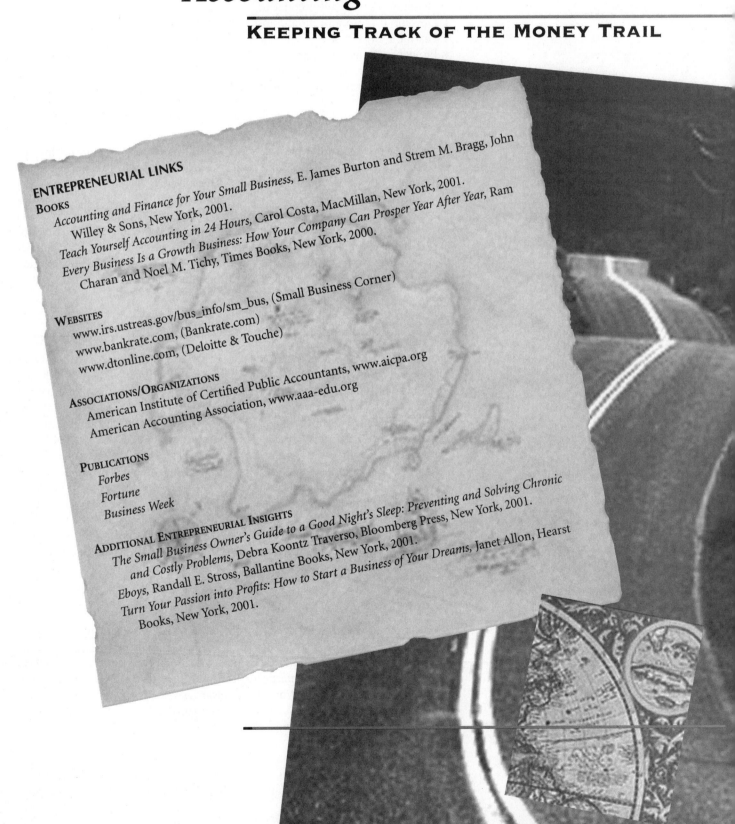

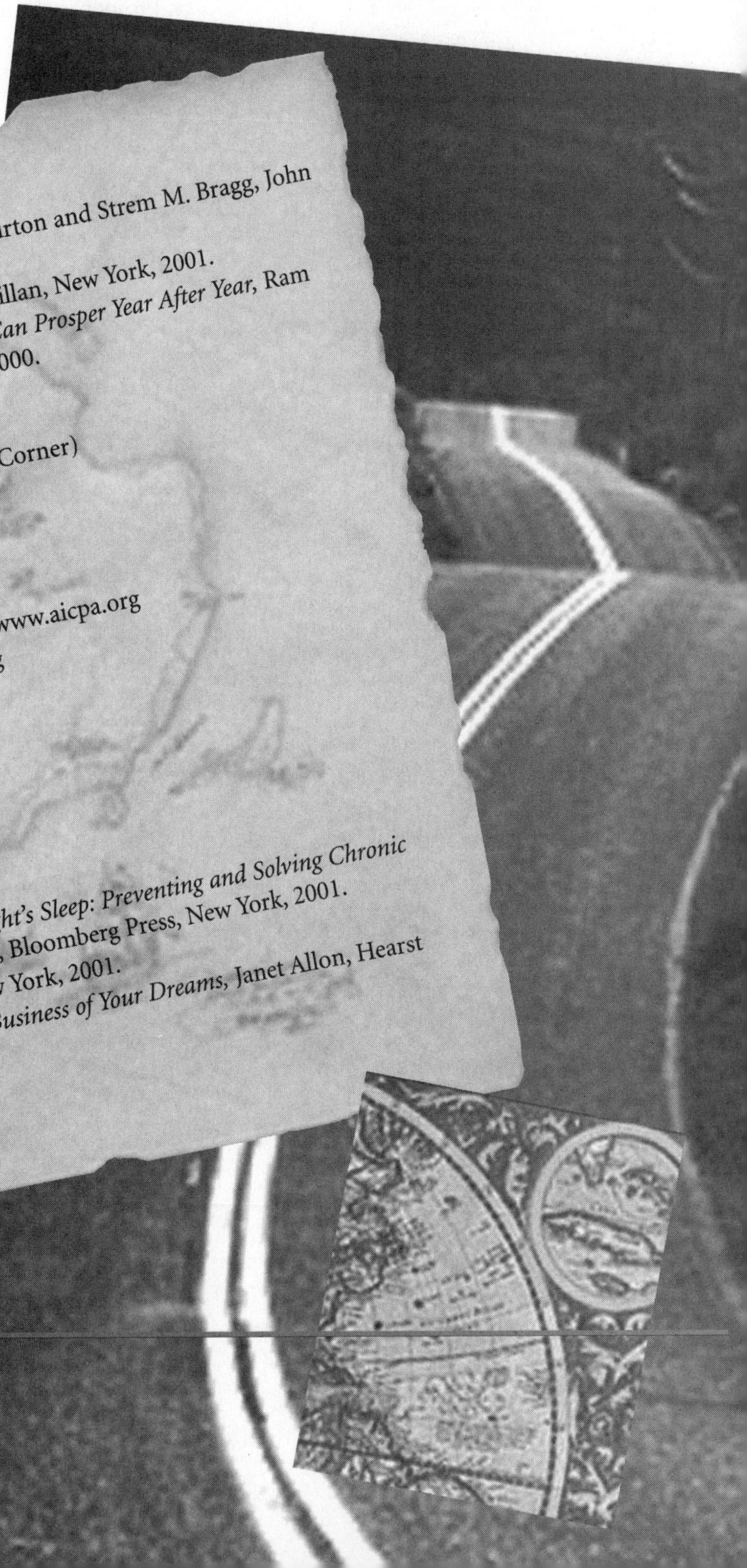

ENTREPRENEURIAL LINKS

Books

Accounting and Finance for Your Small Business, E. James Burton and Strem M. Bragg, John Willey & Sons, New York, 2001.

Teach Yourself Accounting in 24 Hours, Carol Costa, MacMillan, New York, 2001.

Every Business Is a Growth Business: How Your Company Can Prosper Year After Year, Ram Charan and Noel M. Tichy, Times Books, New York, 2000.

Websites

www.irs.ustreas.gov/bus_info/sm_bus, (Small Business Corner)

www.bankrate.com, (Bankrate.com)

www.dtonline.com, (Deloitte & Touche)

Associations/Organizations

American Institute of Certified Public Accountants, www.aicpa.org

American Accounting Association, www.aaa-edu.org

Publications

Forbes

Fortune

Business Week

Additional Entrepreneurial Insights

The Small Business Owner's Guide to a Good Night's Sleep: Preventing and Solving Chronic and Costly Problems, Debra Koontz Traverso, Bloomberg Press, New York, 2001.

Eboys, Randall E. Stross, Ballantine Books, New York, 2001.

Turn Your Passion into Profits: How to Start a Business of Your Dreams, Janet Allon, Hearst Books, New York, 2001.

Learning Objectives

- Learn how to keep score with numbers.
- Determine start-up costs.
- Discover ways to boot-strap your business.
- Develop sales projections.
- Determine seasonality scenarios.
- Develop proforma profit and loss statements.
- Learn the importance of cash flow.
- Project monthly cash flow.
- Learn how to use industry financial ratios and benchmarks.
- Determine return on investment (ROI).

In this chapter we urge you to move beyond your start-up plans and venture out into the uncertain future. It's time to set some numerical goals for your first year of operation. Running out of money in business is the end of the business. This chapter will show you how to avoid running out of money, develop your start-up costs, and prepare you for capital searching. Numbers work is time consuming and frustrating, but without it you will be sure to fail. Many entrepreneurs put all their passion into selecting a site and developing marketing plans. Unless you watch your finances passionately, however, all your other plans may never come to fruition. Use the measuring devices we present, not just once, but several times, and continue to revise as you acquire additional information.

Chart Your Business Future with Numbers

Your first step is to ask questions about the financial state of your business. What will your start-up costs run? Which months will be strong in your particular business? Which ones weak? What will be your gross sales the first year? the second? the third? How much profit will you make? How much money will you lose? Can you project cash flow? bank loans? lines of credit? vendor credit? How many employees will you need? Will shipping costs affect your profit? Can you add some people to the team who will bring in some cash? What will your cash picture look like when your start-up dollars are spread over a full year?

How fast will your business grow? How will rapid growth affect your cash picture? Have any of your life experiences prepared you for handling money in business? What steps should you take to prepare yourself for handling your business's finances?

Your next step is to begin building a business budget. Generally, there are four things you need to consider before you plunge into the numbers of business management: start-up costs, proforma income and cash flow statements, seasonality scenarios, and financial ratios.

Start-up Costs

It's important to determine your costs before proceeding. For some businesses start-up costs will be minor; for others, major. A service business may be up and going with only $5,000 in expenses, whereas a retail store may incur more than $300,000 in start-up expenses alone; manufacturing firms can incur costs of more than $3 million. What can you buy used? What are the advantages of leasing versus buying? How can you conserve cash? Money saved during start-up will help cash flow later.

Sales Projections

Research and good guesstimates based on information gained from talking with competitors, associations, and suppliers will help determine your sales projections.

INCREDIBLE RESOURCE

FEDMARKET.COM

Key to a $700 Billion Market

Fedmarket.com, an online community for government buyers and vendors on the web since January of 1996 and owned by Wood River Technologies, Inc., is singled out as a top government contracting resource by public and private organizations throughout North America. Free site content includes news, expert advice, "how to" articles, a highly focused bid search engine, and the world's largest database of U.S.-based government vendors. Federal, state, and local governmental agencies spend a mere $700 billion a year!

Fedmarket.com carefully maintains and updates a database of over 8,000 federal, state, local, and international procurement URLs and has a proprietary system in place to capture and catalog the hundreds of new bid notices posted daily at government sites. This unique capability puts Fedmarket.com in a position to provide rich business opportunity content to subscribers and vertical industry portal clients.

Vertical industry portals find that bid notices are an important source for driving vendor traffic and jump-starting use of their e-commerce systems. In providing custom bid collection services, they get to know the client's industry, leverage the power of the bid collection system, and bring to the project knowledge of public bidding.

www.Govcommerce.net was launched to provide a safe, secure, and easy-to-use purchasing system for government buyers and vendors. Buyers pay nothing to use the service; though winning vendors pay a 2% transaction fee.

An excellent primer, "Sizing up the Federal Opportunity," may spur your interest further. For additional information on how to do business with the government and government sources, check out Chapter 13's Incredible Resource.

SOURCE: **www.fedmarket.com** (accessed March 28, 2001).

COMMUNITY RESOURCE

Resources for Women Entrepreneurs

Today, the growth of female entrepreneurs is twice the rate of men. And the growth of minority female entrepreneurs is even higher. According to the National Foundation for Women Business Owners, 9.1 million women-owned businesses employing 27.5 million people generated more than $3.6 trillion in 1999 sales. More than one million minority women-owned businesses produce more than $180 billion in sales. We have included a few helpful organizations and websites to get you started. Most of these organizations have local chapters and centers to help you directly in your own community. Finding other women dreaming the same dream and possible mentors may be an incredible boost to your business.

- American Women's Economic Development Corporation (AWED) provides telephone counseling and coaching to members nationwide.
  (800) 222-2933
- National Association of Women Business Owners (NAWBO)
  www.nawbo.org
  (800) 55-NAWBO or (202) 347-8686
- Columbia College Center for Women Entrepreneur
  www.businessforwomen.com
- National Foundation for Women Business Owners (NFWBO)
  www.nfwbo.org
  (202) 638-3060
- Organization of Women in International Trade (OWIT)
  www.owit.org
- Office of Women's Business Ownership (Small Business Administration)
  (202) 205-6673
- Small Business Administration (SBA) women's site (a complete listing of special programs and opportunities)
  www.sba.gov/womeninbusiness
- Women's Business Centers (listing of centers state by state)
  www.sba.gov/womeninbusiness/wbcs.html

Proforma Income and Cash Flow Statements

Before you jump into a business, you need to figure out how much income and profit it will generate in a given period of time. You can pull together a first-year forecast by combining information on sales from business owners and trade associations. Projections should be completed monthly for the first year and quarterly for the next three to five years.

For many businesses there is no time lag between delivering goods to receipt of payment. For others, a time lag of 15 to 60 days may exist. Find out what your selected industry standard is and develop your cash flow proforma accordingly. You will have to expend cash for labor, taxes, rent, utilities, inventory, and other expenses. If your business is to stay afloat in the interim, you're going to have to know where every dollar is going. You must make arrangements for financial infusions long before the money stops trickling in.

Unless you are an exception to the rule, you are not going to make lots of money your first year in business and, if you do get rich, it will happen slowly. A proforma income statement tells you when you should start making a profit—which has to happen before you can start getting rich.

Seasonality Scenarios

Most businesses experience peaks and valleys. What will be your best month? Worst? Attempt to develop a seasonality scenario for the first year of your business.

Financial Ratios

Lenders will evaluate and compare your financial ratios to others in your selected industry. Their lending decisions are based on how you stack up. Ratios also provide a tool for maintaining your firm's finances. Financial ratios will be discussed later in this chapter.

Start-up Costs

When successful entrepreneurs are interviewed and asked what surprises they had not anticipated when they started, they can usually list quite a few. In almost every case it cost more and took longer than they had anticipated. We want you to get started in the planning process and make the best estimates so you are not caught off guard.

To begin, we have provided three worksheets that cover start-up costs, start-up concerns, and office supplies. Each worksheet will need to be adjusted to fit your business operation. Review and complete as necessary.

START-UP CONCERNS WORKSHEET

Here's a checklist of some obvious start-up concerns. Add to this list as you think of things.

I. Taxi Squad (People who can help you)
   - A. Lawyer
   - B. Banker
   - C. Accountant/bookkeeper
   - D. Insurance agent
   - E. Commercial real estate agent
   - F. Mentor
   - G. Consultant(s)
   - H. Suppliers
   - I. Chamber of Commerce
   - J. SBA, SCORE
   - K. Partners, board members

II. Organization
   - A. Federal ID number
   - B. DBA ("Doing business as" fictitious business name)
   - C. Partnership agreement
   - D. Corporation
   - E. Employees

TABLE 8.1
SBA Start-up Worksheet

Estimated Monthly Expenses			
Item	**Your Estimate of Monthly Expenses Based on Sales of $ ______ Per Year**	**Your Estimate of How Much Cash You Need to Start Your Business (See Column 3)**	**What to Put in Column 2 (These Figures Are Typical for One Kind of Business. You Will Have to Decide How Many Months to Allow for in Your Business.)***
	Column 1	Column 2	Column 3
Salary of owner-manager	$	$	2 times column 1
All other salaries and wages			3 times column 1
Rent			3 times column 1
Advertising			3 times column 1
Delivery expense			3 times column 1
Supplies			3 times column 1
Telephone and telegraph			3 times column 1
Other utilities			3 times column 1
Insurance			Payment required by insurance company
Taxes, including Social Security			4 times column 1
Interest			3 times column 1
Maintenance			3 times column 1
Legal and other professional fees			3 times column 1
Miscellaneous			3 times column 1
Starting Cost You Only Have to Pay Once			Leave column 2 blank
Fixtures and equipment			You can save a great deal by buying used equipment
Decorating and remodeling			Talk it over with a contractor
Installation of fixtures and equipment			Talk to suppliers from whom you buy these
Starting inventory			Suppliers will probably help you estimate this
Deposits with public utilities			Find out from utility companies
Legal and other professional fees			Lawyer, accountant, and so on
Licenses and permits			Find out from city offices what you have to have
Advertising and promotion for opening			Estimate what you'll use
Accounts receivable			What you need to buy more stock until credit customers pay
Cash			For unexpected expenses or losses, special purchases, etc.
Other			Make a separate list and enter total
Total Estimated Cash You Need to Start with		$	Add up all the numbers in column 2

*Contact associations and fellow entrepreneurs to determine costs.

SOURCE: **www.sba.gov**

III. Licenses, Permits
   A. Business license
   B. Resale permit
   C. Department of health
   D. Beer, wine, liquor
   E. Fire inspection permit
   F. Other
IV. Location
   A. Lease review (lawyer)
   B. First and last month's rent (Rent usually has to be paid while making improvements. Estimate time needed to do improvements.)
   C. Security deposit (last month's)
   D. Leasehold improvements
   E. Insurance
   F. Security system
   G. Utilities, deposits, estimated monthly costs
      1. Electric
      2. Gas
      3. Water
      4. Phone installation
   H. Other
V. Auto (Consider new, used, leased)
   A. Auto(s)
      1. New/used
      2. Lease/purchase
   B. Truck(s)
      1. New/used
      2. Lease/purchase
   C. Insurance
   D. Maintenance, repairs
VI. Equipment
   A. Office
   B. Retail space
   C. Warehouse
   D. Manufacturing area
   E. Kitchen
   F. Dining area
   G. Communication
   H. Other
VII. Fixtures
   A. Tables
   B. Chairs
   C. Desks
   D. File cabinets
   E. Workbenches
   F. Storage cabinets
   G. Display cases
   H. Lighting
   I. Shelving/storage
   J. Computers
   K. Printers
VIII. Supplies
   A. Business cards
   B. Pencils
   C. Pens
   D. Notepaper
   E. Tape
   F. Letterheads
   G. Dictionary
   H. Calendar
   I. Appointment book
   J. Coffee

- K. Tea
- L. Soft drinks
- M. Bottled water
- N. Other

IX. Inventory (What are the minimum/maximum average inventory requirements needed on hand in order to do business on your first day?)

X. Advertising/Promotion
- A. Signs
- B. Business cards
- C. Fliers/brochures
- D. Displays
- E. Ad layouts
- F. Media costs (newspaper, radio, other)
- G. Name tags
- H. Other

XI. Banking
- A. Checking account
  1. Check charges
  2. Interest on account
- B. Savings/money market account
- C. Credit
  1. Credit cards
  2. Personal lines of credit
  3. Loans
  4. Credit from suppliers/vendors

XII. Employees
- A. Application/employment forms completed
- B. Training program
- C. Tax forms

OFFICE SUPPLIES WORKSHEET

Following is a list developed by the founders of a solar energy business (installation of hot water systems). They did not require any start-up inventory because they would purchase the solar equipment after selling the system.

Desk chair
Two guest chairs
Lamp and table
Potted plant
Credenza
Secretary desk and chair
Locking file, two-drawer
File systems, folders
Insurance
Business license
Air-postal-post-zone rates
Telephone directory
Supplies
Letterhead
Personal size pager
Envelopes/letterhead
Business cards
Second sheets for letterhead
Copy paper
Invoices/letterhead
Mail register
Organizer for mail
Printer toner/ink
Pencils, pens
Computer/software/printer
Copier
Facsimile machine
Phone
Rolodex file
335 tickler file
In & out box (2)
Pager
Instruction booklet
Tax deduction tables
Federal employer ID number
State employer ID number
Bank account
Checkbook
One-write checking/bookkeeping system
Utilities—telephone, water, gas, electricity
Hole punch (2/3 hole)
Scissors
Colored tabs
Erasers, paperclips
Telephone message pads
Minute book for corporation
Pocket appointment book
Desk appointment book

ACTION STEP 38

ATTACH PRICE TAGS TO STARTING YOUR BUSINESS

Sit down at your desk and look around with new eyes.

A. List the items on your desk. Pencils, paper, telephone, typewriter, microcomputer, business cards, calendar, and so on. List the desk itself, the lamp, chair, bookcase, filing cabinet, coffee machine. Now go through the drawers, writing down every item you use to make your work run easier and smoother.

B. List your expenditures for things you cannot see, some of which you might take for granted. These include such things as insurance protection, rent, utilities, taxes, legal services, accounting services, and so on.

C. Beside each tangible item and each intangible expense, write down how much it will cost.

D. Discover all start-up costs and fill in SBA start-up sheet. Note that the SBA differentiates costs as either start-up expenses or operating expenses. This is an easy way to think about costs.

As you gather more information, you'll be able to refine the numbers on this sheet.

Pencil holders
Tape
Stapler and staples
Staple remover
Rulers
Answering machine
Petty cash box
Postage meter (application for permit)
Postage scale
Coffee machine
Miscellaneous
Post office box
Dictionary
Reference book
Calendars
Long-distance call record
Clients and projects directory
Steno pads
Scratch paper
Coffee supplies
File folders and labels
Mileage log
Local area wall map
Local area map for truck

If you get into the habit of making lists, doing mind maps, and writing everything down, you'll improve your chances of surviving in small business. Action Step 39 will help you anticipate potential surprises.

BOOKSTORE START-UP COSTS

The American Booksellers Association (ABA) provides start-up expenses for a 2,000-square-foot bookstore with 1,800 square feet allocated for selling space. According to the ABA, start-up inventory required for a bookstore will depend on:

- price point
- ratio of hardcover to trade
- ratio of paper to mass market
- number of titles
- number of copies per title
- store layout

In addition to the previous, one's financial resources will determine investment in inventory. The ABA estimates inventory at $30 to $110 per square foot of allocated selling space. Again, you need to research and work with your professional association to determine appropriate start-up costs for your business.

In addition to outfitting your office, retail store, or manufacturing operation, there will be costs for computers, cash registers, professional organization dues and publications, deposits and fees for utilities, security deposits, advertising and promotion costs, grand opening expenses, and fees for professional help.

If you go over budget on your start-up costs your first year will be very difficult. This is the time to boot-strap. Think of every way you can save: buy used, borrow, barter, or beg. Conserve cash at all times. Sam Johnson, owner of 5 successful businesses and worth more than $5 million, demands his staff check the local library before purchasing any books. Cash is king! Especially at the beginning, do not squander cash. Complete Action Step 38 using the Small Business Administration (SBA) Start-up worksheet.

Summary of Bookstore Preopening Capital Needs

$90,000	Opening inventory (1,800 sq. ft. at $50 per sq. ft.)
20,000	Leasehold improvements (2,000 sq. ft. at $10 per sq. ft.) (based on space improvements not complete building of new facility)
40,000	Furniture and fixtures (2,000 sq. ft. at $10 per sq. ft.)
15,000	Computerized cash registers and software
6,000	Professional consultants
4,000	Supplies
6,000	Deposits, registrations, fees, memberships
8,000	Preopening salaries
3,000	Training and conventions
10,000	Preopening advertising and promotion
202,000	Subtotal
23,000	Contingencies (10%)
$225,000	Total Preopening Costs (Before anticipated first-year operating loss)

SOURCE: Kate Wholey, Linda Miller, and Rosemary Hawkins, editors, *Manual on Bookselling: Practical Advice for the Bookstore Professionals,* 5th edition, American Booksellers Association, Tarrytown, NY, 1996. **www.bookweb.org/edu/676.html.**

Small businesses are especially vulnerable at start-up time because that's when they're least able to afford surprises. If Ginny Henshaw had anticipated possible surprises, she'd have been better prepared for what happened to her.

The reason I decided to start a daycare center was because I really loved children and my experience as a preschool teacher and camp administrator lead me to believe I could do it. I talked it over with my family and they said they would help out if I got in over my head. If only they would have known!

I think we planned things pretty well. We found a good location—smack in the middle of a neighborhood of young families with an average 2.3 children—and then spent weekends painting and fixing up. We worked hard, but it was fun, and it made us feel a part of something important. We spent many hours making sure we complied with the laws and regulations required of daycare centers.

Well, about 3 weeks before our opening, we called the light and power people to ask them to turn on the lights. "Sure thing," they said. "Just send us a check for $3,000, and the lights will be on in a jiffy."

"What?" I asked. "Did you say $3,000?" We had around $4,000 in the kitty, but that was earmarked for emergencies.

"That's right. You're a new commercial customer with a good credit rating. That's the reason the figure's so low."

"You think $3,000 is low?" I asked, shocked.

"For your tonnage," they said, "it's right on the money."

"Tonnage? What tonnage?"

"Your air conditioner," they said. "You have a 5-ton unit on your roof. Figure you run it for a month, that's $1,100. The other $400 is for lights and gas."

"But we're not planning to run it!" I said. "The breeze here is terrific. We don't need the air conditioner."

"Sorry, ma'am. Our policy is pretty clear. As I said, sometimes we get three months' deposit, but for your business, we'll only require the two. Is there anything else I can help you with today?"

"No," I said. "Nothing."

Complete Action Step 39 as you explore possible start-up surprises.

ACTION STEP 39

PREPARING YOUR CHECKLIST

Now that you've got your business well in mind, take a few minutes to brainstorm a list of surprises that could cost you money or time and thus threaten the survival of your business. Use our checklist to help you get started. Talk to business-people in your industry. Ask them to tell you how they handled unfortunate surprises. Once you select a site, ask the neighbors what has happened to them and how they're doing in this location. Talk to vendors, suppliers, customers, and insurance brokers. Ask. Probe.

When you finish your list, put a checkmark beside each item where you may incur costs. Determine the potential costs. How will you cover unforeseen expenses? How much money should you put aside?

BOOT-STRAPPING

It's no secret that start-ups are expensive, and those first few months can be a make-or-break time for the entrepreneur. When you are out of money, you are out of business! This is definitely the time to care passionately about each and every dollar that comes in and goes out of your business. Guard each dollar with a passion! You want to make your dollars work efficiently. Here are some tips:

1. Find out who you have to pay right now.
2. Find out who can wait a while.
3. Keep asking what you're getting for your money.
4. Conserve cash.
5. Buy used.

How to Save Money

If you work the dollars you do have, you won't have to shake the money tree so hard. Here are some tips that could save you money. Read through the list. How many of these ideas have you thought of? How many are new to you?

1. Ask your customers for **cash deposits** when they place orders.
2. Persuade vendors to give you more **trade credit** or **dating** and more time to pay.
3. Lease your equipment.

Cash Deposits Funds paid in advance of delivery

Trade Credit or Dating A vendor's extension of the payment term into the near future

4. Run a lean operation; do not waste anything.
5. Work out of your home if you can for as long as you can.
6. Get your landlord to make **on-site improvements** and finance the cost over the term of the lease.
7. Keep track of everything. Try to resell whatever waste or by-products you have in your business.
8. Take markdowns quickly on **dead goods**.
9. Use as little commercial space as you can.
10. If your customers do not visit your business facility, it does not have to be highly visible or attractive.
11. When you have to borrow money, shop around. The most expensive cash is the cash you have never planned for.
12. Make sure your **liquid cash** is earning interest.
13. Shop **nonbank lenders** like commercial credit firms.
14. Do not collateralize your loans unless you have no other alternative.
15. Survey your friends and relatives for loans. They might lend you money at rates higher than they would get in the money markets but lower than you would have to pay institutional lenders.
16. Add employees carefully.

Getting Advice

There's a boatload of surprises awaiting every entrepreneur who enters the marketplace. We've talked about Plan B, formulating your strategy, checking and double-checking your market, and peering into the future to see what lies ahead. There's another angle to planning; it's called seeking advice.

Think for a moment about where you are right now on your road to the marketplace. You're halfway through this book. You've analyzed your skills and needs. You've probed your past and surveyed your friends. You've discovered what success means to you, and you've plotted trends and found your industry segment. You've profiled your target customer, studied the demographics, and developed a promotional campaign. You've examined the competition. You've used your new eyes to find a dynamite location. Now you need to locate several **small-business gurus** for financial advice.

Where might you find a business guru? Well, what about your banker? Many people come to him or her for money—some of them carrying business plans, others not

Passion

Passion for a One-Man Show

After 30 years working in a Boston leather factory, Aaron Burke was out of work. His old company had failed because it could no longer compete with cheaper foreign imports.

Aaron loved the leather business and he did not want to give it up. He had worked long and hard for others and now it was time for him to shine. Although he wanted to own his own business, he despised the thought of supervising employees or taking on a partner. Wanting freedom to travel and not be beholden to anyone but himself and his customers, he knew he desired to be a one-man show! So he decided to establish a "virtual company" that could compete.

He created a high-quality line of upscale leather goods that included wallets, belts, and briefcases. At key industry trade shows he showed his designs and took orders. He personally selected the best leather, contracted with short run manufacturers (some of whom were former co-workers), and arranged for a public warehouse to ship the goods to leather stores and high-end gift shops.

Aaron Burke had developed a "virtual company;" he had no employees, factories, or overhead. All the people who were brought together for this undertaking were independent and had a passion to pull together for mutual benefit. The headaches, strains, stresses, joys, fears, and profits were all his, and he loved every minute!

On-site Improvements Modifications to real estate to accommodate the special needs of the business

Dead Goods Merchandise no longer in demand

Liquid Cash Funds that are immediately available, usually held in checking or other accounts

Nonbank Lenders Institutional lenders other than banks

Small-business Guru A wise person on the sidelines who can help you with advice and counsel

GLOBAL VILLAGE

EXPORTING AND IMPORTING OPPORTUNITIES

The following graphs detail the principle commodity groups that make up U.S. trade with its top Organization for Economic Cooperation and Development (OECD) partners. Percent of total exports or imports and the top commodities are shown for each partner country.

Canada is the largest OECD market for U.S. exports and the largest supplier of U.S. imports. Transport equipment includes non-road vehicles such as aircraft, ships and boats, and railway vehicles. The category of specialized machinery can include agricultural machines such as ploughs and tractors, construction equipment such as bulldozers, and machines for sewing, weaving, and food processing.

International opportunities abound for the entrepreneur who is willing to reach beyond his or her country's border and comfort zone.

SOURCE: **www.usaid.gov/economic_growth/trdweb/oecd** (accessed February 1, 2001).

U.S. Exports to OECD in 1998
Country Distribution and Top Commodities

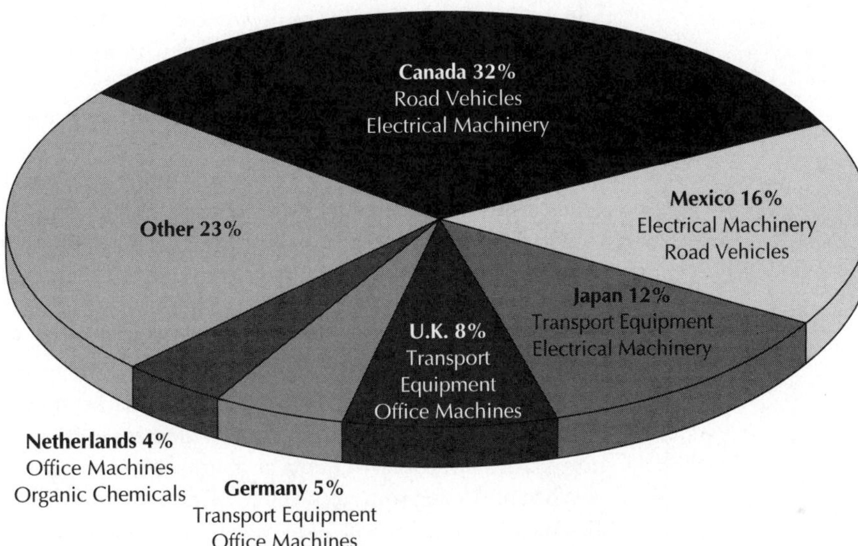

U.S. Imports to OECD in 1998
Country Distribution and Top Commodities

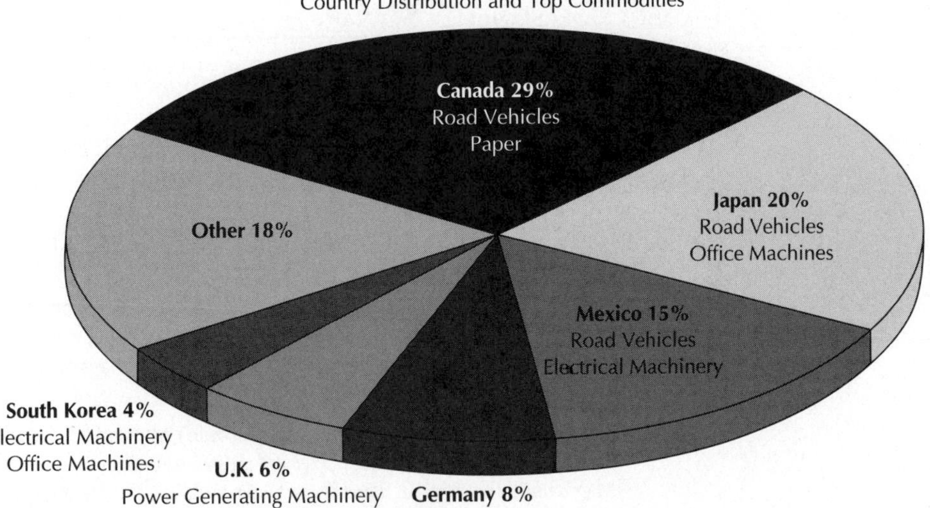

knowing a spreadsheet from a bed sheet. What about your accountant? What about the real estate broker who helped you with your search for a location? What about your business insurance specialist? What about your lawyer? What about your distributors? What about your competitors?

You can use your network to find other people who may help you. Show them your list of potential surprises and ask for their advice. Ask them for their ideas about what other surprises might be in store for you. If one of these persons gives you wonderful advice, consider putting him or her on your board of directors.

Sales Projections

One of the most challenging, and often the most difficult, steps in preparing financial statements is estimating sales for the first year of a new business. The thirteenth month becomes more manageable because you have a year of experience.

Marketing research is the key. The financial community wants to make sure that you spend a lot of time on your projections because it drives everything else. You also want to minimize surprises—even "good surprises" can raise havoc with a well-thought-out plan—if, for example, you receive ten times the orders you expected and simply don't yet have the resources to deal with them.

You have already conducted an industry overview. You may have identified total sales internationally, nationally, statewide, and in your service area. After factoring industry and local growth, determine which part of the market you can reasonably expect to penetrate in the first, second, third, fourth, and fifth years. Annual issues of trade magazines, census data, suppliers, and major newspapers often have already performed your secondary research. For your business plan, attach any appropriate printed data to your market research section in the appendix to prove and support your numbers. Fine-tune these numbers by showing your own research and including notes from industry experts that support your assumptions on projected sales. Each and every number you present in your business plan should have back-up support. When you list your competitors, estimate their market share and the part of their market that you have targeted.

Projections are well-documented estimates. A third party's estimate will have more value than yours, so quote as many sources as you can to prove your numbers.

When projecting your sales, you may want to consider doing high, low, and medium sales projections. This will allow you to make plans for your expenses and revenues based on various scenarios. Continuing on with our bookstore example, the ABA has provided average first-year bookstore projections and the following advice (Table 8.2):

Seasonality Scenario

Determining the inventory for the bookstore Know It All was fairly easy based on the information provided by the ABA. But now the owners of Know It All need to complete a seasonality scenario to determine monthly profit and loss and cash-flow projections. They talked with a local bookstore owner and he shared the following:

January (6.5 percent)

"January is an anticlimax to Christmas, but it's still busy because of gift certificates and exchanges. I run some good specials at the end of January, prior to taking yearly inventory. Even though sales are slowing down, I have to order new titles because publishers (our suppliers) are giving me advance notice on their spring lists."

February (4.5 percent) and March (5 percent)

"Very quiet. I take inventory, weed out stuff that didn't sell, send it back, and usually feel bad when I see the restocking fees. I meet publishers' reps who are out on the road pushing new titles. On March fifteenth, I have an Ides of March sale. Next year I'm planning a St. Patrick's Day tie-in."

April (5 percent)

TABLE 8.2

ABA Bookstore

Proforma Profit & Loss—Three Scenarios

	Low	Medium	High
Sales per square foot	$ 100	$ 125	$ 150
Sales Revenue	180,000	225,000	270,000
Less: Cost of Goods Sold*	108,000	135,000	162,000
Gross Margin	72,000	90,000	108,000
Less: Expenses			
Wages (1st year, 18%)	32,400	40,500	48,600
Rent ($14/square foot)	28,000	28,000	28,000
Advertising	3,600	4,500	5,400
Insurance	1,500	1,500	1,500
Postage	1,000	1,200	1,400
Conventions	1,000	1,000	1,000
Supplies	1,200	1,300	1,400
Telephone	1,200	1,300	1,400
Utilities	1,400	1,400	1,400
Taxes, Licenses, Fees	1,000	1,200	1,200
Depreciation	15,000	15,000	15,000
Payroll Taxes	2,500	3,200	3,850
Bank/Card Fees (1% of sales)	1,800	2,250	2,700
Professional Services	2,000	2,000	2,000
All Other Expenses	5,000	5,000	5,000
Total Expenses	$ 98,600	$109,350	$119,850
Net Profit or Loss	($ 26,600)	($ 19,350)	($ 11,850)

*NOTE: Assuming 40% discount.

It can be seen that even under the best sales projection, the first-year bookstore has an operating loss of $11,850; the loss with a medium sales projection would be $19,350; while under the worst scenario there is an anticipated loss of $26,600. In planning capital needs for a new bookstore, the anticipated operating losses during the first year should be taken into consideration. After a store has experienced an operating loss is not a good time to seek additional outside sources of capital, whether or not that loss is quite normal and anticipated. The bookstore owner must plan in advance how the capital depletion from the first year's operating loss will be covered. Cash-flow analysis gives a more accurate picture of what proportion of the first year's bottom-line loss must be replaced as working capital. For purposes of illustration, however, let us assume that the high sales projection's loss of $11,850 needs to be replaced. If this amount of capital is added to the preopening capital, the total amount of capital to be raised is:

(Preopening Capital) + (Year 1 Operating Loss) = (Total Capital)

$225,000 + $11,8505 = $236,850

SOURCE: Kate Wholey, Linda Miller, and Rosemary Hawkins, editors, *Manual on Bookselling: Practical Advice for the Bookstore Professionals,* 5th edition, American Booksellers Association, Tarrytown, NY, 1996.

"Still slow. We get a slight jump in sales after the tenth, mostly because spring vacations give some people time to read."

May (8 percent) and June (8 percent)

"Two holidays—Mother's Day and Father's Day—plus weddings and graduations give us our second-busiest season. Art books and gift editions do well, also encyclopedias and how-to's."

July (6 percent) and August (7 percent)

"We're not in a tourist area, and summers for us are slow. We sell mostly easy-to-read paperbacks and lots of Oprah Winfrey's book selections. Our minds, though, are on ordering books for Christmas."

September (9 percent)

"Back-to-school purchases. We're interviewing people for Christmas jobs and making last-minute purchases of gift items."

October (10 percent) and November (12 percent)

"The start of the busy season. Customers sense it, and we can feel the momentum. The rush is just around the corner. We usually hire more sales help at this time."

December (19 percent)

"The crush. Our computer does a great job of tracking sales. It's different every year, but with two years of great data gathering behind me, I am getting a feel for what really happens. And that helps us plan ahead for the next year."

After the first year of business, seasonal sales forecasting will become easier. Keep very careful records that first year, so that you'll know how your own peaks and valleys correlate with the seasonality of your selected industry. Many businesses are seasonal, and you'll need to develop strong control systems to manage your financial resources. Start now to identify alternative sources of credit and find ways to collect cash from customers before all your products or services are delivered.

PROFORMA MONTHLY INCOME AND CASH FLOW STATEMENTS

Income statements track revenue and expenses but don't tell the whole story. (Even a documentary movie is shot from only one angle at a time.) It's nice to watch paper profits, but you must also be alert to what is happening to real cash. Figure 8.1 shows the typical pattern of cash flows.

Income statements tell you when you're going to make a profit on paper. A cash-flow projection tells (1) whether or not you can pay bills, and (2) when you'll need cash infusions to keep going. Both of these projections are essential to the survival of your business. Some SBA worksheets include both on one statement.

More than sales are involved in projections; you also need to project times of collection and other time lags so you can get a feel for the way cash will flow through your business. You need to discover all expense categories involved with your business to be able to make proper projections. Forecasting your income is like project-

FIGURE 8.1
Cash Flow

This simple cash-flow diagram shows the typical time lag between paper profits and the flow of real profits. Plan ahead for this lag.

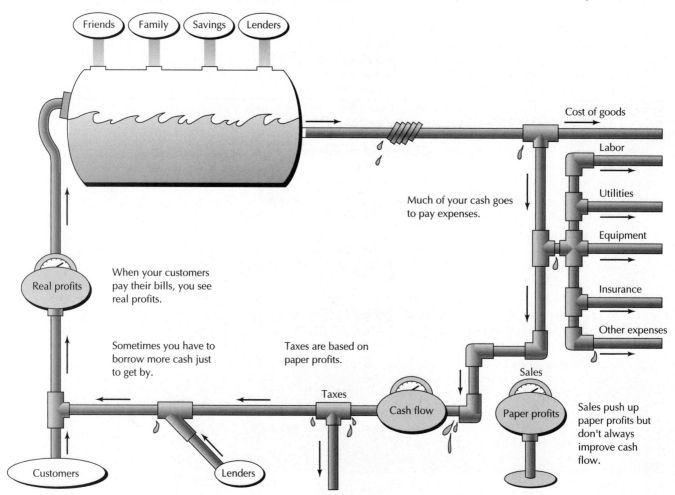

ing a moving picture of your business. If you're careful in how you prepare your numbers, that movie will be reasonably accurate.

Know It All's projections are based on ABA figures and local research. Advertising expenses are greater because of several very tough competitors. No salary or payroll expenses are included because Know It All will be managed by the owner who will not take a salary—"sweat equity." Please review how notes have been added to Know It All's proformas to explain the figures. Be sure you do the same on your proformas.

Review Know It All's projected monthly proforma income statement (Table 8.3) and quarterly forecasts for the second through fifth years (Table 8.4). Action Step 40

TABLE 8.3
Know It All Proforma Profit & Loss (Monthly)*

	July	Aug	Sept	Oct	Nov	Dec	Jan	Feb	Mar	Apr	May	June	Total
Sales	7,800	9,100	11,700	13,000	15,600	24,700	8,450	5,850	6,500	6,500	10,400	10,400	130,000
Cost of Goods Sold	5,070	5,915	7,605	8,450	10,140	16,055	5,495	3,800	4,225	4,225	6,760	6,760	8,450
Gross Profit	2,730	3,185	4,095	4,550	5,460	8,645	2,955	2,050	2,275	2,275	3,640	3,640	45,500
Expenses													
Rent		1,875	1,875	1,875	1,875	1,875	1,875	1,875	1,875	1,875	1,875	1,875	20,625
Utilities	200	200	200	200	200	200	200	200	200	200	200	200	2,400
Adv./PR/4%	310	365	470	520	625	990	340	235	260	260	415	415	5,205
Insurance	75	75	75	75	75	75	75	75	75	75	75	75	900
Supplies/1%	80	90	115	130	155	245	85	60	65	65	105	105	1,300
Misc./5%	390	455	585	650	780	1,235	425	295	325	325	520	520	6,505
Credit card fees	70	80	105	120	140	225	75	55	60	60	95	95	1,180
Loan interest													
Total Expenses	1,125	3,140	3,425	3,580	3,850	4,845	3,075	2,795	2,860	2,860	3,285	3,285	38,125
Net Profit/Loss	1,605	45	670	970	1,610	3,800	2120	2745	2585	2585	355	355	7,375

*Sales: the first-year forecast of $130,000 is based on industry information gathered by the owners ($10,031,300 sales space).
Cost of Goods Sold: Estimated at 65% of sales (includes all shipping).
Rent: 1.25 cents per square foot x 1500 square feet; no rent charged for the first month; the owners used the first month to get ready for their opening.
Utilities: Figures are estimates from the local utility company.
Advertising and Promotion: Estimated at 4% of sales based on information from other bookstore owners.
Insurance: $900 per year is the rate quoted by owners' insurance agent.
Supplies: Estimated at 1% of sales based on interviews.
Miscellaneous: Estimated at 5% of sales based on interviews; added a fudge factor to cover unexpected expenses.
Loan Interest: This represents interest on the line of credit at 1% per month of the unpaid balance.
Credit Card Fees: Projected on the basis of 30% of sales being credit-card sales; the credit card company charges 3%.

TABLE 8.4
Know It All Proforma Profit & Loss, 2nd-5th Years*

			2nd Year			3rd Year	4th Year	5th Year
	1st Qtr	2nd Qtr	3rd Qtr	4th Qtr	Total	Total	Total	Total
Sales	34,320	63,960	24,960	32,760	156,000	201,175	210,800	237,200
Cost of Goods Sold	22,310	41,575	16,225	21,295	101,405	137,020	137,020	154,180
Gross Profit	12,010	22,385	8,735	11,465	54,595	64,155	73,780	83,020
Expenses								
Rent	5,905	5,905	5,905	5,910	23,625	24,805	26,045	27,350
Utilities	630	630	630	630	2,520	2,645	2,780	2,920
Adv./PR	1,375	2,545	1,000	1,310	6,230	7,330	8,430	9,490
Insurance	235	235	235	240	945	990	1,040	1,090
Supplies	345	640	250	330	1,565	1,835	2,110	2,370
Misc.	1,785	3,200	1,250	1,640	7,875	9,215	10,540	11,860
Credit card fees	310	575	225	295	1,405	1,650	1,900	2,135
Loan interest								
Total Expenses	10,585	13,730	9,495	10,355	44,165	48,470	52,845	57,215
Net Profit/Loss	1,425	8,655	2760	1,110	10,430	15,685	20,935	25,805

*2nd year: 20% growth
3rd year: 17.5% growth
4th year: 15% growth
5th year: 12.5% growth

ACTION STEP 40

COMPLETE A PROFORMA PROFIT AND LOSS SCHEDULE

Write the scenario for a typical year in your business.

You can do part of the scenario with new eyes—just look around at obvious forces such as weather, heat, cold, time, and expense—and relate these to the life-cycle stage of your product, location, and competition.

You will have to glean other information from other small-business owners and from trade associations.

When does your selected industry collect money? (Before the sale? during? after? long after?) When will you have to pay for your inventory? What is the shortest time lag you could see between the time you pay for inventory and the time you receive money (payment, hard dollars) for the sale of that inventory?

What is the *longest* time lag? When will you declare a lag a bad debt?

If you are in manufacturing and have to alter, reshape, or rebuild raw materials into a product, what kind of time lag will there be?

Adapt Tables 8.5 and 8.6 for this action step. Generate your numbers for the year as follows:

1. Using data from trade associations and small business owners, forecast your sales for the year.
2. Figure your cost of goods sold and subtract that figure from sales. This gives you your gross profit.
3. Add up all expenses and subtract them from gross profit. This gives you the net profit before taxes.
4. Subtract taxes. (Uncle Sam uses what we might call "old eyes." You will be taxed on paper profit, so you have to build in this figure.) The figure you arrive at is your net profit after taxes for the year.

leads you through a monthly proforma income statement. Be sure to include several cash flow and proforma scenarios.

Cash-flow projections are a tool used to help you control money. The lifeblood of any business is cash flow. Many businesses are profitable but fail because of cash-flow problems. Without completing proforma cash flows, entrepreneurs can truly underestimate their cash needs and fail early on.

Table 8.7 illustrates Know It All's proforma cash flow for 12 months. Action Step 41 asks you to project your firm's cash flow. Table 8.8 will help you to complete your cash-flow proforma.

Review Know It All's proformas. What would you recommend to the entrepreneur? Could the owners increase sales dramatically to improve cash flow and income? Could they provide additional services to increase cash flow such as renting out the store in the evening for book or investment clubs? Could they sublet the premises for after-hours private speakers to conduct seminars? Could the owners run a special youth reading and arts program in the afternoon to bring in additional cash? To increase cash flow, look beyond the initial product or service and extend your facilities and products.

Are you willing to put in sweat equity? Are your projections realistic? Would you be able to forego taking a salary for a few months if serious cash flow problems occur? When you have completed your projections, show the results to an expert. Ask him or her if they look accurate. It's better to know the truth now, while you're working on paper; paper truth is a lot easier on the pocketbook than reality.

BREAK-EVEN ANALYSIS

Knowing a few key numbers can help to avoid painful surprises. If you know your costs (variable and fixed) and your gross sales, you can use a break-even formula that will tell when you will start making money. A break-even analysis is useful at start-up time, when you have completed your income and expense projections, and when you are considering launching a new product or service (Figure 8.2).

A small manufacturing company was completing a plan for its second year of operation. Its first-year sales were \$177,000, and a sales breakdown for the last three months of their first year looked like this:

October	\$24,000
November	29,000
December	15,000
	\$68,000

The owners took a look at the numbers and called in a consultant to help. The consultant gathered information from sales reps, owners, and customers and then projected that sales for the second year would be a whopping \$562,000. The owners reacted with disbelief.

"You're crazy," they said. "That's more than three times what we did last year."

The consultant smiled. "Didn't you tell me you were going to add three new products?"

"Yes."

"And new reps in March, June, and September?"

"Yes, but—"

"And what about those big promotions you've got planned?"

"Well, sure, we've planned some promotions, but that doesn't get us anywhere near three times last year."

"All right," the consultant said. "Can you do \$275,000?"

The owners got into a huddle. Based on the fourth quarter, they were sure they could stay even, and four times \$68,000 (the fourth-quarter sales) was \$272,000. They knew they had to do better than last year.

"Sure, no problem. We can do \$275,000."

"All right," said the consultant, rolling out his break-even chart. "I've just projected \$562,000 in sales for the year. To break even, you only need \$275,000."

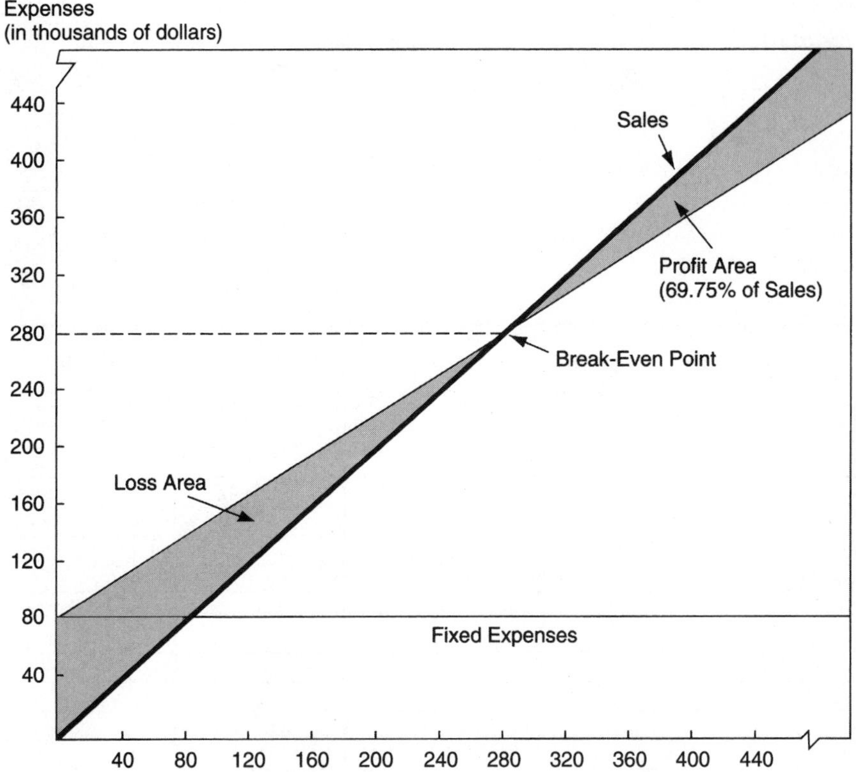

FIGURE 8.2

A simple break-even chart like this may be all it takes to convince your banker that a small loan now means big profits later.

Projected sales:	\$562,000
Projected fixed expenses:	\$82,750
Projected variable expenses:	\$392,000
Total sales needed to break even:	$\text{Fixed Expenses} \div \left(1 - \frac{\text{Variable expenses}}{\text{Sales}}\right)$
	$\$83{,}000 \div \left(1 - \frac{\$392{,}000}{\$562{,}000}\right)$
	\$83,000 ÷ (1 – .6975)
	\$83,000 ÷ .3025
	\$274,380
Break-even range:	\$270,000 to \$280,000

"Hey," the owners said, "we're projecting \$90,000 the first quarter."

"I'm glad you're thinking my way," the consultant said. "Because if you don't believe you can reach a goal, you'll never get there." He paused, then said, "By the way, that \$90,000 is three times what you did your first quarter last year!"

"Just tell us what to do," the owners said.

Based on a careful cash-flow analysis, the consultant determined that the company would need to borrow money. The owners knew their business—industry trends, product line, competitors, sales and promotion plans—but what banker would believe such growth? The key to getting the loan would be to convince the banker that the company could do better than break even. The consultant prepared a break-even chart on the \$562,000 sales figure (see Figure 8.2). Note in the chart that after \$280,000 in sales, the firm will have passed its break-even point and will be earning a profit.

Their banker granted the loan, realizing the company could pass the break-even point with room to spare. The key, as usual in business, was a combination of numbers and human confidence.

TABLE 8.5A
Proforma Profit & Loss (Worksheet)

($)	Month 1	Month 2	Month 3	Month 4	Month 5	Month 6
Net Sales						
COST OF SALES:						
Goods/Materials						
Production Exp						
Direct Labor						
Gross Profit						
Expenses:						
GENERAL & ADMIN						
Payroll Expense						
Payroll Taxes						
Travel/Entertainment						
Rent/Util/Tel						
Ins/Legal/Acct						
Office & Supply						
Equipment Exp						
Credit/Collect						
Maintenance						
Auto/Truck Exp						
Other						
SELLING EXPENSE						
Payroll Expense						
Sales Commission						
Advertising						
Travel/Entertainment						
Auto Expenses						
Other						
OTHER EXPENSES						
Interest						
Depreciation						
Total Expenses						
OTHER INCOME						
Interest Income						
Other						
PROFIT (LOSS)						
Income Taxes						
NET PROFIT/LOSS						

TABLE 8.5B
Proforma Profit & Loss (Worksheet)

($)	Month 7	Month 8	Month 9	Month 10	Month 11	Month 12	First Year Totals
Net Sales							
COST OF SALES:							
Goods/Materials							
Production Exp							
Direct Labor							
Gross Profit							
Expenses:							
GENERAL & ADMIN							
Payroll Expense							
Payroll Taxes							
Travel/Entertainment							
Rent/Util/Tel							
Ins/Legal/Acct							
Office & Supply							
Equipment Exp							
Credit/Collect							
Maintenance							
Auto/Truck Exp							
Other							
SELLING EXPENSE							
Payroll Expense							
Sales Commission							
Advertising							
Travel/Entertainment							
Auto Expenses							
Other							
OTHER EXPENSES							
Interest							
Depreciation							
Total Expenses							
OTHER INCOME							
Interest Income							
Other							
PROFIT (LOSS)							
Income Taxes							
NET PROFIT/LOSS							

ACTION STEP 41

PROJECTING CASH FLOW

If you don't have access to a computer and an electronic spreadsheet program, use the spreadsheet shown in Table 8.8 to project your cash flow across the first year of your business.

1. Write down the amount of cash you'll start the year with as the amount on hand (or in the bank) at the beginning of the first month.
2. For each month, enter the amount of cash you'll receive from sales or accounts receivable.
3. Enter any loans in the month you receive the cash from the lender.
4. Total the previous items to learn how much cash will be available each month.
5. List all disbursements (cash going out). Spread these out, too.
6. Subtract disbursements from cash available for each month. This gives you a monthly cash flow. Carry this figure forward (to point one for each succeeding month).

Now examine your work. Have you explored the quirks of seasonality? Have you discovered the minimum and maximum time lags between when you make a sale and when you get paid (in cash) for that sale? Does the picture look accurate? Have an expert check it for you.

Try the "what-if" test: If your cash flow picture looks good, introduce a couple of what-ifs. What surprise expenses could throw a monkey wrench into your new business?

TABLE 8.6

Proforma Profit & Loss Second Year/Summary (Worksheet)

	Second Year				
($,000's)	**Quarter 1**	**Quarter 2**	**Quarter 3**	**Quarter 4**	**Year Total**
Net Sales					
COST OF SALES:					
Goods/Materials					
Production Exp					
Direct Labor					
Gross Profit					
Expenses:					
GENERAL & ADMIN					
Payroll Expense					
Payroll Taxes					
Travel/Entertainment					
Rent/Util/Tel					
Ins/Legal/Acct					
Office & Supply					
Equipment Exp					
Credit/Collect					
Maintenance					
Auto/Truck Exp					
Other					
SELLING EXPENSE					
Payroll Expense					
Sales Commission					
Advertising					
Travel/Entertainment					
Auto Expenses					
Other					
OTHER EXPENSES					
Interest					
Depreciation					
Total Expenses					
OTHER INCOME					
Interest Income					
Other					
PROFIT (LOSS)					
Income Taxes					
NET PROFIT/LOSS					

TABLE 8.7

Proforma Cash Flow for Know It All

	July	Aug	Sept	Oct	Nov	Dec	Jan	Feb	Mar	Apr	May	June
Cash on hand	1,900	3,945	100	145	610	5,715	21,070	20,990	20,360	22,030	21,200	20,950
Sales	7,800	9,100	11,700	13,000	15,600	24,700	8,450	5,850	6,500	6,500	10,400	10,400
Less: Credit fees	270	280	2105	2120	2140	2225	275	255	260	260	295	295
Loan												
Total	9,360	12,965	12,965	13,025	16,070	30,190	29,445	26,785	26,800	28,470	31,505	31,255
Disbursements												
Book purchases	4,255	9,800	9,305	8,030	6,720	4,575	5,080	3,760	2,045	4,545	7,440	8,420
Rent		1,875	1,875	1,875	1,875	1,875	1,875	1,875	1,875	1,875	1,875	1,875
Utilities	200	200	200	200	200	200	200	200	200	200	200	200
Adv./PR/4%	310	365	470	520	625	990	340	235	260	260	415	415
Insurance	450											
Supplies/1%	80	90	115	130	155	245	85	60	65	65	105	105
Misc./5%	390	455	585	650	780	1,235	425	295	325	325	520	520
Interest				10								
Loan payment				1,000								
Total	5,685	12,865	12,550	12,415	10,355	9,120	8,455	6,425	4,770	7,270	10,555	11,535
Net Cash Flow	3,945	100	145	610	5,715	21,070	20,990	20,360	22,030	21,200	20,950	19,720

TABLE 8.8A
Proforma Cash Flow (Worksheet)

($)	Month 1	Month 2	Month 3	Month 4	Month 5	Month 6
Cash Sources:						
FROM OPERATIONS						
Cash Sales						
A/R Collections						
Other Cash Collections						
OTHER SOURCES						
Interest Income						
Loan from Bank						
Investment						
Subtotal						
Cash Uses:						
TO OPERATIONS						
Accts Payable						
Goods/Materials						
Services						
Petty Cash						
Payroll Expense						
Sales Commission						
Travel/Entertainment						
Rent/Util/Tel						
Advertising						
Auto/Truck Exp						
Maintenance						
Equipment Exp						
Ins/Legal/Acct						
Miscellaneous						
OTHER USES						
Interest Exp						
Dividends						
Loan Payoff						
Investor Payoff						
Reserve for Tax						
Subtotal						
Cash Incr/Decr						
Beginning Bal						
Ending Balance						

LEAVING A PAPER TRAIL

If you're the typical entrepreneur, you're not real big on details and you're very busy; nonetheless, you know it's important to keep good records. One solution for a short period of time is shoebox accounting—a simple procedure that will give your accountant or bookkeeper a chance to put together financial statements and prepare your tax returns. The point of this system is to leave a paper trail. Be sure to order *Starting a Business and Keeping Records*, Publication 583 from the IRS.

How to Implement the System

Open a business checking account—even if you are just doing business under your own name. Deposit all business income into this account, making a note in the checkbook (or check register, or computerized check-writing program) as to the source of the deposit; for example, "Sat., 10/21, Swap Meet Sales." Write a check for

TABLE 8.8B
Proforma Cash Flow (Worksheet)

($)	Month 7	Month 8	Month 9	Month 10	Month 11	Month 12	First Year Totals
Cash Sources:							
FROM OPERATIONS							
Cash Sales							
A/R Collections							
Other Cash Collections							
OTHER SOURCES							
Interest Income							
Loan from Bank							
Investment							
Subtotal							
Cash Uses:							
TO OPERATIONS							
Accts Payable							
Goods/Materials							
Services							
Petty Cash							
Payroll Expense							
Sales Commission							
Travel/Entertainment							
Rent/Util/Tel							
Advertising							
Auto/Truck Exp							
Maintenance							
Equipment Exp							
Ins/Legal/Acct							
Miscellaneous							
OTHER USES							
Interest Exp							
Dividends							
Loan Payoff							
Investor Payoff							
Reserve for Tax							
Subtotal							
Cash Incr/Decr							
Beginning Bal							
Ending Balance							

TABLE 8.8C
Proforma Cash Flow (Worksheet)

	Second Year			
	Quarter 1	Quarter 2	Quarter 3	Quarter 4
Cash Sources:				
FROM OPERATIONS				
Cash Sales				
A/R Collections				
Other Cash Collections				
OTHER SOURCES				
Interest Income				
Loan from Bank				
Investment				
Subtotal				
Cash Uses:				
TO OPERATIONS				
Accts Payable				
Goods/Materials				
Services				
Petty Cash				
Payroll Expense				
Sales Commission				
Travel/Entertainment				
Rent/Util/Tel				
Advertising				
Auto/Truck Exp				
Maintenance				
Equipment Exp				
Ins/Legal/Acct				
Miscellaneous				
OTHER USES				
Interest Exp				
Dividends				
Loan Payoff				
Investor Payoff				
Reserve for Tax				
Subtotal				
Cash Incr/Decr				
Beginning Bal				
Ending Balance				

each business expenditure, even if it's only $1. Enter what the check was for. Get a receipt and write the check number on the receipt. During the first few weeks, toss everything into a shoebox. When the shoebox begins to fill up, purchase an alphabetical file folder—such as a brown accordion-style folder—and file all receipts there according to some system. (Ask your accountant or bookkeeper.)

If you must pay for items with cash, use a petty cash box or a bank bag. Get a receipt for every cash purchase also, and clip all the receipts for cash purchases together. When you have accumulated enough cash purchases—perhaps $10 to $20—write yourself a check, being careful to record the check number on each cash receipt.

Together, the business checkbook and the file folder are the paper trail you leave for your accountant or bookkeeper—and the IRS. This trail could save your neck in an IRS audit. The system is a step up from the "pocket" system—that is, in one pocket and out the other—and only a stop-gap for a very short time until you move into a one-write or computerized bookkeeping system such as Quikbooks.

Financial Ratios

Calculating a few simple ratios will help you analyze how your venture compares with other businesses in your selected industry. Lenders use ratios as measuring devices to determine the risks associated with lending.

To the entrepreneur, ratios are control tools for maintaining financial efficiencies.

Current Ratio

Does the business have enough money to meet current debt? Have you anticipated a safety margin for losses resulting from uncollectible funds owed to the business? Most start-up ventures are undercapitalized.

The current ratio is computed from the balance sheet. Divide current assets by current liabilities. If current assets are $200,000 and current liabilities are $100,000, you have a current ratio of 2.

Many lenders see this as a minimum, and like to see that you have at least twice as much invested as you owe. The current ratio is the most widely used method to determine the financial health of a business.

Liquidity Ratio

The liquidity ratio tells you if you have cash on hand or assets that can be converted into cash quickly to pay your debts. The more liquidity, the better. An untapped credit line will help beef up your liquidity.

Return on Investment

Return on investment (ROI) is the favorite tool of investors and venture capitalists. This ratio shows the return expressed as a percentage of their investment. Investors and entrepreneurs want the highest profit (return) for the least amount of money invested.

Most bankers use the ratio studies published by Robert Morris and Associates. Every lending officer has a current copy, as do most business libraries. This publication, considered the bible for statement analysis, covers more than 200 types of businesses. Also in your library or available at a nominal cost is *Dun & Bradstreet Business Information Systems.* This annual publication provides key ratios on more than 100 businesses. The U.S. Small Business Administration has key ratio reports for several industries. Trade associations often provide the most comprehensive work on financial ratios. Some are a bit out of date, but most provide specific and very valuable data. Additional financial ratios are shown in Table 8.9.

TABLE 8.9
Financial Ratios

Ratio Name	How to Calculate	What It Means in Dollars and Cents
Balance Sheet Ratios		
Current	Current Assets / Current Liabilities	Measures solvency: the number of dollars in current assets for every $1 in current liabilities *Example:* A current ratio of 1.76 means that for every $1 of current liabilities, the firm has $1.76 in current assets with which to pay it.
Quick	Cash + Accounts Receivable / Current Liabilities	Measures liquidity: the number of dollars in cash and accounts receivable for each $1 in current liabilities *Example:* A quick ratio of 1.14 means that for every $1 of current liabilities, the firm has $1.14 in cash and accounts receivable with which to pay it.
Cash	Cash / Current Liabilities	Measures liquidity more strictly: the number of dollars in cash for every $1 in current liabilities *Example:* A cash ratio of 0.17 means that for every $1 of current liabilities, the firm has $0.17 in cash with which to pay it.
Debt-to-worth	Total Liabilities / Net Worth	Measures financial risk: the number of dollars of debt owed for every $1 in net worth *Example:* A debt-to-worth ratio of 1.05 means that for every $1 of net worth the owners have invested, the firms owes $1.05 of debt to its creditors.
Income Statement Ratios		
Gross margin	Gross Margin / Sales	Measures profitability at the gross profit level: the number of dollars of gross margin produced for every $1 of sales *Example:* A gross margin ratio of 34.4% means that for every $1 of sales, the firm produces 34.4 cents of gross margin.
Net margin	Net Profit before Tax / Sales	Measures profitability at the net profit level: the number of dollars of net profit produced for every $1 of sales *Example:* A net margin ratio of 2.9% means that for every $1 of sales, the firm produces 2.9 cents of net margin.
Overall Efficiency Ratios		
Sales-to-assets	Sales / Total Assets	Measures the efficiency of total assets in generating sales: the number of dollars in sales produced for every $1 invested in total assets *Example:* A sales-to-assets ratio of 2.35 means that for every $1 dollar invested in total assets, the firm generates $2.35 in sales.
Return on assets	Net Profit before Tax / Total Assets	Measures the efficiency of total assets in generating net profit: the number of dollars in net profit produced for every $1 invested in total assets *Example:* A return on assets ratio of 7.1% means that for every $1 invested in assets, the firm is generating 7.1 cents in net profit before tax.
Return on investment	Net Profit before Tax / Net Worth	Measures the efficiency of net worth in generating net profit: the number of dollars in net profit produced for every $1 invested in net worth *Example:* A return on investment ratio of 16.1% means that for every $1 invested in net worth, the firm is generating 16.1 cents in net profit before tax.
Specific Efficiency Ratios		
Inventory turnover	Cost of Goods Sold / Inventory	Measures the rate at which inventory is being used on an annual basis *Example:* An inventory turnover ratio of 9.81 means that the average dollar volume of inventory is used up almost ten times during the fiscal year.
Inventory turn-days	360 / Inventory Turnover	Converts the inventory turnover ratio into an average "days inventory on hand" figure *Example:* An inventory turn-days ratio of 37 means that the firm keeps an average of 37 days of inventory on hand throughout the year.
Accounts receivable turnover	Sales / Accounts Receivable	Measures the rate at which accounts receivable are being collected on an annual basis *Example:* An accounts receivable turnover ratio of 8.00 means that the average dollar volume of accounts receivable are collected eight times during the year.
Average collection period	360 / Accounts Receivable Turnover	Converts the accounts receivable turnover ratio into the average number of days the firm must wait for its accounts receivable to be paid *Example:* An average collection period ratio of 45 means that it takes the firm 45 days on average to collect its receivables.
Accounts payable turnover	Cost of Goods Sold / Accounts Payable	Measures the rate at which accounts payable are being paid on an annual basis. *Example:* An accounts payable turnover ratio of 12.04 means that the average dollar volume of accounts payable are paid about 123a year.
Average payment period	360 / Accounts Payable Turnover	Converts the accounts payable turnover ratio into the average number of days a firm takes to pay its accounts payable. *Example:* An accounts payable turnover ratio of 30 means that it takes the firm 30 days on average to pay its bills.

SOURCE: *Entrepreneurship: A Contemporary Approach,* Donald Kuratko. © 1998. pp. 280-282. Reprinted with permission of Thomson Learning.

Summary

Not surprisingly, many entrepreneurs find it difficult to project numbers for their businesses. There are several explanations for this:

They're action people who are in a hurry; they don't think they have time to sit down and think.

They're creative; their strengths are greater in the innovation area than in the justification area.

They tend to think in visual terms, rather than in terms of numbers or words.

They believe they can't fail.

Nonetheless, business is a numbers game, and despite the entrepreneur's feelings about numbers and projections, survival in the marketplace depends on having the right numbers in the right color of ink. This chapter should help you get those kinds of numbers down on paper.

The point behind projecting numbers is to make the numbers as realistic as possible. You need to relate each projection to your specific business and to industry standards, and then to *document* them (tell where they came from) in your business plan. The case studies and examples in this chapter will help you make your projections believable to your banker and to yourself.

That is the key. Your numbers may seem reasonable to you, but you must make them seem reasonable to others as well. You make them believable by keeping them realistic and by documenting them properly.

What you don't need during the start-up phase is expensive surprises that knock you and your business for a loop. So, before you open your doors, you need to have anticipated as many potential unpleasant surprises as possible and have a plan of action for each one of them. For example, what will you do if...

your anchor tenant leaves?

your Yellow Pages ad stinks or you miss the deadline?

the customer that accounts for 75 percent of your business declares bankruptcy?

Expecting and *planning for* the unexpected can make the difference between life and death in business. Looking closely at your present assets and liabilities—by developing a personal financial statement—and calculating the opportunity costs of going into business for yourself will help you eliminate some surprises and may even cause you to question whether you're truly ready to take the plunge. Just remember two things: No one can anticipate everything, and it will probably cost more and take longer than your planning indicates.

Think Points For Success

- It's cheaper to make mistakes on a spreadsheet before you go into business.
- When you work out numbers for your business plan, hit the return-on-investment section with underlines.
- When you visit your banker to ask for money, make sure you know how much you're going to need for the long run.
- Projecting will help control the variables of your business—numbers, employees, promotion mix, product mix, and the peaks and valleys of seasonality.
- At the very *least* leave a "shoebox" paper trail of your business dealings so that a professional accountant or bookkeeper can bail you out if you get into trouble. Hire an accountant as soon as possible. He or she will save you money!
- Cash flow is king!
- Walk away if it isn't going to work financially. There will always be new opportunities.

Key Points from Another View

Deciding to Grow—Street Smarts

When a business is successful, it's only natural to want to expand it, but be careful: bigger isn't always better.

I've often noted that failure is a great teacher. When you fail in business, you can look back, see what you did wrong, and learn the appropriate lesson.

Success is another matter. It's often difficult, if not impossible, to figure out why a particular business concept clicks. You may be able to list a number of important factors, but you still won't necessarily know exactly what combination of them came together at the right moment and in the right proportions to make the business take off.

That's worth bearing in mind when you're deciding how you're going to take your business to the next level in sales. If you don't really know what's driving your success, you have to be careful about the strategy you adopt. There's a risk, after all, that you may accidentally undermine whatever made your company successful in the first place.

Consider a friend of mine who owns one of the hottest little stores around these days. For purposes of the column, I'll call him Seymour and his store Hot Pants. It's a tiny shop—about 1250 square feet—located in a suburban strip mall; it specializes in jeans and casual clothing, mainly for young women and teenaged girls. From that one location, Seymour racks up several million dollars a year in sales, giving him one of the highest sales-per-square-foot figures in his segment of the retail clothing industry.

For Seymour, the shop has been a dream come true. A self-taught businessman, he'd had several previous ventures that did well enough, but none of them took off the way Hot Pants did following its launch in 1994. His plan, he says, is to grow the business and sell it in five years or so. Toward that end, he's opened a second Hot Pants, in a town about 60 miles away from the first store. He also has a discount store, where he sells his old and discontinued inventory.

A couple of months ago I got a call from Seymour, who said he had to see the big opportunity that had come along, and he wanted my advice.

It turned out that the space next to the original Hot Pants was becoming vacant. Seymour wanted to lease it, knock down the wall, and double the size of his store. He figured he could generate between $1 million and $2 million in additional sales pretty much overnight. What did I think?

Now, you have to understand that Hot Pants is a very crowded place. On most days there are lines at the cash registers and the dressing rooms. Somehow, Seymour has managed to generate tremendous buzz among middle-class girls a certain age—say, 13 to 18 years old—and large numbers of them show up on a regular basis, not only to shop but to socialize with their friends.

That's good for the buzz, but Seymour thought he was losing a significant amount of business from customers who didn't want to wait in line or deal with the crowds. He figured he could solve the problem by expanding.

I was skeptical. For one thing, I wasn't sure he could make enough additional profit to justify the investment. "What does the landlord want?" I asked. Seymour said the landlord wanted him to give up his old lease and sign a new one for the combined space at the current market rate. Because rates have increased since he signed his original lease, he'd wind up paying about 25 percent more on his old space, in addition to the rent for the new space. He'd also have to put up "key money"—a sort of signing bonus for the landlord. Then there was the cost of fixing up the new space, carrying additional inventory, and hiring more staff.

"You have to look at the effect on your margins," I said. Seymour agreed. Seymour went through the numbers. It quickly became clear that he'd need more than $1 million in additional sales just to break even on his investment.

And could he, in fact, count on getting those sales? I had my doubts. A specialty-clothing store is not a restaurant. When a would-be diner walks out of restaurant because the wait is too long, that sale is probably lost. Why? Because it almost always goes to a competitor. I wasn't convinced, however, that the same thing happened when Seymour's customers decided against waiting. When you have a hot store, people come partly because they want to say they bought from you. They're looking for prestige and merchandise. My guess was most Hot Pants' customers who left because of the crowds would simply return when the store was less busy.

In that case, I pointed out, Seymour was losing few, if any, sales because of overcrowding. He'd saturated his marketplace. Everybody who wanted to shop at Hot Pants already did. "Well, then, maybe I'll bring in new lines," Seymour said "like for young guys."

That's what I was afraid of. To justify his investment, Seymour might be tended to change his concept. "You're talking about a whole new business," I said. "You could be jeopardizing what you already have. Maybe the girls want to be alone."

The truth is, Seymour doesn't know why his business is so successful, and nor do I. It could be the music he plays or the quality of his staff or the store's name or his own personality. Most likely, it's some combination of those things and a dozen other factors—perhaps even the lack of space. The kids may like being jammed together. They may not mind waiting in line to use a dressing room. All Seymour knows for sure is that right now he's blowing away all the standard projections for a business of his type, size, and location. His sales are two and a half times the amount anyone would have predicted for a jeans store in a strip mall with limited foot traffic.

You can't explain that kind of success. You can only recognize it, respect it, and handle it with care. Seymour's most valuable asset is the brand he's created; by doubling the size of his store, he's taking a chance that he'll inadvertently devalue the brand. It's a risk that, in my view at least, is way out of proportion to the potential reward.

I'm not saying that Seymour shouldn't grow his business. He already has a second Hot Pants up and running. It hasn't yet matched the performance of the first store, but it probably just needs time.

So what should Seymour do? I urged him to think about starting a third Hot Pants. I suggested he choose a location near enough to the original store that local kids would have heard the buzz but far enough away that they wouldn't already be regular customers. If the new store did well, Seymour would have a proven concept that he could sell in five years to someone interested in taking it national. If the spin-off failed, well, at least he wouldn't have damaged his core business.

But Seymour wasn't looking for that type of advice. He mainly wanted to know whether I thought he was crazy to double the size of the original Hot Pants. "Do you think I'll got out of business?" he asked. "No," I said, " but I think you'll hurt yourself."

Seymour didn't care—or maybe he simply disagreed. In any case he plans to go ahead with his expansion, and that may be the right decision for him personally even if it's wrong for the business. It's much easier to expand an existing store than to start a new one. It's also less expensive. Seymour already works 6 to 7 days a week, putting in long hours, and he's a guy who likes to have a direct control of operations. So he may be happier with a larger main store than with a third smaller one.

I'm just afraid he'll lose some of the value he's worked so hard to build. The one time I hope I'm wrong.

SOURCE: Norm Brodsky, **www.inc.com/incmagazine/columns/streetsmarts** (accessed May 30, 2001).

CHAPTER 9

Shaking the Money Tree

Locating Hard Cash

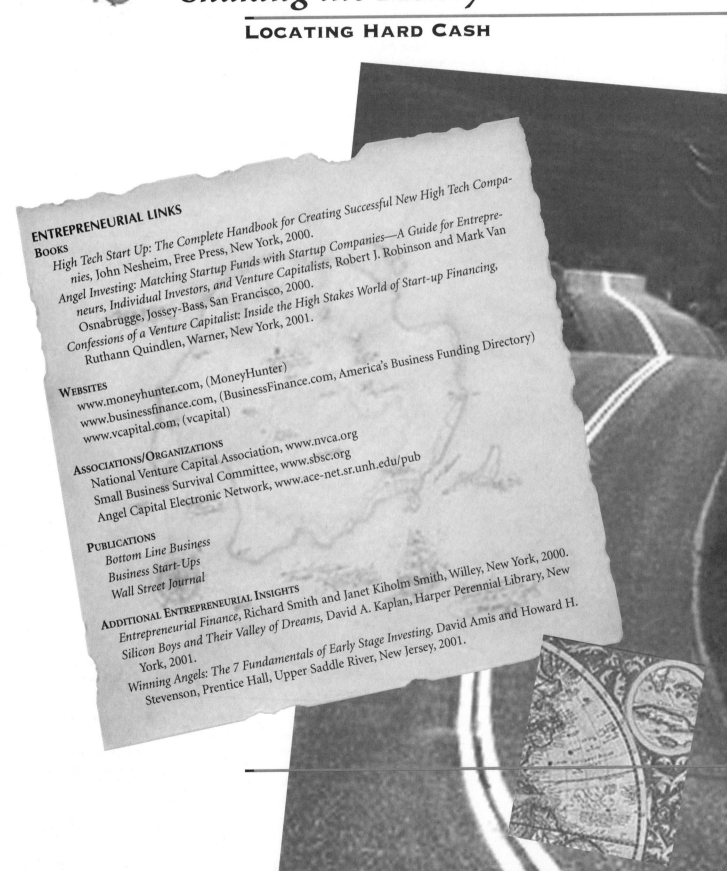

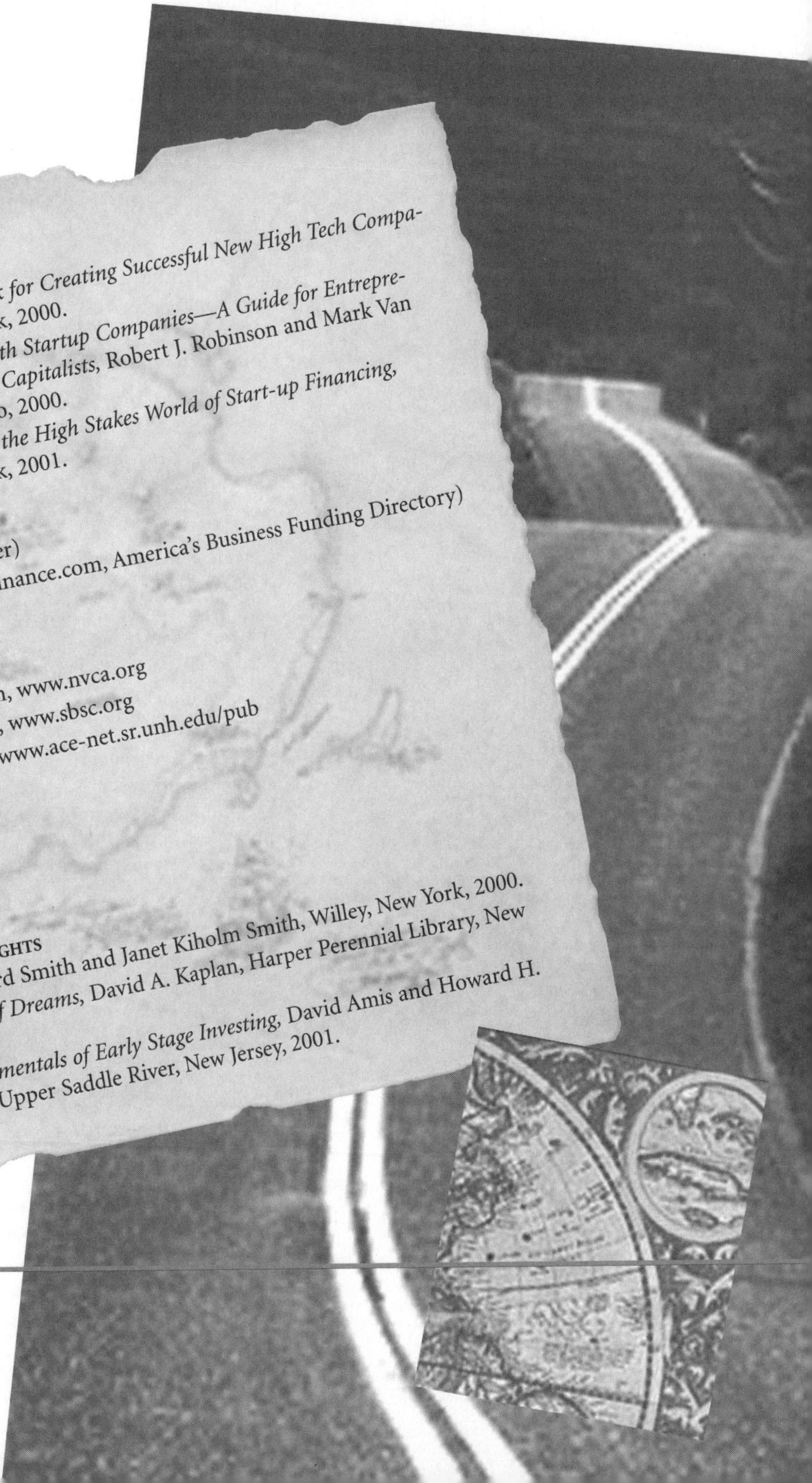

ENTREPRENEURIAL LINKS

Books

High Tech Start Up: The Complete Handbook for Creating Successful New High Tech Companies, John Nesheim, Free Press, New York, 2000.

Angel Investing: Matching Startup Funds with Startup Companies—A Guide for Entrepreneurs, Individual Investors, and Venture Capitalists, Robert J. Robinson and Mark Van Osnabrugge, Jossey-Bass, San Francisco, 2000.

Confessions of a Venture Capitalist: Inside the High Stakes World of Start-up Financing, Ruthann Quindlen, Warner, New York, 2001.

Websites

www.moneyhunter.com, (MoneyHunter)

www.businessfinance.com, (BusinessFinance.com, America's Business Funding Directory)

www.vcapital.com, (vcapital)

Associations/Organizations

National Venture Capital Association, www.nvca.org

Small Business Survival Committee, www.sbsc.org

Angel Capital Electronic Network, www.ace-net.sr.unh.edu/pub

Publications

Bottom Line Business

Business Start-Ups

Wall Street Journal

Additional Entrepreneurial Insights

Entrepreneurial Finance, Richard Smith and Janet Kiholm Smith, Willey, New York, 2000.

Silicon Boys and Their Valley of Dreams, David A. Kaplan, Harper Perennial Library, New York, 2001.

Winning Angels: The 7 Fundamentals of Early Stage Investing, David Amis and Howard H. Stevenson, Prentice Hall, Upper Saddle River, New Jersey, 2001.

Learning Objectives

- Discover your risk tolerance.
- Determine your credit situation.
- Explore credit card usage and risks for your business.
- Understand inherent risks in borrowing from friends and family.
- Scour the lending arena for money to fund your new business.
- Review strategies for approaching bankers.
- Explore SBDC, SBA, state, and local lending programs.
- Locate angels.
- Explore vendor financing.

Would it sound too easy if we told you to go out and simply shake a money tree to secure financing for your business? Yes, of course. You know it will not be that easy. First you must become familiar with the world of money. Then you must learn to tell the forest from the trees. And then you must find the right branch. Once you've accomplished these things, you might be surprised how money turns up when you shake the right branch.

Looking for Money: Hawkins Case Study—Surgery Shunt

The Prototype

Don Hawkins started his work life as a model maker in a large medical manufacturing firm. Don had talent. His fellow workers both envied and admired him because, although they fussed around with trial and error, he got it right the first time.

Margo McKay, a product manager at Don's firm, often sought out Don when she needed help on a glitch that slowed production. One day, over a cup of coffee, Margo confided in Don.

"I've got this customer," Margo said. "He wants a special design."

"What's the gizmo?"

"A wound drainage device."

"Hmm. What size?"

"Five millimeters."

"Who's the customer?" Don asked.

"He's a surgeon. A friend of mine."

"If it's microsurgery," Don said. "I'm way behind."

"Are you interested?"

"Let me do some reading, see what I can come up with."

It took Don four days to comb through the literature on microsurgery. It took him three days to develop the prototype. A week later, they had coffee, and Don revealed the prototype to Margo. She was wild with joy. Because she understood a winner when she saw one, Margo revealed her plan: They would quit their jobs; they would put together a venture team; they would make millions.

The Team

In the next few weeks they recruited Bob Bernstein, a production supervisor, and Nancy Jones, the best salesperson in the company. Before they got too deep into dreams and celebrations, Margo warned the group they'd need cash. To get cash, they needed investors. To get investors, they needed a Business Plan.

Margo, who had put together several marketing plans, was weak on finance. Bob Bernstein, the production man, was weak on marketing and sales. Nancy understood people, but, as she admitted over a cup of coffee: "I'm confessing. I need a videotape to tell me how to program my videocassette recorder."

To keep the weak spots to a minimum and to maximize their strengths, all four members of the venture team enrolled in a college course titled "The Weekend Entrepreneur: Writing Your Business Plan." The system worked. Over the next six weekends, they cranked out a Business Plan. It was bulletproof. It gave them the confidence they needed.

Don, especially, was amazed at how much they already knew. Writing the plan helped them pull together their ideas. Organizing on paper made them realize they would need $1,000,000 in start-up capital to make it through the first 12 months of their venture.

The Money

Each partner had to come up with $250,000, a quarter of the first-year's seed money. Margo McKay refinanced her house. Don tapped his Uncle Marvin, who was worth several million. Nancy got two investments of $125,000 each from a couple of go-getter doctors. Bob Bernstein borrowed from his credit union and cashed in two life insurance policies.

On a sunny day in June they said goodbye forever to the corporate womb. Their destination was a small warehouse. The rent was cheap; the security great. The microsurgery trade show was 62 days away. For a piece of the corporate pie, a shrewd attorney waived his fee for doing the patent work. With the "patent pending" in hand, production began on Don's prototype.

The trade show proved to be a goldmine. On opening day, their booth was swamped. News got around about their device. By the end of the first day, orders for the device exceeded their first-year sales forecast.

The best deal came from Surgery Unlimited, an old-line medical manufacturer, and small competitor of their former employer. Surgery Unlimited's president offered them $1,500,000 for a 2-year deal on exclusive distribution of the device.

Before she deposited the check for $1,500,000, Margo McKay interviewed bankers to find and establish a good working relationship.

The Niche

Encouraged by success, the partners explored the marketplace for more product possibilities. Bob Bernstein was put in charge of the surgery shunt's production, and the other three partners became marketplace detectives. As they developed new products, they were careful not to operate in the same arena as their former employer.

Their niche was microsurgery.

In their third year, Don, the inventor, discovered the solution to a problem that had confounded two generations of optical surgeons. To get FDA approval would take two to three years. With such a long lag time between production and sales, developmental costs would hurt the firm, maybe even take it under.

Then their CPA introduced them to Dream Funds, Inc., a venture capital group in Minneapolis. This was Dream Funds' deal: In return for 60 percent of the company's stock, Dream Funds would deposit $10 million in the company's bank account. The deal closed in a short time.

Two years later, with FDA approval, Don's invention took off. The numbers caught the eye of the second largest firm in the medical products industry. The firm made an offer they couldn't refuse: $50 million in cash for their company, of which they now owned 40 percent.

Guess what?

They took the money.

After paying off all debt, each partner came away with $4 million and change. Because of their positive experience in the big world of small business, they founded a new start-up—a venture capital firm. They named it The Honey Pot, with each member contributing $1 million to the fund.

"Hey," said Margo. "Why not? We worked for a big company. All of us did that. Our big discovery was how much fun it was to do start-ups. With Honey Pot funds, we can help start one a month. I can't believe I wasted all that time working for someone else."

BEFORE COMMITTING MONEY

Don and his colleagues put up their *own money first.* Committing your own nickel is essential for all entrepreneurs. Lenders and investors will make sure you have committed your own resources before they will commit theirs. You've already completed Action Step 3 from Chapter 1, which asked you to complete a budget and a personal financial statement, and the Actions Steps in Chapter 8, which asked you to determine your start-up costs and cash-flow requirements, so you now know the amount you need to start and the amount you have to do it with. Now it's time to reconcile and determine how to fund the difference.

Because the vast majority of small businesses are self-financed in the start-up stage, you must first consider your risk tolerance, your credit history, and the availability of your own cash.

What Is Your Risk Tolerance?

How much are you willing to risk? $10,000? $20,000? $200,000? $2,000,000? Are you willing to go deeply in debt for your venture? A sushi vendor worked for more than seven years and spent millions of dollars before he hit on a successful way to flash freeze his product.

Are you willing to give up a successful career with benefits for the unknown? If you lose your house, will you be devastated, or will you pick yourself back up and start again like a true entrepreneur? Jim LaMoss, a home-builder from South Carolina, was a millionaire at age 22 and lost it; a millionaire again at age 28, and lost it! And a millionaire again at 35!

Remember, you must also consider the risk tolerance level of the members of your family and any persons you partner with.

What Is Your Credit History?

Loan officers will look first at your credit report. If it doesn't pass, you are sunk at the bank! Take action to determine your credit history.

CREDIT REPORTING AGENCIES—WHAT DO THEY KNOW ABOUT YOU?

Credit reporting agencies keep track of all your financial moves—the good, the bad, and the ugly—including bill paying, credit (requested and denied), payment of utility bills, and loans, liens, and legal judgments. Information is retained for 7 years and bankruptcies for 10 years.

If you have released financial statements previously, these may also appear as part of a credit report. Credit inquires from potential lenders, which also will show up on a credit report, let others know where you might currently be seeking credit.

Be warned: What might appear minor to you—like one missed or late payment—may not appear minor to potential lenders.

Because most entrepreneurs will depend on their own credit history as they reach out for money, it is essential that your credit report be perfectly clean! Mistakes are very common. It costs less than $10 to check your credit report; do this before moving forward. If there is a problem, go to the Internet and research the steps you need to take to clear up problems as quickly as possible. Or call the credit reporting firm and talk directly with them.

A credit scoring system has been developed. Request your score from the sources listed here. Future lending opportunities and interest rates may be based on your specific score, so take the time early on to complete your research and correct problems.

To receive a copy of your credit report and FICO score, contact:

- Equifax
  1-888-532-0179
  www.equifax.com
- Experian
  1-888-397-3742
  www.experian.com
- Trans Union Corporation
  P.O. Box 2000
  Chester, PA 19022
  1-800-888-4213
  www.transunion.com

Availability of Cash and Credit

Looking at your personal financial statement from Action Step 3 in Chapter 1, how much money are you able to commit? Are you able to sell any of your assets? Take a second or a third mortgage on your house, or a home equity loan? Refinance your car? Sell your baseball card collection? Take a loan from your 401K?

Reviewing your budget from Action Step 3, how much extra in your budget can you commit to the venture? How much do you need to live on each month? Are you willing to change your lifestyle? Are you willing to rent? Share an apartment? Live in your parents' home? Are you willing to go without healthcare and disability benefits? (If you have answered yes, please rethink!) Can you dine out less? Buy a cheaper car?

What sacrifices are you willing to make for your dream? Can you get a part-time job to help support your dream? Can you hang on to your present job and start your new venture part-time? Do you need to find a partner who has some cash? Can you start in your basement? Living room? Garage?

Find out how much unsecured credit you have. This will give you a general picture of how the financial world rates you at this time. Once taken, this step can help you determine if there are any untapped sources of funds for your start-up, or fall-backs and emergency sources for your business or personal expenses. Use Table 9.1 to determine your credit limits on charge accounts. Look at your last statement to discover available credit. You may need to call or write to several businesses for this information. When you've filled in the amounts for each of your credit accounts, add them up. Surprised? Few people are aware of how much credit they do have.

However, before you tell your boss what she can do with your job, there are a few additional concerns you might want to address. For example:

1. Get complete medical checkups for your entire family. You might ask to read through your medical files to make sure there are not any statements that might preclude you from obtaining health insurance in the future. Examples might include "possible problems with drinking or drugs." In addition, pre-existing conditions, such as uncontrolled high blood pressure, can be a major roadblock to securing affordable health insurance.
2. Check out the costs and possibility of continuing your present health insurance or purchasing new insurance. If you are unable to qualify for a private insurance plan, a group plan might be available through a business trade association or possibly through a state program. Many entrepreneurs find they must maintain one member of their family working for a company that provides insurance that will cover the family.

TABLE 9.1
Your Current Untapped Financial Sources

Source	Amount/Limit
Department Stores	
Sears	
JC Penney	
Others	
Oil Companies	
Exxon	
Standard Oil	
Mobil	
Texaco	
Shell	
Others	
Bank Credit Cards	
American Express	
Diner's Club	
Visa	
MasterCard	
Discover Card	
Others	
Personal Lines of Credit	
Bank	
Savings & Loan	
Credit Union	
Others	
Home Equity	
Total Available Credit	

3. Apply for additional credit cards. Check with **www.bankrate.com** for cards with the best terms. Use cards only for business expenses. Pay bills as they come due with a company check. Banks don't care who writes the check, as long as it clears. In addition, it will give you good documentation for your bookkeeper and the IRS. Plus, you will have some additional credit for your business. You may need it!
4. Consider applying for a personal **line of credit**. Usually, depending on the **Four Cs** of credit (your capital, character, capacity, and collateral), you can obtain anywhere from $5,000 to $50,000 of unsecured credit at very attractive rates. If you have a personal line of credit, you are in a much more flexible position for your new business. If you need it to finance the new business, it's available. If not, it can be your security blanket, to be there for you if unexpected expenses should pop up—and they will.
5. Explore the possibility of a home equity loan or home equity line of credit.

With regard to points 3 and 4, bankers are much more relaxed about extending credit to a "steady citizen"—a person with steady employment income. However, you would be making arrangements for the money when you don't need it, and bankers tend to like lending money to people who don't really need it.

Don't quit your job until you've finished your Business Plan and checked with your banker. You need to have enough money to withstand setbacks. Don't be surprised when your business does not support you (right away) in the manner to which you've become accustomed or would like to be accustomed to!

Your Bottom Line

You are not risking your own capital and providing sweat equity for *just* an immediate paycheck or return. You are building your business's potential. If you only consider the income from the first year or two, you will not be able to justify risking capital or putting in 12- to 14-hour days. You must look ahead three to five years. Money is a strong motivating factor; just thinking about it will help you keep your business on the success track. Here are additional thoughts to consider as you explore the bottom line for starting and building your business:

- **Income stream.** What can you count on from your business? Salary? Profit? Benefits? Company car? Insurance? Travel? Retirement fund?
- **Profit from sale of business.** What is the potential profit if the business is sold? What could you make if you took the company public via a stock offering? What will you leave to your children?
- **Profit life cycle.** How long will it take for your business to move from start-up to a profit position? Many businesses take two years, even three, to show a profit. What happens to your investment if you project the shift to profit-making status to be 5 to 10 years down the road?
- **The rule.** *Your business should provide you with two sources of financial return: an income stream and growing equity. If you have income without equity, you are just replacing your former income. If you have equity without income, you could starve to death.*

SHAKING THE MOST FRUITFUL BRANCHES FIRST

Shaking the money tree takes effort for most entrepreneurs. Many resources are available, but they *all* come with strings attached. Type of company, control of the business, family and friends' emotions, your risk tolerance, and taxation are all issues that should play a part in determining which branches of the money tree you can and should shake. Sitting down with a knowledgeable small-business accountant or

Line of Credit An unsecured lending limit

Four Cs Capacity, collateral, character, and capital

attorney will give you great insight. Although there are many funding opportunities available to entrepreneurs, more than 90 percent of start-up capital comes from self-financing, friends, and family. That means banks provide less than 10 percent of start-up capital!

If you bootstrap your company as we suggest, you may find yourself on *Inc.'s* Annual Listing of the 500 Fastest Growing Businesses in the United States because more than half of the businesses on 2000's list started in the home, and the overall list had an average start-up cost of only $25,000. It doesn't always take large amounts of capital to launch your business, but it will take enormous amounts of risk-taking, time, energy, and passion.

SELF-FINANCING

Your Money and Your Credit

We have discussed several ways to tap into your financial resources. Many individuals can't tap retirement, home equity, stock, or bond funds; therefore credit cards may come to the rescue. For many entrepreneurs, credit cards are the standard way of accessing capital to keep the doors open and the fires burning. More than 34 percent of entrepreneurs use credit cards routinely in their businesses. However, it is *always* safer to use cold hard cash to start and support your business, if possible, before depending on credit cards.

Many large credit card companies, such as American Express, **www.americanexpress.com**, court small-business owners. Unfortunately, many of the small-business credit cards, which provide excellent recordkeeping, are available only to businesses with a two-year track record.

When selecting cards, consider the following:

- Payment dates. If you have several cards, with varying closing and payment dates, you may be able to creatively manage your cash flow by using the cards in tandem as follows:

Card	Closing Date of Billing Cycle	When to Use Start	Stop	Time from Purchase to Payment
Visa	4th of the month	5th	19th	Charge July 5th Pay Sept 3rd (60 days)
Discover	19th of the month	20th	4th	Charge July 20th Pay Sept. 18th (60 days)

- Annual Percentage Rate (APR). Check your newspaper or Bank Rate Monitor (**www.bankrate.com**) for the lowest current credit card rates. If you have a card and are paying too high of an APR, call the credit card company and request that they lower the rate. Yes, this can work!
- Annual fees.
- Maximum credit limits. Call your current credit card issuers and request an increase in your credit line. Many times all it takes is a phone call.
- Additional fees. Make sure any "extras" you receive with the card are worth paying for.
- Grace periods. This is extremely important if you are using the card to manage cash flow.
- Late fees. *Never* incur late fees. In the past, credit card companies did not balk if you were up to 30 days late. Today, a payment that is one day late may incur high late fees, show up on your credit report, and possibly increase your interest rate by 25 to 30 percent.

Judicious use of credit cards can be a lifesaver for many entrepreneurs. They help you track your expenses and help to build a financial history. But unless you realize that the credit card bills need to be paid on time and there are spending limits, you may find yourself in over your head and your business underwater. In addition, if you are using credit cards, make sure to include in your Business Plan repayment of this debt.

CREDIT CARDS—KNOW THE RISK

Using credit cards is a very risky way to finance your company. You have the huge bill to face every month, instead of several smaller ones that can be juggled. Once you max out, you can't pay your other bills any more. And the interest payments on carrying a balance can make a grown entrepreneur cry. Also, funding businesses with a credit card violates the consumer-cardholder agreement although it's a standard practice for thousands of company owners.

For more information, visit **www.inc.com/incmagazine/archives/02980501.html.**

FRIENDS AND FAMILY

For many entrepreneurs, heading to Mom and Pop is the first branch to shake. If you plan on making it your first stop, think again! According to many experts, parents may be the largest single source of start-up capital in the United States, but having a banking relationship with your parents is fraught with potential problems. Before continuing further, ask yourself, "Is money for this venture worth damaging or losing my relationship with my parents?" At the moment, you may just be thinking about speeding ahead with your venture, and all you can see is success; the reality is, however, you could fail. You might not be able to pay back your parents in a timely fashion—or ever!

Consider your parents' emotional tie to money. Especially if your parents or grandparents are in their seventies or eighties and lived through the Depression, money means security. If you borrow money, they may never truly feel secure until you have completely paid it back. Also, if you take a trip to Paris while you still owe them money, will they make you feel guilty? Will you feel guilty if you purchase a new car? Will you truly be secure in expanding your business if you are not secure in your lending relationship?

If you are borrowing money from friends or family, be sure that the loss of that money will not affect the lenders' future or lifestyle. Borrowing Grandma's last $20,000 is not fair to Grandma.

In addition to borrowing money directly from parents, you may consider asking them to co-sign loans. Remember, that legally obligates them to the debt. Also, your parents, friends, or relatives may be more willing to loan you money if you put up your house, car, or jewelry as collateral.

Remain at your job and save for another year before striking out on your own rather than risking the capital of those you love. Mixing money and personal relationships is never easy and with family it tends to be even more emotional and volatile. Long-running family issues come into play and brother–sister relationships may also be harmed. There are unseen and unknown issues for both parties. How will you deal with them? If your folks get sick, will you be able to pay back the loan? If your dad and mom want to be part of the business to oversee their investment, how will you feel? Do you want your parents only as lenders, or will you consider taking them on as partners and investors?

If you are still willing to borrow from friends and family after reviewing potential issues and problems, here are a few things you can do to alleviate some of the difficulties.

- Put everything in writing.
- Make it a business loan, not a personal loan. Have loan papers drawn up. State the amount, payments, time period of loan, interest rate, payment date, collateral, and late payment penalties.

- A provision in the loan should be included for repayment in case of emergencies. This will alleviate a lot of stress and concern for both parties.
- Discuss thoroughly with your lenders the company's goals. Make sure they understand that the loan will need to be for a certain length of time. If the business starts to be profitable, it will still require their cash infusion for working capital.
- Discuss your fears for potential problems and encourage your lenders to discuss their issues as well. Putting feelings and concerns out on the table early may stem future problems.

One family we know lends to all their adult children in a bank-like fashion. To purchase a home, one son might receive a $50,000 loan at 7 percent interest. A daughter purchasing a franchise might receive a loan of $50,000 with an 11 percent interest rate. The youngest son, starting a high-tech business with two of his out-of-work and not-very-well-respected friends, will be required to pay 15 percent interest. All understand the Mom and Dad Bank is only operating on the basic investment principal of risk versus return, resulting in the various interest rates. If payments are late, a call goes out, and payment is expected immediately. Just like a bank!

One son kept forgetting to pay on time. The Mom and Dad Bank requested post-dated checks for the next six months to secure payments in a timely fashion. No comments about loans or the children's spending habits are made to the children. After 35 years, there are no hurt feelings and strong, stable personal relationships remain. In addition, several flourishing entrepreneurial ventures continue to grow with the assistance of the Mom and Dad Bank.

It can be done! But it's hard work and takes exceptional people with good relationships who have no axes to grind. *Tread lightly and carefully. Friends and family cannot be bought or replaced.*

BANKS

Most new ventures begin with an entrepreneur's own capital. If you have other sources of income and collateral—such as home equity, stocks, or bonds—you may be able to borrow against your assets for funding. Although banks are in the business of lending money, they also have a responsibility to their depositors. Therefore bankers tend to choose the safest deals. They want to help businesses expand, but they have to be picky. Banks can help you in many areas, but they are neither investors nor venture capitalists, so don't expect them to take risks. Your chances to receive a bank loan increase substantially after being in business several years; then you can demonstrate to the bank you are a viable business by providing them with your past sales records and tax returns.

A small local community bank, where the chief loan officer may be a part owner, may be an excellent choice for small business banking. You're hunting for a permanent relationship, not merely a place to park your money, and are more likely to find it in a small community bank. Contact the Independent Bankers Association of America to access the names of more than 5,000 community banks. Bear in mind though that your business could outgrow a small bank and some firms need support services (such as import–export assistance) that only a large bank can offer.

Few bankers are thrilled about lending money to start-ups. Nonetheless, bankers are people, so seek a banker who understands you, your selected industry, and your needs. Network with your attorney, your accountant, the Chamber of Commerce, civic clubs, and people in your industry for recommendations. Be prepared to spend a lot of time on this search. Once you have located several good banks, ask your accountant to accompany you as you make your introductory visits to the banks.

Several large banks such as Chase and Fleet Bank provide assistance to fledgling businesses with big plans. Also, creative leasing programs may be available through these larger banks.

Microlending programs, which generally refer to business loans less than $100,000, are available through various banks and economic development programs. These small loans are giving new hope to entrepreneurs. According to SBA research, more than 500 banks participated in microlending programs, providing $17 billion in 1997.

Bankers' Expectations

In general, bankers tend to not make start-up loans without home equity or stocks to secure the loan. When they do, they expect:

1. A very solid Business Plan with good projections and supporting data. Numbers are king! Bankers use the Annual Statement Studies published by Robert Morris Associates to determine operating ratios. Make sure you are in line. Back-up and support each assumption and number in your plan.
2. Experience in managing a business.
3. Background in the industry.
4. Enough other assets for the borrower to live on while the business is growing.
5. Your personal financial commitment to be a major part of the financing.
6. Possibly a co-signer who guarantees your loan.
7. A second salary in the family.
8. Generally at least two to three years of successful operations. Once again, unsecured bank lending is rare to start-ups without collateral.
9. Income statements that demonstrate you are willing to take a reasonable salary or no salary in the beginning.
10. Detailed explanation of what you are going to do with the funds and how repayment will be made.
11. A compelling product or service with strong management.
12. Capacity to repay the loan in a timely fashion.

Unsecured bank loans or lines of credit may not be available to an entrepreneur even after three to five years of successful business operations. Your personal assets and your business assets are therefore intertwined for a very long time whether you like it or not.

Strategies

Bankers can lead you to money sources you may have not considered and may be one gateway to the world of money. Seek your banker's advice on pulling your Business Plan together. If you ask for your banker's input, he or she will have a harder time refusing help later on.

In the SBA section that follows, a paperwork checklist is provided for SBA loans; a similar checklist will be required by most banking institutions for any loan.

Bring your banker into your **information loop** and involve him or her in your business idea. People lend money to people. Stop thinking about a banker as someone who will lend you an umbrella only on a sunny day. *You* would not lend money to a stranger, so make sure your banker knows exactly what you are up to.

Some strategies for dealing with bankers are as follows:

- Never ask directly for money; ask initially for *advice* and *information.* Ideally, a banker will *tell you* when it is the right time to seek money.
- A bank may seem very formidable, like a medieval fortress or a modern cathedral. Try to ignore these impregnable symbols by looking at the bank with new eyes. Do not just drop in. Make an appointment. Dress conservatively. Ask lots of questions.
- Lure a banker to **your turf** if you have a retail or manufacturing operation. Say, "It's difficult to explain to you exactly what my shop is like. Why not come out for a look? We could have lunch. How's Thursday around noon?" On your own turf, you will be in a stronger position. You should feel more at ease, and communication will probably flow more easily for both parties.
- Keep in touch with your banker. Continue to position yourself on the ladder in your banker's mind.
- Comparison shop for money just as you would shop for any major purchase. The deals could surprise you. But like any major purchase, price is only one factor to consider.
- Negotiate for your line of credit or loan while you are still employed. A personal line of credit is often reviewed annually. You may have to prove that you are still a good credit risk after you are in your own business. If you keep up a good credit rating, however, the chances are good that you will be able to keep the personal lines of credit.

Keep a running list of questions to ask prospective bankers. The following questionnaire will help get you started.

QUESTIONS FOR YOUR BANKER

What are your lending limits?

Who makes the decisions on loans?

What are your views on my industry?

What experience do you have in working with businesses like mine?

Could you recommend a highly qualified lawyer? Bookkeeper? Accountant? Computer consultant? Advertising consultant? Patent attorney?

Are you interested in writing **equipment leases**?

What kind of terms do you give on **accounts receivable** financing?

Does your bank offer businesses Visa and MasterCard accounts?

What credit limit could I expect for my business credit cards?

What handling charge would I have to pay on credit card receipts?

What interest can I earn on my business checking account?

Do you have a merchants' or commercial window?

Do you have a night depository?

If you can't lend me money, can you direct me to people who might be interested in doing so?

Do you make **SBA-guaranteed loans**?

If I open up a business checking account here, what else can you do for me?

What will you be looking for in my Business Plan?

Would you describe the loan approval process?

Information Loop A network of people who need to be kept informed about your business

Your Turf One's place of business or the place one feels most comfortable

Equipment Lease Long-term arrangement with a bank or leasing company for renting capital equipment

Accounts Receivable What is owed to a firm

SBA-Guaranteed Loans Loans in which up to 90 percent of borrowed funds are insured by the federal government

Make Your Banker a Member of Your Team

A helpful banker can be an entrepreneur's best friend and a member of his or her auxiliary management team or "taxi squad." Business growth demands money from external sources. The more successful you become, the more likely you will need a close bank relationship to help you finance prosperity. If you grow more than 25 percent a year, you will most likely need financing help. Manufacturers get into trouble fast, but even service firms have to wait for their customers to make payments. Your creditors and employees will want their money when it's due them. So keep your banker in your information loop. Bankers are more willing to help if they understand your needs and know you are trying to anticipate them.

Now read about how Steve White handled his cash flow problems by helping a banker understand the business he was in.

Banker to the Rescue

Things went really well our first year. My third invention—a battery-operated fuel monitor for diesel turbos being made in Germany—was selling like hotcakes, and I'd found a great production manager to keep things going down on the line.

Then cash flow troubles developed.

It happened in February of our second year when a couple of the big carmakers—customers that purchased at least half of our product—slowed down on their payments. Some payments were more than 90 days past due.

I stay pretty much in the lab and the shop because that's the fun part of the business for me, so I didn't find out about the cash problems for almost three weeks. When I did find out, we invoiced the customers again. Still no money. The first week in March, I had trouble meeting the payroll. The second week I had to pay a couple of crucial supplier accounts. The third week, except for petty cash, the company was almost out of money.

I gave my banker a call. We were on good terms, and I had four accounts at her bank. When I told her my problem, she simply asked me how much I needed and for how long. Instant line of credit. What a relief!

Well, we got that squared away, and when things were rolling smoothly again, my banker sat down with me and the company books, and we worked out a strategy for bridging the gap between billing and customer payment.

Numbers bore me. Recognizing their importance, I started looking around for someone to help out with accounting. My banker helped here, too, with advice and recommendations about what kind of person would be best at keeping track of the firm's finances.

When I worked for someone else, I never thought of a banker at all. Since I've been in business, I've come to realize a banker can be a businessperson's best friend.

Action Step 42 will help you get started in developing your relationship with a banker.

If you have tapped out your own resources, investigated borrowing from friends and family, and made a few bank inquiries—and there is still not enough in the money pot, look to other sources.

SBA Programs

One of the first stops many people make is the Small Business Association with its myriad of lending programs. During 2000, more than 5,600 different commercial lenders made more than $10.5 billion in SBA-backed small business loans. Extensive information on SBA programs can be accessed at **www.sba.gov/financing**. Several major SBA programs are as follows:

- The 7 (A) Program is the most flexible because it can provide financing for a variety of general purposes, such as to acquire or start a business, or to meet

Action Step 42

Befriend a Banker

Money creates its own world. There are several doorways into that world. Your banker sits at the threshold of one of those doors.

Start with a familiar place, the bank where you have your checking account. Make an appointment to talk to the chief officer (president, vice-president, or branch manager).

Use Questions for Your Banker as a guide.

If you are happy with your banker's answers, talk over the possibility of opening a business account for your business. If you have money tucked away in life insurance or a money market fund somewhere, ask about the bank's money market accounts.

Check out checking and bank fees and compare to other banks.

very specific financing needs such as contract or export financing. Recent changes raise the guaranty percentage to 85 percent for loans up to $150,000 and greatly simplify the guaranty fee structure, making these loans easier for lenders and thus for small business owners. The maximum loan size is $2 million.

- The Certified Development (or 504) program can finance a portion of a business's fixed asset acquisition with a fixed interest rate loan in combination with third-party financing and equity up to $1 million. For loans that meet certain public policy goals, the maximum loan size was increased to $1.3 million.
- The Microloan program provides loans under $35,000 to eligible businesses needing limited amounts of borrowed funds. The SBA provides its funds to a microlender who, in turn, makes the actual loan to the business. If the borrower also secures financing from another source, the combined loans can go up to $105,000.
- The Small Business Investment Companies (SBIC) are private lenders licensed by the SBA to provide equity capital to small businesses. The recipients may give up some ownership, but not necessarily control, in exchange for the funds. Offering both debt and equity financing, the SBICs expect to recoup their investment in five to seven years. Access **www.sba.gov/INV** for further information.

COMMUNITY RESOURCE

Small Business Development Centers (SBDCs)

Federal funds are awarded to state universities and economic development agencies to establish Small Business Development Centers at universities, chambers of commerce, and community colleges. These 58 centers with almost 1,000 service locations provide assistance in marketing, finance, and management to entrepreneurs. During 1999 the SBDC's trained approximately 600,000 clients. To access the SBDC sites in your area, click on **www.sba.gov.sbdc** or **www.asbdc-us.org**. These programs will not fund your venture, but will provide assistance and prepare you to seek funding.

Specialty programs exist within each state to meet the changing needs of each state's economy and to exploit the assets of each area. For example New York State offers the following: Veterans' Business Outreach Program, Manufacturing and Defense Development Center, Self-Employment Assistance Program, and the International Business Program.

To address the needs of entrepreneurs in Florida, the SBDCs offer the following:

USA*Japan Trade Expansion Center (JTEC), the nation's first trade expansion center to be funded by both the USA and Japan, expressly promotes U.S. exports to Japan. JTEC provides direct market assessment and company matchmaking through offices located in Japan, conducts a series of national seminars on doing business with Japan, and conducts an annual "U.S. Export Matchmaker Trade Mission" each fall for promoting U.S. exports to Japan.

Defense Transition Assistance Center assists companies affected by Defense cuts created to retrain for high-wage employment.

Florida Procurement Technical Assistance Center provides consulting and technical assistance to firms who are pursuing contracts with the Department of Defense and state and local government programs.

Check out your state's SDBC programs. In addition, if you have specific needs, which are not met by a program in your state, contact other state programs to see how they can assist you. Free SBDC counseling may prove to be more helpful than you could ever imagine. One of the best reasons to use these centers is to access the contacts that they have developed through the years.

- The Small Business Innovation Research (SBIR) program provides direct funding for development efforts. The SBIR offers ventures for an opportunity to develop innovative ideas that meet the research needs of the federal government while hopefully opening the door to future commercialization. For further information, contact the SBA for their publication *Proposal Preparation for Small Business Innovation Research.* Contact the SBA at (202) 205-6450 or **www.sba.gov/sbir/indexsbir_sttr.html** for further information.

The SBA has two major categories of loans: guaranteed and direct. Banks and non-bank lenders make the SBA guaranteed loans. The direct loans are made directly to businesspeople by the federal government. Direct loans are scarce.

The guarantee is between the SBA and the bank. If the business goes under, the government repays a majority portion of the loan. Real estate loans are a major component of the SBA loan portfolio because they are collateralized and more secure than other loans. Banks lending in cooperation with the SBA like to see at least a 30 percent commitment of personal funds before they loan money. Your local SBA office will give you a list of the major SBA-guaranteed lenders in your area. It is a good idea to use one of these banks for their expertise and experience in dealing with government red tape.

The following checklist of required papers for SBA/bank financing applicants gives a fair idea of the *major* paperwork necessary for applying for a loan. SBA's Standard Application Package following provides a list of requirements for the SBA's Standard Application Package. SBA 4 is included in Appendix B. Additional forms are available on the Web and at local SBA offices. For further information contact the SBA Answer Desk at (800) U ASK SBA (827-5722) or **www.sba.gov**.

*Checklist for SBA/Bank Financing**

1. SBA Form 4, 4I — Application for Business Loan
2. SBA Form 413 — Personal Financial History
3. SBA Form 912 — Statement of Personal History
4. Detailed, signed Balance Sheet and Profit & Loss Statements current (within 90 days of application) and last three (3) fiscal years Supplementary Schedules required on Current Financial Statements.
5. Detailed one (1) year projection of Income & Finances (please attach written explanation as to how you expect to achieve same).
6. A list of names and addresses of any subsidiaries and affiliates, including concerns in which the applicant holds a controlling (but not necessarily a majority) interest and other concerns that may be affiliated by stock ownership, franchise, proposed merger or otherwise with the applicant.
7. Certificate of Doing Business (If a corporation, stamp corporate seal on SBA form 4 section 12).
8. By Law the Agency may not guarantee a loan if a business can obtain funds on reasonable terms from a bank or other private source. A borrower therefore must first seek private financing.

   A company must be independently owned and operated, not dominant in its field and must meet certain standards of size in terms of employees or annual receipts. Loans cannot be made to speculative businesses, newspapers, or businesses engaged in gambling.

   Applicants for loans must also agree to comply with SBA regulation that there will be no discrimination in employment or services to the public, based on race, color, religion, national origin, sex, or marital status.
9. Signed Business Federal Income Tax Returns for previous three (3) years.

*Source: **www.sba.gov/gopher/Financial-Assistance/reg6.txt** (accessed March 8, 2001).

INCREDIBLE RESOURCE

GE SMALL BUSINESS COLLEGE

With a 30-hour program focusing on rapidly expanding businesses, GE Small Business College offers an incredible resource for learning, personal advisement by GE associates, and networking opportunities with other successful entrepreneurs. According to GE, "the content addresses key management issues owners face, such as how to increase sales, access capital, beat the competition, and use technology effectively. It is designed to provide practical information and tools business owners can implement right away." A good deal of time is spent learning 1) how to access capital and 2) how to become a supplier to large entities in a confidential environment.

You must be in business for three years, have three or more employees, and have gross annual revenues of $1 million or more to qualify for the program with its nominal cost. Scholarships are available.

A few success stories follow:

- Daycare provider given financing to enlarge facility and serve more teenage mothers.
- Construction firm met Port Authority representatives at the College and, subsequently, became certified contractor.
- Engineering firm approved for favorable procurement status by the SBA.

For further information contact **www.financiallearning.com/ge/home.jsp**.

SOURCE: **www.financiallearning.com/financial_life_events/own_business/basics.html** (access date March 7, 2001).

10. Signed Personal Federal Income Tax Returns of principals for previous three (3) years.
11. Personal Resume including business experience of each principal.
12. Brief history of the business and its problems: Include an explanation of why the SBA loan is needed and how it will help the business.
13. Copy of Business Lease (or note from landlord giving terms of proposed lease).
14. For purchase of an existing business:
    a. Current Balance Sheet and Profit and Loss Statements of business to be purchased.
    b. Previous two (2) years Federal Income Tax Returns of the business.
    c. Proposed Bill of Sale including: Terms of Sale.
    d. Asking Price with schedule of:
        1. Inventory
        2. Machinery and Equipment
        3. Furniture and Fixtures

STATE PROGRAMS AND LOCAL DEVELOPMENT AUTHORITIES

Contact you local SBA office for a copy of *The State and Small Business: A Directory of Programs and Activities.* Local development authorities are very helpful and interested in securing financing for growing businesses, and can be extremely flexible in their financing programs.

ANGELS

While Janice was sharing her Business Plan with her best friend Sally, Sally's mother, Josie, popped in and said, "That sounds like a great idea. Tell me more." After a few hours, the "Angel Josie" invested $100,000 for a 40 percent share of the business. In addition Josie offered to have dinner meetings once a week and provide business counseling. Her 30 years in various healthcare management positions made her a great mentor for Janice's home healthcare agency.

Angels may just appear, but that's unlikely. You will need to search out potential investors. The first step is to tell all your friends and family about your business idea and ask them if they have any possible contacts for you. Your research may unearth potential investors. Always follow up on anyone who expresses an interest. Research shows that a business angel interested in your venture very often lives within 10 miles.

Angels come in many different sizes and types—from the small investor who just came into money to the professional investor who wants to help others follow their passion. Most angels like to invest in companies in industries where they have knowledge and experience. Hopefully, your angel will not only support the financial part of your business but will also offer their contacts and experience; in the end this aid may be far more important to your success than investment capital.

Specific industries and some communities offer angel networks, some of which offer a matchmaking process for investors and entrepreneurs.

Angel Capital Electronic Network (ACE-Net), sponsored by the SBA, offers a way for people to find each other online. ACE-Net exists for businesses seeking $250,000 to $5 million in capital. Use the SBA site to access ACE-Net.

In some communities private or college-sponsored investors' forums are offered, where individuals are given 10 to 15 minutes to present their idea to potential investors. Forums are an excellent place to sell your ideas, receive feedback, and hopefully find financing. SBA research reports 250,000 angels provide more than $20 billion annually to 300,000 new and expanding businesses each year. Your chance to find an angel may be better than you thought!

VENDOR FINANCING

An often-overlooked technique for reducing your capital requirements is to probe your vendors (major suppliers) for the best prices and terms available. Professional buyers and purchasing agents ask their vendors to fill out an information sheet that forces them to write down the terms and conditions of their sales plans. This is a good idea for you as well.

A small business must buy professionally, and a **vendor statement** will help you do just that. With this form, your vendors' verbal promises become written promises. How well you buy is as important as how well you sell because every dollar you save by "buying right" drops directly to the bottom line. To compete in your arena, you need the best terms and prices you can get. The vendor statement will help you negotiate the best.

Personalize your vendor statements by placing your business name at the top. Then list the information you desire and provide blanks for the vendors to write on. The following list provides the basics for a vendor statement:

1. vendor's name
2. vendor's address and phone number
3. sales reps name (800 number)
4. business phone / email / fax / cell phone / pager
5. amount of minimum purchase
6. existence of quantity discounts (how much? requirements to earn?)
7. availability of dating or extended payment terms
8. advertising/promotion allowances
9. policies on returns for defective goods (who pays the freight?)
10. delivery times
11. assistance (technical, sales, etc.)
12. product literature available
13. point-of-purchase material provided
14. support for grand opening (will supplier donate prize or provide other support?)

Vendor Statement A personally designed form that allows one to negotiate with each vendor from a position of informed strength

GLOBAL VILLAGE

RESOURCES FOR INTERNATIONAL BACKGROUND INFORMATION

World FactBook, available online at **www.cia.gov/cia/publications/factbook**, is an excellent, free online resource for conducting background research on a country. Country profiles cover the following:
Geography: map, climate, natural resources, environmental concerns, land use, etc.
People: population, age structure, growth rate, life expectancy, ethnic divisions, languages, literacy, etc.
Government: type of government, legal system, governmental structure, political parties, etc.
Economy: summary of past and current economic status, GDP, inflation rate, profile of labor force, unemployment rate, major industries, agriculture, exports, etc.
Transportation: railways, highways, waterways, pipelines, airports, etc.
Communications: telephone, radio, television, etc.
Military: manpower, budget.

International Market Research Reports are provided by ***Strategis***, a service of the Canadian government. This site, **strategis.ic.gc.ca**, is superb for gathering market information about industries, products, or other aspects of a country's economy. After entering your subject of interest or selecting a country and industry, you will receive a market research report. Although many of the reports are written in terms of economic relationships between Canada and the chosen country, general data may be obtained.

For example, when "Information Technologies and Telecommunications" for Germany was selected, ten documents were posted. One of them, "Germany—Computers and Peripherals," included the following information: trade analysis (country's population, level of computer literacy and spending on information technology according to specific categories of computer hardware and software) and German computer hardware and software manufacturers.

World Competitiveness Yearbook, prepared by Professor Stéphane Garelli at the University of Lausanne, Switzerland, provides an analysis of 49 major world economies and their current competitive status, including relative strengths and weaknesses in the world market. If you want more details about the yearbook, such as the factors considered in preparing the analysis, or want to review the competitiveness rankings for a country, visit the yearbook's homepage, **www.imd.ch/wcy**.

USATrade.gov is an excellent source of market research data, industry specific sector analyses, country commercial guides, and customized research. In addition, webcasts present market opportunities and insights on how to do business in specific countries.

15. nearest other dealer handling this particular line
16. special services the sales rep can provide
17. vendor's signature, the date, and agreement that you will be notified of any changes to the above immediately

Remember, the information the vendor writes on this statement is the starting point for negotiations. You should be able to negotiate more favorable terms with some vendors because these people want your business. Revise your application form as you learn from experience how vendors can help you. If you are a new business, you will most likely be required to *personally* guarantee in writing payment of your purchase.

A Vendor Success Story

Rich Cameron was a Marketing VP working for a large firm when he decided to go into a retail business for himself. He attended seminars, interviewed owners, walked neighborhoods, and read trade journals for quite a while before opening his toy store.

The store opened in May, but Rich knew from doing industry research that he would have to start placing orders for the Christmas season right away. The problem was that although his store could hold $300,000 worth of toys, Rich only had $180,000 to use for inventory. He knew he would have to be well-stocked by Thanksgiving, or he would miss out on the profitable holiday business.

The unwritten rule in a new business is that suppliers want you to pay cash up front—for everything. You are a new account, unproven in the grand arena of trade and commerce. They want to wait and see how well you do before they extend credit.

Rich found a way to get around this. He showed his Business Plan to his suppliers' credit managers.

What happened?

"They were amazed," Rich says. "They'd been dealing with toy store owners for years, and mine was the first Business Plan they'd seen from a toy store owner. I showed them everything in black and white—industry trends, projections, marketing plan, management team statistics, promotion strategy, everything—and when they had read it, they willingly extended dating terms."

The Business Plan didn't do all Rich's work for him. He also bought merchandise for his store very carefully and developed his own personalized vendor statement to use when he spoke to sales reps.

"A vendor statement really helps," Rich says, "because the survival items are written down. It puts sales reps on the spot. If they want your business to succeed, they have to deal with the questions.

"When I brought out my vendor statement form, I got some strong resistance. One guy spent 30 minutes long distance, telling me why he wouldn't sign it. He wanted all cash up front for the first sale, 75 percent cash for the second, 50 percent for the third, and 30 percent of net after that. But using the statement, backed by my Business Plan, I was able to negotiate him into dating, which means I bought toys in early summer and didn't have to pay for them until December 10. Dating saved my business."

Rich smiles as he recalls those early days. "The interesting thing about negotiating is that it gets you in close enough so you can ask for other assistance. A lot of my advertising and promotion comes free through the vendors because they want my store to be a success. If I hadn't gone in to deal, they wouldn't have known I was going to be a major customer for the long run. And I couldn't have moved confidently without that vendor form."

If you're a new account, flash them your Business Plan. Then flash them your vendor form. Show them you're going to be a very important customer soon.

Now it's time to prepare your own vendor statement form. Action Step 43 will help you.

ACTION STEP 43

DESIGNING A VENDOR STATEMENT FORM

One of the best ways to save money is to ask for help from your vendors/suppliers. To do that, you will need to create your own special form that specifies, in writing, the terms to be negotiated.

Be firm. Be pleasant. Be tough.

Personalize this form by placing the name of your business at the top. Prepare your list of needed information using the list of 17 suggestions we've given you.

The vendor form provides talking points. Most vendors hold something back; design your form to help you learn what those things are and get the best deal for your business.

Before negotiating, determine the standard terms offered in the industry. During negotiations, use a lot of open-ended questions like "What else can you do for me?"

Remember, vendors will ask you for detailed information.

Remember, dating and credit may be very limited for new accounts.

VENTURE CAPITAL FIRMS

With venture capital firms we enter the world of high rollers and higher flyers. Unlike banks that lend money that is secured (usually by real estate), venture capitalists don't lend money; they buy a piece of the business. They gamble on the business's rapid growth, hoping to reap a 300- to 500-percent return on their investment within 3 to 5 years. Venture capitalists provided more than $36 billion to entrepreneurs in 2000. The payoff for most venture capital firms occurs when the company interests enough investors in an initial public offering of common stock (IPO) or when the company they're invested in is purchased by another business. When the business "goes public" or is sold, the venture capital people take out their original investment and, hopefully, profits.

Venture capitalists vary but most prefer to enter the financial picture at the second stage of a firm's development—when the business has proven its potential and needs a large infusion of cash to support growth. Currently, they tend to prefer high-tech concepts in embryonic industries with high growth potential.

Venture capitalists come in lots of shapes. For example, there are family firms (Rockefeller), industrial firms (GE), banks, and other firms (insurance companies, finance companies). Venture capitalist firms exist that target specific industries such as health care, biotechnology, Internet, software, and telecommunications.

There's an excellent list of names and addresses of venture capital firms in *Pratt's Guide to Venture Capital Sources* and the *Directory of Venture Capital,* available in most public libraries. Local newspapers sometimes compile names of local and regional venture capitalists. Use these sources to determine which firms are interested in your selected industry and to determine the firms' minimum and maximum investment levels.

Passion

Passion for VC Dollars
How I Got VC Money

PRESIDENT: Brian Brittsan
COMPANY: Water Management Services Inc., in San Diego
BUSINESS: Designs and installs water-conserving upgrades in buildings
FOUNDED: 1996
NUMBER OF EMPLOYEES: 20
1999 REVENUES: $2 million
STAGE OF FINANCING: First
VENTURE-CAPITAL FIRMS: Nth Power Technologies, Early Stage Enterprises, the Calvert Group (a mutual-fund firm)
AMOUNT: $2.6 million
EQUITY TAKEN BY VCS: 30.76 percent total
ACE IN THE HOLE: Structured company with an eye toward attracting VC money; had revenues before seeking financing

"From the beginning, my founding partner, Wade Smith, and I had a strategy for the company that called for establishing the "right" profile of our management team and board and making sure that our image and business model were appropriate for both VC funding and a future initial public offering.

"Less than three weeks after incorporating, we pulled together a trio of high-net-worth individuals who gave us investment advice and legal counsel in exchange for equity. Not only did those advisers help us put together a business plan, navigate the capital markets, and attract to our board Wall Street–savvy folks like the senior financial analyst for General Motors; they also allowed us to delay payment of our early legal expenses—close to $100,000.

"Next we rounded out our management team. At the same time, we enlisted a broker to put together a private placement for us. We decided not to pursue venture capital at that point, because we wanted a very small placement in order to limit the dilution of the company. The broker raised some $700,000 from seven accredited investors and in return took a commission of about 8 percent. As I see it, an Achilles' heel in the financing process is that owners whose core skills are not in financing pull themselves out of the operations of the business to do something that they're not very good at, and everything unravels. We chose instead to put our financing in the hands of others so that we could continue to add value to the business.

"We did that, in part, by forming a strategic partnership with a plumbing subcontractor, who invested $250,00 in us. And we brought in sales: some $84,000 in our first year and about $1.9 million in our second. Having revenues was a critical component to our financing; investors like to see their money going for business-development initiatives rather than to crack your monthly nut. Because it's very difficult for VCs to get their arms around the upside of a service-only company, we were also very conscious about developing a technology to act as an enabler for our service business: an Internet-based water-meter-reading system for tenants of apartment buildings.

"Finally, in late 1997 we felt ready to plunge into the capital markets. We hired an investment banker with a focus on the energy industry—Boston-based EnCapital—for a monthly retainer plus commission. All told, we must have talked to 50 VCs—it was like a dog-and-pony show. Yet even with EnCapital advocating for us, it took nearly two years to close a deal. Why? Partly because most VCs have a minimum amount they want to invest and we were looking for only $2 million, again to limit dilution of our holdings while we went about building value.

"Ironically, at the end of the day, the VCs that invested in us were all brought to the table by in-house management. Still, I'm not sorry that we hired EnCapital, because of its contribution in recasting our business plan, determining our valuation, and advising us in how to negotiate."

SOURCE: "How I Got VC Money, Interview with Thea Singer," *Inc.*, September 2000, p. 55.

For additional financing options, visit Idea Café's superb Financing Your Business Website, **www.ideacafe.com/getmoney/FINANCING.shtml.** The site also has several interesting self-exams that help you to explore your "financing psyche."

The following additional websites provide excellent listings of venture capitalists—**www.vfinance.com** and **www.kennedyinfo.com/wsj/vcs_db.html.** Follow one entrepreneur's quest for venture capital funds on page 202.

After thoroughly reviewing all your financing options, it is time to test the waters with Action Step 44.

ACTION STEP 44

PREPARE TO MEET YOUR LENDERS

Know who your potential lenders are and why they should want to help you.

Part A. List potential lenders and investors. Begin with your family and friends and move on to business acquaintances and colleagues. Don't forget institutional lenders.

Part B. Now list reasons why lenders should want to invest in your business. What inducements are you offering potential investors? If you're offering them a very small ROI, what are you offering that will offset that?

Think about the legal form of your business. Would you attract more investors if you incorporated?

Part C. Test your tactics by talking to a few friends. Tell them: "This is just a test, and I'd like your reactions to my new business venture." Watch their reactions, and make a list of the objections they give you—the reasons why they cannot loan money to you.

Using your list of friends' objections, write down your answers to those objections. Are there any you cannot answer? What does this mean for your business?

Part D. Time to go out and meet with lenders and shake the right branches of the money tree. Good luck!

SUMMARY

Few start-up firms have access to venture capital markets, bank financing, vendor credit, or angels at the beginning. The majority of ventures start from the bottom up—bootstrapping their venture and using capital from friends and family.

Keep excellent financial records. When investors come calling, you will be prepared with vital financial documents. Cultivate your banker while you are growing your business.

Be prepared to put in sweat equity for at least the first few years. Learn how to conserve capital and manage debt and accounts receivables. If you are fulfilling your customers' needs and keeping your nose to the grindstone, your day will come.

Money creates its own world. It has its own customs, rituals, and rules. Before you start asking people for money for your business, research the world of money. Read *Barrons, Inc., Forbes, Fortune, Business Week,* and the *Wall Street Journal.* Find someone who knows more about money than you do. Ask questions! Listen!

As you continue to work on your Business Plan, remember what lenders are looking for:

capacity and timeframe of repayment

character and commitment of borrower

strong idea with identifiable Target Market in a growing market

collateral

background and experience of management team

THINK POINTS FOR SUCCESS

- Your banker can be a doorway to the world of money. Use that door.
- Conserving capital is essential in the beginning.
- Take as little capital out of your business as you can.
- In dealing with bankers and vendors, use lots of open-ended questions like "What else can you do for me?"
- Become operational as fast as you can.
- Aim for break even and strong cash flow as soon as possible.

KEY POINTS FROM ANOTHER VIEW

Why Start-ups Fail

By Norm Brodsky

Entrepreneurs usually put the blame of failure on lack of capital. But more often, the problem is how they use the capital they have.

You always hear that the vast majority of new businesses fail because they're undercapitalized. I don't buy that. It's true in maybe 550 percent of the cases—no more. I'll give you an example from the software company I do business with in California. Two of its employees left to start a competing business. They contacted me because I was a potential customer and they wanted me to help finance them. They had a plan of sorts, built around signing up 60 percent to 70 percent of their old employer's customers in the first year. I wasn't interested, but I kept in touch. I think in the end they raised about $200,000.

So what was the first thing they did? They rented a beautiful office suite and filled it with lavish furnishings. Understand, at least 90 percent of their prospective customers were outside California, so they were never going to see the company's offices. Soon I received a brochure the new company had done up. It was elegant, and so was the stationery. When I called the guys up, I said, "That sure is beautiful stationery you have, great logo." They said, "Oh yes, our PR people did it for us." I laughed. Then I got an invitation to their grand opening, a really extravagant party. Of course, almost none of their customers could attend it.

A couple of months later, I was at an industry meeting, and I ran into the old employer. He was very upset with these guys. I said, "Don't worry, Tim. They're going to fail." He said, "How can you be so sure?" I said, "Trust me." They were out of business within a year. I called them up and asked what had happened. They said they were undercapitalized. Baloney. They'd raised $200,000 and thrown $120,000 out the window.

That's a very common story. People who fail on their first venture always say they were undercapitalized, and I suppose they're right in the sense that their capital ran out. But it's *not* because they didn't have enough capital to start out with. It's because they didn't use their capital wisely.

So why does that happen? Part of the problem, I believe, has to do with optimism. When people go into business for the first time, they have wonderful, wonderful dreams. They think they're going to be successful in the first year and make a ton of money. They're wildly optimistic, and at the same time they're scared to death. They're thinking, "Oh, God, I'm never going to make it." Meanwhile, they're projecting 10 times more sales than they can possibly do.

It's weird, but those two things—fear and overoptimism—almost always go together. I guess people use optimism to overcome their fear. They do everything they can to bolster their confidence. They believe that they'll improve their chances if they just act the part. So they rent a fancy office in the most expensive part of town. Or they join an exclusive country club. Or they invest in a computer system they won't need for two years—if they're lucky. Or they do what I did—drive around in a brand-new Mercedes. When I later read about Sam Walton and his beat-up old pickup truck, it dawned on me that the truly successful entrepreneurs don't need those symbols of success.

I eventually realized that you can always tell when people are going into business fresh, without a plan, without knowing what they need to do to survive. All you have to do is check out their offices. Are there drapes on their windows? Did they upgrade the carpeting? Are the walls painted or papered? Did they rent more space than they need? Is the reception area too big for a company whose customers rarely come in? Those are all potential signs of trouble. When you see them, watch out—especially if people are asking you to give them credit.

Of course, if you happen to be one of those first-time entrepreneurs, I can only say this: Forget about image. Forget about making a splash. Forget about everything except getting your capital to last until you don't need it anymore. You don't have to give up your dreams. Dreams are important. Just wait until you can afford them.

Norm Brodsky is a veteran entrepreneur whose six businesses include a former Inc. 100 company, a three-time Inc. 500 company, and a start-up that he hopes will become eligible for the list in 1996. His column, Street Smarts, will appear every other month. Readers are encouraged to send him questions care of Inc.

Norm Brodsky's column, while it may be from 1995, certainly covers and details the excesses of what were to come in the dot.com feeding frenzy of 1999 and 2000.

SOURCE: *Inc.*, December 1995, p. 27.

Legal Issues

STAYING OUT OF COURT

ENTREPRENEURIAL LINKS

BOOKS

American Bar Association Legal Guide for Small Business: Everything a Small Business Person Must Know, from Start-up to Employment Laws to Financing, American Bar Association, Chicago, 2000.

Patents and How to Get One: A Practical Handbook, United States Department of Commerce, Washington, D.C., 2000.

Nolo's Patents for Beginners, David Pressman and Richard Stein, Nolo, Berkley, Cal, 2000.

WEBSITES

www.nolo.com, (Nolo Law for All)

www.umass.edu/fambiz, (University of Massachusetts Family Business Center)

www.uspto.gov/web/offices/com/iip/indextxt.htm, (Independent Inventor Resources)

ASSOCIATIONS/ORGANIZATIONS

Family Firm Institute, www.ffi.org/forums.html

Federal Trade Commission, www.ftc.gov

U.S. Patent and Trademark Office, www.uspto.gov

PUBLICATIONS

Family Business, www.familybusinessmagazine.com

Inventor's Digest

IP-The Magazine of Law Policy for High Technology, www.ipmag.com

ADDITIONAL ENTREPRENEURIAL INSIGHTS

Keeping the Family Baggage out of the Family Business: Avoiding the Seven Deadly Sins that Destroy Family Businesses, Quentin J. Fleming, Fireside, New York, 2000.

Small Time Operator: How to Start Your Own Business, Keep Your Books, Pay Your Taxes and Stay Out of Trouble (Small Time Operator, 25th Ed), Bernard B. Kamoroff, Bell Springs, Willits, Cal., 2000.

How to Register Your Own Trademark: With Forms (How to Register Your Own Trademark, 3rd Ed), Mark Warda, Sourcebooks, Naperville, Ill., 2000.

Learning Objectives

- Understand the importance and necessity of professional legal advice.
- Decide which legal form is best for your business.
- Explore the good, the bad, and the ugly of partnerships.
- Review the advantages of forming a Limited Liability Company.
- Recognize the importance of documenting everything.
- Understand legal escape routes.
- Protect your business with a buy-sell agreement.
- Review patent protection.
- Understand copyright laws.
- Take action to protect your trademark or service mark.
- Review rules for advertising within safe, legal limits.
- Explore family business issues.

In your interviews of successful entrepreneurs, you've probably run across the four main legal forms for small business: sole proprietorship, partnership, corporation, and limited liability company. Which is the right form for you? It's common, although not always advisable, for a small business to start out as a sole proprietorship or a partnership and then to **incorporate** later.

It Pays to Look Ahead

How will you exit a partnership? Is your insurance in place? Are you aware of taxes due? Who is your lawyer?

Imagine that you are in a great business with a partner you trust and respect. When should you incorporate or sign a partnership agreement? Perhaps sooner than you think. That's what Phil Johnson would tell you now.

Sail Away

The power sailer was my idea. My partner, Steve Savitch, said it would break us, and I should have listened to him. Steve's an engineer and inventor. He's great with numbers and computers, but he doesn't know much about people, which is my department. We'd been friends for at least a dozen years and we'd been partners—Savitch and Johnson, Business Consultants—for the past three. This year we were going to each clear more than $200,000.

Steve's tight with a nickel. I knew he'd sock his money away in a money market fund at a conservative rate. But I had this idea that we could buy a boat for the partnership, write off the down payment as an expense, and do our company image a world of good.

"Image, Steve," I said. "Image."

"Uh-oh," Steve said. "Here we go with the immeasurable intangibles."

"It's not intangible when you think about those prospects coming from Chicago next week," I said. "A cruise to Sanibel Island should soften them up, don't you think?"

The first payment wasn't due for a month, and when Steve and I took the boat out with our wives, I tell you, I felt like a prince of the sea. We'd pulled off a smooth deal, and I patted myself on the back every time I thought about the ***write-offs****.*

Our boat, Sunbiz, *boosted business, just like I'd thought it would. We closed the Chicago deal and were busy on a couple of other deals that looked promising. We*

Incorporate Form an artificial, immortal business entity

Write-offs Legitimate business deductions accepted by the IRS *made the first payment with no trouble, and when Steve* ***countersigned*** *the check, he admitted he was beginning to like the boat.*

For a couple of weeks, Steve took his laptop and slept on the Sunbiz. I didn't recognize this early sign. We took Sunbiz out one weekend, with four prospects from St. Louis, and Steve seemed preoccupied. I closed the deal with them Sunday, 15 minutes before putting them on the plane for home. But when I called Steve's house to tell him the good news, his wife, Mary, told me he was still at the boat.

Monday, Steve didn't come to work until almost noon. He looked tired, but he handed me his projections and we got on with planning our strategy for the next couple of weeks.

"Anything wrong, partner?" I asked. "You seem a little far-off today."

"Sorry," Steve said. He was never one to admit to having problems. "My mind wandered a bit there. Where were we?"

On Thursday Steve still didn't make it to work after missing Wednesday. I called his house in the morning. No answer. I thought of driving down to the dock to check the boat, but didn't. When I arrived at the dock with clients around 4:30 that afternoon, there was no Sunbiz. Someone on the next dock said Steve had taken off early that morning.

Then Joey, the guy who pumps gas, came up waving a gas bill for $800—one I'd thought Steve had paid. And the bad news didn't end there. The next day, a fellow who sells radar equipment called me with a $2,000 bill.

I was in shock. There I stood, with two clients in deck shoes and shorts.

My cell phone rang. It was Mary, Steve's wife, wanting to know where Steve was.

Now my stomach was really hurting. My partner Steve was gone—no one knew where—and I was going to have to cover all his business debts, including the payments on the Sunbiz. Terrific!

The problem was that Steve and I had never seen the need for having anything in writing. We were both men of good faith. We had each pulled our weight in the business, and we had balanced each other's skills.

Now that Steve was gone, I felt lost, angry, and betrayed. For the first time in 22 years of business, I made an appointment to talk to a lawyer. He just shook his head.

"You should have come to me sooner, Phil," he said. "A lot sooner."

Last week when I was closing the business down and preparing to return to work for my old boss, I received a postcard from Steve, from Tahiti. "Sorry, Phil," it read. "Didn't mean to run out on you. It was the only way I could handle it. These things happen. Your partner, Steve."

INCREDIBLE RESOURCE

LEGAL RESOURCES ONLINE

As suggested throughout the text, using online legal resources and books does not eliminate, and should *never* be used solely as, legal advice. Legal online sources *do* provide an excellent starting point to gather information and begin your initial research, though. You may be able to perform a great deal of preliminary legal research and determine appropriate questions to ask your lawyer. In addition, many of the sites provide guidelines on how to select legal counsel, which may be of great service—especially if you need to locate a specialized attorney such as a trademark specialist. *Always* use experienced legal counsel.

The following sites provide excellent research starting points:

www.lawsource.com/also, LawSource, Inc., covers U.S., Canada, and Mexico

www.hg.org, Hieros Gamos, provides comprehensive listings of legal and government sources

www.findlaw.com, includes listings of federal, state, and national laws and an excellent search engine

Countersigning A situation in which two or more signatures are required before action can occur

ACTION STEP 45

ENTERTAIN A LAWYER

Network your business contacts for the names of three to five attorneys with experience in forming small business corporations and partnerships. Concentrate on those who have worked in your industry.

Check them out on the phone and then take the most promising candidates to lunch or breakfast.

The first thing you're looking for is someone you can get along with. Then look for experience in the world of small business. A hot trial lawyer may have a lot of charisma, but you want a nuts-and-bolts small-business specialist who can save you time, pain, and money.

During your meeting, find out about fees and costs. Compare the cost, for example, of having your lawyer draw up a complex partnership buy-out agreement with the cost of setting up a corporation. This chapter contains a list of questions to start you off in your discussions with your prospective attorney.

A good lawyer will offer perspectives that will be helpful in the formation of your business. You may have to search for a while, and it may cost you some dollars up front, but there's no substitute for good legal help.

Product Liability Legal exposure if customer becomes ill or sustains injury or property damage

Trademark A word, phrase, logo, or design, or anything used to identify goods or services and differentiates from competitors

Copyright Protects the expression of an idea

Patent Right to make, sell, offer for sale, use, or import an invention

Bankruptcy Legal and financial process if a debtor's financial obligations are greater than his or her assets

Exit Strategy A plan to disengage from business at a future point in time

Buy–sell Agreement An advance contractual agreement that determines how a business is to be valued if one or more partners buys out another

Taxi Squad Human resources outside one's business that can be called on as needed

Retainer Fee An agreement to secure the services of an attorney for a fixed fee for a given period of time or for a specific legal problem

LOCATE AND HIRE AN EXPERIENCED ATTORNEY FROM THE BEGINNING!

A good *small business attorney* can help:

- Create the right business structure for a partnership or a corporation—a structure that gives the protection and flexibility you'll need.
- Review advertising and marketing materials to ensure no laws are violated.
- Organize your human resources department to keep you outside the courtroom; hiring and firing of employees is problematic to say the least—improper handling of even one employee may cause you to lose your business.
- Research and protect you in regards to **product liability**.
- Review all contracts and agreements before you sign.
- Protect you through proper use and development of **trademarks**, **copyrights**, and **patents**.
- Handle collection and possible **bankruptcy** problems.
- Help you plan your **exit strategy**.
- Write partnership agreements and **buy–sell agreements**.

Network your contacts for a lawyer with experience in your selected industry. This is not the time to save money by using your niece who just passed the bar examination. Large law firms may prove very advantageous for rapidly growing technology firms. These firms have access to many specialists who can provide answers quickly. Intellectual property, biotechnology, and manufacturing all have very specific legal issues where expertise is vital for initial and continued success.

One of the most important roles an attorney plays is to provide you entrée to his or her contacts throughout an industry and to bankers, investors, advertising agencies, and accountants. No amount of money can buy you such access.

You need to have a good lawyer, accountant, banker, and insurance agent on your **taxi squad**. Their support and expertise can keep you on track, out of jail, and protected from realized and unforeseen circumstances.

Develop an attorney–client relationship before an employee or customer sues you or your partner leaves for Tahiti. Preventive legal fees are far less costly than clean-up fees if one is sued.

After you have networked to find a lawyer you believe to be right for you, make an appointment with him or her. You are looking for someone you are comfortable with and someone who understands the needs of your business. Many attorneys will not charge for an initial half-hour meeting.

Prepare for your meeting. If you're organized, you will be able to gather a great deal of information in a short time. Complete Action Step 45.

Understanding How Lawyers Charge and Operate

Lawyers either charge by the hour for services they render or work on a **retainer fee**. Or you may have access to a prepaid legal plan in which you receive a variety of services for a flat annual fee. In addition, in the high-tech world, some lawyers are willing to work for stock options. Legal fees range from $100 to more than $500 an hour. Specialized attorneys such as patent or copyright experts may have even higher hourly charges.

To benefit from each appointment with your lawyer, arm yourself first with basic legal research you conduct using the library or Internet. Be thoroughly organized for each meeting, with your questions ready. This will cut down the time you spend with the lawyer and thus cut your fees.

Alternative Legal Forms of Business

You can start doing business as a sole proprietorship with a minimum of hassle. You might need only a city license, a resale license, and perhaps a Doing Business As (DBA) statement (for a fictitious name). It is also advisable to obtain an employer's identification number (EIN) from the federal government (see Appendix C).

The legal paperwork for a partnership is sometimes as simple as sole proprietorship if all agree on basic concepts. Although you can form a partnership with a handshake and dissolve it without a partnership agreement if you're very lucky, hire a lawyer to prepare an agreement if you decide a partnership is right for you; it will protect you against trouble. Don't be left high and dry on the dock like Phil. Less than 10 percent of the small businesses in the United States are partnerships; select your partner(s) wisely and carefully.

A limited liability company (LLC) may be ideal for closely held firms. It offers limited personal liability protection to all owners (termed members) and is treated like a partnership or **Subchapter S corporation** on members' individual tax returns. This avoids the double taxation of income (tax on business profits and individual income) and is usually less costly to form than a corporation. An LLC operating agreement (see Figure 10.2) must be filed with the state.

Forming a corporation takes the most paperwork but gives you more flexibility and a shield that may protect you in case your business harms someone.

If you are forming or currently operating a business with your spouse, the following may provide insight for you. For a detailed review of the correct structure of a family business venture read the "Key Points from Another View" article at the end of the chapter. Also, the Community Resource box on this page provides family business resources.

Community Resource

Family Businesses

Who Can Help?

A wealth of information and assistance is available in your community for your family business adventure. Begin your search for a family business center and consultants in your area at the Family Firm Institute's site, **www.ffi.org**. The site provides listings internationally and nationally by state including private business counselors, accounting firms, lawyers, and therapists who deal with entrepreneurs in family businesses. In addition, listings of most of the family

Source: **www.fambiz.com** (accessed March 14, 2001).

Subchapter S Corporation Legal entity that may provide positive tax treatment for small business

business centers available at colleges throughout the nation are included. Consulting, coaching, seminars, research, legal advice, and roundtables for family entrepreneurs are available at many family business centers for reasonable fees. Following are a few sources from the Illinois state listings:

Crowe Chizek LLP
Family and Owner Managed Business Services
Contact: Edwin A. Hoover, Ph.D., CMC
One MidAmerica Plaza
P.O. Box 3697
Oak Brook, IL 60522-3697
www.crowechizek.com

Crowe Chizek LLP provides educational and consultative resources to families in business and their professional advisors, through internationally recognized staff and faculty. Programs provide insights and tools for managing family relationships, business priorities, and ownership concerns. Educational programs include Family Business Basics, a four-part series for families in business that covers the essential elements for running a successful family company; the Successors' Group, a monthly educational and support roundtable for successors; and the Presidents' Forum, a monthly discussion, accountability, and advisory group for family business CEOs. Crowe Chizek LLP also provides educational workshops and seminars to trade and professional organizations focusing on the management and psychology of family business.

Loyola University of Chicago
Family Business Center
Contact: Andrew D. Keyt
820 North Michigan Avenue
Chicago, IL 60611
www.gsb/luc.edu/centers/fbc

The Loyola Family Business Center is a resource to the universe of family firms, their advisors, and researchers. The Center has the nation's largest collection of family business materials and it is available to the public. Programming is offered for larger, multi-generational family firms and the Center responds to inquiries from anyone interested in the field of family business. Loyola's Family Business Center is one of the nation's leading family business research centers.

Southern Illinois University of Edwardsville
Family Business Forum
Contact: Pamela Hastings-Burlingame
School of Business
Edwardsville, IL 62026-1251

The mission of SIUE's Family Business Forum is to be an evolving educational and networking venue for family business principals. Our commitment is to focus on the special challenges and opportunities inherent in family enterprises. Our goal is to improve the survival rate of family-owned businesses by enhancing family harmony, strengthening their business, and promoting communion between the two. Our process draws on University academic resources, family business service professionals in sponsorship roles, quarterly seminars by nationally recognized experts, and the experience and personal resources of the member families.

Publications that might prove useful to your family business venture include the following:

Family Business Review (quarterly)
Family Business Advisor (monthly)
Family Business (quarterly)

Family businesses present their own set of challenges, so seek out others who have tread the same path for their expertise and experience. Participate in monthly forums with others and send out professionals experienced in dealing with family enterprises.

SOURCE: **www.ffi.org** (accessed March 1, 2001).

FOR COUPLES WORKING TOGETHER, SETTING GROUND RULES IS A MUST

By Carol Sorgen

You married your beloved **for better or for worse**, in sickness and in health, for richer or for poorer.

But **for profit or for loss?** If you're in business together, that's about the size of it.

Take David and Sharon Nevins, for instance.

David Nevins credits much of Owings Mills-based **Nevins and Associates'** success to his wife. Sharon Nevins joined the 10-year-old public relations, marketing, advertising, and customer service firm 2 years ago and **started the company's advertising division**.

But David Nevins, whose firm had capitalized local billings of $6 million last year, admits the partnership—the business one—**isn't necessarily a "forever" thing**. "It's advantageous now, but we have no long-term plans," he says.

That's not because the two don't work well together. They do, and it's because **they've established certain rules that they follow**, he says.

Having **individual lines of authority** is essential for a successful business partnership, say family business experts.

"You need a **clear definition of responsibility**," says **William Ross Adams**, president of Baltimore's Baker-Meekins Co., financial advisers to owners of family and private businesses.

That advice is **echoed by Harsha Desai**, professor of management and director of the Loyola Center for Closely-Held Firms at Loyola College.

"A couple **has to have different areas of expertise**, so you don't run into each other's area," Desai says. "One of you has to be a boss. You can take turns—one is boss for six months, then the other one is—but **someone has to defer to someone else**. One person has to have the final decision-making responsibility."

Leaving Some Room

One tip Nevins offers other married business partners is to **give each other space—literally**.

"Sharon has an office down the hall. Other than the times we meet with a client together, she runs her division and **we don't see that much of each other**. If we were in the same room or meeting together all the time, that would be too much of a good thing," he says.

Another policy both Nevins and Susana V. Ptak, co-owner of Gascoyne Laboratories Inc., recommend is **leaving work at the office**.

Ptak, who co-owns the Baltimore environmental testing lab with husband Francis, agrees: "Two things have helped us not to kill each other," she says, laughing. "One is that **we don't do the same thing** (Francis is a chemist and handles the analytic end of the company; Susana takes care of the business side), and the other is that **we don't talk business at home**. In the car, yes, but once we're actually at home, we just talk family stuff.

"Don't confuse your business with your family," Ptak continues. "If you do, you'll go berserk."

Handling Conflict

To make the business work, a couple must **recognize that the company has specific needs**, says Patrick O. Ring, Baker-Meekins' managing director. "Make a plan, examine your goals, and build in some mechanism to achieve those goals and to resolve conflicts."

The overriding issue to be addressed is, **"What makes sense for the business?** How is the business going to grow? In which direction is it going to grow? How can you make it grow?" Ring adds.

"You need to explicitly talk about such issues," says Desai. **"You can't wait until a crisis occurs** to make a decision."

In times of conflict, **keep the argument between yourselves**. "Don't put the employee, or the business itself, in the middle," Adams advises.

"It's important to **be fair to your workers**," agrees Susana Ptak, whose lab has 61 employees. "Be careful that your employees see you and your spouse as a united front."

Of course, **not all partnerships work out as successfully** as the Nevins' and the Ptaks'.

Sometimes couples get divorces, just as sometimes business partnerships fail. That's an eventuality couples should be prepared for, says Adams.

He recommends that spouses **make an agreement at the beginning** that one partner can buy out the other in case of divorce. Without an agreement, you could spend time and money in litigation.

"Life's too short to **spend all that energy on disputes**," he says.

While arguments are bound to crop up, whether in a marriage or a business partnership, **they don't have to destroy either relationship**.

"Money breeds all sorts of snarling snakes," Adams says, "but you can work out your problems. **It just requires discipline and a willingness** not to let a disagreement destroy a marriage—or a business."

SOURCE: **www.NMQ.com** (accessed March 1, 2001).

WHICH FORM OF BUSINESS IS BEST FOR YOU?

Only you, your lawyer, your business advisor, and your accountant will know for sure what form is best for you and your particular situation. You and your taxi squad should consider the following before making the determination.

- international exposure
- tax implications
- liability issues
- litigiousness of customers, employees, and businesses in your state
- plans for business growth
- family structure and involvement in the business
- relationship with potential partners
- exit strategy

Spend time and money consulting with your taxi squad to determine what is best for you early on because there are many pitfalls and change can be costly. Let your taxi squad help you avoid major errors.

The legal form of your business is just that—a form, a shape. To your customers, the particular form you choose may not be obvious; but to you, the right shape is absolutely essential. You want your business to be rock-solid, stable, and protected—and you want to be able to change its form if the first choice doesn't work.

Beyond the mental images we have of these forms of ownership, there are business realities—and various amounts of paperwork—that you should know about. Table 10.1 summarizes the differences.

Sole Proprietorships

Most small businesses begin as sole proprietorships. If you start a business on your own—without partners—you are a sole proprietor unless you form an LLC or corporation. If this form is your choice, the paperwork will be relatively easy. Check with your local city offices to determine which licenses will be needed. If you are a service business, you may be required to purchase a license to do business in each city in which you operate. In some cities inspectors visit work sites to ensure that all businesses are in compliance. Get your required licenses! Fines are considerably more expensive than licenses.

You will also need to discuss tax requirements with your accountant, insurance matters with an insurance representative, and legal issues with an attorney before you open your doors.

TABLE 10.1
S Corp., C Corp., or No Corp., Choice of Business Entities—A Comparison

Applicable Factor	Sole Proprietor	Partnership	Limited Liability Company*	S Corporation	C Corporation
Formation					
Method	None	Partnership agreement	Articles of Organization filed in state recognizing LLCs	Articles of Incorporation	Articles of Incorporation
Owner Eligibility Number of Owners	One	Two or more for limited partnership; one or more general and one or more limited for general partnership	No limit	35	No limit
Type of Owners	Individual	No limitation	No limitation	Individuals and certain trusts	No limitation
Affiliate Limits	No limitation	No limitation	No limitation	No subsidiaries	No limitation
Capital Structure	No stock	No limitations (multiple classes)	No limitation	Only one class of stock	No limitations (multiple classes permitted)
Liability	Unlimited	General partners jointly and severally liable. Limited partners are generally limited to capital contributions.	Limited to member's capital contribution	Limited to shareholders' contributions	Limited to shareholder's capital contributions
Operational Phase					
Tax Year	Calendar year	Generally calendar year	Generally calendar year	Generally calendar year	Generally any year permitted (limit for personal service corporation)
Tax on Income	Individual level	Owner level	Member level	Owner level	Corporate level
Allocation of Income/ Deductions	N/A	Permitted if substantial economic effect	Permitted if substantial economic effect	Not permitted (except through debt/equity structure)	Not permitted (except through multiple equity structure)
Character of Income/ Deductions	Flow-through to individual	Flow-through to partners	Flow-through to members	Flow-through to shareholders	No flow-through to shareholders

*Some states (New York, for example) use the term LLP—Limited Liability Partnership.

If you are conducting a business in a name other than your own, the Uniform Commercial Code requires that you publish notice in your community newspaper to notify customers and creditors of who owns the business. Corporations are usually exempt. Contact your newspaper for the DBA (doing business as) forms, fill out the forms, and send a check (usually for less than $100) to the newspaper to complete the process.

Partnerships

A partnership, as lots of people find out too late, is only an accounting entity. It does not shield one from trouble. It won't make your business immortal or continuous, and it is taxed the same as a sole proprietorship. One plus about a partnership is that it allows the financial and moral support of a teammate.

A partnership is made up of at least two parties. There can be more—six, ten, a baker's dozen—but the more partners a business has, the trickier the decisions. Think of a ship with a dozen captains. Who makes the decisions?

In a limited partnership—composed of two or more limited partners and one general partner—the general partner assumes both managerial duties and the downside risk. A limited partner's liability is limited to the *amount* of his or her original investment as long as he or she has had no role in management decisions. *Do not proceed in such a partnership without legal advice.*

You *can* form a partnership with a handshake, and dissolve it without one; however, it is not advisable to proceed with *any* partnership without benefit of an attorney's counsel.

A partnership is somewhat of a paradox. In a legal sense the partnership doesn't do much for you, but as many partners admit, there are sound psychological and financial reasons for going into business with someone else.

What are some of those reasons? Let's say you've analyzed your personal skills, and realize you need balance in a couple of critical areas. For example, you may be an engineer who can come up with 20 original ideas a day but couldn't sell ice in Florida in the summer. Or perhaps you don't have much money so you need a partner who can supply your new business with capital. Or maybe you get along with people and love to sell and need to team up with an inventor/producer who can supply you with products to sell. Many successful business owners could never have started or succeeded in a business without a partner.

Before committing to a partnership, realize that friendship alone will not resolve business problems. All involved partners need to decide what exactly each brings to the table and then decide if what is brought is worth the complications of a partnership. There will be many unspoken fears and needs of all involved parties. Keeping the lines of communication open is essential for survival.

Business counselors run a lucrative business trying to work out the problems of warring partners. To reduce problems, do your research before starting a partnership and talk continually to keep the partnership successful. You must trust your partner(s) and have confidence in their decisions. A partnership is like a marriage, without the love. You may very well spend more time each week with your business partner than your marriage partner. During tough times in a marriage, duty, commitment, and children may hold the partnership together. What will hold your business together during the rocky times?

Following are several areas that should be discussed with your potential partners.

Questions for Partner Discussion

- **Management and control.** Who will make the final decisions on both small and large issues? Who will have control and responsibility for each area of the business? In one partnership the owners take turns each year trading off being the president and final decision-maker.
- **Dispute resolution.** How will disputes be resolved? Will you use mediation or arbitration if you reach a stalemate?
- **Financial contributions.** How much will you each contribute? It is necessary to determine not only initial contributions but also possible future contributions. An initial 50-50 partnership may turn into a 75-25 partnership if capital needs arise. How will you each of you deal with this change? How will profits and responsibilities change if the financial commitments change?
- **Time contributions.** How much time will each partner commit? Are these contributions considered equal? If you commit 20 hours and the other partner(s) 40, will profit distributions reflect this variance?
- **Demise of the partnership.** If the partnership is to be dissolved, how will the ending be dealt with? What is the buy-out procedure? Who and how will the valuation of the business be determined in the event of death, disability, or sale? What steps should you take to protect the business and its transfer?
- **New partners.** Can new partners be added? If so, what will the process be to include new partners? What number of partners are you willing to take on? Do partners have veto power?
- **Participation of family members as employees and their input into the business.** See Key Points from Another View at the end of the chapter for additional information.

On the surface partnerships make a lot of sense. Two or more entrepreneurs face the unknown together and pool their skills. They can raise more capital than one person could alone. But forming a good *partnership* can be more difficult than forming a good *marriage*.

After the previous questions are answered, you may be ready to review the sample partnership agreement in Figure 10.1 for further discussions with your partners. The

FIGURE 10.1

Sample Partnership Agreement Provided by Internet Legal Resource Guide

NOTE: THE FORMS AVAILABLE THROUGH THIS WEB SITE ARE NOT A SUBSTITUTE FOR THE ADVICE OF AN ATTORNEY. LEGAL ADVICE OF ANY NATURE SHOULD BE SOUGHT FROM COMPETENT, INDEPENDENT, LEGAL COUNSEL IN THE RELEVANT JURISDICTION. ABSOLUTELY NO WARRANTIES ARE MADE REGARDING THE SUITABILITY OF THESE FORMS FOR ANY PARTICULAR PURPOSE.

PARTNERSHIP AGREEMENT

This PARTNERSHIP AGREEMENT is made on ___________, 20__ between ____________________ and______________ of __________.

1. **NAME AND BUSINESS**. The parties hereby form a partnership under the name of ________________ to conduct a ____________________. The principal office of the business shall be in __________________.

2. **TERM.** The partnership shall begin on ___________, 20__, and shall continue until terminated as herein provided.

3. **CAPITAL**. The capital of the partnership shall be contributed in cash by the partners as follows: A separate capital account shall be maintained for each partner. Neither partner shall withdraw any part of his capital account. On the demand of either partner, the capital accounts of the partners shall be maintained at all times in the proportions in which the partners share in the profits and losses of the partnership.

4. **PROFIT AND LOSS**. The net profits of the partnership shall be divided equally between the partners and the net losses shall be borne equally by them. A separate income account shall be maintained for each partner. Partnership profits and losses shall be charged or credited to the separate income account of each partner. If a partner has no credit balance in his income account, losses shall be charged to his capital account.

5. **SALARIES AND DRAWINGS**. Neither partner shall receive any salary for services rendered to the partnership. Each partner may, from time to time, withdraw the credit balance in his income account.

6. **INTEREST**. No interest shall be paid on the initial contributions to the capital of the partnership or on any subsequent contributions of capital.

7. **MANAGEMENT DUTIES AND RESTRICTIONS**. The partners shall have equal rights in the management of the partnership business, and each partner shall devote his entire time to the conduct of the business. Without the consent of the other partner neither partner shall on behalf of the partnership borrow or lend money, or make, deliver, or accept any commercial paper, or execute any mortgage, security agreement, bond, or lease, or purchase or contract to purchase, or sell or contract to sell any property for or of the partnership other than the type of property bought and sold in the regular course of its business.

8. **BANKING**. All funds of the partnership shall be deposited in its name in such checking account or accounts as shall be designated by the partners. All withdrawals therefrom are to be made on checks signed by either partner.

9. **BOOKS**. The partnership books shall be maintained at the principal office of the partnership, and each partner shall at all times have access thereto. The books shall be kept on a fiscal year basis, commencing ______ and ending _______, and shall be closed and balanced at the end of each fiscal year. An audit shall be made as of the closing date.

10. **VOLUNTARY TERMINATION**. The partnership may be dissolved at any time by agreement of the partners, in which event the partners shall proceed with reasonable promptness to liquidate the business of the partnership. The partnership name shall be sold with the other assets of the business. The assets of the partnership business shall be used and distributed in the following order: (a) to pay or provide for the payment of all partnership liabilities and liquidating expenses and obligations; (b) to equalize the income accounts of the partners; (c) to discharge the balance of the income accounts of the partners; (d) to equalize the capital accounts of the partners; and (e) to discharge the balance of the capital accounts of the partners.

11. **DEATH**. On the death of either partner, the surviving partner shall have the right either to purchase the interest of the decedent in the partnership or to terminate and liquidate the partnership business. If the surviving partner elects to purchase the decedent's interest, he shall serve notice in writing of such election, within three months after the death of the decedent, on the executor or administrator of the decedent, or, if at the time of such election no legal representative has been appointed, on any one of the known legal heirs of the decedent at the last-known address of such heir. (a) If the surviving partner elects to purchase the interest of the decedent in the partnership, the purchase price shall be equal to the decedent's capital account as at the date of his death plus the decedent's income account as at the end of the prior fiscal year, increased by his share of partnership profits or decreased by his share of partnership losses for the period from the beginning of the fiscal year in which his death occurred until the end of the calendar month in which his death occurred, and decreased by withdrawals charged to his income account during such period. No allowance shall be made for goodwill, trade name, patents, or other intangible assets, except as those assets have been reflected on the partnership books immediately prior to the decedent's death; but the

FIGURE 10.1
Sample Partnership Agreement Provided by Internet Legal Resource Guide—cont'd

survivor shall nevertheless be entitled to use the trade name of the partnership. (b) Except as herein otherwise stated, the procedure as to liquidation and distribution of the assets of the partnership business shall be the same as stated in paragraph 10 with reference to voluntary termination.

12. **ARBITRATION**. Any controversy or claim arising out of or relating to this Agreement, or the breach hereof, shall be settled by arbitration in accordance with the rules, then obtaining, of the American Arbitration Association, and judgment on the award rendered may be entered in any court having jurisdiction thereof. In witness whereof the parties have signed this Agreement.

Executed this ____________ day of ______________, 20_____ in [CITY], [STATE].

____

____

SOURCE: Internet Legal Resource Guide, **www.irlg.com/forms/partnership-agreement.html** (accessed March 12, 2001).

sample is provided to serve as a starting point and is *not meant* to be your partnership agreement. Reviewing the issues in this chapter and the sample agreement will give you a fair idea of what you should be discussing with your attorney and partners. **Remember to consult your attorney before signing any agreement.**

Corporations

There are at least six good reasons for incorporating. In general, we think most owners of small businesses fail to incorporate because they don't see the signals their businesses are giving. Ask yourself if there is any chance your employees, customers, or suppliers might sue you. The truth is that for almost all firms a great deal of risk exists; therefore incorporating in a LLC, S, or C Corporation should be seriously considered.

Employees driving your vehicles, customers being harmed in some way by a product or service (in ways you would never believe or consider), and customers or employees slipping and falling are just a few of the potential litigious situations that may occur. Consider the following reasons for incorporation:

1. ***You Limit Your Liability***. A corporation may act like a shield between you and the world. If your business fails, your creditors can't come after your house, your condo, your Porsche Boxster, your first-born, or your hard-won collectibles—provided you've done it right. And that is the key. To keep your corporate shield up, make sure you: (a) hold scheduled board of directors' meetings, (b) keep up the minute's book, and (c) act as if you are an employee of the corporation.

   The fact is almost all entrepreneurs use most of their personal assets as collateral for their business loans and thus the limited liability provided by a corporation may only limit your risk of personal financial loss. Ask your attorney how to reduce personal liability issues within your firm's operations. Safety precautions, disclaimers on products, having your employees covered by very high liability policies on their own cars, and proper hiring and firing methods are just a few ways to reduce your risks.
2. ***To Change Your Tax Picture***. Consult the current IRS schedule and ask a CPA for advice.
3. ***To Upgrade Your Image***. What does the word *corporation* mean to you? IBM? Intel? TWA? GM? Let's look at that word. It comes from the Latin *corpus*, which means, "body." To *incorporate* means to make, form, or shape into a body. Looked at from that angle, *incorporating* starts to sound creative. As a corporation, you may enjoy more prestige, attract better employees, and have more clout in the world.
4. ***To Have the Opportunity to Channel Some Heavy Expenses***. Medical and insurance premiums and FICA payments become business expenses.
5. ***To Guarantee Continuity***. If one owner goes to Australia, dies, or becomes ill, the corporation keeps on chugging. That's because you've gone through a lot of red tape and planning to set it up that way.

6. ***To Offer Internal Incentives.*** When you want to reward special employees or retain your best ones, you can offer stock or a promotion (for example, a vice-presidency) in addition to (or in place of) pay raises. Becoming a corporate officer carries its own special excitement, and this gives you flexibility.

According to Nolo.com, a corporation may be advised over a LLC if the following factors exist:

1. You expect to have multiple investors in your business to raise money from the public.
2. You want to set up a single-member LLC, but you live in a state that requires two or more members.
3. You'd like to provide extensive fringe benefits to owner-employees.
4. You want to entice or keep key employees by offering stock options and stock bonus incentives.
5. Your accountant has reviewed the issue with self-employment taxes and weighs in on the decision.

Limited Liability Company

Most states have recently allowed a Limited Liability Company (LLC) to be an acceptable form of business. This entity does not limit the number of investors, allows profits to be distributed in a manner other than investors' capital contribution as a "pass through" tax entity, and limits liability. It is expected that LLCs will be the entity of choice for closely held businesses in the near future. LLCs are designed to provide the tax flexibility and ownership of partnerships with the limited liability features of corporations.

The operating agreement sets out the company's membership and operational rules. In addition, the agreement states how members' profits and losses are shared.

LLCs provide the flow-through tax treatment that has been available to partnerships and subchapter S corporations. The required documentation, known as "articles of organization," is less detailed than articles of incorporation and is usually less costly. See Figure 10.2 for a sample state registration application for articles of organization.

The articles of organization contain an "operating agreement" that resembles a partnership agreement. LLC members may manage the business themselves or delegate such authority to active managers.

Most state statutes require that identifying information such "Limited Liability Company" or "LLC" appear in the name of the company to notify others as to the limited liability enjoyed by the organization. The IRS has ruled that such organizations will be taxed at the individual rate. Be careful! If an LLC is not properly structured, it will be taxed as a corporation.

LLCs generally will not be appropriate for existing corporations or businesses that have or want to raise capital through the public or venture capital markets. If you are considering converting to an LLC, be aware there may be significant tax consequences. It is vital that you consult competent tax, legal, and accounting advisors.

A few states have LLPs (Limited Liability Partnerships), which contain liability exceptions for certain professional service firms (doctors, architects, engineers, etc.). Check the laws in your state.

Subchapter S Corporations

In addition to the standard C corporations, there are subchapter S corporations, which are semicorporate bodies that limit an owner's liability while still allowing a pass-through of business losses to the personal income statements of the owners, founders, and others. Subchapter S refers to the section of the 1958 IRS code that describes the way the corporation will be taxed.

FIGURE 10.2
Limited Liability Company Act

Form **LLC-5.5** January 2000	**Illinois** **Limited Liability Company Act** **Articles of Organization**	**This space for use by Secretary of State**
Jesse White Secretary of State Department of Business Services Limited Liability Company Division Room 359, Howlett Building Springfield, IL 62756 http://www.sos.state.il.us	**SUBMIT IN DUPLICATE** Must be typewritten This space for use by Secretary of State	
Payment must be made by certified check, cashier's check, Illinois attorney's check, Illinois C.P.A.'s check or money order, payable to "Secretary of State."	Date Assigned File # Filing Fee $400.00 Approved:	

1. Limited Liability Company Name: ______________________________

   ____

   (The LLC name must contain the words limited liability company, L.L.C. or LLC and cannot contain the terms corporation, corp., incorporated, inc., ltd., co., limited partnership, or L.P.)

2. If transacting business under an assumed name, complete and attach Form LLC-1.20.

3. The address of its principal place of business: (Post office box alone and c/o are unacceptable.)

   ____

   ____

4. The Articles of Organization are effective on: (Check one)

   a) ______ the filing date, or b) ______ another date later than but not more than 60 days subsequent to the filing date: ______________________ (month, day, year)

5. The registered agent's name and registered office address is:

   Registered agent: ______________________________
   First Name *Middle Initial* *Last Name*

   Registered Office: ______________________________
   Number *Street* *Suite #*
   (P.O. Box and c/o are unacceptable) ______________________________
   City *ZIP Code* *County*

6. Purpose or purposes for which the LLC is organized: Include the business code # (IRS Form 1065).
   (If not sufficient space to cover this point, add one or more sheets of this size.)

   "The transaction of any or all lawful business for which limited liability companies may be organized under this Act."

7. The latest date, if any, upon which the company is to dissolve ______________________ .
   (month, day, year)

   Any other events of dissolution enumerated on an attachment. (Optional)

LLC-4.5

FIGURE 10.2
Limited Liability Company Act—cont'd

LLC-5.5

8. Other provisions for the regulation of the internal affairs of the LLC per Section 5-5 (a) (8) included as attachment:
If yes, state the provisions(s) from the ILLCA. ☐ Yes ☐ No

9. a) Management is by manager(s): ☐ Yes ☐ No
If yes, list names and business addresses.

b) Management is vested in the member(s): ☐ Yes ☐ No
If yes, list names and addresses.

10. I affirm, under penalties of perjury, having authority to sign hereto, that these articles of organization are to the best of my knowledge and belief, true, correct and complete.

Dated ______________________________ , __________
(Month/Day) (Year)

Signature(s) and Name(s) of Organizer(s)	**Business Address(es)**
1. ______________________ *Signature*	1. ______________________ *Number* *Street*
______________________ *(Type or print name and title)*	______________________ *City/Town*
______________________ *(Name if a corporation or other entity)*	______________________ *State* *ZIP Code*
2. ______________________ *Signature*	2. ______________________ *Number* *Street*
______________________ *(Type or print name and title)*	______________________ *City/Town*
______________________ *(Name if a corporation or other entity)*	______________________ *State* *ZIP Code*
3. ______________________ *Signature*	3. ______________________ *Number* *Street*
______________________ *(Type or print name and title)*	______________________ *City/Town*
______________________ *(Name if a corporation or other entity)*	______________________ *State* *ZIP Code*

(Signatures must be in ink on an original document. Carbon copy, photocopy or rubber stamp signatures may only be used on conformed copies.)

LLC-4.5

SOURCE: **www.sos.state.il.us** (accessed March 5, 2001).

The number of stockholders is limited to 35, and corporate income (or loss) is allowed to be passed directly to the stockholders. There is no corporate tax. The IRS has specific time requirements for filing, and some states do not recognize the tax aspects of the Subchapter S category. Verify your state laws. Your attorney can assist you. In a subchapter S corporation, you cannot have any corporate stockholders, partnership(s) stockholders, or trusts as investors. Thus most S corporations lose their S status when venture capital firms invest.

You will be required to supply each of your stockholders with a "K-1" tax report by April 15 of each year. You must follow a calendar tax year with few exceptions. You can drop your S corporation status if you find there are tax advantages to being a regular corporation, but timing is important.

PROTECT YOURSELF

If you don't use a good lawyer to help structure your business, you probably won't have a plan to handle **contingencies**, and unforeseen events can take you by surprise and cost you dearly. If Paul Webber had used his imagination to look ahead, his story might have turned out differently.

A Partner's Unforeseen Death

Paul Webber was a software game developer when he met MaryAnn Dominic. MaryAnn, a likable woman, had four years experience designing game software and was a dynamite salesperson. They got together and formed "Gamestar."

Their first year was okay—they netted more than $50,000 apiece—and their second year was looking even better.

By May of their second year their projections told them they could make $75,000 each before the end of the summer. They thought it felt great to have cash, and to celebrate, they went out to dinner.

At dinner MaryAnn passed out and was pronounced dead by the paramedics on their arrival. At 32 years old MaryAnn Dominic was dead of a heart attack. Two weeks after the funeral, Paul was on the phone with a customer when MaryAnn's widower, Jason, walked in. Jason had just inherited MaryAnn's half of the business.

Paul didn't like Jason being his partner but there was nothing he could do. He knew he would have to break his back to teach him the business. Game software was fast track and competitive—it changed before you could take a breath—and Jason would have to learn an awful lot in a short time.

Passion

Passion for Saving Lives—*It Was a Fatal Accident*

George Loke's best friend died unexpectedly. George was furious! His friend had been hospitalized for a minor surgical procedure and a healthcare worker accidentally brushed against a poorly attached intravenous (IV) line, disconnecting it and subsequently causing George's friend's death.

When George heard the news by phone, he tried to throw the phone across the room, and it snapped back. Angrily he inspected the cord and observed that a simple "click lock" attached it. If only his friend's IV tube had been attached by such a "click lock," his friend would still be alive. Within weeks he designed a workable prototype of an "IV click lock." He soon had a patent issued, and today his IV click lock has become the world standard for IV delivery. Anger and frustration are great motivational factors for innovation. George's passion for his friend and his passion to never allow the same thing to happen again are the driving forces behind his successful product and business.

Contingencies Steps taken to protect one against unforeseen future events

Paul was a good guy, so he tried. The first month, he was extra tired because he was handling his own customers while also spending long hours trying to teach Jason the business. The second month, two of Paul's customers kept on hold defected to a competitor. Paul heard about it through the grapevine. The third month, the company almost ran out of cash, and Paul had to dump in $5,000 from his personal account to keep suppliers happy.

Jason wasn't learning the business. He was getting in Paul's hair, and was spending money. Jason wasn't able to hold up his end, and there was no improvement in sight.

Paul hung on for another week. Then he did the only thing he could do for his own survival: He took what customers he had left and rented an office six blocks away in an attempt to keep going. He figured he had paid his dues to MaryAnn. It wasn't long before Jason's lawyer came calling, though, making Paul nervous and unsure of the consequences and future.

Buy–Sell Agreements

Many small business owners ignore the need for buy–sell agreements, or having a will drawn up. They keep putting if off. A buy–sell agreement would have solved Paul's problems after MaryAnn's death.

When forming your partnership, one of the major contingencies to consider is the **dissolution of the partnership**. Partnerships can end as a result of death, illness, divorce, lack of interest, financial or philosophical differences, or desire for a change in lifestyle. Protect your business, yourself, and your loved ones.

These agreements are often funded by a "key man" life insurance policy on the owners, so that if one dies, the business or other owners can collect the life insurance policy's proceeds and use those funds to buy out the deceased's interest in the business.

For dissolving the partnership under other circumstances, your buy–sell agreement should include who will evaluate the business and how payment will be made by the remaining partners and over what time period. As your business grows and changes, you will want to reevaluate your agreement.

When partners split up, and most eventually do, a buy–sell agreement may keep the dissolution out of court. Think of it as a prenuptial agreement.

Legal fees to draw up a buy–sell agreement and key man insurance premiums are probably two of the best financial investments you and your partners will ever make. A sample buy–sell agreement, available online, should only be used as a starting point for discussions with your partners. **No buy–sell agreement should ever be undertaken without advice of legal and financial counsel.**

COPYRIGHTS, PATENTS, AND TRADEMARKS

Copyrights, patents, and trademarks are important elements of your business. Without protecting them, (1) you may lose your business, (2) your ideas may be stolen, or (3) your products may be copied. The following material on patents, trademarks, and copyrights is published by permission from the copyright holder: Knobbe, Martens, Olson, and Bear, LLP.

Because Intellectual Property laws are subject to change, consult with your Intellectual Property counsel rather than relying on this material for legal advice. The information following provides an excellent starting point for a discussion with your lawyer.

Ten Things You Should Know to Protect Your Inventions

1. **What Is a Patent?**

   A patent is a right granted to inventors by the government to exclude others from making, selling, offering for sale, using, or importing an invention.

Dissolution of a Partnership The separation of partners, an eventuality that needs to be prepared for with intricate planning and much thought

The U.S. Government has issued more than 5,000,000 patents during the past 200 years. These patents cover many types of inventions and discoveries, including machines, compositions of matter, methods, computer software, plants, microorganisms, and designs. Three types of patents are available in the United States. The first, called a utility patent, covers inventions and discoveries, which are defined in the claims of the patent. A utility patent expires 20 years from the day a regular patent application is filed for the invention. In addition to the claims, a utility patent must include a written description of the invention and drawings, where applicable. A second type of patent, a design patent, gives the patent owner the right to exclude others from the nonfunctional, ornamental designs shown and claimed in the patent. This type of patent expires 14 years from the date it issues. The third type of patent is a plant patent, which gives the patent owner the right to exclude others from asexually reproducing a patented plant, or from selling or using an asexually reproduced patented plant. Plants that are sexually reproduced (i.e., through seeds) can be protected under separate, non-patent protection, available under the Plant Variety Protection Act.

2. **What Is the Test for Getting a Patent?**

   To obtain a utility patent, the invention defined in the patent claims must be new and nonobvious to a person of ordinary skill in the field of the invention. Many patents are for combinations of previously existing parts combined in a new, nonobvious way to achieve improved results. A design patent requires a new, nonfunctional, ornamental design that is nonobvious to an ordinary designer in the field of the invention. In all cases the initial evaluation and patentability decision will be made by an Examiner at the United States Patent and Trademark Office. Only the first and original inventor(s) may obtain a valid patent. Thus you cannot obtain a patent in the United States for an invention you saw overseas because you are not the first or the original inventor. Similarly, someone who sees your invention cannot obtain a valid patent on it because that person is not the first or original inventor. But someone else could improve your invention, and patent the improvement. It typically takes about one year from filing the U.S. application before the Examiner sends the initial evaluation of patentability although the process can be expedited with additional effort and cost.

3. **What Is a Patentability Search?**

   When a U.S. patent application is filed, the Patent Office will conduct a search of the patents on file in the U.S. Patent and Trademark Office in Washington, D.C. and a smaller selection of foreign patents and non-patent references. Inventors can have a similar patentability search conducted in order to better evaluate the cost and probability of obtaining patent protection for their invention. Evaluating patentability search results is complex, requiring not only an understanding of the pertinent technology but also of patent law. The U.S. Patent Office tests and authorizes persons with appropriate technical backgrounds to file and prosecute patent matters before the Patent Office. You should consider contacting a registered patent attorney authorized to practice before the U.S. Patent and Trademark Office to assist with your evaluation.

4. **What Is a Patent Notice?**

   A product or accompanying literature is typically marked with a patent notice such as "Patent 5,000,000" or "Pat. No. 5,000,000" when the product, or the method used to produce the product, is patented. Marking the patent number gives notice of the patent rights to potential infringers. The term: "Patent Pending" means a patent has been applied for, but has not yet issued.

5. **When Must I Apply for a Patent?**

   An application for a patent must be filed in the United States within one year of the first date that the invention is (1) disclosed in a printed publication,

(2) publicly used, or (3) offered for sale. In most foreign countries a patent must be filed before any public disclosure is made anywhere in the world. The rules for determining when an invention is publicly disclosed, used, or offered for sale are complex, and you should seek the advice of a patent attorney if you have a question in this regard. By treaty with most, but not all, foreign countries, if a U.S. application is filed before any public disclosure is made, a foreign patent application may be filed up to one year after the U.S. filing date. Thus, if a U.S. patent application is filed before any public disclosure of the invention, the option to pursue foreign patent rights in many foreign countries is preserved for one year. Filing a U.S. patent application after a public disclosure, however, usually prevents filing in most foreign countries.

Recent amendments to the patent laws created a "provisional patent application" that enables an informal and less expensive filing to preserve patent rights for 12 months. It also extends the term of the patent one year. The provisional application is not examined and lapses after 12 months. Accordingly, a regular patent application must be filed within those 12 months in order to claim the benefit of the provisional application's filing date and to have the patent claims examined and issued. Likewise, foreign applications must be filed within those 12 months in order to claim the benefit of the provisional application filing date.

6. **What Is a World-Wide Patent?**

There is no single, world-wide patent. Each country has different laws. Thus a patent covers only the country or countries issuing the patent. For example, a U.S. patent can prevent an infringing product that is made overseas from being sold in the United States, but will not prevent it from being sold in a foreign country. There are several international treaties which enable much of the patent prosecution to be consolidated for many countries, provided there was no public disclosure before the U.S. application was filed. Ultimately, however, the patent application must be translated and filed in each country where a patent is sought. The Patent Cooperation Treaty allows the additional cost of translating and filing in each foreign country to be delayed for up to 33 months from the U.S. filing date. During this 33-month period, it is often possible to test the market for the product and better judge the potential benefits of pursuing foreign patent protection.

7. **Does a Patent Guarantee My Right to Sell My Product?**

A patent gives its owner the right to exclude others from practicing the patented invention for the duration of the patent. It does not give the owner the right to make the patented invention. It is thus possible to have an improved and patented product that infringes a prior patent. For example, one person obtains a patent for a chair. Later, a second person obtains a patent for a rocking chair. The first person could stop the second person from selling rocking chairs because they incorporate the original chair and thus infringe the first person's patent.

8. **What Is an Infringement Study?**

An infringement study determines whether an unexpired patent has claims that might encompass a product or method that is being made, used, or sold without authorization by the patent owner. If it is determined that a product or method may infringe someone else's patent, the design may be altered to avoid infringement, or a license may be negotiated with the patent owner.

Infringement studies require an ability to understand and apply the pertinent technology to the applicable patent law.

You should consider contacting an experienced patent attorney for such infringement studies. If a defendant is found guilty of willfully infringing another's U.S. patent, the court can treble the damage award and require the payment of the patent owner's attorneys' fees. Thus questions of patent infringement should not be taken lightly.

9. **Are Patents Worth the Costs?**

   For many years, courts often held patents invalid or not infringed, making it difficult to enforce them. That changed dramatically with the creation of a single Court of Appeals that now decides the appeals from all patent cases throughout the United States. Patent law is now applied much more uniformly. A presumption of patent validity is being upheld, fewer patents are invalidated, and more patents are found infringed. Patents can be a significant source of income. Texas Instruments Inc. is reported as having received $600 million dollars in patent royalties over a four-year period.

   Polaroid's lawsuit against Eastman Kodak shut down Kodak's entire instant-camera facility, and the damages awarded were nearly a billion dollars. The bottom line is that patents are now easier to enforce.

   While that is good for patent owners, it also means that those accused of patent infringement must take prompt steps to minimize their exposure.

10. **Where Can I Get More Information on Patents?**

    Additional information on patents may be obtained from the U.S. Patent and Trademark Office, Washington, D.C., 20231. Patents from the 1970s on are accessible over the Internet from the U.S. Patent Office and from IBM. Patent Depository Libraries containing the text of many of the more than 5,000,000 issued U.S. patents are available in major libraries.

Ten Things You Should Know to Protect Your Artwork, Ads, Writings, and Software

1. **What Is a Copyright?**

   Copyright exists in any original "expression" of an idea that is fixed in any physical medium such as paper, electronic tapes, or floppy disks. Copyrights cover such diverse things as art, songs, technical and architectural drawings, books, computer programs, and advertisements. Copyright protects only the expression, not the idea itself; it does not protect facts, words, short phrases, or slogans.

2. **What Protection Does a Copyright Give?**

   Copyright protection encompasses a bundle of exclusive rights that include: (1) the right to reproduce the work; (2) the right to make derivative works; (3) the right to distribute copies by sale, lease, or rental; (4) the right to publicly perform certain works such as plays or audiovisual works; and (5) the right to publicly display certain works such as pictorial or sculptural works.

   These rights may be licensed or transferred together or separately. For example, an author may grant a book company the rights to reproduce a book, may grant a movie studio the rights to make a movie derived from the book, and may grant foreign distribution rights to other companies.

3. **How Long Does a Copyright Last?**

   U.S. Copyright protection for works created after January 1, 1978, will last for the life of the author plus 70 years after his death. If the work was created for an employer by an employee within the scope of his or her employment, the copyright protection will last for 95 years from the date of first publication, or 120 years from the date of creation, whichever is shorter.

   If a U.S. work was created before January 1, 1978, and the copyright was not forfeited so as to place the work in the public domain, then the copyright can last for a total of 75 years, provided that any necessary renewals are made in a timely manner. Determining precisely when the term of the copyright ends, and who owns any renewal rights, are complex matters for which legal advice should be sought.

4. **Can I Copyright Factual Information?**

   Compilations of factual data, like names or part numbers, may be copyrightable, but the protection is limited to such things as the selection and arrangement of the information. Facts by themselves cannot be protected by copyright, even if considerable time and expense went into compiling the facts. In appropriate cases trade secret protection may be available for the factual information.

5. **If I Change 10 Percent, Can I Use Copyrighted Works?**

If the portion taken is the heart of the copyrighted work, or from a widely recognized portion of the work, then infringement can exist even though less than 10 percent of the copyrighted work is taken. The test for copyright infringement is whether the accused work is copied from, and "substantially similar" to, the copyrighted work. Thus there is no "rule" or fixed amount with respect to the portion of a work which one must change in order to avoid infringement.

6. **Must Copyrights Be Registered?**

Under current law, a copyright need not be registered until a U.S. citizen wants to file a lawsuit against an infringer. Registration, however, offers the copyright holder some significant advantages. For example, if a work is registered before an infringement commences, then the infringer may be liable for statutory damages up to $150,000 for each copyright that is infringed, and may also have to pay the attorney's fees incurred by the copyright owner in the lawsuit.

7. **Do I Need a Copyright Notice?**

For U.S. works first published after March 1, 1989, a copyright notice is not necessary to maintain copyright rights. But using a copyright notice makes it difficult for other people to claim that they are "innocent" infringers who were misled by the absence of a copyright notice.

For U.S. works first published between 1978 and 1989, the omission of copyright notice from published works could result in the loss of copyright rights unless certain steps were taken in a timely manner. For U.S. works first published before 1978, omission of copyright notice from published works usually resulted in the loss of any copyright protection.

A copyright notice consists of the copyright symbol ©, the year a work is first published, and the name of the copyright owner, (e.g., © 2001 Knobbe, Martens, Olson & Bear, LLP). If a sound recording is copyrighted, use ℗ along with the first publication date and owner. If the copyrighted material is revised, add the year of the revision to the copyright notice. It is also advisable to add "All Rights Reserved."

8. **Do I Own Copyrights I Pay Others to Create?**

You probably do not own the copyright in material you pay independent contractors to prepare, unless you have a written agreement transferring the ownership of any copyrights.

While a business usually owns the copyrights in works created by full time employees within the scope of their employment, the business has only limited rights to use copyrightable works created by independent contractors. Ownership of works created by employees, but not in their normal course of employment, varies with the facts of each case.

Ownership issues are often complex. An attorney should be consulted on such issues.

9. **Do Foreign Countries Protect Copyrights?**

The United States has long been a member of the Universal Copyright Convention through which copyright protection may be obtained in many foreign countries. In 1988 the United States joined the Berne Convention through which copyright protection may be obtained in the vast majority of foreign countries.

Obtaining and enforcing copyrights in foreign countries requires complying with the laws and treaties of each individual country. An attorney knowledgeable in copyright law should be consulted about any specific needs.

10. **Where Can I Get More Information on Copyrights?**
    Information on copyright registrations may be obtained from the Register of Copyrights, Library of Congress, in Washington, D.C, **www.loc.gov.**

Ten Things You Should Know to Protect Your Product and Business Names

1. **What is a Trademark?**
   A trademark is usually a brand name for a product. However , it can be a word, phrase, logo, design, or virtually anything that is used to identify its owner's product and distinguish it from competitors' products. CHEVROLET®, BMW "The Ultimate Driving Machine," and logos are trademarks.
   A trademark represents the goodwill and reputation of a product and its source. Its owner has the right to prevent others from trading on that goodwill by using the same or a similar product in a way that is likely to cause confusion as to the source, origin, or sponsorship of the products.
   A service mark is just like a trademark, except it is used to identify and distinguish services rather than products. American Express® is a service mark for retail store services.
   The terms trademark or "mark" are often used interchangeably to refer to either a trademark or service mark.
2. **How Should a Mark Be Used?**
   If used incorrectly, the rights to a mark may be lost, allowing anyone to use the mark. For example, these rights can be lost if the mark becomes the generic name for the product. Because competitors need to use generic words to describe their products, no one can own trademark rights to generic terms. Kerosene, corn flakes, and nylon were once trademarks, but are now generic names.
   To prevent loss of trademark or service mark rights, the generic name for the product should appear after the mark, and the mark should appear visually different from the surrounding text. Use different type size, type style, color, or quotation marks for the trademark or service mark, as in **KODAK®** cameras, iMac® computers, or "Carl's Jr.®" restaurant services. You may also use an asterisk (*) after a mark where the asterisk refers to a footnote explaining the ownership of a mark.
   Marks should be used only as proper adjectives, and never as nouns or verbs.
   Referring to a XEROX® brand copier is fine, but it is improper to say you "bought a XEROX" or that you want to "XEROX a paper."
   If a mark is registered with the U.S. Patent and Trademark Office, then the federal registration symbol ® should be used next to the mark, such as **XEROX®**. If the mark is not federally registered, the letters TM may be used to indicate a trademark, or SM to indicate a service mark.
3. **What Is a Trade Name?**
   A trade name is the name of a business. Unlike trademarks, a trade name can be used as a noun, and is not required to be followed by generic terms.
   It is permissible to use all or a portion of a trade name as a trademark or service mark. While "XEROX Corporation" is a trade name, **XEROX®** is a trademark when used on copying machines, and may be a service mark when properly used with a copy machine rental, repair, and maintenance service.
4. **Does My Incorporation or Fictitious Business Name Statement Give Me the Right to Use My Name?**
   Most businesses form a corporation or file a Fictitious Business Name statement. Neither the Certificate of Incorporation nor the Fictitious Business Name statement gives a business the right to use in commerce a trade name which is likely to cause confusion with a trade name, trademark, or service mark that was previously used by someone else in the same area of trade.

The state or county agencies that issue the Certificates of Incorporation and Fictitious Business Name statements do not perform searches sufficient to ensure that your use would not infringe another's prior rights.

A court's determination of trademark infringement will override any Fictitious Business Name statement or any Certificate of Incorporation. Further, the legal test that the courts apply to determine the right to use trade name, trademarks, or service marks does not require that the names or products be identical: it requires only enough similarity to cause a likelihood of confusion. Thus neither of these filings means that you have the right to use your name in the advertising, promotion, or sale of goods or services.

5. **Must Trademarks Be Registered?**

There is no requirement to register your mark, but there are many advantages to doing so. A federally registered mark is presumed to be a valid mark and the registrant is presumed to have the exclusive right to use the trademark throughout the United States on the goods or services listed in the registration. After five years the registration may become incontestable, which significantly limits the grounds on which competitors can attach the registration. A registered mark will also be revealed in searches conducted by other businesses in their effort to avoid selecting marks that may conflict with those of others. Finally, only federally registered trademarks or service marks may use the ® symbol in the United States.

An application for a federal registration may be filed before a mark is ever actually used in commerce, provided that the applicant has a good faith intent to use the mark. Marks may also be registered in one or more of the 50 states, with the advantages of a state registration varying according to the laws of each state. A registration with the California Trademark Unit is usually obtained faster, cheaper, and with less difficulty than a federal registration. It also allows its owner to sue infringers under several California statutes that offer advantages not available under federal law. You must actually use a mark before applying for a California State trademark registration.

6. **What Is a Trademark Search?**

There are a number of professional search services that may be used to help ensure that your mark or trade name does not conflict with the existing rights of another business. The goal of such searches is to avoid spending time, effort, and money promoting a product name or business name only to have to change it at a later date because it conflicts with someone else's rights.

These searches are typically performed through attorneys because the search report is evaluated to determine whether there is an actual or potential conflict with another name or mark, and this evaluation depends on the consideration of numerous legal factors and case-law decisions.

7. **Is My Product's Shape or Packaging Protectable?**

The non-functional features of a product's shape or packaging (its "trade dress") are being protected with ever-increasing frequency. The appearance of a "C" clamp, of Ruger's 22 caliber pistol, a fingernail polish bottle, and the red border and format of **TIME®** magazine, have all been protected against look-alike competitive products. To help achieve this type of protection, non-functional and distinctive product features or packaging should be selected, and then promoted through "image advertising" so that customers recognize the product shape or packaging and associate it with a single source.

8. **Can I Register My Trade Dress?**

If your trade dress is non-functional, and is either inherently distinctive or has acquired customer recognition from sufficient promotion of the protectable features, it may be registered as a trademark. For example, the shape of the **WEBER®** barbecue grill and the clear tip of a **SHAKESPEARE®** fishing rod have been registered with the U.S. Patent and Trademark Office.

9. **What about Protection in Foreign Countries?**
   Trademark owners who have not registered their marks in foreign countries may find that the mark has been appropriated by a third party who was the first to register in that country as the true owner of the mark, even if it is a pirate who saw the mark in the United States and appropriated it. This pirate may even be a trusted foreign distributor of the trademarked product.
   Foreign pirates may be able to prevent the original U.S. owner of the mark from using it in one or more foreign countries. In some cases it may be possible to recover the mark, but the U.S. owner may face expensive litigation or exorbitant demands from the pirate.
   Generally, if a U.S. product is sold overseas, care must be taken to ensure the U.S. federal registration symbol ® is not used unless the mark is registered in the foreign country where the mark is used.
   Some countries have both civil and criminal penalties for using the ® symbol with a mark not registered in that country. Improper use of the ® symbol may also make the mark unenforceable in some countries.
10. **Where May I Get Information on Protecting Product and Business Names?**
   Information on trademarks may be obtained from the Trademark Unit of your Secretary of State's Office. Information on federal registrations may be obtained from the U.S. Patent and Trademark Office in Washington, D.C., **www.uspto.gov**.
   The assistance of an attorney experienced in trademark matters can help avoid problems before they arise.

SOURCE: Knobbe, Martens, Olson and Bear, L.L.P. Use of company names and trademarks is solely for the purpose of examples, and does not imply sponsorship, affiliation, or endorsement by respective trademark owners.

GLOBAL VILLAGE

INTERNATIONAL INTELLECTUAL PROPERTY LAWS

Legal details are a concern to a growing number of U.S. exporters because of the increasing technological and informational content of our products. Before conducting business abroad, familiarize yourself with the appropriate patent, trademark, copyright, and licensing laws of the country. Use the Internet for your initial search and then work directly with international intellectual property attorneys. There are a number of ways of protecting your product in a foreign market, and each has its own merits according to circumstance and country.

Patent laws vary from country to country and a few countries do not have patent laws. Keeping your trade secrets to yourself often works well overseas, except that others may be able to copy your product on the open market. Consider selling patent rights or granting licenses in a foreign market.

To track down information on international laws use the following sources:

www.lcweb2.loc.gov/law/GLINv1/GLIN.html, The Global Legal Information Network (GLIN)

www.ili.org, International Law Institute, an excellent resource page for both national and international law

www.wulaw.wustl.edu/Infores/Library/Guides/intellectual-sem.html, Research Guide to International Intellectual Property Law, an online guide by Washington University School of Law

ADVERTISING WITHIN THE RULES

Beware of the many state and federal laws that oversee advertising, as misleading or deceptive ads may land your business in a courtroom. Legal counsel should review *all* advertisements. The Federal Trade Commission is in charge of taking action in the event unlawful advertising has been alleged by your competitors or customers. State consumer protection laws may also provide consumers with the right to sue for deceptive advertising.

According to Nolo.com, a leading source of legal self-help books, the following rules will help keep your ads within safe, legal limits.

Rule 1: Be Accurate

Make sure your ads are factually correct. Don't show a picture of this year's model of a product if what you're selling is last year's model, even if they look almost the same.

Be truthful about what consumers can expect from your product. Don't say ABC pills will cure headaches if the pills offer only temporary pain relief. Don't claim a rug shampooer is a wizard at removing all kinds of stains when there are some it won't budge.

"Waterproof" or "fireproof" means just that—not water resistant or fire resistant under some circumstances. The term "polar," when describing winter gear, suggests that it will keep people warm in extreme cold, not just in temperatures near freezing.

Rule 2: Get Permission

Does your ad feature someone's picture or endorsement? Does it quote material written by someone not on your staff or employed by your advertising agency? Does it use the name of a national organization such as the Boy Scouts or Red Cross? If so, get written permission.

Under U.S. copyright law, the "fair use" doctrine allows limited quotations from copyrighted works without authorization from the copyright owner. In some circumstances this doctrine provides legal justification for the widespread practice of quoting from favorable reviews in ads for books, movies, and plays—and even vacuum cleaners. However, with the exception of brief quotes from product or service reviews, you should always seek permission to quote protected material. For more on the fair use doctrine and many other aspects of copyright law and practice, see *The Copyright Handbook: How to Protect and Use Written Works*, by Stephen Fishman (Nolo).

Rule 3: Treat Competitors Fairly

Don't knock the goods, services, or reputation of others by giving false or misleading information. If you compare your goods and services with those of other companies, check your information to make sure that every statement in your ad is accurate. Then check again.

Rule 4: Have Sufficient Quantities on Hand

When you advertise goods for sale, make every effort to have enough on hand to supply the expected demand. If you don't think you're able, state in your ad that quantities are limited. You may even want to state the number of units on hand. State law may require merchants to stock an advertised product in quantities large enough to meet reasonably expected demand, unless the ad states that stock is limited. California, for example, has such a law. In other states merchants may have to give a rain check if they run out of advertised goods in certain circumstances. Make sure you know what your state requires.

Rule 5: Watch Out for the Word "Free"

If you say that goods or services are "free" or "without charge," be sure there are no unstated terms or conditions that qualify the offer. If there are any limits, state them clearly and conspicuously. Let's assume that you offer a free paintbrush to anyone who buys a can of paint for $8.95 and that you describe the kind of brush. Because you're disclosing the terms and conditions of your offer, you're in good shape so far. But there are pitfalls to avoid.

- If the $8.95 is more than you usually charge for this kind of paint, the brush clearly isn't free.
- Don't reduce quality of the paint that the customer must purchase or the quantity of any services (such as free delivery) that you normally provide. If you provide a lesser product or service, you're exacting a hidden cost for the brush.
- Disclose any other terms, conditions, or limitations.

Rule 6: Be Careful When You Describe Sales and Savings

You should be absolutely truthful in all claims about pricing. The most common pitfall is making doctored price comparisons with other merchants or with your own "regular" prices.

Rule 7: Observe Limitations on Offers of Credit

Don't advertise that you offer easy credit unless it's true. You don't offer easy credit if:

- You don't extend credit to people who have a poor credit rating.
- You offer credit to people with marginal or poor credit ratings, but you require a higher down payment or shorter repayment period than is ordinarily required for creditworthy people.
- You offer credit to high-risk customers, but once all the fine print is deciphered, the true cost of credit you charge exceeds the average charged by others in your retail market.
- You offer credit to high-risk customers at favorable terms but employ draconian (although legal) collection practices against buyers who fall behind.

If you advertise specific credit terms, you must provide all relevant details, including the down payment, the terms of repayment, and the annual interest rate.

SOURCE: Copyright © Nolo.com, Inc., 2000, **www.nolo.com** (accessed March 1, 2001).

SUMMARY

It is important that every entrepreneur be familiar with basic legal concepts and with some of the special problems that can arise in particular areas of his or her business. Determining your legal form of business should be undertaken with the advice of your attorney, accountant, and business advisor. As your firm grows and changes, reassess your decision.

Partnerships can be a rocky road. Therefore evaluate your need for a partner and your choice of partner thoroughly. Do not enter into a partnership without legal assistance.

Protecting yourself through copyrights, trademarks, and patents requires the assistance of intellectual property attorneys. You will be able to do a great deal of preliminary research using data from the Internet. Because these issues are significant and have many nuances and complications, you should not skimp on finding the best legal advice available.

THINK POINTS FOR SUCCESS

- We only remember what we want to. Get *everything* in writing.
- If your business is small and you like it that way, keep it simple—like your hobby.
- Most growth businesses need outside infusions of cash. Your business structure may hinder or enhance your ability to reach out for money.
- Don't pay Uncle Sam more than you have to and make sure you pay what is due. Have your accountant structure your business according to your needs.
- When you create corporate stock in your by-laws, think about creating at least ten times more than you intend to sell at start-up.
- Even if you incorporate, a banker may still want a personal guarantee for loans. And this guarantee may be in place for years to come.
- The increase of lawsuits should encourage most businesses to at least consider incorporating or establishing a limited liability company.

Key Points from Another View

Which Business Form Is Best for Your Family Business?

by Paul and Sarah Edwards

If you're working with your spouse or a family member, you might be wondering if you should go through the trouble and expense of forming a partnership or a corporation. The answer to this question depends on your own needs, the tax implications, and the laws in the state where you live. Here are the issues you may want to consider.

Your Own Needs

If your business started as a sole proprietorship and your spouse or a family member has decided to join your already ongoing concern, the easiest solution may be to simply hire your relative as an employee. Any salary you pay may be deductible as a business expense to you. In fact, hiring your children can prove to be a tax bonus because their salaries are a deductible business expense to you while their earnings will in most cases be taxed at a lower rate than your own.

When hiring an employee, however, you will need to comply with many federal and state regulations on employees. This means two things:

1. If your business is home based and your city has a zoning code forbidding employees to work in your home, you could run into a problem if the employee is a family member other than your spouse or children.
2. When you become an employer, you must maintain payroll records and file and pay many tax items. For more information about payroll taxes, try Handling Your Payroll, or from the IRS website, visit Alternative Methods for Figuring Withholding.

All this record keeping can be a headache for some people, and if that's the case for you, it might be easier to have your spouse or family member work on a volunteer basis—without pay.

In some cases, however, the better choice is to make your spouse or family member a co-owner (partner) in your business, complete with a written partnership agreement. A partnership agreement and the Uniform Partnership Act provide both you and your relative with some form of protection in the event of a disagreement or dispute that might eventually force you to divide up the business.

Of course, if you've decided to form a C corporation, S corporation, or LLC, you won't have any choice about how you handle your spouse or family members who co-own the company with you. In using these forms of business you still need to file papers with your state listing them as directors or officers of the company.

Tax Implications

There are specific tax implications to be aware of when a partnership or corporation is owned by members of the same family. For example, if you try to include your child as a partner in your family partnership with the intention of transferring a portion of the partnership income to him or her (thereby reducing all the partners' shares of income and hence their taxes), the current income tax laws dealing with children and earned income make this option less worthwhile. Such an outright transfer of partnership income to a child may arouse IRS scrutiny.

However, hiring your child is feasible and has some advantages as long as you pay him or her a "reasonable" wage for actual work done. In this way your child's wages are deductible business expenses to your partnership, and the child's earnings will likely be taxed at a lower rate than your own. In addition, if your child becomes an employee in your business, he or she is entitled to open an IRA and put up to $2,000 in earned income per year toward his or her retirement. However, no business deduction is allowed to the partnership or a partner for any contribution you make toward your child's IRA.

There are also ways of setting up a limited partnership or LLC in such a way that your children, by working for the family business over a number of years, increase their percentage ownership by means of nontaxable "gifts" each year from parents, who continue to receive a steady stream of income until they formally retire from the business. The documents necessary to create such entities must comply strictly with the estate-planning provisions of the Internal Revenue Code and can be quite complex; usually you will need the assistance of a tax attorney who specializes in "succession planning" for small businesses.

Be aware that there are many special IRS regulations affecting family members who are owners/employees of a C or S corporation. These regulations are intended to prevent families from shifting expenses among family members to create losses (through making sales of corporate assets to one another at a so-called loss, or from taking a loan from their corporation at "special low" rates for example). In short, if you are choosing to start a C or S corporation that includes your spouse or other family members, be sure to see an accountant so you can properly plan how to best divide the ownership of the company.

Your State Laws

Spouses have a legal interest in the business matters of their mates. This is especially true in the "community property states" of Arizona, California, Idaho, Nevada, New Mexico, Texas, Washington, and Wisconsin, where each spouse automatically owns one-half of all community property. This is also true in those common-law states in which divorce proceedings require an equitable division of property. In some states personal agreements between spouses as to how they will divide their interests in a family business on divorce or separation are not enforceable, and the family court is required to divide the business ownership based on the state's rules of equitable distribution. This does not preclude you from writing a partnership agreement with your spouse to use as the basis for your working relationship, however, if you desire. In fact, we think it can be a good idea.

Paul and Sarah Edwards have written eight books and hundreds of articles covering a range of home-office and self-employment issues. They have also produced and broadcast their show "Working From Home" on the Business News Network since 1988. You can learn more about Paul and Sarah by visiting their Website **paulandsarah.com**. This tip came from their book: *Teaming Up: The Small Business Guide to Collaborating.*

SOURCE: **www.quicken.com** (accessed June 3, 1999).

Build a Winning Team

TEAMING WITH PASSION

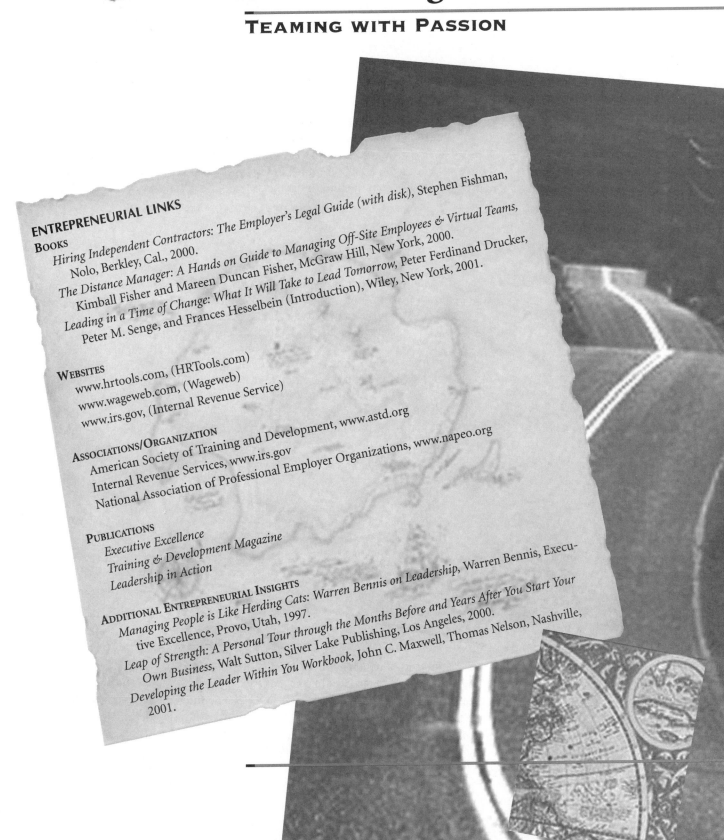

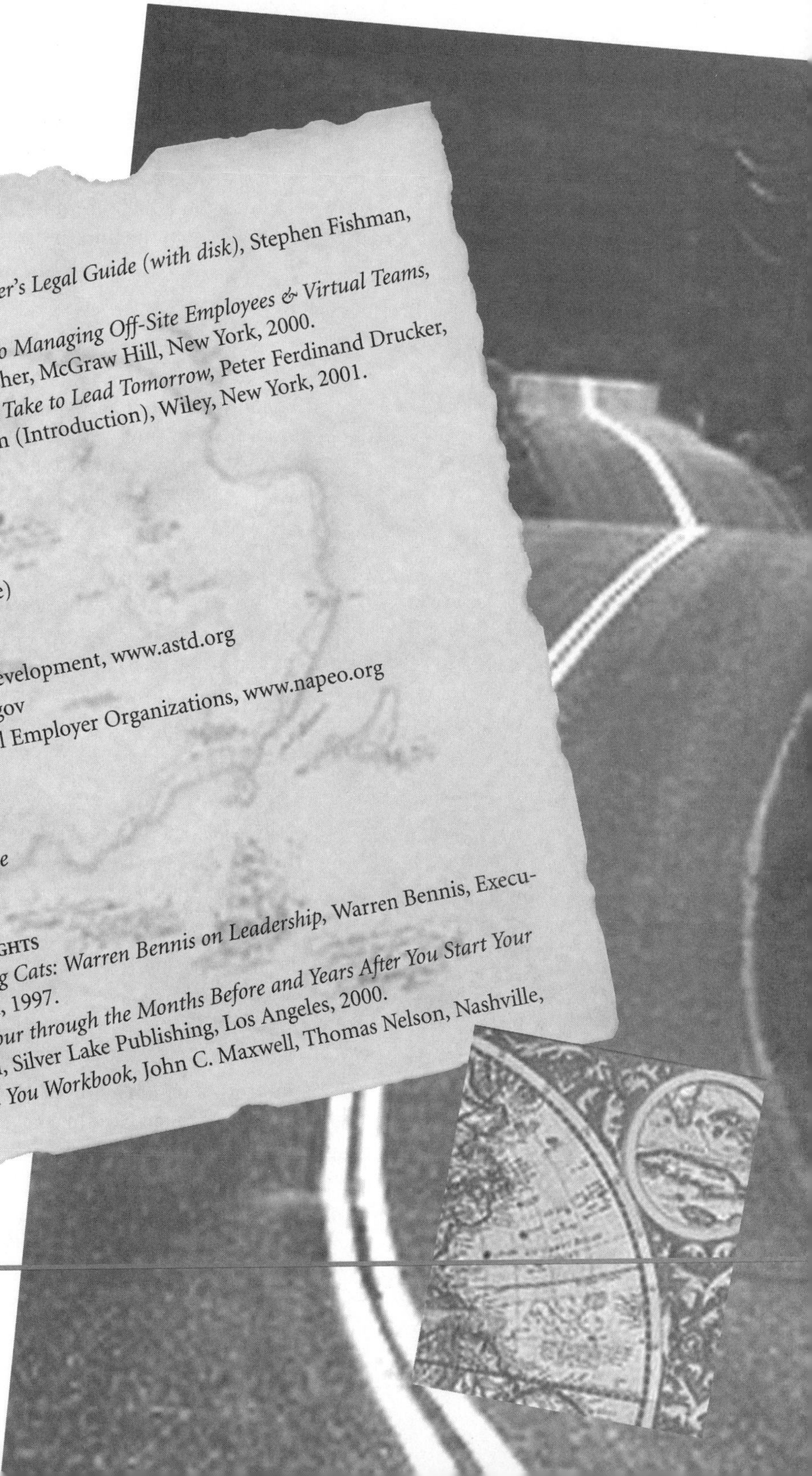

ENTREPRENEURIAL LINKS

BOOKS

Hiring Independent Contractors: The Employer's Legal Guide (with disk), Stephen Fishman, Nolo, Berkley, Cal., 2000.

The Distance Manager: A Hands on Guide to Managing Off-Site Employees & Virtual Teams, Kimball Fisher and Mareen Duncan Fisher, McGraw Hill, New York, 2000.

Leading in a Time of Change: What It Will Take to Lead Tomorrow, Peter Ferdinand Drucker, Peter M. Senge, and Frances Hesselbein (Introduction), Wiley, New York, 2001.

WEBSITES

www.hrtools.com, (HRTools.com)
www.wageweb.com, (Wageweb)
www.irs.gov, (Internal Revenue Service)

ASSOCIATIONS/ORGANIZATION

American Society of Training and Development, www.astd.org
Internal Revenue Services, www.irs.gov
National Association of Professional Employer Organizations, www.napeo.org

PUBLICATIONS

Executive Excellence
Training & Development Magazine
Leadership in Action

ADDITIONAL ENTREPRENEURIAL INSIGHTS

Managing People is Like Herding Cats: Warren Bennis on Leadership, Warren Bennis, Executive Excellence, Provo, Utah, 1997.

Leap of Strength: A Personal Tour through the Months Before and Years After You Start Your Own Business, Walt Sutton, Silver Lake Publishing, Los Angeles, 2000.

Developing the Leader Within You Workbook, John C. Maxwell, Thomas Nelson, Nashville, 2001.

Learning Objectives

- Accept that you can't do everything well.
- Write a profile of the founding team.
- Understand the importance of balance to the survival of your business.
- Explore new ways of putting together a team, including the virtual organization.
- Look back and see if there's anyone who could work with you in this venture.
- Review using independent contractors.
- Explore hiring practices, legal issues, and setting salaries.
- Understand the true cost of an employee.
- Review employee leasing.
- Locate a mentor to help guide you.
- Use a personality profile system to identify who you are and the types of people you need for a balanced team.

Building a winning team can be one of the most enjoyable tasks you face, but it will be challenging. This is *your* turn to build the team of *your* dreams. To do so, first look at yourself objectively, and then build a team that will fulfill business, psychological, and financial needs. That's what the successful entrepreneur does. This chapter will show you various ways to build a winning team to fulfill your passionate dream.

Build a team composed of people who have a common purpose and specific goals. In a small venture it is important to share the rewards of success with your team players. Remember, each employee in a small business plays a significant role in its success. As you grow, consider stock ownership for your employees. In good economic times stock ownership can be a key to keeping your best and brightest. As the leader of your company, you must represent and live by the mission you have set forth for your firm. Inspire your employees with your passionate behavior.

It is fun being an entrepreneur. You're on your own, doing your own thing, running your own show. And one of the toughest things you have to admit is that you can't perform all business tasks with the same success. Once you know where you need help, today's options to find assistance are vast.

In this chapter we touch on how to build a team and stress the importance of internal understanding for a stronger team. Balance, proportion, the right materials, and the structural forces of personality are equally important in building a winning team.

The Founding Team

Your Business Plan reader will be most impressed by a founding team with industry-related experience, complementary skills, and a record of achievement. Investors want you to learn on *your* dime and time, not theirs. They will be evaluating your background in depth. You will need to prove to investors that your team has the experience, ability, and pedigree to ensure success. Information about the founding team is the most-read section of any Business Plan.

The following management team examples are not full-blown résumés, but brief biographies that demonstrate that the founder or founders understand what they are doing. Vendors, bankers, and investors believe past success is the greatest indication of future success.

Manufacturing Team Example

Bill Jones and Lee Gray spent more than 11 years in the fitness business, Bill as a product designer and Lee as a sales representative. Bill developed and patented the Velopedical, an exercise bicycle that burns energy faster than a Stair Climber, and has sold more than 10,000 units. Lee has been in the top 10 percent of Acme Exercise Equipment's sales force for the past four years and has been personally responsible for more than $8 million in sales.

Bill has hired Lee to be Vice President of Sales. A recently retired manufacturing manager of Sport Tech, Ed Riggs, has been hired to serve as the Vice President of Manufacturing. Ed has an Operations Management degree from Purdue University and has managed a light assembly manufacturing plant for more than 20 years. He also teaches quality management classes part-time at two universities.

Jan Wilkes, a retired CPA with manufacturing experience, has agreed to serve as CFO on a part-time basis.

Restaurant Team Example

Dorothy Foltz won many prestigious awards as Executive Chef of the Carlton Hotel and is well known in the community. As one of the founders of Éclair, she will work full-time and serve as President. Ms. Foltz is certified as a Master Pastry Chef and trained in Paris at the Culinary Institute. She will supervise the kitchen and own a majority interest in the limited liability company.

Leslie Perk was, until December, a training manager for the French Connection restaurant chain. Ms. Perk will act as general manager under the direction of Ms. Foltz.

Pat Watter is a minority investor. Ms. Watter intends to retain her position as Food and Beverage Manager of Crooked Stick Country Club, but will be available as needed to monitor inventory and accounting activities.

Internet Team Example

Nancy Hipp (a graphic artist) of Indianapolis, Indiana, will develop the Internet site for a children's bookstore, Annie Gail's.

Cindy Barn, who recently retired from a New York management position in publishing, will serve as the fulfillment manager for all Internet orders. She will continue living in New York.

Three teachers—Pat Tran in Arizona, Casey Duke in Florida, and Troy Ball in Iowa—will answer all customer inquiries and review all new books.

Fran Shue and Amy Peters, both children's librarians, will pen book descriptions and reviews.

No matter how you begin your business, at some point in time you will find yourself needing the assistance of others. The previous examples illustrate solutions found to round out a team. As you look to fulfill your business needs, remember to find other people who will balance your skills and personality.

FIGURE 11.1

Seven Keys to Shaping the Entrepreneurial Organization

According to Michie P. Slaughter, chairman of the Kauffman Center for Entrepreneurial Leadership, "The entrepreneurial organization may look like any other firm. Yet it thrives on attitude toward growth that exists only when a team spirit is fostered among the associates and with the suppliers and customers of the firm."

Shaping the entrepreneurial organization is not a difficult process when growth, strongly supported by the founders and the top management team, is well planned and constantly reinforced. These seven steps are:

1. Hire self-motivated people.
2. Help others be successful.
3. Create clarity in the organization—clarification of purpose, direction, structure, and measurement.
4. Determine and communicate your own values and philosophies.
5. Provide appropriate reward systems.
6. Create an experimental learning attitude.
7. Celebrate your victories.

SOURCE: *Seven Keys to Shaping the Entrepreneurial Organization*, **www.entreworld.com** (accessed June 12, 2001).

In one firm the owner, Sam, had poor customer-relation skills; he scared off all but the heartiest customers and employees. His brother was one of those employees and realized that the business was headed for disaster. Taking a chance, he approached Sam. They agreed that the front office and customers should be off limits for Sam. Several months later the business was back on track and the employees and customers were relieved and much happier.

Do what you do best and hire the rest!

Now let's discuss various ways to get the help you need to grow your business.

THE VIRTUAL ORGANIZATION

The virtual organization has become a buzzword. It is often called a virtual company or virtual corporation.

A virtual organization allows the little guy to compete with larger firms without sacrificing scale, speed, or agility. It is much like forming an all-star team to exploit a market opportunity.

Let's back up and examine how the old motion picture studios used to work. They owned real estate, studios, equipment, performers, and a lot of other fixed assets with which they cranked out movies both good and bad. Most of the old giants have gone the way of the dinosaurs.

In their place are project teams of highly creative people hired "just-in-time to make a great picture" who disband after the project until the next opportunity presents itself. They rent everything they need and are never left with any overhead between projects.

An advertising agency may consist of a single person who presents the client with an idea. Once the idea is approved, the single person assembles freelance graphic designers, copywriters, photographers, models, performers, and media experts to produce the package. The virtual advertising agency has no overhead but can bring together the best talent to provide the client with a high-quality campaign at lower cost.

A general contractor pulls together a team of subcontractors who can be trusted to build a high-quality building. If the job goes well, there will be other opportunities for this team of specialists.

Suppose you have an idea for a new widget. You develop a prototype, demonstrate it at a trade show, and take orders. Why build a factory or hire workers? You can find

GLOBAL VILLAGE

WORLD TRADE INSTITUTE'S SCHOOL OF INTERNATIONAL TRADE AND COMMERCE

Through Pace University's online education program, **www.paceonline.edu**, the World Trade Institute offers an array of courses for exporters and importers. Following is a list of their offerings:

- Introduction to World Trade
- Import Regulations and Documentation
- Customs Entry Preparation Workshop
- Customs Law Issues for Importers
- Export/Import Letters of Credit
- Customhouse Brokers License Preparation
- Importing Techniques
- Import Transportation Management

These courses allow one to gather a thorough knowledge of importing and exporting techniques. If you are not prepared to take courses on the Internet or at your local college, we suggest you mine Internet sites and the myriad of books that cover international business. As we have discussed previously, the federal government and many state offices provide extensive detailed information on global opportunities.

other partners who can do almost anything. The big firms call this *outsourcing*. By using SIC codes and industry sources you can almost always find assemblers, packagers, box makers, food mixers, toolmakers, public warehouses, sales agents, and whatever else, just as you need them.

At another level, consider as partners firms with special capabilities that will share your risk in bringing a product or service to market. These partners are often called *strategic partners*. A team that includes retailers or end users may solve your marketing problems.

A sales agent who represents paper mills gathers specifications from retail stores to supply private-label napkins, toilet paper, and allied paper products to be packaged with the retailer's name. The price is negotiated with the supplier, and the agent pockets a commission.

A local printer discovered that her sales ability exceeded her ability to produce. She redefined herself as a "Printer's Broker" and used her knowledge to select from a wide variety of printers available for the most appropriate product. She sold her own small shop to an employee and increased her income several times over by providing assistance to customers who knew little about printing. Her virtual organization had just-in-time access to more than 500 experienced printers.

With continued corporate downsizing comes mushrooming opportunities to alert "virtual organization" entrepreneurs. The benefits include:

- having access to the skills and experience of proven experts in their field.
- paying only for services needed.
- obtaining variable production quantities.
- gaining higher reliability.
- achieving better quality and consistency.
- having lower internal developmental costs.
- locating a customer who is pre-sold.
- maintaining flexibility to instantly address new market opportunities.

The virtual organization needs to be customer-driven and opportunity-focused. There must be agreement and a shared vision among all the participants.

Partners and opportunities must be selected with care. Performance standards are critical. The virtual organization might exist for weeks or years—and then, when the opportunity has been fully exploited, be prepared to disband quickly. Action Step 46 will help you explore the virtual organization alternative.

Although it is wise to build a web of complementary business associations to ensure the success of the virtual company, the day may come when you need an employee—or several.

ACTION STEP 46

CONSIDER A VIRTUAL ORGANIZATION

Make a list of people or firms who might assist your efforts on an as-needed basis. To keep your overhead to an absolute minimum, ask and shop around, and look for those people who share your vision. Compile your list using a pencil so you can make adjustments as you continue to explore.

INDEPENDENT CONTRACTORS

Many people misunderstand the rules on independent contractors. If you tell the worker when to start and stop work, and if you supply the tools or office equipment, you have an employee. On the other hand, if the work assignment is task-driven, if the worker sets his or her own hours, if you pay by the job and not by the hour, and if most of the work takes place away from your office using the worker's resources, then you *may* have an independent contractor relationship.

You may save money if your workers are independent contractors—no Social Security, Medicare, workers' compensation insurance, healthcare insurance, retirement benefits, paid holidays, vacations, sick days, and so on. Most employers can locate workers who will work without mandated benefits—but sooner or later they will get hurt, apply for unemployment, or attempt to collect Social Security benefits. When they do, the government will come back to the employer with high fines and penalties. *Review independent contractor rules with a CPA and labor attorney because the IRS rules are rigid.* In addition, independent contractor status receives a high level of IRS scrutiny (Figure 11.2).

Be aware state employment laws may differ from federal rules.

Make sure your independent contractors carry their own insurance; if they don't have their own liability coverage you'll be responsible under *your* worker's compensation. If a window washer being paid cash by your store falls through your windows, guess who pays!

FIGURE 11.2
Employee or Independent Contractor

IRS Guide

An employer must generally withhold income taxes, withhold and pay Social Security and Medicare taxes, and pay unemployment tax on wages paid to an employee. An employer does not generally have to withhold or pay any taxes on payments to independent contractors.

Common-Law Rules

To determine whether an individual is an employee or an independent contractor under the common law, the relationship of the worker and the business must be examined. All evidence of control and independence must be considered. In any employee-independent contractor determination, all information that provides evidence of the degree of control and the degree of independence must be considered.

Facts that provide evidence of the degree of control and independence fall into three categories: behavioral control, financial control, and the type of relationship of the parties as shown below.

Behavioral control. Facts that show whether the business has a right to direct and control how the worker does the task for which the worker is hired include the type and degree of—

Instructions the business gives the worker. An employee is generally subject to the business' instructions about when, where, and how to work. All of the following are examples of types of instructions about how to do work:

- When and where to do the work
- What tools or equipment to use
- What workers to hire or to assist with the work
- Where to purchase supplies and services
- What work must be performed by a specified individual
- What order or sequence to follow

The amount of instruction needed varies among different jobs. Even if no instructions are given, sufficient behavioral control may exist if the employer has the right to control how the work results are achieved. A business may lack the knowledge to instruct some highly specialized professionals; in other cases, the task may require little or no instruction. The key consideration is whether the business has retained the right to control the details of a worker's performance or instead has given up that right.

Training the business gives the worker. An employee may be trained to perform services in a particular manner. Independent contractors ordinarily use their own methods.

Financial control. Facts that show whether the business has a right to control the business aspects of the worker's job include:

The extent to which the worker has unreimbursed business expenses. Independent contractors are more likely to have unreimbursed expenses than are employees. Fixed ongoing costs that are incurred regardless of whether work is currently being performed are especially important. However, employees may also incur unreimbursed expenses in connection with the services they perform for their business.

The extent of the worker's investment. An independent contractor often has a significant investment in the facilities he or she uses in performing services for someone else. However, a significant investment is not necessary for independent contractor status.

The extent to which the worker makes services available to the relevant market. An independent contractor is generally free to seek out business opportunities. Independent contractors often advertise, maintain a visible business location, and are available to work in the relevant market.

How the business pays the worker. An employee is generally guaranteed a regular wage amount for an hourly, weekly, or other period of time. This usually indicates that a worker is an employee, even when the wage or salary is supplemented by a commission. An independent contractor is usually paid by a flat fee for the job. However, it is common in some professions, such as law, to pay independent contractors hourly.

The extent to which the worker can realize a profit or loss. An independent contractor can make a profit or loss.

Type of relationship. Facts that show the parties' type of relationship include:

Written contracts describing the relationship the parties intended to create.

Whether the business provides the worker with employee-type benefits, such as insurance, a pension plan, vacation pay, or sick pay.

The permanency of the relationship. If you engage a worker with the expectation that the relationship will continue indefinitely, rather than for a specific project or period, this is generally considered evidence that your intent was to create an employer-employee relationship.

The extent to which services performed by the worker are a key aspect of the regular business of the company. If a worker provides services that are a key aspect of your regular business activity, it is more likely that you will have the right to direct and control his or her activities. For example, if a law firm hires an attorney, it is likely that it will present the attorney's work as its own and would have the right to control or direct that work. This would indicate an employer–employee relationship.

IRS help. If you want the IRS to determine whether a worker is an employee, file **Form SS-8,** Determination of Worker Status for Purposes of Federal Employment Taxes and Income Tax Withholding, with the IRS.

SOURCE: **www.irs.gov** (accessed May 1, 2001).

Team Members

Action Step 47 uses the idea of balance to scout potential team members. If you're able to imagine how each candidate will work in your new venture, you'll be well on your way to building a winning team.

Building a dream . . . working 60 to 80 hours . . . spending more time together than with your family . . . the reality of a new venture team working together. How do you keep the employer–employee relationship? It is one of the toughest parts of the job for many an entrepreneur. To understand the potential pitfalls and to explore ways to avoid problems review the following advice.

BOSS VS. BUDDY

It's human nature to want people to like you, but separating the roles of boss and buddy can help head off management headaches.

That doesn't mean you need to chuck compassion when you become a manager. Warmth and openness are valuable elements of an effective working relationship. Nor do you need to adopt an aloof attitude that says, "I'm above all the grunt work that I hired you to do." New companies especially are finding that nonhierarchical structures where managers and employees work together can be productive and morale-boosting.

"Those issues are separate from treating people differently based on how well you get along with them," contends Susan Stites, a human resources consultant with Management Allegories, Madison, Wisconsin.

The two foremost risks of befriending employees are the potential conflict of interest (and discomfort level) in giving job performance feedback to friends and the perception of unfairness.

The latter pitfall surfaces regularly when a work group plans after-hour outings or social gatherings around activities some employees aren't interested in or can't join in. For instance, some employees may have family commitments that limit their spare time.

Because of this potential conflict, a good rule of thumb is to plan social activities that everyone enjoys at a time when everyone can attend.

Another issue is the interplay of personalities in the workplace. Effective managers need to get along with people with varied approaches to life and work. Stites cites the example of companies that suffer when the presidents "hire themselves." They end up with a staff that supports their strengths—and magnifies their weaknesses.

"A manager needs to be a role model in accepting diversity in work and thinking styles and in capitalizing on that diversity," she suggests. Building on everyone's strengths is a foolproof recipe for success and for turning personality differences into complementary assets.

To learn more about personalities in the workplace, Stites suggests that managers look into seminars on personality profiling by Myers-Briggs, Social Styles, and DISC. They can be expensive, but are well worth the money, even for managers in small companies, she says.

Good books include *Personal Styles and Effective Performance* (based on the Social Styles program) by David W. Merrill and Roger H. Reid and *People Smart* (based on the DISC program) by Tony Alessandra and Michael J. O'Connor.

"Coach" or "mentor" may be a better title than "friend" to strive for when you become a boss. "There's been a lot of recent emphasis on those terms," Stites adds, "but I think good business leaders—even back in the 1920s when everything was autocratic—have always been good mentors."

Source: **www.nfibonline.com** (accessed March 1, 2001).

Action Step 47

Brainstorm Your Ideal Team

What do you need to win at the game of small business? Money, of course. And energy, tremendous energy. (You've got that or you wouldn't have read this far.) You also need footwork, a terrific idea, intensity, the ability to concentrate, a sense of industry and thrift, and the curiosity of Sherlock Holmes.

And you need people. People to support your effort. People to balance your skills. People to take up the slack. People to help you with tasks you find distasteful or don't understand.

So analyze yourself first. What do you like to do? What are you good at? What do you hate to do? What does your business need that you cannot provide yourself? Who can fill that need for you?

Start on building your ideal team.

After you've taken the time to do some research into your own personality (especially your strengths and weaknesses—refer back to the Action Steps you've already completed), you'll begin to get the feel for what kind of help you need in your venture. Is there anyone out there who can balance some of your skills?

Now that you have the idea of balance firmly in mind, network your vendors and your competitors for potential team members. Whenever you meet someone new, keep asking yourself: "How would this person work out in my new business?"

Keep looking for your future team with new eyes.

Make a list of all potential team members, the role they could play, and their strengths and weaknesses. What will it take to have them join your team?

The First Employees

When to hire your first full-time employee is a question often asked. You may require people immediately, but many small firms do well using part-time or temporary workers until the owners have a strong feel for what needs to be done and who is best suited to do the job.

If the first worker needs to provide a high level of technical skill or is a person who can take your organization to the next level, you may need to provide an extra carrot, such as profit-sharing or stock options. Talented workers may prefer the entrepreneurial adventure to big business bureaucracy and will work for less if they share your vision and passion for entrepreneurship.

As you continue to add people, you must understand that competence is not the only criterion to consider. You are assembling a venture team that wants to see growth and prosperity as much as you do. It is impossible to grow and expand until you have people who are not only capable but also motivated to ensure success.

The quest for new employees begins with a written job description. You may not find a perfect fit so don't fence yourself in with too many specifications. Define the duties to be performed and the skills needed to perform them. A small business cannot afford a misfit or an unproductive person. If one person in a four-person organization doesn't work, you have lost 25 percent of your efficiency. Hiring and keeping good people is a critical factor in a firm's success.

If experience is not critical when hiring, consider vocational, trade, and professional schools. Local colleges and high schools also have placement offices. There are many programs offered through social agencies that might subsidize the training of workers. Check out public and private employment agencies. In addition, temporary agencies may be able to locate short-term help. Hiring through a temporary agency allows you to "check out" the person before actually hiring him or her for full-time employment.

What *is* critical in hiring is your efforts to make sure you have investigated the applicants to the best of your ability within legal parameters. Unfortunately, firing employees can trigger lawsuits—justified or not, they will cost you an incredible sum of money. Be sure you have a qualified and experienced attorney on call at all times.

Be prepared: you *will* have employee turnover in the beginning. Either they will quit or you will decide to terminate their employment. Suggestion for restaurants and retail—overhire for opening.

You will need to develop personnel policies to cover hiring, firing, and managing your employees. One source, which allows you to develop policies using online software, is located at **www.hrtools.com**. Because of the potential problems inherent in the hiring and employment process we highly suggest you use a firm such as ADP to assist you in managing required legal paperwork. The following list of employment forms provided by HRTools is an indicator of the many legal issues involved with employees:

Recruitment Forms

A Summary of Your Rights under the FCRA
Adverse Employment Action Notice
Applicant Acknowledgement Letter
Applicant Rejection Letter
Application for Employment
Credit Report Disclosure and Authorization Form
Hiring Checklist
Job Posting Application
Pending Adverse Employment Action Notice
Reference Release Form
Telephone Reference Check

Employment

Employee Acknowledgment Form
Model California Inventions Agreement
New Employee Orientation Checklist

Non-compete Agreement
Offer Letter
Work-Made-for-Hire Agreement

Employee Relations Forms

Acknowledgment of New or Revised Policy
Ergonomics Training Completion Form
Ergonomics Worksite Evaluation Form
Matching Gifts Request Form
Relocation Assistance Form
Repetitive Motion Injury Report Log
Request for Flexible Work Schedule
Request for Leave of Absence
Sample Peer Review Procedure
Suggestion Forms

Discipline and Termination Forms

Certificate of Group Health Plan Coverage
Employee Exit Interview
Employee Termination Checklist
Employee Warning Notice
Special Notice of Health Coverage Documentation
Termination Notice Forms

SOURCE: HR Tools, Inc., **www.hrtools.com** (accessed March 1, 2001).

If the previous list scares you, good! It should! Employment law requires legal advice at every step of the way. Remember, any form you take from the Internet should be reviewed by your lawyer before use.

STAY OUT OF COURT

Review Table 11.1 and the questions following before conducting your first interview.

Ask the Right Questions

Use open-ended questions to start the applicant talking. Develop a list of questions appropriate to the position you want to fill. Affirmative action laws make it important to ask each applicant the same questions. You might consider using similar questions on an application form for screening purposes. The following questions will help get you started on preparing your own list.

1. How did you prepare for this meeting?
2. What are some of the obstacles you have overcome?
3. Can you work independently without close supervision?
4. What gives you satisfaction in a job?
5. What do you like and dislike about this kind of work?
6. What have been your most pleasant work experiences?
7. Have you ever organized an event?
8. What did you like or dislike about your last job?
9. How well do you handle change and uncertainty?
10. Are you a team player?
11. How do you evaluate yourself?

TABLE 11.1
Legal and Illegal Pre-employment Inquiries

The chart following outlines the type of information you can ask for in applications and during job interviews as specified in federal laws. The chart may also be sufficient for complying with the laws of your state, but double check with your state's civil rights department to be sure.

Subject	Lawful Pre-employment Inquiries	Unlawful Pre-employment Inquiries
Name	Applicant's full name. Have you ever worked for this company under a different name?	Original name of an applicant whose name has been changed by court order or otherwise. Is any additional information relative to a different name necessary to check work record? Applicant's maiden name.
Address or Duration of Residence	How long have you been a resident of this state or city?	
Birthplace		Birthplace of applicant. Birthplace of applicant's parents, spouse, or other close relatives. Requirements that applicant submit birth certificate, naturalization, or baptismal record.
Religion or Creed		Inquiry into an applicant's religious denomination, religious affiliations, church, parish, pastor, or religious holidays observed.
Race or Color		Complexion or color of skin.
Photograph		Any requirement for a photograph prior to hire.
Height		Inquiry regarding applicant's height.
Weight		Inquiry regarding applicant's weight.
Gender		Mr., Miss, or Mrs. or an inquiry regarding gender. Inquiry as to the ability to reproduce or advocacy of any form of birth control. Requirement that women be given pelvic examinations.
Disability		Inquiries regarding an individual's physical or mental condition that are not directly related to the requirements of a specific job and that are used as a factor in making employment decisions in a way that is contrary to the provisions or purposes of the Civil Rights Act.
Citizenship	Are you a citizen of the United States? If not a citizen of the United States, do you intend to become a citizen of the United States? If you are not a United States citizen, have you the legal right to remain permanently in the United States? Do you intend to remain permanently in the United States? To avoid discrimination based on national origin, the questions above should be asked after the individual has been hired even if it is related to the federal 1-9 process.	Questions below are unlawful unless asked as part of the federal 1-9 process. Of what country are you a citizen? Whether an applicant is naturalized or a native-born citizen; the date when the applicant acquired citizenship. Requirement that an applicant produce naturalization papers or first papers. Whether applicant's parents or spouse are naturalized or native-born citizens of the United States: the date when such parent or spouse acquired citizenship.
National Origin	Inquiry into language applicant speaks and writes fluently.	Inquiry into applicant's lineage; ancestry; national origin; decent; parentage or nationality. Nationality of applicant's parents or spouse. Inquiry into how applicant acquired ability to read, write, or speak a foreign language.
Education	Inquiry into the academic, vocational, or professional education of an applicant and public and private schools attended.	
Experience	Inquiry into work experience. Inquiry into countries applicant has visited.	
Arrests	Have you ever been convicted of a crime? Are there any felony charges pending against you?	Inquiry regarding arrests that did not result in conviction. (Except for law enforcement agencies.)
Relatives	Names of applicant's relatives already employed by this company.	Address of any relative of applicant, other than address (within the United States) of applicant's father and mother, husband or wife, and minor dependent children.
Notice in Case of Emergency	Name and address of person to be notified in case of accident or emergency.	Name and address of nearest relative to be notified in case of accident or emergency.
Organizations	Inquiry into the organizations of which an applicant is a member, excluding organizations the name or character of which indicates the race, color, religion, national origin, or ancestry of its members.	List all clubs, societies, and lodges to which you belong.

SOURCE: Copyright © Nolo Press, 1998; **www.nolo.com** (accessed March 1, 2001).

A Team of Part-Timers

Charlene Webb has built a winning team of part-time employees. After Charlene Webb sold her gourmet cookware shop, she opened a women's specialty clothing store. The shop is small—about 2,000 square feet—and is located within a small shopping center in an upscale community of about 60,000 people.

Charlene discovered that her ideal employees were local women who were active in community life and who preferred to work only one day a week. Monday's saleswoman is a golfer whose country-club friends come in to visit and buy from her on her day of work. Tuesday the tennis player is on, and her friends have followed her to the store. Wednesday is the yacht club member; Thursday, a leader of hospital volunteers; Friday, a well-known club woman; and Saturday, an attorney's wife. All of them are friendly women who know a lot about fashion and have a lot of energy. They never tire from the routine, and they are excellent customers and employees. Also, they serve as walking store models at all times.

Charlene, who writes a society column (as free PR) in the community newspaper, has positioned herself as a social force, and many women have come to view her shop as the one to buy from for formal events at the country clubs and the nearby Ritz Carlton Hotel.

Passion

Passion for Employees
Rachel Hubka Proves "Doing Right" Pays Off

Rachel Hubka has no illusions about the many accolades she has received for her business achievements and innovative employee programs. She is convinced that her success in transforming people into conscientious workers with self-esteem, a strong work ethic, a sense of pride, and an intense desire to excel is simply an expected outcome of her belief in the people themselves. Besides, she'll tell you, it's just good business!

Rachel's Bus Company is a metaphor for all that is good about people who combine social conscience with sound management practices. Rachel Hubka "walks the walk" with the people who work for her, locating her business in one of Chicago's poorest inner-city neighborhoods: "I needed reliable part-time drivers, and I wanted to tap a neglected labor pool," she says.

She hires disadvantaged workers from the community; gives new drivers comprehensive training, professional pride, and an incentive program; then guides them into positions of increasing responsibility. She has formed partnerships with local schools to teach employees computer skills and help her drivers earn their GEDs. Her motivational program teaches her employees pride and confidence in their appearance and capabilities—qualities that don't come easily "on the street!"

An amazing transformation usually takes place. Her staff members become role models within the community. They catch her entrepreneurial spirit and she is right there with support. When one of her employees developed a software program to handle her charter business, she helped him through the hurdles of starting his own consulting business, then became his first client.

And doing good really is good business! Rachel's Bus Company has grown into a $5 million enterprise in little more than a decade. She has built a team of committed drivers, a supportive staff, and a solid reputation for service, safety, and professionalism.

Her success is a tribute to her strong personal commitment to Chicago's schoolchildren, her love affair with people, and her dedication to the advancement of all her employees.

SOURCE: *Wise Women, Success Strategies for Women Entrepreneurs*, Bank One.

What Do Employees Really Cost?

If you plan on hiring individuals on an employee basis, consider *all* the costs associated with hiring, training, and retaining an employee.

- Ad placements (very expensive)
- Recruiting and hiring
- Salary
- Employment taxes—Social Security, Unemployment, and Medicare
- Worker's Compensation Insurance
- Benefits—health, retirement, dental, vacation, sick leave
- Space, furniture, equipment
- Additional management time
- Any additional perks you might offer—childcare, car allowance, etc.
- Training

It is estimated that each employee will cost you 130 to 200 percent of his or her salary. Employees in an entrepreneurial venture need to pull *more* than their own weight. Select wisely. If you find an excellent employee, encourage him or her to send his or her friends. For many companies, finding "friends of employees" is their main recruiting avenue.

To keep abreast of salaries and wages use salary comparison information from the following Internet sites:

www.wageweb.com

www.monster.com

www.careerjournal.com

www.salary.com

www.jobstar.org

Maintaining Compliance

Ignorance is not an acceptable defense if you are charged with breaking labor laws. Check with all government agencies to be sure that you do not overlook any legal requirements. Again, lawyer time! The penalties for failure to comply may be very stiff. Many firms have lost their businesses because of non-compliance.

Contact the following federal organizations to learn about your legal responsibilities:

- Occupational Safety and Health Administration (OSHA) **www.osha.gov**
- Equal Employment Opportunity Commission (EEOC), **www.eeoc.gov/small/index.html**
- Department of Labor, **www.dol.gov**
- Internal Revenue Service (IRS), **www.irs.gov**
- U.S. Department of Justice, Americans with Disabilities, **www.usdoj.gov/crt/ada/adahom1.htm**
- Immigration and Naturalization Service, **www.ins.usdoj.gov/graphics**

In addition to the previous federal offices, you will need to contact your state offices for further employment law information. Review the short description of selected employment statutes most applicable to new ventures on page 246.

Also, check to see that all employees can legally work in the United States and have them fill out an Employment Eligibility Verification form (I-9 in Appendix C).

Know requirements for complying with the Americans with Disabilities Act (Figure 11.3) before you complete your tenant improvements for your new office or retail complex and before conducting any interviews or hiring.

FIGURE 11.3
Ten Steps to ADA Compliance

Since the Americans with Disabilities Act (ADA) may pose potential liability, as well as potential opportunity for employers, it's important to know and understand the requirements of the law. The following concrete steps can be taken to prepare for ADA compliance.

1. Train Your Interviewers

People often need training in "disability etiquette" in order to feel comfortable interviewing applicants with disabilities. Because it is illegal to make pre-employment inquiry into an applicant's disability, it is essential that interviewers be trained not to ask prohibited questions such as: "Have you ever had a back problem?" Instead, interviewers should ask essential function-related questions. The qualified applicant with a disability should have input regarding possible accommodations on his or her behalf.

2. Revise Applications & Other Forms

Any inquiry that is prohibited when made orally is also illegal if made in writing. It is important to remove any illegal inquiries contained on forms, such as applications. For example, a common question found on many application forms, "Do you have any physical or mental disabilities that would affect your ability to perform the job? should be avoided. Any question that seeks information about an applicant's physical or mental condition prior to a job offer being made could result in liability.

3. Avoid Judgments Based on Myths, Fears, or Stereotypes

Many employees may reject applicants with readily apparent disabilities as a result of a good faith belief that the applicant will be unable to "do the job." The person with the disability should be allowed to respond to how he/she can perform the essential functions. Employers should avoid drawing conclusions based on myths, fears, and stereotypes.

4. Revise Job Descriptions

While not required by the ADA, an employer's written job descriptions are considered evidence of the essential functions of a job if the job description existed before the job was advertised, or if the applicant/employee was interviewed for the job, or considered for promotion, before a job-related action was taken. It is important that the essential job-related functions can be defined. As a preventive measure, all essential job-related functions of a position should be contained in the job description.

5. Review Job Standards Criteria

In addition to intentional discrimination, employees and applicants can prove disability discrimination by showing that a job criterion, which appears to be neutral, actually has a disparate impact on individuals with disabilities. To avoid this problem, use only job standards or criteria that are job-related and consistent with business necessity (i.e., essential to the performance of the job). The use of non-essential job criteria (such as lifting, hearing, eyesight, driver's license, etc.) that have the effect of screening out applicants with disabilities may result in liability. EEOC regulations (and KnowledgePoint's Descriptions Now! software for writing job descriptions) will assist you in the classification of job standards criteria.

6. Review Medical Examinations

Traditional pre-employment medical examinations are prohibited under the ADA. Medical examinations can only be administered after a conditional offer of employment is made (that is, in the "post-offer, pre-employment" stage). All employees in that job class must be required to take the examination.

7. Centralize Your Applicant/Employee Screening System

In order to ensure that consistent, lawful employment practices are followed, it is best that one person with knowledge of the many employment laws has final review authority over hiring and other employment decisions. In addition, all levels of staff involved in the hiring process should be trained in ADA-related policies.

8. Develop Procedures for Maintaining & Disclosing Confidential Medical Records

Employers who maintain medical examinations and records must develop appropriate procedures for maintaining the confidentiality of medical records. The ADA requires that medical records be kept separate from any other personnel information.

9. Modify Drug Testing Programs

While drug tests are allowed under the ADA at any point in the application or employment process, existing drug testing programs may require modification. For example, a test to determine an individual's blood alcohol level would be considered a "medical exam," and could only be administered in accordance with the medical exam requirements of the ADA.

It should be noted also that tests for the illegal use of drugs may also reveal the presence of lawfully used drugs. If a person is excluded from a job because the employer erroneously "regarded" him or her to be an addict currently using drugs illegally based on that drug test, the employer would be liable under the ADA.

10. Train Supervisors on Reasonable Accommodation for Employees Returning to Work

Current employees returning to work from disability leave may require a reasonable accommodation. Special issues arise where the return to work involves workers' compensation. Supervisors must be adequately trained on how to handle employees returning to work under these conditions.

This material is reprinted from the Cornell University National Materials Development Project on the ADA Employment provisions as published in the "Pacific Disability and Business Technical Assistance Center Update."

SOURCE: **www.knowledgepoint.com** (accessed June 12, 2001).

Be aware of overtime laws and those laws pertaining to employment of anyone under 18. Post a copy of the labor laws conspicuously—where everyone can read them. If you have even *one* non-English-speaking employee, also post the laws in that employee's language.

In addition to complying with state and federal labor laws, you must also comply with all federal and state tax laws. See Chapter 12 for a brief review of employee taxes.

We suggest you hire a payroll services company to prepare payroll and to ensure compliance with all employment and tax laws. The cost of these services such as those offered through ADP is a fraction of the cost of the time it would take you to become an expert on labor law or the fines for non-compliance.

U.S. DEPARTMENT OF LABOR STATUTES

The U.S. Department of Labor administers and enforces more than 180 federal laws. These mandates and the regulations that implement them cover many workplace activities for about ten million employers and 125 million workers.

The following is a brief description of the principal statutes most commonly applicable to businesses. *The intent is to acquaint you with the major labor laws and not to offer a detailed exposition of laws and regulations enforced by the Department of Labor. For the fuller requirements of these statutes, see information sources at* **www.dol.gov.**

Wages and Hours

The Fair Labor Standards Act prescribes standards for wages and overtime pay, which affect most private and public employment. The act is administered by the Wage and Hour Division of the Employment Standards Administration. It requires employers to pay covered employees the federal minimum wage and overtime of one-and-a-half times the regular wage. It prohibits certain types of work in an employee's home. It restricts the hours that children under 16 can work and forbids their employment in certain jobs deemed too dangerous. Wage and Hour Division also enforces the workplace provisions of the *Immigration and Nationality Act* that apply to aliens authorized to work in the United States.

Workplace Safety and Health

The *Occupational Safety And Health Act* (OSH) is administered by the Occupational Safety and Health Administration (OSHA). Safety and health conditions in most private industries are regulated by OSHA or OSHA-approved state systems. Employers must identify and eliminate unhealthful or hazardous conditions; employees must comply with all rules and regulations that apply to their own workplace conduct. Covered employers are required to maintain safe and healthful work environments in keeping with requirements of the law. Effective OSHA safety and health regulations supersede others originally issued under these other laws: the *Walsh-Healey Act,* the *Services Contract Act,* the *Contract Work Hours and Safety Standards Act,* the *Arts and Humanities Act,* and the *Longshore and Harbor Workers' Compensation Act.*

Pensions and Welfare Benefits

The *Employee Retirement Income Security Act (ERISA)* regulates employers who offer pension or welfare benefit plans for their employees. It preempts many similar state laws and is administered by the Pension and Welfare Benefits Administration (PWBA). Under the statute, employers must fund an insurance system to protect certain kinds of retirement benefits, with premium payments to the federal government's *Pension Benefit Guaranty Corp.* Pension plans must meet a wide range of fiduciary, disclosure, and reporting requirements. Employee welfare plans must meet similar requirements. PWBA also administers reporting requirements for continuation of health-care provisions, required under the *Comprehensive Omnibus Budget Reconciliation Act of 1985 (COBRA).*

Unions and Their Members

The *Labor-Management Reporting and Disclosure Act* (also known as the *Landrum-Griffin Act*) deals with the relationship between a union and its members. It safeguards union funds and requires reports on certain financial transactions and administrative practices of union officials, labor consultants, etc. The act is administered by the Office of Labor-Management Standards, which is part of the Employment Standards Administration.

SOURCE: **www.dol.gov/dol/opa/public/aboutdol/lawsprog.htm** (accessed June 1, 2001).

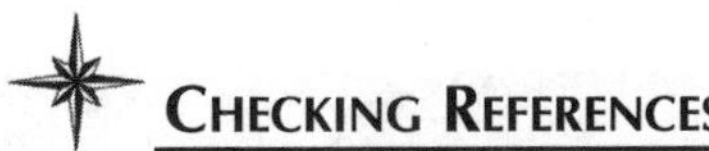

CHECKING REFERENCES

If you have any doubt of the significance of checking references, review Avert's 1999 report on more than 1,100,000 job applicants (Figure 11.4).

Professional payroll services firms will perform reference checking for you, saving you time, money, and paperwork and ensuring your compliance with the law. The following information again stresses the importance of reference checks.

The U.S. Chamber of Commerce and American Management Association cites that 30 percent of all business failures are caused by employee theft and related forms of dishonesty. (See Chapter 12 for further information.)

The Immigration and Naturalization Services (INS) reports that inadvertently hiring an illegal alien can result in fines ranging from $250 to $10,000.

Rutgers University Graduate School of Management discovered that direct and indirect turnover costs an average 1½ times the annual salary of the position in question, in addition to the position remaining open for an average of 10 weeks.

The Workplace Violence Research Institute reports action against an employer for negligent hiring is becoming increasingly common. The average award in security negligence cases is $1 million.

SOURCE: **www.adp.com** (accessed March 5, 2001).

Because of potential libel lawsuits, past employers are very reluctant to provide information about past employees. This makes it necessary to delve deeper into potential employees' backgrounds another way. Professionals will be able to review the following: driving records, credit reports, education and credential checks, employment and personal reference checks, warrants, etc. If the credit report shows a potential employee is deeply in debt, would you reconsider him or her as a potential employee? If a driving record shows four moving violations in the last year would you reconsider? If the person has relocated 10 times in the past 7 years would you reconsider? If he or she has lied about a degree would you reconsider? Not reconsidering may cost you a great deal! Spend the money to hire correctly and firing will not be as necessary.

Check out two sites on the Internet for employment screening services **www.order.choicepointinc.com** and **www.avert.com,** but before using any screening services, consult your attorney.

FIGURE 11.4
Avert Hiring Index

10%	**Criminal Records**—10% had a criminal record in the last seven years
10%	**Workers' Compensation Claims**—10% had a previous Workers Compensation claim
12%	**Driving Records**—12% had four or more moving violations, a DUI or DWI, or had a suspended driver's license
15%	**Employment Records/Reference Checks**—15% misrepresented their employment records
25%	**Credit Records**—25% had credit records showing a judgement, lien, or bankruptcy, or had been turned over to a collection agency
27%	**Driving Records**—27% had one or more accidents or moving violations on their driving records
29%	**Employment Records/Reference Checks**—29% misrepresented their education, credential, and/or employment records

SOURCE: *Avert, Inc.,* **www.avert.com/hrindex/hrindex99.htm** (accessed May 1, 2001).

INCREDIBLE RESOURCE

IRS! YES, THE IRS!

Contact the IRS now!

800-829-3676 for publications

800-829-1040 to talk with a Taxpayer Education Coordinator

www.irs.gov for downloads of many IRS publications

The following publications may be of interest:

- Form SS-4—Application for Employer Identification Number (see Appendix B)
- Publication 334—Tax Guide for Small Business (for individuals who use Schedule C or C-EZ)
- Publication 560—Retirement Plans for Small Business
- Publication 587—Business Use of Your Home
- Publication 509—Tax Calendars
- Publication 583—Starting a Business and Keeping Records

Employee Leasing

Consider employee leasing as a way to reduce administrative costs, paperwork hassles, legal issues, and costly benefits. Not unlike leasing physical property, in this instance you will be leasing people (employees) whose leasing organization handles payroll and most, if not all, of the human resources functions.

The leasing firm will help you stay in compliance with the myriad of federal, state, and local employment laws. California and federal labor codes run more than 460 pages! Keeping in compliance is a full-time job.

For your protection, we suggest you use only a firm that has a strong track record and a sound financial background. Many new ventures are unable to offer employees health insurance benefits and retirement programs and thus lose out on top employees. Because of economies of scale, large leasing firms are able to provide these benefits to your "leased employees." The National Association of Professional Employer Organizations, **www.napeo.org** or 703-836-0466, can provide further information on employee leasing.

Employee leasing may appear to cost more initially, but it allows for additional benefits, such as:

- Background screening checks are completed by the leasing organization.
- If you don't like the employee you can send him or her back, thereby eliminating termination issues.
- Leasing organizations reduce turnover.
- Such arrangements nearly eliminate costs of hiring (advertising, interviewing time, reference checks, turnover, etc.).

Find Mentors

If you're starting up a business for the first time, there's a good chance you need mentors—people who can give you advice and encouragement. Perhaps you have mentors already. If not, how can you find such help? First, network with your friends, co-workers, and business associates. Tell them what you're looking for—that is, successful businessowners with a good track record. The perfect mentor would be one with experience in your particular segment. Second, join the chamber of commerce and one or more civic clubs. Third, keep your new eyes peeled for a mentor appearing on the horizon. If your community has a chapter of Service Corps of Retired Executives (SCORE), contact them to see if you can find a match.

Once you've located several candidates, develop a set of questions and arrange a meeting. You want to pick the brains of all the candidates. Here are some things to consider when selecting a mentor:

Do you feel comfortable with this person?

Can you trust him or her?

Is he or she easy to communicate with?

Does he or she have experience and contacts that can help your new business?

Once you've made your choices and the people have agreed to help you, keep in close contact. See the people at least once a month, and use phone calls or e-mail to smooth out rough spots. Your mentors may be able to help you establish banking connections and vendor–supplier relationships. A good mentor can be invaluable for checking your leases, contracts, and marketing materials.

Here's a story that illustrates the kinds of assistance mentors can provide.

Mine the Riches of the Experienced

Dick Knox is now the proud owner of a seven-year-old, $3 million company, Logo Shirts. He started selling t-shirts from his garage and moved to a warehouse facility after two years. He had the energy but not the knowledge to expand his small business, so he kept his eyes open for a mentor.

Enter Bob Redman. A Fortune 1000 company had just purchased Bob's clothing firm. When Dick approached him with the mentor offer, he jumped at it. He loved being associated with a start-up, and the day he left his president's chair he was ready to step into his own business—a five-person clothing firm. (Mentoring works both ways, you see. Dick gave Bob a new angle on a tired life; Bob gave Dick almost a million dollars in sales leads.)

Dick's second mentor was Mickey McCarthy, a wild and crazy entrepreneur who had sold his last venture for $10 million. Mickey was tired. Starting businesses took energy and he was ready to retire to a cabin in the mountains. Before he packed his bags, however, he agreed to be a mentor to Dick.

A month later Dick was having cash-flow problems. Although he was meeting payroll, he had not taken a salary himself for three months. The cupboard was bare, and Dick had lost 18 pounds.

Over the next couple of months Mickey worked with Dick on a complete Business Plan/bank package with projections for the next five years. With projections in hand Dick met with Mickey's banker. Three weeks later he had a credit line of $500,000 and the provision that he could expand it to $750,000 when he needed it.

With mentors like Bob and Mickey, how could Dick lose?

Rounding Out the Personalities of Your Team

If you are an entrepreneur, you like to move fast. You want quick answers and quick action. You've studied the marketplace. You've found your market niche. You didn't think you'd need much of a team, but now you're growing so quickly that you have to do some team building. You're an entrepreneur, so you want to move fast building this team. To do so, you need a key to human behavior. You want people who can help you, not harm you, because *every* person counts in small business. A test—called an assessment instrument in the training field—might help you locate the key that unlocks the door behind which your team awaits.

We would like to point out that the search for the key to human behavior is not a recent phenomenon. In the earliest civilizations astrologers and stargazers tried to explain human behavior based on the four elements: earth, air, fire, and water. In the fourth century B.C. Hippocrates, who gave us the Hippocratic Oath, kept the

Community Resource

Chat Away with Like-Minded Entrepreneurs

A worldwide community of entrepreneurs is available at your fingertips. Many entrepreneurial sites on the web contain chat rooms, forums, moderated chats with professionals, and newsletters all focused on a particular area of small business. For example, the Entrepreneur Center, **www.ecenteronline.org**, a joint venture of Cisco and the SBA, recently offered the following online chats.

Affordable Ways of Drawing Customers to Your Website

Whether you are currently doing business on the web or are considering creating a website, it is imperative that you are strategic about using your limited finances to get the most for your web advertising dollars. After all, most small business owners can't afford full-page ads in the *Mercury News* or The *SF Chronicle*. That doesn't mean that there are not other very effective ways to get free media to advertise your company. You just need the right tools!

The chat will cover how to harness the marketing ability of the web to attract and retain clients when you don't have a Fortune 500 advertising budget. Learn the difference between effective web-based marketing, such as banners vs. buttons vs. e-mail, as channels to acquire and retain customers online. Questions such as how should you make the best investment and how do you evaluate the success of a web marketing campaign will be answered.

Choosing the Right Internet Professional

Ready to dive into the Internet revolution? Picking a web professional to work with may be the single most important aspect of ensuring your success online. Without a knowledgeable team who understand the complexities of how to succeed online, you could end up like more than 90 percent of all new online ventures—unsuccessful. But what criteria should you look for as you assess potential web development teams? Learn about selecting the best web professionals for your business from top web strategy consultants who can help you make the right technological and strategic choices that meet your mission and budget!

Financing Oops: Having Trouble Getting a Loan?

Looking for financing? Have you been turned down by banks because the financing you need does not fit their traditional loan portfolio/lending requirements? You are not alone; in fact, most small-businesses owners obtain their financing by tapping family, friends, credit cards, and even home equity as opposed to using bank funds. This chat topic will describe how entrepreneurs can access needed capital when their businesses do not meet traditional lending criteria of commercial lending institutions. Maryl Curran is the Program Director of Lending at Lenders for Community Development (LCD), one of the South Bay's leading microlenders, which is also located on-site at the Entrepreneur Center. LCD, which specializes in making micro-loans, was developed in response to community credit needs. LCD's mission is to complete the cycle of reinvestment by investing local bank deposits in community-oriented ventures through a microloan program. Its lending programs are administered in partnership with community organizations, and involve community representatives in the management of our business activities.

In addition to online chats, many of the entrepreneurial sites, such as **www.about.com/smallbusiness**, have online professionals who respond to questions on a daily basis. By posting on a site's forum you will receive input from a wide variety of voices. Following is a list of several excellent sites for entrepreneurial schmoozing on the Internet:

www.ideacafe.com has discussions for and about work-at-home moms, GenX Biz, Tech Talk, and e-commerce

www.about.com/smallbusiness, with discussions and sites for arts and crafts, businesses, franchises, Canadian small business, business software, etc.

www.inc.com, with discussions for going global, customer service, and ethics in business

These are just the tip of the iceberg. For each entrepreneur, specific sites dealing with science, technology, and biotechnology are widely available covering areas pertinent to your specific industry. Click away!

---

four-part framework developed by the astrologers but changed the labels: choleric, phlegmatic, sanguine, and melancholic.

The four-part grid continued into the Middle Ages, where physicians treated patients based on which of the Four Humors—blood, phlegm, choler, and black bile—dominated the bloodstream.

As this century comes to a close, we find other behaviorists renaming the quadrants again, calling them driver, expressive, amiable, and analytical. Or, controller, organizer, analyzer, and persuader.

Our advice is to leave name-calling to the experts and to get help building your team. If you are an entrepreneur, there's a good chance you are either a Dominant Driver–Controller or an Expressive Inducer–Persuader. In either case you're busy leading and charging, so you need help with details and organization. Find a simple test. Take it yourself. Use it to build your team. Check with your attorney to be sure that the test is legal as a screening or evaluation device. Access these sources for help:

1. The counseling–testing center of your local community college.
2. The Internet under "Human Resource Training" or **www.keirsey.com** for an abbreviated Myers-Briggs Inventory Test

Now it's your turn. Action Steps 48 and 49 are to be completed once you have built your team. It's your chance to brainstorm for ways to win. Make the most of all the creative human resources you've just brought on board! We think these Action Steps are a great way to end this chapter on team building and to start your new business.

Summary

An entrepreneur's venture team often goes beyond bankers, lawyers, and accountants. A single-person entrepreneur may never need to hire an employee to grow and prosper. Many of today's successful firms use strategic partners and customer alliances for almost everything.

But if you grow beyond current capacity, and need to hire employees, hire wisely, train carefully, and encourage greatly. Remember, very few employees will ever have the "fire in their belly" for your business as you do. If you expect them to believe in your dream as much as you do, you may be very disappointed. Remember this is "your baby" and unless you are willing to share the financial successes, your employees are not likely to share the same dream.

Consider the costs of hiring an employee full time. Review your options of hiring part-timers, independent contractors, and employee leasing. Build the best team you can under the current constraints.

You have the right and responsibility to build a culture for your firm and its employees. What kind of environment do you want to provide for your employees? Strict and by the law? Easy-going and free-flowing? Open door? Jeans and t-shirts? Three-piece suits? Employees who can rise from inside the firm? Hiring from outside? Offering the best benefits around? Child-friendly policies? Hiring cheap? Friday bashes?

You wanted your own business. Now passionately build the environment you want to work in.

Action Step 48

Tap Your Team's Strengths by Brainstorming

Before you sign a lease, go into the hole for $50,000 of equipment, hire a lot of people, or spend $2,000 for a six-line telephone service, round up your new team and brainstorm the organization and objectives of your new business. A whiteboard is a handy tool here, so that everyone can follow the track of the session. One way to begin is to ask every member of your team to write down a list of objectives for the business.

You've found some good people, and that's taken hard work. Make that work pay off by tapping your human resources. Brainstorming will get you going, and you'll be surprised at what develops.

Action Step 49

Who's in Charge?

Time to Impress Your Business Plan Reader

Investors or vendors are often more interested in the founders than in the Business Plan itself. Experience in the same type of business and former businesses are powerful positive components of the plan. You will need to focus on past responsibility and authority. Present balance and diversity of your founding team.

Several paragraphs in the Business Plan may be sufficient for each key founder. If experience is lacking, discuss consultants or committed strategic partners who will bring balance to the management team and contribute experience and special skills. You may also want to include an organizational chart in your Business Plan's appendix.

Write short, strong bios for each member of your team. Full résumés will need to be completed later for the appendix of your Business Plan.

Think Points for Success

- People tend to "hire themselves." How many more "like you" can the business take?
- A winning team may lurk in your network.
- Look to your competitors and vendors for team members.
- Your company is *people.*
- Balance the people on your team.
- Have each team member write objectives for his or her responsibilities within the business. Set up your own internal management by objectives system.
- You can't grow until you have the right people.
- How much of your team can be comprised of part-timers and moonlighters?
- Consider a virtual organization.
- Consider independent contractors.
- Consider employee leasing.
- Find a mentor.

Key Points from Another View

Seven Characteristics of Highly Effective Entrepreneurial Employees

By Joe Hadzima with George Pilla

Fast-growing, entrepreneurial organizations need employees who regularly demonstrate entrepreneurial characteristics and work habits. Management of entrepreneurial companies must work diligently to recognize, identify, and attract this type of employee during the recruitment process to ensure a steady stream of the people with the "Right Stuff" to fuel growth of the venture.

Employees come in all shapes and sizes with all sorts of different skills and quirks. Their outlook and approach has been tempered by past experiences, good or bad. In the relatively short period that you have to do hiring, you have to cut through the prospective employee's résumé and verbal statements and figure out if he or she has the "Right Stuff." This is really important because just as "a bad apple will spoil the barrel," an employee with the "Wrong Stuff" will drag your whole effort down. It would be one thing if a Wrong Stuff employee simply didn't contribute, but it is worse than that—he usually sucks up scarce management time, creates diversions for Right Stuff employees—you get the picture.

So what are the characteristics of highly effective "Right Stuff" entrepreneurial employees? Here are a few to keep in mind as you interview potential new hires; you probably can think of others.

Ability to Deal with Risk

An entrepreneur has to operate effectively in an environment filled with risk. The Right Stuff employee can deal with risk and uncertainty. He or she is able to make progress toward goals and is able to make decisions when lacking one or several critical resources or data.

Results Oriented

The Right Stuff employee is results oriented—he or she takes control to get the task done. He or she is a "can do" person who demonstrates common sense in decisions and actions and is able to cut through and resolve problems that divert others. His or her business judgment is sound and becomes stronger with each experience, decision, or recommendation. While supervisors and managers may disagree with her ultimate recommendation, they usually agree that the presented alternatives are reasonable for the situation at hand.

Energy

The Right Stuff employee has high levels of enthusiasm and energy; he or she consistently generates output that is higher than could be reasonably expected. He or she is fully committed to the organization, its goals, and overall success. Not only does he or she desire to make a contribution to results, he or she needs to see the results of contributions quickly, not measured in years! He or she will seek out an organization that solicits and acts on his or her ideas, gives credit where credit is due, and points out errors and poor decisions quickly and clearly. He or she performs effectively with limited supervision and is able to self-motivate and set priorities with minimal guidance.

Growth Potential

The Right Stuff employee's reach exceeds her or his grasp today. Today's Right Stuff employee is often next year's supervisor and a department manager soon thereafter. She or he is willing to accept much higher levels of responsibility than is the norm for the position, title, experience level, or salary. She or he acts as a strong role model, trains and coaches others, and soon begins to assume supervisory responsibilities, again much earlier than would be expected in a normal corporate environment.

Team Player

The Right Stuff employee is a true team player; she or he recognizes how her or his role contributes to the overall effort and success of the organization. She or he accepts accountability and ownership for the area of responsibility and expects others on the team to do the same. She or he also recognizes the roles and contributions of others and applauds their efforts sincerely.

Multitasking Ability

The Right Stuff employee is flexible to accept new duties, assignments, and responsibilities. He or she can perform more than one role until the incremental duties and functions assumed can be assigned to co-workers in newly defined roles. He or she is also willing to dig in and do grunt work tasks that eventually will be performed by lower-level employees.

Improvement Oriented

The Right Stuff employee is more than willing to challenge, in a constructive way, existing procedures and systems; to her or him, the status quo is temporary. She or he suggests changes and improvements frequently and encourages others to do so also.

Right Stuff employees are easier to manage in some ways but require a higher level of management involvement in others. Ordinary (average) employees will not produce extraordinary results over time; Right Stuff employees will generally produce extraordinary results consistently over time. Unfortunately, unless properly motivated, managed, and rewarded, Right Stuff employees could perform at lower levels and only produce ordinary results. So what makes a Right Stuff manager?

First of all, the Right Stuff manager must have the characteristics of the Right Stuff employee. Beyond that she or he must have the basic skill set of sound business judgment, practical hands-on experience, general management skills, and common sense. She or he must be committed to and contribute to the organization's vision and mission and must convey this commitment in multiple ways: written, verbal, and by actions. She or he needs an awareness, understanding, and interest in the technology trends that affect the venture and its customers.

Externally, the Right Stuff manager must be able to identify and build creative strategic relationships, especially for partnering opportunities in areas of limited resources. Internally, he or she must effectively produce and manage change as the organization evolves, gaining enthusiastic support for change and improvements from the Right Stuff employees in the ranks.

So when you interview each new employee or manager, look beyond the mere facts of the resume and ask yourself: Is this a "Right Stuff" person? You are most likely interviewing the person because of the résumé. Now is the time to put the résumé aside and focus on the "Right Questions."

SOURCE: **web.mit.edu** (accessed June 1, 2001).

Protecting Your "Baby" and Yourself

Fulfilling Your Duties: Insurance, Taxes, Ethics

Entrepreneurial Links

Books

The Good, The Bad, and Your Business: Choosing Right When Ethical Dilemmas Pull You Apart, Jeffrey L. Seglin and Norman R. Augustine, Wiley, New York, 2000.

J.K. Lasser's Tax Deductions for Your Small Business, Barbara Weltman, Wiley, New York, 2000.

J.K. Lasser's Taxes Made Easy for Your Home-Based Business, Gary W. Carter, Wiley, New York, 2000.

Websites

www.internationalinsurance.org, (Insurance Information Institute)
www.isquare.com, (Small Business Advisor)
www.zdnet.com/smallbusiness, (ZD Net Small Business Advisor)

Associations/Organizations

Research Institute for Small and Emerging Businesses (RISE), www.riseb.org
Josephson Institute, www.josephsoninstitute.org
Insurance Information Institute, www.iii.org

Publications

Business Ethics, www.business-ethics.com
Business Ethics Resource Directory
Making Ethical Decisions (from Josephson Institute)

Additional Entrepreneurial Insights

How to Win Friends and Influence People, Dale Carnegie, Dorothy Carnegie (Ed.), and Arthur R. Pell, (Ed.), Pocket Books, 1994 (reprint).

Longaberger, An American Success Story, Dave Longaberger, Harper Business, 2001.

Good to Great: Why Some Companies Make the Leap . . . and Others Don't, James C. Collins, Harper Collins, New York, 2001.

LEARNING OBJECTIVES

- Understand the importance of protecting your assets through insurance.
- Explore insurance needs for your specific business.
- Investigate and initiate loss prevention strategies for both internal and external crime.
- Recognize the need to file all tax forms in a timely matter.
- Understand the importance of tax planning not just tax filing.
- Prepare for your exit at the beginning.
- Recognize that ethical behavior is first and foremost required of the owner before any expectations of ethical behavior can be expected of the employees.
- Understand the ethical dilemmas entrepreneurs face on a daily basis.
- Review the ethical principles for entrepreneurs.
- Learn the five steps to principled reasoning.

You will work incredibly hard to start and grow your business, but you must take steps to protect the business, which has become your "baby." Using insurance wisely, paying taxes as required, negotiating effectively, and following ethical principles will keep your business on track for success. The Internal Revenue Service (IRS) and lawyers are formidable foes.

In addition, you need to plan for the future by planning for the finish. In other words, when you begin your business you need to plan for how you will exit your business. When reviewing your exit strategy, we will ask you to return to the questions in Chapter 1, which asked you to assess your reasons for starting a business.

Protecting your business also includes financial planning. In Key Points from Another View we present a couple who not only have grown a wonderfully successful franchise organization, but have protected their personal lives as well.

In the Action Steps we ask you to take steps to protect your "baby" and yourself.

Passion

Passion for Others Leads to Change

People called Sharon Shore "a silent hero." She turned her care and concern for homeless people into a business—HOM, Inc. (Housing Operations and Management)—that is one of the first companies in the nation to privatize the delivery of government-assisted housing services. Her watchwords are empowerment and human dignity in dealing with customers and employees. Her commitment has made HOM the largest rental assistance provider in the nation for people with mental illness.

SOURCE: *Wise Women, Success Strategies for Women Entrepreneurs*, Bank One.

INSURANCE

Managing Risk

Can I forego insurance? If not, what type of insurance should I carry? How much coverage should I have? First consider:

- The size of any potential loss.
- The probability of loss.

- The resources available to meet a loss if one occurs.
- The probability of lawsuits (some industries and areas are heavily targeted).

Can you eliminate all risks? Doubtful! Can you reduce some risks? Yes, but you also *must* assume some risk.

How do you decide whether a particular risk should be transferred to an insurance company or personally assumed? Calculate the maximum potential loss that might result. If the loss would force your company into bankruptcy or cause serious financial damage, *recognize the risk and purchase insurance to help protect your assets.*

Losses that occur with predictable frequency such as shoplifting and bad debts can usually be absorbed by the business and are often budgeted as part of the normal costs of doing business; the cost of the loss is incorporated into the price. Where probability of loss is high, a more effective method of controlling the loss is to adopt appropriate precautionary measures and purchase better-than-adequate insurance. The key to purchasing insurance (and all risk management) is: *Do not risk more than you can tolerate losing.*

Insurance Planning

First consider all of the insurable risks faced by your business. In general, the following risks can be covered by insurance if you have followed the law:

- Personal injury to employees and the general public. Some retail stores have become targets for slip and fall claims. Certain businesses have higher personal injury claims and you need to protect accordingly.
- Employment practices such as hiring, firing, sexual discrimination, libel, and so on.
- Loss to the business caused by the death or disability of key employees or the owner—an essential coverage needed to protect your business.
- Loss or damage of property—including merchandise, supplies, fixtures, and building. A standard fire insurance policy pays the policyholder only for those losses directly caused by fire. Make sure when dealing with your insurance agent that you understand your policy thoroughly.
- Loss of income resulting from interruption of business caused by damage to the firm's operating assets (storms, natural disasters, electrical blackouts).

Other indirect losses, known as consequential losses, may be even more important to your company's welfare. You can protect yourself against these losses by obtaining business-interruption insurance. Consequential losses include the following:

- Extra expenses of obtaining temporary quarters.
- Loss of rental income on buildings damaged or destroyed by fire, if you are a landlord.
- Loss of facility use.
- Continuing expenses after a fire—salaries, rents paid in advance, interest obligations, and so on.
- Loss of customer base.

Do not fail to provide safe equipment and working conditions, hire competent employees, and warn employees of any existing danger. In every state an employer must insure against potential workers' compensation claims. However, employee coverage and the extent of the employer's liability vary from state to state. The cost of workers' compensation varies greatly by occupation and risk involved. Worker's compensation can cost up to 42 cents on every dollar you pay your employees! Ask your insurance company if they have any loss-prevention services and use them to the fullest extent. If your employees speak several different languages, you need to make sure *everyone* understands the safety rules.

General liability covers any kind of nonemployee bodily injury except that caused by automobiles and professional malpractice. In some cases this coverage may even extend to trespassers. As a businessowner, you may also be liable for bodily injuries to customers, pedestrians, delivery people, and other outsiders—even in instances in which you have exercised "reasonable care." In highly litigious states you may need substantial liability coverage to protect your business.

Vehicle use is a major source of liability claims. Under the "doctrine of agency," a business can be liable for injuries and property damage caused by employees operating their own or someone else's vehicle while on company business. The company may have some protection under the employee's liability policy, but the limits are probably inadequate. If it is customary or convenient for employees to use their vehicle while on company business (e.g., salespeople on the road or covering a route), you should purchase nonownership liability insurance.

The best form of general liability insurance for the small business consists of a comprehensive general liability policy combined with a comprehensive auto liability policy and a standard workers' compensation policy.

One retail store owner recently discovered that the merchandise she transported in her van from store to store was not covered while she was in transit. An additional rider had to be added to her policy to provide insurance protection. Sitting down and going through various scenarios with your insurance agent is one of the best ways to make sure you are protecting *all* areas of your business. To provide an additional layer of protection, consider an umbrella policy.

Types of Coverage

You can purchase insurance to cover almost any risk. Businessowners most commonly protect themselves with the following types of coverage.

1. **Fire and general property insurance**—protects against fire loss, vandalism, hail, and wind damage.
2. **Consequential loss insurance**—covers loss of earnings or extra expenses when business is interrupted because of fire or other catastrophe (see also item 4 following).
3. **Public liability insurance**—covers injury to the public, such as customer or pedestrian injury claims.
4. **Business-interruption insurance**—coverage in case the business is unable to continue as before.

GLOBAL VILLAGE

ISO IN BRIEF

The International Organization for Standardization (ISO) develops International Standards over almost the entire range of technology. Its membership comprises the national standards institutes of some 130 countries.

ISO is a non-governmental organization and the standards it develops are voluntary. However, a certain percentage of its standards—mainly those concerned with health, safety, or environmental aspects—have been adopted in some countries as part of their regulatory framework.

ISO standards are market-driven. They are developed by international consensus among experts drawn from the industrial, technical, or business sectors, which have expressed the need for a particular standard. These may be joined by experts from government, regulatory authorities, testing bodies, academia, consumer groups, or other organizations with relevant knowledge, or which have expressed a direct interest in the standard under development.

Although ISO standards are voluntary, the fact that they are developed in response to market demand, and are based on consensus among the interested parties, ensures widespread compliance.

International Standards are increasingly important to business. They are essential to global communication, technology transfer, and international trade.

To increase your competitiveness in the international market, learn more about ISO standards at **www.iso.ch**.

Source: **www.iso.ch**

5. **Crime insurance**—protects against losses resulting from burglary, robbery, and so forth. Fidelity bonds provide coverage from employee theft.
6. **Malpractice insurance**—covers against claims from clients who suffer damages as a result of services that you perform.
7. **Errors and omissions insurance**—covers against claims from customers who suffer injury or loss because of errors you made, things you should have done but failed to do, or warnings you failed to supply.
8. **Employment practices liability insurance (EPLI)**—covers against claims from employees for employment practices: sexual harassment, wrongful discharge, discrimination, breach of contract, libel, and so on.
9. **Key man insurance**—covers the life, death, dismemberment, or physical disability of owner(s) or key employee(s).
10. **Product liability insurance**—covers injury to the public, such as customer use or misuse of product.
11. **Disability insurance**—covers owner and employees against disability and usually allows for payments to be continued during rehabilitation. Disability for an owner is a much greater risk than death and few owners insure themselves adequately.
12. **Life and health insurance for employees.**
13. **Workers' Compensation insurance**—protects employees if they are injured while on the job.
14. **Extra equipment insurance**—covers specialized equipment not covered in standard policies.
15. **Directors' and Officers' liability insurance**—if company stock is held by outside investors, directors and officers should be protected.

ACTION STEP 50

PROTECT YOUR VENTURE

Network your way to a business insurance salesperson. Discuss your Buisness Plan with him or her and complete the insurance worksheet on this page. Discover the cost of insuring your business for the first year. If you are a home-based business, review the information on pages 258–261 and discuss with your agent or broker.

According to the Insurance Information Institute, **www.iii.org**, about 40 percent of small business owners carry no insurance at all because of cash concerns. If you cannot afford minimal insurance coverage, rethink your Business Plan and delay starting your business until you *can* afford adequate coverage. One mishap or incident can destroy everything you have worked for. Do not let this happen to you. Complete Action Step 50 using the Insurance Planning Worksheet (Figure 12.1) to discover your insurance needs and costs.

FIGURE 12.1
Insurance Planning Worksheet

Required Insurance Types	Yes	No	Annual Cost ($)
1. Personal liability	☐	☐	
2. General and public liability	☐	☐	
3. Product liability	☐	☐	
4. Errors and omissions liability	☐	☐	
5. Malpractice liability	☐	☐	
6. Key man insurance	☐	☐	
7. Directors and Officers	☐	☐	
8. Term life	☐	☐	
9. Health	☐	☐	
10. Workers Compensation	☐	☐	
11. Crime Insurance	☐	☐	
12. Vehicle	☐	☐	
13. Business interruption	☐	☐	
14. Extra equipment	☐	☐	
15. Consequential loss	☐	☐	
16. EPLI	☐	☐	
17. Fire and theft	☐	☐	
18. Business loan	☐	☐	
19. Bonds (fidelity, surety)	☐	☐	
20. Other	☐	☐	
Total Annual Cost			

HOME-BASED BUSINESS INSURANCE

If you're working at home—STOP—and review your insurance coverage. Your homeowners insurance probably doesn't cover your business. A typical homeowner's policy provides only $2500 coverage for business equipment, which is usually not enough to cover all of the business property. You also need coverage for liability and business interruption.

To insure your business, you have three choices—endorsements to the homeowner's policy, an in-home business policy, or a small businessowner's package policy.

Endorsements

Depending on the type of business you operate, you may be able to add an endorsement to your existing homeowner's policy. For as little as $14 a year, you can double your standard homeowners policy limits for business equipment from $2,500 to $5,000.

Some companies have begun offering endorsements that include property and limited business liability coverage. Endorsements are typically only available for businesses that generate $250,000 or less in annual receipts. They are available in most states.

In-Home Business Policy

The insurance industry has responded to the growing number of home-based businesses by creating in-home business insurance policies. For about $200 per year you can insure your business property for $10,000. General liability coverage is also included in the policy. A business owner can purchase anywhere from $300,000 to $1 million worth of liability coverage. The cost of the liability coverage will depend on the amount purchased.

If your business is unable to operate because of damage to your house, your in-home business policy will cover lost income and ongoing expenses such as payroll for up to a year. The policy also provides limited coverage for loss of valuable papers and records, accounts receivable, off-site business property, and use of equipment.

In some cases the companies that offer these policies require that you purchase your homeowners and automobile insurance policies from them as well.

Businessowner's Package Policy

Created specifically for small businesses, this policy is an excellent solution if your home-based business operates in more than one location or manufactures products outside the workplace. A businessowner's package policy, like the in-home business policy, covers business property and equipment, loss of income and extra expenses, and liability. However, these types of coverage are on a much broader scale than an in-home business policy.

Automobile Coverage

If you are using your automobile for business activities—transporting supplies or products or visiting customers—you need to make certain that your automobile insurance will protect you from accidents that may occur while on business.

To get insurance coverage that will not overlap with your homeowner's policy or leave any exposures, you should consult with an insurance professional with experience in this field. To find an expert, contact your home insurer, other professionals with similar businesses, or other home business owners.

SOURCE: Insurance Information Institute, *Home-Based Business Insurance*, **www.iii.org** (accessed March 1, 2001).

CRIME: BE PREPARED, TAKE PREVENTATIVE STEPS!

Thirty percent of small-business failures can be attributed to employee theft, according to the U.S. Chamber of Commerce. A sobering statistic, no doubt, for any entrepreneur. You must be prepared and take preventative steps not to be in this 30 percent. Seeing your hard work and money go down a rat hole because of employee theft is enough to crush even the hardiest entrepreneur. You must be knowledgeable of both internal crime and external crime and train for both events. Your trade organization may be very helpful in providing you with loss prevention information pertinent to your industry. In addition, large insurers offer specialists to work with industry-specific issues.

Potential issues you will face:

- Credit card fraud
- Check deception
- Shoplifting
- Cash register vulnerability with employees shortchanging customers
- Cash handling
- Bookkeeping theft
- Fraudulent refunds
- Counterfeit money
- Fitting room theft
- Burglary
- Robbery
- Bomb threats
- Theft of items from stock room, layaway, and displays
- Computer fraud
- Sabotage
- Theft of private information
- Manipulation of time card data
- Illegal use of company time
- Fraudulent trip expense reports
- Sweethearting (discounts for family and friends)

Take action promptly when any of the previous take place in your firm. We have seldom met an entrepreneur who has not experienced one or more of the previous problems. Make it known throughout your firm that none of these actions will be tolerated. Don't look the other way and believe crime cannot occur in your organization. Keep your eyes and ears wide open. Explain to your employees the financial consequences of shoplifting and employee theft. Josie Rietkerk, owner of Caterina's, recently wrote the following note to her employees.

> Theft in our store is a serious problem. For each \$2.00 candy bar stolen in our store, we pay 20 percent of our gross sales to our landlord. The cost of the candy bar is 86 cents, and we have a 10 percent additional overhead on gross sales. Thus our costs are \$1.46. Therefore we need to sell more than three \$2.00 candy bars (with a net profit at 54 cents each) to cover the loss of one candy bar just to break even. Please keep your eyes on our customers. In addition, please understand that the employee policies in regards to free food and sweethearting are there to protect our business and your job.

A recent FMI Library Video, *Preventing Front End Losses*, shared the following:

10 Warning Signs of Retail Employee Theft

1. Small calculators or notepads near cash drawers.
2. Employees who clip a lot of coupons.

3. Cashiers who bend down to pick things up a lot.
4. Associates who move their display screen out of sight.
5. Cashiers who frequently have excessively long lines.
6. Associates who insist on taking customers out of one line and into their own.
7. Journal tapes that are often jammed, torn, or damaged.
8. Cashiers with a high amount of no-sales.
9. Chronically low scanning percentages.
10. A drawer that is balanced to the penny for every shift.

SOURCE: Denise Purcell, "Employee Theft: How to Stop It," *Specialty Food Magazine.*

An excellent restaurant manager we know always insisted on closing out the register every night, never took a vacation, and never missed closing; everyone, including the owners, was thrilled to have such a conscientious employee. That is until they realized the reason he did these things was that he was stealing. In fact, Jerry Gallon, owner of the restaurant, shared, "We think he stole more than $110,000 in two years. We trusted him like he was our own son and thought he loved the restaurant as much as my wife and I. But we found out what he really loved was the cash drawer!"

Pre-employment testing, background checks, drug testing, mystery shoppers, awareness training, and employee hotline programs can reduce, but not eliminate, retail theft. In addition, surveillance technology and well-designed point-of-sale software can limit theft. Shifting managers around to different stores and to different shifts will also serve as another check on your employees.

Make sure your business establishes a code of conduct that new employees sign and review. According to O'Brien and Associates, Ontario-based loss prevention consultants, "The code of conduct should clearly state that the taking of merchandise or cash without payment or management authorization—or helping others to do so—are violations that may result in disciplinary action up to and including termination of employment and possibly criminal charges."

THE TAX MAN COMETH!

What are the laws? What forms do I have to fill out? If I am audited, how can I protect myself? These are just a few of the questions answered in IRS Publication 334, "Tax Guide for Small Business." See the Incredible Resource box (in Chapter 11) for further IRS information. Table 12.1 lists the most common tax forms businesses are required by law to file.

Schedule C and Schedule C-EZ for sole proprietors are provided in Appendix C.

A tough tax for many sole proprietors to absorb is the self-employment tax. As of 2001, the tax is 15.3 percent of the first $80,400 of income and 2.9 percent on anything above that amount. Use Schedule SE in Appendix C to calculate your tax.

In addition to federal taxes, you will also be responsible for state, county, and local taxes. State and federal rules do not always mesh. Be careful to understand both systems. An *experienced* CPA who specializes in your selected industry will be able to keep you on track with what is acceptable practice to the IRS.

The best thing you can do for your business is to keep excellent records of *all* transactions. Recently one of our colleagues was audited and the audit took one day instead of the usual three—the result of excellent record-keeping and no problems! The IRS and your accountant will tell you exactly what is required.

While preparation is essential, your CPA can be of most assistance to you in *tax planning*. Tax preparation is sometimes too late! Keep your accountant abreast of any major business changes. *Make your accountant part of your team.*

TABLE 12.1
Which Forms Must I File?

If You Are a:	You May Be Liable for:	Use Form:
Sole proprietor	Income tax	1040 and Schedule C[1] or C-EZ (Schedule F for farm business[1])
	Self-employment tax	1040 and Schedule SE
	Estimated tax	1040-ES
	Employment taxes:	
	• Social security and Medicare taxes and income tax withholding	943 for farm employees 941 for all others
	• Federal unemployment (FUTA) tax	940 or 940-EZ
	• Depositing employment taxes	8109[2]
	Excise taxes[4]	See *Excise Taxes*
Partnership	Annual return of income	1065
	Employment taxes	Same as sole proprietor
	Excise taxes	See *Excise Taxes*
Partner in a partnership (individual)	Income tax	1040 and Schedule E[3]
	Self-employment tax	1040 and Schedule SE
	Estimated tax	1040-ES
Corporation or S corporation	Income tax	1120 or 1120-A (corporation) 1120S (S corporation)
	Estimated tax	1120-W (corporation only) and 8109[2]
	Employment taxes	Same as sole proprietor
	Excise taxes	See *Excise Taxes*
S corporation shareholder	Income tax	1040 and Schedule E[3]
	Estimated tax	1040-ES

[1]File a separate schedule for each business.

[2]Do not use if you deposit taxes electronically.

[3]Various other schedules may be needed.

[4]Contact IRS for information on excise taxes (which are additional taxes for the environment, communications, fuel, luxury, etc.).

SOURCE: *Starting in Business & Keeping Records*, Publication 583, IRS, Washington, DC, 2001.

Employment Taxes

You will be responsible for corporate or personal income taxes, employment taxes, sales taxes, and property taxes. If you have employees, you will need to file an Application for Employer Identification Number (EIN), Form SS-4 (both found in Appendix C). Keeping up with employee taxes and laws are a headache for most employers. As recommended in Chapter 11, use a payroll service. Some employers pay their employees cash in an illegal attempt to save on taxes and worker's compensation. If an employee gets injured, the deception will be discovered and fines are very heavy. In addition, if an angry employee calls the IRS to report you, the IRS *will* call you! Another scenario is when a competitor turns you in to the IRS for suspected tax evasion. Tax laws and regulations are a burden but they are *not* to be avoided or taken lightly at any time.

If you have employees, be sure to order Publication 15, Circular E, Employer's Tax Guide. According to the IRS, "The term, 'employment taxes' describes several federal, state, and local taxes that employers have the responsibility to manage. Some of these taxes apply only to the employer, some are levied on employees, and some apply to both employer and employees. Federal employment taxes are: 1) Federal income tax withholding, 2) Social Security and Medicare taxes, and 3) Federal unemployment (FUTA) tax."

If you are not heeding our advice to use a payroll service who will retain your rewards, the IRS recommends you retain the following employment records for at least four years for possible IRS review:

- Your employer identification number.
- Amounts and dates of all wage, annuity, and pension payments.

COMMUNITY RESOURCE

Small Business and Self Employed COMMUNITY

www.irs.gov/smallbiz

The IRS's new effort to build community sites on the Web is an excellent source for entrepreneurs to locate tax-related information pertaining to a specific industry. One excellent source on this site is the "Audit Technique Guide," which specifies what the IRS auditor will be looking for if and when your business is audited. Information like this gives you a leg up and time to prepare for an audit. Better yet, read it when you open your business, act on its suggestions, and maybe you will avoid an audit! The front page of the "Restaurant Community" follows:

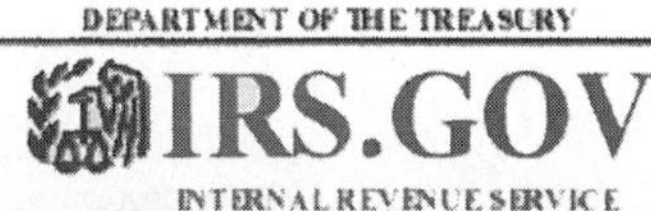

IRS.gov | Digital Daily | Business Co
Business Communities> Restaurant>
Restaurant Community
News & Events
Tax Tips
Avoiding Problems
Audit Tech. Guides
Calendar
Related Links
Financ. Resources
Tax Laws and Regs
Trends and Stats
Coming Soon!
Practitioners
Products & Forms
Helpful Resources
Contact SB Expert
Tax Library
SB Workshops
IRS Links
Tax Tips
Learn about tax issues related to your business
Avoiding Problems
Avoid costly mistakes made by others in your tax situation
Audit Technique Guides
Get into the mind of an IRS auditor before you file
Tax Calendar
This calendar has important due dates for all types of businesses
Related Links
Get a leg up on the latest tax changes that may impact your business
Financial Resources
How to create and maintain a successful organization
Tax Laws and Regulations
Review and comment on rules that impact you
Trends and Statistics
Data about your industry
News and Events
Remain up to date in what's happening in your profession or industry

SOURCE: **www.irs.gov/smallbiz/restaurants/index.htm?industry=Restaurant** (accessed June 14, 2001).

- Amounts of tips reported.
- The fair market value of in-kind wages paid.
- Names, addresses, social security numbers, and occupations of employees and recipients.
- Any employee copies of Form W-2 that were returned to you as undeliverable.
- Dates of employment.

- Periods for which employees and recipients were paid while absent because of sickness or injury and the amount and weekly rate of payments you or third-party payers made to them.
- Copies of employees' and recipients' income tax withholding allowance certificates (Forms W-4, W-4P, W-4S, and W-4V).
- Dates and amounts of tax deposits you have made.
- Copies of returns filed.
- Records of allocated tips.
- Records of fringe benefits provided, including substantiation.

ACTION STEP 51

1. Contact the IRS through the Internet or with a visit to your local office to collect and review all the appropriate tax forms that you will need in your business. If you are not sure which forms you will need, read up on the IRS website and use the publications mentioned in the text to guide you. Contact the office for additional help or an appointment.
2. a) Review Action Steps 1–5.
   b) Make changes.
   c) Develop an exit strategy to be included in your Business Plan.

Sales Taxes

For sales tax and resale numbers, contact your State Board of Equalization. Do not forget to remit your collected sales tax! Many small businessowners attempt to avoid reporting sales taxes for cash transactions. The IRS has many ways to determine your true sales figures. For example, they look at the number of disposable cups you purchased and used to determine how much coffee you sold, or review your electric and water bills to estimate how many loads your Laundromat washed and dried.

If you are starting up, don't overestimate projected sales. If projections are high, you will be required to post a higher bond to get a resale number and permit.

Final Tax Thoughts

Fines are considerable. Once audited, the chance to be audited again increases. Realize that everyone is audited some time or other. Be prepared with excellent record-keeping, a payroll services firm to support you, and an excellent, experienced accountant to represent you. Excellent records will be of great benefit to you when you decide to sell your business and keep the IRS at bay. Complete Part 1 of Action Step 51.

EXIT STRATEGY

Return to the first five Action Steps in Chapter 1 and your notebook and review your answers. Have they changed since you began your adventure? If so, make the relevant changes and then proceed. Business plans usually include a section referred to as the "Exit Strategy." One's exit should be based on the reasons and purposes one started the business. For some, they will pursue a small business to create long-term capital appreciation. For others, they dream of leaving a successful viable business to their children. To protect your business, you need to discuss your potential exit strategy with your legal and accounting team as changes to the legal form of the business may have a large impact on tax consequences on the firm's sale or transfer.

Potential exit strategies include the following:

- Selling all or a portion of the business.
- Going out of business sale.
- Handing down the business to family members (either slowly or all at once).
- Franchising your business.
- Selling to an Employee Stock Ownership Plan (ESOP).
- Taking the company public.
- Merging with another firm or being acquired.
- Buyout by a partner in the business.

If you are seeking investment capital, your investors will need to know your personal financial goals and anticipated time frames. Venture capitalists and angel investors are looking at investing for usually three to five years. In addition to your personal and financial goals, a realistic exit plan should include your particular industry, competitive

INCREDIBLE RESOURCE

HELP FOR SOCIALLY RESPONSIBLE BUSINESSES

By Kate O'Sullivan

If you're looking for capital for your socially responsible business, you're in luck. A growing number of funds are providing financing for companies that address societal needs, whether they do so by providing environmentally friendly products or services or by the way they run their business. Some of the funding sources profiled here target companies that create jobs for low-income workers, while others facilitate investments in specific sectors such as education, energy, or health care. All of them, however, hold the same high standards for their socially responsible investments as they do for other ventures. Although they may not expect quite the same level of financial return, they look "first and foremost for sustainable businesses," says Jerry Colonna, managing partner at Flatiron Partners. Because we limited our list to funding sources for socially responsible for-profit companies, we did not include organizations that offer funding for nonprofits or those that focus solely on community development.

Coastal Ventures LP

Founded: 1996, a subsidiary of Coastal Enterprises

nc. Location: Portland, Maine

Fund size: $5.5 million; CEI Ventures hopes to raise $20 million for the new fund in the first quarter of 2001.

Mission: "The three Es: employment, equity (social justice), and economics (profitability)," says CEI Ventures president Nat Henshaw.

Investment criteria: Looks for companies that create jobs for low-income people. Most of the companies in the fund's portfolio provide socially responsible products and services, focusing on areas like health care, education, and the environment. The fund also seeks companies that engage in progressive management techniques like incentive compensation, including employee ownership. Portfolio companies receiving an investment must sign an agreement to fill 50 percent to 75 percent of new jobs with low-income workers referred through Maine's job-training programs.

Average investment: $200,000 with current fund; aiming for $1 million with new fund.

Average equity stake: 10 percent.

Environmental Capital Network

Founded: 1995.

Location: Ann Arbor, MI.

Fund size: Not a fund. The network facilitated more than $82 million worth of investments in 2000.

Mission: ECN is a network of 200 members including entrepreneurs in the environmental and energy fields and the angels and venture-capital firms who want to invest in them.

Investment criterion: Looks for early-stage companies whose founders want to commercialize their environmental or energy products and have at least a rough Business Plan.

Average investment: Ranges from less than $1 million to $20 million.

Average equity stake: NA.

Flatiron Future Fund

Founded: April 2000 by Flatiron Partners, a venture-capital firm focused on Internet investing.

Location: New York City.

Fund Size: From $2 million to $5 million.

Mission: To spread social awareness among entrepreneurs and to fund for-profit ventures that promote technology for a greater social good. Flatiron Partners also formed the Flatiron Foundation to make grants to nonprofit organizations.

Investment criteria: Will invest in companies involved in computer and high-tech education for children and in female- and minority-owned businesses.

Average investment: Ranges from $250,000 to $1,000,000.

Average equity stake: Will be minority stakeholders. Investors' Circle

Founded: 1992.

Location: San Francisco.

Fund size: Not a fund. Has facilitated more than $70 million in investments to date.

Mission: Investors' Circle is an organization of 130-plus members that matches angel investors and venture-capital funds with early-stage socially responsible businesses.

INCREDIBLE RESOURCE—CONT'D

Investment criteria: Focuses on businesses in the health, education, environment, energy, and community-development sectors; also seeks out female- and minority-led businesses.

Average investment: $600,000.

Average equity stake: Investors take a minority stake.

Sustainable Jobs Fund LP

First fund closed: 1999.

Location: Durham, N.C., and Philadelphia.

Fund size: $17 million.

Mission: To fund companies that will create jobs in economically distressed regions of the eastern United States

Investment criteria: The fund's companies must create jobs; SJF also focuses on manufacturing and environmental companies such as recycling and renewable-energy businesses. Requires entrepreneurs receiving an investment to sign a "community-development covenant" stipulating the number of jobs they will create and which of those are targeted to low-income workers. They must also agree to provide health insurance and a living wage.

Average investment: $500,000.

Average equity stake: Ranges from a few percent up to 30 percent. If you'd like to learn more about this topic, read "Can Business Still Save The World?" in the April 2001 issue of *Inc.* magazine.

SOURCE: *Inc.*, April 2001.

environment, management needs, and business life cycle. According to Tom Richman, when he looked at the exit strategy for a potential business venture he shared, "I was forced to think about myself as an entrepreneur the way a venture capitalist thinks about his money: How much will I have to invest and over what time period before I can get out with a decent return? Only in my case, I was the capital, and the exit strategy we worked out suggested I'd have to invest a lot more of myself and for a good many more years than I thought I could. So I decided to get out before I got in. Creating an exit strategy helps one visualize not just the start and bailout points for a nascent enterprise but also the distance and journey between them."

According to Jennifer Lawton, "There is plenty to fear about continuing to work in entrepreneurial nirvana with no consideration of its end or change: The reality is that unless you define that end or change, your business may change in a way that wasn't in your plan." Lawton suggests you consider the following words of wisdom:

1. **Know why you're in the business** and what is most important to you. Know this in parallel tracks—the personal and the professional—and also know where the two can merge.
2. **Educate yourself through listening, reading, and interacting** to know what others strive for, both in like-minded and not so like-minded businesses.
3. **Communicate your goals and intentions**, include people in them, and enlist support.
4. **Understand that your exit strategy may be that you will never leave,** or alternatively, that you will sell high and retire early.
5. **Do what's right for you.**

SOURCE: Jennifer Lawton, "Exit Strategies: What's Yours?" **www.entreworld.org** (accessed August 11, 2001).

Write your exit strategy down. Have a road map with a start and a finish. Know how to answer the "What is your exit strategy?" question, but also know that you're really answering the "What are your vision and goal?" question. And realize that, through identifying your exit strategy, you have a chance to preserve and control your own entrepreneurial nirvana. Complete part 2 of Action Step 51.

ACTION STEP 52

1. Respond to the Ethical Issues in Business questions on page 268. Next, have potential partners complete the questionnaire as well. Then sit together over a very long cup of coffee and discuss your answers. Do you see any potential problems? If so, how will you work the problems out? Is this someone you want to be in business with? In addition, discuss the Ethical Principles for Entrepreneurs (see Figure 12.3). Which areas do you agree and disagree on? How will you solve your differences when you disagree on an issue from an ethical standpoint?
2. Develop your firm's Code of Conduct. Use The Center for the Study of Ethics in the Professions at the Illinois Institute of Technology's website at **www.csep.iit.edu/codes/index.html** to help you complete this action step.

ETHICS

You will be confronted with many ethical issues in running your business. How you react will set the tone for your employees and the future of your company. Figure 12.2 lists potential ethical issues and dilemmas entrepreneurs face. Review these issues on your own to determine where you stand. If you have partners, ask them to review the issues and then meet to discuss your thoughts. Knowing what your partner truly believes and where he or she stands ethically can prevent potential problems

FIGURE 12.2
Ethical Issues for Entrepreneurs

How important is each of the following to you?

4=Very important, 3=Important, 2=Not very important, 1=Not important

1. _____ Expecting a "full day's work for a full day's pay" work ethic.
2. _____ Not allowing petty theft (i.e., supplies, telephone, photocopying, etc.)
3. _____ Not cheating on expense accounts.
4. _____ Not allowing employee acceptance of gifts or favors from vendors.
5. _____ Not distorting or falsifying internal reports.
6. _____ Not allowing cheating or overreaching on benefits (sick days, insurance, etc.)
7. _____ Sexual or racial non-discrimination in hiring, promotion, or pay.
8. _____ Invasion of employee privacy.
9. _____ Providing safe and healthy working conditions.
10. _____ Providing honest, fair, and timely work appraisals.
11. _____ Not recruiting for employee's replacement without telling employee being replaced.
12. _____ Not allowing strategies or technical justifications to deny employees' earned benefits.
13. _____ Dealing fairly with employee complaints.
14. _____ Having fair expectation of paid staff.
15. _____ Providing adequate compensation.
16. _____ Providing adequate recognition, appreciation, or other psychic rewards to staff.
17. _____ Promoting "healthy" competition among employees.
18. _____ Promoting "good" communication.
19. _____ Promoting mutual support and teamsmanship.
20. _____ Fair product pricing.
21. _____ Commitment to honest and truthful marketing and advertising.
22. _____ Providing and ensuring safe and healthy products.
23. _____ Fair handling of customer complaints.
24. _____ Providing truthful tax reports and financial statements.
25. _____ Protecting the environment.
26. _____ Avoidance of bribes, payoffs, or "grease" to union or public officials.
27. _____ Doing business in countries with inhumane or anti-American policies.
28. _____ Community involvement and philanthropy.

SOURCE: Josephson Institute, Marina Del Ray, Cal.

for your business. Complete Action Step 52 to determine where possible conflicts may lie regarding ethical issues among your partners.

In addition, we have included an entrepreneur's code of ethical principles (Figure 12.3), which can be a guide as one faces difficult issues and problems while operating a business. By knowing where one stands and what one believes, making the hard decisions is much easier. Guidelines such as those presented in Figure 12.3 and the Josephson Institute's Five Steps to Principled Reasoning (Figure 12.4) assist individuals to act in the best interest of others.

FIGURE 12.3

Ethical Principles for Entrepreneurs

Ethical values, translated into active language, establish standards or rules describing the kinds of behavior an ethical entrepreneur should and should not engage in. The following list of principles incorporates the characteristics and values that most people associate with ethical behavior. Ethical decision-making systematically considers these principles.

1. **HONESTY.** Ethical entrepreneurs are honest and truthful in all their dealings and they do not deliberately mislead or deceive others by misrepresentations, overstatements, partial truths, selective omissions, or any other means.
2. **INTEGRITY.** Ethical entrepreneurs demonstrate personal integrity and the courage of their convictions by doing what they think is right even when there is great pressure to do otherwise; they are principled, honorable, and upright; they will fight for their beliefs. They will not sacrifice principle for expediency or be hypocritical or unscrupulous.
3. **PROMISE-KEEPING AND TRUSTWORTHINESS.** Ethical entrepreneurs are worthy of trust, they are candid and forthcoming in supplying relevant information and correcting misapprehensions of fact, and they make every reasonable effort to fulfill the letter and spirit of their promises and commitments. They do not interpret agreements in an unreasonably technical or legalistic manner in order to rationalize non-compliance or create justifications for escaping their commitments.
4. **LOYALTY.** Ethical entrepreneurs are worthy of trust, demonstrate fidelity and loyalty to persons and institutions by friendship in adversity, and display support and devotion to duty; they do not use or disclose information learned in confidence for personal advantage. They safeguard the ability to make independent professional judgments by scrupulously avoiding undue influences and conflicts of interest. They are loyal to their employees and colleagues. They respect the proprietary information of their former employer, and refuse to engage in any activities that take undue advantage of their previous position.
5. **FAIRNESS.** Ethical entrepreneurs are fair and just in all dealings; they do not exercise power arbitrarily, and do not use overreaching nor indecent means to gain or maintain any advantage nor take undue advantage of another's mistakes or difficulties. Fair persons manifest a commitment to justice, the equal treatment of individuals, and tolerance for and acceptance of diversity and are open-minded; they are willing to admit they are wrong and, where appropriate, change their positions and beliefs.
6. **CONCERN FOR OTHERS.** Ethical entrepreneurs are caring, compassionate, benevolent, and kind; they live the Golden Rule, help those in need, and seek to accomplish their business objectives in a manner that causes the least harm and the greatest positive good.
7. **RESPECT FOR OTHERS.** Ethical entrepreneurs demonstrate respect for the human dignity, autonomy, privacy, rights, and interests of all those who have a stake in their decisions; they are courteous and treat all people with equal respect and dignity regardless of sex, race, or national origin.
8. **LAW ABIDING.** Ethical entrepreneurs abide by laws, rules, and regulations relating to their business activities.
9. **COMMITMENT TO EXCELLENCE.** Ethical entrepreneurs pursue excellence in performing their duties, are well informed and prepared, and constantly endeavor to increase their proficiency in all areas of responsibility.
10. **LEADERSHIP.** Ethical entrepreneurs are conscious of the responsibilities and opportunities of their position of leadership and seek to be positive ethical role models by their own conduct and by helping to create an environment in which principled reasoning and ethical decision making are highly prized.
11. **REPUTATION AND MORALE.** Ethical entrepreneurs seek to protect and build the company's good reputation and the morale of it's employees by engaging in no conduct that might undermine respect and by taking whatever actions are necessary to correct or prevent inappropriate conduct of others.
12. **ACCOUNTABILITY.** Ethical entrepreneurs acknowledge and accept personal accountability for the ethical quality of their decisions and omissions to themselves, their colleagues, their companies, and their communities.

SOURCE: *Ethical Obligations and Opportunities in Business: Ethical Decision Making in the Trenches,* Josephson Institute, Marina Del Ray, Cal.

FIGURE 12.4
Five Steps to Principled Reasoning

1. **Clarify**

   Determine precisely what must be decided.

   Formulate and devise the full range of alternatives (i.e., things you could do). Eliminate patently impractical, illegal, and improper alternatives. Force yourself to develop at least three ethically justifiable options. Examine each option to determine which ethical principles and values are involved.

2. **Evaluate**

   If any of the options require the sacrifice of any ethical principle, evaluate the facts and assumptions carefully.

   Distinguish solid facts from beliefs, desires, theories, suppositions, unsupported conclusions, and opinions that might generate rationalizations. Take into account the credibility of the sources of information and the fact that self-interest, bias, and ideological commitments tend to obscure objectivity and affect perceptions about what is true. With regard to each alternative, carefully consider the benefits, burdens and risks to each stakeholder.

3. **Decide**

   After evaluating the information available, make a judgment about what is or is not true and about what consequences are most likely to occur.

   If there is not an ethical dilemma, evaluate the viable alternatives according to personal conscience, prioritize the values so that you can choose which values to advance and which to subordinate, and determine who will be helped the most and harmed the least. It is sometimes helpful to consider the worst case scenario. In addition, consider whether ethically questionable conduct can be avoided by modifying goals or methods or by consulting with those likely to be affected in order to get their input or consent. Finally, you may want to rely on three "ethics guides":

   Golden Rule—Are you treating others as you would want to be treated?

   Publicity—Would you be comfortable if your reasoning and decisions were to be publicized? How would you feel about seeing it on the front page of tomorrow's papers?

   Kid-on-Your-Shoulder—Would you be comfortable if your children were observing you? Are you practicing what you preach?

4. **Implement**

   Once a decision is made about what to do, develop a plan of *how* to implement the decision in a way that maximizes the benefits and minimizes the costs and risks.

   Remember that any decision or act, however ethical, is bound to be weakened by a sanctimonious, pious, judgmental, or self-righteous attitude.

5. **Monitor and Modify**

   An ethical decision-maker should monitor the effects of decisions and be prepared and willing to revise a plan or take a different course of action, based on new information.

   Because most decisions are based on imperfect information and "best effort" predictions, it is inevitable that some of them will be wrong. Those decisions will either fail to produce the consequences anticipated or they will produce unintended or unforeseen consequences. The ethical decision-maker is willing to adjust to new information.

SOURCE: Michael Josephson, *Making Ethical Decisions*, Josephson Institute, Marina Del Ray, Cal., 1997.

SUMMARY

Protect your "business baby" and yourself throughout your entire venture, by insuring against losses, paying taxes on time, and acting ethically. It is not worth taking unnecessary or unethical risks after all the effort you have taken to create your baby.

Discover your insurance needs early and pay to protect your business and personal investment. Work with an experienced agent in your selected industry who is qualified as a business insurance broker.

Work with your accountant (CPA) and payroll service to be sure you are complying with *all* federal, state, and local tax laws. Tax planning is an important element in the financial success of your business. Your accountant not only will keep you in compliance with the laws but can also help you look toward the future as well.

Protect your business from internal and external crime. Take all feasible loss prevention measures and insure as needed as well. Establish a code of conduct for your firm and discuss it openly and frequently with your employees.

Work with your accountant to not only complete your taxes but most importantly to tax plan. An experienced accountant must be part of any entrepreneurial team.

Plan your exit strategy early on because it will guide you throughout your venture. Your exit strategy may well determine the form of business you should undertake (corporation, LLC, or sole proprietorship).

Act ethically and responsibly; your actions will set the example for your employees.

Think Points for Success

- Protect your investment with insurance.
- Reduce risk of employee theft and crime with loss prevention strategies.
- Find and hire an expert tax accountant or consultant.
- Pay taxes on time.
- Keep impeccable, organized records. They will help you survive an audit.
- Keep personal and business funds separate.
- Plan your exit strategy.
- Follow the "golden rule."

Key Points from Another View

Run Your Company—and Have a Life

By Michael S. Hopkins

Most company presidents don't fill out time cards. Then again, Pete and Laura Wakeman are no ordinary business executives.

In the November 2000 issue of *Inc.* magazine, Executive Editor Michael Hopkins introduces us to the Wakemans and their company, Great Harvest Bread Co., in an article titled "Zen and the Art of the Self-Managing Company." The Wakemans are cofounders and copresidents of Great Harvest Bread, a franchiser of retail bread bakeries that they launched in 1976.

"After 24 years we're still fresh—we still love our business," notes Laura Wakeman in the Inc. story. "How many company owners can say that?"

How many, indeed? To find out more about the way the Wakemans manage the pressures of an entrepreneurial business—one with 137 franchised stores—while avoiding burnout, Hopkins followed up with Pete Wakeman in an e-mail conversation. The Wakemans have some very innovative techniques for living a balanced life—from taking time off to keeping time cards.

Inc.: *At the very beginning, when you started your bakery in the 1970s, did you have a clear idea about how you would balance your work with whatever else was in your life? How many hours did you work each week? How much time did you take away from the business at a stretch?*

Pete Wakeman: I like this question because it goes right to something important—which is the simple fact that we've been like this all our lives. It's not uncommon for people to want to believe they're trapped, and often those people will do the "must be nice" thing with us—"Must be nice to have a company, so you can take the whole summer off" or "Must be nice to have enough money to go to Bolivia." The assumption is that the way we live is a rich-people thing, an arrived-people thing, something few can afford (and by afford, I mean in time, as much as in money).

We wish we could show people our younger selves, the Pete and Laura who had no money and were building things from scratch. We were surprisingly the same as the way we are now.

Before the bakery, I graduated from college a year before Laura and worked on a dairy farm. We were both working too hard, she on her schooling, I milking cows. I talked my boss into one 3-day weekend a month away, to go rock climbing with friends. We really looked forward to that weekend; we needed it badly.

When the long weekend finally arrived, off we went to the Schwanagunks for some camping and rock climbing. Well, it rained like crazy, all weekend long. Our friend—who basically lived at the climbing area and climbed every day of the week—was in a great mood. He was happy while it rained and let his climbing calluses soften a bit.

Something snapped in Laura and me that weekend, something deep—the very word "Schwanagunks" still has this Waterloo meaning for us, even today. That Sunday night, driving home in the rain, we vowed that no weekend would ever be that precious to us, ever again. We vowed to live more like our friend the climbing bum, rich in time.

In the early days of the business I remember we had simple rules, but we followed them like religion. One was the **2-day weekend**. We never violated that, no matter what. It was a line we were afraid to cross, as if lightning would strike us down if we did.

We worked about 50 hours per week, for the two of us. We didn't talk about work at home; that was a rule. That's especially important. When we left the bakery, we were gone until we came back.

In fact, for our first seven years in business we lived 12 miles out of town, then another five miles further on gravel after that. We had no phone. No phone and a gravel road for seven years are wonderful things for teaching basic work and home separation habits.

Those things are what we have always called "handrails"—**physical** things that make it almost impossible **not** to live the way we want. But the biggest handrail of all was what we used to call our "**3-week trips**."

Sometimes the trips were longer than three weeks, but they were never less. We **never** skipped them. In the early years they were mostly wilderness trips; later we often went to Latin America.

We worked so we could take trips. We loved our work, but we worked so we could take trips. Later, as the business got more intense, it was easy to get confused and begin to think the trips were to refresh us so that we could work better. We fought that thought like the poison that it is. The trips were and are their own justification . . .

It was the **inviolate** nature of these weekends and trips that forced us to hire right, and train right, and invent systems for our people, as the business grew. The business grew up around this belief system, adjusted to it. That was fabulous for the business. Imagine a little bakery, or a just-beginning two-employee franchise company, whose people knew they had to do Sundays alone, Mondays alone, August alone—and that there was no way to call if they got in trouble.

Laura and I work on ourselves, read success stuff, write in our journals, build habits, break habits — if that's what it takes to have a great life, we're into it. But we really believe that it's the physical solutions that work, not the mental.

The physical act of leaving has tremendous power. That sounds so obvious. It even sounds easy. And in fact, it is easy, once you get the hang of it.

Inc: *I know your work habits have evolved since the start-up. Do you have a routine now, in terms of both weekly hours and time away? What is it?*

Wakeman: We like strong lines between things. We carry time cards, and we punch in and punch out, to the nearest five minutes. We know when we're working. We get paid by Great Harvest by the hour.

I keep an Excel spreadsheet; we make a conscious decision about how many hours we will work, each year. We work less now than we used to. In 1993 we worked 2,986 hours. That's for the two of us, so if you figure that about 2,080 hours is full-time (52 40-hr weeks), we were each working about three-quarters time. In 1996 we made a conscious decision to go to 1000 hours each—basically half-time. The last four years have been controlled, by time card, at exactly that.

Aside from the 1000-hour rule, we vary our schedule any way we want. Last winter I worked an 18-hour day followed by a 24-hour day, against a deadline, straight through the night. I love the intensity of being on a roll, when it happens. Other days we'll drive in for a single meeting and clock less than two hours.

To some extent, this 1000-hour rule has replaced the rigidness we used to have about weekends and vacations. Right now, for example, I'm billing. It's Sunday, I'm on a lawn chair by the Jefferson River in strong Montana sun, camped really nowhere, 50 miles outside Dillon.

I live the life they like to show in the computer ads. Difference is, I have my 1000-hour spreadsheet and when my year is done, it's done. I know when I'm working and when I'm not. Writing by a river is nicer than writing inside, but it's still more like writing, less like river.

You can see, by fast-forwarding from then to now, that what works for us with a 100-plus bakery franchise is what worked for us with a single retail store: simple, physical handrails. Handrails we set, then follow without further questioning.

All the good systems, all the good habits, derive from this simple act of partitioning. In the old days working on a Sunday would have been taboo. But the partition between work and play is just as simple and clear today as it was back then.

Source: Michael S. Hopkins, "Run Your Company—and Have a Life," *Inc.*, October 24, 2000.

Buying a Business

Maneuvering Through the Pitfalls

Entrepreneurial Links

Books

In and Out of Business…Happily, Ted Burbank, Business Book Press, Niantic, Conn., 2001.

Secrets of Buying and Selling a Business, Ira N. Nottonson, PSI Research–Oasis, Central Point, Ore., 1999.

The 2001 Business Reference Guide, (with software, VALUware Business Valuation Software for the Non-Financial Professional), Tom West, Business Book Press, Niantic, Conn., 2001.

Websites

www.enterprise.org/enet, (EntrepreNet)

eweb.slu.edu/Default.htm, (St. Louis University eWeb)

www.BizBuySell.com, (BizBuySell.com in alliance with *The Wall Street Journal's* StartupJournal.com)

Associations/Organizations

Institute of Business Appraisers

Appraisal Foundation

American Society of Appraisers

Publications

Industry Week Growing Companies, www.iwgc.com

Fortune Small Business, www.fsb.com/fortunesb

Buyer's Workbook, available online at www.BizBuySell.com

Additional Entrepreneurial Insights

Beyond Entrepreneurship: Turning Your Business into an Enduring Great Company, James C. Collins and William C. Lazier, Prentice Hall, Upper Saddle River, N.J., 1995.

Filling the Glass: The Skeptic's Guide to Positive Thinking in Business, Berry Maher, Dearborn Trade, 2001.

Spare Room Tycoon: The Seventy Lessons of Sane Self-Employment, James Chan, Nicholas Brealey, London, 2000.

LEARNING OBJECTIVES

- Explore the advantages and disadvantages of buying a business.
- Locate businesses for sale.
- Evaluate a business from the outside.
- Understand the role attorneys, brokers, appraisers, business educators, and accountants play in purchasing a business.
- Explore inside a business to determine if the numbers are accurate.
- Understand how a business broker operates.
- Learn how to protect yourself from a dishonest seller.
- Assess the market value of a business for sale.
- Evaluate goodwill.
- Learn how to use an earn-out to save cash at the beginning.

In this chapter you'll learn ways to evaluate businesses for sale. Although we focus on ongoing, independent operations, many of the tactics are the same for evaluating franchise opportunities. However, we'll discuss franchising more specifically in Chapter 14. Purchasing the "right" business requires great effort on your part and a tremendous amount of skepticism at all times.

When you buy an ongoing business, you're buying an income stream. You may also be buying inventory, a location, goodwill, and an agreement that the seller will not compete with you. When you buy a franchise, you're primarily buying the right to use a name. In addition, you may also be buying a training program, a Business Plan, advertising assistance, lease negotiation assistance, and purchasing advantages.

Enough emphasis cannot possibly be given to warn you of the traps that are inherent in purchasing a business. Thus informed, experienced advisors familiar with your industry are essential and no purchase should be undertaken without ***extreme*** *diligence and legal representation.*

As you begin your search for a franchise or business to purchase, make sure that you do not fall in love with a "deal" but fall in love with a business that hopefully will fulfill your needs and desires. Return back to the beginning Action Steps in Chapter 1, where you explored your interests, strengths, weaknesses, and "Your Inc. Plan." Review your thoughts. You will be expending a great deal of your time, energy, and emotion so choose wisely based on intuition and factual information. Trust your instincts and research, and follow your passion.

Investigate the deal thoroughly and completely. Make sure you stress the importance of finding the "right opportunity" first and the "right price" second.

Spend time searching for an opportunity that feels right. Will this be something you will enjoy doing day in and day out? Can you visualize yourself at work each day and improving the business? Are the customers the type of people you want to interact with on a daily basis? Are the employees the type of individuals you want to supervise and work with each day? Does this look like fun? Are you passionate about the business?

Make sure the business opportunity will be able to show a profit and a return on your investment. If you purchase an ongoing business, someone else has already taken the risk and high cost of starting a business from scratch. Your goal is not to pay too much for their risk-taking.

One entrepreneur, Sarah Berry, loved the idea of buying struggling businesses. She improved each business and tried to resell within 12 months. Entrepreneurs like Sarah become "serial entrepreneurs," purchasing and improving businesses and then selling for a profit. Some people enjoy the start-up phase but do not enjoy the

GLOBAL VILLAGE

TEST YOUR EXPORT QUOTIENT

TEST YOUR E.Q. (EXPORT QUOTIENT)	YES	NO
1. Are you entrepreneurial?	❑	❑
2. Do you have a reliable service-oriented character?	❑	❑
3. Are you a natural networker, building and maintaining relationships?	❑	❑
4. Do you see yourself as highly organized and research oriented?	❑	❑
5. Have you a sense of "mission" . . . ?	❑	❑
6. Do you possess good communication skills?	❑	❑
7. Is a sales, marketing, or distribution background featured in your résumé?	❑	❑
8. Do you excel in finance and business-related subjects?	❑	❑
9. Do you pride yourself in your strong negotiating skills?	❑	❑
10. Are you experienced in handling complex documentation?	❑	❑
11. Are you an avid follower of global politics?	❑	❑
12. Do you have the ability to speak and write more than one language?	❑	❑
13. Are you sensitive to different cultures?	❑	❑
14. Do you consider yourself able to adopt ideas easily, even under pressure?	❑	❑
15. Are you well-traveled or curious about other cultures?	❑	❑

Total (award 1 point for every "yes"):

Evaluating Your Score

1–6 Although you have acquired some skills related to exporting, you need further assessment to find out if you are suited to this field.

7–10 You show a keen interest in the subject. However, you should consider increasing your knowledge, language, and technical trading skills training.

11–15 You have a high rating in the critical factors that make companies and individuals successful in the exciting field of global trade.

SOURCE: Excerpt from *Global Entrepreneurship Skills,* Module 1, p. 206. Copyright Forum for International Trade Training. Used with permission.

management phase of operating a business. Determine which type of entrepreneur you are before making the leap.

By now you're far enough along on your quest to sense the atmosphere of the marketplace and it is time to explore businesses for sale. Talking to sellers is just one more step to expand your entrepreneurship education.

Have fun, but leave your checkbook at home.

WHY PURCHASE AN ONGOING BUSINESS?

The overwhelming reason for buying an ongoing business is money, primarily the ongoing income stream. *If* you do your research and *if* you strike a good deal, you may start making money the day you take over an ongoing business. Because most start-ups must plug along for months (even years) before showing a profit, it's smart to consider this doorway to business ownership. Other things to consider when buying an existing business may include the following:

1. If you find a "hungry seller," you should be able to negotiate good terms. You might be able to buy into a business for very little up-front cash, and might also negotiate seller financing.
2. Fixtures and equipment will be negotiable. Be sure the equipment is in good working condition and has been well maintained. Ask to see service records.
3. Training and support may be available through the seller and can sometimes be negotiated. If the seller is financing, he or she will have a stake in your success. Many banks like to see some seller financing because they believe it secures the seller's interest and thus the bank's interest. Request the owner

continue to work in the business for a short time to help you adjust and to serve as a bridge with the customers.

4. An established customer base should be in place. You will need to determine how loyal the customers are and whether there is goodwill or ill-will. If the customer base is not strong or loyal, consider this fact strongly in your price negotiations.
5. Relationships with suppliers and distributors are in place. Make sure you spend time talking to the suppliers and distributors to determine the status of the relationship. They should provide great insight.
6. The location may be excellent and not easily duplicated. Determine if the lease can be reassigned to you. Have your lawyer review the lease and determine if the owner of the building has other goals for the location.
7. Employees may possess specialized knowledge that can benefit your business immensely. In high-technology industries, purchasing businesses for brainpower is common practice. You will have no guarantee, though, that the employees and their expertise will remain—you must also consider the possibility that key employees may leave and compete.
8. Existing licenses and permits may be difficult to replicate. Check with your attorney or licensing agencies to determine the availability and process of transfering licenses and permits before proceeding with any purchase.
9. The uncertainties of a start-up business are reduced.
10. You will be able to see actual financial data and tax-reporting forms. Investigate! Investigate! Investigate! Assume they may have two sets of books and ask to see both. Some firms have three sets!
11. An inside look into the business operation will determine if using advanced technology could increase operational effectiveness and thus profits.

How to Buy and How Not to Buy

Smart buyers scrutinize everything about a business with a microscope, Geiger counter, computer analysis, clipboard, and sage advice from business gurus. They do not plunge into a business for emotional reasons. For example, you may have eaten lunch around the corner at Millie's Cafeteria with your pals for years, and when the place goes up for sale, nostalgia may make you want to write out a check for it on the spot. That would be a wrong reason to buy. *Don't* buy a business that way.

In purchasing an ongoing business, you will need to use the expertise of experienced **business brokers**, accountants, small business attorneys, and business appraisers. As when searching for all professionals, use your eyes and ears to search out the best. *Their fees are minimal when compared to their invaluable expertise and experience!*

Reach business appraisers through the Institute of Business Appraisers, **www.instbusapp.org**, 954-584-1144, or 954-584-1184 (fax).

FranNet and VR Business Brokers are the largest franchised business brokerage firms. In addition, independent brokers can serve your needs. Business brokers have helped thousands of individuals find their dreams and meet their financial goals. A business broker's expertise can be very helpful in your search. Always remember, though, brokers work for the seller and that is where their allegiance lies.

Locate an attorney with expertise in business sale transactions and an accountant who thoroughly understands the tax implications involved in the transfer of a business. A good accountant may be able to turn up some interesting loopholes that will benefit both buyer and seller. Experienced industry accountants will also know where owners hide their problems.

Keep in mind, every business in the country is for sale at some time. Deals are like planes. If you miss one, another one will be along soon.

Business Broker A real estate broker who specializes in representing people who want to sell businesses

Good buys are always available to the informed and careful buyer, but they may be difficult to discover. Seeking the right business to buy is much like an employment search: the best deals are seldom advertised. In contrast, the worst business opportunities are advertised widely, usually in the classified sections of newspapers. When you see several advertisements for a particular type of business, you know where the unhappy businesspeople are.

Running your own advertisement can be a good idea, however. A man ran the following advertisement in the business section (not the classifieds) of a large-circulation Midwestern newspaper:

> Sold out at 30. Tired of retirement. Ready to start again. Want to buy business with more than 1 million dollars in annual sales? Write to Box 4050, Naperville, Ill., H.G.

H.G. received more than 100 replies and said reading the proposals was one of the most educational and entertaining experiences he's ever had.

ACTION STEP 53

PREPARING A LETTER OF INQUIRY

Write a form letter of inquiry and send it to three to five firms that you may be interested in buying. Keep it open-ended; let them make the disclosures.

It's best to learn of businesses for sale by networking, but you can find some of the most eager sellers by their advertising in the newspaper classified section.

Leave your checkbook right where it is for now. This action step will cost you practically nothing. The goal is to learn what's out there and how sellers talk about their businesses.

Getting the Word Out

Once you're ready to look for a business to buy, you'll need to learn what's for sale. These tips will help:

1. Spread the word that you are a potential buyer.
2. Contact everyone you can in your chosen industry—manufacturers, resellers, agents, dealers, trade associations, and so on; let them know you are looking.
3. Ask your network of bankers, attorneys, CPAs, and community leaders to help you in your search.
4. Advertise your desires in trade journals. In addition, trade associations may rent their member lists; you can use them to send query letters to their members.
5. Send letters of inquiry to potential sellers you have identified (see Action Step 53).
6. Knock on doors.
7. Check with business brokers.
8. Talk with firms that deal in mergers and acquisitions.
9. Don't allow yourself to be rushed; time is your ally, and the deals will get better.
10. Check out businesses you would like to operate and buy. Ask the owners if they would consider selling.
11. Look for owners who want to retire or sell for other reasons such as partnership disagreements, illness, boredom, or divorce.
12. Look for businesses that aren't doing well that you believe your expertise and energy could improve. Make sure the business is not in a shrinking marketplace.
13. Check out businesses with a great product but possibly bad marketing or location. Would a new location or a great marketing campaign help the business take off? If it is a manufactured product, could reducing the costs of production by moving the facility reduce costs enough to make the business profitable?
14. Visit **www.BizBuySell.com** and other sites on the Internet for businesses that are for sale.
15. Review classifieds in your local and city papers.

Action Step 53 will help you get the word out. It will be quite interesting and informative to read the letters you receive in response to your request.

INVESTIGATE THE BUSINESS FROM THE OUTSIDE

Once you've found a business that looks promising, check it out by playing marketplace detective. This section suggests some techniques that will make you feel like a superspy. After investigating the business from the outside, you'll be ready to move inside, to check the books, and talk to the owners in an attempt to learn the real reasons they are selling. But the first step is to get your telescope and your telephoto camera and gather as much information as you can from the exterior. Unfortunately, Ben and Sally Raymundo didn't do this, and learned about fraud the hard way.

A Horror Story from the Suburbs

Ben and Sally Raymundo bought a women's sportswear store, BeeBees, in a thriving community about two miles from a regional shopping mall. They learned too late that the seller had a more profitable store in another part of the county and that she had used that store's records to misrepresent the store they bought. Here are the particulars:

1. *The seller moved the cash registers from the higher-volume store to the store she wanted to sell so that the store's sales were greatly inflated.*
2. *The price was fixed at inventory plus $10,000 for goodwill. This seemed a bargain for a store whose cash register records showed it was grossing $500,000 per year at a 40 percent average gross margin.*
3. *Ben and Sally paid full wholesale value ($100,000) for goods that had been shipped there from the other store. The "dead goods" were already shopworn and out of date and eventually had to be marked down to less than $20,000.*
4. *Ben and Sally assumed the remainder of an iron-clad lease at $6000 per month, and the landlord made them sign a personal guarantee that pledged their home as security on the lease.*
5. *The location proved to be a dead foot-traffic location in a marginally successful center.*

Fortunately, Ben had kept his regular job. Sally worked at selling off the unwanted inventory and replaced it with more salable stock hoping to survive. They spent another $30,000 for advertising during the 12 months they stayed in business. It was another year before the landlord found a new tenant and Ben and Sally could get out of the lease. BeeBee's was a tough and very expensive mistake for Ben and Sally.

Learn from Others' Mistakes

What could Ben and Sally have done to avoid this fiasco? Many things. They could have asked the mall merchants how well the shopping center was doing. They could have spent some time observing the store and the shopping mall before they committed. They could have insisted that Sally be allowed to work in the store prior to or during the escrow period, with a clause that would have allowed them to bail out.

Ben and Sally were honest, hardworking people who took the seller at face value—a huge mistake! A talk with suppliers might have uncovered the seller's fraud. They are now suing. The CPA and attorney they have *now* hired could have helped them *before* they purchased the business. It's only going to get more expensive for them, and their chance of recovery is slim.

Some sellers don't count the value of their own time as a cost of doing business. This makes the firm show an inflated return on investment (ROI). Let's say such a firm earns $100,000 per year and has an inventory of $200,000. This could be a bad buy if the seller, his spouse, and their two children work a total of 200 hours per week and if a $200,000 investment could earn 10 percent or more per year in high-yield bonds.

Look at each deal from the viewpoint of what it would cost to hire a competent manager and help at market wage rates. In this case let us suppose you had to pay $40,000 a year for a manager, $30,000 a year for an assistant, and $30,000 a year for two hourly employees. You would have spent $100,000 and lost the opportunity to earn another $20,000 on your investment. Yes, this would be a "no-brainer," but a lot of businesses are bought with even less going for them.

It's time now to go out and investigate a business on your own. Remember what you've learned from Ben and Sally's bad experience, and take along your new eyes and your camera. You'll be surprised how much there is to see. Action Step 54 tells you how to do it.

Know When You Need Outside Help

We've already discussed the need for a team of small business gurus to help you realize your dream of small business ownership. When you evaluate a small business for purchase, however, you may need a special kind of outside help. If you have any lingering doubts about the business you are researching, you may need the perspective of someone who is more objective than one of your team players. If you're not the Sherlock Holmes type yourself, hire someone who is. Your dream may be shattered by this kind of investigation, but you'll save money in the long run.

Georgia Webster had some doubts about the business she and her husband were considering. See what you can learn from the Websters' experiences.

Saved by a Bulldozer

I'd worked for a large ad agency in New York for 12 years before I gave it up and moved west to Charleston, South Carolina. I couldn't believe it—no snow, no grey-black winter slush, no icicles in April—and I soon became a sports freak to make up for all the years I'd spent indoors. I took up tennis, then racquetball, then biking, then volleyball, then hiking.

I met Fred on the tennis court. It was love at first sight for both of us, and we were married six months later. Fred is really creative, and he'd always wanted to have a business of his own. Because we both loved sports, we decided to look around for a sporting goods store to buy.

We found the perfect store by networking with our sports-minded friends. It was called The Sports Factory, and it was located a block from a complex of tennis courts, three blocks from a new racquetball club, and a quarter mile from a park where volleyball tournaments are held every other month.

A friend of ours, who's an accountant, checked over the books. He said they looked perfect. "Great P and L," he said, "and accounting ratios you wouldn't believe for this business. If you get the right terms, you could clear 50 Gs every quarter, and that's *only the beginning. This guy doesn't even advertise."*

We learned that the owner wanted to sell the store because he was tired of it—the long hours, being tied down, and so on. He'd been at it for a dozen years and he wanted to start enjoying life.

I asked around—networking again—and located a community college professor who knows a lot about small business. His name is Harry Henkel, and he had written a book about going into small business. I called him, and he listened very patiently when I told him our story. Then we made an appointment to talk some more. After 15 minutes he told me he'd be glad to check things out for us for a small fee. I told him to go ahead, but I didn't tell Fred about it.

Two days later, my marketplace detective called and said he had some news.

"Oh?" I said. "So soon?"

"Yes. Do you remember seeing a bulldozer working across the street from The Sports Factory?"

"No, I don't. What *bulldozer?"*

"It started grading last week. Right across the street."

"We were just there Sunday," I told him, "and we didn't notice anything like that."

"Well," he said, "I talked to the driver on his lunch break. It seems a developer is putting in a seven-store complex, and one of the stores is going to be a discount sporting goods store." He paused.

"Oh, no," I said. "Are you sure?"

He explained that the store going in was part of a monster chain. I could see that we would have a hard time competing with them. I asked him if the owner knew and if maybe that's why he's so "tired."

"Yes, I believe so," Harry said. "I double-checked at the city planning office and the building permit was issued six weeks ago." And he paused again.

ACTION STEP 54

STUDY A BUSINESS FROM THE OUTSIDE

Let's say you've got your eye on a business you think is a real money machine. What can you do to find out more about it without tipping your hand and driving up the asking price?

1. Make sure the business fits into the framework of your industry overview. You want a business that's in the sunrise phase, not the sunset phase, of the life cycle.
2. Diagram the area. What's the location and how does the area fit into the city/county planning for the future? What is the life-cycle stage of the community? Where is the traffic flow? Is there good access? How far will your Target Customers have to walk? Is parking adequate? Is the parking lot a drop-off point for car poolers? What is the employee pool of the area?
3. For retail, take some photographs of the exterior. Analyze them carefully. Is the building in good repair? What are the customers wearing? driving? buying? What can you deduce about their lifestyle? Take photographs on different days and at different times of day.
4. Ask around. Interview the neighbors and the customers. What do the neighbors know about the business? Will the neighbors help draw Target Customers to your business? Be up front with the seller's customers because they may soon be your customers. What do they like about the store? Is the service good? What changes would they recommend? What services or products would they like to see added? Where else do they go for similar products or services?
5. Check out future competition. Do you want to be close to competitors (like Restaurant Row, Mile of Cars, and other such successful business areas), or do you want to be miles away? Could a competitor move in next door the day after you move in?

Studying the business from the outside will tell you if you should go inside and probe more deeply. Adjust these five steps for manufacturing or service businesses.

This marketplace detective work cost us $475, but it saved us thousands of dollars and years of heartache. Armed with what we learned through that experience, we examined almost 20 businesses before we found the right one for us. It pays to investigate.

Georgia and Fred Webster came very close to buying the wrong business. The outsider's perspective helped them avoid making a terrible mistake. As valuable as these outside perspectives are, however, you have to have an inside look to truly get a feel for the business you are investigating.

INVESTIGATE THE BUSINESS FROM THE INSIDE

Once you've learned all you can from the outside, it's time to cross the threshold for a look at the interior. This is an important, time-consuming process, and it's an important milestone in your quest.

There are two ways to get inside the business: either contact the owner yourself, or get assistance from a business-opportunity broker. We recommend that you use a broker because brokers have access to all the listings. You can locate these brokers in the Yellow Pages under *Real Estate* or *Business Brokers* and in the newspaper classifieds. However, it would be best to locate a good broker through networking.

Call several brokers to learn of listings in your area of interest and check out the ones that appear interesting. Be prepared for disappointment. You will probably look at a great many businesses before you find anything close to your requirements. Nevertheless, you will learn from the experience.

Dealing with Brokers

Business-opportunity brokers are active in most communities and play an important role in matching up sellers with buyers. Their level of competency ranges from specialists who know as much about fast-food franchises as McDonald's, to part-timers who know so little about business that they will only waste your time. A good broker can save you time and be very helpful in playing a third-party role in negotiations.

A broker has a **fiduciary** responsibility to represent the seller and is not paid unless he or she sells something. Typically, the broker's commission is around 10 percent, but it's less on bigger deals, and everything is open to negotiation. You may prefer a buyer's broker (but they are rare) whose first responsibility is to you—but the seller will still pay the commission.

Some sellers list with brokers because they do not want it generally known (to their customers, employees, competitors) that they want to sell their business. Many sellers who list with brokers, however, do so out of desperation because they've already tried to sell their business to everyone they know. Probably nine out of ten fall into this category.

Spending time with a skilled broker can be a fascinating educational experience. If you want a particular type of business and are able to examine a half-dozen that are on the market, you will probably end up with a better grasp of the business than the owners. Network your business contacts to locate a competent broker. Ask brokers for referrals from their former clients. Quiz their business knowledge. (Can they explain a cash-flow forecast, an **earn-out**, the bulk sales law?) And as we've said so many times before, leave your checkbook at home. Don't let anyone rush you.

According to American Express' Small Business Exchange, a good broker provides the following services:

MATCHES BUYERS AND SELLERS

If you're a seller, a broker can do the first phase of evaluation of buyers and only bring qualified buyers to you. If you're looking to buy a business, a good broker will ask you lots of questions and know exactly what you're looking for. He or she may even be able to help you decide what kind of business might be best for you to purchase, given your resources, abilities, and interests.

Fiduciary Primary obligation is owed to the person who is paying (the seller)

Comes up with a fair market value

If you're selling, you might want a broker who has a strong working relationship with a business appraiser. If you list your business exclusively with the agent, they will often pick up the cost of the appraisal.

Facilitates the negotiating process

Because selling a business is at least as emotionally charged as selling a home, you'll benefit greatly from a go-between who can handle all aspects of the transaction while keeping each party cool. A broker can speak more candidly to each party involved in the transaction than they could manage on their own.

Shields you from publicity

A good broker will be discrete about the sale of your business. Employees may get nervous if they learn that a business is for sale. Suppliers and creditors may also want to stop doing business with you if word gets out that you are selling.

Untangles red tape

An experienced broker will know the most efficient way to acquire all the necessary permits and licenses and will know how to locate financing and a reputable escrow company. This helps to eliminate many potential risks to you.

SOURCE: American Express, Small Business Exchange, **www.home3.americanexpress.com/smallbusiness//resources/starting/bizbroker.shtml** (accessed March 18, 2001).

The following provides sample broker listings available from **www.BizBuySell.com**, affiliated with the *Wall Street Journal:*

SAMPLE OF BUSINESS BROKERS' LISTINGS

Wholesale Cake Bakery New York Metro

New York City, New York
Asking: $1,800,000
Gross: $2,000,000
Cash Flow: $300,000
Summary Description

A fresh baked box cake line sold in supermarkets, club stores, and mom+pop shops through direct warehouse programs, and direct store distribution. We are currently but not limited to the tri-state market where we have established good brand recognition through quality in product and service. This business can be grown independently or merged with a similar project.

General Information
Year Established: 1995
Employees: 16

Facilities: 13,000 sq. ft. wholesale bakery with two double bay loading docks fully equipped to produce 200,000 lbs. of goods weekly. The lease has 4 years remaining with rent of $75,000 per year.

Market Outlook

Competition: Only one major player, which has 95%+ of the market. Great growth potential.

Growth and Expansion: Currently offer 30 to 40 products to the supermarket and mom+pop trade along with 8 items for food service accounts. Both markets have great growth potential with more product and customer development.

About the Sale
Financing: 50%

Support/Training: Principle and staff will stay on as long as needed to insure smooth transition.

Reason Selling: It has outgrown me.

Contact Information
Contact:
Phone: (718) 555-1234
Write: Reply to this ad

Bicycle Sales & Services

Downers Grove, Illinois
Asking: $100,000
Gross: $150,000
Cash Flow: $55,000
Summary Description

Bicycle sales and service located in western suburb of Chicago. Twenty-five years at same location and same ownership/management. Loyal customer base. High school nearby for potential customers and employees. Shopping center 90% occupied. Located at major intersection of n/s tollway and e/w interstate highway within 5 miles. Population of hometown and surrounding communities approx. 500,000.

General Information
Year Established: 1975
Employees: 3

Facilities: 2400 sq ft store lease of $1205 per month includes taxes and maintanence. All fixtures and tools included to support service (approx. value 15,000.)

Market Outlook

Competition: Two similar business approximately 5 miles away. Established business in 1975 and have good repeat customers and large customer database.

Growth and Expansion: Other athletic products available.

About the Sale
Financing: 50% down, 50% financed
Support/Training: 60 day training support and part time employees willing to stay
Reason Selling: Have other business interest in unrelated field.
Contact Information
Contact: Rich
Write: Reply to this ad

The information in these listings has been provided by the seller or broker stated previously. BizBuySell has no stake in the sale of these businesses and has not independently verified any of such information and assumes no responsibility for its accuracy or completeness.

SOURCE: **www.BizBuySell.com** (accessed March 1, 2001).

How to Look at the Inside of a Business

Once you have wedged your foot in the door and established yourself as a potential buyer, you will be able to study the inner workings of the business. Take full advantage of this opportunity and don't stop till you have investigated the business thoroughly and all your questions are answered.

Study the Financial History

What you need to learn from the financial history is where the money comes from and where it goes. Ask to see all financial records, preferably audited, for at least five years back if they're available, and take your time studying them. Hire an accountant with industry experience to review the records. Your aim in buying an ongoing business is to step into an income stream. The financial records give a picture of how fast the stream is flowing and where there might be dams along the way.

Before reviewing financial documents, most sellers and brokers will screen and qualify you as a potential buyer. They want to make sure only buyers with financial ability to purchase are shown company financial data. You will be required to present your personal financial data to the seller or broker. In addition, signing a nondisclosure agreement assures the seller that you will not talk to employees, suppliers, or customers until an appropriate agreed on time. You will also be required not to disclose any information about the business to others except your advisors (who also must not disclose any information).

You may also be requested to sign a nonpiracy agreement, which prevents you from pirating the business's system, products, or ideas.

Look at the history of cash flow, profit and loss, and accounts receivable and payable. If the seller has a stack of accounts receivable a foot high, remember that:

After three months, the value of a current account's dollar will have shrunk to 90 cents.

After six months, it will be worth 50 cents.

After a year, it will be worth 30 cents.

Review every receipt you can find. If a tavern owner tells you he sells 600 hamburgers per week, ask to see the receipts from the suppliers. If none are offered, ask permission to contact the suppliers for records of shipment. Make him prove to you what he has bought from suppliers. You can then accurately measure sales. If the seller won't cooperate, run—don't walk—away; he's hiding something. You can use this technique with any firm that is buying and marking up material or merchandise.

Evaluate closely any personal expenses that are being charged to the business. (Your CPA will help you determine a course of action that will keep you out of trouble.) This allows you to get a clearer picture of the firm's true profits.

It's also a good idea to review canceled checks, income tax returns (probably for the last five years), and the amount of salary the seller has been paying himself or herself. If your seller was stingy with his or her own salary, decide whether you could live on that amount.

Many cash businesses will be very difficult to evaluate. Owners many times skim cash off the top and do not report it to the IRS. Beware of cash-only businesses.

If the seller brags that she doesn't pay her taxes, ask yourself, "Can you trust her?" If she's willing to lie to the IRS, who can put her in jail, she will more than likely be willing to lie to you.

Make sure the owner has not been paying his employees in cash. If he is, employee costs will be underestimated. Explore if family members are working in the business and not getting paid. If so, projected employee costs will need to be revised. Many owners also underestimate the number of hours they work. If you will be hiring a manager to run the business, you may need to hire a full-time manager and an assistant to cover the number of hours the owner has been willing to devote to the business. Small family-run businessowners are notorious for underestimating hours spent working in the business.

The following provides a list of items you need to review with the owner, your accountant, your lawyer, and the business broker before finalizing your purchase of any business. Following the steps we have outlined in Chapter 13 may take you several weeks or months. Do not skip any steps in your haste to start your business.

DUE DILIGENCE—ITEMS FOR REVIEW

Accounting services contract

Accounts payable records (if not being paid within 60 days be on alert!)

Accounts receivable records (aging?)

Advertising agreements with media companies (usually not assumable)

Agreements (franchise, other)

Appraisals

Asset list including: maintenance records, warranties, invoices, title, encumbrances, operating instructions, manuals

Bank account statements including: deposit receipts, checking account statements with canceled checks

Contributions and dues records

Corporate minutes book

Credit card company agreements (hardly ever assumable)

Customer agreements (wholesale)

Employment contracts (oral or written)

Equipment lease agreements (check to see if assumable—they seldom are—if so, what will it take to assume?)

Equipment suppliers list

Financial statements for past three years, profit and loss statement, balance sheet

Insurance policies including: property, liability, medical, business interruption (beware of potential large increases)

Inventory list (current or out of date?)

Labor union problems

Leasehold agreements and options to renew

Legislation or pending legislation which might affect business

Licenses and fees

Liens

Maintenance records/receipts and agreements

Non-compete agreements

Patents

Payroll records

Personal and financial affairs of sellers (private investigators can perform research for you)

Personnel policies including: vacation, sick leave, maternity, commissions, deferred compensation, pensions, stock options, and profit sharing

Recipes

Records of litigation and notice of litigation pending against the business or anyone associated with the business such as the leasor

Supplier agreements and contracts

Taxes including: personal property taxes, IRS returns, municipal, sales, employment

Travel and entertainment details

Utility bills including telephone (consider possible utility changes which might adversely affect business—i.e., skyrocketing electric costs)

Word of mouth

Zoning (potential changes)

Compare What Your Money Could Do Elsewhere

How much money will you be putting into the business? How long will it take you to make it back? Have you figured in your time?

Let's say you will need to put $100,000 into this business, and that the business will give you a 33.3 percent return, which is full payback in 3 years. Are there other investments you could make that would yield the same amount on your $100,000?

If you will be working in the business, you need to add in the cost of your time; that's $40,000 per year (your present salary) over the 3-year period, or $120,000 (assuming no raises). In three years the business would need to return $220,000 after expenses and taxes to cover the risks involved with your $100,000 investment and to compensate you for the loss of $40,000 in annual salary.

INCREDIBLE RESOURCE

BENCHMARK BEFORE YOU PURCHASE WITH KAUFFMAN'S BUSINESS EKG

According to the Kauffman Center for Entrepreneurial Leadership, "Benchmarking is the process of comparing your company's performance on key financial and operational indicators with the most appropriate standard in your industry." Indicators evaluated using their free financial benchmarking service include the following:

- Annual net profits or losses
- Average annual percentage change in sales
- Employees
- Estimated annual sales
- Net worth
- Total assets
- Asset turnover
- Ave. annual growth rate
- Profits per employee
- Return on equity
- Return on assets
- Return on sales
- Sales per employee

By providing a comprehensive assessment of a firm's financial vital signs, you may discover insights into the company's financial well-being and how it compares to the "best of the class" in your industry. The assessment can be completed online at **www.businessekg.com** in only a few minutes. The detailed financial review you will receive truly stands out as an incredible resource for helping you assess a potential firm's price and potential.

Evaluate the Tangible Assets

If the numbers look good, move on to assess the value of everything you can touch, specifically real estate, equipment and fixtures, and **inventory**.

1. **Real Estate** Get an outside professional appraisal of the building and the land. Review deeds, titles, liens, and title insurance.
2. **Equipment and Fixtures** Remember, these are used! You can get a good idea of current market values by asking equipment dealers and reading the want ads. Scour your area for the best deals because you don't want to tie up too much capital in equipment that's outmoded or about to come apart. Suppliers have lots of leads on used equipment, so check with them. If you're not an expert in the equipment field, seek help from someone who is.
3. **Inventory** Count the inventory yourself, and make sure the boxes are packed with what you think they are. Make certain you specify the exact contents of shelves and cabinets in the purchase agreement. Don't get careless and write in something vague like: "All shelves are to be filled." Specify what goes on the shelves.

   Once you've made your count, contact suppliers to learn the current prices. If you find merchandise that is damaged, out of date, out of style, soiled, worn, or not ready to sell as is, don't pay full price for it. *Negotiate.* This is sacrifice merchandise and it should have a sacrifice pricetag.
4. **Lease/Location** How important is location to success? Parking? Walk-in or drive-by traffic? Transportation? Signage? Storage space? Expansion capabilities?

Ensure closing is based on satisfactory inspection of all building, inventory, fixtures and equipment.

Tangible Assets Things that can be seen and touched

Inventory Items carried in stock

Talk to Insiders

There's no substitute for inside information. Every detective takes it seriously.

Suppliers Will suppliers agree to keep supplying you? Are there past difficulties between seller and supplier that you would inherit as the new owner? Remember, you're dependent on your suppliers.

Employees Identify the key employees early. In small business, success can rest on the shoulders of one or two persons, and you don't want them to walk out the day you sign the papers and present the seller with a fat check. Usually business owners will forbid you from talking with employees until the sale is finalized. You must honor this request no matter how difficult it may make your decision. If and when you are able to talk with the employees drill them for all the information you can. You may need to provide incentives to keep the key employees.

Competitors Identify the major competitors and interview them to learn what goes on from their perspective. Expect some bias, but watch for a pattern to develop. (Review Chapter 5 for competitor research clues.)

Customers Who are the major customers? What percentage of sales are generated from the major players? Is their loyalty to the business or specifically to the owner?

Obtain a Noncompete Covenant

Once you buy a business, you don't want the seller to set up the same kind of business across the street. Customers are hard to come by, and you don't want to pay for them and have them spirited away by a cagey seller. So secure an agreement, in writing, that the seller will not set up in competition with you—or work for a competitor, or help a friend or relative set up a competitive business—for the next five years. You need a lawyer to make sure all loopholes are closed.

Be sure to specify the exact amount you're paying for the noncompetition covenant. That way, the IRS will allow you to deduct it against ordinary income over the life of the covenant. Appendix C provides further discussion and a sample noncompete agreement.

Analyze the Seller's Motives

People have all kinds of reasons for selling their businesses. Some of these reasons favor the buyer, and others favor the seller. Here are some reasons for selling that can favor the buyer:

1. Retirement
2. Too busy to manage—seller has other investments
3. Divorce, family problems
4. Disgruntled partners
5. Expanded too fast—out of cash
6. Poor management
7. Burned out, lost interest
8. Ill health
9. Change in lifestyle
10. Wants new challenge

Beware of the following reasons that may lead a seller to want to get out of the business:

1. Local economy in a decline
2. Specific industry declining
3. Intense competition
4. High insurance costs
5. Increasing litigation

6. Skyrocketing rents
7. Technological obsolescence
8. Problems with suppliers
9. High-crime-rate location
10. Lease not being renewed
11. Location in a decline

Examine the Asking Price

Many owners view selling their firms as they would view selling their homes; that is, they are emotionally attached to the business and therefore overvalue its worth. Pride also plays a role: they might want to tell their friends that they started from scratch and sold out for millions. If you run into irrational and emotional obstacles, walk away or find a professional who can intervene and develop a fair agreement.

One quick source for a cursory evaluation can be found at **www.BizBuySell.com**. Valuations can be determined by valuators trained by the National Association of Certified Valuation Analysts (NACVA), **www.nacva.com**. The following information from NACVA details why you might want to use the services of a business valuation analyst.

BUSINESS VALUATION ANALYST

Preparing an accurate assessment of value for any business, enterprise, or intangible asset requires in-depth specialized knowledge. Valuation professionals have this special skill. Valuation professionals from the National Association of Certified Valuation Analysts (NACVA) have practical experience as Certified Public Accountants (CPAs), or practice in business evaluation or performing evaluations while working for the government. Their experience in accounting, tax, auditing, finance, insurance, economics, and investments, combined with NACVA's training in valuation theory, practical application, and litigation support, prepares them to provide you a comprehensive analysis and competent valuation.

Numbers, facts, figures, balance sheets and financial statements by themselves are not accurate measures of the true fair market value of your assets. There is much more to the process of determining value. Different approaches and methods of valuation analysis should be reviewed and selectively matched to the business being valued—your business. Determining the most appropriate methodology—along with various analyses, sophisticated mathematical calculations, ratios, industry comparisons, economic and market analyses, business risk assessments—is needed for a competent valuation of your business.

SOURCE: **www.nacva.com** (accessed March 1, 2001).

For another source, contact The Institute of Business Appraisers to find a qualified appraiser. Private firms such as BIZCOMPS collect and analyze business sales data and market the information through their services on the Web and through the mail. Table 13.1 illustrates BIZCOMPS use of data to determine the valuation and selling prices of Printing Businesses throughout the central United States. Reach BIZCOMPS at **www.bizcomps.com** or 858-457-0366 to determine comparisons for your area and selected industry. Reports cost less than $150.

Some industries have rule-of-thumb pricing. For example, a retail firm might be priced at three times its earnings or four times cash flow. One of the most important formulas for you to consider is the return on your effort (ROE):

$$\text{ROE} = \text{hours spent} \times \text{value of your time per hour}$$

If you can earn 10 percent without sweating on high-grade bonds, you should earn at least a 20 percent return on a business that will make you sweat.

You should be willing to pay a higher price for a firm with above-average growth potential than one that is declining. In fact, you should not buy a declining business unless you believe you can purchase it cheaply and turn it around or dispose of its assets at a profit.

TABLE 13.1
Sample Page of BIZCOMPS Data Base Report

Exhibit #12 - All Central States Printing Businesses

Sic #	NAISC #	Bus Type	Ask Price (000)	Ann Gross (000)	SDCF (000)	SDCF/ Gross Sales	Sale Date	Sale PR (000)	% Down	Terms	Sale/ Sales	Sale/ SDCF	Inv Amt	FF & E (000)	Rent/ Sales	Days on MKT	Fran Royalty	Area
2752	323114	Printer-Commercial	193	469	127	.27	12/31/99	187	26%	5 yrs. @ 10%	.40	1.5	7	226	10%	300		Texas
2752	323114	Printer-Laminating	1,500	2,136	267	.12	10/19/99	1,002	80%	8 yrs. @ a0%	.47	3.8	7.5	875	N/A	90		Central Kentucky
2752	323114	Printing Shop	480	707	194	.27	4/1/99	572	100%	N/A	.81	2.9	0	78	5.7%			Madison, WI
2752	323114	Printer-Commercial	325	1,358	145	.11	4/21/98	325	100%	N/A	.24	2.2	25	400	N/A	180		Central Iowa
2752	323114	Printer-Commercial	2,450	3,000	924	.31	1/31/98	2,180	90%	5 yrs @ 0%	.73	2.4	150	1M	N/A	210		Temple, TX
2752	323114	Printer-Commercial	1,525	3,500	750	.21	1/31/98	1,525	75%	3 yrs @ 10%	.44	2.0	75	1M	N/A	270		Texas
2752	323114	Print Shop-Franchise	435	386	121	.31	7/18/97	360	100%	N/A	.93	3.0	15	260	4%	98	5%	Louisville, KY
2752	323114	Printer-Commercial	147	262	34	.13	6/9/97	142	100%	10 yrs @ 8.5%	.54	4.2	3	100	6%	349		Grand Rapids, MI
2752	323114	Printing Shop	216	295	110	.37	5/8/97	178	15% SBA	7 yrs @ Pr.+2.5	.60	1.6	2	67	5.3%	28		North Texas
2752	323114	Printing Shop	54	92	33	.36	11/27/96	38	100%	N/A	.41	1.2	2	18	9%			Southern Iowa
2752	323114	Printer-Commercial	182	214	57	.27	11/15/96	148	47%	5 yrs @ 9%	.69	2.6	3	39	5.5%	50		Knoxville, TN
2752	323114	Printing Shop	218	296	110	.37	11/8/96	178	100%	N/A	.60	1.6	2	58	8.5%			Dallas/Ft. Worth
2752	323114	Printing Shop	220	200	50	.25	10/31/96	113	100%	N/A	.56	2.3	10	30	N/A			Austin, TX
2752	323114	Printer-Commercial	160	164	60	.37	2/28/96	155	19%	7 yrs @ 9%	.95	2.6	2	100	7.6%			Cincinnati, OH
2752	323114	Printer-Commercial	162	390	90	.08	4/24/95	102	50%	6 yrs @ 9%	.26	3.4	18	105	7%			Madison, OH
2752	323114	Printing Shop	120	136	39	.29	1/16/95	96	N/A	N/A	.71	2.5	10	90	N/A	255		Minnesota
2752	323114	Printing Shop	105	360	40	.11	12/31/94	105	100%	N/A	.29	2.8	5	50	7%			Minneapolis, MN
2752	323114	Print & Copy Shop	150	320	95	.30	11/10/94	160	47%	5 yrs @ 8%	.50	1.7	2	122	6.4%	44		Texas
2752	323114	Printing Shop	65	120	24	.20	8/31/94	55	55%	5 yrs @ 10%	.46	2.3	1	48	8%			Austin, TX
2752	323114	Printing Shop	81	192	48	.25	6/30/94	68	100%	N/A	.35	1.4	3	67	4%			North Illinois
2752	323114	Printer-Commercial	240	306	72	.24	6/30/94	219	50%	7 yrs @ 8%	.72	3.0	10	165	10%			Minneapolis, MN
2752	323114	Printer-Commercial	350	630	188	.30	2/28/94	340	26%	10 yrs @ 10%	.54	1.8	15	385	1.9%			Houston, TX

All Printing Businesses in Data Base Sold for an Average of 93.3% of Asking Price

Average Sale Price Divided by Gross Sales=.54 (i.e.: Sale Price Was 53% of Gross Sales)<

Median=.54

Average Sale Price Divided by SDCF=2.2 (i.e.: Sale Price Was 2.2 Times SDCF)
Median=2.1

*Key to Headings
SIC = Small Business Industry Classification Number
NAISC = North American Industry Standard Code
BUS TYPE = Best Description of Subject Business
ASK PRICE = Asking Price (000) (Does not include inventory)
ANN GROSS = Annual Gross Sales (Normally Net of State Sales Tax)
SDCF = Seller's Discretionary Cash Flow (Net Profit Before
Taxes AND ANY COMPENSATION TO OWNER plus Amortization, Depreciation, Interest,
Other Non-cash Expense and Non-Business Related Expense. (SDCF Assumes One Working Owner)
SDCF/GROSS SALES = Seller's Cash Flow Divided by Gross Sales
SALE DATE = Actual Date of Sale
SALE PRICE = Actual Sale Price (in 000's) (Inventory has been deducted if it was in Sale Price)
% DOWN = Down Payment as a Percent of Sale Price
TERMS = Terms of New or Assumed Encumbrance
SALES/SALES = Sale Price Divided by Gross Sales
SALE/SDCF = Sale Price Divided by Seller's Cash Flow
INV = Inventory At The Time of Sale. (in 000) (Inventory is not included in Sale Price)
RENT/SALES = Rent as a Percent of Sales
DAYS ON MKT = Actual Number of Days Business Was on Market
FRANCHISE ROYALTY = Actual Royalty Less Advertising Percentage
FF&E = Estimate of Value of Furniture, Fixtures & Equipment
AREA = Region of Geographical Location of Business

Rev 10/00

Source: **www.bizcomps.com** (accessed June 1, 2001).

When evaluating a business for sale, reconsider the list of reasons to purchase a firm that we've already discussed and the following:

- Terms—interest rate, down payment, length of note
- Operating profit
- Buyer's income
- Lease, location, equipment, competition, and customer base
- Return on investment
- Employees
- Growth potential
- Potential tax advantages

Buyers determine the true selling price of a business. During slow economic times, prices decrease; with a rising economy, business prices rise as well. Be sure to purchase a business that meets your income needs. If you pay too much, there may not be enough left to pay yourself an adequate salary. If this happens, you will sour on the business early and may not be willing to put in the effort required for success.

Tax Issues

Tax issues, as follow, should be considered in negotiating any business purchase.

Major Considerations in Structuring a Business Transaction are the Tax and Accounting Consequences to Both the Buyer and Seller

Like other terms of the agreement, the structure that is best for the buyer from a tax or accounting standpoint may not be optimal for the seller, and vice versa. Unlike some other elements of the negotiation, however, taxes and accounting considerations provide opportunities for the buyer and seller to work together to improve the economics of the total transaction.

From a tax standpoint, the best strategy is to minimize the total taxes paid on the transaction, taking into account both your taxes and the taxes that the buyer will ultimately pay. By minimizing the combined taxes, value is added to the transaction. The buyer and seller can then negotiate how they will share that added value.

The buyer will also be concerned with the accounting treatment of the transaction (and if you and some or all of your management team will be joining the newly merged organization, you will also want to be aware of how the transaction is reported financially). Depending on how it is structured, the transaction may be recorded using either the *pooling of interest* or the *purchase* method, or it may even be recorded as a recapitalization. Each yields very different financial statement results.

As the seller, structure the sale so as to minimize the taxes on the gain from the sale. A related concern is the timing of the taxable gain. If you provide financing by accepting payments in installments or by accepting the purchaser's stock, structure the transaction so that the tax to be paid on the gain is delayed until receipt of the installment payments or the proceeds from the ultimate sale of the stock are received.

A second related issue is the character of the gain—whether it is capital gain or ordinary income. For individuals, the tax rate on capital gains is less than the tax rate on ordinary income, making characterization as a capital gain more desirable.

SOURCE: **www.dtonline.com** (accessed April 1, 2001).

Determine Whether Bulk Sales Escrow Is Required

You need to know if any inventory you would buy is tied up by creditors. If it is, the instrument you'll use to cut those strings is a bulk sales transfer, a process that will transfer the goods from the seller to you through a qualified third party. In most states bulk sales transfer is specified under a series of regulations known as the Uniform Commercial Code.

If there are no claims by creditors, the transfer of inventory should go smoothly. If there are claims, you'll want to be protected by law. Either consult an attorney who has experience in making bulk sales transfers, or arrange for an **escrow company** to act as the neutral party in the transfer. The quickest way to find an escrow company is to look in the Yellow Pages under *escrow*. A *better* way is to ask your banker, broker, or CPA to recommend one. Try to find one who specializes in **bulk sales escrows**.

Negotiate the Value of Goodwill

If the firm has a strong customer base with deeply ingrained purchasing habits, this has value. It takes a while for any start-up to build a client base, and the wait for profitability can be costly.

Some firms have built up a great deal of **ill will**—customers who have vowed never to trade with them again. A large proportion of the businesses on the market have this problem. If the amount of ill will is great, the business will have little value; it may be that *any* price would be too high. Ill will is very difficult and sometimes impossible to turn into **goodwill**. Do *not* assume you can change ill will to goodwill. It might not happen regardless of the expense and effort you expend.

A smart seller will ask you to pay something for goodwill. Thus you'll need to play detective and find out *how much* goodwill there is and *where* it is. For example, consider the seller who has extended credit loosely. Customers are responding, but there's no cash in the bank. If you were to continue that policy and keep granting easy credit, you will be sacrificing your source of cash flow. Or maybe the seller is one of those very special people who is loved by everyone and will take the goodwill with him or her—like a halo—when he or she walks out the door.

So negotiate.

Let's say the asking price for the business you'd like to buy is $200,000 and that its tangible assets (equipment, inventory, and so on) are worth $125,000. In other words, the seller is trying to charge you $75,000 for goodwill. Before you negotiate, do the following:

1. Compare the goodwill you're being asked to buy to the goodwill of a similar business on the market.
2. Figure out how long it will take you to pay that amount. Remember, goodwill is intangible; you'll be unhappy if it takes you years to pay for it. Even the most cheerful goodwill comes out of profit.
3. Estimate how much you could make if you invested that $75,000 in T-bills.

This gives you a context in which to judge the seller's assessment of the value of goodwill, and you can use the hard data you have generated to negotiate a realistic—and no doubt, more favorable—price.

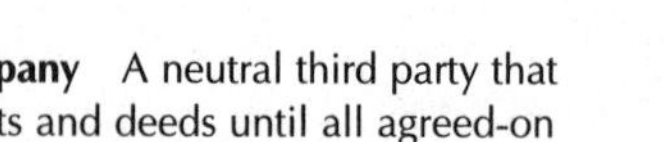

EARN-OUT: EARN YOUR WAY TO SUCCESS

Larry Drumon demonstrates below how to successfully purchase a business where the seller agrees to an earn-out. Usually the seller agrees to a reasonable down payment with a percentage of future earnings designated as quarterly or yearly payments.

An Earn-Out Success Story

Larry Drumon held several key human resource executive positions in large manufacturing firms after receiving his MBA in the 1980s. His last position was as president of a

Escrow Company A neutral third party that holds deposits and deeds until all agreed-on conditions are met

Bulk Sales Escrow An examination process intended to protect buyers from unknown liabilities

Ill Will All the negative feelings about a business; the opposite of goodwill

Goodwill An invisible commodity used by sellers to increase the asking price for a business often its worth the price *medium-size U.S. firm with branch offices throughout the world. When a large conglomerate purchased the firm and moved the headquarters to London, Larry was squeezed out.*

After freelance management consulting for a year, Larry arranged to purchase an executive search firm that specialized in finding engineering talent in the aerospace industry. Buying the business seemed like a good idea to Larry because the business had been profitable for more than 20 years. The key personnel agreed to stay with the firm, which had loyal customers and a solid reputation. Larry knew it would take him years to build a similar business from scratch, even though he understood the business.

He purchased the business for no cash down and agreed to pay off the entire purchase price from the earnings over the next five years. (This is called an **earn out.***) The seller was an older man who had known of Larry's reputation as a winner. Larry was one of the few prospective buyers who was willing to pay full price for the business and seemed qualified to continue the growth of the firm. The business did prosper, but its growth was somewhat limited to what could be achieved while keeping a watchful eye on cash flow. Larry had to pay the salaries long before he received payment from clients.*

Larry worked in the firm 2 to 3 days a week, and monitored activities by daily reports. He had plenty of time to run another business, but it would have to be a type of business whose cash flow was "front-loaded;" rather than "back-loaded" like the search firm. Front-loaded businesses are those whose customers pay cash up front before the product or service is delivered. They include such businesses as hotels, bed and breakfast inns, bridal shops, custom printers, magazine publishers, and so on.

Larry chose to purchase a travel agency. He found a medium-sized firm that had five excellent travel agents but was only slightly profitable. He purchased it for a low six-digit figure on a no-money-down, earn-out basis.

The travel agency cash flow was positive, and Larry saw some opportunities to make the firm more profitable. Observing that many travel agencies are run by "hobbyists" who know little about marketing and management, he refocused the agency efforts on exotic cruises and upscale vacation adventures. The agency was located in a very affluent area, and yet none of the competitors were specializing like this. He also knew that volume is the key to profit; some of the large chain agencies were earning 17 percent commissions on trips that paid small firms only 10 percent. Larry is now in the process of purchasing four more good agencies on an earn-out basis so that he can take advantage of the larger commissions.

Buying a business on an earn-out basis is an option only if the seller has great confidence in the buyer's skills and knowledge of the business. Therefore the burden of convincing the seller to agree to such terms is on the buyer. It's necessary to show the seller that the business will continue to show a profit.

Larry Drumon developed a detailed Business Plan and demonstrated to the sellers that he was competent, and his track record and references backed him up.

Community Resource

Where to Find Federal Contract Opportunities

The federal government buys just about anything a small business can offer. Its unending need for goods and services covers everything from catering to trash hauling to computer equipment and training to plumbing supplies.

The challenge is finding out what's on Uncle Sam's shopping list so you can decide whether it's worth your company's time and effort to pursue this market. The good news is the government makes this information readily accessible through a wide range of outlets, many of which are free. Here are some of the most common methods to learn about opportunities to bid on government contracts:

Earn Out The seller agrees to accept (a portion of) his payment for the business from the business's future earnings

- Read ***Commerce Business Daily***
- Register with Pro-Net
- Introduce yourself to your customers
- Use your local Procurement Technical Assistance Center
- Attend procurement seminars
- Don't overlook subcontracting and supplier opportunities.
- Consider using VANs

Read *Commerce Business Daily (CBD)*

The CBD is published Monday through Friday by the Department of Commerce and is the most common method of advertising contracting opportunities for purchases over $25,000. You can subscribe to the CBD by calling the Government Printing Office at 202-512-1800 and paying the $324 annual subscription fee. Or, you can get the CBD for free and in a more timely fashion by accessing it on the web at **www.cbdnet.access.gpo.gov**. Be aware that the CBD reflects only a fraction of the government's total needs, so read it faithfully, but make it only one part of your government marketing strategy.

Register with Pro-Net

Help procurement agents find you by registering with this free online database. Pro-Net is the largest small business database in the world. It is operated by the U.S. Small Business Administration, and is designed to be a one-stop-procurement shop for government purchases. You can use it as a marketing tool by profiling your business on it. Government contracting officers use it as a search engine when they're interested in making a purchase. For more on how to register with Pro-Net, call the SBA at 800-827-5722.

Introduce yourself to your customers

Federal government purchases under $25,000 are made directly by the end users in each agency—so get to know the people at each agency who might be interested in your product. Send brochures and letters introducing yourself, and follow up with a phone call to make an appointment. Like any of your customers, government purchasers prefer doing business with people they know and trust. Remember that selling to the government still means selling yourself and your business to people.

Use your local Procurement Technical Assistance Center

These centers (sometimes called PTACs or programs) are another free resource designed to assist local businesses in marketing and selling to federal and local governments. There are about 60 PTACs located around the country. Call 409-886-0125 or 703-767-1650 for the one nearest you.

Attend procurement seminars

Various federal agencies offer briefings, conferences, and seminars to teach interested firms about doing business with government. In addition to learning how to engage in the process, you are likely also to find out about specific procurement opportunities. As an added bonus, you'll have an opportunity to network and make important contacts with procurement officers. Get in touch with individual government agencies, your nearest PTAC, or your local SBA office to find out about upcoming events.

Don't overlook subcontracting and supplier opportunities

Market your business to prime contractors, emphasizing your interest in becoming a subcontractor or supplier. The SBA publishes the Subcontracting Directory, which lists several prime contractors for multiple agencies. The GSA publishes the GSA Subcontracting Directory twice a year and the Department of Defense annually publishes Subcontracting Opportunities with DoD. In addition, many agencies publish procurement forecasts that can help identify future subcontracting opportunities, giving your business lead time to prepare a proposal.

Consider using VANs

Value Added Networks (VANs) are private companies that gather and sort government procurement opportunities and match them with individual businesses. Some VANs are better than others, so ask each for references and samples of the types of opportunities they might pair you with before you sign up and pay for the service. Some VANs are certified by the government for electronic commerce using electronic data interchange (EDI). This certification does not guarantee the quality of the information they provide. Call the Electronic Commerce Resource Center at 800-231-2772 to get information about your nearest VANs.

ACTION STEP 55

STUDY A BUSINESS INSIDE OUT

Looking at a business from the inside enables you to determine its real worth and to see what it would be like to own it. Make an appointment—or have a business-opportunity broker arrange it—to take a serious inside look at the business you think you want to buy. Before you go, review everything we've explained in this section and write down a list of things you hope to learn while you're there. Don't allow anyone to rush you. Leave the checkbook at home; this fun is free.

THE DECISION TO BUY

Too many people purchase businesses emotionally. They buy a business as if it were a home, a car, or a suit. They are drawn to businesses that they think will enhance their image—that will impress their friends and relatives. Physically attractive businesses are often the worst investments because "image-conscious" buyers allow sellers to bid the price up to an unreasonable figure. The "ugly" business or the "invisible" business often provides the best return on time and investment.

Many people view buying a business as buying a *job*; they look at it as providing them with "employment." (Larry's experience demonstrates that this is a narrow view.) Such people lack the experience to make a good choice, and often invest their life savings in ventures that demand 70 to 100 hours per week to run and often pay them less than their 40-hour-week jobs did.

Does the thought of walking into someone's business for the purpose of "snooping" around, looking at the books, and asking the owner probing questions fill you with anxiety and make you nervous? It shouldn't. Sellers expect prospective buyers who are seriously looking for a business to buy to do those things. You are now ready for Action Step 55, *prepared* to investigate a business close up—and to enjoy it.

If you think you're ready to make your decision, do it—but not yet. Read the checklist that follows first for important details you might have overlooked. Even if you *know* you've found your dream business, complete this checklist before you sign the papers.

FINAL CHECKLIST

________ How long do you plan to own this business?
________ How do you plan to exit this business?
________ How old is this business? Can you sketch its history?
________ Is this business in the embryonic stage? the growth stage? the mature stage? the decline stage?
________ Has your accountant reviewed the books and made a sales projection for you?
________ How long will it take for this business to show a *complete* recovery on your investment?
________ What reasons does the owner give for selling?
________ Will the owner let you see bank deposit records? (If not, why not?)
________ Have you calculated utility costs for the first 3–5 years?
________ What does a review of tax records tell you?
________ How complete is the insurance coverage?
________ How old are receivables? (Remember, age decreases their value.)
________ What is the seller paying him or herself? Is it low? high?
________ Are there any unpaid employees?
________ Have you interviewed your prospective landlord?
________ What happens when a new tenant takes over the lease?

Action Step 56

Probe the Depths of Ill Will

How many products have you vowed never to use again? How many places of business have you vowed never to patronize again? Why?

Make a list of the products and services you won't buy or use again. Next to each item, write the reason. Does it make you sick? Does it offend your sensibilities? Was the service awful?

After you've completed your list, ask your friends what their negative feelings about particular businesses are. Take notes.

Study the two lists you've made. What are the common components of ill will? How long does ill will last? Is there a remedy for it, or is a business plagued by ill will cursed forever?

Turn your attention to the business you want to buy. You need to learn as much as you can about the ill will that exists toward that business.

Have fun with this step, but take it seriously—and think about the nature of ill will when your seller starts asking you to pay for goodwill.

________ Have you made spot checks on the currency of the customer list?
________ Who are the top 20 customers? Top 50?
________ Is the seller locked into less than four major customers who control the business?
________ Are you buying inventory? If so, how much is the seller asking?
________ Have you checked the value of the inventory with vendors?
________ Have you checked the value of the equipment against the price of used equipment from another source?
________ Who does your seller owe money to?
________ Has your attorney checked for liens on the seller's equipment?
________ Do maintenance contracts exist on the equipment you're buying? Can you assume the contracts?
________ Has your attorney or escrow company gone through bulk sales escrow? Is there any pending litigation?

Have you made certain that:

________ you're getting all brand names, logos, trademarks, and so on, you need?
________ the seller has signed a noncompete covenant?
________ the key lines of supply will stay intact when you take over?
________ the key employees will stay?
________ the seller isn't leaving because of stiff competition?
________ you aren't paying for goodwill but taking delivery on ill will?
________ you're getting the best terms possible?
________ you're buying an income stream?
________ all utility bills have been paid?

Prepare for Negotiations

Let's say you know you're ready to buy. You've raised the money, and the numbers say you can't lose, so you're ready to start negotiating. (If you're an experienced entrepreneur, you already know how to negotiate. If not, read *Getting to Yes: Negotiating Agreement Without Giving In,* by Roger Fisher and William Ury.)

We suggest two things about negotiations. First, when it comes time to talk meaningful numbers, the most important area to concentrate on is *terms*—not asking price. Favorable terms will give you the cash flow you need to survive the first year and then move from survival into success. Unfavorable terms can torpedo your chances for success, even when the total asking price is well below market value.

Second, when the seller brings up the subject of goodwill, be ready for it. Goodwill is a "slippery" commodity; it can make the asking price soar. It's only natural for the seller to attempt to get as much as possible for goodwill. Because you know this ahead of time, you can do your homework and go in primed to deal. Action Step 56 will help you do your homework. When the seller starts talking about goodwill, you can flip the coin over and discuss ill will—which hangs on much longer.

Only you can negotiate a low price caused by ill will or decrease a high asking price for goodwill, the intangible commodity that most sellers believe is worth more than it is. Action Step 56 will help you. Go for it!

Protect Yourself

Evaluate each business opportunity by the criteria we present in this chapter. When you find one you think is personally and financially right for you, and have completed due diligence, start negotiating. Your goal is the lowest possible *price* with the best possible *terms.* Start low; you can then negotiate up if necessary.

When asked to put down a deposit, place the money in an escrow account, and include a stipulation in your offer that says the contract is *subject to your inspection and approval* of all financial records and all aspects of the business.

Doing this gives you an escape hatch so that you can get your deposit back—and back out of the deal—if things aren't what they should have been.

One of the best things you can do to protect yourself is to work within the business for a few weeks with the option to back out if you have a change of heart. Sondra Butra fell in love with a retail photography business. Her husband suggested she work in the business for free for several weeks to determine if they should explore the business further. She discussed the arrangement with the seller. While reluctant at first, he gave in to Sondra.

After three weeks, Sondra knew working with fussy children, crabby parents, and stressed-out brides and grooms brought her little joy. This was not the business for her! She continued on her search and recently purchased an established Sylvan Learning franchise after working there free for four weeks.

Working in a business allows one to see the daily routine, employee interaction, atmosphere, and potential issues one may be faced with. The cost is zero and the return incredible! If at all possible, try before you buy.

Expect Some Pleasant Surprises

Well, you've come a long way and you've worked hard on your research. You may be wondering if the digging was worth it. Only you can answer that. There *are* bargains to be found out there—businesses like Woolett's Hardware. For hunter–buyers with vision and persistence, beautiful opportunities are waiting behind ugly facades.

What a Find!

I heard about Woolett's being up for sale more than a year ago. I'd just opened up my second store at the time—it's also in the hardware line—and it took me just about a year to streamline the paperwork. Thanks to an incredible retail computer system and a good manager, my sanity remained intact.

Woolett's had been on the market a year and a half or so. One look from the street, and I could see why.

The store was a mess. The building was pre-World War II, and so was the paint. Out front, the sign was sagging. The parking lot needed lots of work; there were potholes six-inches deep. The entryway was littered with scraps of paper, and the front door was boarded up.

Inside, things weren't much better. The floor needed a good sweeping. The merchandise was covered with dust. And all around there was this feeling of mildew, age, and disuse. It was dark—like a cave. It was tough finding a salesperson, and when you did, you couldn't get much help. Yet there were customers all over the place.

After you've been in retailing a while, you develop a sort of sixth sense about things. And the minute I stepped into the store, I knew there was something special about it—something hidden, something the eye couldn't see right off. I knew I had to dig deeper.

A visit to the listing real estate broker didn't help much. "Make us an offer," he said. "We just dropped the price yesterday to $400,000."

"What do the numbers look like?" I asked.

He dug into a slim manila folder. "Last year," he said, "they grossed just under $800,000. The net was around $100,000."

"What about inventory?" I asked. "What about loans and ***liens*** *and accounts receivable? When can I interview the manager? And why is the owner selling?"*

"Are you just asking that," he said, "or is this for real?"

"This is for my son," I said. "He's new to the business, and we don't want a lot of surprises."

"Like I said, make us an offer."

"Let me check the books," I said.

Lien A legal obligation filed against a piece of property

I deposited $500 with an escrow company, making sure I got my usual escape clause—a deposit receipt saying my offer for the business was contingent on my inspection of all assets and my approval of all financial records. Doing this has saved me tons of heartburn over the years.

The minute they got wind of a buyer, the manager and two of the employees up and quit. The back office was a mess, and it took me three days of searching to find something that would tell me I was on the right track. I found a supply of rolled steel. It was on the books at $12,000, but I knew it was worth $40,000. I took that as a buy signal.

The next day, I made an offer—$12,000 down, with the balance to be paid out of profits over the next five years. The owner accepted, and we cleared escrow in 60 days.

The first thing we did was clean the place up. We surfaced the parking lot with asphalt, added a couple of coats of paint, fixed the door, and added lighting.

Business picked up right away. My son, newly married, was settling down and learning the business. He seemed to have managerial talents.

Then we found another set of records that had been hidden away in a safe. They showed us that the Woolett Corporation owned a bank account containing $30,000 and five acres of land, mostly along the road leading to town, right in the path of future growth! We had bought the whole corporation.

The first year we did just over a million dollars in sales. And there was every indication that we would do better from then on.

People who come into the store now hardly recognize the place. We've spent some more money on new lighting fixtures and we've added a large kitchen section. And in the summer we're staying open until eight.

Passion

Passionate Leap

The Tricky World of Purchasing a Business

The postage center store seemed like a great opportunity for Mitch and Carolyn Jones. The owner was ready to bail out and they could take it over for just $10,000 plus $98,000 in equipment and inventory. The owner offered to finance the $98,000 if they would offer their house as collateral.

They asked Uncle Joe, an experienced entrepreneur, what he thought. "You have to see the books, interview the previous owner thoroughly, and talk to everybody in the center and in the business. Then, complete a total evaluation of the location. When you are done with all that, come see me!" he shared.

The next day Mitch and Carolyn made the deal—Uncle Joe went nuts! The second day they were open a big truck backed up to their back door and removed all the copy machines. It seems that they were leased and the payments had not been made in six months. This was only the start!

A year later they were broke and their house was gone!

Even passionate leaps require due diligence!

SUMMARY

There are two good reasons to explore businesses for sale: You'll learn a lot by exploring the marketplace, and you might find a gem like Woolett's Hardware—a business that will make money right from the start.

If the seller is "hungry," you may be able to obtain terrific terms. For example, let's say you find a business for sale with an asking price of a $300,000. Its net profit last year was $50,000. You and the seller agree on

$20,000 down

A no-interest loan of $280,000

Payments of 20 percent of net profits each year until the loan is paid off

Your loan payment would be 20 percent of $50,000 a year. You would have a profit of $40,000 left each year. After 10 years, you would have paid the owner upwards of $100,000, and your profit would have been a minimum of $400,000 if sales and profit did not even increase (hope that doesn't happen). With such good terms you wouldn't need to worry about paying off the loan.

Trained and experienced lawyers, accountants, and bankers are necessary for you to complete a business purchase transaction. Sellers are tied emotionally to their business and you are tied emotionally to your dream. You need impartial third parties to keep the sale on a rational basis.

Accountants will be able to evaluate financial statements to determine where the owners are hiding money, bad debt, employee theft, and countless other problems, which you might never discover on your own.

Keep your checkbook at home as you initially explore. Make sure once you have entered into any negotiations that you do not sign *anything* without your lawyer's review. If at all possible, work in the business before signing a final purchase agreement.

Buy a business that fits your personal and financial needs. Finally, remember always to follow your passions.

Think Points for Success

- Stick to what you know.
- Do not buy a business you know nothing about.
- If your seller looks absolutely honest, check him or her out anyway. Private detectives can run a thorough background check for very little money—a wise investment!
- Worry less about price; work harder on terms.
- Most good businesses are sold behind the scenes, before they reach the open market.
- Make sure you're there when the physical inventory takes place. Look in those boxes yourself.
- Get everything in writing. Be specific. Don't sign anything without understanding every word and getting your lawyer's OK.
- Buying a corporation is tricky. Have an experienced corporate attorney assist you.
- Be ready to hold your own through the negotiation process but do not nit pick. Look at the whole picture.
- Income stream is vital. Be sure it is there and that your interest payments will not take it all away from you.

Key Points from Another View

Valuation Methodologies

Strictly speaking, a company's fair market value is the price at which the business would change hands between a willing buyer and a willing seller when neither are under any compulsion to buy or sell, and both parties have knowledge of relevant facts. This is a somewhat circuitous statement because it asks the question, "How do buyers and sellers arrive at this value?"

Arriving at the transaction price requires that a value be placed on the company for sale. The process of arriving at this value should include a detailed, comprehensive analysis that takes into account a range of factors including the past, present, and most importantly, the future earnings and prospects of the company.

Valuing a business is not an exact science. The valuation process involves comparing several different approaches and selecting the best method, or a combination of methods, based on the analyst's knowledge and experience. Generally, there are several different methodologies that practitioners use to value businesses. These are:

1. Asset-based valuation
2. Comparable transactions analysis

3. Comparable public company method
4. Discounted cash flow

In applying these methodologies to determine the value of a business, one or more of the following factors are generally reviewed and analyzed:

1. The nature of the business and its operating history
2. The industry and economic outlook
3. The book value and financial condition of the company
4. The company's earnings and dividend paying capacity
5. The value of the company's intangible assets
6. Market prices of public companies engaged in similar lines of business
7. Transaction prices of other companies engaged in similar lines of business

Throughout the valuation process, it is important that the purpose of the valuation be kept in mind. Although a valuation can serve many purposes, if the aim is to sell the business, then the valuation should objectively determine the fair market value of the business. This objective market valuation should also take into account the synergies and fit that the business may have with potential buyers. In addition to valuing a business for an impending sale, a business valuation can also be required for legal proceedings, estate planning, shareholder disputes, and capital raising.

SOURCE: US Business Exchange, **www.usbx.com** (accessed May 1, 2001).

Investigating and Buying a Franchise

Reading Between the Lines

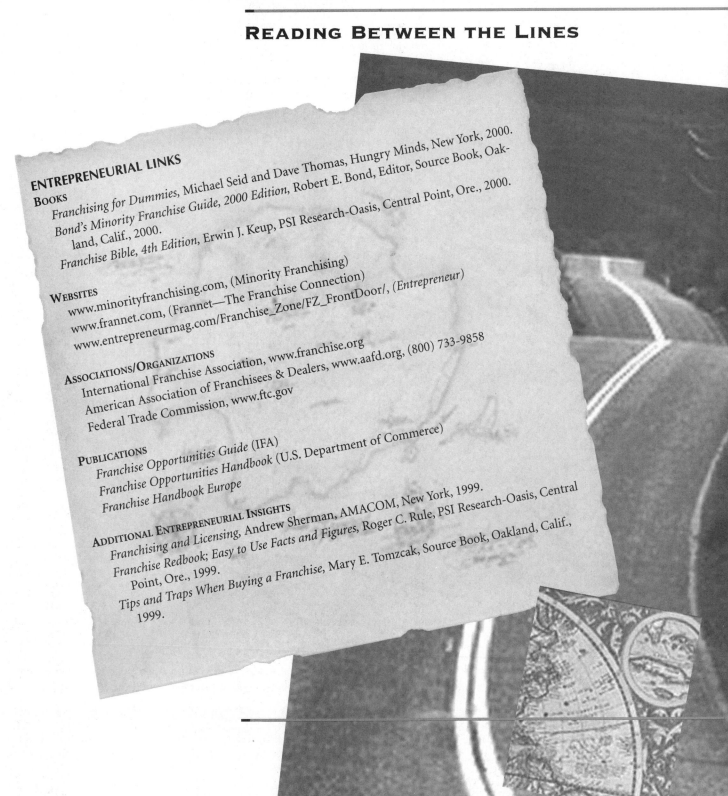

ENTREPRENEURIAL LINKS

Books

Franchising for Dummies, Michael Seid and Dave Thomas, Hungry Minds, New York, 2000.

Bond's Minority Franchise Guide, 2000 Edition, Robert E. Bond, Editor, Source Book, Oakland, Calif., 2000.

Franchise Bible, 4th Edition, Erwin J. Keup, PSI Research-Oasis, Central Point, Ore., 2000.

Websites

www.minorityfranchising.com, (Minority Franchising)

www.frannet.com, (Frannet—The Franchise Connection)

www.entrepreneurmag.com/Franchise_Zone/FZ_FrontDoor/, (*Entrepreneur*)

Associations/Organizations

International Franchise Association, www.franchise.org

American Association of Franchisees & Dealers, www.aafd.org, (800) 733-9858

Federal Trade Commission, www.ftc.gov

Publications

Franchise Opportunities Guide (IFA)

Franchise Opportunities Handbook (U.S. Department of Commerce)

Franchise Handbook Europe

Additional Entrepreneurial Insights

Franchising and Licensing, Andrew Sherman, AMACOM, New York, 1999.

Franchise Redbook; Easy to Use Facts and Figures, Roger C. Rule, PSI Research-Oasis, Central Point, Ore., 1999.

Tips and Traps When Buying a Franchise, Mary E. Tomzcak, Source Book, Oakland, Calif., 1999.

LEARNING OBJECTIVES

- Learn how your daily life is influenced by the franchise system.
- Explore franchising as an alternative doorway.
- Gain an overview of how the franchise system works.
- Develop techniques for examining franchises.
- Evaluate the pros and cons of being a franchisee.
- Understand risk–reward factors in "ground floor" opportunities.
- Learn why a franchise may not be for you and why some people should consider *only* franchises.
- Recognize the advantages of owning multiple franchises.
- Understand why the true entrepreneur is always the franchisor.
- Understand what you need to look for in the Uniform Franchise Offering Circular (UFOC).

Your walk-through of opportunities in small business is almost finished. Decision time approaches. If you've followed the Action Steps, you've spent several months gathering data and talking to people in small business. You have spent time exploring businesses that are up for sale and talking to sellers. If you wanted to write a Business Plan now, you could sit down and do it. Before you do that, however, there is one other doorway to explore, the doorway to a franchised business.

DOING BUSINESS WITH A FRANCHISE

Did you scarf down an Egg McMuffin on your way to work? Did your kids lead you to Burger King or Taco Bell for dinner last night? On your way from Tacoma to Taos, did you stop at a Perkins for pancakes? When you bought your last piece of real estate, did you happen to check out properties with Prudential?

When was your last trip to a 7-Eleven store? What do you think of the advertisements for Sir Speedy, the instant printer? If you want a business of your own, but do not feel strong enough to strike out on your own without a support net, check out a Play It Again Sam sports equipment **franchise**, an educational franchise called Sylvan, or any other franchise of your choice.

If you had money from an early retirement buyout package, a minimum of $100,000 liquid assets, and a minimum $350,000 net worth, would you purchase an Alphagraphics' franchise? Would you search the marketplace for an El Pollo Loco outlet that still had some legs? Or would you opt for a clever business like Takeout Taxi—delivering gourmet meals to upscale diners at home?

Whether or not you personally patronize franchises (it is almost impossible not to, with the franchise market including almost everything American—burgers, real estate, printing, tax preparation, equipment rental, travel agent, soft drinks, and used cars, to name a few)—the franchising game is big.

According to estimates from the International Franchising Association (IFA), there are more than 2,000 franchisors in the country and approximately 600,000 franchisees. Ask yourself the following questions as you enter the franchise door:

Franchise Authorization granted by a manufacturer or distributor to sell its products/services

IS A FRANCHISE RIGHT FOR ME?

Franchising can produce great personal success, but it's not right for everyone. The best way to start is by objectively assessing your own strengths, weaknesses, and goals in regard to franchising.

Ask yourself:

- ✓ What do you enjoy doing in a work environment? What are your strongest skills? Make a list of your strengths and the things you like doing.
- ✓ What tasks do you dislike? What frustrates you? Make another list of the tasks that, even if you were able to perform them, you wouldn't be happy doing. The negative aspects of owning a franchise include loss of control, binding contract, and franchisor problems, which also become your problem.
- ✓ How do you feel about managing employees? Are you effective at creating and sustaining a work environment that people want to work in? Have you had experience recruiting and retaining employees in the past? This is a critical management skill necessary for success with most franchises.
- ✓ How do you feel about risk? What's the most financially risky thing you've ever done?
- ✓ How much risk can you assume and still sleep comfortably at night?
- ✓ Is status an important issue in picking a business? Does it matter to you what the product or service of the franchise is or just whether the business can meet your goals?
- ✓ How much capital do you have to work with? How much can you reasonably invest in your start-up without leaving yourself financially strapped?
- ✓ What are your financial and lifestyle goals? How do you see your life changing in the next few years as a result of owning your own business?
- ✓ How do you feel about implementing someone else's system? This last point is especially critical. A good franchisor is not looking for innovation from a new franchisee. They have a proven operating system and are looking for people who have the capital and managerial talent to execute their system and produce predictable results. If that doesn't seem attractive to you, you might be better off doing something else.

After you've answered these questions, you'll know whether a franchise is right for you. If so, the next step is to start looking at opportunities and evaluating them based on your answers. It may take some work, but don't compromise. Look for an opportunity that's the right match for your talents, goals, and passions.

SOURCE: Modified from Jeff Elgin, "Is a Franchise Right for Me?," **www.entrepreneur.com** (accessed August 13, 2001).

SURFING THE NET FOR FRANCHISING BASICS

The Internet has volumes of material on franchising. If you type in "buying a franchise," you'll narrow down the options to information you can use to locate and evaluate a franchise. The steps that follow walk you through some websites that can save you time.

1. **FAQs.** Start with answers to Frequently Asked Questions, an Internet staple, at **www.afww.com**. Questions include: What kind of franchise should you buy? Is financing available? What's a **Union Franchise Offering Circular (UFOC)?** Who provides the location? Do you need professional help?
2. **Terminology.** If you are new to franchising, you would be smart to acquire some of its specialized vocabulary. Check out the glossary of terms at **www.franchisearchitects.com**. The glossary begins with "Advertising Co-op" and ends with "Waiver." One of the key terms you'll need to know is "UFOC"—a disclosure document provided by the franchisor to the prospective franchisee. If you reach this step in your dream search—receiving a UFOC—consult an attorney who specializes in franchising.
3. **Searching Yourself.** The Internet bristles with tools to help you know yourself better. Tools for the franchisee come in two forms: admonitions (do this, do this, don't do that) and questions on tests (Can you work long hours and not whine? Are you averse to aggressive sales techniques?). There are a few good franchising tests at **www.afww.com.** If you're averse to tests and prefer admonitions (study hard; don't rush in; peer deeply into the marketplace), go to the U.S. Government Gopher website at **www.sba.gov/gopher**. You will find a workable definition of franchising: ". . . a legal and commercial relationship between the owner of a

UFOC (Uniform Franchise Offering Circular) Franchise information outlining 23 tightly defined terms required by FTC to be disclosed to prospective franchisees before any fees are paid or contracts signed

ACTION STEP 57

WEB SEARCH

Take a couple of hours to check out some of the e-links listed. As with any web search, you'd be smart to set a timer—the Internet eats time—and to make a checklist of what you're after:

FAQs—Do you need more than one set of frequently asked questions?

Glossary—Print out the glossary of franchising terms instead of trying to commit the whole thing to memory in a single gulp. Take along a page to study over coffee or while you're waiting for the bus.

Hot Franchises for Sale—Use the Internet to start your comparison-shopping. For example, if you're handy in the kitchen and leaning toward a food franchise, compare a Perkins (each unit has its own in-house bakery) to a Bagel House.

Tips to Make You Smarter—Keep a list of the good ideas gleaned from reading about franchises. The owners of Takeout Taxi, a gourmet food delivery service, cranked a lot of money and design effort into their menus.

Legal Beefs—The Internet is such a happy place of sizzling super-hype, you might not find much information about which unhappy franchisee is suing which corporate franchisor. But file this image away—the Unhappy Franchisee Stung by Shrewd Franchisor—and bring up the question when you do field interviews. See Action Step 59.

trademark, service mark, trade name, or advertising symbol and an individual or group seeking the right to use that identification in a business."

4. **Franchising with Smarts**. A must read for any incipient franchisee is a dated but excellent *Inc. Magazine* piece (Nov. 1, 1995) called "The Smartest Franchisees in America," by Jay Finnegan. This online essay at **www.inc.com/incmagazine/archives** explores the survival tactics of savvy entrepreneurs who came to franchising with money, experience, and education.

   For example, to increase his used car sales, a savvy franchisee for J.D. Byrider Systems launched his own brand of Road Show. First, the cars were repaired and warranteed. Then they were transported to an outlying town too small to support a major car dealer, where 60 vehicles were parked in a large lot (arrangements were made with Wal-Mart, for example, to use their lot), next to a country band performing on a flatbed truck. A Road Show cost the franchisee $5,000 and unit sales doubled.

   This essay, with its excellent examples, demonstrates what can be done with smart marketing.

   On this same *Inc. Magazine* website, you'll find links to other articles on franchising: management, customer feedback, research, scoping out the future, and so on.

5. **Searching the World**. For a super-positive view of franchising in the world, check out the website for the IFA at **www.franchise.org**. The IFA offers multitudes of services to members at only $100 a year.

6. **A Mouse Click Away, Opportunities Abound**. How about those opportunities you encountered by typing *franchise* in your search engine?

   If you haven't run across the website for *Entrepreneur*, it's time to access **www.entrepreneur.com**. If you don't bypass all the interesting stuff and go directly to the Franchising Channel, you'll stay here for weeks. Visit pages in the Franchise Channel like "Low-Investment 150" and "International 200"—but make sure you set your alarm clock to remind you when its time to leave!

7. **Litigious Gloom**. The wonderful world of franchising is not all rosy sunsets and profits made easy. A dour U.S. government website at **www.ftc.gov** leads you to case summaries involving franchisors and creative business developers who landed in court for attempting to sell opportunities that either: (a) did not exist, or (b) were misrepresented by these creative businesspersons. Franchising is a very litigious business. Lawyers get rich over the problems associated with deceptive or irresponsible franchising. People who buy franchises have to do things *exactly* the way they are laid out in the franchise agreement. They can't deviate from the system. When people do try to deviate from the system, they often end up in court.

Franchise agreements are airtight and *always* favor the franchisor.

The franchise industry is enormous. If you were to buy or rent a car tomorrow morning, put gas in it, and then drive it to a fast-food restaurant for lunch, you might be supporting a franchise at every stop.

It is time for you to explore franchising through the Internet. Log on and search. After reading for several hours, using the websites at the beginning of the chapter as a starting point, locate several franchises that interest you. Visit their web pages and explore their franchise opportunities. In the past one would need to request a franchise information packet, but most of the franchisors' web pages now include most of the information you will need to conduct preliminary research. Complete Action Steps 57 and 58 as you do your Internet research.

BEWARE OF SCAMS

Unfortunately, many scammers and schemers ply their wares to unsuspecting dreamers. We cannot emphasize enough the importance of conducting due diligence and

INCREDIBLE RESOURCE

FRANCHISING WORKSHOP

To explore franchising further on the Internet check out the SBA's Franchise Workshop online at **www.sbaonline.sba.gov/workshops/franchise**. The workshop has worksheets and exercises covering the following areas:

- Is Franchising for Me?
- What is Franchising?
- Identifying the Franchisors Responsibilities
- Determining What the Franchising Packet contains
- Understanding the Franchise Contract

ACTION STEP 58

FRANCHISE INFORMATION PACKET

Using the insights gained from searching out franchises on the Internet, in magazines, or from a franchise directory, your next step is to request information from selected franchisors.

At this point you're the prospective buyer. You have the funds, the drive, and the will to succeed. The franchisor has a product to sell, which will be represented by the franchise information packet.

Write, call, or e-mail to request several packets.

Take time to study and compare: Subway to Blimpie's, Ace Hardware to True Value . . .

Addresses are on the web. Type in your franchise choice at the search engine site. Then mouse click your way to "corporate." When you have examined the online packets, write a page or two summarizing what you have learned. Focus on the need, the uniqueness, and the advantages of the franchise format.

Advantages should include economies of scale in advertising and bulk buying and the established "goodwill" of the name, proven track record, and reputation of franchisor.

using a lawyer throughout the purchasing process. Remember, salespeople hawking franchises only make money when they close a sale. And yours is the one they want to close today!

HOW TO SPOT A SCAM

The Top 10 Warning Signs of a Shady Franchise or Business Opportunity
By Andrew A. Caffey
March 12, 2001

If you're in the market to buy a business, protect yourself by being on the lookout for these 10 warning signs of a franchise or business opportunity scam.

1. **The Rented Rolls-Royce Syndrome**. The overdressed, jewelry-laden sales representative works hard to impress you with an appearance of success. These people reek of money—and you hope, quite naturally, that it will rub off on you. (Motto: "Don't you want to be like me?") Antidote: Check the financial statements in the Uniform Franchise Offering Circular; they're required to be audited.
2. **The Hustle**. Giveaway sales pitches: "Territories are going fast!" "Act now or you'll be shut out!" "I'm leaving town on Monday afternoon, so make your decision now." They make you feel that you'd be a worthless, indecisive dreamer not to take immediate action. (Motto: "Wimps need not apply.") Antidote: Take your time, and recognize The Hustle for the crude closing technique that it is.
3. **The Cash-Only Transaction**. An obvious clue that companies are running their programs on the fly: They want cash so there's no way to trace them and so you can't stop payment if things crash and burn. (Motto: "In God we trust; all others pay cash.") Antidote: Insist on writing a check—made out to the company, not to an individual. Better yet, walk away.
4. **The Boast**. "Our dealers are pulling in six figures. We're not interested in small thinkers. If you think big, you can join the ranks of the really big money earners in our system. The sky's the limit." And this was in answer to your straightforward question about the names of purchasers in your area. (Motto: "We never met an exaggeration we didn't like.") Antidote: Write your Business Plan and make it realistic. Don't try to be a big thinker—just a smart one.
5. **The Big-Money Claim**. Most state authorities point to exaggerated profit claims as the biggest problem in business opportunity and franchise sales. "Earn $10,000 a month in your spare time" sounds great, doesn't it? (Motto: "We can sling the zeros with the best of 'em.") If it's a franchise, any statement about earnings (regarding others in the system or your potential earnings) must appear in the Uniform Franchise Offering Circular. Antidote: Read the UFOC and find five franchise owners who have attained the earnings claimed.
6. **The Couch Potato's Dream**. "Make money in your spare time. . . This business can be operated on the phone while you're at the beach . . . Two hours a week earns $10,000 a month." (Motto: "Why not be lazy and rich?") Understand this and understand it

now: The only easy money in a deal like this one will be made by the seller. Antidote: Get off the couch, and roll up your sleeves for some honest and rewarding work.

7. **Location, Location, Location**. Buyers are frequently disappointed by promises of services from third-party location hunters. "We'll place these pistachio dispensers in prime locations in your town." (Motto: "I've got 10 sweet locations that are going to make you rich.") Turns out all the best locations are taken and the bar owners will not insure the machines against damage by their inebriated patrons. Next thing you know, your dining room table is loaded with pistachio dispensers—and your kids don't even like pistachios. Antidote: Get in the car, and check for available locations.
8. **The Disclosure Dance**. "Disclosure? Well, we're, uh, exempt from disclosure because we're, uh, not a public corporation. Yeah, that's it." (Motto: "Trust me, kid.") No business-format franchisor, with very rare exception, is exempt from delivering a disclosure document at your first serious sales meeting or at least 10 business days before the sale takes place. Antidote: "Disclosure: Don't let your money leave your pocket without it."
9. **The Registration Ruse**. You check out the franchisor with state authorities, and they respond, "Who?" (Motto: "Registration? We don't need no stinking registration!") Franchisors are required to register in 15 states; in Florida, Nebraska, and Texas, franchisors may file for exemption. Antidote: If you are in a franchise registration state and the company is not registered, find out why. (Some companies are legitimately exempt.)
10. **The Thinly Capitalized Franchisor**. This franchisor dances lightly around the issue of its available capital. (Motto: "Don't you worry about all that bean-counter hocus-pocus. We don't.") Antidote: Take the UFOC to your accountant and learn what resources the franchisor has to back up its contractual obligations. If its capitalization is too thin or it has a negative net worth, it's not necessarily a scam, but the investment is riskier.

SOURCE: Andrew A. Caffey, "The Top 10 Warning Signs of a Shady Franchise or Business Opportunity", **www.entrepreneur.com** (accessed March 12, 2001). Andrew A. Caffey is a practicing franchise attorney in the Washington, DC, area; an internationally recognized specialist in franchise and business opportunity; and former general counsel of the International Franchise Association.

WHY BUY A FRANCHISE?

Now that you know how to protect yourself from the scams, consider the overwhelming reason for buying a franchise: to benefit from name recognition and brand loyalty. Consumers grow to trust brand-name products and services. Look at the places where you do business. Do you drink Coca-Cola? The Coca-Cola headquarters are in Atlanta, but the beverage is bottled by regional franchisees. Do you buy gas at a Mobil, Texaco, Exxon, or Shell? They're franchises, too. If you buy milk at 7-Eleven, buy hamburgers at Burger King, or use a Century 21 Realtor, you're into the franchise system. Franchised products and services are predictable and reliable. Many consumers go out of their way to do business with franchisors and this customer loyalty is worth paying for.

What the Franchisee Receives

Let's examine what you can expect when you pay money to a **franchisor** for a franchise—that is, when you become a **franchisee**. A franchise can provide:

Franchisor A firm that sells the right to do business under its name to another for a fee, but continues to control the business

Franchisee An individual who, for a fee, is licensed to operate a business under the franchisor's rules and directives

1. Brand-name recognition. If you ask the right questions and pick the right franchise, the marketing boost you get from the name of your franchise might be worth what it will cost you.
2. Support. Corporate support services may include help with selecting a site, employee training, inventory control, vendor connections, a corporate-produced Business Plan, and more.

3. Training. The franchisor will teach you the business (two days to four weeks), and training is continuous. You may have to pay additional for training, though. Be sure to check out what is covered—training, materials, housing, airfare, and meals.
4. Money. The franchisor may also provide financing or assistance in locating financing.
5. Planning. You are buying a proven Business Plan (although in buying a franchise start-up, this will not be the case).
6. Bargains. Collective buying power may bring economies of scale in purchasing goods, services, and promotion.
7. Psychological handholding and field visits from the franchisor (support varies greatly).
8. Assistance in layout and design.
9. Site selection.
10. Reduced odds of failure.
11. Pretested products and promotion.
12. The possible opportunity to buy another franchise in your area. Area franchises can lead to riches.
13. Assistance of a store-opening specialist. This person may help get you off to a running start and help with your grand opening.
14. Operations manuals.
15. Sales and marketing assistance.
16. National or regional advertising.
17. Standardized products and operating and financial systems.
18. Territory protection.
19. Assistance in selling or exit strategy.
20. Advertising support.
21. Creative single-message commercials.
22. Brand loyalty of customers.

Please see Key Points from Another View for vital legal information concerning the franchise contract, which spells out the previous items. Do not ever consider purchasing a franchise without legal representation.

What the Franchisor Receives

Franchisors earn money in several ways:

1. They collect a one-time, up-front, non-refundable **franchise fee** for the rights to use their name and system. This ranges from $3,000 for a small service firm to more than $1,000,000 for a well-established name such as that of a hotel, auto dealership, or major restaurant.
2. They collect a **royalty fee**, which ranges from 2 percent to 15 percent of gross sales.
3. They may make a profit on items they sell to franchisees.
4. They may make additional money through sales of training materials and fees for training classes.

In addition, franchisees commonly pay franchisors advertising, creative, and promotion fees. These generally range from 2 percent to five percent of a franchise's gross sales.

Some of the fees may be open to negotiation—especially with a new franchisor. For example, it might be possible to delay the royalty fee for six months or until the franchise is profitable. It's always a good idea to ask for concessions. Advice from your lawyer and accountant will provide back-up data to reinforce your negotiating points.

Franchise Fee One time up-front fee paid to a franchisor

Royalty Fee Ongoing obligation to pay a franchisor a percentage of gross sales; may or may not include advertising fee

GLOBAL VILLAGE

A FRANCHISE OVERSEAS?

Let's say you like to travel. You speak three languages—one of them is French—and your friends say you could pass for a Parisian in Nice in August. You'd like to spend some time overseas, so you think of running a business instead of working for someone else. If you latch on to a business that's already up and running, your chances for success look better.

You've seen the news on TV about McDonald's in Red Square, so you think "How about a franchise?" You think Paris, and then you locate the home page for *Entrepreneur Magazine* at **www.entrepreneurmag.com** and click the International 200 box under the Franchise Channel and a new idea floats into view.

China

The Great Wall

Genghis Khan

Tianamen Square

A teeming market of 1.2 billion.

Before you scale that formidable wall, you can read all about franchising in China on the Internet. McDonald's operates more than 250 McDonald's in China. The key essay from the Franchise Channel, "Spotlight On . . . China," leads the eager entrepreneur through the basics of small business—the same basics that form the journey of this book—location, Target Customer, legal hurdles, and finding good help.

Before you buy a franchise in China, or Paris, or Tibet, check out the top 10 global franchisors according to *Entrepreneur International Magazine* in a recent article about the top 200 global franchisors.

FRANCHISOR	U.S. FRANCHISEES	OUTSIDE U.S. FRANCHISEES
McDonald's	10,678	8,929
Yogen Fruz Worldwide	1,765	3,477
Subway	11,840	2,052
RadioShack	1,957	1,197
Snap-on Tools	3,187	136
Kumon Math & Reading Centers	1,000	23,256
Mail Boxes Etc.	3,099	712
Domino's Pizza	3,907	1,806
GNC Franchising Inc.	1,289	234
Dunkin' Donuts	3,594	1,550

SOURCE: "America's Top 200 Global Franchise Ranking," *Entrepreneur International Magazine*, February/March 2000.

INVESTIGATING FRANCHISE OPPORTUNITIES

Franchising is a major force in the U.S. economy. You can learn a lot about small business by investigating franchises. We recommend that you talk with franchisors and franchisees to get a feel for the world of franchising. Also, talk to franchisees that have left the system. Their phone numbers are in the UFOC. The following discussion points should aid you in evaluating any earnings-potential figures presented in the UFOC or those provided by franchisees. The Key Points article on page 316 will assist you as well in understanding the UFOC.

EARNINGS POTENTIAL—EVALUATE IN DEPTH

You need to know approximately how much money you can make if you invest in a particular franchise system. Be careful. Earnings projections can be misleading. Insist on written substantiation for any earnings projections or suggestions about your potential income or sales.

Franchisors are not required to make earnings claims, but if they do, the FTC's Franchise Rule requires franchisors to have a reasonable basis for these claims and to provide you with a document that substantiates them. This substantiation includes the bases and assumptions on which these claims are made. Make sure you receive and review the earnings claims document if one is available. Consider the following in reviewing any earnings claims.

Sample Size. A franchisor may claim that franchisees in its system earned, for example, $50,000 last year. This claim may be deceptive, however, if only a few franchisees earned that income and it does not represent the typical earnings of franchisees. Ask how many franchisees were included in the number.

Average Incomes. A franchisor may claim that the franchisees in its system earn an average income of, for example, $75,000 a year. Average figures like this tell you very little about how each individual franchisee performs. Remember, a few, very successful franchisees can inflate the average. An average figure may make the overall franchise system look more successful than it actually is.

Gross Sales. Some franchisors provide figures for the gross sales revenues of their franchisees. These figures, however, do not tell you anything about the franchisees' actual costs or profits. An outlet with high gross sales revenue on paper actually may be losing money because of high overhead, rent, and other expenses.

Net Profits. Franchisors often do not have data on net profits of their franchisees. If you do receive net profit statements, ask whether they provide information about company-owned outlets. Company-owned outlets might have lower costs because they can buy equipment, inventory, and other items in larger quantities, or may own, rather than lease their property.

Geographic Relevance. Earnings may vary in different parts of the country. An ice cream store franchise in a southern state, such as Florida, may expect to earn more income than a similar franchise in a northern state, such as Minnesota. If you hear that a franchisee earned a particular income, ask where that franchisee is located.

Franchisee's Background. Keep in mind that franchisees have varying levels of skills and educational backgrounds. Franchisees with advanced technical or business backgrounds can succeed in instances where more typical franchisees cannot. The success of some franchisees is no guarantee that you will be equally successful.

SOURCE: **www.ftc.gov/bcp/conline/pubs/invest/buyfran.htm** (accessed May 8, 2001).

ACTION STEP 59

INVESTIGATE THE FRANCHISE SYSTEM

Franchises are everywhere...

To learn more about the system, interview people on both sides of a franchise agreement.

Part A—Franchisors. Leave your checkbook at home and interview at least three franchisors. Here are some questions to start you off:

What's included in the franchise fee?

What's the duration of the agreement?

How can the agreement be bought back?

What are the royalty fees and other assessments?

What level of training and service can I expect?

Is the territory well defined?

What are the minimum volume requirements?

How much help can I expect with advertising and promotion?

Part B—Franchisees. Now interview several franchisees. Ask them the same questions.

It may be that you would not be comfortable operating by the rules and regulations set down by franchisors—many entrepreneur-types are not. Nonetheless, it makes good sense to check out franchise opportunities (especially those in your selected industry) because it will give you a better picture of the marketplace and your competition. Complete Action Step 59 to expand your horizons about this option.

Franchise Problems

Some notable pitfalls plague franchising in general:

1. Competition is becoming intense among franchisors. Franchisors of fast-food outlets, quick-printing shops, and specialty retailers often oversaturate markets. This causes many failures. Be sure you talk with current and past franchisees to get their reactions on this extremely important point. Some very successful franchisees have found their sales and profits have plummeted when faced with competition from within their organization.
2. Many of the training programs are poor or nonexistent. Check the training materials out if possible and talk with past trainees. Also, make sure you understand exactly what is being offered and at what cost, and make sure you receive this information in writing.
3. Multilevel distributorships and pyramid sales schemes oftentimes only benefit the promoters.
4. The best opportunities are seldom offered to outsiders.

Beware of "ground-floor" franchise opportunities; it's pretty risky to be an early franchisee. A franchisor offering such an "opportunity" would be experimenting with *your money.* You want to buy a recognized brand name, a proven Business Plan,

ACTION STEP 60

VISIT A FRANCHISE EXPOSITION

Most major cities have at least one franchise show a year. Attend one and visit with the exhibitors. Learn what you can from their sales presentations.

Collect their literature and select one that seems worth a second look. Compose a brief summary of your findings and present to your colleagues. Have your colleagues evaluate the franchise along with you.

Remember, it's usually the small and new franchisors that exhibit at the shows, and their salespeople work on commission. Don't allow yourself to be pursuaded; you are there to observe and evaluate. You are probably not yet ready to buy.

excellent field support, and experience that demonstrates the particular franchise will work in your location.

Voluntary chains—such as True Value and Ace hardware stores—are often a more desirable option. Members of voluntary chains remain independent and pay no royalty or franchise fee. Look for more such organizations in the near future.

A Franchising Success Story

Susan Moore and her husband were lucky when it came time to investigate franchises; they had a source of inside information right in the family. They were also lucky because the franchisor they chose provided excellent support. Corporate support, which varies greatly among franchisors, was more important than name-brand recognition to Susan and her husband.

Three years ago, my husband had to travel a lot in his job and I was working very hard for a large company. While we were both drawing good salaries, we felt we had what it took to succeed in small business. We decided to go the franchising route.

We were both interested in the printing industry, and we chose a medium-sized national chain that seemed to have a franchise package we could live with. We did have some inside information on this particular franchisor. My brother had been with them for three years, in the Pacific Northwest area, and he was making a good living.

While we were interested in the quick-print industry, we weren't experts, so the two weeks of intense training was incredibly valuable. In addition, the people from corporate helped us with site selection, market analysis, negotiating the lease, and the layout and design of our shop. There are so many details to think of when you're starting a business; it's very helpful to have experts take over some of the tasks.

Another good feature of this franchise is that corporate will allow you to finance up to 80 percent of your start-up costs. This particular franchise can run as high as $200,000 up front, so that helped us.

We opened a second shop last January, and both stores are doing nicely. We print stationery, business cards, fliers, invitations—and we're developing a reputation for being on time in an industry known for being perpetually late.

A good way to learn a lot about franchising in a short time is to attend a franchise exposition. You can learn when and where they are to be held in your area by watching for announcements in major newspapers or checking websites. If a franchise exposition is available in your area, complete Action Step 60. Keep your checkbooks at home because this is not the time to make any commitments. Up-front franchise fees are very profitable for franchisors, and an incredibly hungry and aggressive force of franchise salespeople can part you and your money quite easily. They know that many people looking for franchises are eagerly awaiting the lift-off of their dreams, and thus many people are vulnerable. Don't be one of the vulnerable!

Follow Demographic Trends When Evaluating Opportunities

As you look for a good franchise opportunity, bear in mind that the best opportunity may lie with a young franchise that has proven its concept, has 50 to 60 winners, and is looking for growth in an area with which you are familiar. Many of these franchises currently are capitalizing on providing services such as home health care, tutoring, meal preparation and delivery, diet and fitness coaching, cleaning, handyman, party planning, catering, teen activities, computer training or repair, and website development with monitoring. As you analyze franchise opportunities, review Chapters 2 and 3, which helped you spot overall trends. Which of your franchise selections are capitalizing on these changing trends and demographics?

Voluntary Chain Organization (consortium) formed by individual wholesalers or retailers to gain purchasing power and other economies of scale

Evaluating a Franchise

Evaluating a franchise opportunity is much like evaluating any other business that's up for sale, but because of the nature of franchisors, you need to ask some additional questions. For example:

How long has this franchise been in business?

Who are the officers? What is their track record in franchising?

Is there any pending litigation?

What is the history of franchisees whose agreements have been terminated?

Is there any history of bankruptcy in the backgrounds of any of the founders? (You would be surprised!)

How many franchise outlets are currently operational?

How well does this franchise compete with similar franchises?

How many support people are assigned to my area and how often will they provide one on one service?

Who will be providing the actual training and what is their experience?

Where is this franchise in its life cycle?

What will this franchise do for me?

Table 14.1 provides Subway's franchise capital requirements and Table 14.2 discusses Subway's financing, equipment leasing, royalties and fees, potential market, and profit potential. We've included Subway because we know there are few readers who are unfamiliar with their sandwiches, which are served in more than 23,000 outlets in 109 countries. Similar information would be included in a franchise packet or on a website for other franchisors. It's now time for you to complete Action Step 61.

In Chapter 13 we presented a checklist to use in evaluating an ongoing business you are considering buying. That checklist applies to franchises as well. To supplement it, we're giving you a checklist prepared specifically for evaluating franchise opportunities (see Table 14.3). The questions will help you generate a profile of the franchise and make a wise decision. In franchising you are not only investigating the actual franchise you are purchasing, but the franchisor as well.

Typically, current franchisees are offered new locations before they are offered to outsiders. Rarely is a new player offered a sure thing. New players are offered those that have already been passed over. Read about Myron Bailey's introduction to franchising.

ACTION STEP 61

WRITING ABOUT A DREAM FRANCHISE

A franchise costs money.

The franchisee (that's you) pays money to the franchisor (a corporate entity like Coke, Subway, Century 21, or Sir Speedy) for the right to a specific niche in the marketplace. In the case of Sir Speedy the niche is fast printing. In the case of Century 21 the niche is real estate.

Because the corporate franchisor wants you to succeed, to make more money for the corporate entity, a great deal comes bundled with the niche: a big-time logo, a Business Plan, a thick disclosure document, and so on.

After you have perused several information packets from various franchisors, take up your pen and write a couple of paragraphs. What do you like? What do you dislike? Do you need more information? Is this the franchise for you? Is there a number you can call for more information?

Include a single paragraph description, then detail initial license fee, royalties, other fees, all other capital costs, training, location, accounting and reporting requirements, terms, duration, renewability, and termination conditions. Use one to two pages.

Don't be afraid to share your feelings with yourself: "I love this franchise because . . ." or "This franchise packet gives me the shakes because . . ."

Three Wins, One Loss

By the time Myron was 29 years old he'd made a lot of money in the stock market, but he felt he was too young to retire. After making several attempts to purchase one of the better-known fast-food franchises and waiting almost a year, he was offered a location in another state.

The store had been open for three years and had not yet turned a profit. Other franchise owners had already turned down the opportunity to take over the operation. Myron liked what he saw and made an offer. The unsuccessful franchisee welcomed his offer as a graceful exit, and the franchisor could hardly wait to see if a new franchisee could turn the loser around.

Myron is a "people person" and a strong manager. His employees followed his enthusiastic leadership, and new customers came in droves. In less than a year the store became very profitable, and the franchisor offered Myron three new locations, all of which he accepted.

Myron's touch was magic; two of the three new stores also became very successful. But try as he would, he couldn't make money on the third one. After three more years,

(continued on p. 312)

TABLE 14.1

Subway Franchise Capital Requirements

General Breakdowns For:	Lower Cost Store	Moderate Cost Store	Higher Cost Store	When Due
Initial Franchise Fee	$10,000	$10,000	$10,000	On signing Franchise Agreement
Real Property**	2,000	5,000	12,000	On signing Intent to Sublease
Leasehold Improvements	25,000	55,000	80,000	Pro rata during construction
Equipment Lease Security Deposit**	2,500	2,500	2,500	Before equipment is ordered
Security System (not including monitoring costs)	—	1,500	2,000	Before order is placed
Freight Charges (varies by location)	2,000	2,900	3,400	On delivery
Outside Signs	2,000	4,000	8,000	Before order is placed
Opening Inventory	2,300	3,300	4,300	Within 1 week of opening
Insurance	500	1,250	2,000	Before opening
Supplies	500	750	1,000	Before opening
Training Expenses (including travel and lodging)	700	1,700	2,500	During training
Legal and Accounting	500	2,500	4,500	Before opening
Opening Advertising	2,000	2,000	2,000	Around opening
Miscellaneous Expenses (Business Licenses, Utility Deposits, Small Equipment, And Surplus Capital)	4,000	6,000	8,000	As required
Additional Funds - 3 Months	11,000	26,000	41,000	As required
Total Investment**	65,000	124,400	183,700	N/A

	Country	Lower Cost	Moderate Cost	Higher Cost
The costs, inclusive of any and all taxes,	United States	$97,000	$159,800	$222,800
including sales taxes/GST, are estimated at:	Canada	$128,400	$180,150	$241,850

*This amount is the estimated deposit of 2 months rent payable upon signing the Intent to Sublease (does not include "key" money).

**If you do not select the equipment leasing program or it is not available, you should substitute the costs for Equipment Lease Security Deposit with $37,140 to $44,840 U.S./$51,600 to $62,900 Canadian (including U.S. buffer 10% /Canadian buffer 15%). The amount of Additional Funds for the 3 months operating expenses would also be adjusted to reflect that you will not have to make 3 monthly equipment lease payments. This will cause your total initial investment to be substantially higher.

THESE FIGURES ARE ESTIMATES OF THE COMPLETE INVESTMENT IN SETTING UP A SUBWAY RESTAURANT AND OPERATING IT FOR 3 MONTHS. IT IS POSSIBLE TO SIGNIFICANTLY EXCEED COSTS IN ANY OF THE AREAS LISTED ABOVE.

Some costs will vary in relation to the physical size of the restaurant. A lower-cost restaurant is one that would require fewer leasehold mprovements, less seating, and fewer equipment expenditures. Moderate- and higher-cost restaurants may require extensive interior renovations, extensive seating, and additional equipment. If you are purchasing a franchise for another location opportunity, such as a non-traditional, satellite or school lunch program location, the above listed capital requirements may vary and could be substantially lower depending upon the necessary equipment you must acquire or changes in leasehold improvements you must make. The above figures do not include extensive exterior renovations.

SOURCE: **www.subway.com/development/investment/capital_regs/usa.html** (accessed August 11, 2001).

TABLE 14.2

Subway Cash Flow Information

Initial Investment

Your total initial investment will depend on many factors. Some of those factors include: location, rent, size of unit, and equipment. An estimate of total cost to open a franchise including the franchise fee can be found in the back of this brochure. The franchise agreement is for 20 years and renewable for 20 years.

Our start-up costs are exceptionally low for a franchise of our size and stature. You can often purchase dependable brand name restaurant equipment at reasonable prices through our purchasing power. As leasehold improvements are only a small portion of the total capital requirements, you are not putting a lot of valuable cash into non-recoverable fixed assets.

Also, take note that most stores are only 500-1,500 square feet (50-150 square meters) in size, and may be opened in a wide variety of building styles. The small amount of space required to open a Subway unit reduces your overhead costs.

Financing

An important consideration in purchasing your first Subway store is how to finance your investment. A good arrangement is to have 50% of the total capital requirements available in cash and sufficient collateral to obtain funding for the balance. Your Development Agent or Regional Manager can provide guidance in selecting a qualified financing source.

Equipment Leasing*

In addition to providing guidance to potential franchise owners in securing financing for a Subway restaurant, we make available to franchisees an equipment leasing program. Please note that capital requirements for major equipment can be reduced by taking advantage of the equipment leasing program.

Royalties and Fees

Royalties and fees are based on gross sales minus sales tax. The royalty is 8% to the company. A 3.5% advertising fee is paid to the Subway Franchise Advertising Fund Trust, also known as SFAFT. Franchisees in some markets may vote to increase the marketing fee percentage for local advertising purposes.

High Reinvestment
We are extremely proud that more than half of all new franchises are awarded to existing owners who are expanding.

Potential Market
We feel it is important to gain as much market share as possible. Our mission is to equal or exceed the number of outlets operated by their largest fast food company in every market that we enter. Since McDonald's is the largest fast food company in the world and the largest in most individual markets, it is useful to use their distribution and growth as a benchmark. McDonald's currently operates over 23,000 outlets in 109 countries, and they are currently projecting the addition of over 2,000 units per year to their chain.† With our system and operational strengths, low capital requirements, simple operation and low overhead, as well as a dedicated field and headquarters staff, there is reason to believe the Subway franchise will continue to grow as a dominant force in the world market.

Profit Potential
The potential sales and profitability of a Subway restaurant is naturally of major interest to any prospective franchisee. To determine this information, we encourage you to contact as many existing owners as you wish and question them on how they are doing. We will provide you with the name and phone number of any franchise owner that we have operating around the world, after you complete and return the application.
We have a policy that no employee of the company can provide you with projections as to your potential sales, earnings, and profitability. This policy eliminates possible misunderstandings and leads to a better long-term relationship.
Of course, it is not mandatory for franchisees to provide exact figures, but most of them are willing to give you a good idea of how they are doing and state if they are satisfied with their Subway franchise.

*Equipment leasing is presently only available in the United States, Canada, Guam, and Australia.

SOURCE: 1997 McDonald's Annual Report, **www.subway.com/development/investment/investment_main.html** (accessed August 11, 2001).

TABLE 14.3
Franchise Evaluation Checklist (Federal Trade Commission)

General

	yes	no
1. Is the product or service:		
a. considered reputable?	______	______
b. part of a growing market?	______	______
c. needed in your area?	______	______
d. of interest to you?	______	______
e. safe,	______	______
protected,	______	______
covered by guarantee?	______	______
2. Is the franchise:		
a. local?	______	______
regional?	______	______
national?	______	______
international?	______	______
b. full-time?	______	______
part-time?	______	______
possible full-time in the future?	______	______

3. Existing franchises
   a. Date the company was founded______________
      Date the first franchise was awarded ______________
   b. Number of franchises currently in operation or under construction
      ____
   c. References______________
      Franchise 1: owner ______________
      address ______________
      telephone ______________ date started ______________
      Franchise 2: owner ______________
      address ______________
      telephone ______________ date started ______________
      Franchise 3: owner ______________
      address ______________
      telephone ______________ date started ______________
      Franchise 4: owner ______________
      address ______________
      telephone ______________ date started ______________
   d. Additional franchises planned for the next twelve months______
      ____

4. Failed franchises
   a. How many franchises have failed?______________
      How many in the last two years? ______________
   b. Why have they failed? ______________
      Franchisor reasons:______________
      Better Business Bureau reasons:______________
      Franchisee reasons: ______________
5. Franchise in local market area
   a. Has a franchise ever been awarded in this area?______________
   b. If so, and if it is still in operation: ______________
      owner______________
      address______________
      telephone ______________ date started ______________
   c. If so, and if it is no longer in operation:
      person involved______________
      address ______________
      date started ______________ date ended ______________
      reasons for failure ______________
   d. How many inquiries have there been for the franchise from the area in the past six months? ______________
6. What product or service will be added to the franchise package
   a. within 12 months? ______________
      ____
   b. within 2 years? ______________
      ____
   c. within 2 to 5 years? ______________
      ____
7. Competition
   a. What is the competition? ______________
      ____
8. Are all franchises independently owned?
   a. Of the total outlets, _____ are franchised, and _____ are company-owned. ______________
   b. If some outlets are company owned did they start out this way, _____ or were they purchased from a franchisee?______________
   c. Date of most recent company acquisition______________

9. Franchise operations
   a. What facilities are required, and do I lease or build?

	build	lease
office	______	______
building	______	______
manufacturing facility	______	______
warehouse	______	______
______________________	______	______
______________________	______	______

   b. Getting started—Who is responsible for:

	franchisor	franchisee
feasibility study?	______	______
design?	______	______
construction?	______	______
furnishings and equipment?	______	______
financing?	______	______
employee training?	______	______
lease negotiation?	______	______

Franchise Company

1. The company
   a. Name and address of the parent company, if different from the franchise company:
      name ______________________
      address ______________________
   b. Is the parent company public or private? ______________
   c. If the company is public, where is the stock traded?
      New York Stock Exchange ______
      American Stock Exchange ______
      over-the-counter ______
2. Forecast of income and expenses can only be presented in UFOC. The franchisor should not give you any other estimates.
3. What is the best legal structure for my company?
   proprietorship ______
   partnership ______
   corporation ______
   limited liability company ______
4. The franchise contract
   a. Is there a written contract? ______ (Get a copy for lawyer and accountant to review.)
   b. Does it specify

	yes	no
franchise fee?	______	______
termination?	______	______
selling and renewal?	______	______
advertising and promotion?	______	______
patent and liability protection?	______	______
home office services?	______	______
commissions and royalties?	______	______
training?	______	______
financing?	______	______
territory?	______	______
exclusivity?	______	______

For additional review questions, see **www.ftc.gov/bcp/conline/pubs/invest/buyfran.htm.**

SOURCE: Federal Trade Commission

Myron decided that the one loser was draining much of his time, energy, and capital. He called the franchisor and asked for assistance in unloading it. They found several prospective buyers and chose the one they thought was the best. He wasn't able to turn it around either. Myron now devotes all his time to working with his winners.

Reasons for Not Buying a Franchise

Many entrepreneurs have decided against buying franchises. Here are some of the reasons they have given:

1. I know the business as well as they do.
2. My name is as well known as theirs.
3. Why pay a franchise fee?
4. Why pay a royalty fee and advertising fee?
5. My individuality would have been stifled.
6. I didn't want others to tell me how to run my business.
7. I didn't want a ground-floor opportunity where I'd be the guinea pig.
8. It felt like I would have been committed for the rest of my life.
9. There were restrictions on selling out.
10. If I didn't do as I was told, I would lose my franchise.
11. The specified hours of business did not suit my location or desires.
12. The franchisor's promotions and products did not fit my customers' needs or tastes.
13. They offered no territory protection.
14. I would not be in control of my business.

If you can develop a winning formula, you can become a franchisor yourself. Many entrepreneurs have done this. This is another reason to learn all you can about franchising now.

PURCHASING A FRANCHISE

If you have explored and investigated franchising and believe it is the right fit for you, the process truly begins. First you must contact the franchise development office of the franchises you are exploring. They will ask you several questions attempting to pre-qualify you. If they think there might be a fit, a franchise packet will be sent to you. The packets are full of marketing pieces meant to sell you on the franchise. Try to read between the lines. Keep in mind you are reading advertising at this point and you are at the start of the process. Many of the packets will include an application form that you fill out and return.

If the franchise is large, a local sales manager or area franchisee will contact you after reviewing your application. You will meet and discuss requirements and locations further. At this point you should be exploring the franchisor and franchisees, current and past, in depth. Spend time and ask questions.

The franchisor may help you with site selection and demographic information. Deposits may be required before site selection begins. According to law, before any funds are exchanged, you will receive the UFOC. Your lawyer, who specializes in franchising, should be reviewing the circular with you and answer any questions you might have. Also, if you are beginning to look at offices or retail space, involve your attorney immediately.

An accountant should also be called in to review material and point out financial issues, which need to be discussed with the franchisor. Your accountant will help you assess the financial possibilities and feasibility of the venture.

With the advice of your accountant, lawyer, and banker, you are finally ready to negotiate with the franchisor to complete the sale. Be sure you understand your role and the franchisor's responsibilities. Good luck!

CAN YOU FRANCHISE YOUR IDEA AND *BECOME* THE FRANCHISOR?

Paul and Lori Hogan have built a network of more than 300 Home Instead franchises (see Passion Box) throughout the United States providing caregivers to the elderly, allowing them to remain independent. From their first office in Paul's mother's house in 1994, they knew they had a successful formula and could meet a growing need for home-care assistance. With previous experience in franchising they searched out passionate franchisors interested in caring for others as they built Home Instead. Their focus on a rapidly growing market has propelled them to be named as one of the top 100 franchise companies by *Success* and *Entrepreneur* magazines.

Passion

Passion for Seniors

Home Instead Franchisee Fulfills Her Dream

Altruism, honed through 15 years in the heath care industry and two years as administrator of finance for her church, led April Moon Willingham to seek a franchise that would allow her to express her need to help others and make a profit at the same time. After reviewing several franchise opportunities, she selected a Home Instead franchise, which specializes in providing non-medical care services to seniors. Companionship, meal planning and preparation, coordinating household activities, light housekeeping, and help with transportation to doctors are just a few of the services offered by her caregivers.

Even with unemployment running below four percent, April was able to recruit excellent caregivers by tapping into an untapped market of 50- to 70-year-olds who choose to work part or full time and enjoy helping others. Each visit lasts a minimum of three hours, and visits can be arranged to meet the needs of the clients with once a week to daily visits.

A great deal of April's time is spent in the community visiting senior centers, assisted living centers, and nursing homes to discuss the firm's services with professionals who can recommend Home Instead to their clients as they transition. In addition, April meets each client personally to complete a need's assessment and returns once again to introduce the caregiver she has selected. If the match between caregiver and receiver does not work out for any reason, a new caregiver will be assigned.

Her franchise fee of $17,500 and a royalty fee of five percent, in her opinion, are well worth the cost. As long-term insurers now cover services such as those provided by Home Instead, April foresees continued and steady growth. In addition, Home Instead is developing alliances with senior organizations throughout the United States that provide additional clientele.

April's passion for helping seniors has been realized through her Home Instead franchise.

For additional information on becoming a franchisor, read *The Wall Street Journal*'s excellent online article, "Turning Your Business Into a Franchise Can Pay Off" by Dan Morse. Morse, *The Wall Street Journal*'s franchising guru, provides the following information for "wannabe" franchisors.

1. Build a successful model first and make sure it makes money.
2. Don't prop up your franchisees financially.
3. Open up the checkbook; franchising takes a "boatload of money."
4. The concept has to be repeatable and not interwoven with the franchisor's personality.
5. Keep it simple. Be able to teach your tricks of the trade in 3–6 weeks.
6. Remember that not all concepts are transferable to other locations.
7. Be able to inspire others to invest in your vision.

SOURCE: **startupjournal.com/franchising/** (accessed August 13, 2001).

FRANCHISING TRENDS AND FINAL THOUGHTS

If you're really interested in making money as a franchisee, do some research on becoming an area franchise. A franchisor may sell area franchises, which would allow the franchisee to open multiple outlets within a certain territory. The territory could be as small as a section of town or as large as several states. Many individuals with strong business backgrounds have found area franchises to be quite lucrative. If you truly believe in the company's concept and have experience, explore the possibility of an area franchise. One Kentucky Fried Chicken franchisee now owns more than 50 stores.

Another growing trend in franchising today is the operation of "mega-franchisees," where multiple franchises are housed and operated under the same roof. To research these, interview key people at several multiple franchise operations. Save yourself time, money, and maybe even some heartache by spending time visiting several successful and unsuccessful "mega-franchises."

Selling franchises is a numbers game. You, the potential franchisee, are a "lead." You will be told what you want to hear.

If you have few business skills, or perhaps little business experience, then your chances of succeeding are far greater as a franchisee. A franchisor with a well-developed Business Plan will keep you on track. Ask to see it. Even if the franchisor has a well-developed Business Plan, you still need to complete one for your particular franchise location.

The key here is gut feeling. If you should decide to buy a franchise and then feel like an employee of the franchisor, strike out on your own. Develop your own plan, and go for it. Look at franchising as an option—an example to learn from—and then blend that knowledge into a unique business that explores the gaps exposed in Chapter 2 and 3, "Spotting Trends and Opportunity Selection."

COMMUNITY RESOURCE

Bartering Becomes Mainstream

With more than 400,000 firms conducting more than $9 billion in transactions per year through more than 1,600 barter exchanges, bartering has definitely gone mainstream. In addition, several firms, such as **www.bigvine.com** and **www.tradefirst.com**, operate online barter exchanges. Just about any business with surplus capacity or inventory can take advantage of bartering. According to American Express, bartering allows you to: 1) trade your idle assets for goods and services you would normally pay cash for, 2) free cash flow by bartering for things your business needs, and 3) reach new customers and markets. There are two associations that represent the barter industry: the International Reciprocal Trade Association (IRTA), **www.irta.com;** and the National Association of Trade Exchanges (NATE), **www.nate.org.** Both organizations have Websites that allow you to discover more about trade exchanges in your area. Use IRTA's "Checklist to Join a Barter Exchange" below to research your local barter exchange.

Checklist to Join a Barter Exchange

- ✓ Can you get what you need for the use of your business? Prepare a list of your wants, and check whether the barter exchange can provide any of them.
- ✓ Ask for a referral list of clients and check with them to see if they are satisfied.
- ✓ Inquire as to how many clients are currently trading, and how many are on standby or reserve (they are unwilling to take barter business until they have spent the trade dollars they have).
- ✓ Check the barter prices to see if products and services are priced fairly and competitively.
- ✓ Check the geographic coverage of the exchange's client base, and the proximity of suppliers of goods and services you want.
- ✓ Does the company provide consulting service on use of barter, in addition to brokerage and management services?
- ✓ Compare the barter contracts, costs, and services of other barter exchanges in order to evaluate the best deal for you.
- ✓ Barter sales are taxable income. In the USA barter exchanges annually report the barter income of each client to the tax authorities. Don't do business with anyone who sells barter as a tax dodge.
- ✓ Make the usual business reference checks on the barter exchange (i.e., Better Business Bureau, Chamber of Commerce, etc.).
- ✓ Be sure the barter exchange is a member of and is regulated by the International Reciprocal Trade Association.

SOURCE: International Reciprocal Trade Association, **www.irta.net/checklist_to_join.html** (accessed March 30, 2001).

If you're not ready to be totally on your own yet or just want the assurance and support, franchising may be the way for you to start.

SUMMARY

There are two good reasons to consider buying a franchise: (1) if the brand name is respected, you'll already be positioned in the marketplace; and (2) if the franchisor is sharp, you'll inherit a Business Plan that works. Examine the franchise's appeal with consumers carefully; you want to get a marketing boost from the name. Depending on the franchise, you may also receive other services for your money (for example, help on site selection, interior layout, and vendor connections), but the main thing you're buying is brand-name recognition.

The franchisor cannot promise anything, and earnings claims are not legal unless in the Uniform Franchise Offering Circular.

Just as if you were investigating an ongoing, independent business, study the opportunity thoroughly. Examine the financial history, and compare what you'd make if you bought the business to what you'd make if you invested the same money elsewhere or started a similar business without the franchise.

Buying a franchise does not ensure success. The ultimate responsibility for success or failure of the business lies with the franchisee. You are purchasing a name brand and a system to follow. Follow it carefully.

Think Points for Success

- Avoid ground-floor opportunities. "Grow with us" can mean *caveat emptor* ("Let the buyer beware").
- Talk to franchisees, especially ones that have left the system. Franchisees who have left the fold are listed in the UFOC. Keep in mind, current franchisees sometimes receive a "finders fee;" therefore they may not be totally honest with a potential buyer.
- Remember you are purchasing a "job" and *have* to do it their way, not your way.
- The franchisor gets a percentage of gross sales for advertising and royalty fees whether or not the franchisee is profitable.
- Do you really need the security blanket of a franchise?
- Read the proposed agreements carefully. They are airtight, favor the franchisor, and are usually nonnegotiable
- Would you be comfortable relinquishing your independence?
- If you like to break rules, be creative, and stretch things to the limit, don't buy a franchise—you will very likely end up in court.

Key Points from Another View

Attorney Contract Review

By Kay Marie Ainsley and Michael H. Seid

Not sure about signing on the dotted line? Our Franchise and Business Opportunities experts suggest you have your attorney take one more look at that contract.

Q: I've been approved for a franchise I really want to buy. They've given me the UFOC and the contract. The franchise salesperson told me it was a standard contract and not negotiable. Because I can't change it, do I really need to pay an attorney to read it?

A: If you've reached the legal age of majority, you can sign any contract you wish to sign. However, remember the old adage. He who acts as his own attorney has a fool for a client. We believe this saying justly describes those who don't have their franchise agreements reviewed by a professional before they sign them.

Regardless of what has been said or implied during your discussions with the franchisor or with other franchisees in the system as you go through the approval process, what's written in the contract is what will rule your relationship with the franchisor. The value of having an attorney review a franchise contract lies not in their ability to beat up the franchisor and "get a better deal" for you, but in their ability to make sure you fully understand what you're getting into when you sign the contract. They can explain the different provisions, compare the provisions in the contract you're about to sign to what are considered "best practices" in the industry, and tell you how the courts have interpreted similar provisions in other cases.

Everything in the franchise agreement is important. However, we suggest you pay particular attention to the following:

"Regarding territory" clause. Does the contract grant you an exclusive territory? How close can the franchisor establish another unit? Does the franchisor reserve the right to sell the same product through different channels such as the Internet?

"Regarding supplies" clause. What must you buy from the franchisor? What can you buy from other suppliers?

"Your right to sell the business" clause. Does the franchisor have the right of first refusal? Do they have the right to approve a potential buyer? If so, what criteria are used to evaluate a candidate?

What happens to your business in the case of your death or disability?

What support must the franchisor provide and what may they provide?

Under what circumstances can the agreement be terminated, and what are the effects of termination?

A word of caution: Having an attorney review your franchise agreement doesn't absolve you of the responsibility to read it thoroughly before you sign it. In fact, we recommend you read it and make a list of your questions. Then give them to your attorney.

Franchise law is a legal specialty. Therefore the most efficient way to conduct the contract review is to use a franchise attorney rather than the attorney who reviewed the purchase agreement for your house or who drew up your will. If you need a referral for a franchise attorney, contact the International Franchise Association's Council of Franchise Suppliers at **www.franchise.org**.

Source: Kay Marie Ainsley and Michael H. Seid, "Attorney Contract Review," **www.entrepreneur.com**, July 17, 2000 (accessed August 1, 2001).

Pull Your Plan Together

LAUNCHING YOUR PASSION

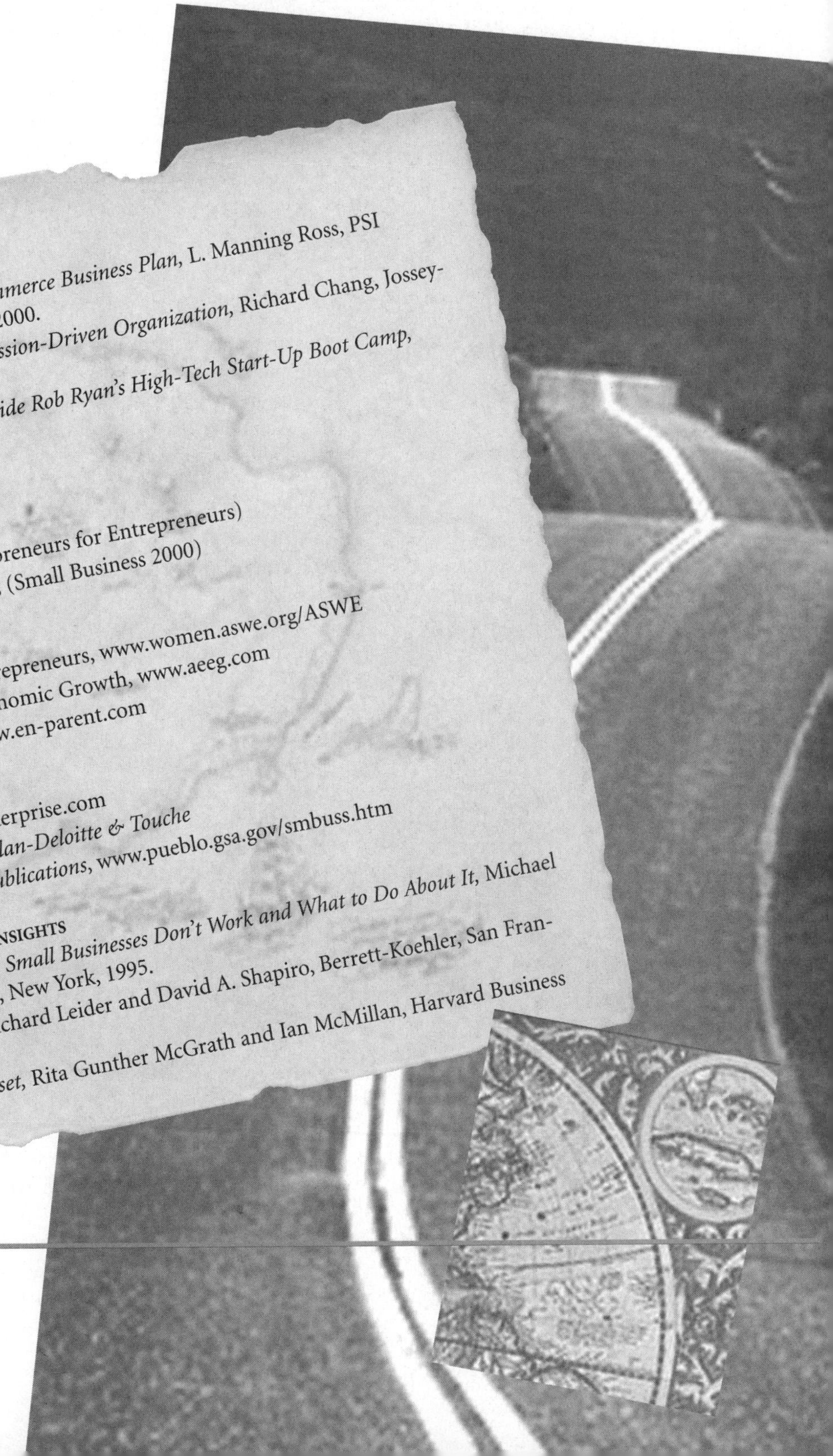

ENTREPRENEURIAL LINKS

BOOKS

Businessplan.com: How to Write an E-commerce Business Plan, L. Manning Ross, PSI Research-Oasis, Central Point, Ore., 2000.

The Passion Plan at Work: Building a Passion-Driven Organization, Richard Chang, Jossey-Bass, San Francisco, 2001

Entrepreneur America: Lessons from Inside Rob Ryan's High-Tech Start-Up Boot Camp, Harper Business, New York, 2001.

WEBSITES

www.growthink.com, (GrowThink)

www.morebusiness.com, (By Entrepreneurs for Entrepreneurs)

SmallBusiness2000.org/home.html, (Small Business 2000)

ASSOCIATIONS/ORGANIZATION

American Society of Women Entrepreneurs, www.women.aswe.org/ASWE

American Entrepreneurs for Economic Growth, www.aeeg.com

The Entrepreneurial Parent, www.en-parent.com

PUBLICATIONS

Asian Enterprise, www.asianenterprise.com

Writing an Effective Business Plan-Deloitte & Touche

Small Business Government Publications, www.pueblo.gsa.gov/smbuss.htm

ADDITIONAL ENTREPRENEURIAL INSIGHTS

E-Myth Revisited: Why Most Small Businesses Don't Work and What to Do About It, Michael Gerber, Harper Business, New York, 1995.

Whistle While You Work, Richard Leider and David A. Shapiro, Berrett-Koehler, San Francisco, 2001.

The Entrepreneurial Mindset, Rita Gunther McGrath and Ian McMillan, Harvard Business School, Boston, 2000.

Learning Objectives

- Pull all your information together into one coherent unit, which becomes a portable showcase for your business.
- Understand the importance of YOU completing the Business Plan.
- Review the advantages and disadvantages of Business Plan software.
- Review a sample Business Plan to discover how one pair of entrepreneurs defined and showcased their business.
- Understand that words can talk but numbers show it can be done.
- Review the Notes section for the financial information.
- Recognize the importance of providing all backup data for your readers.
- Match or surpass the sample Business Plan in power and effectiveness.
- Complete a PERT chart to organize the work ahead.
- Put your finished Business Plan to work.

You may be closer to completing your Business Plan than you think. If you have completed the Action Steps in the preceding chapters, you *already* have the major components of your plan. If you have *not*, return to Chapter 1 and work through the Action Steps. Through the past chapters you have found gaps in the market, researched your Target Customer, defined your business, developed marketing and promotional ideas, and completed basic financial research. As you develop your Business Plan using the Action Steps you've compiled, you may recognize areas that need further attention and research. Chapter 15 provides you with the structure to put your facts, figures, ideas, dreams, and intuition into a workable plan.

Your Business Plan could be one of the most important documents you have ever pulled together. If you need to get started with your business immediately, consider using the Fast-Start Business Plan in Appendix A. Particularly if your business is less complex and has low capital needs, this may be the alternative for you.

With a completed Business Plan in hand you will have something to show to the people who are important to your business: banker, lenders, relatives, venture capitalists, vendors, suppliers, key employees, friends, the SBA, and others. The plan is portable and you can make as many copies as needed to share with people who can help you succeed. You can either mail it to contacts across the country or post it on the various Internet sites that link investors with entrepreneurs.

Planning is hard work. You will stay up nights, lose lots of sleep, and miss too many meals, but in the end you will have saved time. Just as a pilot would not consider a flight without a plan, neither should you consider a business venture without a Business Plan.

Occasionally on completion of the plan, one may decide the costs in terms of money, time, effort, stress, and risk are not justified. If this happens to you, congratulations! You have learned a valuable lesson and it has only cost you time, not money!

Your plan should become a working, breathing, living document for your business dreams. Share your plan with others; they may have ideas, insights, and recommendations. Review this input and revise your plan if necessary. Business Plan reviewers sometimes ask for further details or back-up data that, when added to your plan, will make it stronger and more effective. Sometimes we become so close to our Business Plans we omit important and relevant details and information.

Passion

You're in the (Entrepreneurial) Army Now

By Cynthia L. Webb

A voice boomed from a rainbow-lit stage, a man clad in black gestured wildly to a crowd, delivering one-liners about how to kick start a new business.

"Be passionate," he said. "You have to talk about what matters." For an executive summary, "if you can't do it in three pages, it's too damn long."

It wasn't motivational guru Anthony Robbins, but Bill Joos, head of business development for Garage.com, a Silicon Valley venture capital investment bank that helps start-ups land funding. Some 500 entrepreneurs paid up to $795 to attend the firm's two-day "Bootcamp for Start-ups" held at the Ronald Reagan International Trade Center Wednesday and today.

Joos was one of a slew of featured speakers, including venture capitalists and CEOs, giving how-tos on pitching a business to investors and shaping a start-up. The ideal number of slides for hawking your Business Plan? According to Joos, no more than 14.

Learning What It Takes

Joos, who has worked in sales and marketing for IBM and Apple Computer, said an elevator pitch should take 45 seconds and formal presentations 15 minutes. A good pitch "must change the pulse rate." He told attendees to "kill the MBA speak" and geek-speak, such as using jargon like "end-to-end" and "solution," to explain their business.

Attendees listened to discussions on exit paths for businesses, giving polished presentations, and finding talented employees. During a talk on start-up blunders, Trevor Chaplick, co-managing partner of law firm Wilson, Sonsini, Goodrich, & Rosati, said companies need to be realistic. One pitfall is not anticipating a company's financial needs and cash-burn rate.

Panelists advised entrepreneurs to get funding from some investors who are close to home base to get hands-on help. "You need local attention in VC deals," said Mike Levinthal, general partner of the Mayfield Fund.

The Camp's Roots

Guy Kawasaki, Garage.com's chief executive and former Apple Computer Inc. executive, said the camps are a way to scope out potential business.

Garage.com might consider potential deals in the Washington region involving the telecom sector.

The company links start-ups with funding from outside venture capitalists and provides services, such as shaping a Business Plan and recruiting an executive team. Since 1999 Garage.com has helped about 60 companies raise more than $200 million in venture capital through its wholly owned broker-dealer subsidiary.

None of its portfolio companies have gone public yet, Kawasaki said. He said the "lion's share of our revenue is from events and our investment banking fees."

Older Crowd, but Same Innovation

The company's 11th boot camp was the first one to hit Washington. Others have been held in cities including Boston, Austin, and New York.

Since the first event the audience has changed.

"This crowd is older," Kawasaki said. Gone, he said, is just "a clever idea with a cute domain name." A dropping Nasdaq and closed IPO market has added to the shift.

But the innovation is the same. "I still believe that small teams are going to do it." The concept for the next hot business could come from two people working in a garage, he said.

Building Confidence

Abbe Buck might be the poster child for the changing attendee list. The 39-year-old entrepreneur took time off from her Northern Virginia company, HighViz Consulting Group, which she runs out of her basement, to get business advice.

She said the event gave her confidence to try and secure between $750,000 and $1 million in seed financing from strategic investors. Her three-person firm will need outside capital to hire more workers to keep up the demand for her consulting services and to get an office. She left her job working with IBM/Lotus about a year and a half ago to pursue her own business. Buck brings in about $15,000 a month from consulting gigs.

"I know how to make a pitch now, " she said. "Now I have the courage to go forward."

Making the Pitch

After the conference, while other attendees nibbled on Thai chicken kabobs and other appetizers at a reception, Buck went to find one of Garage.com's "pitch me" booths to practice.

"Where are the pitch people?" she asked. An organizer pointed to two tables: "Those two gentlemen are waiting to hear you."

John D. Ko, president and CEO of software company Cincro Communications in Falls Church, Va., also gave a practice pitch. He said the seminar was helpful.

"You just realize the fact that this is not really a game," said Ko, 35, who has run his firm for about four years and said juggling payrolls, having a handful of employees, and adapting a business to changing market conditions are difficult.

He describes his business as a "bootstrapped" effort that brings in $700,000 to $800,000 a year. He said the conference gave him some pointers, such as how to go after venture capital. Ko wants to land $4 million to $5 million in a first round of funding, but has yet to have a sit-down meeting with an area firm. He has hired an attorney from Shaw Pittman to help introduce him to VCs.

"It's sobering," Ko said of the event. "It's realistic."

SOURCE: **www.LocalBusiness.com** November 16, 2000 (accessed May 5, 2001).

HOW TO START WRITING YOUR BUSINESS PLAN

It is now time for your passion to come to the forefront and spill out into every section of your Business Plan. If your plan doesn't shout passion, you can't expect your Business Plan readers to go further than the executive summary. Before you begin, gather in one place all your completed Action Steps and back-up data. Outline your plan, fill in the information from your Action Steps, refine the plan, ask a knowledgeable person to review your plan, refine further, and prepare to present the plan to potential investors or lenders.

Remember, your reader is looking at where you are now, where you are going, and how you are going to get there. Planning is an ongoing process. Your Business Plan is a roadmap, but it should represent a fast-growing area where new roads and new opportunities and challenges constantly present themselves.

If you're a creative thinker, chances are your thought processes don't always follow a linear sequence. That's great—it will help you as an entrepreneur! Nonetheless, the Action Steps in Chapter 15 do follow a linear sequence; the sequence of the parts of a completed Business Plan. This is a matter of convenience—you will see an example of each part as it would appear in the finished product. Bear in mind, however, that we don't expect you to sequentially write each part.

The best way to begin writing a Business Plan is to start with the material with which you feel most comfortable. For example, if you really enjoyed interviewing Target Customers, you might begin with "The Market and the Target Customers."

In Chapter 15 the Action Steps will serve as a checklist for keeping track of which parts of the plan you have written. For example, in practice you would probably write the cover letter last although that is the first Action Step we present. Think of the writing of this first cover letter as a valuable exercise. After completing Chapter 15 and your Business Plan, rewrite your cover letter. The more cover letters you write, the easier it becomes to write them effectively.

To jump-start your writing skills, review the Business Plans for "Yes, We Do Windows" (Appendix A) and "Annie's" (Appendix B). In addition, you can log on to the Internet and access a wide variety of Business Plans online. A great deal of assistance and advice on the referenced sites will help you write a winning Business Plan. One of the best sites, **www.bplans.com**, offers a wide selection of sample Business Plans.

Three-Part Structure: Words, Numbers, and Appendixes

Your Business Plan tells the world what kind of business you are in and where you are going. For ease of handling, divide your plan into two sections, and provide the needed documentation in appendixes at the end.

In Section I use *words*: introduce your strategies for marketing and management. Try to "hook" your reader with the excitement of creating a business, assessing the competition, designing a marketing plan, targeting customers, finding the right location, and building a team—all those human things that most people can relate to, even if they're not in business. Clearly point out your firm's uniqueness and ability to compete and handle change.

In Section II and the appendix present *numbers*: Proforma income statements, cash flows, and balance sheets. This section is aimed primarily at bankers, credit managers, venture capitalists, vendors, small business investment companies, and commercial credit lenders. Proforma income statements for three to five years are usually included in the appendix. At the same time you must also make it accessible to the casual reader who searches for the bottom line.

Support Sections I and II with *appendixes*. This is where you place résumés, maps, diagrams, photographs, tables, reprints from industry journals, letters from customers, letters from vendors, credit reports, personal financial statements, bids from contractors, and other documentation that demonstrates the viability of your plan.

Note that in most cases, material in the appendixes comes from existing sources. You are not stating anything new here; you are merely supporting what you have already said.

Appendixes vary for each type of business; *for that reason sample appendixes are not included in this book.*

If you follow and complete the Action Steps in this chapter and in the past chapters, you will have in hand all the components you need to write a winning Business Plan.

Business Plan Software

Freeware, shareware, and "payware" for Business Planning are widely available on the Internet. This type of software only serves as a guide. Only through completing an incredible amount of work such as you have done through the Action Steps will you be able to "fill in the blanks" of a software program. The following sources are available on the Internet:

www.moneyhunter.com, Money Hunter provides free downloadable Business Plan templates.

www.sba.gov/starting/indexbusplans.html, SBA offers sample Business Plans and templates.

www.virtualrestaurant.com, Virtual Restaurant displays sample restaurant Business Plans.

www.toolkit.cch.com, Business Owner's Toolkit offers a sample Business Plan for small manufacturers, solo service providers, and retailers.

www.bplans.com, PaloAlto software offers the Business Plan Pro software program and the site displays more than five dozen sample plans and a free template.

www.business-plan.com, Automate Your Business Plan software, published by Out of Your Mind....and Into the Marketplace provides downloadable software for under $100.

www.inc.com, Inc.'s excellent sites will link you to online business planning software and a wealth of Business Plan information.

www.bizplanit.com, BizPlanIt provides online Business Plan software.

www.jian.com, BIZPLANBuilder and BIZPLANExpress are two of the most popular business planning programs.

www.brs-inc.com/pwrite.html, PlanWrite for Business is an award-winning software program published by Business Resource Software, Inc.

www.icbb.com/plana/planabus.html, Plan-A Business Plan & Financing Software are available.

www.planmaker.com, PLANMaker is available in both Macintosh and Windows format.

www.adamsmedia.com/software, Adams Streetwise Business Plan is part of the Adams Streetwise Series.

Software programs like those listed previously facilitate Business Plan preparation, but they do not replace the work required. They serve as a consultant as you write your plan, suggesting appropriate websites, prodding you for further explanation, and posing relevant questions. Business planning software is a standardized tool; you must tweak it to make your plan appear unique.

There is no one magic Business Plan program or template that guarantees success. Only your hard work and an element of luck can do this.

Outside Assistance in Writing a Business Plan

Many people ask, "Should I hire a pro to write my Business Plan?" Our response is always, "*You* are the pro!" If you do not want to put the time and effort into writing your own Business Plan, it is doubtful that you will have the energy and drive to develop a business. Also, no other person but *you* can put the passion you feel into your plan.

With the vast amount of resources available—books, Internet, and software—you have enough help to put you well on your way to developing a complete Business Plan. We do suggest that on finishing your initial plan you look for several business owners and possible investors to review it. In addition, attorneys, marketing specialists, accountants, and manufacturing experts may improve your plan with their review; they will show you what areas need additional clarification or support data. Take all of their comments to heart and rework your plan where necessary.

Hiring a business consultant to refine your plan is acceptable, but do not allow him or her to dream your dream! If you do not have total control over input to your plan, you may embarrass yourself by not being able to explain the details of your plan to investors and bankers.

Reminders

Completing a Business Plan helps reduce the risk of failure. No plan can guarantee success or eliminate failure, but a well-researched plan will help acknowledge issues, anticipate problems, and determine resources.

The plan should be easy to read, with each number and figure well documented. Use bullets, graphs, and appendixes to support the plan's strongest points. Be sure there are no misspelled words and that the plan is well written. If you are not comfortable with your writing skills, hire an editor to review your plan.

Focus on the potential opportunities the business provides for investors. Tie together—with a clear, consistent message—all elements of the plan. Include possible risks as well; the business without risks does not exist.

The plan should consist of about 20 to 40 pages with additional pages for appendixes. Make the plan easy for your reader to write notes on and include how the reader can reach you—fax, e-mail, address, telephone, pager, and so on.

Chapter 15 illustrates the steps involved in completing a Business Plan along with providing you samples of each step for The Entrepreneurs' Software Training Center. The Center has been in operation for six months and has been self-financed by the owners, who are now seeking to expand and need additional outside financing. Read Chapter 15 through once and then reread, completing the Action Steps. Although the Action Steps appear in the order they would be included in your Business Plan, you should complete Action Steps 64 to 73 first, then Action Step 63, which focuses on the Executive Summary, and finally complete Action Step 62, the cover letter.

Cover Letter

To aim your plan so it will achieve the most good, focus your cover letter. Each time you send the plan to someone, write a special cover letter addressed to that specific reader and his or her interests and needs. The cover letter introduces the excitement of your plan and tells the person specifically why you have chosen to send it to him or her. This may be your only shot at making the reader want to review your Business Plan, so make your letter strong—prove you know who you are, where you are going, and how you are going to get there.

Read the sample cover letter for The Entrepreneurs' Software Training Center.

47 Dogwood Lane, Ste. 108-9
Oak Ridge, TN 37953
Jackson@net.com
865/555-5555

June 5, 2001

River Bank
Ms. Nancy Hopp
Vice-President, Lending
1400 Market Lane
Knoxville, TN 37944

Dear Ms. Hopp,

Thank you for the insight you shared with me on reviewing my Business Plan. Your thought-provoking questions in the marketing area led me to research additional advertising avenues. In addition, I have revamped the financial section by adding additional notes to the pro formas and reworking several of the figures. Your suggestions and the consequent changes we have made make our plan much stronger. Everyone here at The Entrepreneurs' Software Training Center appreciates the care you took reading over earlier drafts of our Business Plan.

The positive response to our entrepreneurial software training service over the past six months requires the school to expand to serve our entrepreneurs better. As the economy slows, consumers with substantial severance checks and retirement plan funds in hand are reaching out for the dream of owning a business. To help make their dreams come true as quickly as possible, we provide our Fast-Start software training on the most popular small business software programs. Most of our clients have a good working knowledge of computers and basic software but seek advanced training that focuses on an entrepreneur's needs.

We feel passionate about our business and our entrepreneurs. We have watched several of our clients open up websites through our eCommerce courses and have aided in the preparation of more than 30 Business Plans to date. We serve not only the start-up businesses in the community but also have found a market for our services among entrepreneurs whose businesses have been open two to four years and are now interested in expanding or making their business more professional.

Each of the founders has contributed $100,000 to launch The Entrepreneurs' Software Training Center.

We are currently in the market for a loan of $60,000 to be used for tenant improvements. The location we have in Oak Ridge is built out but will require additional cabling, electrical wiring, furniture, and appropriate lighting to enable us to provide a second classroom. We would appreciate your guidance concerning sources of capital available through your bank or additional avenues.

Action Step 62

Write a Cover Letter for Your Plan

Address your letter to a specific person who can help your business. Be brief; aim for about 200 words.

State the reason you are sending the plan. If you are asking for money, tell the person what you want it for, how much you need, and how you will repay the loan. Several well-written paragraphs should be all you need to do this.

Your purpose in writing the cover letter is to open the door gently and prepare the way for further negotiations. The cover letter is bait on your hook.

If you are putting money into the business, or if you have already contributed, indicate how much.

The tone you are after in this opening move is confident and slightly formal. You want to appear neat, bright, organized, and in control of your venture.

Refer to The Entrepreneurs' Software Training Center's sample letter.

We plan to repay our loan from profits generated over the next three years as we grow to full capacity. For more information, please refer to the financial section.

Again, thank you very much for your help and advice. We couldn't have done it without you.

Cordially,
Danielle Jackson
Chief Executive Officer

Let's summarize what's good about our sample cover letter. We can see that:

1. The writer is making use of a previous contact.
2. The writer tells the reader—the manager of a bank—that she is in the market for a loan. She does not put her on the spot by asking for money. Instead, she asks for advice on where to find sources of capital.
3. She shared her passion for her business and her customers with the reader.
4. The writer struck the right tone. (This requires several revisions.)

You can do as well or better—and it's worth the effort! As you draft your cover letter, remember that the reader will pass judgment on your Business Plan (and on your business ability) on the basis of the letter. Do you want your small business to appear profitable? Attractive? Welcoming? Your cover letter needs to give the same impression. A well written cover letter will make its readers want to become involved in your venture. Action Step 62 will help you write your cover letter. (Complete it after the entire plan including the executive summary are finished.)

Elements of a Business Plan

The Table of Contents

Our sample table of contents provides a quick overview of a finished Business Plan. In practice, the table of contents is prepared last.

THE ENTREPRENEURS' SOFTWARE TRAINING CENTER
Table of Contents

Executive Summary
I. Description of the Business
  A. The Service We Provide
  B. Industry Overview and Target Customers
  C. The Competition
  D. Marketing Strategy
  E. Our Facility/Location
  F. Management and Personnel
  G. Exit Strategy
II. Financial Section
  A. Pro Forma Income/Cash Flow Statement
  B. Balance Sheet
III. Appendixes*
  A. Market Research
  B. Quotes from Hardware and Software Suppliers
  C. Personal Résumés
  D. Personal Financial Statements
  E. Pro Forma Cash Flows Forecasted for Three Years
  F. Letters of Reference
  G. Bids from Contractors

H. Floor plan for Dogwood Lane location expansion
I. Map with Competitors' Locations
J. Census Data
K. Pro Forma Income Statements forecasted for three to five years
L. Break-even Analysis
M. Furniture Estimates

*The need for specific appendixes varies greatly from Business Plan to Business Plan. For that reason, we have not included sample appendixes. As you draft your plan, you will recognize items that require further documentation to substantiate your business strategies; the most logical place for this kind of documentation is in appendixes. In addition, include the names of references, consultants, or technical advisors who have assisted you.

EXECUTIVE SUMMARY

The executive summary serves as an introduction to the Business Plan. Its function is similar to that of a preface in a book. It is written to (1) acquaint the reader with the subject matter of the material that follows, (2) direct the reader's attention to whatever strengths the author (entrepreneur) wants to emphasize, and (3) make the reader want to turn the pages and keep reading. Because the executive summary reviews the entire Business Plan, it must be written last. After the plan is completed, condense the information to two to three pages. Pay special attention to the *business description, current position and future outlook, management, uniqueness* and, if you need financing, *funds sought, how they will be used, when they will be repaid,* and *how they will be repaid*. This summary appears right after the table of contents and should be able to stand on its own.

As a preview to your plan, the executive summary should excite, entice, and draw the reader into the plan. A well-written executive summary captures the reader's attention and makes him or her eager to explore further. Because many readers never go further than the executive summary, it's important to expend a great deal of effort to make your executive summary an excellent selling tool. It may be your only chance!

As you write your executive summary, remember that lenders prefer "hard," numerical data and facts. Therefore such phrases as "30 percent return on the original investment" and "secured training agreements from three retail computer stores in the area" make the following example *a strong* executive summary. The words help to paint a picture of good management and solid growth for The Entrepreneurs' Software Training Center.

You, too, can write an effective executive summary. Action Step 63 will help you decide which facts and numbers portray you and your business venture as credible and promising and then to summarize them in writing. Finish Action Step 63 on completion of your Business Plan.

ACTION STEP 63

WRITE AN EXECUTIVE SUMMARY

Imagine you had two minutes to explain your business venture to a complete stranger. This gives you an idea of what information you need to put into writing for your executive summary.

Practice explaining your venture to friends and strangers, limiting yourself to two minutes. Ask them to raise questions, and use their questions to guide you as you revise and hone your presentation.

When you are satisfied with your oral summary, write it down and type it up. It should not exceed three typed pages. (The Entrepreneurs' Software Training Center's executive summary that serves as our example was less than one single-spaced page.) This may constitute a very small portion of your Business Plan, but it could be the most important part.

Rewrite your executive summary again after completing your Business Plan.

EXECUTIVE SUMMARY

The Entrepreneurs' Software Training Center is a user-friendly, state-of-the-art software, eCommerce, and small-business training center. We are tapping into the growing need for entrepreneurs to have software classes focused specifically on their entrepreneurial needs. Our market area is growing quickly today because of the expansion of the following consumer groups:

- People retiring early and starting new businesses.
- Entrepreneurs who are ready to expand their current businesses.
- Individuals wanting to take advantage of opportunities the Internet can provide.
- Young people who see small business as an alternative to working in a corporate world.
- Increasing number of people who run a business in addition to their full-time jobs.

We will market our training classes exclusively to entrepreneurs. All classes will focus on the use of computer programs in small business and all examples will be taken from the classroom participants. The Entrepreneurs' Software Training Center's sophisticated electronic classroom provides "hands-on" education. Adapting packaged software to meet each participant's needs will be the goal of classroom instruction.

We are currently operating with one classroom and hope to add an additional classroom within the next six months. This expansion will allow us to attain sales of $660,000 by the end of fiscal year 2002. At that time our pretax profits will have reached almost $168,000.

According to our research, our entrepreneurs have an insatiable appetite for software application knowledge and Internet training. They generally have strong computer backgrounds and thus are attending our classes for advanced training. We anticipate an annual sales growth rate of 30 percent over the next three years.

Our competitors continue to train in the traditional classroom style and currently show no sign of copying our unique instructional approach. At this point none of our competitors are focusing on small business owners, and we hope to capitalize on this gap in the market.

We not only plan to offer software training but hope to become an Entrepreneurial Hub for our clients. We have contacted many individuals who will offer special courses at our center to include:

- Patent Protection
- Selling to the Federal Government
- Bringing a Product to Market
- Pricing Strategies
- ECommerce Solutions

Throughout the past six months, we have demonstrated that we can offer superior training at competitive prices. Our plans for the future include developing additional training centers. Research and customer surveys indicate that we have just begun to tap the ever-increasing need for entrepreneurial education and services.

Danielle Jackson will continue to focus on sales and marketing in addition to developing and teaching courses with Robert Bennett. Curriculum for more than twenty courses has been developed with another ten courses in development. As the needs of our students change, we will be able to adapt and meet their needs. If we are unable to develop a course, contract teaching professionals will be hired. Robert Bennett also manages the technical aspects of keeping the hardware and software up-to-date and online.

We are seeking funding of $60,000 to cover remodeling costs required to equip an additional classroom. Funds will also be used for license fees, furniture, and equipment costs for our second classroom. The appendix contains contractor, computer, and furniture estimates. We plan to purchase refurbished classroom furniture at a potential cost savings of $15,000 to $20,000.

Bank loans will be paid back from the operating profits of the business over the next three years.

SECTION I

Description of the Business

Marketing, Location, and Management

How well do you know your business? You need to prove it with words and numbers. By the time your reader finishes reading your Business Plan, you should have an ally on your side. To give you examples to follow, we provide key sections from the Business Plan for The Entrepreneurs' Software Training Center, a business that is seeking financing for remodeling and equipment expenses. Regardless of whether your business is ongoing or just starting up, the goals of Section I and II are the same: to demonstrate that you know your business and you are a winner.

The Service We Provide

Review how The Entrepreneurs' Software Training Center tackled this part. The Center is likely to receive its funding because the writer of the plan proves that his business is a winning concern. The writer has:

ACTION STEP 64

DESCRIBE YOUR PRODUCT OR SERVICE

Excite your reader about your business. Excitement is contagious. If you can get your reader going, there's a good chance you'll be offered money. Investors love hot ideas.

If this is a start-up, explain your product or service fully. What makes it unique? What industry is it in? Where does the industry fit in the big picture?

Mention numbers wherever you can. Percentages and dollar amounts are more meaningful than words like *lots* and *many*.

If this is an ongoing business, your records of sales, costs, and profit and loss will substantiate your need for money.

Keep the words going and the keyboard smoking. You need to convince the reader to keep reading.

INCREDIBLE RESOURCE

FREE ONLINE SMALL BUSINESS AND INTERNET COURSES

The following free online courses are offered at **www.sba.gov/classroom/courses.html**:

- The Business Plan
- How to Start a Small Business
- Self Assessment
- Building Your Business
- Business Mentoring
- How to Raise Capital for Small Business
- What is an IPO and is it Right for Your Small Business?
- Small Business Opportunities in Federal Procurement

In addition, the SBA and Cisco have entered into cosponsorship of the following eCommerce courses:

- Internet Economy
- Internet Basics
- E-Commerce Basics
- E-Business Basics
- Web Marketing

- Let the facts speak for themselves.
- Supported all claims with numbers.
- Avoided hard-sell tactics.
- Refused to puff the product.

The writer does a terrific selling job. Now it's your turn. Complete Action Step 64.

THE SERVICE WE PROVIDE

The Entrepreneurs' Software Training Center is an entrepreneurial software training school and hub in Oak Ridge, Tennessee, near the rapidly growing area of West Knoxville. The vast number of scientists and engineers in the area make it ripe for entrepreneurial activity.

We train entrepreneurs on computer software, which increases their productivity. Because of their power, these programs are complex; training is desirable to get the maximum value out of the software as quickly as possible..

Students are drawn to our teaching method because it gives them hands-on experience and because it's fast. Our entrepreneurs are busy, and a student can upgrade a given software skill by 50 percent in four hours. Slow learners are guaranteed a second try, and a third, at no cost.

Most of our courses can be completed in either four hours or one day. In contrast, the average college course (which emphasizes concepts, rather than hands-on experience) takes 12 to 18 weeks. Our price is $99 for most four-hour courses, which is about 10 percent lower than our competitors' offerings. All of our competitors' classes are one or two day offerings and none focus specifically on an entrepreneur's needs. Our customers are very computer savvy. Unlike the students at many of our competitors, our students only require software training, not computer training. In addition, our entrepreneurs are usually unable to sit for more than a four-hour stretch because they have business to attend to.

The Entrepreneurs' Software Training Center's courses are able to teach concepts and techniques more quickly than traditional methods through the use of a sophisticated electronic teaching system.

As a service business we sell seats, skills, and information. We constantly survey our current customers for additional classes they would like to see offered.

We are open Monday through Thursday from 8 A.M. to 10 P.M. and Saturdays from 8 A.M. to 5 P.M. This allows us to offer single-day, eight-hour courses, and short four-hour evening courses, thus maximizing the use of our facility. Seminars and guest speakers will

ACTION STEP 65

DESCRIBE THE MARKET AND THE TARGET CUSTOMERS

Bring all your marketing research into this section and wow your reader with a picture of your Target Customers just sitting there waiting for your product or service.

Use data from secondary sources to give credibility to the picture you are painting.

Provide any back-up research data in the appendix.

also be offered to our customers throughout the year. Local community colleges cannot meet the demand for weekend courses and suggest our classes to their students.

The Entrepreneurs' Software Training Center is in the business of increasing productivity by providing the following:

- Sales force automation software training.
- Manufacturing software training.
- Inventory control software training.
- Assistance with writing a Business Plan using the most popular software programs.
- Database, word processing, accounting, and presentation software training.
- Web page and Web store design.

The demand for our classes will increase dramatically when we sign training contracts with the leading area computer stores. As a sales promotional tool, we plan to offer free training to several salespeople from each of the major stores. The salespeople in turn will likely refer their customers to us for training. Computer retailers have learned they can sell upgraded systems if they can provide or offer software training. Although one store in our area offers in-house training, the training is generic and students as young as 10 participate in the classes.

They are in the business of selling systems and we are in business of training.

Our equipment is top quality. Our staff combines excellent training skills with attention to people and their needs. We have launched a solid start-up in a heated growth industry, and plan to continue our growth and success.

INDUSTRY OVERVIEW AND TARGET CUSTOMERS

Knowledge is power, especially in the Information Age. The Entrepreneurs' Software Training Center—an information business—capitalized on expert knowledge to define the marketplace. In the same way, if your research is sound, your niche will be evident in your writing.

Use your industry research from the Action Steps in Chapters 2 and 3 to give your reader an overview of the industry. The reader needs to know the size of the market, trends in the marketplace, how the industry is segmented, where the industry is headed, and what specific part of the market you are aiming your product toward. In addition, briefly discuss technological advances that are changing the industry and how you will capitalize on these changes.

Prove to your reader that you understand the market and are meeting a customer need. Discuss market segmentation. Define your Target Customers in great detail. Provide research data to back up your assumptions on demographics, psychographics, market size, and buying patterns. Return to your Action Steps from Chapter 4 to assist you in describing your Target Customers.

The reader should have a clear idea as to how your product or service will be capable of capturing a unique position in the marketplace. An in-depth explanation should be provided in the competition section of your Business Plan.

Action Step 65 gives you a chance to show that you know the industry and your Target Customers. Review what the Business Plan for The Entrepreneurs' Software Training Center says about its industry and Target Customers. Be sure to use secondary sources (documents, tables, quotes) to lend this section credibility.

INDUSTRY OVERVIEW AND TARGET CUSTOMERS

Industry Overview

Today's powerful computers and software are fueling a constant need for upgrading and training on new or updated versions of popular and new software programs. Many entrepreneurs need to learn programs quickly and expect to be productive in a short time.

With the sales flurry of hardware and emphasis on speed, many are being left behind because they don't know how to fully use the software. A computer can be your best friend, but only if you learn how to maximize its capabilities. This makes training people to use computers a booming industry, and The Entrepreneurs' Software Training Center is on the leading edge of a major growth segment.

Target Customers

Geographically, our target area encompasses Knoxville, Oak Ridge, and Harriman. Realistically, most of our customers originate within a 25-mile radius of our location. We are looking ahead to possible future expansion throughout Eastern Tennessee over the next five years. Kingsport and Chattanooga are two areas we are especially interested in exploring.

Anderson County's population is expected to grow an additional 20 percent over the next five years. Our entrepreneurial students are primarily college educated, are ages 25 to 55, and have annual incomes of $40,000 to $90,000. Our area has one of the highest concentrations of PhDs in the United States. Several of the leading scientists and researchers from the Oak Ridge National Laboratory have taken courses at our school and have completed excellent Business Plans and are currently seeking funding. The Tennessee Valley Authority employs a large group of engineers and biological scientists, many of whom are interested in developing their expertise into a profit-making venture. Our research indicates that 50 percent of our Target Customers will be women and 100 percent will have a computer in their own home with primarily broadband Internet access.

Our entrepreneurs, split fairly evenly between manufacturing, service, and retailing businesses, are dreamers first and foremost—our job is to help make their dreams come true as quickly as possible. We have found through our experience that entrepreneurship can be very lonely as others may not be dreaming the same dream. We hope to reduce the loneliness by providing opportunities for our entrepreneurs to gather together and share their dreams.

All sales and marketing efforts are tracked, which aids us in refining our Target Customer profile and focusing our marketing efforts on the strongest and most profitable markets.

Action Step 66

Describe Your Major Competitors

Briefly profile the businesses that compete with you directly. Try to be objective as you assess their operations.

What are their strengths? Weaknesses? What can you learn from them?

After you've described your competitors, indicate how you're going to ace them out of the picture or develop a niche you can own.

Provide back-up data in the appendix.

The Competition

Obviously, if you know who your competitors are and how they fail to meet market needs, you are well on your way to developing your niche. You need to persuade your reader how great your competitive tactics are. Reread Chapter 5 and review your Action Steps.

If your competitive strength derives from patents, copyrights, or trademarks, include information about them in this area. Provide copies of any patents or copyrights received or pending in the Appendix.

How tough do your competitors look? As you read The Entrepreneurs' Software Training Center's assessment of its competition, note that the writer takes a cool, objective look at the competition. He does not belittle them, and certainly does not underestimate them.

The Entrepreneurs' Software Training Center's plan leaves no doubt that management is exploiting a market gap that is ignored by the competition: software training for entrepreneurs.

This is more than a matter of writing skill. Early on, the entrepreneurs who founded The Entrepreneurs' Software Training Center did the right research so they could make decisions ahead of time—just as you were asked to do in the earlier chapters.

How will you handle your competition? Your readers will expect you to provide an honest appraisal of each of your major competitors.

Now you are ready to complete Action Step 66.

THE COMPETITION

While there is considerable computer training available in the Oak Ridge/Knoxville area, we hope to capitalize on the need for *entrepreneurial software training,* which our competitors are not currently providing. On reviewing our competitors, we discovered the

ACTION STEP 67

DESCRIBE YOUR MARKETING STRATEGY

Now that you've profiled your Target Customers and assessed your competition, take time to develop the thrust of your market strategy.

Which techniques will reap the best and most cost-effective response?

Because pricing is such an important consideration, you might start with what your Target Customers see as a good value, and then develop your marketing mix.

Prepare back-up data for the appendix.

major players in the industry have developed specific niches in the marketplace. A brief review of our four major competitors follows:

- **Trayhart Schools.** Our oldest, most entrenched competitor with three locations in East Tennessee. Trayhart conducts primarily six-hour classes on database and word-processing software. Their primary Target Market consists of upgrading secretarial skills for local employees. Classes are offered only during the day, Monday through Friday. Average two day courses cost $500.
- **Big Micro Instruction.** Excellent classroom facilities located in Knoxville, with easy freeway access. All instruction is free if you purchase your hardware from Big Micro; otherwise, courses generally cost around $200 for six- to eight-hour classes. The instructors try hard, but Big Micro is really in the business of pushing hardware. No eCommerce courses are offered. The classes are aimed at the novice user and classes tend to have users as young as 10.
- **Your Micro and You (YMAY).** Developed by professional educators, their local facility in the southern part of Knoxville is 25 miles from our site. The atmosphere of YMAY is excellent. They offer a normal range of classes and one course in using the computer in a small business; each two-day course costs about $375. Their market seems to be divided between adults with a casual interest in computers and children between the ages of 10 and 15. If YMAY chooses to expand their offerings, they could pose a small threat to our school.
- **Max Software Training.** A professional high-tech facility aimed at providing Microsoft, Oracle, and Novell training and certification. Specializes in retraining people to become advanced software technicians. Max has done it right by offering week-long and month-long courses.

Our business is geared to offering $99 courses and to have entrepreneurs proficient on specific business software in a very short time. Most of our competitors' class offerings take two days in contrast to our four-hour and single-day training offerings, and none focus on entrepreneurs.

MARKETING STRATEGY

Now it is time to describe your marketing strategy. Need a reminder? Look back at your work from Chapter 6.

The marketing strategy example from The Entrepreneurs' Software Training Center's Business Plan demonstrates a carefully reasoned approach, and describes conscious marketing policies that will help this small business be competitive. If you were to read a Business Plan in which the writer does not demonstrate this care and deliberation, how much faith would you have in the writer's business abilities?

Note that The Entrepreneurs' Software Training Center uses a three-pronged approach to reaching the public. This business understands the importance of finding a good promotional mix.

The entrepreneurs who own The Entrepreneurs' Software Training Center will stay on top of the changing market picture by:

- Looking to radio and TV exposure.
- Logging calls and gathering information on callers and students to maintain a base of up-to-date information on their Target Market.
- Tracking our customers.

In your Business Plan include the distribution channels, selling methods, public relations, and methods of customer retention. If your firm has plans to sell products or services internationally, discuss those plans in this section. Present a list of potential customers/clients and sales forecasts. Action Step 67 will help you refine your marketing strategy. Continue to focus your marketing strategy on your Target Customers.

MARKETING STRATEGY

We use a wide range of strategies to let our customers know about our class offerings, including mass-media advertising, special promotions, personal selling, and networking. We are in the productivity and information business, and toward that end we are presently developing an Internet site that will provide a community for Knoxville area budding entrepreneurs. A new entrepreneur will be highlighted each week on our site. New class offerings will also be posted. In addition, we are considering posting, on clients' request, Business Plans online for potential angel investors to review.

Networking

Each owner belongs to four professional trade organizations focusing on small business owners within a 20-mile radius. In addition, each owner has joined a local chamber of commerce organization to network. Both owners serve as guest speakers to civic and educational organizations. A discount program will be designed for entrepreneurs in venture-training programs such as SBDCs.

Mass-Media Advertising

We plan to host and sponsor a five-minute show each morning during drive time on the local radio station, KBIC. Our show will be called Tips for Entrepreneurs. The Entrepreneurs' Software Training Center will initially place advertisements in the *Knoxville Business Journal*, *Knoxville Sentinel*, and the *Oak Ridge News* as soon as the second classroom is available.

Personal Selling

Fortunately, our owners have experience and talent in the area of personal selling. Each owner spends five to 15 hours per week talking with potential entrepreneurs. In addition, phone selling is an important aspect of our business. Converting phone queries into sales is a major goal of each and every person answering the phone. Logging all calls and making sure they are followed up on in a timely matter is essential for our success.

Center training programs are being developed for local stores such as Staples and Office Max to offer at a discount to their business customers.

Creative Promotions/Free Ink

We will sponsor a yearly Business Plan competition for the Junior Achievement (JA) chapters in the Oak Ridge/Knoxville area each year. In addition, we will sponsor one Business Plan competition for our clients each year. The prizes will include classes at our center and a small scholarship for the JA winner. We may offer the Business Plan competition in conjunction with Roane State Community College or The University of Tennessee.

Once a month we will have special speakers onsite free for our current and potential customers.

GEOGRAPHICAL FACTORS AND SITE SELECTION/ FACILITY LOCATION

The next part of your Business Plan concerns location, site selection, and physical facilities. You may want to review your work from Chapter 7 now.

If you are planning a retail establishment, this area is critical and should include extensive research data to back up your site-selection decision. Discuss the accessibility and visibility of the site and the demographics and psychographics of the surrounding population. Download graphics from the many online databases showing roads, competition, and potential customers for support data, which should be placed in the Appendix but referenced in the text.

For a retail business to be located in a shopping center or strip center, discuss the retail market mix and how it will help draw customers into your store. Drawings of

ACTION STEP 68

SHOW OFF YOUR LOCATION

The great thing about a location is that it's so *tangible*. A potential lender can visit your site and get a feel for what's going on.

Bankers often visit a client's business site. That's good news for you because now the banker is on your turf.

Clean up the place before your banker arrives.

In this section you want to persuade potential lenders to visit your site. Describe what goes on there. Use photographs, diagrams, and illustrations to make it feel almost like home.

the actual facility and store layout may help your reader visualize the store as well. Use digital photographs to enhance your Business Plan.

If you are planning a manufacturing firm, facility layout and equipment will need to be discussed thoroughly.

You need to paint an attractive picture of your business site and, at the same time, keep your reader interested by inspiring confidence in your choice. Location takes a tremendous amount of analyses. The Entrepreneurs' Software Training Center writer gives himself a subtle pat on the back by describing the lease arrangements and by identifying the need for a second classroom.

Your plan will become very real when you showcase your physical facility. Read how The Entrepreneurs' Software Training Center shows off its location and complete Action Step 68.

OUR FACILITY

The Entrepreneurs' Software Training Center has secured a five-year lease at 47 Dogwood Lane, Oak Ridge, Tennessee. The facility is all on the ground floor and occupies 1,500 square feet. The area, which is zoned for business use, is near a hotbed of high technology and entrepreneurial activity. Within a 10-mile radius of the facility are two computer superstores, one computer furniture store, a Staples, and an Office Max.

The location has easy freeway access, is close to the rapidly growing West Knoxville area, and offers well-lit and abundant parking.

During our lease negotiations, we persuaded the landlord to make extensive improvements to the interior, and to spread the cost out over the five-year term of the lease. The decor—blue carpet, white walls, and gray furniture—gives the effect of a solid, logical, somewhat plush business learning environment.

The building is divided into four areas currently: a reception and lounge area (150 square feet), a director's office (150 square feet), a classroom (600 square feet), and a storage area (600 square feet).

The principals envision the storage area as a future second classroom (see diagram in the Appendix) and are requesting funds to expand into this area.

MANAGEMENT

Management will make or break a small business. You are a member of the management team, and you want this Business Plan to inspire confidence in your team for investors. Writing this section will help you focus on your management team members. If you need a refresher, review your work from Chapter 11. Many plan reviewers read the management section first. They want to have confidence not only in the business idea but also in the team who will take the concept to reality.

Now is the time to discuss the legal form of business you have chosen as well. Include applicable agreements or legal papers dealing with partnerships or corporations in the Appendix..

Read how The Entrepreneurs' Software Training Center introduced its management team. The Center's team demonstrates balance, diversity, experience (some interesting track records), and the will to succeed. Danielle Jackson's experience in training and entrepreneurship combined with Robert Bennett's extensive curriculum development are strong selling points.

Highlight the balance and experience of your team with short résumés. Longer and more detailed résumés should be included in the Appendix.

The reader looks for someone with financial skills, marketing skills, and management and entrepreneurial experience. In addition, many readers will focus on the teams' people skills.

The Entrepreneurs' Software Training Center was wise to include short résumés of the directors. In this case the background of the directors enhances the balance of the team. All have admirable depth in their business careers, sharing a combined 45 years of experience in the corporate world.

The listing of the legal counsel, accounting firm, insurance broker, and advertising agency also adds to the impression of solid business practices. We have referred to these people as the taxi squad, but in a Business Plan, the language is more formal.

Nothing is more important than the people who will make your business successful. Present their pedigrees, and focus on their track records and accomplishments as you complete Action Step 69.

For a start-up business, you are peering into the future with confidence—doing informal job analyses for key employees who will help you to succeed. For an ongoing business, you need to list your present employees and anticipate your future personnel needs. If you currently employ five people but want to indicate growth, try projecting how many jobs you will be creating in the next three years.

When you start thinking about tasks and people to do them, review your work from Chapter 11. Preparing this part of your plan is important because it gives you one more chance to analyze job functions before your begin interviewing, hiring, and paying benefits—all of which are expensive.

Note that The Entrepreneurs' Software Training Center gives a very brief rundown of the personnel situation. In describing their lean operation the entrepreneurs who run The Entrepreneurs' Software Training Center keep their job descriptions lean as well. They show good sense when they express a commitment to hold down operating costs. Their decision reflects business discipline and foresight. If you were a potential investor in this business, wouldn't you appreciate some tight purse strings and sweat equity?

Every person on your team is important. Action Step 69 will help you to describe the kinds of people you will need and how you will help them to become productive.

ACTION STEP 69

INTRODUCE YOUR MANAGEMENT TEAM AND PERSONNEL

Almost every study you read on small business failure places the blame on management. Use this section to highlight the *positive* qualities of your management team.

Focus on quality first—their experience, accomplishments, education, training, flexibility, imagination, tenacity. Be sure you weave in experience that relates to your particular business.

Remember—dreamers make terrific master-builders, but they make lousy managers. Your banker knows this, and potential investors will sense it. A great team can help you raise money.

The key to a great team is balance. Describe the kinds of people you will need as employees and how they fit into your plan.

What skills will they need? How much will you have to pay them? Will there be a training period? If so, how long? What fringe benefits will you offer? How will you handle overtime?

If you haven't yet written job descriptions, do that now. Job descriptions will help avoid potential problems with the people who work for you although they are not necessary for your Business Plan.

MANAGEMENT AND PERSONNEL

Owners

Danielle Jackson was born in Shaker Heights, Ohio, in 1960. She earned her BS degree in Industrial Engineering at Purdue University. After graduation, she spent eight years in the Marine Corps, where she was a flight instructor and check pilot. While in the service, Jackson completed her MBA at the University of California in Irvine.

Following military service, Jackson was employed as a pilot for United Airlines for five years. Wanting a change, she purchased a firm exporting software and sold it four years later for $1 million. Serving on regional training committees and as a Director of a local Small Business Development Center, she recognized a need for a center for entrepreneurial support and training focused on software training.

Robert Bennett was born in Dallas, Texas, in 1965. He has a BS degree in Information Science from the University of Oklahoma. After graduation, he worked for Proctor and Gamble for several years. For eight years he worked developing curriculum and training materials and presented classes for Microsoft, Quest, and Oracle. For the past two years, he developed specialized small business programs for Microsoft. His vast exposure to entrepreneurs and their psyche will be an invaluable asset to The Entrepreneurs' Software Training Center.

Directors

Cheryl Hughes Smith, born in Corpus Christi, Texas, has an MBA from Harvard and a law degree from the University of Texas at Austin. Ms. Smith is a partner in Smith, Jones, and Schultz, a Knoxville law firm. She is the author of numerous articles in the field of small business planning and taxes.

Phil Carpenter was born in Duluth, Minn332esota, in 1963. He graduated from Purdue University with a BS in Management and a minor in Operations Management.

Mr. Carpenter then worked for one of the big-six accounting firms for five years before returning to Indiana University for his MBA. His research projects during his Master's program focused on small business ventures. Mr. Carpenter is currently Professor of Business at Roane State Community College, a general partner in two businesses, and a small-
business consultant. He has written and lectured widely in the area of small business.

Other Available Resources

The Entrepreneurs' Software Training Center has retained the legal firm of Farney and Shields and the accounting firm of Hancock and Associates. Our insurance broker is Sharon Mandel of Fireman's Fund. Our advertising agency is Friend and Associates.

Personnel

During our first six months of operations, we only had one full-time employee, but we have found another employee is necessary for our expansion to become a reality and to serve our customers properly. Most of the classes will be taught by one of the owners. Additional instructors will be hired on a contract basis. We need to run a lean operation and the owners are willing to put in sweat equity.

Exit Strategy

As discussed earlier many readers of your plan will be interested in your exit strategy. The more money involved the more likely they will want to know your particular plans. The Entrepreneurs' Software Training Center founders plan on continuing for at least five years in their business.

EXIT STRATEGY

After we build out our Oak Ridge location, we hope to build two additional locations in East Tennessee over the next five years. On successful completion and when we are able to show a strong profit in each center, we plan to sell all three training facilities, either to the managers running the individual centers or to one entrepreneur wishing to run a small chain of centers.

Section II

Financial Section

Good Numbers

The financial section is the heart of your Business Plan. It is aimed at lenders—bankers, credit managers, venture capitalists, vendors, SBICs, commercial credit lenders—people who think and dream in numbers. Lenders are professional skeptics by trade; they will not be swayed by the enthusiasm of your writing in Section I. Therefore your job is to make your numbers do the talking. This is easier than you may believe.

In Chapter 8 you projected cash flow and income. You have tested your numbers on real lenders in the real world. If you have not already done so, you need to organize your numbers into standard instruments:

1. Pro forma income statements
2. Balance sheet

Community Resource

School Ties Heavenly for Angel Investors

By Donna Howell

When Harvard University graduate Rebecca Bass needed funding for her high-tech start-up, she turned to some old-school ties—and the Internet.

Bass found financial backing for her Atlanta-based expense management software firm Galileo Development Systems LLC through UniversityAngels.com—a new service that pairs entrepreneurs and investors with $25,000 to $250,000 to put up.

Grew out of Reunion

"I've been on it from the first rumor," Bass said of the funding program. "I heard through the proverbial grapevine that someone was getting together the 'Crimson Angels.'"

That "someone" was Rick Sasner and three Harvard Business School chums—James Marcus, Charles Sanford, and Todd Klein.

The four originated University Angels Inc. at a reunion of the class of 1994, during which they marveled how fast high-tech firms were popping up. "We were lamenting that so much is happening in the world, sometimes you feel it's evolving around you," Sasner said.

To help fellow alumni ride the business bandwagon, Sasner and friends took to the Internet. Their idea: to provide an online place for start-ups to network with investors, with both from top schools.

School Spirit

The White Plains, N.Y. firm launched its Crimson Angels site—dedicated to Harvard and named for the school's color—at the beginning of the year.

"A huge level of entrepreneurs and investing" already exists among the business school's 60,000 alumni, Sasner said. So it made sense to bring it online.

In April University Angels launched 24 more sites, ranging from BeaverAngels.com for the California Institute of Technology to WolverineAngels.com for the University of Michigan. It's shooting for 100 sites by year's end.

Going online helped software developer Bass find funding quickly. With limited competition for her company's product, she said she needed to "get funded and get out now."

"Speed to market is important," Bass said. "In the Internet world it's life or death."

Sasner wanted to make the matchmaking process easy for entrepreneurs such as Bass.

"She registered at the site," he said. "She never had to go on a plane to meet someone."

At UniversityAngels.com students and alumni post information about their businesses. Prospective angel investors sign up, browse, and back a start-up they like—or pool their resources toward one.

University Angels gets a cut, usually about four percent of the proceeds, plus a stake in the firm to the tune of 10 percent equity raised.

700 Investors

Among those who have decided to back Bass' company is angel investor and longtime investment banker Robert Hanson.

"I happen to be sitting in Wyoming," he says, and "would never have heard of Rebecca's business" without the Internet.

Hanson is a graduate of Yale University who found out about University Angels through an alumni magazine advertisement. The Cody, Wyoming, man is now scouting out other deals online.

"What it's done is made efficient what in the past was an inefficient process. Angel investing heretofore was pretty much a word of mouth idea," he said.

About 700 investors have signed up with the service. To qualify, a prospective backer must have net worth of $1 million or more, or a minimum $200,000 in annual income.

Around 400 Business Plans seeking funding have been put online.

"I would have thought we'd have more from students, but 70 percent are from alumni," Sasner says. "They're people who graduated in the 1970s and have upward of 20 years of industry experience."

Nationwide, more than 250,000 individual investors provided more than $20 billion in funding for 30,000 companies last year, the U.S. Small Business Administration says.

Sasner hopes school ties could make start-up investing attractive to those who haven't considered it.

"There are roughly 8 (million) to 10 million millionaires who would qualify to be investors, and about three percent have made early-stage investments before," Sasner said. "Why not more?"

Some lack access to deals; others are uncomfortable funding someone's proposal without knowing more about the person and the opportunity.

School affiliations lend credibility and a common ground for both investors and start-ups. Without an Internet forum like this, Sasner says, they would have a hard time finding each other.

MORE THAN ALUMS

Knowing a Business Plan came from students or alumni of a respected school "does give me some comfort," says angel investor Robert Hanson.

"The investors I've had privilege to talk with from University Angels have been very sophisticated," Bass said. Among them is "a person who's currently employed by Goldman Sachs at a high level," who is also a retired managing partner from a Big Five accounting firm.

"Through this net of wealthy alumni from top schools, we're getting people from companies all over the country in top positions," Sasner said. To an entrepreneur who needs business advice, that, he says, is "someone I'd like to be able to phone."

SOURCE: Donna Howell, "School Ties Heavenly for Angel Investors," *Investors Business Daily*, May 10, 2001.

Examples from The Entrepreneurs' Software Training Center will serve as models for you; adapt them to suit your business type.

The idea is to know where every dime is going. You need to show when you will make a profit and appear neat, orderly, in control, and conservative. You will know you have succeeded when a skeptical lender looks up from your Business Plan and says, "You know, these numbers look good."

Good Notes

One way to spot a professional lender is to hand over your Business Plan and watch to see which sections he or she reads first. Most lenders first study the notes that accompany income and cash-flow projections. Knowing this allows you to be forewarned. Use these notes to tell potential lenders how you generated your numbers (for example, "Advertising is projected at five percent of sales") and to explain specific entries (for example, "Leased Equipment—monthly lease costs on IBM microcomputers"). Make these notes easy to read, with headings that start your readers off in the upper-left-hand corner and march them down the page, step by step, to the bottom line. Some projections use tiny footnotes, on the same page. We recommend *large* notes on a separate page with a heading "Notes." Notes are important, so they should be big.

Creating your Business Plan takes a lot of time. It is only natural for you to hope that lenders will read it, become enthusiastic, and ask questions. The notes to your plan can help you accomplish that, even if you have not as yet started up and the numbers are projections into the future.

If your business has been going for some time, a detailed financial history should be included. For those seeking funding, the financial statements will be significant. You need to describe which type of funding you are seeking and specific details on how that funding will be used and repaid. Completing your financial statements requires business finance and accounting knowledge.

Proforma Income/Cash Flow Statement

Your next task is to put together your pro forma income statement (also called a "profit and loss" statement). With the information you have gathered so far, it should not be too difficult. In fact, it will be enjoyable if the numbers look good. If they don't, reconsider before you commit.

Review The Entrepreneurs' Software Training Center's pro forma income/cash flow statement and the careful documentation of each item. Action Step 70 will help you project your own monthly profits and losses for 12 months. You should also include a pro forma income statement for the next two to five years for your business. The Entrepreneurs' Software Training Center's pro forma income/cash flow statement will help you in developing your statements.

Action Step 70

Project Your Income/Cash Flow Statement(s)

What you're driving at here is *net profit*—what's left in the kitty after expenses—for each month and for the year.

First, figure your *sales*. The first big bite out of that figure is the *cost of goods sold*. (In a service business the big cost is labor.) Subtracting that gives you a figure called *gross margin*.

Now add up all your *expenses* (rent, utilities, insurance, etc.), and subtract them from gross margin. This gives you your *net profit before taxes*. (Businesses pay taxes in quarterly installments.)

Subtract taxes.

There's your net profit.

In the Center's example in the text, the Income Statement and Cash Flow Statement have been combined as one. In many instances two separate statements will be used. Either format is usually acceptable.

Global Village

INTERNATIONAL SMALL BUSINESS CONSORTIUM

Honored by Microsoft as a "Technology Success Story," the International Small Business Consortium (ISBC), **www.isbc.com**, provides support, information, and advice on international marketing, cyberspace law, and using the Internet for business. ISBC's goal is to help small businesses make international connections.

The website has several excellent moderated discussion groups. In addition, a database of international business opportunities and contacts is available for searching. ISBC focuses on international community building.

If you want to develop contacts and find a community of international business entrepreneurs, ISBC will meet your needs. ISBC reduces the barriers for new entrepreneurs and opens the doors to almost six billion customers.

Balance Sheet

Professional lenders look at your balance sheet (also called a "statement of financial position") to analyze the state of your finances at a given point in time. They are looking at things like liquidity (how easily your assets can be converted into cash) and capital structure (what sources of financing have been used, how much was borrowed, and so on). Professional lenders use such factors to evaluate your ability to manage your business.

The Entrepreneurs' Software Training Center (Table 15.2) did not provide notes to its balance sheets because in their case no notes were needed. In conjunction with the income statement in the body of the text and cash flow projections in the appendix, all the entries in the balance sheet will make sense to professional readers. Under some circumstances, you would want to note unusual features of a balance sheet for an actual fiscal year, but in most cases—and in most projections—this won't be necessary. Complete Action Step 71 to help you prepare and include a balance sheet in your Business Plan.

TABLE 15.1
Entrepreneurs' Software Proforma Income Statement

	Total	1st Month	2nd	3rd	4th	5th
Sales Revenue	$607,329.22	$46,570.00	$47,268.55	$47,977.58	$48,697.24	$49,427.70
Expenses						
1. Advertising - 7%	$42,513.05	$3,259.90	$3,308.80	$3,358.43	$3,408.81	$3,459.94
2. Licenses/fees - 6%	$36,439.75	$2,794.20	$2,836.11	$2,878.65	$2,921.83	$2,965.66
3. Payroll Taxes - 10%	$4,159.20	$346.60	$346.60	$346.60	$346.60	$346.60
4. Salaries	$38,126.00	$3,466.00	$3,466.00	$3,466.00	$3,466.00	$3,466.00
5. Bank Charges - 0.4%	$18,219.88	$1,397.10	$1,418.06	$1,439.33	$1,460.92	$1,482.83
6. Dues and Subscriptions	$600.00	$50.00	$50.00	$50.00	$50.00	$50.00
7. Insurance	$18,000.00	$1,500.00	$1,500.00	$1,500.00	$1,500.00	$1,500.00
8. Janitorial - 0.7%	$4,251.30	$325.99	$330.88	$335.84	$340.88	$345.99
9. Office Supplies - 3.5%	$21,256.52	$1,629.95	$1,654.40	$1,679.22	$1,704.40	$1,729.97
10. Phone/Cable - 3%	$18,219.88	$1,397.10	$1,418.06	$1,439.33	$1,460.92	$1,482.83
11. Professional Fees	$12,000.00	$1,000.00	$1,000.00	$1,000.00	$1,000.00	$1,000.00
12. Rent	$46,680.00	$3,890.00	$3,890.00	$3,890.00	$3,890.00	$3,890.00
13. Repairs & Maint. - 3%	$18,219.88	$1,397.10	$1,418.06	$1,439.33	$1,460.92	$1,482.83
14. Travel & Entertain -1%	$6,073.29	$465.70	$472.69	$479.78	$486.97	$494.28
15. Interest - 9%	$5,400.00	$450.00	$450.00	$450.00	$450.00	$450.00
16. Utilities - 3.0%	$18,219.88	$1,397.10	$1,418.06	$1,439.33	$1,460.92	$1,482.83
17. Misc. Expense - 3.0%	$6,443.93	$1,397.10	$425.42	$431.80	$438.28	$444.85
18. Lease Equipment	$24,000.00	$2,000.00	$2,000.00	$2,000.00	$2,000.00	$2,000.00
19. Contract Instructors (3)	$96,567.05	$7,200.00	$7,344.00	$7,490.88	$7,640.70	$7,793.51
20. Depreciation	$12,000.00	$1,000.00	$1,000.00	$1,000.00	$1,000.00	$1,000.00
Total Expenses	$450,855.60	$36,363.84	$35,747.12	$36,114.51	$36,488.14	$36,868.13
Net Income Before Taxes	$156,473.61	$10,206.16	$11,521.43	$11,863.07	$12,209.10	$12,559.57

NOTES FOR PROFORMA INCOME STATEMENT

Sales Revenue. The seventh month we expect to sell 470 workshops to individuals at $99 each. Sales grow at 1.5% each month.
Advertising. Based on 7% of sales.
Licenses/fees. Software license fees estimated at 6% of sales.
Payroll Taxes. 10% of salaries.
Salaries. 2 full-time secretarial employees earning $9 per hour.
Bank Charges. 75% of sales will be charged to credit cards at a cost of 4% of sales.
Dues and Subscriptions. Subscriptions for owners and classrooms.
Insurance. Quote provided by our insurance broker, Sharon Mandel of Fireman's Fund.
Janitorial. Cleaning will be provided by janitorial service for less than the normal rate as the owner has traded janitorial services for software training.
Office Supplies. 3.5% of sales.

6th	7th	8th	9th	10th	11th	12th
$50,169.12	$50,921.65	$51,685.48	$52,460.76	$53,247.67	$54,046.39	$54,857.08
$3,511.84	$3,564.52	$3,617.98	$3,672.25	$3,727.34	$3,783.25	$3,840.00
$3,010.15	$3,055.30	$3,101.13	$3,147.65	$3,194.86	$3,242.78	$3,291.42
$346.60	$346.60	$346.60	$346.60	$346.60	$346.60	$346.60
$3,466.00	$3,466.00	$3,466.00	$3,466.00	$3,466.00	$3,466.00	$3,466.00
$1,505.07	$1,527.65	$1,550.56	$1,573.82	$1,597.43	$1,621.39	$1,645.71
$50.00	$50.00	$50.00	$50.00	$50.00	$50.00	$50.00
$1,500.00	$1,500.00	$1,500.00	$1,500.00	$1,500.00	$1,500.00	$1,500.00
$351.18	$356.45	$361.80	$367.23	$372.73	$378.32	$384.00
$1,755.92	$1,782.26	$1,808.99	$1,836.13	$1,863.67	$1,891.62	$1,920.00
$1,505.07	$1,527.65	$1,550.56	$1,573.82	$1,597.43	$1,621.39	$1,645.71
$1,000.00	$1,000.00	$1,000.00	$1,000.00	$1,000.00	$1,000.00	$1,000.00
$3,890.00	$3,890.00	$3,890.00	$3,890.00	$3,890.00	$3,890.00	$3,890.00
$1,505.07	$1,527.65	$1,550.56	$1,573.82	$1,597.43	$1,621.39	$1,645.71
$501.69	$509.22	$516.85	$524.61	$532.48	$540.46	$548.57
$450.00	$450.00	$450.00	$450.00	$450.00	$450.00	$450.00
$1,505.07	$1,527.65	$1,550.56	$1,573.82	$1,597.43	$1,621.39	$1,645.71
$451.52	$458.29	$465.17	$472.15	$479.23	$486.42	$493.71
$2,000.00	$2,000.00	$2,000.00	$2,000.00	$2,000.00	$2,000.00	$2,000.00
$7,949.38	$8,108.37	$8,270.54	$8,435.95	$8,604.67	$8,776.76	$8,952.30
$1,000.00	$1,000.00	$1,000.00	$1,000.00	$1,000.00	$1,000.00	$1,000.00
$37,254.58	$37,647.60	$38,047.32	$38,453.84	$38,867.29	$39,287.79	$39,715.45
$12,914.54	$13,274.05	$13,638.16	$14,006.92	$14,380.38	$14,758.60	$15,141.63

Professional Fees. Estimates received from our attorneys, Farney and Shields, and our accounting firm of Hancock and Assoc.
Rent. Based on $2.57 per square foot.
Repairs and Maintenance. 3% of sales.
Travel and Entertainment. 1% of sales and includes dues for professional and service organizations.
Utilities. 3% of sales. Based on discussions with utility providers and past experience.
Misc. Indirect Expense. 3% of sales.
Lease Equipment. Set monthly rate estimate provided by vendors.
Contract Instructors. Three instructors each working 60 hours per month at $40 per hour.
Interest. 9% per year on $60,000; 12 payments per year.
Depreciation. Depreciation charges estimated by accountant

ACTION STEP 71

COMPLETE YOUR BALANCE SHEET

A balance sheet is a snapshot in time of your financial position.

1. Add up your assets. For convenience, divide these into *current* (cash, notes receivable, etc.), *fixed* (land, equipment, buildings, etc.), and *other* (intangibles like patents, royalty deals, copyrights, goodwill, contracts for exclusive use, and so on). You'll need to depreciate fixed assets that wear out. As value, show the net of cost minus the accumulated depreciation.
2. Add up your liabilities. For convenience, divide these into *current* (accounts payable, notes payable, accrued expenses, interest on loans, etc.), and *long-term* (trust deeds, bank loans, equipment loans, balloons, etc.).
3. Subtract the smaller figure from the larger one.

You now have a picture of your net worth. Are you in the red or in the black?

TABLE 15.2
The Entrepreneurs' Software Training Center

Balance Sheet

	ACTUAL (After first 6 months)
Current Assets	
Cash	$3,970
Books/Materials	2,500
Total Current Assets	$6,470
Leasehold Improve	91,000
Furniture	15,100
Equipment	40,600
Total Fixed Assets	$146,700
Other Assets	
License	25,000
TOTAL ASSETS	$178,170
Debt and Equity	
Current Debt	
Accounts Payable	7,060
Accrued Wages	2,500
Loan Payment	
Total Current Debt	$9,560
Long Term Debt	
Bank Loan	0
TOTAL DEBT	$9,560
Equity:	
Owners Net Worth	$168,610
TOTAL DEBT & EQUITY	$178,170

EPILOGUE

Act on What You Know

Well, do you feel like you are ready? You are. You have thoroughly researched your product or service, your market and Target Customers, your competition, marketing strategy, and location. You have discovered how to prepare for surprises you cannot afford; how to handle numbers; how to pursue financing; when and why you should incorporate; how to build a winning team; and whether you should buy, franchise, or start on your own. And you have written it all up in a beautiful showcase: your winning Business Plan.

Before you take off running, we want to give you one more tool we believe every entrepreneur should have—a tool to help you put your Business Plan to work. It is called PERT—Program Evaluation and Review Technique—and is often used to establish schedules for large projects. PERT was pioneered in military research and development as an aid for identifying activities and their optimal sequence and then monitoring progress. The aerospace industry, the construction industry, and other big businesses that must plan complicated projects use PERT charts, and so can you.

Using a PERT chart (Table 15.3) is advisable if you feel overwhelmed by the tasks of starting up and don't know where to begin. If you are a person who sometimes tries to do everything at once, PERT will help you focus your energy on the right job at the right time. A sample PERT chart is provided. Yours will need to be bigger and more detailed. You can use days, weeks, or months to plot the tasks ahead.

Action Step 72 is the last Action Step for Chapter 15. It is the end, yes, but also the beginning.

TABLE 15.3
Sample PERT Chart

Task	Week 1	2	3	4	5	6
Befriend banker	X	X	X	X	X	X
Order letterhead		X				
Select site	X					
Get fictional name statement	X					
Bulk mail permit			X			
Ad agency	X					
Lunch, lawyer			X			
Appointment, accountant				X		
Vendor statement					X	
Utilities deposits					X	
Review promotional material					X	
Survey phone system			X	X	X	
Order phone system						X
Open house						X

ACTION STEP 72

CONSTRUCTING A PERT CHART

Rehearsal is over. Now it's time to step onto the stage and get the drama under way. One way to shift from planning into action is to develop your own personal PERT chart. A PERT chart will serve as a script for you. It also will tell you and the other members of your team how long certain jobs should take.

List the tasks you need to accomplish—befriending a banker, filing a fictitious name statement, taking a lawyer to lunch, ordering business letterhead, selecting a site, contacting vendors, and so on—and set your deadlines.

As you already know, a successful package is made up of many, many details. If you take the details one at a time, you'll get there without being overwhelmed. The sample PERT chart in Table 15.3 can guide you.

All our best wishes go with you as you embark on your great adventure. We hope that this book and its Action Steps have convinced you that you can achieve success—whatever it means to *you*—and have *fun* at the same time. Good luck! Work smart, and enjoy your adventure with passion!

SUMMARY

It has been a long haul, and you are now ready to create your Business Plan—a portable showcase for your business. When you visit vendors, bankers, and potential lenders you can take along a copy of your Business Plan to speak for you, to demonstrate to all that you have a blueprint for success.

Begin writing by starting with the material you feel most comfortable with. Once you have completed one portion of the plan, the other parts will fall into place more easily. Fortunately, your work in earlier chapters has prepared you for each section.

Make sure your Business Plan has answered the following questions:

- What is your mission?
- How are you going to market your product or service?
- Who is going to purchase your product or service?
- How will you reach your Target Customers?
- What makes your firm unique?
- How will you support the financial needs of your growing firm?

After you have completed the plan, rewrite your executive summary, highlighting the most relevant information and data for your readers. Personalize each cover letter. Go for it!

THINK POINTS FOR SUCCESS

- The executive summary should read like advertising copy. Keep revising it until it is tight and convincing.
- Section I should generate enthusiasm for your business.
- Section II should substantiate the enthusiasm with numbers.
- Be sure to use footnotes sufficient to explain the numbers in your financial statements.
- Do not inflate numbers to impress.
- Use your Business Plan as a road map to success.
- Your Business Plan is a working, living document.

KEY POINTS FROM ANOTHER VIEW

35 Biz Planning Tips—Best Practices for Practical Success

By Richard Benner

1. Clearly define your business idea and be able to succinctly articulate it. Know your mission.
2. Develop a personal financial evaluation. Determine your net worth and your annual, personal cash flow needs.
3. Examine your motives. Make sure that you have a passion for owning a business and for this particular business.
4. Be willing to commit to the hours, discipline, continuous learning, and the frustrations of owning your own business.
5. Understand that your primary responsibility is the proper use of capital and that you are in business to make a profit.
6. Test the economics of your product or service. Make sure that it is profitable and that the gross profit percent is in line with that of the industry.
7. Determine who your customers are, and what their wants or needs are. Know how your product or service satisfies their wants or needs.
8. Know how customers will buy from you. Plan how you will make your product or service available to them—wholesale, retail, direct, or Internet.
9. Know how you will finance your business. Visit lenders (banks) prior to seeking financing to gather information. Ask your lenders what they will want to see before you apply for a loan.
10. Conduct a competitive analysis in your market, including products, prices, promotions, advertising, distribution, quality, and service, and be aware of the outside influences that effect your business.
11. Test the reality of your business—know why it will work and how you will make it work. Think your business through step by step.
12. Write a Business Plan with a complete financial and marketing plan.
13. Determine your primary business unit—units sold, customers sold, average order, hours billed, etc. Know what drives your business.
14. Develop meaningful sales forecasts in terms of basic business units. Predict weekly sales for the first few months and monthly sales for the first year. Consider possible scenarios such as a 10 percent rise or fall in sales.
15. Develop realistic financial forecasts for income statements, cash flow, and balance sheets for three years. Forecast monthly for the first year.
16. Establish an annual operating plan. Review it and update it monthly with appropriate employees.
17. Carefully select your place of business. Review guidelines for locations on type of business, customer convenience, traffic, safety, etc.
18. Develop profiles for your products or services, customers, and markets.
19. Conserve capital. Do not commit cash or capital until necessary. Don't buy services before you need them. Lease instead of buy when possible.
20. Carefully determine your inventory needs. Don't overstock or get oversold by eager vendors.
21. Know and use your suppliers, including your banker. They can be a great source of training, information, and support.
22. Select the proper business structure for your business. Consider taxes, liability, capital needs, costs, entry, and exit. Know the benefits and drawbacks of your legal structure.
23. Seek help from other small businesses, vendors, professionals, government agencies, employees, trade associations, and trade shows. Be alert, ask questions, and visit your local SCORE office!
24. Advertising is expensive so know why you are advertising and what you want to accomplish. Evaluate your advertising carefully and measure its effectiveness.
25. Develop appropriate sales promotion tools such as flyers, brochures, and signs. Carefully review each item for it's effectiveness and evaluate what these tools say about your business.
26. Establish an accurate, timely, and meaningful accounting and financial system to enable proper management of the business.
27. Maintain strict separation of personal and business accounts.
28. Employees are your most important assets, so hire the best, provide training and growth opportunities, and recognize good performance.
29. Examine your own skills carefully. Know your strengths and weaknesses and hire to compliment your skills, not duplicate.
30. Have a meaningful, concise, realistic job description for each employee. Make sure you review it with the employee and that it is understood.
31. Be sure employees know what is expected of them. Establish high standards of performance and morality but be realistic and practical and communicate effectively.
32. Instill and practice the concept of continuous quality improvement and quality customer service as a way of life in your business.
33. Study your business and stay abreast of what's going on in your industry. Read newspapers, periodicals, trade journals, etc.

34. Get involved in your community. Join the Chamber of Commerce, business organizations, service clubs, and charities. Network yourself and keep your antennae up.
35. Allow three to four hours every week for thinking and planning. Do not allow anything to interfere with this time. You run the business. Don't let it run you.

Provided by SCORE Business Counselor Richard Benner. Benner of Kansas City, Missouri, is an experienced strategic and business manager.

SOURCE: **www.score.org/35ann/success.html** (accessed August 13, 2001).

APPENDIX A
Fast-Start Business Plan

The Fast-Start Plan lets you get going *now*! It's great if you've been in business before and know the footwork of entrepreneurship. With the Fast-Start Plan, you're using the business as a probe into the marketplace. You can start quickly because you have an instinct for beating out the competition. You have a sense of the market. You have a good feel of the business you are starting.

The Fast-Start Plan is *not* a substitute for preparing a full-fledged plan. Use the Fast-Start Plan for a specific venture that is easy to start, carrying minimal risk. Also use it for a business that's breaking new ground, where there is little data available and speed to the market is imperative.

In addition, to check out a business idea quickly one can prepare a Fast-Start Business Plan and then complete a full-fledged plan if the Fast-Start Plan looks promising. Read through the "Yes, We Do Windows" Business Plan at the end of Appendix A before you start writing your Fast-Start Plan.

But first you need to make sure the Fast-Start Plan is the right start for you. If you're going it alone, with money you can afford to lose ($1,000; $5,000; $10,000; $100,000), and if the loss of that money won't jeopardize your loved ones and make wolves howl at your door, use the Fast-Start Plan.

If other people are involved—investors, bankers, advisors, company officers—then return to Chapter 15 and write a comprehensive plan.

The comprehensive plan gives you a blueprint to follow month by month through the first year. It tracks your business through seasonal ups and downs. It allows for contingencies.

Gather up all the information from your past action steps. For assistance use one of the online Business Plan templates discussed in Chapter 15 or develop the Fast-Start Plan on your own.

QUICK CHECKLIST

Here's a quick checklist for implementing the Fast-Start Plan:

1. Can you afford to lose your dollar investment? How much money can you afford to lose at the slots in Reno or Las Vegas or Atlantic City? Can you lose $100? $500? $1,000? $25,000? more? What's your deductible on your car insurance, your boat insurance, or your major medical insurance? Write down the amount you can afford to lose. If you have excess money to speculate with, then the Fast-Start Plan may be for you.
2. How easy is it to enter this business? Is it easy to talk to other owners? Are role models in great abundance? Do the prospective customers have a clear understanding of the goods and services provided? Examples of businesses with wide doors include window washing, auto detailing, landscape maintenance, vacation pet-sitting, and house-sitting.
3. Can you start this business on a part-time basis? Starting part-time decreases your risk. You have a chance to prove the business. You see how much you really like it. You keep a running tally of customer responses. You keep your other job and the income it provides.
4. How tough is it to gather needed data to formulate a Fast-Start Business Plan? In breaking new ground, be careful. In a venture like this the market is not clearly defined. There are very few competitors. Pricing is not clear. You must make certain you've got a market out there.
5. Can you start using only your own funds? Bill Gates, the founder of Microsoft, could use the Fast-Start Plan for a business start-up costing tens of millions. A single parent of two with rent and a car loan to pay can afford much less. Be honest with yourself. Be honest with your family.

Structuring Your Plan

Use these questions and all of the Actions Steps you have completed to structure your Fast-Start Plan:

How do you describe your business?
What business are you really in?
Who is your competition and how are they doing?
What is your pricing strategy?
Who is your Target Customer?
Why should Target Customers buy from you?
How will you advertise?
What are your start-up costs?
What are your sales goals for the first three months?
What are your operating expenses for the first three months?
If you crash and burn, what can you salvage for cash?
What have you forgotten?

A Great Dream Can Equal Great Business

It's night. The family's gone to bed. The house is quiet. The pets are snoozing. A business dream separates your business from everyone else.

You're proud of being in business. You care. The customer cares that you care. Remember people like to do business with people who care about what they're doing. Such people take pride in a job well done and it shows.

Your dream gives you a jump-start. Now you need to add in the details.

Who Are Your Competitors?

This is a good time to try out your new eyes. How much can you learn from your competitors? How do you find them?

If you're hunting for retailers or restaurant owners, hop in your car and drive around. But how do you find a home-based word-processing business? How do you find a home-based cleaning service? How do you find a mobile auto detailer?

You know a business must communicate with potential customers, so tune in your entrepreneurial radar. Check Yellow Pages and area newspapers; look for business cards in copy services, in service stations, in local food stores, and on kiosks.

Once you find your competitors, take a closer look. Were they easy to find? How visible was their advertising? As you study their advertising strategy, what kind of a customer profile can you draw? Are they spending a lot on their advertising? Are they working on a shoestring?

What can you tell from their pricing? Are prices firm? Are they negotiable? Are they high? Low? Competitive? What kind of customer will go for these prices? Who will get shut out? Do your competitors understand the marketplace? Is their pricing structure positioned properly?

Are your competitors zeroed in on a specific Target Customer, or are they using the shotgun approach? Just for practice, profile the Target Customer of your competitors.

Which of your competitors are successful? Can you tell why? Which are just hanging in there? Why? If a business has been operating for some time, there's a good chance the owner's doing something right. What is it? Nose around. What customer benefits do they offer? Fast service? Quality work? Free delivery and pick up? Low prices?

Even the most successful business overlooks something. Find out what they missed. Did they overlook a market segment? Did they get sloppy with their advertising? Is their range of services actually limited? Is their inventory sparse? Thousands of businesses have been built on the weaknesses of competition.

Take the time to chat with the customers of your competitors. Are they satisfied? If not, why not? How do they see the competition? What image does the competition project? How do customers feel about price, quality, and timeliness?

Take the time to chat with competitors outside your area. Is there a gap no one has thought to close?

How Much Should You Charge?

Pricing is key. Don't be misled by thinking you can whisk customers away from established competitors by charging less for the same thing. It didn't work for now-bankrupt department stores. It won't work for you.

Find out what is important to the customers. It's probably time or dependability or quality or convenience. Then learn to see the value of your product or service through your customers' eyes. The question is: "What is the customer's perception of value?"

Profile Your Target Customer

Who will receive the biggest benefit from your business? Who can pay the price? Who can you target? Where do they live? What's their income range? What do they need? What work do they do? Are they married, single, divorced, or retired?

To profile your customers, become a marketplace detective. To practice, study the customers that buy from your competitors.

Do women outnumber men? What's the average age? What cars do they drive? How are the customers dressed? How expensive are their shoes? If you can get inside, check out methods of payment. Do they use cash? Checks? Credit? How expensive are the items they're buying?

Practice trains your new eyes to consider the person as a prospect.

How Do You Make That Customer Connection?

Before you spend a bundle on a TV advertisement, or three months knocking on doors of houses along Golf Course Drive, take some time to put together a message.

What image do you want to project? How do you want the marketplace to receive your product or service? What position do you want to assume among your competitors? What are the key benefits your business will offer customers? How soon do you want to start? How many autos can you detail—or homes can you clean—in one day?

Once you answer these questions, design your business card. Use a logo that offers an insight into your business. If you're starting a word-processing business, use something along the lines of "On Time Quality Service." If you're thinking of house cleaning: "Only Sparkle—Not a Speck of Dust." Always carry lots of business cards. They're inexpensive memory seeds, handy reminders, and often your most cost-effective advertising.

Once your business cards are done, research ways of reaching customers. Do they gather at church, at school, at football games, or at Little League? What do they read, watch, and listen to? Could you reach them best through the Yellow Pages, radio, or billboards? What can you afford? Match that amount with the most effective communications channel.

Stay visible. If your Target Customers gather in groups, try to reach them there. Attend their meetings. Get on their list of speakers. Give a demonstration. Hand out business cards. Offer a freebie.

If you must find your customers one at a time, spend a few hours each day knocking on doors. Telephone prospects. Work your mailing list. If you use mail contacts, be sure you do phone follow-ups.

Join the local chamber of commerce. If you're lucky, your chamber will run a short piece about you, the newcomer, in their newsletter. Stay visible at chamber meetings. Don't get pushy with your business cards, but have them handy.

While you're connecting with customers, don't overlook organizations that might act as your sales force. For example, let's say you've found a school where the parents' group is trying to raise funds to support an athletic endeavor. Put together a flyer for students to take home. In return for each sale from the flyer, your business will donate 10 percent to 15 percent to the fund-raising group. Consider the donation a part of your promotional budget.

What Are Your Start-up Costs?

At your local office supply store, make these purchases: a mileage log, an expense journal, and a folder to hold receipts. You can deduct mileage and expenses related to your business start-up.

List everything that you need to get started. Don't worry if the list would cost a bundle. You're brainstorming at this point. The key here is not to overlook anything. A visit to your competitors will add ideas to your list. An interview with an owner will trigger new items. When you're chatting with businesspeople, ask questions: What kind of computer register do you use? What computer system and software do you have? What's the cost of start-up inventory? When your list is fat, add price tags.

When you start purchasing, check the large discount stores. Also investigate mail-order houses, especially for personal computers. If one company in your area can supply most of your needs, focus on trying to get a package deal and develop a long-term relationship.

On equipment items, save by buying used. Used equipment might be scratched or dented, but you stand to save 50 percent to 90 percent. Check the newspaper classifieds under "Equipment for Sale" or "Office Furniture." Talk with potential suppliers—they usually know someone who's going out of business. You can find good deals from an owner who's folding.

You should also consider leasing your equipment. Leasing costs more in the long run, less when you're getting started. As your business grows, and your leases expire, you can decide whether to replace by buying new or used. Leasing provides you a lot of up-front flexibility.

Divide your start-up list into two columns. Column 1 contains items that are absolutely necessary. Column 2 contains "nice-to-haves."

Check Column 1. Is there anything you can borrow from home, parents, or friends? Scrape to the bottom of the barrel here. Your goal is to cut costs so you'll have cash to run the business.

Charting Your Sales Goals for the First Three Months

How much would you like to sell the first month, the second, and the third? How much can you afford to sell? What is a realistic target for your new business?

Sales goals provide the information you need to forecast your variable expenses—those expenses forced to change in relation to sales volume. If you are selling a product, sales goals will allow you to estimate the cost of goods sold.

Sales goals provide the driving force for you and your team. They help you focus on your target for the month. When the month is finished, compare how you did with your initial sales goals. Did you make it? If not, why not? Did you exceed your goal by 25 percent? Why? What worked well? What didn't? As you evaluate, decide how to improve next month, and how to keep improving.

To chart a reasonable sales goal, focus on three factors:

1. **The weight of your marketing program.** Do you plan a wide-area campaign? Will you start by calling on friends and neighbors, counting on them to spread the word slowly? How much energy are you putting into this? Will you start full-time? Will you keep your job? If you're in school, will you stay enrolled?
2. **The experience of entrepreneurs in businesses like yours who operate in a noncompeting area.** How much effort does Entrepreneur A have to put out to make a $100 sale in his or her area?
3. **The capacity you have to deliver the product or service.** What do you need to make this venture go? If it costs you $500 for materials to build one computer cabinet and you only have $500 worth of capital, then you will be limited to building one cabinet at a time. You have to get paid before you can build a second cabinet.

Or let's say you're starting a part-time business detailing automobiless. Detailing one automobile takes three hours. In addition, driving, collection, and scheduling take approximately one hour per car. Your maximum sales activity per week will be based on the number of hours you can devote to your business after you put in your hours at your full-time job. If you can devote 24 hours a week, then your sales would be 24 hours, divided by time per car, multiplied by your charge. Let's try that:

$$24 / 4 = 6 \text{ autos per week}$$
$$\text{your charge per auto} = \$120$$
$$6 \times \$120 = \$720 \text{ per week}$$

Make a list of your friends and relatives. Find out how many of them have their cars detailed. Add the repeat factor. How often do they want detailing—once a month, once every quarter, or once a year? When your list is finished you have 24 prospects. You have a realistic shot at 18 of those prospects. For your business, that's enough for a start-up.

As a wise entrepreneur, you know that your first few jobs will take longer than later ones. You're new. You're learning the business. You want to make sure you do a super job. You have four prospects who want monthly detailing. You have six who want it quarterly. Start with these ten prospects and lay out a chart. (Table A1).

TABLE A.1
Proforma Sales—Auto Detailing

	1	2	3	4	5	6	7
1							
2	First Sales Forecast						
3							
4		1st Month		2nd Month		3rd Month	
5	Monthly Detailing (1)	480		480		480	
6	Quarterly Detailing (2)	240		240		240	
7	Rest of 18 prospects (3)	240		480		720	
8	Need to Find (4)	240		480		720	
9	Sales (5)	1200		1680		2160	
10							
11							
12							

TABLE A.1
Proforma Sales—Auto Detailing—cont'd

Assumptions for Proforma Sales—Auto Detailing

1. Four monthly customers already committed.
2. Six quarterly customers already committed/two each month.
3. Assume add one new monthly customer and one quarterly customer each month from current prospects.
4. Take action and secure two new monthly customers.
5. This assumes all customers are retained.

EXPENSE FORECAST

List everything you'll need to pay for on a regular basis to operate your business: for example, telephone, supplies, truck, advertising/promotion. Next, list everything you can think of under each heading. Here's a partial example:

Supplies	Truck
rags	gas
soap	oil/maintenance
wax	insurance
cleaner	car signs
cotton-tipped swabs	

Now consider each specific item. Which ones can you tie to the detailing job? For example, for each detailing job, you use two packages of rags, one-half can of wax, one-quarter can of cleaner, 10 cotton-tipped swabs, $4 for gas, and so on.

Add these expenses to your first sales forecast. Also add expense items that don't change. See Table A2.

TABLE A.2
Proforma Income Statement—Auto Detailing

	1	2	3	4	5	6	7
1	First Income Statement Forecast						
2							
3		1st Month	2nd Month	3rd Month			
4	Sales:						
5	Monthly	480	480	480			
6	Quarterly	240	240	240			
7	Original Prospects	240	480	720			
8	Need to Find	240	480	720			
9							
10	Sales Total	1200	1680	2160			
11							
12	Expenses:						
13	Phone (1)	100	100	100			
14	Gasoline (2)	80	96	112			
15	Oil/Maint (3)	80	80	80			
16	Insurance (4)	200	200	200			
17	Supplies (5)	150	210	270			
18	Ad/Promotion (6)	220	220	220			
19	Taxes (7)	180	252	324			
20	Miscellaneous (8)	150	150	150			
21							
22	Expense Total	1160	1308	1456			

(continued)

TABLE A.2
Proforma Income Statement—Auto Detailing—cont'd

23	Profit	40	300	704
24				
25				

Assumptions for Table A2
1. Phone: monthly basic rate, plus pager and cell phone.
2. $40 per month, plus $4 per job.
3. $80 per month toward oil change, tires, and vehicle maintenance.
4. $2,400 per year/$200 per month.
5. Estimated at $15 per job.
6. Yellow Page ad at $70 a month, plus $50 a month for four-line ad in weekly paper, and $50 for flyers and $50 for magnet business cards each month.
7. Set aside for taxes 15% of sales.
8. Miscellaneous.

THINGS TO DO LIST

Now that your plan is complete, act on it. Your first step is to compile a list of things that need doing. You need this list for at least three reasons:

1. It gives you easy steps to follow.
2. It keeps you on target.
3. It gives you a sense of getting there at last.

Following is a sample "things to do" list for a car detailing service.

List of Necessities Before Opening Day—Car Detailing Service
1. Talk with experienced car detailers.
2. Prepare Fast-Start Plan.
3. Stay organized.
4. Choose a business name.
5. File for fictitious business name.
6. Determine specific geographical area to service.
7. Have business phone installed. Purchase answering machine or voicemail and cell phone.
8. Check out several banks because fees and services vary. Set up business checking account.
9. Locate, evaluate, and select suppliers.
10. Check city and county business license regulations and apply.
11. File for a federal ID number—needed by all employers.
12. Locate an insurance agent and purchase insurance.
13. Hire employees. Decide on full-time or part-time and how many. Make sure to obtain all information: Social Security number, correct name and address, telephone number, citizenship. Develop application form. Have each employee fill out a W-4 and I9.
14. Complete advertising next and schedule to run in Penny Saver.
15. Join a discount warehouse club.
16. Business cards should be ordered and ready to hand out.
17. Preprint billing statements for customers who do not pay upon receipt. Preferably ask for money up front.
18. Record all income and expenses daily in a ledger.
19. Find a bookkeeper to prepare financial statements. Check out computerized accounting systems.

20. Hire an attorney.
21. Network with friends, relatives, and other detailers.
22. Join chamber of commerce.
23. Project profit and loss statements for three months.
24. Contact Yellow Pages.
25. Order signs for vehicles.

YOUR TURN NOW!

The key to any business, and to any Business Plan, is how well you understand the needs of your Target Customer. Find an itch that isn't being scratched and you can ace your competitors. You have read through the We Do Windows Business Plan, completed many of the Action Steps, and read the instructions for a Fast-Start Plan.

Now, write your own Fast-Start Plan. Keep it handy. Refer to it often. Use it to keep your business on track in those early months of operation. When you've been in business for three months, use your Fast-Start Plan as a launching pad for your next nine months of operation. For your second year, write a full-fledged Business Plan.

Your Business Plan is your pathway to success.

Congratulations!

Ten Commandments from Sam Walton

1. Commit to your business.
2. Share your profits.
3. Motivate your partners.
4. Communicate all that you know.
5. Appreciate what your associates do.
6. Celebrate your success.
7. Listen to everyone in your company.
8. Exceed your customers' expectations.
9. Control your expenses better than competitors.
10. Swim upstream and avoid conventional wisdom.

SOURCE: Guerilla Marketing Communiquee, **www.gmarketing.com**.

YES, WE DO WINDOWS

Model Fast-Start Business Plan

1. Business definition
2. What business am I really in?
3. Competition
4. Pricing
5. Target Customer
6. Ad/sales program
7. Start-up costs
8. Sales goals/expenses/first three months
9. "To do" list

1. **Business definition.**

   I have been a window washer for three years. For two years, I worked for Windowlite Ltd., a large organization with more than 250 satellites across three states. For the next year, I worked for a local operator who owned a truck and three squeegees. I think that I know the business from both ends.

   My plan—and the subject of this plan—is to do window and house cleaning.

Window cleaning: I will clean windows, screens, and window casings.

House-cleaning: I will vacuum, dust, polish/wax, mop. I will do bathrooms, mirrors, kitchens, range tops, and ovens.

A customer may contract for one or more services. House cleaning will be offered on a once-a-week or once-every-two-weeks basis. Window cleaning will be offered monthly, quarterly, twice a year, or as needed.

2. **What business am I really in?**

   Pride of ownership—a home is a person's most expensive investment. Keeping it clean makes the customer proud.

   Timesaving—homeowners work hard to pay for their investment; many homes today are supported by double incomes; few homeowners have the time to do their own cleaning.

   Preserving the value of the investment—dirt and grime damage the home. Cleaning on a regular basis enhances and preserves the value of the home.

   Comfortable, healthy living area—a clean home is a healthier home. Who wants to live with dirt?

   The business I am really in: "providing a clean and healthy environment while at the same time preserving the value of an investment and deepening pride of ownership."

3. **Competition**

   At this time there are 5 window cleaning services and 10 housecleaning services listed in my area Yellow Pages.

   Taking the time to make phone calls to these competitors made me feel even better about my idea for a business. Many of these firms did not return calls, did not seem interested, and were unable to provide phone bids.

   I can see two "musts" for the business: (a) my bids must be firm, and (b) my phone skills must be customer-oriented. If I can't answer the phone, I must find a phone person who can fulfill these two musts. The image we're presenting here is "We aim to please. We're interested in servicing your home."

   One question I asked was: "Will the same person be in my home each visit?" A mere 6 percent said yes. The other responses were vague. That indicated a problem in scheduling.

   Measuring the competition has given my start-up a real advantage. Since I'll be doing all the work myself, I can gather customer data as I work. As I expand, I shall match employees to homeowners. A home is a private place. It's a place where one goes to escape from the day. You don't want it invaded by different strangers every week. My plan is to expand only when I find the right employees.

   My strategy is to price my services just slightly higher than the current competitors' rates. Every three months, to stay current, I will survey the competition.

Basic Rates for Housecleaning
Checksheet Items Only

Square Feet	*Price*
	1st Cleaning
1000	$ 50
1000–1500	75
1500–2000	100
2000+	100 + $25 per 1000 sq. ft.
	Weekly Cleaning
1000	$ 35
1000–1500	55
1500–2000	75
2000+	75 + $30 per 1000 sq. ft.
	Bi-monthly
1000	$ 45
1000–1500	70

1500–2000	90
2000+	90 + $30 per 1000 sq. ft.
Window Washing	
One-Story House	
Up to 15 windows	$ 25
Each additional 5 windows	10
Two-Story House	
Up to 25 windows	$ 60
Each additional 5 windows	10

4. **Target Customer**

I can classify three types of Target Customers for my business:

Customer A—Family dwelling. A married couple with one or more children. The household income is $60,000 or more. Two vehicles. Both parents work. Reason for the service: Spare time is at a premium for child-care, recreation, and entertainment. Parents cannot spare the time to do windows or other cleaning.

Customer B—Single-person condo. A single or divorced person living alone, usually in an apartment or waterside condo. Age range from 28 to 40. The income here runs from $30,000–$40,000. Time is at a premium. Customers are seldom at home on nights or weekends.

Customer C—High roller. Customer C is distinguished by incomes in the six-figure range. Home values start at $400,000 and move up the scale to $1.0 million. Customer C has high standards and wants a spotless home. Has zero desire to perform menial tasks. As long as the work is excellent and they feel they're not getting ripped off, price is no object. As my business grows, I will concentrate on this segment of the market.

5. **Ad/Sales Program**

- I will maintain an image of high visibility. My white truck is washed daily. If there is mud on the tires after a job, the mud is washed off before the next job. I wear a white polo-type shirt and khakis that bear the company logo. My employees will wear similar outfits. Footgear is white tennis shoes; they're easy on the feet and look professional, almost a sporty image.
- My business cards are white with blue lettering. On the reverse side is a list of my services. I make it a habit to get a business card whenever I hand one out. Data from these cards are entered into a computer. Names are added to a master list.
- Flyers will be placed door to door in target neighborhoods. I plan to do one neighborhood of 100 to 200 homes, and then evaluate the response. I survey each person who calls in response to the flyer: What did he or she like? What was missing? From this marketing survey, I'll redesign the flyer before approaching a second neighborhood.

I make a habit of leaving flyers and business cards at all day-care centers in the area. In exchange for each customer I gain, I donate to a fund for schoolbooks or toys.

6. **Start-up Costs**

Insurance	700
Truck (used white)	8000*
Ladder rack (custom-made)	550
Ladders	612
Supplies—windows	400
Supplies—housecleaning	1000
Signs for new truck	295
Advertising	500
Answering machine	75
Phone and pager installation	200

*I should be able to buy this for $1000 down and $250 to $275 per month for 36 months. Thus start-up cash may be as low as $6548.

P.O. box per month—first and last month	40
Chamber of commerce	300
Fictitious business name	85
Business license	155
Used desk and chair	375
Desk calendar	6
Date book, home	65
Date book, truck	15
Rolodex, supplies, file system	50
Bank account	125
Total Estimated Start-up Expenses	13,548

7. **Sales Goals and Expenses, First Three Months**
   I plan to work six days per week for the first year. Until I gain experience, I can work a maximum of three jobs per day. On the schedule at present, I have four weekly customers and two bi-monthly scheduled for the third week. When not on the job, I plan a strong marketing effort, so that I can add one customer per week until I'm up to 18 customers, my maximum for the week. At that time I will evaluate my ability to add additional customers and hire a part-time employee (Table A3).

"Things to Do" List

File for fictitious business name

Design business logo, cards, and flyer

Order phone installation

Purchase cell phone

Lease pager

Set up bank account

Order business cards

Set up post office box

Locate source of supplies

Purchase supplies

Purchase truck

Order signs for truck

Purchase answering machine

Buy ladder rack for truck

Buy ladders

Join chamber of commerce

Purchase desk, chair, and office supplies

TABLE A.3

Proforma Income Statement—Yes, We Do Windows

	1	2	3	4	5	6	7
1	Sales Goals and Expenses						
2							
3		1st Month	2nd Month	3rd Month			
4							
5	Sales (1)	1087.50	2580	3500			
6							
7	Expenses:						
8	Gas (2)	80	80	100			
9	Maintenance (3)	100	100	100			
10	Insurance (4)	200	200	200			
11	Phone (5)	75	75	75			
12	Advertising (6)	105	105	105			
13	Supplies (7)	65	155	175			
14	Truck Loan Interest	250	250	250			
15	Credit Card (8)	300	300	300			
16	Expense Total	1175	1265	1305			
17	Profit	(87.50)	1315	2195			

Assumptions for Table A3

1. Average customer will own a one-story house of 2000 square feet with 15 windows. Month 1=4 weeks. Month 2=4 weeks. Month 3=5 weeks. Every other new customer bi-monthly. All window-washing contracts on a quarterly basis. First 2 weeks marketing and second 2 cleaning for Month 1.
2. Gas, $20 per week.
3. Maintenance—mainly a reserve for tires, repairs, oil changes, $25 per week.
4. Auto insurance and bonding, $1,500 per year.
5. Basic phone, pager, post office box.
6. Approximately 400 flyers per month come to $55, plus $50 for distribution.
7. Approximately $5 per job.
8. Credit card payment for start-up expenses.

Annie's Business Plan Proposal

Cover Letter for Annie's

Business Plan Proposal for Specialty Chocolates and Candy Concession at Sea World

Annie's
27898 Palm Tree Lane
Escondido, CA 92677

May 6, 2001

Sea World
Ms. Janet Wilkes
2 Sea World Drive
San Diego, CA 92888

Dear Ms. Wilkes,

We are pleased to offer our proposal to operate a chocolate and candy concession at Sea World opening in August. With six years of retailing experience throughout San Diego and our excellent reputation as a provider of one of the largest selections of candies and chocolates, we believe Annie's will be an excellent addition to Sea World's concession offerings.

Annie's is thrilled to offer your national and international tourists the opportunity to shop at San Diego's finest chocolate and candy store. Sea World's long and successful run as one of the premiere attractions in San Diego offers Annie's great opportunity to expand our business.

Our firm is self-financed, and our strong balance sheet allows Annie's to expand into Sea World without further financing. Thus we will be able to open within eight weeks following acceptance of our proposal.

On review of our proposal, please contact us to clarify any points. We look forward to a long and profitable association with Sea World.

Sincerely,

Kathy Johnson
Annie's Owner

Annie's Business Plan Proposal

Business Plan Contents

Note: Due to the fact this Business Plan is a proposal for operating a concession within Sea World, primary emphasis is on store operations, experience, and product. Location is clearly defined, marketing is limited primarily to in-store promotions, and competition is limited to other concessionaires, none of whom are direct competitors.

EXECUTIVE SUMMARY

Annie's specialty shop will feature fine chocolates and candy as a concessionaire for Sea World. Annie's unique store strives to create an atmosphere that is entertaining and fun for the customer to browse and shop in, upscale yet casual, and a place where employees enjoy working. We are known to provide high-quality, fresh products and intimate customer service. Annie's owners like it when people get excited in their stores, and remember Annie's as a place that they want to return to. As owners we are customer-driven and love retailing.

We have been successful candy retailers for the past six years and believe we do an excellent job selling bulk candy, chocolates, and candy gift packages. Few other operations offer such a complete selection of confections from hundreds of manufacturers under one roof. Many of the items offered for sale are very different and unusual. Because of this wide selection, the Company is able to offer many different price points to meet the needs of most customers. Your customers will also consider our candies and chocolates as ideal gifts.

Our proposal for a candy concession at Sea World comes after thorough research into the make-up of the other vendors and our belief that Annie's will complement the other stores and not cannibalize sales. Candy is considered an "extra," one that tourists and families gladly splurge on during their vacations. Many tourists will pass our store as they exit Sea World and will want something sweet before they get on the road back to their homes or hotels.

Upon Sea World's acceptance of our proposal, we could be open within eight weeks. Our strong balance sheet and available cash will allow us to act immediately. Annie's staff will thoroughly train all Sea World store staff in our other stores prior to opening in Sea World. On opening day, we will offer trained personnel ready and willing to serve Sea World's customers with our legendary customer service.

Our creative store layout is designed to accommodate a large number of customers at one time, and at the busiest times of the day and year we will be able to operate two cash registers. Through our six years in business, we have refined our store layout to best serve our customers and employees.

We believe our retail experience, strong balance sheet, excellent reputation throughout the Southern California area, and tasty chocolate product offerings will be a wonderful addition to Sea World.

MANAGEMENT AND STAFFING

Retail Experience and History

Since its inception in 1995, Annie's has been a successful retailer of bulk candy and chocolates, top-of-the-line gourmet boxed chocolates and truffles, domestic and foreign product lines, sugar-free products, novelty and nostalgia candies, dried fruit gifts, gourmet, fancy food gifts, gift baskets, Kosher confections, difficult-to-find items, seasonal merchandise, and related gift items that complement the packaged food products. Annie's is well known by consumers in Southern California as having the largest and most complete selection of confections in the area at the five store locations.

Through the years the owners have identified the best sources for over 2000 SKUs. They not only know where and how to get the merchandise, they also know, for each item, the turnover when reasonably priced, the shelf life, and the gross margin. They know how to purchase in both large and small quantities, depending on the candy, the weather, the store location, and the time of year. They know which vendors are able to keep freight costs under control and pack without excessive damage. The company "cherry picks" the best from many distributors and manufacturers. It also carries nearly the entire line of those who do an excellent job; for example, Lindt, Joseph Schmidt, Asher's, Ghiradelli, Goelitz, Laymon, and so on.

Annie's does not manufacture any of its own chocolates. In the store, employees dip strawberries and other fresh and/or glazed fruit, Oreo cookies, pretzels, fudge, Rice Krispie treats, Gummi bears, and so on in chocolate. Sometimes employees mold chocolate roses and other chocolate items, or make gift baskets, and the customers have great fun watching this.

Our five store locations throughout Southern California include Dana Point, Carlsbad, Fallbrook, Escondido, and downtown San Diego. We have opened one store each year with our own funds. All stores are profitable and we have more than 30 employees on the payroll.

Annie's opened in 1995 as an LLC in Escondido, California. The principal member and manager of this company is Kathy Johnson. Kathy's three adult children all play a major role in the management and daily operations of the business. Annie's owns the service mark and trademarks.

Management

1. Kathy Johnson (see resume) began working in her aunt's 15,000 square foot retail department store business at the age of 13. Through the years working in this third-generation business, she learned many of the fine details of operating a successful retail business. She opened her own branch store at 22.

   Kathy worked her way through the ranks at several retail chains, Sears, and The Gap. In addition, she completed her undergraduate degree in business at the University of California in Santa Barbara. Ms. Johnson serves as a guest lecturer at several colleges and is a frequent guest speaker at retail association meetings.
2. Troy Johnson is currently site manager. He monitors inventory levels, develops staffing schedules, deals with day-to-day operational issues, and supervises personnel. He worked for several years as a shift supervisor for Cheesecake Factory. He has been actively involved in all aspects of Annie's since its inception.
3. Samantha Johnson, an English graduate of Indiana University, helped develop all Annie's operation manuals. With six years of retail experience at Hallmark, K-Mart, and Nordstrom, Samantha brought wide exposure to various training methods and rules. Samantha aided in the store layout and design and is responsible for all ad layouts.
4. Casey Johnson holds a Chemical Engineering degree from UC Riverside. His primary focus with Annie's has been computer operations and information systems. He has assisted with all new store start-ups and has a thorough working knowledge of all aspects of the company.

If awarded this concession, Kathy Johnson will be directly involved in the day-to-day operations of the business. Troy Johnson will provide on-site management under the close supervision of Kathy Johnson. Other company members may also provide on-site management and support with members of the company reporting directly to Kathy Johnson. Troy Johnson will assist with store start up. Day and evening charge persons will be hired and trained.

Staffing Plan

1. Organizational chart for proposed operations:
   a. Kathy Johnson: Responsible for the operations and management of the concession.
   b. Troy Johnson: Responsible for on-site, 24-hour management and supervision of the concession. Reports to Kathy Johnson.

c. Casey, Troy, and Samantha Johnson: Consultation and support.
d. Day charge person (to be hired), reporting to Troy Johnson.
e. Evening charge person (to be hired), reporting to Troy Johnson.
f. Four additional sales people will be hired.

2. Staffing plan: There will be two employees to service the customers at all times. During busy seasons there will be three to four employees. This number includes the charge person.
3. Resumes: see Business Plan Appendix.

Exit Strategy

Kathy Johnson and her children will continue to run Annie's as a family company. The company will stay in the family when Ms. Johnson retires in 5 to 10 years. The company has been developed to support and provide a good living for the entire family. Each of the children enjoys retailing and finds opening and running new stores an exciting part of the business. Kathy and her family hope to grow Annie's to 10 stores within the next 5 years.

STORE OVERVIEW

Floor Plan

A Ghirardelli merchandising tower will be near the right front window and a floor standing sucker rack near the left window. These may be moved to other areas of the store periodically. Window displays will be seasonal and kept low to enhance visibility into the store. As the customers enter the store, they will face an 8-foot curved glass chocolate showcase merchandised with truffles, turtles, pecan rolls, English toffee, and similar chocolate items. On both sides of the chocolate case there will be various sucker and change maker displays.

Both the right and left walls will be mirrored. Along the lower right wall will be acrylic Jelly Belly dispensers. Above these dispensers will be staggered glass shelves to display gift items. Along the back wall will be custom made acrylic bulk candy bins. Gift items will be displayed along the top shelves of these bins. The rear wall will be painted white. Neon will be installed across the rear wall above the bulk candy. Across from the bulk candy bins, on the back side of the service counter, will be shelves for novelty candy items and bins filled with taffy along the top shelf.

The left wall will have open cabinet shelves, the highest being 36 inches, for boxed chocolates. Above these shelves will be staggered glass shelves for display of gift items. In the center of this wall will be an 8-foot section of custom slat wall to hang packaged items.

The service counter will be in the center of the store. There will be a 6-foot long, 36-inch high, flat glass counter showcase on both the right and left sides of the service area. The left side will hold sugar-free chocolates and the right side will hold fudge and other bulk chocolates. A center island will be used to do chocolate dipping, construct baskets, and so on. There will be one register and one scale on each side of the service counter.

Behind the rear wall of the store is the required hand sink, three-basin sink, mop sink, water heater, microwave, small refrigerator, and shelving. It is estimated that this area is approximately 140 square feet.

Floor Space

There is approximately 250 square feet of floor space allocated to merchandise fixtures. Based on this area, the estimated square footage for each category is:

1. Bulk candy	approximately 84 sq. ft
2. Bulk chocolates	approximately 38 sq. ft
3. Edible gift	approximately 66 sq. ft

4. Sugar-free and/or fat-free approximately 15 sq. ft
5. Non-edible gifts approximately 10 sq. ft
6. Novelty candy approximately 37 sq. ft

However, because there are multiple levels of shelves, the percentage of products carried to actual square footage would be quite different. For example, the right wall would have 22 square feet of Jelly Belly Bean fixtures but above the beans there would be four levels of glass shelves, with approximately 15 square feet for each level, for packaged gift items. It is estimated that 90 percent of all revenue would be from edible food and gift products and less than 10 percent from non-edible gift products. Aisles would be 5 feet wide to allow for wheelchair access, back packs, and comfortable movement for the customers.

See floor plan drawings in the appendix.

Visual Presentation of Merchandise

The colorful world of candy always lends itself to great displays and store designs. The stores are merchandised and decorated to reflect the numerous holidays and seasons throughout the year. The summer season is followed by Fall, Halloween (great fun!), Thanksgiving, Hanukah, Christmas, Valentine's Day (the prettiest), St. Patrick's Day, Easter, teachers, graduation, and the 4th of July. Colors and store decor are changed to match these events. Organdy and other beautiful ribbons are used to dress up packages and displays. Gift wrap paper is changed to match the seasons/holidays.

With the exception of very high-turnover products, and products that are always carried, few single items are purchased in large quantities. Rather, many different items are purchased in smaller quantities, thus giving the customer a wider selection of products to choose from and giving the company the ability to bring in new merchandise and change displays often. Most importantly, this ensures freshness of the products.

Unique gift items are incorporated into the merchandising themes. Many times the company purchases their own supplies to create these unusual gifts. For example, the employees may take small watering cans painted with sunflowers, insert cello bags printed with sunflowers, fill the bags with bulk lemon drops, and tie a silk sunflower into the organdy bow or attach a small plush item or sunflower button doll. All of the Easter baskets sold by Annie's are custom.

Bulk chocolates, including sugar-free items, are sold from the chocolate cases. Through the years the company has identified those items that are in high demand and those companies who manufacture the best products. Annie's knows who makes the best truffles, the best turtles, the best honeycomb, and so on.

The bulk candy bins are very colorful; the customers love them—and they generate nice revenue. The bins will be segmented by types of candy such as licorice, sour, gummi, sugar-free, and so on. Approximately 10 percent of the bulk bin space is allocated to candies that have a lower demand, such as horehound lumps and Bit O' Honey. Annie's believes that they maintain a competitive edge by carrying some of these more difficult-to-find items.

Individual shelves within the store may be merchandised with different themes, for example, all golf-related gifts, or all teacher gifts, or all dried fruit packages. A certain shelf for example may be merchandised with the 101 Dalmatians theme, including such items as suckers and stick candy by Kencraft with a Dalmatian on them, a plush Dalmatian, a fire engine tin shrink wrapped with Jelly Belly Jelly Beans to match, an Applause Dalmatian mug and straw filled with candy, and firemen button babies. Product displays are changed frequently so that things don't become boring.

Products

The product lists in the appendix are examples of many products we carry and are arranged by merchandise category. Not all items are carried at all times because new

Companies such as Joseph Schmidt never repeat their seasonal packaging from year to year and they frequently change their product lines. Annie's is vigilant about staying on top of the market. For example, War Heads were the rage yesterday and Raven's Revenge is the rage today. Tomorrow it will be something different.

There are six major merchandise categories:

1. Bulk candy in self-serve bins
2. Bulk chocolates in the chocolate cases
3. Packaged, edible gift items (boxed chocolates, mugs filled with candy, etc.)
4. Sugar-free and/or fat-free (incorporated throughout the store)
5. Non-edible gift items (collectible plush bears, candy dishes, candy tins, etc.)
6. Packaged novelty candy (War Heads, Pop Rocks, etc.)

Estimate of quantities:

1. Bulk candy	approximately 175 bins including 18 taffy and 54 Jelly Belly
2. Bulk chocolates	approximately 500 different pieces
3. Edible gifts	approximately 500 to 600 different items
4. Sugar-free	approximately 100 different items
5. Non-edible gifts	approximately 200 different items
6. Packaged novelty	approximately 300 to 400 different items

Pricing

Most packaged and gift items are now street priced at a 39% to 42% margin, which is monitored on the computer with every invoice. Since this was done, the average ticket increased (customers feel they can afford to purchase more?). Customers are happier now, product turnover is higher, and the problems with transferring product among stores has decreased significantly.

Estimate of price ranges:

1. Bulk candy	\$1.79 ¼ lb.
2. Bulk chocolates	\$1.00 to \$5.00 each, average \$2.25 each
	\$2.98 ¼ lb. to \$4.98 ¼ lb., average \$3.98 ¼ lb.
3. Edible gifts	\$1.00 to \$150.00, average \$10 to \$30 range
4. Sugar free and/or fat free	Same as 1, 2, and 3 above
5. Non-edible gifts	\$1.00 to \$150.00, average \$10 to \$30 range
6. Packaged novelty candy	\$0.39 to \$25.00, average \$1.00 to \$3.00 each

MARKETING

Retail Trends

To keep abreast of retail trends, Annie's frequently attends the following trade shows:

1. The International Fancy Food Show—twice yearly
2. The Philadelphia Candy Show
3. The LA Gift Show
4. The Denver Gift Show
5. The Phoenix Gift Show
6. The New York Gift Show
7. The Seattle Coffee Fest

Annie's subscribes to trade journals and is in constant communication with both vendors and customers. Annie's frequently visits all competitors to monitor prices and look for new items.

Customer Service Philosophy/Programs

The customer service goal of Annie's is to assist the customer in getting his/her needs met in the most efficient and pleasant manner possible. The employees are expected to do whatever is necessary to make the purchase easy for the customer. This may mean gift wrapping a package, wrapping an item in bubble wrap so that it doesn't break, holding an item for a customer, or processing a special order.

Annie's accepts all credit cards for customer convenience.

Returns are processed cheerfully, efficiently, and without question. The customer is offered replacement merchandise or a refund. A refund/complaint form is completed and all employees have the authority to process refunds so that the customer is taken care of immediately.

Customers are often in a hurry and like their purchases processed quickly. This requires employees who are well-trained and know the merchandise and who are swift, accurate, helpful, friendly, and courteous, especially when under pressure. Annie's occasionally employs mystery shoppers and uses this feedback for coaching employees. Feedback on employee behavior is solicited from regular customers, employees from other businesses, business acquaintances, and friends whenever possible. Annie's business card is always out on the counter for customers who wish to call.

Employees are taught the following concepts of customer service:

a. Always, whenever possible, acknowledge the customer as they enter the store.
b. Offer assistance but also respect their wishes to be left alone.
c. Smile—all the time.
d. Do not ignore customers or turn your back on them.
e. Do not talk/gossip among yourselves when customers are in the store.
f. Do not talk badly abut any customer, especially in front of other people, not even outside of work hours.
g. Do not complain about anything, or talk about personal problems, religion, or politics to customers or among yourselves when customers are in the store. Save this chatter for after hours when you are away from the workplace.
h. Try to never leave a customer once you are engaged in a transaction.
i. Process refunds and/or complaints cheerfully and efficiently. Don't argue. Listen and hear the customer out. Resolve the problem on the spot whenever possible.
j. Always say thank you.
k. The customer is your real boss so treat him/her accordingly.

Employees are taught about candy and chocolate because they are expected to be knowledgeable and conversant. They are also taught how to gift wrap, tie bows, construct gift baskets, dip chocolate, process special orders, process charges, etc. They are trained to handle cash accurately. They all learn how to process shipments from invoices and price products.

Blue bib aprons with the store logo in pink across the front are worn by all employees and name tags are required at all times.

Marketing Plan

1. An advertisement will be placed in the local yellow pages candy section of the major area phone books. This advertisement will promote corporate/quantity orders and special orders.
2. Entertainment retail: most customers find it very entertaining just to browse the store. Employees dip chocolate-covered strawberries, caramel apples, and other items where customers can watch. Customers like to watch the employees mold chocolate items (Easter Bunnies, etc.). They also tend to stand and watch gift baskets being made.

3. Employees often dress up as Mr. Jelly Belly, or as a witch at Halloween or an Easter Bunny at Eater time, and so on.
4. Face painting has been done in the past, as well as demonstrations showing how to make chocolate roses.
5. At Christmas time Annie's may construct a gingerbread house.
6. Controlled food sampling is used to promote sales.

Store Operations

Stocking

Food products will be stored in the shop and nonfood items will be stored in the storeroom. The storeroom area is inadequate and unsafe to store food products that are not sealed in cans or glass bottles. The temperature is too warm and it would be nearly impossible to have adequate pest control. There are storage shelves under the bulk candy bins, under the chocolate bins, and under the service counters. There is limited storage area near the sinks.

Bulk candy bins and other products will be replenished during slow periods or off hours by employees. Each candy bin is removable and can be replaced with a bin that is full. Pricing and stocking will be done by employees daily during quiet periods. During busy periods, such as Christmas, Valentines, and Easter, an employee will be brought in to adjust the price of merchandise and/or replenish shelves. All items will be individually priced, even if bar coded.

The owners may find it necessary to rent off-site storage. If this occurs, a part-time stocker will be hired to accept deliveries at the off-site location and price merchandise before transporting it to the store. During hot weather, merchandise will be transported at night.

Logistics and Frequency of Deliveries

1. Delivery schedule of new goods: Most goods are delivered by UPS or similar common carrier. UPS can deliver as often as daily. These shipments are generally not very large. The on-site manager will be responsible for coordinating deliveries. Large freight shipments will come in approximately every 10 days and may have to go to off site storage for processing. Most manufacturers only ship out UPS on Monday or Tuesday so that product doesn't sit in a UPS warehouse over the weekend.
2. Replenishment of on-site stock: Par levels are established for items that are carried all of the time (e.g., malt balls). Orders are placed at least weekly and more often if needed. Seasonal items are replenished only if they turn over quickly and early. It is impossible to get replacement candy late into the holiday season. While stores are selling Christmas, the manufacturers are processing Valentine orders, and so on.

Facility Maintenance Plan

1. Policy for maintenance and repairs: A preventative maintenance program will be implemented for the refrigerated chocolate case and the under counter refrigerator per manufacturer's recommendations. All repairs will be made in a timely manner and as needed.
2. Frequency of cleaning: Glass shelves are cleaned daily except for Friday and Sunday. The floors are mopped nightly by employees. The floors are professionally cleaned quarterly. Windows are washed weekly and touched up daily. The store is dusted daily. It is management's expectation that the store be kept spotless.
3. Disposal of trash: At least five times per day and sometimes more often.
4. Replacement of equipment, displays, fixtures, and carpeting: No replacement is anticipated during the life of this lease. If the need occurs, items will be replaced accordingly.

Financial Management and Financials

System of Internal Control

Sales and Cash Receipts

a. Cash registers—Two point-of-sale registers, which are capable of recording sales by stock-keeping units (SKUs), will be used. They will be equipped with sales totalizer counters for all sales categories in which the counters are locked, constantly accumulating, and which cannot be reset. Beginning and ending sales totalizer counter readings will be recorded daily.

b. Sales will be entered into one of five departments:
   Bulk Candy (self serve out of the bins)
   Chocolates/Candy (all other food and/or items containing food)
   Non-food Gifts
   Gift Certificates
   Shipping Costs

c. Sales transactions will be either cash, credit card, or traveler's checks. No other checks will be accepted. Credit cards will be processed through one of two terminals for electronic authorization and capture. All transactions will be entered into the cash registers.

d. At the end of each day the daily journals (Z tapes) will be removed from the registers and placed with the cash receipts for the day. A $200.00 bank will be left in each register and a coin bank of $300.00 will be maintained on the premises. Each morning, for the previous day, Troy Johnson (or his designee) will prepare the night drop deposit and deposit it at the bank.

e. The information from the daily journal tapes will be entered onto the weekly sales summary form. At the end of each week, the weekly totals will link to the monthly sales summary form. All Z tapes and any other paper transactions pertinent to the gross and/or net sales for each day (void slips, refund forms, cash paid out receipts, employee discount receipts, credit card batch slips, deposit slips, etc.) will be attached together by day and stored by month in the storeroom.

f. Weekly and monthly records will be faxed to the CPA, who will prepare the monthly compiled financial statements for the location. The original Z tapes and other paper transactions will be submitted to the CPA who will prepare the annual audited sales report. Once returned by the CPA, the original Z tapes and report forms will be stored in the storeroom.

g. The CPA performing the annual audit will review the system of internal control semi-annually.

h. Gross sales will only be offset by customer refunds, voids (documented employee errors during sales transactions), shipping expenses when an item is shipped for a customer (customer will only be charged actual cost of shipping), and Annie's employee discounts.

i. Annie's employees are allowed a 30 percent discount on all purchases daily and a 50 percent discount on Christmas Eve, Christmas Day, and Easter Sunday. All employee purchases will be entered into the registers by management. The sales receipt will be initialed by the manager and the employee and placed with the daily cash receipts. If management is not available, purchases will be documented in the "Tab Book" and paid for by the employee at a later date. Employees will not be allowed to ring up their own purchases.

j. Sea World employees will be allowed a discount of 10 percent on any total sale of $5.00 or more. The employee must be in uniform or be able to show some form of proof that he is an employee. The person receiving the discount must write where he works on the receipt and sign it. This receipt is placed with the daily cash receipts.

k. Employees are not allowed to make change from the register without a sale. There is no exception to this rule. Change is also only made up to the amount of cash amount tendered to complete the transaction.

l. Cash is bled from the cash drawers at frequent intervals throughout the day and transferred to a locked, built-in cash drop drawer.
m. Voids: The cash register receipt tape showing the void will be stamped with the void stamp and initialed by the person making the error. Sometimes the customer just changes his or her mind after a sale is rung up. This is also treated as a void. The void slips are placed with the daily cash receipts.
n. Refunds/Returns: The refund/return form will be completed. The merchandise and proof of purchase must be presented by the customer. The receipt will be attached to the refund/return form. If the item was charged, a credit will be processed. If the customer paid cash, a cash refund will be given. If there is no proof of purchase, but it can be determined that it was a valid purchase from Annie's, a refund will still be given. If the customer eats the merchandise and then attempts to get a refund, the request will be denied.
o. Discounts: It is not anticipated that any promotional discounts will be given.
p. Keys: One set of Annie's storeroom keys will be kept on a large key ring in the store and a key log will be used. One set of keys will also be issued to Kathy Johnson and Troy Johnson for a total of three keys. Store keys will be issued to those hired to open and close the store. Delivery or other persons will never be left unattended in the store room.
q. Badging: Only key personnel will be badged, such as the day and evening charge persons and Annie's management.
r. Secret Shoppers: To be used periodically. Employees will be informed of this when they are hired. Video cameras may be installed.

Inventory and Accounts Payable

a. Shipments will be checked at delivery for evidence of damage. Any damage will be documented with the carrier. Shipments will be checked against the packing slip/invoice. Internal damage and/or shortages will be documented and the vendor notified immediately.
b. Extensions on all invoices, including computer-generated invoices, will be checked before payment. Amounts for damaged merchandise will be deducted from payment.
c. COD shipments are not accepted by Annie's under any circumstances. It is anticipated that all purchases will be paid for by check or credit card and not by cash on hand.
d. All invoices for payment will be approved by Kathy Johnson. Checks will be prepared and signed by Kathy Johnson or other Company members in her absence. Invoices will be paid when due and stored, by month of payment, in Annie's storeroom.
e. Inventory counts will be completed twice yearly, in May and September.
f. A review of the actual cost of physical inventory will be compared to the inventory on the financial statement. Any significant variations will be investigated, especially for theft of inventory.
g. Transfer of inventory among the Annie's locations will be documented, at cost, on a duplicate transfer form. A copy of each transfer form will be kept at both the sending and receiving store. These forms will be stored in Annie's storeroom.

Annie's Projected Rental Revenues and Annual Minimum Guarantee

Proposer's Name	Annie's
Store Concept	Full line bulk & packaged chocolates, novelty candy, related gift packaged fancy food, gift baskets, related gifts, bulk candy
Merchandising Theme	Fine Chocolates and Candy

Established Tenant Rental Rate: 12.5%

Projected Gross Sales ($)		Percentage Rent	Projected Rental Revenues	Rental Revs. Per Sq. Ft.
A. Year 1	$600,000	12.5%	$75,000	$71.43
B. Year 2	$660,000	12.5%	$82,500	$78.57
C. Year 3	$726,000	12.5%	$90,750	$86.43
D. Year 4	$798,600	12.5%	$99,825	$95.07
Total Four Years	$2,784,600		$348,075	

Proposed Minimum Annual Guarantee: Year 1 $75,000 $71.43
(Not less than $55.00 per sq. ft. and not greater than Year 1's rental revs./sq/ft.)

Annie's Estimated Capital Investment

I. Retail Opportunity
- A. Proposer's Name — Annie's
- B. Store Concept: — Full line bulk and packaged candy and chocolates, related gift packaged fancy foods, gift baskets and gifts
- C. Merchandising Theme — Fine Chocolates and Candy

II. Proposer's Estimated Capital Investment		
A. Architectural & Engineering Fees		$ 5,000
B. Equipment, Furnishings & Fixtures$_{(1)\ (2)}$		20,000
C. Leasehold Improvements$_{(2)}$		40,000
D. Working Capital		15,000
E. Initial Inventory		25,000
F. Improvements Completion Bond		2,500
G. Total Investment (Sum of II-A. through II-F.)		$107,500
III. Source of Investment		
A. Amount Financed	$75,000	70%
B. Cash	32,500	30%
C. Total Investment (III-A. + III-B.) (Should equal II-G. above)	$107,500	100%
IV. Facility Improvements/Sq. Ft. (II-B. + II-C.)/I-D.		$ 57.14

(1) Items removable at end of lease term.

(2) The sum of these two categories (Equipment, Furnishings & Fixtures and Leasehold Improvements) shall not be less than $55 per square foot.

ANNIE'S

Projected Annual Income and Cash Flow Statements for Proposed Store

Proposer's Name	Annie's
Store Concept	Packaged & bulk confections & related gift & food items
Merchandising Theme	Fine Chocolates & Candy

	Year 1		Year 2		Year 3		Year 4	
Category	**Amount**	**% of Gross Sales**	**Amount**	**% of Gross Sales**	**Amount**	**% of Gross Sales**	**Amount**	**% of Gross Sales**
Gross Sales	$600,000.00		$660,000.00		$726,000.00		$798,600.00	
Cost of Goods	$216,000.00	36%	$237,600.00	36%	$261,360.00	36%	$287,496.00	36%
Gross Profit	$384,000.00	64%	$422,400.00	64%	$464,640.00	64%	$511,104.00	64%
Operating Expenses:								
Salaries/Wages/Benefits	$ 84,000.00	14.0%	$ 92,400.00	14.0%	$101,640.00	14.0%	$ 11,804.00	14.0%
Utilities and Telephone	$ 1,200.00	0.2%	$ 1,320.00	0.2%	$ 1,452.00	0.2%	$ 1,597.00	0.2%
Maintenance/Cleaning/Supplies	$ 14,400.00	2.4%	$ 15,840.00	2.4%	$ 17,424.00	2.4%	$ 19,166.00	2.4%
Insurance	$ 6,000.00	1.0%	$ 6,600.00	1.0%	$ 7,260.00	1.0%	$ 7,986.00	1.0%
Marketing/Advertising	$ 6,000.00	1.0%	$ 6,600.00	1.0%	$ 7,260.00	1.0%	$ 7,986.00	1.0%
Licensing Fees	$ 18,900.00	3.2%	$ 20,790.00	3.2%	$ 22,869.00	3.2%	$ 25,156.00	3.2%
Rent	$ 75,000.00	12.5%	$ 82,500.00	12.5%	$ 90,750.00	12.5%	$ 99,825.00	12.5%
General & Administration	$ 36,000.00	6.0%	$ 39,600.00	6.0%	$ 43,560.00	6.0%	$ 47,916.00	6.0%
Interest Expense	$ 9,600.00	1.6%	$ 9,600.00	1.5%	$ 9,600.00	1.3%	$ 9,600.00	1.2%
Other Misc. Expenses	$ 1,800.00	0.3%	$ 1,980.00	0.3%	$ 3,630.00	0.5%	$ 3,993.00	0.5%
Total Expenses	$252,900.00	42.2%	$277,230.00	42.1%	$305,445.00	42.1%	$335,029.00	42.0%
Depreciation	$ 7,600.00	1.3%	$ 7,600.00	1.3%	$ 7,600.00	1.3%	$ 7,600.00	1.3%
Net Income	$123,500.00	20.6%	$137,570.00	20.8%	$151,595.00	20.9%	$168,475.00	21.1%
Add Back: Depreciation	$ 7,600.00		$ 7,600.00		$ 7,600.00		$ 7,600.00	
Cash Flow From Operations	$131,100.00	—	$145,170.00	—	$159,195.00	—	$176,075.00	—
Beginning Cash Balance	$ 10,000.00		$131,100.00		$251,170.00		$385,365.00	
Plus: Cash Flow from Operations	$131,100.00		$145,170.00		$159,195.00		$176,075.00	
Minus: Debt Service (Principal only)	$ 10,000.00	—	$ 25,000.00	—	$ 25,000.00	—	$ 15,000.00	—
Minus: On-Going Annual Capital Expenditures	$ —	—	$ —	—	$ —	—	$ —	—
Ending Cash Balance Available to Proposer	$131,100.00	—	$251,170.00	—	$385,365.00	—	$546,440.00	—

See list of assumptions made to create these sales projections and figures on the following pages.

Assumptions Used In Developing Sales Projections and Figures

1. Statistics for this store are similar to the statistics for other stores in similar locations.
2. Five-year historical sales record for the former See's candy concession.
3. Current monthly sales should closely parallel historical record of former See's candy concession.
4. Growth projections provided by owner.
5. Historical record of growth.
6. Current economic growth.
7. Price increases in product over time.
8. U.S. Department of Commerce Confectionery Report shows a steady, consistent increase in per-capita consumption of candy (in pounds) since 1984.
9. Confection sales are predominantly impulse purchases; therefore, the higher the foot traffic, the higher the sales.

Annie's Appendix*

A. Balance Sheet
B. Break-even Analysis
C. Store Layout
D. Facility Design
E. Complete Store Design Details
F. Resumes
G. Legal References
H. Business References
I. Product Lists
J. Market Research Statistics

(*Appendices A–J would be provided to Sea World but are not included in the text.)

Forms, Forms, Forms

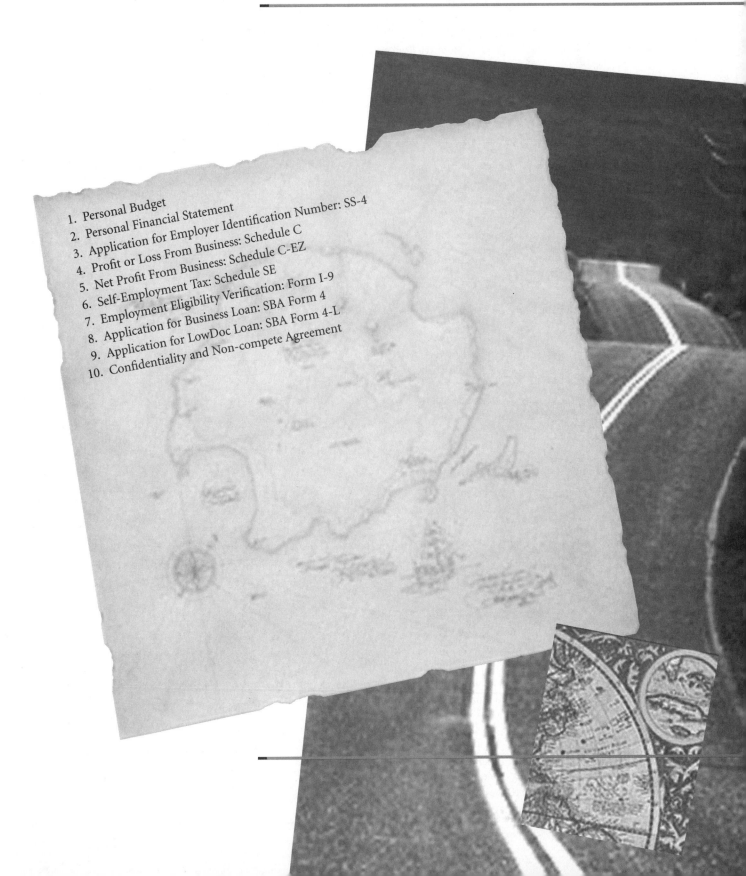

1. Personal Budget
2. Personal Financial Statement
3. Application for Employer Identification Number: SS-4
4. Profit or Loss From Business: Schedule C
5. Net Profit From Business: Schedule C-EZ
6. Self-Employment Tax: Schedule SE
7. Employment Eligibility Verification: Form I-9
8. Application for Business Loan: SBA Form 4
9. Application for LowDoc Loan: SBA Form 4-L
10. Confidentiality and Non-compete Agreement

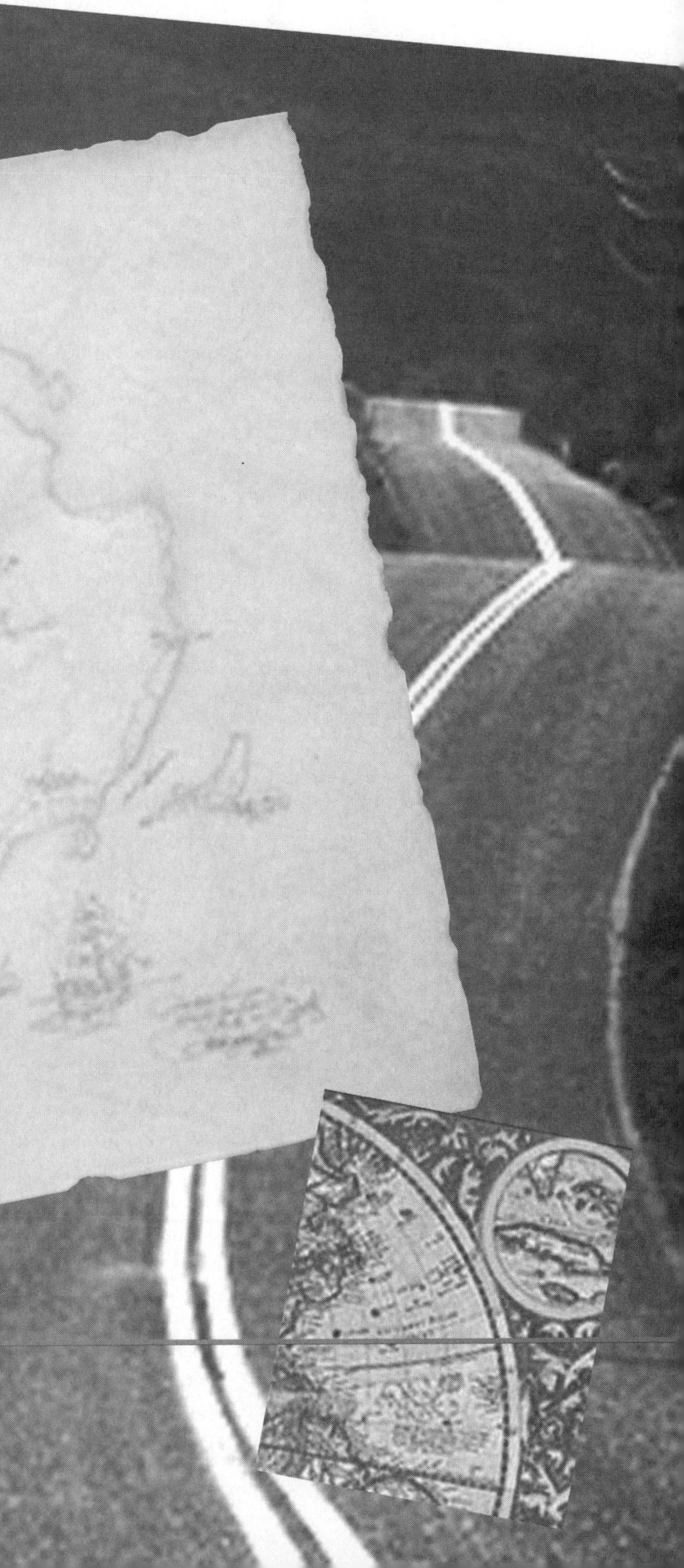

PERSONAL BUDGET

	AMOUNT
Food	
At home	______
Away from home	______
Housing	
Rent or Mortgage Payments	______
Property taxes	______
Maintenance	______
Insurance	
Life	______
Health	______
Car	______
House	______
Other	______
Credit Card Payments	______
Loan Payments	______
Clothing	______
Transportation	
Loan/Lease Payment	______
Gas/Oil	______
Maintenance	______
Licenses	______
Public transportation	______
Child Care	______
Health Care	
Insurance	______
Medical Services	______
Dentist	______
Drugs/Supplies	______
Entertainment	
Weekend/Dates	______
Hobbies	______
Other	______
Personal Care	______
Education	______
Charitable Contributions	______
Utilities	
Phone	______
Electricity	______
Gas	______
Cable	______
Water/garbage	______
Spending money	______
Miscellaneous	______
Children's allowances	______
Gifts	______
Vacations	______
Retirement Contributions	______
Savings	______
Taxes	
Social Security	______
Federal	______
State and local	______
Other	______
TOTAL	______

PERSONAL FINANCIAL STATEMENT

U.S. SMALL BUSINESS ADMINISTRATION

As of ______________, 19 ____

Complete this form for: (1) each proprietor, or (2) each limited partner who owns 20% or more interest and each general partner, or (3) each stockholder owning 20% or more of voting stock, or (4) any person or entity providing a guaranty on the loan.

Name | Business Phone

Residence Address | Residence Phone

City, State, & Zip Code

Business Name of Applicant/Borrower

ASSETS	(Omit Cents)	LIABILITIES	(Omit Cents)
Cash on hands & in Banks	$	Accounts Payable	$
Savings Accounts	$	Notes Payable to Banks and Others (Describe in Section 2)	$
IRA or Other Retirement Account	$	Installment Account (Auto)	$
Accounts & Notes Receivable	$	Mo. Payments $	
Life Insurance-Cash Surrender Value Only (Complete Section 8)	$	Installment Account (Other)	$
Stocks and Bonds (Describe in Section 3)	$	Mo. Payments $	
		Loan on Life Insurance	$
Real Estate (Describe in Section 4)	$	Mortgages on Real Estate (Describe in Section 4)	$
Automobile-Present Value	$	Unpaid Taxes (Describe in Section 6)	$
Other Personal Property (Describe in Section 5)	$	Other Liabilities (Describe in Section 7)	$
Other Assets (Describe in Section 5)	$	Total Liabilities	$
		Net Worth	$
Total	$	Total	$

Section 1. Source of Income		Contingent Liabilities	
Salary	$	As Endorser or Co-Maker	$
Net Investment Income	$	Legal Claims & Judgments	$
Real Estate Income	$	Provision for Federal Income Tax	$
Other Income (Describe below)*	$	Other Special Debt	$

Description of Other Income in Section 1.

*Alimony or child support payments need not be disclosed in "Other Income" unless it is desired to have such payments counted toward total income.

(Use attachments if necessary. Each attachment must be identified as a part of this statement and signed.)

Name and Address of Noteholder(s)	Original Balance	Current Balance	Payment Amount	Frequency (monthly,etc.)	How Secured or Endorsed Type of Collateral

Section 3.

Number of Shares	Name of Securities	Cost	Market Value Quotation/Exchange	Date of Quotation/Exchange	Total Value

Section 4. (List each parcel separately. Use attachment if necessary. Each attachment must be identified as a part of this statement and signed.)

	Property A	Property B	Property C
Type of Property			
Address			
Date Purchased			
Original Cost			
Present Market Value			
Name & Address of Mortgage Holder			
Mortgage Account Number			
Mortgage Balance			
Amount of Payment per Month/Year			
Status of Mortgage			

Section 5. (Describe, and if any is pledged as security, state name and address of lien holder, amount of lien, terms of payment and if delinquent, describe delinquency)

Section 6. Unpaid Taxes. (Describe in detail, as to type, to whom payable, when due, amount, and to what property, if any, a tax lien attaches.)

Section 7. Other Liabilities. (Describe in detail.)

Section 8. Life Insurance Held. (Give face amount and cash surrender value of policies - name of insurance company and beneficiaries)

I authorize SBA/Lender to make inquiries as necessary to verify the accuracy of the statements made and to determine my creditworthiness. I certify the above and the statements contained in the attachments are true and accurate as of the stated date(s). These statements are made for the purpose of either obtaining a loan or guaranteeing a loan. I understand FALSE statements may result in forfeiture of benefits and possible prosecution by the U.S. Attorney General (Reference 18 U.S.C. 1001).

Signature: Date: Social Security Number:

Signature: Date: Social Security Number:

PLEASE NOTE: The estimated average burden hours for the completion of this form is 1.5 hours per response. If you have questions or comments concerning this estimate or any other aspect of this information, please contact Chief, Administrative Branch, U.S. Small Business Administration, Washington, D.C. 20416, and Clearance Officer, Paper Reduction Project (3245-0188), Office of Management and Budget, Washington, D.C. 20503.

Form **SS-4**
(Rev. April 2000)
Department of the Treasury
Internal Revenue Service

Application for Employer Identification Number

(For use by employers, corporations, partnerships, trusts, estates, churches, government agencies, certain individuals, and others. See instructions.)

▶ Keep a copy for your records.

EIN

OMB No. 1545-0003

Please type or print clearly.

1 Name of applicant (legal name) (see instructions)

2 Trade name of business (if different from name on line 1)

3 Executor, trustee, "care of" name

4a Mailing address (street address) (room, apt., or suite no.)

5a Business address (if different from address on lines 4a and 4b)

4b City, state, and ZIP code

5b City, state, and ZIP code

6 County and state where principal business is located

7 Name of principal officer, general partner, grantor, owner, or trustor—SSN or ITIN may be required (see instructions) ▶

8a Type of entity (Check only one box.) (see instructions)
Caution: *If applicant is a limited liability company, see the instructions for line 8a.*

☐ Sole proprietor (SSN) ______
☐ Partnership
☐ REMIC
☐ State/local government
☐ Personal service corp.
☐ National Guard
☐ Farmers' cooperative
☐ Estate (SSN of decedent) ______
☐ Plan administrator (SSN) ______
☐ Other corporation (specify) ▶ ______
☐ Trust
☐ Church or church-controlled organization
☐ Federal government/military
☐ Other nonprofit organization (specify) ▶ ______ (enter GEN if applicable) ______
☐ Other (specify) ▶

8b If a corporation, name the state or foreign country (if applicable) where incorporated — State — Foreign country

9 Reason for applying (Check only one box.) (see instructions)
☐ Started new business (specify type) ▶ ______
☐ Hired employees (Check the box and see line 12.)
☐ Created a pension plan (specify type) ▶
☐ Banking purpose (specify purpose) ▶ ______
☐ Changed type of organization (specify new type) ▶ ______
☐ Purchased going business
☐ Created a trust (specify type) ▶ ______
☐ Other (specify) ▶

10 Date business started or acquired (month, day, year) (see instructions)

11 Closing month of accounting year (see instructions)

12 First date wages or annuities were paid or will be paid (month, day, year). **Note:** *If applicant is a withholding agent, enter date income will first be paid to nonresident alien. (month, day, year)* . . . . ▶

13 Highest number of employees expected in the next 12 months. **Note:** *If the applicant does not expect to have any employees during the period, enter -0-. (see instructions)* . . . . ▶

Nonagricultural	Agricultural	Household

14 Principal activity (see instructions) ▶

15 Is the principal business activity manufacturing? . . . . ☐ **Yes** ☐ **No**
If "Yes," principal product and raw material used ▶

16 To whom are most of the products or services sold? Please check one box. ☐ Business (wholesale)
☐ Public (retail) ☐ Other (specify) ▶ ☐ N/A

17a Has the applicant ever applied for an employer identification number for this or any other business? . . . . ☐ **Yes** ☐ **No**
Note: *If "Yes," please complete lines 17b and 17c.*

17b If you checked "Yes" on line 17a, give applicant's legal name and trade name shown on prior application, if different from line 1 or 2 above.
Legal name ▶ Trade name ▶

17c Approximate date when and city and state where the application was filed. Enter previous employer identification number if known.

Approximate date when filed (mo., day, year)	City and state where filed	Previous EIN

Under penalties of perjury, I declare that I have examined this application, and to the best of my knowledge and belief, it is true, correct, and complete.

Business telephone number (include area code) ( )

Fax telephone number (include area code) ( )

Name and title (Please type or print clearly.) ▶

Signature ▶ Date ▶

Note: *Do not write below this line. For official use only.*

Please leave blank ▶	Geo.	Ind.	Class	Size	Reason for applying

General Instructions

Section references are to the Internal Revenue Code unless otherwise noted.

Purpose of Form

Use Form SS-4 to apply for an employer identification number (EIN). An EIN is a nine-digit number (for example, 12-3456789) assigned to sole proprietors, corporations, partnerships, estates, trusts, and other entities for tax filing and reporting purposes. The information you provide on this form will establish your business tax account.

Caution: *An EIN is for use in connection with your business activities only. Do **not** use your EIN in place of your social security number (SSN).*

Who Must File

You must file this form if you have not been assigned an EIN before and:

- You pay wages to one or more employees including household employees.
- You are required to have an EIN to use on any return, statement, or other document, even if you are not an employer.
- You are a withholding agent required to withhold taxes on income, other than wages, paid to a nonresident alien (individual, corporation, partnership, etc.). A withholding agent may be an agent, broker, fiduciary, manager, tenant, or spouse, and is required to file **Form 1042,** Annual Withholding Tax Return for U.S. Source Income of Foreign Persons.
- You file **Schedule C,** Profit or Loss From Business, **Schedule C-EZ,** Net Profit From Business, or **Schedule F,** Profit or Loss From Farming, of **Form 1040,** U.S. Individual Income Tax Return, **and** have a Keogh plan or are required to file excise, employment, or alcohol, tobacco, or firearms returns.

The following must use EINs even if they do not have any employees:

- State and local agencies who serve as tax reporting agents for public assistance recipients, under Rev. Proc. 80-4, 1980-1 C.B. 581, should obtain a separate EIN for this reporting. See **Household employer** on page 3.
- Trusts, except the following:

1. Certain grantor-owned trusts. (See the **Instructions for Form 1041,** U.S. Income Tax Return for Estates and Trusts.)

2. Individual retirement arrangement (IRA) trusts, unless the trust has to file **Form 990-T,** Exempt Organization Business Income Tax Return. (See the **Instructions for Form 990-T.**)

- Estates
- Partnerships
- REMICs (real estate mortgage investment conduits) (See the **Instructions for Form 1066,** U.S. Real Estate Mortgage Investment Conduit (REMIC) Income Tax Return.)
- Corporations
- Nonprofit organizations (churches, clubs, etc.)
- Farmers' cooperatives
- Plan administrators (A plan administrator is the person or group of persons specified as the administrator by the instrument under which the plan is operated.)

When To Apply for a New EIN

New Business. If you become the new owner of an existing business, **do not** use the EIN of the former owner. **If you already have an EIN, use that number.** If you do not have an EIN, apply for one on this form. If you become the "owner" of a corporation by acquiring its stock, use the corporation's EIN.

Changes in Organization or Ownership. If you already have an EIN, you may need to get a new one if either the organization or ownership of your business changes. If you incorporate a sole proprietorship or form a partnership, you must get a new EIN. However, **do not** apply for a new EIN if:

- You change only the name of your business,
- You elected on **Form 8832,** Entity Classification Election, to change the way the entity is taxed, or
- A partnership terminates because at least 50% of the total interests in partnership capital and profits were sold or exchanged within a 12-month period. (See Regulations section 301.6109-1(d)(2)(iii).) The EIN for the terminated partnership should continue to be used.

Note: *If you are electing to be an "S corporation," be sure you file **Form 2553,** Election by a Small Business Corporation.*

File Only One Form SS-4. File only one Form SS-4, regardless of the number of businesses operated or trade names under which a business operates. However, each corporation in an affiliated group must file a separate application.

EIN Applied for, But Not Received. If you do not have an EIN by the time a return is due, write "Applied for" and the date you applied in the space shown for the number. **Do not** show your social security number (SSN) as an EIN on returns.

If you do not have an EIN by the time a tax deposit is due, send your payment to the Internal Revenue Service Center for your filing area. (See **Where To Apply** below.) Make your check or money order payable to "United States Treasury" and show your name (as shown on Form SS-4), address, type of tax, period covered, and date you applied for an EIN. Send an explanation with the deposit.

For more information about EINs, see **Pub. 583,** Starting a Business and Keeping Records, and **Pub. 1635,** Understanding Your EIN.

How To Apply

You can apply for an EIN either by mail or by telephone. You can get an EIN immediately by calling the Tele-TIN number for the service center for your state, or you can send the completed Form SS-4 directly to the service center to receive your EIN by mail.

Application by Tele-TIN. Under the Tele-TIN program, you can receive your EIN by telephone and use it immediately to file a return or make a payment. To receive an EIN by telephone, complete Form SS-4, then call the Tele-TIN number listed for your state under **Where To Apply.** The person making the call must be authorized to sign the form. (See **Signature** on page 4.)

An IRS representative will use the information from the Form SS-4 to establish your account and assign you an EIN. Write the number you are given on the upper right corner of the form and sign and date it.

*Mail or fax (facsimile) the signed Form SS-4 **within 24 hours** to the Tele-TIN Unit at the service center address for your state.* The IRS representative will give you the fax number. The fax numbers are also listed in Pub. 1635.

Taxpayer representatives can receive their client's EIN by telephone if they first send a fax of a completed **Form 2848,** Power of Attorney and Declaration of Representative, or **Form 8821,** Tax Information Authorization, to the Tele-TIN unit. The Form 2848 or Form 8821 will be used solely to release the EIN to the representative authorized on the form.

Application by Mail. Complete Form SS-4 at least 4 to 5 weeks before you will need an EIN. Sign and date the application and mail it to the service center address for your state. You will receive your EIN in the mail in approximately 4 weeks.

Where To Apply

The Tele-TIN numbers listed below will involve a long-distance charge to callers outside of the local calling area and can be used only to apply for an EIN. **The numbers may change without notice.** Call 1-800-829-1040 to verify a number or to ask about the status of an application by mail.

If your principal business, office or agency, or legal residence in the case of an individual, is located in:	**Call the Tele-TIN number shown or file with the Internal Revenue Service Center at:**
Florida, Georgia, South Carolina	Attn: Entity Control Atlanta, GA 39901 770-455-2360
New Jersey, New York (New York City and counties of Nassau, Rockland, Suffolk, and Westchester)	Attn: Entity Control Holtsville, NY 00501 631-447-4955
New York (all other counties), Connecticut, Maine, Massachusetts, New Hampshire, Rhode Island, Vermont	Attn: Entity Control Andover, MA 05501 978-474-9717
Illinois, Iowa, Minnesota, Missouri, Wisconsin	Attn: Entity Control Stop 6800 2306 E. Bannister Rd. Kansas City, MO 64999 816-926-5999
Delaware, District of Columbia, Maryland, Pennsylvania, Virginia	Attn: Entity Control Philadelphia, PA 19255 215-516-6999
Indiana, Kentucky, Michigan, Ohio, West Virginia	Attn: Entity Control Cincinnati, OH 45999 859-292-5467

Kansas, New Mexico, Oklahoma, Texas	Attn: Entity Control Austin, TX 73301 512-460-7843
Alaska, Arizona, California (counties of Alpine, Amador, Butte, Calaveras, Colusa, Contra Costa, Del Norte, El Dorado, Glenn, Humboldt, Lake, Lassen, Marin, Mendocino, Modoc, Napa, Nevada, Placer, Plumas, Sacramento, San Joaquin, Shasta, Sierra, Siskiyou, Solano, Sonoma, Sutter, Tehama, Trinity, Yolo, and Yuba), Colorado, Idaho, Montana, Nebraska, Nevada, North Dakota, Oregon, South Dakota, Utah, Washington, Wyoming	Attn: Entity Control Mail Stop 6271 P.O. Box 9941 Ogden, UT 84201 801-620-7645
California (all other counties), Hawaii	Attn: Entity Control Fresno, CA 93888 559-452-4010
Alabama, Arkansas, Louisiana, Mississippi, North Carolina, Tennessee	Attn: Entity Control Memphis, TN 37501 901-546-3920
If you have no legal residence, principal place of business, or principal office or agency in any state	Attn: Entity Control Philadelphia, PA 19255 215-516-6999

Specific Instructions

The instructions that follow are for those items that are not self-explanatory. Enter N/A (nonapplicable) on the lines that do not apply.

Line 1. Enter the legal name of the entity applying for the EIN exactly as it appears on the social security card, charter, or other applicable legal document.

Individuals. Enter your first name, middle initial, and last name. If you are a sole proprietor, enter your individual name, not your business name. Enter your business name on line 2. Do not use abbreviations or nicknames on line 1.

Trusts. Enter the name of the trust.

Estate of a decedent. Enter the name of the estate.

Partnerships. Enter the legal name of the partnership as it appears in the partnership agreement. **Do not** list the names of the partners on line 1. See the specific instructions for line 7.

Corporations. Enter the corporate name as it appears in the corporation charter or other legal document creating it.

Plan administrators. Enter the name of the plan administrator. A plan administrator who already has an EIN should use that number.

Line 2. Enter the trade name of the business if different from the legal name. The trade name is the "doing business as" name.

Note: *Use the full legal name on line 1 on all tax returns filed for the entity. However, if you enter a trade name on line 2 and choose to use the trade name instead of the legal name, enter the trade name on all returns you file. To prevent processing delays and errors,* ***always*** *use either the legal name only or the trade name only on all tax returns.*

Line 3. Trusts enter the name of the trustee. Estates enter the name of the executor, administrator, or other fiduciary. If the entity applying has a designated person to receive tax information, enter that person's name as the "care of" person. Print or type the first name, middle initial, and last name.

Line 7. Enter the first name, middle initial, last name, and SSN of a principal officer if the business is a corporation; of a general partner if a partnership; of the owner of a single member entity that is disregarded as an entity separate from its owner; or of a grantor, owner, or trustor if a trust. If the person in question is an alien individual with a previously assigned individual taxpayer identification number (ITIN), enter the ITIN in the space provided, instead of an SSN. You are not required to enter an SSN or ITIN if the reason you are applying for an EIN is to make an entity classification election (see Regulations section 301.7701-1 through 301.7701-3), and you are a nonresident alien with no effectively connected income from sources within the United States.

Line 8a. Check the box that best describes the type of entity applying for the EIN. If you are an alien individual with an ITIN previously assigned to you, enter the ITIN in place of a requested SSN.

Caution: *This is not an election for a tax classification of an entity. See "Limited liability company (LLC)" below.*

If not specifically mentioned, check the "Other" box, enter the type of entity and the type of return that will be filed (for example, common trust fund, Form 1065). Do not enter N/A. If you are an alien individual applying for an EIN, see the Line 7 instructions above.

Sole proprietor. Check this box if you file Schedule C, C-EZ, or F (Form 1040) and have a qualified plan, or are required to file excise, employment, or alcohol, tobacco, or firearms returns, or are a payer of gambling winnings. Enter your SSN (or ITIN) in the space provided. If you are a nonresident alien with are a nonresident alien with no effectively connected income from sources within the United States, you do not need to enter an SSN or ITIN.

REMIC. Check this box if the entity has elected to be treated as a real estate mortgage investment conduit (REMIC). See the Instructions for Form 1066 for more information.

Other nonprofit organization. Check this box if the nonprofit organization is other than a church or church-controlled organization and specify the type of nonprofit organization (for example, an educational organization).

If the organization also seeks tax-exempt status, you must file either **Package 1023,** Application for Recognition of Exemption, or **Package 1024,** Application for Recognition of Exemption Under Section 501(a). Get **Pub. 557,** Tax Exempt Status for Your Organization, for more information.

Group exemption number (GEN). If the organization is covered by a group exemption letter, enter the four-digit GEN. (Do not confuse the GEN with the nine-digit EIN.) If you do not know the GEN, contact the parent organization. Get Pub. 557 for more information about group exemption numbers.

Withholding agent. If you are a withholding agent required to file Form 1042, check the "Other" box and enter "Withholding agent."

Personal service corporation. Check this box if the entity is a personal service corporation. An entity is a personal service corporation for a tax year only if:

- The principal activity of the entity during the testing period (prior tax year) for the tax year is the performance of personal services substantially by employee-owners, and
- The employee-owners own at least 10% of the fair market value of the outstanding stock in the entity on the last day of the testing period.

Personal services include performance of services in such fields as health, law, accounting, or consulting. For more information about personal service corporations, see the **Instructions for Forms 1120 and 1120-A,** and **Pub. 542,** Corporations.

Limited liability company (LLC). See the definition of limited liability company in the **Instructions for Form 1065,** U.S. Partnership Return of Income. An LLC with two or more members can be a partnership or an association taxable as a corporation. An LLC with a single owner can be an association taxable as a corporation or an entity disregarded as an entity separate from its owner. See Form 8832 for more details.

Note: *A domestic LLC with at least two members that does not file Form 8832 is classified as a partnership for Federal income tax purposes.*

- If the entity is classified as a partnership for Federal income tax purposes, check the "partnership" box.
- If the entity is classified as a corporation for Federal income tax purposes, check the "Other corporation" box and write "limited liability co." in the space provided.
- If the entity is disregarded as an entity separate from its owner, check the "Other" box and write in "disregarded entity" in the space provided.

Plan administrator. If the plan administrator is an individual, enter the plan administrator's SSN in the space provided.

Other corporation. This box is for any corporation other than a personal service corporation. If you check this box, enter the type of corporation (such as insurance company) in the space provided.

Household employer. If you are an individual, check the "Other" box and enter "Household employer" and your SSN. If you are a state or local agency serving as a tax reporting agent for public assistance recipients who become household employers, check the "Other" box and enter "Household employer agent." If you are a trust that qualifies as a household employer, you do not need a separate EIN for reporting tax information relating to household employees; use the EIN of the trust.

QSub. For a qualified subchapter S subsidiary (QSub) check the "Other" box and specify "QSub."

Line 9. Check only **one** box. Do not enter N/A.

Started new business. Check this box if you are starting a new business that requires an EIN. If you check this box, enter the type of business being started. **Do not** apply if you already have an EIN and are only adding another place of business.

Hired employees. Check this box if the existing business is requesting an EIN because it has hired or is hiring employees and is therefore required to file employment tax returns. **Do not** apply if you already have an EIN and are only hiring employees. For information on the applicable employment taxes for family members, see **Circular E,** Employer's Tax Guide (Publication 15).

Created a pension plan. Check this box if you have created a pension plan and need an EIN for reporting purposes. Also, enter the type of plan.

Note: *Check this box if you are applying for a trust EIN when a new pension plan is established.*

Banking purpose. Check this box if you are requesting an EIN for banking purposes only, and enter the banking purpose (for example, a bowling league for depositing dues or an investment club for dividend and interest reporting).

Changed type of organization. Check this box if the business is changing its type of organization, for example, if the business was a sole proprietorship and has been incorporated or has become a partnership. If you check this box, specify in the space provided the type of change made, for example, "from sole proprietorship to partnership."

Purchased going business. Check this box if you purchased an existing business. **Do not** use the former owner's EIN. **Do not** apply for a new EIN if you already have one. Use your own EIN.

Created a trust. Check this box if you created a trust, and enter the type of trust created. For example, indicate if the trust is a nonexempt charitable trust or a split-interest trust.

Note: ***Do not*** *check this box if you are applying for a trust EIN when a new pension plan is established. Check "Created a pension plan."*

Exception. Do **not** file this form for certain grantor-type trusts. The trustee does not need an EIN for the trust if the trustee furnishes the name and TIN of the grantor/owner and the address of the trust to all payors. See the Instructions for Form 1041 for more information.

Other (specify). Check this box if you are requesting an EIN for any other reason, and enter the reason.

Line 10. If you are starting a new business, enter the starting date of the business. If the business you acquired is already operating, enter the date you acquired the business. Trusts should enter the date the trust was legally created. Estates should enter the date of death of the decedent whose name appears on line 1 or the date when the estate was legally funded.

Line 11. Enter the last month of your accounting year or tax year. An accounting or tax year is usually 12 consecutive months, either a calendar year or a fiscal year (including a period of 52 or 53 weeks). A calendar year is 12 consecutive months ending on December 31. A fiscal year is either 12 consecutive months ending on the last day of any month other than December or a 52-53 week year. For more information on accounting periods, see **Pub. 538,** Accounting Periods and Methods.

Individuals. Your tax year generally will be a calendar year.

Partnerships. Partnerships generally must adopt one of the following tax years:

- The tax year of the majority of its partners,
- The tax year common to all of its principal partners,
- The tax year that results in the least aggregate deferral of income, or
- In certain cases, some other tax year.

See the Instructions for Form 1065 for more information.

REMIC. REMICs must have a calendar year as their tax year.

Personal service corporations. A personal service corporation generally must adopt a calendar year unless:

- It can establish a business purpose for having a different tax year, or
- It elects under section 444 to have a tax year other than a calendar year.

Trusts. Generally, a trust must adopt a calendar year except for the following:

- Tax-exempt trusts,
- Charitable trusts, and
- Grantor-owned trusts.

Line 12. If the business has or will have employees, enter the date on which the business began or will begin to pay wages. If the business does not plan to have employees, enter N/A.

Withholding agent. Enter the date you began or will begin to pay income to a nonresident alien. This also applies to individuals who are required to file Form 1042 to report alimony paid to a nonresident alien.

Line 13. For a definition of agricultural labor (farmwork), see **Circular A,** Agricultural Employer's Tax Guide (Publication 51).

Line 14. Generally, enter the exact type of business being operated (for example, advertising agency, farm, food or beverage establishment, labor union, real estate agency, steam laundry, rental of coin-operated vending machine, or investment club). Also state if the business will involve the sale or distribution of alcoholic beverages.

Governmental. Enter the type of organization (state, county, school district, municipality, etc.).

Nonprofit organization (other than governmental). Enter whether organized for religious, educational, or humane purposes, and the principal activity (for example, religious organization—hospital, charitable).

Mining and quarrying. Specify the process and the principal product (for example, mining bituminous coal, contract drilling for oil, or quarrying dimension stone).

Contract construction. Specify whether general contracting or special trade contracting. Also, show the type of work normally performed (for example, general contractor for residential buildings or electrical subcontractor).

Food or beverage establishments. Specify the type of establishment and state whether you employ workers who receive tips (for example, lounge—yes).

Trade. Specify the type of sales and the principal line of goods sold (for example, wholesale dairy products, manufacturer's representative for mining machinery, or retail hardware).

Manufacturing. Specify the type of establishment operated (for example, sawmill or vegetable cannery).

Signature. The application must be signed by (a) the individual, if the applicant is an individual, (b) the president, vice president, or other principal officer, if the applicant is a corporation, (c) a responsible and duly authorized member or officer having knowledge of its affairs, if the applicant is a partnership or other unincorporated organization, or (d) the fiduciary, if the applicant is a trust or an estate.

How To Get Forms and Publications

Phone. You can order forms, instructions, and publications by phone 24 hours a day, 7 days a week. Just call 1-800-TAX-FORM (1-800-829-3676). You should receive your order or notification of its status within 10 workdays.

Personal computer. With your personal computer and modem, you can get the forms and information you need using IRS's Internet Web Site at **www.irs.gov** or File Transfer Protocol at **ftp.irs.gov.**

CD-ROM. For small businesses, return preparers, or others who may frequently need tax forms or publications, a CD-ROM containing over 2,000 tax products (including many prior year forms) can be purchased from the National Technical Information Service (NTIS).

To order **Pub. 1796,** Federal Tax Products on CD-ROM, call **1-877-CDFORMS** (1-877-233-6767) toll free or connect to **www.irs.gov/cdorders**

Privacy Act and Paperwork Reduction Act Notice. We ask for the information on this form to carry out the Internal Revenue laws of the United States. We need it to comply with section 6109 and the regulations thereunder which generally require the inclusion of an employer identification number (EIN) on certain returns, statements, or other documents filed with the Internal Revenue Service. Information on this form may be used to determine which Federal tax returns you are required to file and to provide you with related forms and publications. We disclose this form to the Social Security Administration for their use in determining compliance with applicable laws. We will be unable to issue an EIN to you unless you provide all of the requested information which applies to your entity.

You are not required to provide the information requested on a form that is subject to the Paperwork Reduction Act unless the form displays a valid OMB control number. Books or records relating to a form or its instructions must be retained as long as their contents may become material in the administration of any Internal Revenue law. Generally, tax returns/return information are confidential, as required by section 6103.

The time needed to complete and file this form will vary depending on individual circumstances. The estimated average time is:

Recordkeeping	7 min.
Learning about the law or the form	22 min.
Preparing the form	46 min.
Copying, assembling, and sending the form to the IRS	20 min.

If you have comments concerning the accuracy of these time estimates or suggestions for making this form simpler, we would be happy to hear from you. You can write to the Tax Forms Committee, Western Area Distribution Center, Rancho Cordova, CA 95743-0001. **Do not** send the form to this address. Instead, see **Where To Apply** on page 2.

SCHEDULE C (Form 1040)

Department of the Treasury Internal Revenue Service (99)

Profit or Loss From Business

(Sole Proprietorship)

▶ Partnerships, joint ventures, etc., must file Form 1065 or Form 1065-B.

▶ Attach to Form 1040 or Form 1041. ▶ See Instructions for Schedule C (Form 1040).

OMB No. 1545-0074

2000

Attachment Sequence No. 09

Name of proprietor | Social security number (SSN)

A Principal business or profession, including product or service (see page C-1 of the instructions) | B Enter code from pages C-7 & 8 ▶

C Business name. If no separate business name, leave blank. | D Employer ID number (EIN), if any

E Business address (including suite or room no.) ▶
City, town or post office, state, and ZIP code

F Accounting method: (1) ☐ Cash (2) ☐ Accrual (3) ☐ Other (specify) ▶

G Did you "materially participate" in the operation of this business during 2000? If "No," see page C-2 for limit on losses . ☐ Yes ☐ No

H If you started or acquired this business during 2000, check here . . . ▶ ☐

Part I Income

1	Gross receipts or sales. **Caution.** If this income was reported to you on Form W-2 and the "Statutory employee" box on that form was checked, see page C-2 and check here ▶ ☐	1	
2	Returns and allowances	2	
3	Subtract line 2 from line 1	3	
4	Cost of goods sold (from line 42 on page 2)	4	
5	**Gross profit.** Subtract line 4 from line 3	5	
6	Other income, including Federal and state gasoline or fuel tax credit or refund (see page C-2)	6	
7	**Gross income.** Add lines 5 and 6 ▶	7	

Part II Expenses. Enter expenses for business use of your home **only** on line 30.

8	Advertising	8		19	Pension and profit-sharing plans	19	
9	Bad debts from sales or services (see page C-3)	9		20	Rent or lease (see page C-4):		
				a	Vehicles, machinery, and equipment	20a	
10	Car and truck expenses (see page C-3)	10		b	Other business property	20b	
11	Commissions and fees	11		21	Repairs and maintenance	21	
12	Depletion	12		22	Supplies (not included in Part III)	22	
				23	Taxes and licenses	23	
13	Depreciation and section 179 expense deduction (not included in Part III) (see page C-3)	13		24	Travel, meals, and entertainment:		
				a	Travel	24a	
14	Employee benefit programs (other than on line 19)	14		b	Meals and entertainment		
15	Insurance (other than health)	15		c	Enter nondeductible amount included on line 24b (see page C-5)		
16	Interest:						
a	Mortgage (paid to banks, etc.)	16a		d	Subtract line 24c from line 24b	24d	
b	Other	16b		25	Utilities	25	
17	Legal and professional services	17		26	Wages (less employment credits)	26	
18	Office expense	18		27	Other expenses (from line 48 on page 2)	27	

28	**Total expenses** before expenses for business use of home. Add lines 8 through 27 in columns ▶	28	
29	Tentative profit (loss). Subtract line 28 from line 7	29	
30	Expenses for business use of your home. Attach Form 8829	30	
31	**Net profit or (loss).** Subtract line 30 from line 29. • If a profit, enter on **Form 1040, line 12,** and **also** on **Schedule SE, line 2** (statutory employees, see page C-5). Estates and trusts, enter on Form 1041, line 3. • If a loss, you **must** go to line 32.	31	

32 If you have a loss, check the box that describes your investment in this activity (see page C-5).
• If you checked 32a, enter the loss on **Form 1040, line 12,** and **also** on **Schedule SE, line 2** (statutory employees, see page C-5). Estates and trusts, enter on Form 1041, line 3.
• If you checked 32b, you **must** attach **Form 6198.**

32a ☐ All investment is at risk.
32b ☐ Some investment is not at risk.

Schedule C (Form 1040) 2000 Page **2**

Part III **Cost of Goods Sold** (see page C-6)

33 Method(s) used to value closing inventory: **a** ☐ Cost **b** ☐ Lower of cost or market **c** ☐ Other (attach explanation)

34 Was there any change in determining quantities, costs, or valuations between opening and closing inventory? If "Yes," attach explanation . . . ☐ **Yes** ☐ **No**

35	Inventory at beginning of year. If different from last year's closing inventory, attach explanation	35	
36	Purchases less cost of items withdrawn for personal use	36	
37	Cost of labor. Do not include any amounts paid to yourself	37	
38	Materials and supplies	38	
39	Other costs	39	
40	Add lines 35 through 39	40	
41	Inventory at end of year	41	
42	**Cost of goods sold.** Subtract line 41 from line 40. Enter the result here and on page 1, line 4	42	

Part IV **Information on Your Vehicle.** Complete this part **only** if you are claiming car or truck expenses on line 10 and are not required to file Form 4562 for this business. See the instructions for line 13 on page C-3 to find out if you must file.

43 When did you place your vehicle in service for business purposes? (month, day, year) ▶ ..../......../........

44 Of the total number of miles you drove your vehicle during 2000, enter the number of miles you used your vehicle for:

a Business .... **b** Commuting .... **c** Other ....

45 Do you (or your spouse) have another vehicle available for personal use? . . . ☐ **Yes** ☐ **No**

46 Was your vehicle available for use during off-duty hours? . . . ☐ **Yes** ☐ **No**

47a Do you have evidence to support your deduction? . . . ☐ **Yes** ☐ **No**

b If "Yes," is the evidence written? . . . ☐ **Yes** ☐ **No**

Part V **Other Expenses.** List below business expenses not included on lines 8–26 or line 30.

48 **Total other expenses.** Enter here and on page 1, line 27	48	

Schedule C (Form 1040) 2000

SCHEDULE C-EZ (Form 1040)

Department of the Treasury Internal Revenue Service (99)

Net Profit From Business

(Sole Proprietorship)

▶ Partnerships, joint ventures, etc., must file Form 1065 or 1065-B.

▶ Attach to Form 1040 or Form 1041. ▶ See instructions on back.

OMB No. 1545-0074

2000

Attachment Sequence No. **09A**

Name of proprietor | Social security number (SSN)

Part I General Information

You May Use Schedule C-EZ Instead of Schedule C Only If You:

- Had business expenses of $2,500 or less.
- Use the cash method of accounting.
- Did not have an inventory at any time during the year.
- Did not have a net loss from your business.
- Had only one business as a sole proprietor.

And You:

- Had no employees during the year.
- Are not required to file **Form 4562,** Depreciation and Amortization, for this business. See the instructions for Schedule C, line 13, on page C-3 to find out if you must file.
- Do not deduct expenses for business use of your home.
- Do not have prior year unallowed passive activity losses from this business.

A Principal business or profession, including product or service

B Enter code from pages C-7 & 8 ▶

C Business name. If no separate business name, leave blank.

D Employer ID number (EIN), if any

E Business address (including suite or room no.). Address not required if same as on Form 1040, page 1.

City, town or post office, state, and ZIP code

Part II Figure Your Net Profit

1	**Gross receipts. Caution:** *If this income was reported to you on Form W-2 and the "Statutory employee" box on that form was checked, see* ***Statutory Employees*** *in the instructions for Schedule C, line 1, on page C-2 and check here* . . . . ▶ ☐	1	
2	**Total expenses.** If more than $2,500, you **must** use Schedule C. See instructions	2	
3	**Net profit.** Subtract line 2 from line 1. If less than zero, you **must** use Schedule C. Enter on **Form 1040, line 12,** and **also** on **Schedule SE, line 2.** (Statutory employees **do not** report this amount on Schedule SE, line 2. Estates and trusts, enter on Form 1041, line 3.)	3	

Part III Information on Your Vehicle. Complete this part only if you are claiming car or truck expenses on line 2.

4 When did you place your vehicle in service for business purposes? (month, day, year) ▶ ..../........./.......

5 Of the total number of miles you drove your vehicle during 2000, enter the number of miles you used your vehicle for:

a Business .... **b** Commuting .... **c** Other ....

6 Do you (or your spouse) have another vehicle available for personal use? . . . . ☐ Yes ☐ No

7 Was your vehicle available for use during off-duty hours? . . . . ☐ Yes ☐ No

8a Do you have evidence to support your deduction? . . . . ☐ Yes ☐ No

b If "Yes," is the evidence written? . . . . ☐ Yes ☐ No

For Paperwork Reduction Act Notice, see Form 1040 instructions. Cat. No. 14374D **Schedule C-EZ (Form 1040) 2000**

(continued)

Instructions

You may use Schedule C-EZ instead of Schedule C if you operated a business or practiced a profession as a sole proprietorship and you have met all the requirements listed in Part I of Schedule C-EZ.

Line A

Describe the business or professional activity that provided your principal source of income reported on line 1. Give the general field or activity and the type of product or service.

Line B

Enter the six-digit code that identifies your principal business or professional activity. See pages C-7 and C-8 of the Instructions for Schedule C for the list of codes.

Line D

You need an employer identification number (EIN) only if you had a qualified retirement plan or were required to file an employment, excise, estate, trust, or alcohol, tobacco, and firearms tax return. If you need an EIN, file **Form SS-4,** Application for Employer Identification Number. If you do not have an EIN, leave line D blank. **Do not** enter your SSN.

Line E

Enter your business address. Show a street address instead of a box number. Include the suite or room number, if any.

Line 1

Enter gross receipts from your trade or business. Include amounts you received in your trade or business that were properly shown on **Forms 1099-MISC.** If the total amounts that were reported in box 7 of Forms 1099-MISC are more than the total you are reporting on line 1, attach a statement explaining the difference. You must show all items of taxable income actually or constructively received during the year (in cash, property, or services). Income is constructively received when it is credited to your account or set aside for you to use. Do not offset this amount by any losses.

Line 2

Enter the total amount of all deductible business expenses you actually paid during the year. Examples of these expenses include advertising, car and truck expenses, commissions and fees, insurance, interest, legal and professional services, office expense, rent or lease expenses, repairs and maintenance, supplies, taxes, travel, the allowable percentage of business meals and entertainment, and utilities (including telephone). For details, see the instructions for Schedule C, Parts II and V, on pages C-3 through C-6. If you wish, you may use the optional worksheet below to record your expenses.

If you claim car or truck expenses, be sure to complete Part III of Schedule C-EZ.

Optional Worksheet for Line 2 (keep a copy for your records)

a	Business meals and entertainment	a			
b	Enter nondeductible amount included on line **a** (see the instructions for lines 24b and 24c on page C-5)	b			
c	Deductible business meals and entertainment. Subtract line **b** from line **a**			c	
d				d	
e				e	
f				f	
g				g	
h				h	
i				i	
j	**Total.** Add lines **c** through **i**. Enter here and on line 2			j	

SCHEDULE SE (Form 1040) Department of the Treasury Internal Revenue Service (99)	**Self-Employment Tax** ▶ See Instructions for Schedule SE (Form 1040). ▶ Attach to Form 1040.	OMB No. 1545-0074 **2000** Attachment Sequence No. **17**

Name of person with **self-employment** income (as shown on Form 1040)	Social security number of person with **self-employment** income ▶	: :

Who Must File Schedule SE

You must file Schedule SE if:

- You had net earnings from self-employment from **other than** church employee income (line 4 of Short Schedule SE or line 4c of Long Schedule SE) of $400 or more **or**
- You had church employee income of $108.28 or more. Income from services you performed as a minister or a member of a religious order **is not** church employee income. See page SE-1.

Note. Even if you had a loss or a small amount of income from self-employment, it may be to your benefit to file Schedule SE and use either "optional method" in Part II of Long Schedule SE. See page SE-3.

Exception. If your only self-employment income was from earnings as a minister, member of a religious order, or Christian Science practitioner **and** you filed Form 4361 and received IRS approval not to be taxed on those earnings, **do not** file Schedule SE. Instead, write "Exempt–Form 4361" on Form 1040, line 52.

May I Use Short Schedule SE or Must I Use Long Schedule SE?

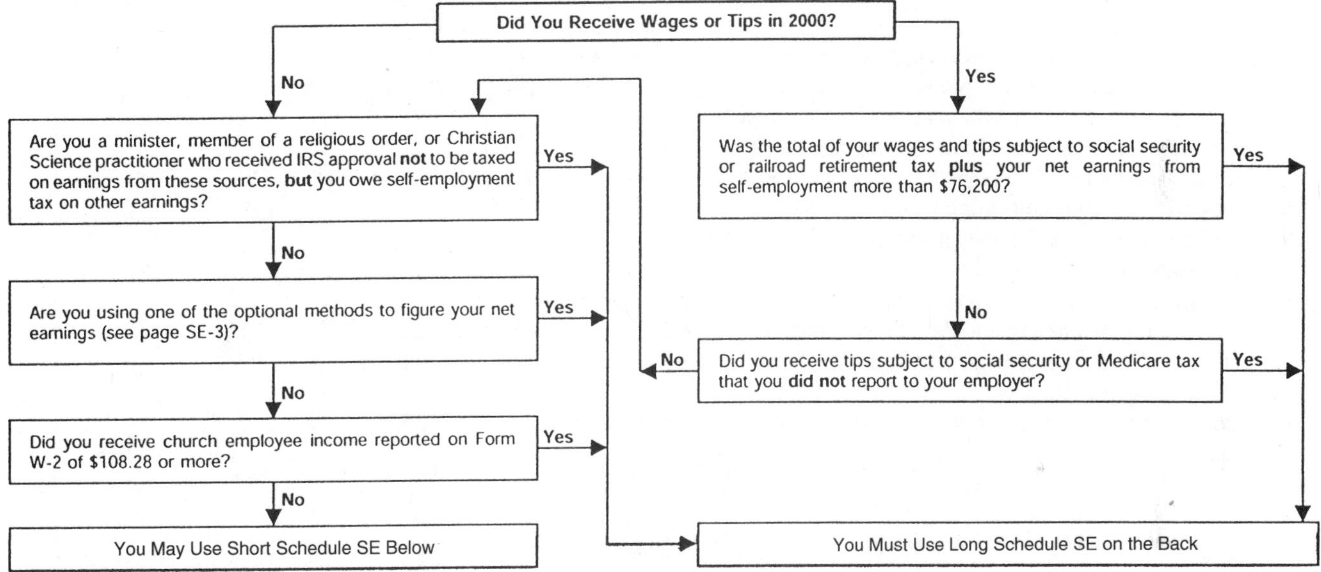

Section A—Short Schedule SE. Caution: *Read above to see if you can use Short Schedule SE.*

1	Net farm profit or (loss) from Schedule F, line 36, and farm partnerships, Schedule K-1 (Form 1065), line 15a	1	
2	Net profit or (loss) from Schedule C, line 31; Schedule C-EZ, line 3; Schedule K-1 (Form 1065), line 15a (other than farming); and Schedule K-1 (Form 1065-B), box 9. Ministers and members of religious orders, see page SE-1 for amounts to report on this line. See page SE-2 for other income to report	2	
3	Combine lines 1 and 2	3	
4	**Net earnings from self-employment.** Multiply line 3 by 92.35% (.9235). **If less than $400, do not file this schedule; you do not owe self-employment tax** . . . . ▶	4	
5	**Self-employment tax.** If the amount on line 4 is: • $76,200 or less, multiply line 4 by 15.3% (.153). Enter the result here and on **Form 1040, line 52.** • More than $76,200, multiply line 4 by 2.9% (.029). Then, add $9,448.80 to the result. Enter the total here and on **Form 1040, line 52.** . . .	5	
6	**Deduction for one-half of self-employment tax.** Multiply line 5 by 50% (.5). Enter the result here and on **Form 1040, line 27** . . . . | 6 |		

For Paperwork Reduction Act Notice, see Form 1040 instructions. Cat. No. 11358Z **Schedule SE (Form 1040) 2000**

Name of person with **self-employment** income (as shown on Form 1040)	Social security number of person with **self-employment** income ▶	

Section B—Long Schedule SE

Part I Self-Employment Tax

Note. If your only income subject to self-employment tax is **church employee income,** skip lines 1 through 4b. Enter -0- on line 4c and go to line 5a. Income from services you performed as a minister or a member of a religious order **is not** church employee income. See page SE-1.

A If you are a minister, member of a religious order, or Christian Science practitioner **and** you filed Form 4361, but you had $400 or more of **other** net earnings from self-employment, check here and continue with Part I . . . . ▶ ☐

Line	Description			Line	Amount	
1	Net farm profit or (loss) from Schedule F, line 36, and farm partnerships, Schedule K-1 (Form 1065), line 15a. **Note.** Skip this line if you use the farm optional method. See page SE-3			1		
2	Net profit or (loss) from Schedule C, line 31; Schedule C-EZ, line 3; Schedule K-1 (Form 1065), line 15a (other than farming); and Schedule K-1 (Form 1065-B), box 9. Ministers and members of religious orders, see page SE-1 for amounts to report on this line. See page SE-2 for other income to report. **Note.** Skip this line if you use the nonfarm optional method. See page SE-3.			2		
3	Combine lines 1 and 2			3		
4a	If line 3 is more than zero, multiply line 3 by 92.35% (.9235). Otherwise, enter amount from line 3			4a		
b	If you elect one or both of the optional methods, enter the total of lines 15 and 17 here			4b		
c	Combine lines 4a and 4b. If less than $400, **do not** file this schedule; you do not owe self-employment tax. **Exception.** If less than $400 and you had **church employee income,** enter -0- and continue ▶			4c		
5a	Enter your **church employee income** from Form W-2. **Caution:** *See page SE-1 for definition of church employee income*	5a				
b	Multiply line 5a by 92.35% (.9235). If less than $100, enter -0-			5b		
6	**Net earnings from self-employment.** Add lines 4c and 5b			6		
7	Maximum amount of combined wages and self-employment earnings subject to social security tax or the 6.2% portion of the 7.65% railroad retirement (tier 1) tax for 2000			7	76,200	00
8a	Total social security wages and tips (total of boxes 3 and 7 on Form(s) W-2) and railroad retirement (tier 1) compensation	8a				
b	Unreported tips subject to social security tax (from Form 4137, line 9)	8b				
c	Add lines 8a and 8b			8c		
9	Subtract line 8c from line 7. If zero or less, enter -0- here and on line 10 and go to line 11 ▶			9		
10	Multiply the **smaller** of line 6 or line 9 by 12.4% (.124)			10		
11	Multiply line 6 by 2.9% (.029)			11		
12	**Self-employment tax.** Add lines 10 and 11. Enter here and on **Form 1040, line 52**			12		
13	**Deduction for one-half of self-employment tax.** Multiply line 12 by 50% (.5). Enter the result here and on **Form 1040, line 27**	13				

Part II Optional Methods To Figure Net Earnings (See page SE-3.)

Farm Optional Method. You may use this method **only** if:

- Your gross farm income[1] was not more than $2,400 **or**
- Your net farm profits[2] were less than $1,733.

Line	Description	Line	Amount	
14	Maximum income for optional methods	14	1,600	00
15	Enter the **smaller** of: two-thirds (⅔) of gross farm income[1] (not less than zero) **or** $1,600. Also include this amount on line 4b above	15		

Nonfarm Optional Method. You may use this method **only** if:

- Your net nonfarm profits[3] were less than $1,733 and also less than 72.189% of your gross nonfarm income[4] **and**
- You had net earnings from self-employment of at least $400 in 2 of the prior 3 years.

Caution: *You may use this method no more than five times.*

Line	Description	Line	Amount	
16	Subtract line 15 from line 14	16		
17	Enter the **smaller** of: two-thirds (⅔) of gross nonfarm income (not less than zero) **or** the amount on line 16. Also include this amount on line 4b above	17		

[1]From Sch. F, line 11, and Sch. K-1 (Form 1065), line 15b.
[2]From Sch. F, line 36, and Sch. K-1 (Form 1065), line 15a.
[3]From Sch. C, line 31; Sch. C-EZ, line 3; Sch. K-1 (Form 1065), line 15a; and Sch. K-1 (Form 1065-B), box 9.
[4]From Sch. C, line 7; Sch. C-EZ, line 1; Sch. K-1 (Form 1065), line 15c; and Sch. K-1 (Form 1065-B), box 9.

OMB No. 1115-0136

Employment Eligibility Verification

INSTRUCTIONS

PLEASE READ ALL INSTRUCTIONS CAREFULLY BEFORE COMPLETING THIS FORM.

Anti-Discrimination Notice. It is illegal to discriminate against any individual (other than an alien not authorized to work in the U.S.) in hiring, discharging, or recruiting or referring for a fee because of that individual's national origin or citizenship status. It is illegal to discriminate against work eligible individuals. Employers **CANNOT** specify which document(s) they will accept from an employee. The refusal to hire an individual because of a future expiration date may also constitute illegal discrimination.

Section 1 - Employee. All employees, citizens and noncitizens, hired after November 6, 1986, must complete Section 1 of this form at the time of hire, which is the actual beginning of employment. **The employer is responsible for ensuring that Section 1 is timely and properly completed.**

Preparer/Translator Certification. The Preparer/Translator Certification must be completed if Section 1 is prepared by a person other than the employee. A preparer/translator may be used only when the employee is unable to complete Section 1 on his/her own. However, the employee must still sign Section 1.

Section 2 - Employer. For the purpose of completing this form, the term "employer" includes those recruiters and referrers for a fee who are agricultural associations, agricultural employers or farm labor contractors.

Employers must complete Section 2 by examining evidence of identity and employment eligibility within three (3) business days of the date employment begins. If employees are authorized to work, but are unable to present the required document(s) within three business days, they must present a receipt for the application of the document(s) within three business days and the actual document(s) within ninety (90) days. However, if employers hire individuals for a duration of less than three business days, Section 2 must be completed at the time employment begins. **Employers must record: 1)** document title; **2)** issuing authority; **3)** document number, **4)** expiration date, if any; and **5)** the date employment begins. Employers must sign and date the certification. Employees must present original documents. Employers may, but are not required to, photocopy the document(s) presented. These **photocopies may only be used for the verification process and must be retained with the I-9. However, employers are still responsible for completing the I-9.**

Section 3 - Updating and Reverification. Employers must complete Section 3 when updating and/or reverifying the I-9. Employers must reverify employment eligibility of their employees on or before the expiration date recorded in Section 1. Employers **CANNOT** specify which document(s) they will accept from an employee.

- If an employee's name has changed at the time this form is being updated/ reverified, complete Block A.
- If an employee is rehired within three (3) years of the date this form was originally completed and the employee is still eligible to be employed on the same basis as previously indicated on this form (updating), complete Block B and the signature block.
- If an employee is rehired within three (3) years of the date this form was originally completed and the employee's work authorization has expired or if a current employee's work authorization is about to expire (reverification), complete Block B and:
  - examine any document that reflects that the employee is authorized to work in the U.S. (see List A or C),
  - record the document title, document number and expiration date (if any) in Block C, and
  - complete the signature block.

Photocopying and Retaining Form I-9. A blank I-9 may be reproduced, provided both sides are copied. The Instructions must be available to all employees completing this form. Employers must retain completed I-9s for three (3) years after the date of hire or one (1) year after the date employment ends, whichever is later.

For more detailed information, you may refer to the INS Handbook for Employers, (Form M-274). You may obtain the handbook at your local INS office.

Privacy Act Notice. The authority for collecting this information is the Immigration Reform and Control Act of 1986, Pub. L. 99-603 (8 USC 1324a).

This information is for employers to verify the eligibility of individuals for employment to preclude the unlawful hiring, or recruiting or referring for a fee, of aliens who are not authorized to work in the United States.

This information will be used by employers as a record of their basis for determining eligibility of an employee to work in the United States. The form will be kept by the employer and made available for inspection by officials of the U.S. Immigration and Naturalization Service, the Department of Labor and the Office of Special Counsel for Immigration Related Unfair Employment Practices.

Submission of the information required in this form is voluntary. However, an individual may not begin employment unless this form is completed, since employers are subject to civil or criminal penalties if they do not comply with the Immigration Reform and Control Act of 1986.

Reporting Burden. We try to create forms and instructions that are accurate, can be easily understood and which impose the least possible burden on you to provide us with information. Often this is difficult because some immigration laws are very complex. Accordingly, the reporting burden for this collection of information is computed as follows: **1)** learning about this form, 5 minutes; **2)** completing the form, 5 minutes; and **3)** assembling and filing (recordkeeping) the form, 5 minutes, for an average of 15 minutes per response. If you have comments regarding the accuracy of this burden estimate, or suggestions for making this form simpler, you can write to the Immigration and Naturalization Service, HQPDI, 425 I Street, N.W., Room 4307r, Washington, DC 20536. OMB No. 1115-0136.

EMPLOYERS MUST RETAIN COMPLETED FORM I-9
PLEASE DO NOT MAIL COMPLETED FORM I-9 TO INS

OMB No. 1115-0136

Employment Eligibility Verification

Please read instructions carefully before completing this form. The instructions must be available during completion of this form. ANTI-DISCRIMINATION NOTICE: It is illegal to discriminate against work eligible individuals. Employers CANNOT specify which document(s) they will accept from an employee. The refusal to hire an individual because of a future expiration date may also constitute illegal discrimination.

Section 1. Employee Information and Verification. To be completed and signed by employee at the time employment begins.

Print Name: Last	First	Middle Initial	Maiden Name
Address *(Street Name and Number)*		Apt. #	Date of Birth *(month/day/year)*
City	State	Zip Code	Social Security #

I am aware that federal law provides for imprisonment and/or fines for false statements or use of false documents in connection with the completion of this form.

I attest, under penalty of perjury, that I am (check one of the following):

☐ A citizen or national of the United States
☐ A Lawful Permanent Resident (Alien # A__________
☐ An alien authorized to work until ___/___/___
(Alien # or Admission #) __________

Employee's Signature	Date *(month/day/year)*

Preparer and/or Translator Certification. *(To be completed and signed if Section 1 is prepared by a person other than the employee.) I attest, under penalty of perjury, that I have assisted in the completion of this form and that to the best of my knowledge the information is true and correct.*

Preparer's/Translator's Signature	Print Name
Address *(Street Name and Number, City, State, Zip Code)*	Date *(month/day/year)*

Section 2. Employer Review and Verification. To be completed and signed by employer. Examine one document from List A OR examine one document from List B and one from List C, as listed on the reverse of this form, and record the title, number and expiration date, if any, of the document(s)

List A	OR	List B	AND	List C
Document title: __________		__________		__________
Issuing authority: __________		__________		__________
Document #: __________		__________		__________
Expiration Date *(if any)*: ___/___/___		___/___/___		___/___/___
Document #: __________				
Expiration Date *(if any)*: ___/___/___				

CERTIFICATION - I attest, under penalty of perjury, that I have examined the document(s) presented by the above-named employee, that the above-listed document(s) appear to be genuine and to relate to the employee named, that the employee began employment on *(month/day/year)* ___/___/___ and that to the best of my knowledge the employee is eligible to work in the United States. (State employment agencies may omit the date the employee began employment.)

Signature of Employer or Authorized Representative	Print Name	Title
Business or Organization Name	Address *(Street Name and Number, City, State, Zip Code)*	Date *(month/day/year)*

Section 3. Updating and Reverification. To be completed and signed by employer.

A. New Name *(if applicable)*	B. Date of rehire *(month/day/year) (if applicable)*

C. If employee's previous grant of work authorization has expired, provide the information below for the document that establishes current employment eligibility.

Document Title:__________ Document #: __________ Expiration Date (if any): ___/___/___

I attest, under penalty of perjury, that to the best of my knowledge, this employee is eligible to work in the United States, and if the employee presented document(s), the document(s) I have examined appear to be genuine and to relate to the individual.

Signature of Employer or Authorized Representative	Date *(month/day/year)*

LISTS OF ACCEPTABLE DOCUMENTS

LIST A

Documents that Establish Both Identity and Employment Eligibility

1. U.S. Passport (unexpired or expired)
2. Certificate of U.S. Citizenship *(INS Form N-560 or N-561)*
3. Certificate of Naturalization *(INS Form N-550 or N-570)*
4. Unexpired foreign passport, with *I-551 stamp or* attached *INS Form I-94* indicating unexpired employment authorization
5. Alien Registration Receipt Card with photograph *(INS Form I-151 or I-551)*
6. Unexpired Temporary Card *(INS Form I-688)*
7. Unexpired Employment Authorization Card *(INS Form I-688A)*
8. Unexpired Reentry Permit *(INS Form I-327)*
9. Unexpired Refugee Travel Document *(INS Form I-571)*
10. Unexpired Employment Authorization Document issued by the INS which contains a photograph *(INS Form I-688B)*

OR

LIST B

Documents that Establish Identity

1. Driver's license or ID card issued by a state or outlying possession of the United States provided it contains a photograph or information such as name, date of birth, sex, height, eye color and address
2. ID card issued by federal, state or local government agencies or entities, provided it contains a photograph or information such as name, date of birth, sex, height, eye color and address
3. School ID card with a photograph
4. Voter's registration card
5. U.S. Military card or draft record
6. Military dependent's ID card
7. U.S. Coast Guard Merchant Mariner Card
8. Native American tribal document
9. Driver's license issued by a Canadian government authority

For persons under age 18 who are unable to present a document listed above:

10. School record or report card
11. Clinic, doctor or hospital record
12. Day-care or nursery school record

AND

LIST C

Documents that Establish Employment Eligibility

1. U.S. social security card issued by the Social Security Administration *(other than a card stating it is not valid for employment)*
2. Certification of Birth Abroad issued by the Department of State *(Form FS-545 or Form DS-1350)*
3. Original or certified copy of a birth certificate issued by a state, county, municipal authority or outlying possession of the United States bearing an official seal
4. Native American tribal document
5. U.S. Citizen ID Card *(INS Form I-197)*
6. ID Card for use of Resident Citizen in the United States *(INS Form I-179)*
7. Unexpired employment authorization document issued by the INS *(other then those listed under List A)*

Illustrations of many of these documents appear in Part 8 of the Handbook for Employers (M-274)

OMB Approval No: 3245-0016
Expiration Date: 9/30/01

U.S. Small Business Administration

APPLICATION FOR BUSINESS LOAN

Individual	Full Address

Name of Applicant Business	Tax I.D. No. or SSN
Full Street Address of Business	Tel. No. (inc. A/C)

City	County	State	Zip

Type of Business	Date Business Established

Bank of Business Account and Address

Number of Employees (Including subsidiaries and affiliates)

At Time of Application ____

If Loan is Approved ____

Subsidiaries or Affiliates (Separate for above) ____

Use of Proceeds: (Enter Gross Dollar Amounts Rounded to the Nearest Hundreds)	Loan Requested		Loan Request
Land Acquisition		Payoff SBA Loan	
New Construction/ Expansion Repair		Payoff Bank Loan (Non SBA Associated	
Acquisition and/or Repair of Machinery and Equipment		Other Debt Payment (Non SBA Associated)	
Inventory Purchase		All Other	
Working Capital (including Accounts Payable)		Total Loan Requested	
Acquisition of Existing Business		Term of Loan - (Requested Mat.)	____ Yrs.

PREVIOUS SBA OR OTHER FEDERAL GOVERNMENT DEBT: If you or any principals or affiliates have 1) ever requested Government Financing or 2) are deliquent on the repayment of any Federal Debt complete the following:

Name of Agency	Original Amount of Loan	Date of Request	Approved or Declined	Balance	Current or Past Due
	$			$	
	$			$	

ASSISTANCE List the name(s) and occupation of anyone who assisted in the preparation of this form, other than applicant.

Name and Occupation	Address	Total Fees Paid	Fees Due
Name and Occupation	Address	Total Fees Paid	Fees Due

Note: The estimated burden completing this form is 12.0 hours per response. You will not be required to respond to any collection of information unless it displays a currently valid OMB approval number. Comments on the burden should be sent to U.S. Small Business Administration, Chief, AIB, 409 3rd St., S.W., Washington, D.C. 20416 and Desk Office for Small Business Administration, Office of Management and Budget, New Executive Office Building, room 10202 Washington, D.C. 20503. OMB Approval (3245-0016).**PLEASE DO NOT SENDFORMS TO OMB. SUBMIT COMPLETED APPLICATION TO LENDER OF CHOICE**

ALL EXHIBITS MUST BE SIGNED AND DATED BY PERSON SIGNING THIS FORM

BUSINESS INDEBTEDNESS: Furnish the following information on all installment debts, contracts, notes, and mortgages payble. Indicate by an asterisk (*) items to be paid by loan proceeds and reason for paying them (present balance should agree with the latest balance sheet submitted).

To Whom Payable	Original Amount	Original Date	Present Balance	Rate of Interest	Maturity Date	Monthly Payment	Security	Current or Past Due
Acct. #'	$		$			$		
Acct. #	$		$			$		
Acct. #	$		$			$		
Acct. #	$		$			$		
Acct. #	$		$			$		

MANAGEMENT (Proprietor, partners, officers, directors, all holders of outstanding stock – (100% of ownership must be shown). Use separate sheet if necessary.

Name and Social Security Number and Position Title	Complete Address	% Owned	*Military Service From	To	*Sex
Race*: American Indian/Alaska Native ☐ Black/African-Amer. ☐ Asian ☐ Native Hawaiian/Pacific Islander ☐ White ☐			Ethnicity* Hispanic ☐ Not Hispanic ☐		
Race*: American Indian/Alaska Native ☐ Black/African-Amer. ☐ Asian ☐ Native Hawaiian/Pacific Islander ☐ White ☐			Ethnicity* Hispanic ☐ Not Hispanic ☐		
Race*: American Indian/Alaska Native ☐ Black/African-Amer. ☐ Asian ☐ Native Hawaiian/Pacific Islander ☐ White ☐			Ethnicity* Hispanic ☐ Not Hispanic ☐		
Race*: American Indian/Alaska Native ☐ Black/African-Amer. ☐ Asian ☐ Native Hawaiian/Pacific Islander ☐ White ☐			Ethnicity* Hispanic ☐ Not Hispanic ☐		

*This date is collected for statistical purpose only. It has no bearing on the credit decision to approve or decline this application.

THE FOLLOWING EXHIBITS MUST BE COMPLETED WHERE APPLICABLE. ALL QUESTIONS ANSWERED ARE MADE A PART OF THE APPLICATION.

For Guarantee Loans please provide an original and one copy (Photocopy is Acceptable) of the Application Form, and all Exihibits to the participating lender. For Direct Loans submit one original copy of the application and Exhibits to SBA.

1. Submit SBA Form 912 (Statement of Personal History) for each type of individual that the Form 912 requires.

2. If your collateral consists of (A) Land and Building, (B) Machinery and Equipment, (C) Furniture and Fixtures, (D) Accounts *Receivable*, (E) Inventory, (F) Other, please provide an itemized list (labeled Exhibit A) that contains serial and identification numbers for all articles that had an Original value of greater than $500. Include a legal description of Real Estate Offered as collateral.

3. Furnish a signed current personal balance sheet (SBA Form 413 may be used for this purpose) for each stockholder (with 20% or greater ownership), partner, officer, and owner. Include the assets and liabilities of the spouse and any close relatives living in the household. Also, include your Social Security Number. The date should be the same as the most recent business financial statement. Label it Exhibit B.

4. Include the financial statements listed below a,b,c for the last three years; also a,b,c, and d as of the same date, – current within 90 days of filing the application; and statement e, if applicable. **Label it Exhibit C (Contact SBA for referral if assistance with preparation is wanted.) All information must be signed and dated.**

a. Balance Sheet
b. Profit and Loss Statement (if not available, explain why and substitute Federal income tax forms)
c. Reconciliation of Net Worth
d. Aging of Accounts Receivable and Payable (summary not detailed)
e. Projection of earnings for at least one year where financial statements for the last three years are unavailable or when

5. Provide a brief history of your company and a paragraph describing the expected benefits it will receive from the loan. Label it Exhibit D.

6. Provide a brief description similar to a resume of the education, technical and business background for all the people listed under Management. Label it Exhibit E.

ALL EXHIBITS MUST BE SIGNED AND DATED BY PERSON SIGNING THIS FORM

7. Submit the names, addresses, tax I.D. number(EIN or SSN), and current personal balance sheet(s) of any co-signers and/or guarantors for the loan who are not otherwise affiliated with the business as Exhibit F.

8. Include a list of any machinery or equipment or other non-real estate assets to be purchased with loan proceeds and the cost of each item as quoted by the seller as Exhibit G. Include the seller's name and address.

9. Have you or any officers of your company ever been involved in bankruptcy or insolvency proceedings? If so, please provide the details as Exhibit H.
If none, check here: [ ]Yes [ ]No

10. Are you or your business involved in any pending lawsuits? If yes, provide the details as Exhibit I.
If none, check here: [ ]Yes [ ]No

11. Do you or your spouse or any member of your household, or anyone who owns, manages or directs your business or their spouses or members of their households work for the Small Business Administration, Small Business Advisory Council, SCORE or ACE, any Federal Agency, or the participating lender? If so, please provide the name and address of the person and the office where employed. Label this Exhibit J.
If none, check here: [ ]

12. Does your business, its owners or majority stockholders own or have a controlling interest in other businesses? If yes, please provide their names and the relationship with your company along with a current balance sheet and operating statement for each. This should be Exhibit K.

13. Do you buy from, sell to, or use the services of any concern in which someone in your company has a significant financial interest? If yes, provide details on a separate sheet of paper labeled Exhibit L.

14. If your business is a franchise, include a copy of the franchise agreement and a copy of the FTC disclosure statement supplied to you by the Franchisor. Please include it as Exhibit M.

CONSTRUCTION LOANS ONLY

15. Include as a separate exhibit (Exhibit N) the estimated cost of the project and a statement of the source of any additional funds.

16. Provide copies of preliminary construction plans and specifications. Include them as Exhibit O. Final plans will be required prior to disbursement

EXPORT LOANS

17. Does your business presently engage in Export Trade?
Check here: [ ]Yes [ ]No

18. Will you be using proceeds from this loan to support your company's exports?
Check here: [ ]Yes [ ]No

19. Would you like information on Exporting?
Check here: [ ]Yes [ ]No

AGREEMENTS AND CERTIFICATIONS

Agreements of non-employment of SBA Personnel: I agree that if SBA approves this loan application I will not, for at least two years, hire as an employee or consultant anyone that was employed by SBA during the one year period prior to the disbursement of the

Certification: I certify: (a) I have not paid anyone connected with the Federal Government for help in getting this loan. I also agree to report to the SBA office of the Inspector General, Washington, DC 20416 any Federal Government employee who offers, in return for any type of compensation, to help get this loan approved.

(b) All information in this application and the Exhibits are true and complete to the best of my knowledge and are submitted to SBA so SBA can decide whether to grant a loan or participate with a lending institution in a loan to me. I agree to pay for or reimburse SBA for the cost of any surveys, title or mortgage examinations, appraisals, credit reports, etc., performed by non-SBA personnel provided I

(c) I understand that I need not pay anybody to deal with SBA. I have read and understand SBA Form 159, which explains SBA policy on representatives and their fees.

(d) As consideration for any Management, Technical, and Business Development Assistance that may be provided, I waive all claims against SBA and its consultants.

If you knowingly make a false statement or overvalue a security to obtain a guaranteed loan from SBA, you can be fined up to $10,000 and/or imprisoned for not more than five years under 18 usc 1001; if submitted to a Federally insured institution, under 18 USC 1014 by Imprisonment of not more than twenty years and/or a fine of not more than $1,000,000. I authorize the SBA's Office of Inspector General to request criminal record information about me from criminal justice agencies for the purpose of determining my eligibility for programs authorized by

If Applicant is a proprietor or general partner, sign below:

By: ______________________________

If Applicant is a Corporation, sign below:

____

Corporate Name and Seal Date

By: ______________________________
Signature of President

Attested by: ______________________________
Signature of Corporate Secretary

SUBMIT COMPLETED APPLICATION TO LENDER OF CHOICE

APPLICANT'S CERTIFICATION

By my signature, I certify that I have read and received a copy of the "STATEMENTS REQUIRED BY LAW AND EXECUTIVE ORDER" which was attached to this application. My signature represents my agreement to comply with the approval of my loan request and to comply, whenever applicable, with the hazard insurance, lead-based paint, civil rights or other limitations in this notice.

Each proprietor, each General Partner, each Limited Partner or Stockholder owning 20% or more, each Guarantor and the spouse of each of these must sign. Each person should sign only once.

Business Name: ______________________________

By: ______________________________ ______________________________

Signature and Title Date

Guarantors:

______________________________ ______________________________

Signature and Title Date

______________________________ ______________________________

Signature and Title Date

______________________________ ______________________________

Signature and Title Date

______________________________ ______________________________

Signature and Title Date

______________________________ ______________________________

Signature and Title Date

______________________________ ______________________________

Signature and Title Date

______________________________ ______________________________

Signature and Title Date

U.S. SMALL BUSINESS ADMINISTRATION

OMB Approval No. 3245-0016

APPLICATION FOR LOWDOC LOAN

Expiration Date: 09/30/01

A. BORROWER

Please Print Legibly or Type (**ALL BLANKS MUST BE COMPLETED,** Use "N/A," if Blank is Not Applicable)

Business Name ____
Trade Name (if different) ____
Type: Proprietorship ☐ Partnership ☐ Corporation ☐ LLC ☐ Other ☐
Address ____
City ____ State __ County ____ Zip ____
Mailing Address (if different from above)____
City ____ State __ County ____ Zip ____
Phone ____ IRS Tax ID #____
Business Bank ____ Checking Balance $ ____

Nature of Business ____
Date Business Established ____
Date Current Ownership Established ____
Number of employees ____
Number of affiliate(s) employees ____
Total number of employees after Loan ____
Exporter? Yes ☐ No ☐ Pre-Qual? Yes ☐ No ☐
Franchise? Yes ☐ No ☐ Name____

B. LOAN REQUEST

AMOUNT $____ Maturity: ____ Purpose:____
Have you employed anyone to prepare this application? Yes ☐ No ☐ If Yes, how much was paid? $____ How much do you owe? $ ____
Name of Packager ____ Packager's Tax ID No. or Social Security No. ____

C. INDEBTEDNESS:

Furnish information on **ALL BUSINESS** debts, contracts, notes and mortgages payable. Indicate by an (*) items to be paid by loan proceeds.

To Whom Payable	Orig. Amount	Orig. Date	Cur. Balance	Int. Rate	Maturity Date	Pmt. Amt.	Pmt Frequency	Collateral	Status
N/A	N/A	N/A	N/A	N/A	N/A	N/A	N/A	N/A	N/A
N/A	N/A	N/A	N/A	N/A	N/A	N/A	N/A	N/A	N/A
N/A	N/A	N/A	N/A	N/A	N/A	N/A	N/A	N/A	N/A

D. PRINCIPALS:

Submit all information in this section for each principal of the business. Use separate attachments for each principal.

D1 Full Name ____ Phone ____Social Security Number ____ Title President
Address ____ City ____ State __ Zip
Date of Birth ____ Place of Birth (City, ST or Foreign Country) ____ U.S. Citizen? **Yes** ☐ **No** ☐ If No, Alien reg. #____

D2 Percentage Owned % | Veteran *: Non-Veteran ☐ Vietnam Era Veteran ☐ Other Veteran ☐ | Gender *: Female ☐ Male ☐
Race*: African American ☐ Puerto Rican ☐ Native American ☐ Hispanic ☐ Asian/Pacific Islander ☐ Eskimo & Aleuts ☐ Caucasian ☐ Multi-Ethnic ☐

***This data is collected for statistical purposes only. It has no bearing on the credit decision. Disclosure is voluntary.**

D3 PERSONAL FINANCIAL STATEMENT: Complete for all principals with 20% or more ownership.

Liquid Assets $____ Ownership in Business $____ Real Estate $____ Assets Other $____ Total Assets $____
Liabilities Real Estate $____ Liabilities Other $____ Total Liabilities $____ Net Worth (less value of business) $____
Annual Salary $____ Other Source of Repayment $____ Source ____ Residence: Own ☐ Rent ☐ Other ☐ Mthly Housing $____

D4 PREVIOUS SBA OR OTHER GOVERNMENT FINANCING: For all owners, principals, partners, and affiliates.

Borrower Name	Name of Agency	Loan No.	Date	Amount	Balance	Status
N/A	N/A	N/A	N/A	N/A	N/A	N/A
N/A	N/A	N/A	N/A	N/A	N/A	N/A

D5 ELIGIBILITY AND DISCLOSURES:

I. Are you or your business involved in any pending lawsuits? **Yes** ☐ **No** ☐ If Yes, provide the details as Exhibit A.

II. Do you or your spouse or any member of your household, or anyone who owns, manages, or directs your business or their spouses or members of their households work for the Small Business Administration, Small Business Advisory Council, SCORE or ACE, any Federal Agency, or the participating lender? Yes ☐ No ☐ If Yes, please provide the name and address of the person and the office where employed. Label this Exhibit B.

III. Affiliates: Do you or the applicant business have any interest in any other business as owner, principal, partner or manager? **Yes** ☐ **No** ☐ **If Yes, Please provide** details to Lender.

IV. Are you: (a) presently under indictment, on parole or probation, **Yes** ☐ **No** ☐ or (b) have ever been charged with or arrested for any criminal offense other than a minor motor vehicle violation (including offenses which have been dismissed, discharged, or nolle prosequi) **Yes** ☐ **No** ☐ or (c) convicted, placed on pretrial diversion, or placed on any form of probation including adjudication withheld pending probation for any criminal offense other than a minor motor vehicle violation? **Yes** ☐ **No** ☐ **If Yes to an "IV" question,** Lender must submit application to local SBA Office for processing under the regular 7(a) program.

V. **I have received and read SBA Form 1261, STATEMENTS REQUIRED BY LAW AND EXECUTIVE ORDER.**

If you knowingly make a false statement or overvalue a security to obtain a guaranteed loan from SBA you can be fined up to $10,000 and/or imprisoned for not more than five years under 18 U.S.C.1001; if submitted to a Federally insured institution, under 18 USC 1014 by Imprisonment of not more than twenty years and/or a fine of not more than $1,000,000. I authorize the SBA's Office of Inspector General to request criminal record information about me from criminal justice agencies for the purpose of determining my eligibility for programs authorized by the Small Business Act, as amended.

VI. Signature________________________ Date________________

E. SIGNATURE

I authorize SBA/Lender to make inquires as necessary to verify the accuracy of the statements made and to determine my creditworthiness. I agree that if SBA approves this loan application I will not, for at least two years, hire as an employee or consultant anyone that was employed by the SBA during the one year period prior to the disbursement of the loan. And, I hereby certify that: (1) as consideration for any Management, Technical, and Business Development Assistance that may be provided, I waive all claims against SBA and its consultants, and (2) all information contained in this document and any attachments is true and correct to the best of my knowledge,

Print Name ________________________ Date ________________________
Signature ________________________ Title ________________________
If Corporation, Attested By: ________________________
Signature of Corporate Secretary

SBA Form 4-L (9-98) Previous Editions are Obsolete

LENDER'S APPLICATION FOR GUARANTEE

F. LENDER

Please Print Legibly or Type (**ALL BLANKS MUST BE COMPLETED,** Use "N/A," if Blank is Not Applicable)

Name of Lender ______________________ Business Name ________________ Applicant SIC Code__________
Lender's Address ____________________ City____________ State ____ Zip ______
Phone _______________ Fax ________________ **750 Agreement Date:** __________

G. LOAN TERMS: The following section should be completed exactly as shown in the LowDoc Program Guide.

SBA Guarantee ____% Loan Amount _____No. of Mos. to Maturity_____Payments: P&I ☐ or P+I ☐ $_____ No. of Mos. Interest Only_____
Initial Interest Rate: ☐ Fixed _____% ☐Variable _____% Initial spread over WSJ Prime_____% Adjustment Period: Mthly ☐ Qtrly ☐ Other ☐ _____
Life Insurance required? **Yes** ☐ **No** ☐ On Whom? _____ How much _____ Stand-by Agreements? **Yes** ☐ **No** ☐ Amounts $_____
If Start-Up or Purchasing of Existing Business, Amount of Applicant Injection**: Cash $_____ Assets $_____ Stand-by Debt $_____ Other $_____
****Equity in home is not considered injection.**

Use of Proceeds:

Amount	Purpose
	Acquire/Renovate Real Property
	Acquire Fixed Assets, Non-RE
	Impact Current Assets/Liabilities
	Refinance SBA Debt*
	Refinance Non-SBA Debt*
	Purchase Existing Business
	Other:
	Total

Collateral:

Type	Description	Market Value	Existing Lien(s)* Lien holder	Balance	Collateral Value

*If use of proceeds is for debt repayment, Lender **must** retain copies of refinanced notes. If for participant bank, debt refinancing may **not exceed 25%** of total loan amount.

H. FINANCIAL STATEMENTS: (Balance Sheet and Current Income Statement must be of the same period)

BALANCE SHEET

☐ Pro Forma ☐ Interim ☐ Year End (As of)

ASSETS		LIABILITIES	
Cash Equivalent		Notes Payable	
Net Trade Rec.		Trade Payable	
Inventory		Current LTD	
Other Curr. Assets		Other Curr. Liab.	
Total Curr. Assets		Total Curr. Liab.	
Net Fixed Assets		Long Term Debt	
Other Assets		Other Liabilities	
Total Assets		Total Liabilities	
		Tangible Net Worth* (*including Stand-by debt)	

INCOME STATEMENT

No. of Interim Mos. / **Date**	**Prior FY**	**Current**	**Projected**
a) Net Sales/Revenue			
b) Cost of Sales			
c) Gross Profit			
d) Owner Comp/Drawings			
e) Rent (if applicable)			
f) Depreciation/Amortization			
g) LongTermDebt Int. Exp.			
h) General & Other Exp.			
i) Net Income after "d" above			
A) Cash Flow (f+g+i)			
B) Term Debt P & I			
Debt Coverage Ratio (A / B)			

I. LENDERS COMMENTS: (Comment on Management's character, and the business' financial strength and repayment ability, including forecast.)

Business Start-Ups and Purchases: Lender **MUST** comment on management qualifications, location, competitive factors and feasibility of business plan.

J. ELIGIBILITY EVALUATION: Refer to program guide. If you have any eligibility questions, please contact the LowDoc Processing Center before submitting an application.

Eligibility Evaluation: To the best of your ability, have you determined that the Borrower meets SBA eligibility requirements as outlined in the "LowDoc Program Guide" and the "Eligibility Checklist?" **Yes** ☐**No** ☐ (Please note, by law, SBA cannot guarantee ineligible loans.)

I submit this application to SBA for approval subject to the terms and conditions outlined above. Without the participation of SBA to the extent applied for we would not be willing to make this loan, and in our opinion the financial assistance applied for is not otherwise available on reasonable terms. I certify that none of the Lender's employees, officers, directors, or substantial stockholders (more than 10%) have financial interest in the applicant. I also certify that our institution has at least 20 qualified commercial loans outstanding demonstrating our significant experience lending to small business concerns.

Lender Officer (Print Name) ______________________________
Signature of Lender Officer ______________________________ Title ____________________ Date ____________

The estimated burden for completing this form is 30 minutes per response. You will not be required to respond if an OMB approval number is not displayed, Any questions or comments can be forwarded to the U.S. Small Business Administration, Chief, AIB, Washington,D.C.20416 or Office of Management and Budget, Clearance Officer, (325-0016), Washington, D.C. 20503.

CONFIDENTIALITY/NON-COMPETE AGREEMENT

The Confidentiality and Non-Compete Agreement is designed to protect you when you work with another party and they learn confidential and/or proprietary information about you and/or your business. For example, another party you are working with on a project you are building. A confidentiality/non-compete agreement may help to prevent that party from disclosing any information he/she may have obtained in the course of doing business with you, and it binds them from competing against you for the same or very similar products or services in the future.

However, keep in mind that unscrupulous people will steal your ideas even if they have signed an agreement. They will risk the chance of being sued if the idea is good enough. With this in mind, reveal only that information that pertains to your working relationship.

Be sure to have the other party sign the confidentiality and non-compete agreement as soon as he/she begins working with you—even when you are in the early stages of discussion about a project. It is a very common form, and nobody should be offended or feel that you don't trust them if you ask them to sign it.

SOURCE: **americanexpress.com/smallbusiness/resources/starting/contracts/confide.shtml**

SAMPLE

CONFIDENTIALITY AND NON-COMPETE AGREEMENT

The undersigned, representing ________________________________ [COMPANY NAME], hereby acknowledges that the nature of the work to be performed for [YOUR COMPANY] involves his/her access to trade secrets, confidential information, files, records and forms of [YOUR COMPANY], collectively Confidential Information. Confidential Information includes, but is not limited to, any information relating to [YOUR COMPANY]'s organizational structure, marketing philosophy and objectives, project plans, data models, strategy and vision statements, business initiatives, business requirements, systems design, methodology, processes, competitive advantages and disadvantages, financial results, product features, systems, operations, technology, customer lists and other information which would give the Company an opportunity to obtain an advantage over its competitors, or which the Company is ethically obligated to protect from unauthorized sources. None of this information shall be deemed to be in the public domain. The undersigned hereby agrees that he/she will not disclose proprietary information acquired pursuant to this meeting or any other discussions he/she has had with ________________________________, representing [YOUR COMPANY] and other [YOUR COMPANY] representative, ot any other party. This agreement shall not apply to any information which was in the undersigned's possession prior to the time of disclosure; in the public domain prior to disclosure; becomes part of the public domain not due to any unauthorized act or omission on the undersigned's part; or, is supplied to the undersigned by a third party as a matter of right. The undersigned agrees that he/she will not now, or at any future time, divulge or appropriate to his/her own use or the use of others, reproduce, transmit or provide information regarding [YOUR COMPANY] business or plans for business or any part thereof to any person or persons not connected with your organization.

The undersigned agrees that he/she will maintain information in strict confidence, and not discuss and/or provide Confidential Information to sources outside of [YOUR COMPANY], including, without limitation, at conferences, seminars, meetings of professional organizations, or by publication in a journal or granting of interviews to journalists and other members of the news media. In addition, the undersigned agrees not to use information gained in this or any other meeting or discussion, to compete with [YOUR COMPANY], or to use the information gained from this or any other meeting or discussion with [YOUR COMPANY], to create a product that is similar to the one that is being discussed.

The undersigned agrees that any work product produced or developed by him/her in the performance of his/her duties hereunder shall be Confidential Information subject to this agreement and such work product is, and shall remain, the property of the Company.

Signed,

____

Representing: ________________________________

Dated: ________________________________

Provided only as a sample agreement. Contact your lawyer for legal advice before using.

SOURCE: **www.americanexpress.com**

Index